# ASSER'S
# LIFE OF KING ALFRED

TOGETHER WITH THE

## ANNALS OF SAINT NEOTS

ERRONEOUSLY ASCRIBED TO ASSER

EDITED WITH INTRODUCTION AND
COMMENTARY BY

## WILLIAM HENRY STEVENSON, M.A.

NEW IMPRESSION
WITH ARTICLE ON RECENT WORK ON
ASSER'S LIFE OF ALFRED
BY
## DOROTHY WHITELOCK
*Elrington and Bosworth Professor of*
*Anglo-Saxon in the University of Cambridge*

OXFORD
AT THE CLARENDON PRESS

Oxford University Press, Great Clarendon Street, Oxford OX2 6DP

Oxford New York

Athens Auckland Bangkok Bogota Buenos Aires Calcutta
Cape Town Chennai Dar es Salaam Delhi Florence Hong Kong Istanbul
Karachi Kuala Lumpur Madrid Melbourne Mexico City Mumbai
Nairobi Paris São Paolo Singapore Taipei Tokyo Toronto Warsaw
and associated companies in
Berlin Ibadan

Oxford is a registered trade mark of Oxford University Press

Published in the United States by
Oxford University Press Inc., New York

© Oxford University Press 1959

Special edition for Sandpiper Books Ltd., 1998

British Library Cataloguing in Publication Data
Data available

ISBN 0-19-821201-1

1 3 5 7 9 10 8 6 4 2

Printed in Great Britain
on acid-free paper by
Bookcraft (Bath) Ltd.,
Midsomer Norton

# PREFACE

THE following pages constitute an attempt to supply one of the great *desiderata* in our early historical literature—a critical edition of the text of the *Life of Alfred*, and an endeavour to decide the question of its authenticity. The difficulty of establishing a text has been greatly enhanced by the destruction of the unique MS., the obviously corrupt nature of that MS., and by the scandalous treatment meted out to the text by the early editors who had access to it. The vexed question of the authenticity of the work itself could obviously be dealt with only by means of a thorough examination of its contents, and the canvassing of the possibility of every statement in it that might throw light upon the question. When I undertook this task, I had little idea of the labour it would involve. The reign of Alfred is a dark period of our history, illuminated only by the Old-English Chronicle and a few charters, preserved in much later chartularies, of a more or less suspicious nature. This paucity of evidence, while it adds greatly to the importance of the Life (if it can be shown to be genuine), renders the task of sifting and checking the statements of the work very difficult. Some little assistance is derivable from Frankish chroniclers of the time and from the papal records. But even then

there remain many statements in the Life that cannot
be corroborated by any documents at our disposal, and
their credibility can only be estimated by a careful
consideration of all details, and by the aid of light
reflected from later evidences. In many cases even
this assistance is denied us. It was probably these
considerations that led so distinguished a scholar as
Reinhold Pauli to express, in his *König Ælfred*,
a doubt whether the Life afforded sufficient material
for establishing its authenticity. The attempt to
weigh its credibility by the aid of later writings and,
where possible, of earlier ones, although it is the only
possible method in many cases, is necessarily somewhat unsatisfactory. Not only must every conclusion
be carefully tested by the aid of views established by
careful collation of later documents, but the applic-
ability of the results to the work under discussion
must always be given in a problematical manner, and
the hypothetical nature of the arguments be constantly made evident to the reader. In endeavouring
to do this I have had to qualify almost every statement or conclusion with a 'possibly,' a 'perhaps,' or
a 'probably.' When, in addition to this, almost every
shred of evidence has to be submitted to a critical
examination, involving research into numerous subordinate questions, it becomes impossible to deal
briefly with the numerous problems that have to be
discussed. The annotation may be, I fear, accused of
going into unnecessary detail, but I have preferred
laying myself open to this charge rather than put
forward definite assertions where the evidence at our
command precludes hard and fast conclusions. For

the minute study of the work I have the support of
Adolf Ebert, who, in his admirable *Allgemeine Geschichte der Literatur des Mittelalters im Abendlande,*
expresses the opinion that a relatively sure result
could be reached only by a careful study of all the
details of the Life. I can hardly flatter myself that
the present work adequately fulfils this requirement,
but the opinion of so sound a scholar is some justification for making the attempt.

In discussing the work I have attempted to
approach it without any bias for or against it, and
throughout my endeavour has been to subject every
portion of it to as searching an examination as my
knowledge and critical powers would permit. The
net result has been to convince me that, although
there may be no very definite proof that the work
was written by Bishop Asser in the lifetime of King
Alfred, there is no anachronism or other proof that
it is a spurious compilation of later date. The serious
charges brought against its authenticity break down
altogether under examination, while there remain
several features that point with varying strength to
the conclusion that it is, despite its difficulties and
corruptions, really a work of the time it purports to
be. This result is confirmed by the important corroboration of some of its statements by contemporary
Frankish chroniclers. Thus the profession of belief
in its authenticity by such eminent historians as
Kemble, Pauli, Stubbs, and Freeman agrees with my
own conclusion.

It would be ungracious to take leave of my task
without thanking those of my friends who have

lightened its burden by their learning, aid, and advice.
I am under great obligations for assistance in O.E.
philology to Professor Napier and to Dr. Henry
Bradley, and in Celtic philology and history to Pro-
fessor Rhys and Mr. Egerton Phillimore. My thanks
are due to the Societies of Corpus Christi College,
Cambridge, and to Trinity College, in the same
University, for the conveniences enjoyed in using
MSS. in their libraries. The invariable courtesy and
patience under many calls upon his time of Mr. C. W.
Moule, Fellow and Librarian of C.C.C., Cambridge,
I most thankfully acknowledge. I must also thank
the Bodleian Librarian, Mr. Falconer Madan, and
Mr. A. E. Cowley of the Bodleian Library, Dr. F. J.
Jenkinson, the Librarian of the Cambridge University
Library, and his assistant Mr. A. E. Rogers, for their
good offices. The Keeper of the Oxford University
Archives has been good enough to grant me special
facilities for consulting the documents under his
charge.

# CONTENTS

|  | PAGE |
| --- | --- |
| INTRODUCTION TO LIFE OF ALFRED . . . | xi |
| RECENT WORK ON ASSER'S LIFE OF ALFRED . | cxxxii |
| ASSERIUS DE REBUS GESTIS ÆLFREDI . . . | 1 |
| INTRODUCTION TO ANNALS OF ST. NEOTS . . | 97 |
| CHRONICON FANI SANCTI NEOTI SIVE ANNALES, QUI DICUNTUR, ASSERII . . . . . . | 117 |
| NOTES TO ASSER . . . . . . . | 147 |
| INDEX . . . . . . . . | 345 |

FACSIMILE OF COMMENCEMENT OF THE LOST MS. OF ASSER, REPRODUCED FROM WISE'S EDITION  xxxii

# INTRODUCTION

1. History of the Text (§§ 1–12), p. xi.   2. Description of the lost MS. (§§ 14–27), p. xxxii.   3. The Transcripts (§§ 28–32), p. li.
4. Excerpts from the work in later Compilers (§§ 33–38), p. lv.
5. The Author.   Internal evidence of the Text (§§ 39–60), p. lxv.
6. The attacks upon the Authenticity of the Work (§§ 61–89), p. xcv.
7. Summary (§§ 90–92), p. cxxv.

## 1. HISTORY OF THE TEXT.

§ 1. THE Life of King Alfred, known to us as the work of Bishop Asser, is one of the most important and at the same time most difficult of the sources of our early history. The work possesses unique literary interest as the earliest biography of an English layman, and as its subject was a very great man, it occupies in English sources much the same position as Einhard's Life of Charles the Great in the history of France and Germany. Probably no work of similar extent has contributed so much to English history. At an early period it was transcribed almost entirely into the continuous chronicles of Florence of Worcester and Simeon of Durham, and by their means it descended to Roger of Howden and the St. Alban's school of writers, whose influence upon mediaeval history-writing in England was all-pervading. But this copying of it into the usual handbooks of the later Middle Ages had the effect, not unusual at that time, of causing the original work to be neglected. When so important a work as the Chronicle of Matthew of Paris ceased to be copied because it was embodied in later compilations[1], we need not

---

[1] Cf. Sir Frederic Madden, preface to Paris's *Historia Anglorum*, i. pp. xxvii, xxxi. So also Bishop Stubbs, preface

be surprised at the oblivion into which the present work fell. It was transmitted beyond the Middle Ages by one copy only, and that a very unsatisfactory one. Owing to its great rarity it was selected by Archbishop Parker as one of the works printed by him in order to preserve them for posterity. His edition was awaited with much interest and received with enthusiasm. The great antiquity and personal interest of the work begot a somewhat exaggerated estimate of its supreme authority for the history of the latter part of the ninth century. It was usually given precedence of the Old-English Chronicle. Modern criticism has revised this estimate, and the process of depreciation set in. It has, in consequence, been denounced as a clumsy and bare-faced forgery of much later times than those of Alfred.

§ 2. The task of deciding upon the authenticity of the Life is by no means an easy one, and it has been rendered more difficult by the total destruction of the unique MS. in 1731. The work is known to us therefore solely through the medium of printed texts and transcripts. Of the four editions through which it has run two only are based upon the MS. The earliest of these is filled with arbitrary alterations and interpolations, which are distinguished in no way from the readings of the original (§ 6). The other affords us much aid in detecting these alterations and interpolations, but it occasionally makes the mistake of repeating as the reading of the MS. alterations in the MS. or misprints in the previous edition (§ 11). Hence we are assailed with constant doubts as to its giving faithfully the reading of the MS. Owing to these interpolations and the imperfect manner in

to Roger of Howden, i. p. xi, states that the publication of Higden's *Polychronicon* in the fourteenth century 'stopped the writing of new books ⟨upon history⟩ and ensured the destruction of the old.' The work bearing the name of Simeon of Durham is preserved in one MS. only.

which they are distinguished in the existing editions, the work has had to bear not only the weight of its own sins, but also those of the authors of the interpolations and of the editors.

§ 3. The first step in our task is obviously to ascertain, so far as the imperfect materials at our command will allow, what was the text of the lost MS. This is the main object of the present edition, in which the interpolations, some of which have become so embedded in our commoner histories that they possess an interest that forbids their being ignored, are for the first time unmistakably distinguished by the use of smaller type[1]. The text has been established by a minute collation of the existing

---

[1] The interpolated matter has not been sufficiently distinguished in the existing texts. Wise marks the interpolations by a footnote only at the beginning of the chapter, and the edition in the *Monumenta Historica Britannica* distinguishes them by enclosing them in square brackets. When the interpolation is a lengthy one, the reader referring to the text is very liable to overlook these important footnotes or brackets. A few instances will show how distinguished historical writers have been thus misled into quoting the interpolated matter as the original text. Dr. Todd, *Wars of the Gaidhil with the Gaill*, p. lvi, note 5, cites c. 54 b as from Asser ' or rather in some copies of it.' Sir Thomas Duffus Hardy, *Descriptive Catalogue of Materials relating to the History of Great Britain and Ireland*, i. 539, note *, quotes the interpolation at the end of c. 53 as the words of Asser. The passage from Matthew Paris, c. 50 c, is treated as coming from Asser by Eduard Winkelmann, *Geschichte der Angelsächsen*, Berlin, 1883, p. 146, who was probably misled by Reinhold Pauli, *König Ælfred und seine Stelle in der Geschichte Englands*, Berlin, 1851, p. 118 note. In this case one has to refer back to the commencement of the preceding chapter in the *Monumenta* to discover the bracket marking c. 50 c as an interpolation. So great a scholar as P. A. Munch, *Det Norske Folks Historie*, Christiania, 1852, i. part 1, pp. 614, 627, note 5, has been misled by the *Monumenta* text into citing c. 54 b as the words of Asser. The like mistake has also been made by J. C. H. R. Steenstrup, *Normannerne*, Copenhagen, 1876, i. 114, and by Sir J. H. Ramsay, *Foundations of England*, i. 240, note 6.

transcripts and editions and of the early compilers who embody matter derived from this work. By the aid of these compilers we are able to get back to twelfth-century texts, which are, in the nature of the case, superior to the printed texts. The foremost place amongst them is occupied by Florence of Worcester, the author of a translation of the O.E. Chronicle with additions. He died in 1118, and is an early writer with a high character for honesty. His readings are of such value that we have deemed it advisable to distinguish the portions copied by him by printing them in Roman type, and to give in italic type the portions that he omitted. Next in importance comes the work that is printed as an appendix to this volume, the so-called Annals of St. Neots. The author of this jejune compilation slavishly copied his originals, and his close reproduction of the passages derived from the Life of Alfred has been the great cause of the corruption of the text of the latter. Parker was so struck with this agreement that he assumed that the Annals were also the work of Asser, and he accordingly interpolated from them, in perfectly good faith, passages that did not occur in the Life, under the impression that they preserved a fuller text of the Life. In the third place we may put the extracts from the Life in the Durham compilations that bear the name of Simeon of Durham, one portion of which may possibly go back to the tenth century (§ 35).

§ 4. Archbishop Parker's edition of the work was published at London in 1574 by his printer John Day. The engraved title-page contains merely the words *Ælfredi Regis Res Gestae*, the title given in Parker's hand to the best transcript (§ 28). Below this title is a portrait of King Alfred [1], and the first four lines

---

[1] The portrait is, of course, entirely imaginary. How little value was assigned to it by Parker may be seen from his use of the same block as a portrait of Richard II, Duke of

of Henry of Huntingdon's verses on the king, which
Parker added to his text (c. 106 c). No mention is
made of the place or date of publication or of the
name of the printer or editor. But the arms of
the Archbishop appear, with his initials M. P., in the
engraved initial letter of the text, which also contains
the first portion of his motto *Mundus transit*[1]. The
text was printed, as mentioned in the preface, in the
Anglo-Saxon letters cut by John Day a few years
before, and the author of the preface records that
he had caused the O.E. gospels to be printed. They
appeared in 1571 under the editorship of John Foxe,
the author of the well-known *Acts and Monuments*,
from the press of John Day, and Foxe states in his
preface that the Archbishop had defrayed the costs
of the edition. The date of publication of the Life
of Asser is established by a letter from Parker to
the Lord Treasurer, William Cecil, Lord Burleigh, in
November, 1574, sending to him a copy of the book[2].
The Archbishop died on May 17, 1575.

§ 5. Parker gives very little information regarding
the manuscript used by him, but, as will be seen
below, it was clearly the Cottonian MS. Otho A xii.
The MS. was, he tells us, written in Latin letters,
but, 'out of veneration for the antiquity of the
archetype,' he caused it to be printed in Anglo-
Saxon characters[3]. His words have been carelessly

Normandy, in his edition of Walsingham's *Ypodigma Neustriae*, issued by John Day in 1574. This was noticed by
Hearne, *Collections*, ii. 78.

[1] His motto in full was *Mundus transit et concupiscentia eius*.
See upon the arms and motto Strype's *Life of Parker*, ii. 428,
523, in Strype's *Works*, Oxford, 1821.

[2] See Strype, ii. 380. Mr. Arber, *Registers of the Stationers'
Company*, v. 91, no. 1864, refers the publication to 1574. There
is no entry regarding it in the Registers.

[3] 'Latina autem cum sint, Saxonicis literis excudi curavimus,
maxime ob venerandam ipsius archetypi antiquitatem, ipso
adhuc (ut opinio fert mea) Ælfredo superstite, iisdem formulis
descriptam ... Sin autem quis requirit, quamobrem cum isthaec

taken to mean that the MS. used by him was written in these characters, and were hence cited to prove that the Cott. MS. was not the one from which he printed [1]. The MS. was, in his opinion, written during the lifetime of King Alfred, and he supported this view by the resemblance of the hand to the MSS. of Alfred's translation of the *Pastoral Care*. These were written in Anglo-Saxon characters, and therefore could not, strictly speaking, very closely resemble the 'Latin' hand of Parker's MS. By 'Latin' writing it is clear that he meant the development of the Caroline minuscule that was introduced into England in the tenth century, and which was used by English scribes in copying Latin after the middle of that century. In Alfred's time an English scribe would have used the Anglo-Saxon characters in writing Latin. The Cott. MS. was in this developed Caroline minuscule (§ 15), but O.E. words and names occurring in it seem to have been in Anglo-Saxon characters. It is, perhaps, these English names that led Parker to compare the hand with that of the MSS. of the O.E. version of the Pastoral Care. There are in existence three MSS. of this version that were the property of Parker [2], and of these the only one that

---

Latinis literis memoriae mandentur, eadem tamen nos Saxonicis typis pervulgari fecerimus, nihil est, quod expedire tam facile possimus.'

[1] For example, by Wise, p. 137.

[2] They are all eleventh-century copies, and are preserved in Cambridge. They are (*a*) Trinity College, MS. R. 5, which bears traces of Parker's use in the shape of red ochre pencillings, and a note in the hand of one of his secretaries that this was the very copy sent by Alfred to Sherborne. It seems to be a copy of the one sent thither, and to have been sent to Parker by Bishop Jewell from Salisbury, whither the see of Sherborne was transferred in the eleventh century (see Wanley, *Catalogus*, p. 168, Dr. M. R. James, *Catalogue of Western MSS. in the Library of Trinity College, Cambridge*, ii. 192). The copy is unfortunately incomplete, the king's prefatory letter, which would have mentioned the name of the bishop to whom

has any resemblance to the facsimile of the burnt Cott. MS. is that preserved in the library of Trinity College, Cambridge, the first hand of which is an early eleventh century one much resembling the Anglo-Saxon characters in the facsimile of the Cott. MS. (§ 15).

§ 6. Parker claims that in this, as in his other editions of historical works, he had faithfully followed his MS., altering or adding nothing. Unfortunately this is as untrue as it is in regard to his other works, in which he took the greatest liberties with the texts, correcting the style and spelling, interpolating from other works, and committing such sins that a modern scholar has been moved to describe his editing as 'wicked' and 'fantastic[1].' Possibly this singular inaccuracy arose from the works being really prepared for press by some of his secretaries, as suggested by Sir Frederic Madden[2]. Parker was in bad health when the present work was published, and the duties of his exalted office in the stirring times of ecclesiastical and political strife in which he lived make it a subject for marvel that he could find any time to devote to such work as text-editing. Yet we know from the appearance of his characteristic red-ochre pencillings in the MSS. that formerly belonged

the original was sent, being missing. (b) Corpus Christi College, No. XII, in large folio, written in a very bold hand. (c) University Library, I, 1, 2. 4, in a large (Canterbury?) hand, addressed to Wulfsige Bisceop. See § 71. The letters from Jewell to Parker pasted in this volume (Wanley, *Catalogus*, pp. 153, 168) seem to refer to *a*, not to this MS.

[1] Luard, preface to *Flores Historiarum*, i. xliv; Matthew Paris, *Chronica Maiora*, ii. xxii; iv. xvii. Similarly Sir F. Madden, preface to Paris, *Historia Anglorum*, i. xx, note 2, describes Parker's edition of the Flores as 'a mere piece of patchwork,' exhibiting 'an utter disregard of the ordinary rules to be observed in publishing an historical work.' Cf. the examples of Parker's treatment of the text given by him at p. xxxiv sqq., and Riley's remarks, preface to Walsingham's *Chronicle*, ii. p. xvii, note 3.

[2] Preface to Paris, *Hist. Anglorum*, p. xxxvii.

to him that he was a diligent student of MSS. His
unparalleled services in rescuing for posterity so many
priceless MSS. must cause his name to be ever held
in honour by the student of English historical materials,
and it is therefore a painful duty to blame him for his
treatment of this and other texts. Textual criticism
had hardly risen to a science in his time, and his
sins in editing are to a very great extent to be
ascribed to the faulty appreciation of differences in
the age and value of MSS. evidence that prevailed
in England long after his day. As a proof of the
accuracy of his texts so wrongly vaunted, he states
that he had willed that the *prima exemplaria* of them
should be preserved in the library of Corpus Christi
College, Cambridge, so that any one comparing his
printed texts with the originals might see that he
had faithfully reproduced the latter [1]. After his death
his MSS. were sent to the College, but, as appears
from a note of his son, Sir John Parker, many of
them had been ' either lent or embezeled,' so that
they could not be delivered to the College [2]. The

---

[1] Taken in conjunction with the terms of the Archbishop's
will (Strype, iii. 338), it is evident that he was referring to an
intended bequest of the MSS. printed by him, and did not mean
to convey that he had already deposited the MS. of the present
work in the College, as stated by Sir T. D. Hardy, *Monumenta
Historica Britannica*, p. 79, § 187 ; *Descriptive Catalogue*, i. 552.
The Archbishop's words are as follows : ' Quod autem ad historiae fidem attinet (lector humanissime), hoc te scire volo,
eam me semper rationem secutum, in omnibus iis libris, quos
divulgavi, nihil ut de meo adiecerim, aut diminuerim, sed cuncta
prout in primis exemplaribus reperiuntur ad verbum expres-
serim. . . . Indicio erunt ipsa prima exemplaria, quae idcirco
Cantebrigiae ⟨*sic*⟩, in bibliotheca Collegii Corporis Christi, ad
sempiternum huius rei testimonium, extare voluimus. Ubi si
quis cum codicibus manuscriptis impressos comparare voluerit,
enimvero nihil nos aut detraxisse aut addidisse inveniet, sed
summam ubique fidem et religionem praestitisse.'

[2] Quoted in the *Dict. of National Biography*, vol. xliii, 260,
from an original list at Corpus Christi College, Cambridge,
which cannot now be found.

MS. of the present work appears to have been one
of the missing ones, for in 1600 it was vainly sought
for in the College (§ 16). There is, however, in the
library the transcript of the present work prepared
for the Archbishop (§ 28), which follows his transcript
of the Annals of St. Neots. The juxtaposition of the
two is significant, for he incorporated from the latter
into his text of the Life all the matter relating to
England during the period covered by the Life [1].
This was, no doubt, done in good faith under the
idea that the Annals preserved a fuller text of the
work, but the result has been most disastrous. No
hint was given of the falsification of the text. He
did not scruple to supply here and there a word or
two of his own in order to connect the interpolated
matter with the text [2]. In accordance with his custom
he changed the spelling of words [3], substituted more
classical words and expressions for those of his original
that displeased him [4], and altered into classical forms

---

[1] The words *Ex Annalibus Asserii*, noted by Wise from the
Cott. MS. at the end of c. 50 d, are conclusive proof of the source
of the interpolations. Cf. also c. 50 b, 4. In one case (c. 31,
note to line 2) Parker interpolated from the Annals a passage
derived by the latter from the Norman Annals. In cc. 68, 3;
70, 6 he interpolated from the Annals of St. Neots later interlinear glosses to the latter.

[2] Thus he adds (c. 17 b) *Anno Dominicae Incarnationis* and
*et nativitatis Ælfredi octavo* to the date in the Annals in order
to harmonize with the style of the Life. Similarly *Dominicae
Incarnationis* appear in Parker's transcript (§ 28) in c. 50 c, 1,
but were omitted in the printed text.

[3] The normalization of the spelling of the original to the Latin
orthography of his age was what might be expected from any
editor of his time. The addition of a final *e* to an English word,
which there is reason to believe occurs occasionally, was also
in accordance with the custom of the time. Thus William
Lambarde, who acted as one of Parker's literary secretaries,
added or omitted final *e*'s at pleasure when copying O.E. MSS.
Cf. Liebermann, *Archiv f. das Studium d. neueren Sprachen*,
vol. cii, p. 269. See below, p. lxxvii, note 3.

[4] Thus he alters *intrans*, c. 82, 5, into *dirigens*; *dispoliatis* into

the local names[1]. In one case he interpolated, in addition to a passage from the Annals, the account of the same event given by Matthew of Paris[2]. By inexcusable carelessness his note at the end of c. 50 b referring to the Annals for further particulars, the interpolation from the Annals and Henry of Huntingdon, cc. 106 b, c (the former of which is a passage from the Annals with an interpolation from Huntingdon), and, worst of all, the abstract from John Bale, c. 106 d, a contemporary and friend of the Archbishop, were printed in Anglo-Saxon characters as part of the original MS. The great carelessness thus shown in preparing the copy for press is also evidenced by the overlooking of errors of tran-

*evaginatis*, c. 97, 9; *subarravit*, c. 29, 6, into *expetivit*; *coeti* (for *coetus*), c. 27, 24, into *capti*; *elimavit*, c. 56, 29, into *elevavit*; *oppido*, c. 37, 11, into *similiter*; *nimirum*, c. 106, 15, into *nec mirum*; *quis*, c. 88, 42, into *queis*; *etiam*, c. 105, 13, into *lucro*. The characteristic *suatim utens* of the original he perverts into *sua ipsius*, c. 56, 18, into *sublevatus est*, c. 74, 21, and into *advocatos*, c. 106, 22. He changed *cultu*, c. 100, 5, 11, into *curto*, and *roborans*, c. 74, 59, into *laborans*. He gives no hint that *inhiabat*, c. 105, 14, and *metuens*, c. 74, 47, did not occur in the MS. The commencement of c. 40 he tacitly omitted. He took like liberties with the interpolated matter, substituting *cymbas* for *cyulas*, c. 50 c, 6.

[1] Thus he changes the regular O.E. Latin *Cantia* into the classical *Cantium*, cc. 3, 9; 5, 4; 6, 3; 18, 5; 20, 9; 66, 5; 67, 2. He has also, obviously, tampered with the form of the name of the Thames. By writing the quasi-Latin *Brechoniae*, c. 80, 11, an impossible form at the date of the writing of the Cott. MS. of the Life, he obscured the Old Welsh *Brecheniauc*, which we have restored to the text. The late spelling *Hynguari*, c. 54, 1, seems to be derived from the Annals of St. Neots. Such a spelling as *Londonia*, cc. 4, 4; 83, 2, could not have occurred before the Norman Conquest. The transcriber is probably responsible for the late spelling *-burgh* in *Eadburgh*, cc. 14, 6; 15, 7, and *Osburgh*, c. 2, 1.

[2] Cc. 50 c, 50 d. Here the making of the interpolation is clearly recorded, for his transcript (§ 28) has a note ' Deest annus 877,' and the interpolated matter is added on an inserted piece of paper. It appears in the body of his printed text.

scription, even in the interpolations[1]. These alterations
and errors have been retained, almost without exception, in all the later editions. Most of the alterations
and interpolations were written in the Cott. MS. by
Parker's secretaries, in accordance with his custom[2].

§ 7. The second edition, published at Frankfort in
1602–3 by William Camden[3], is a mere reprint of

---

[1] Thus *Durngueis*, c. 49, 7, for the valuable form *Durngueir*;
*Gnavewic*, c. 50 c, 19, for *Suanewic*; *Suanavine* for *Suanauuic*,
c. 50 d, 3; *Stemrugam*, c. 17, 2, for *Steningam*; *Amgresbyri*,
c. 81, 22, for *Cungresbyri*; *aprino*, c. 54, 21, for *a primo*;
*Reafau*, c. 54 b, 2, for *Reafan*; *Habbe*, c. 54 b, 3, for *Hubbe*;
*Ine se*, c. 63, 4, for *Mese*; *fulconarios*, c. 76, 5, for *falconarios*;
*dixerit*, c. 78, 3, for *direxit*; *Farlus*, cc. 13, 8; 70, 1, 6; 85, 1,
13, for *Carlus*; *Domnanus*, c. 3, 3, for *Domnaniis*; *habitabile*,
c. 98, 3, for *habile*. *Cleolwulfo*, c. 51, 3; *refiam*, c. 52, 3; *qui*,
c. 57, 4, for *quae* are probably errors of the press. *Humbsensis*,
c. 26, 5, and *sex*, c. 38, 1, clearly arise from a printer's confusion
of the Anglo-Saxon ſ (=*s*) with *r*. *Wihtzur*, c. 2, 6, for *Wihtgar*,
appears to owe its *u* to the transcriber and its *z* to the printer.
*Æscendun*, c. 39, 18, for *Æsces*- (cf. c. 37, 3), and *Nunberctus*,
c. 17 b, 4, for *Hunberchtus* seem to be clerical or typographical
errors.

[2] Many of the MSS. that belonged to Parker have marginalia,
interlineations, glosses, &c., added to them in the hands of his
secretaries. Although he kept in his household 'such as could
imitate any of the old characters well,' and especially one Lyly,
'an excellent writer, and ⟨one⟩ that could counterfeit any
antique writing' (Strype, *Life of Parker*, ii. 5co), the additions
to the Cott. were made in the handwriting of Parker's time (§ 17).
Lambarde records that he made, by the Archbishop's order, an
interpolation in the *Textus Roffensis* (Strype, ii. 518). An interpolation in the Black Book of the Archdeacon of Canterbury
made by Parker led to a fierce protest at the time (*ibid.* 456).

[3] In the volume entitled: 'Anglica, Normannica, Hibernica,
Cambrica, a veteribus scripta: ex quibus Asser Meneuensis,
Anonymus de vita Gulielmi Conquestoris, Thomas Walsingham,
Thomas de la More, Gulielmus Gemiticensis, Giraldus Cam-
brensis: plerique nunc primum in lucem editi, ex bibliotheca
Guilielmi Camdeni. . . . Francofurti, impensis Claudii Marnii,
et haeredum Iohannis Aubrii. Anno M.DCIII.' folio. This
differs from the 1602 edition in having a dedication, lives of the
authors, and the prefixing of Parker's name to his preface. See
British Museum *Catalogue of Printed Books*.

Parker's text in Latin letters [1], as, indeed, he seems to convey [2]. A superficial examination will show that he reprints Parker's texts of the present work and of the other works included in his volume that had appeared under Parker's editorship. Everything in Parker's edition of Asser and Walsingham is reproduced, with the exception of the index to the latter writer. The portraits of kings, the tables, the preface to the O.E. version of the *Pastoral Care* and the interlinear Latin translation, and even the table of Anglo-Saxon letters with their Latin equivalents are reprinted. The sole reason for giving the latter is that Parker's preface to Asser speaks of his printing the text in Anglo-Saxon letters. Camden's printer adds a note that he has used Latin types because he did not possess the necessary O.E. letters, and he did not think it worth while to have them specially cut for so small a work. From this we may conclude that Camden supplied him with Parker's text, and that the printer instructed his compositors to replace the O.E. characters by their Latin equivalents according to Parker's table. A careful collation of Camden's text has revealed no variations from Parker beyond a few errors due, probably, to the printers [3],

---

[1] This was seen by Sir John Spelman, *Life of Ælfred the Great*, ed. Hearne, Oxford, 1709, p. 181, § 35, and Petrie, *Mon. Hist. Brit.*, p. 490 note, col. 2 ; Hardy, *ibid.*, p. 80 (his statement at p. 11, § 28, that the text was 'collated, however, with Camden's MS.' is groundless).

[2] In his preface : 'Anno vero 1575 Alfredi Regis res gestas, ... Historiam brevem Thomae Walsingham ... cum Hypodigmate Neustriae sive Normanniae 1574 publicavit ⟨Parkerus⟩, quos ⟨libros⟩ denuo, cum exemplaria in Anglia rarius inveniantur, Claudius Marnius e suo praelo nunc edit.' He nowhere mentions the MSS. of the works reprinted from Parker, whereas he speaks of the transcripts of the MSS. of the newly published matter.

[3] *Wanading*, c. 1, 3, for *Wanating* ; *Ecgberthi*, c. 1, 7, for *Ecgberhti* ; *Geada*, c. 1, 22, for *Geata* ; *Wicgam-*, c. 3, 4, for *Wicgan-* ; *Scheapieg*, c. 3, 6, for *Sceapieg* ; *Marciam*, c. 7, 6, for *Merciam* ; *Snotengaham*, c. 30, 3, for *Snotengaham* ; *Æthel-*

and one or two obvious corrections, which may have
proceeded from the printer's reader [1]. In addition to
these there are a few changes that have the character
of emendations such as a foreign printer might deem
needful [2]. The whole of Parker's marginal abstracts
and interpolations are reproduced, and his marginal
glosses are incorporated in the text. Even the note
at the end of cap. 50 b and the abstract from Bale
(c. 106 d) are repeated from Parker as if they were
part of the text. It is clear that Camden's text does
not rest upon any independent MS. basis, and that
it is, therefore, valueless for any critical purpose. It
has, however, been collated for the present edition,
and all variants from it noted, so that the reader may
see for himself how trivial are the differences between
Camden's text and that of Parker [3].

§ 8. But although Camden thus merely reproduced
Parker, he inserted in the text, without any explanation,
the famous chapter 83 b. This had previously appeared

---

*berti*, c. 21, 3, for -*berhti*; *Danubio*, c. 21, 5, for *Danubia*;
*Obsbern*, c. 39, 21, for *Osbern*; *Hungari*, c. 54 b, 3, for *Hinguari*; *advocarit*, c. 78, 4, for *advocavit*; *Fernail*, c. 80, 7, for
*Fernmail*. All these errors, except the first and third, are retained by Wise and Petrie. *Fatigatus*, c. 91, 6, for *fatigatur* is
probably due to confusion of the Anglo-Saxon characters for *r*
and *s*. Cf. p. xxi, note 1, above. *Gueryr*, c. 74, 20, for *Gueriir*,
may be an emendation by Camden.

[1] *Tradant*, c. 1, 31, for *tradunt*; *Davidicis*, c. 1, 32, for
*Daviticis*; *Indis*, c. 2, 5, for *Iutis*; *aufugerant*, c. 2, 13, for
*aufugerunt*; *Tamesin*, c. 35, 10, for *Tamesen*; *Healfdenae*,
c. 54, 1, for -*dene*; *Habbae*, c. 54 b, 3, for *Habbe*; the alteration
of *querelaretur* to *querelabatur*, c. 76, 41; *mandari*, c. 16, 11,
for *mandare*; *dividerentur*, c. 16, 29, for *divideretur*; *vasallis*,
cc. 53, 3; 55, 3, for *vassellis*; *liberalibus*, c. 106, 47, for *litteralibus*.

[2] *Centaurios*, c. 3, 8, for *Cantuarios*, must be due to the
foreign printer.

[3] The whole of Parker's alterations of words, &c., given
above, p. xix, note 4, p. xx, note 1, and the errors of Parker's
transcribers and printer mentioned in note 1, p. xxi, above, with
the exception of *refiam*, are reproduced by Camden.

in his *Britannia* in 1600, as *ex optimo manuscripto Asscrii exemplari*. It was intended to prove that there was already in existence at Oxford when Grimbald, one of Alfred's foreign scholars, and his followers are alleged to have begun teaching there, a body of *scholastici*, who resented the changes that Grimbald is asserted to have introduced. After three years of quarrelling the king is made to intervene, as the result of which Grimbald retires to Winchester. Grimbald is also said to have built the church and crypt of St. Peter's-in-the East, Oxford—a twelfth-century Norman church. The object of this interpolation is plain. It was to prove that the University was in existence before Alfred's time, and that it had enjoyed usages sanctioned by St. German, Gildas, Nennius, and Kentigern. It was thus a powerful argument for the Oxford champions who maintained, with a credulity only equalled by that of their opponents, that their University was an older foundation than that of Cambridge. This interpolation was not without its good effects, for the uproar caused by its publication directed attention to the MS. of the present work. Cambridge men pointed out that it did not appear in Parker's text, and denounced it as an interpolation and a forgery. The Oxford reply was that Parker, being a Cambridge man, had suppressed the passage purposely, because it told against the claims of his University, or that the MS. used by him, if it did not contain the passage, was imperfect, &c.[1]. It is needless to go further into this absurd

---

[1] A full account of the arguments and counter-arguments will be found in Wise's *Apologia* for Camden, printed at the end of his edition of Asser, pp. 133–164. Mr. James Parker, *Early History of Oxford*, Oxford Historical Society, 1885, pp. 40–47, also treats of this dispute. An important part of the case of the Oxford scholars who defended the authenticity of the passage was the view that Camden did not print from the Cottonian but from some other MS., and the consequent opinion that the latter was imperfect. The appearance of the words

dispute as to the relative antiquity of the two Universities, for modern criticism has shown that both are much younger than either side believed. The dispute was still rife in Wise's time, and he produced arguments as pitiable as anything advanced by Twyne, Wood, or Hearne to justify this passage. In strong contrast to the childish and disingenuous arguments advanced by these Oxford antiquaries stands the calm and accurate decision of Archbishop Ussher, that the passage was an unjustifiable interpolation by Camden [1].

§ 9. It is difficult to excuse Camden for this falsification of the text, whether he inserted the passage in good faith or not. On February 18, 1622-3, the credulous but well-meaning Brian Twyne succeeded, at an interview with Camden, in extracting a statement from him, which, if Twyne's account is

*probabant et ostendebant, idque indubitato veterum annalium* in the edition of the Life (c. 83 b, 16–17), and their absence from the 1600 edition of the *Britannia* are alone sufficient to throw doubts upon Camden's good faith. They are obviously intended to strengthen the claim put forth in the interpolation, which had been immediately challenged by the Cambridge advocates.

[1] *Britannicarum Ecclesiarum Antiquitates*, c. xi (*Opera*, ed. Elrington, Dublin, 1847, v. 392). Hearne, *Collections*, ed. Doble, i. 229, endeavoured to discount Ussher's evidence by the absurd suggestion that he was biassed in favour of Cambridge, because Trinity College, Dublin, the Archbishop's college, 'was, as it were, a colony from Cambridge.' The first Oxford scholar to estimate this interpolation at its true value was William Smith, Fellow of University College, who informed Hearne in 1705 that the passage was a forgery (Hearne's *Collections*, i. 146), an opinion that he still held when he published his *Annals of University College*, at Newcastle-upon-Tyne, in 1728, pp. 76, 173, 193. In this work he censures 'the nice arguings and sophisms' of Wood in maintaining the early history of the University (p. 53), in which he disbelieved. He exposed the origin of the fiction of the foundation of University College by King Alfred, and was evidently sceptical of the existence of the University in that king's time. With such critical views it is not surprising to find that he was described by Hearne (*Collections*, i. 38) as being 'known to be a man of but little judgment.'

true, throws a dark stain upon his fame[1]. Twyne desired him to state the origin of the passage, so as to clear himself of the charge of having interpolated it, a charge that had been hanging over him for twenty years. Camden's answer was most unsatisfactory. In the first place he said that he had already done so, and then that the charge came from his enemies who had so long persecuted him. and he attempted to fob off Twyne by telling him that his extensive researches into the antiquities of the University would enable him to appreciate the genuineness of the passage, although it must have been obvious that he had failed to convince himself, willing as he was to believe it, that it was true. Finally Camden, after further pressure, said, in answer to the question whether he had received the passage from any one, or whether he had taken it from an approved exemplar, that he had caused 'the whole entire history of Asserius, which I published, to be transcribed out of a manuscript copie, which I had then in my hands, wherein that place now questioned was extant, and in the very same forme as there I found it, and in none other.' This statement is incompatible with the clear proof that he simply reprinted Parker's text. The mysterious MS. alleged by him, which he had called *optimum exemplar* in his *Britannia*, he now stated was written, as he thought, about the time of Richard II. It was a monstrous thing under these circumstances to set

---

[1] From a declaration by Twyne, printed from an attested copy in Wood, *History and Antiquities of the University of Oxford*, ed. Gutch, Oxford, 1792, i. 22. The original declaration was sought in vain among Twyne's papers at Corpus Christi College by Wise (p. 139), but he states that Hearne had seen it there not long before. It occurs, however, among Twyne's MSS. in the University Archives (Twyne MSS. xxii. 385-7), where it is preceded by what appears to be a first draught of the declaration. Camden was probably in bad health at the time of the interview. He was described in the April preceding as being 'much decayed' (Ussher's *Opera*, xv. 173).

up its evidence against that of Parker's MS., which
he could easily have ascertained was much older than
this date. But this mysterious MS. has evaded the
search of all subsequent investigators.

§ 10. Twyne professed himself satisfied with this
explanation, 'forasmuch as some give out, as though
there was never any such copie at all to be seen, and as
though he, who I heare was the owner of that copie,
had been also the author thereof (especially of that
place now questioned), namely one Mr. Henry Savile
of the Banke [1],' &c. Twyne elsewhere records, upon
the authority of Thomas Allen [2], a well-known Oxford
collector of MSS., that Savile lent the MS. from which
the passage was alleged to have been taken to one
Nettleton [3], that Savile proceeded against Nettleton
at law to recover it, but did not succeed, and that
Nettleton's books, at his death, came into the hands
of Savile, a baron of the Exchequer [4], when this
volume alone was found to be missing [5]. It is an

---

[1] Henry Savile, 1568-1617, of Bank, near Halifax, known as
'Long Harry Savile,' is to be distinguished from Sir Henry
Savile, the famous Warden of Merton College, 1585-1621, and
Provost of Eton, 1596-1621, with whom Mr. Parker, *Early
History of Oxford*, p. 43, has confused him. He was a B.A. of
Merton College, taking his M.A. from St. Alban Hall in 1595.
An account of him is given by Wood, *Athenae Oxonienses*,
ed. 2, i. col. 419, and *History and Antiquities of the Uni-
versity*, ed. Gutch, i. 24; *Dict. of National Biography*, l. 369.
He died April 29, 1617.

[2] Of Trinity College and Gloucester Hall. See *Dict. of
National Biography*, i. 312.

[3] Probably Thomas Nettleton, of Thornhill, near Dewsbury,
co. York, a neighbour of the Saviles of Bank.

[4] Sir John Savile, 1545-1607, Baron of the Exchequer, 1598,
brother of the Warden of Merton and a friend of Camden's.
See *Dict. of National Biography*, l. 371. A letter from him to
Camden is printed in Camden's *Epistolae*, ed. Smith, London,
1691, p. 36.

[5] *Antiquitatis Academiae Oxoniensis Apologia*, Oxford, 1608,
lib. ii. p. 144. Thoresby, the Leeds antiquary, seems to have
searched for this alleged Savile MS., for he writes to Hearne, on

unsatisfactory story. Ussher, a friend of Camden's, also refers to the view that the passage in question was derived from a MS. in the possession of Henry Savile[1]. It is to be regretted, as Wise has remarked[2], that Twyne did not follow up the clue before Henry Savile's death. The latter was an accomplished scholar, interested in antiquities, and living in London. He can hardly have failed to learn something of the controversies excited by the publication of the passage, but no utterance of his was known to the persons interested in maintaining its authenticity. It is obviously spurious, and it cannot have been much older than Savile's time, for it employs *divus* for 'saint,' a usage due to the classicalism of the Renaissance scholars[3]. It is noticeable that Henry Savile was suspected of interpolating a passage relating to Oxford University in Ingulph[4].

§ 11. In 1722 the Oxford University Press published an edition of the work by Francis Wise, M.A., Fellow of Trinity College[5], adorned with a portrait of King

16 October, 1708, 'I am sorry the MS. you enquire of, cannot be found at Mr. Savile's' (Hearne's *Collections*, ii. 140).

[1] *Antiquitates*, c. xi (*Opera*, v. 392). Ussher's deliberate statement that Camden never saw the copy whence this passage was alleged to be derived, was, no doubt, founded upon something that Camden had told him.

[2] Page 135. Twyne refers erroneously to Henry Savile as an old man in 1608, probably through confusion with some other Savile.

[3] Cf. Professor Mayor, introduction to Richard of Cirencester's *Speculum Historiale*, ii. pp. cv, clxiii.

[4] Wood, *Athenae*, i. col. 420, *Hist. and Antiqq.*, i. 24. John Jocelyn, in a composite chronicle made by him and preserved in his own writing, Cott. MS. Vitellius E xiv, used a work described in the early seventeenth century table of contents, which is probably copied from one by Jocelyn, as *Per anonimum* (sic) *apud Mr. Savell Eboracensem*. If this was, as Strype thinks (*Life of Parker*, ii. 250), a work commenced by Jocelyn under Parker's directions, the Mr. Savell can hardly be Long Harry Savile.

[5] Wise, who was a sub-librarian of the Bodleian, was an antiquary of some repute. He was a young man in 1722. He

Alfred and admirable vignettes of Parker and Camden
by George Vertue, and other illustrations. It also
included a facsimile of the first fourteen lines of the
first page of the MS. (§ 15). Unfortunately Wise did
not see the MS. himself, but relied upon collations
made for him by his friend James Hill, of the Middle
Temple[1]. It is evident that Hill performed his task
in a very perfunctory manner, for Wise's text reproduces almost all the alterations and errors of Parker's
text that were retained by Camden[2], and also most
of those due to Camden and his printer[3]. Hence it
is clear that Hill used a copy of Camden's text for
the purpose of collating. On two occasions Wise
gives readings from the MS. in chapters that he had
marked as not occurring in it[4]. As the interpolations
were written in the MS. in a Parkerian hand (§ 16),
it is clear that Hill has in these instances failed to
distinguish between the hand of the MS. and the
Parkerian one. This confusion renders it probable
that in other cases the readings given by Wise as
those of the MS. were really alterations by Parker[5].

was born on June 3, 1695, and survived until 1767 (*Dict. of
National Biography*, lxii. 238).

[1] Wise, p. 137 and preface, p. [2]. Hill was a Herefordshire
antiquary. See *Dict. of National Biography*, xxvi. 394. Hill
was also a member of Trinity College, matriculating on May 15,
1713, age 16 (Foster, *Alumni Oxonienses*).

[2] He retains uncorrected the misprints in Parker's edition
noticed above, p. xxi, note 1, under cc. 49, 7; 50 c, 19; 50 d, 3;
81, 22; 76, 5; 70, 1, 6; 85, 1, 13; 51, 3; 57, 4; 2, 6; 39, 18.

[3] All the errors noted at p. xxii, note 3, remain uncorrected
except 1, 22; 91, 6, and also all the alterations mentioned at
p. xxiii, note 1, are reproduced.

[4] See cc. 17 b; 54 b. Petrie, *Mon. Hist. Brit.* 472 note *d*,
481 note *c*, thinks these may have been derived by Wise from
another MS. There are no grounds for this belief.

[5] Wise prints silently Parker's alterations as specified above,
p. xix, note 4 in cc. 97, 9; 56, 18, 29; 74, 21, 59; 106, 22, and the
alterations of *Cantia* into *Cantium* in the seven examples given
at p. xx, note 1. He does not notice that the MS. had *cultu* and
not *curto* in c. 100, 5, 11, where the former reading is supported

Wise, probably relying upon the absence from Hill's collations of any notes to the contrary, occasionally states that the MS. had forms that we have evidence did not appear in it. Thus the word *Indis*, c. 2, 5, which he says occurred in the MS., has no other basis than an error or alteration in Camden's text, for we have the clear evidence of Archbishop Ussher that the reading in the MS. was *Iutis*[1], as in Parker's text and the transcripts. Similarly Wise prints *Wanading*, c. 1, 3, from Camden, whereas his facsimile shows that the MS. had *Uuanating*. In some cases Wise states that the MS. had readings that do not appear in the best transcript, and which seem to be due to the carelessness of Parker's transcribers or printer[2]. There are in addition numerous other passages in which we may well doubt whether the MS. had the readings given by Wise in the body of the text. He makes no note that the passage at the end of c. 53, referring to the Life of St. Neot, was an interpolation of Parker's, as we may conclude that it was from its absence from two transcripts, and from the existence of a note of Parker's in the best transcript, which plainly led him to interpolate this and the succeeding chapter[3]. We are, therefore, unable to endorse the great praise that has been bestowed upon Wise's edition, and hold that for textual purposes its value

by Florence of Worcester, and by its occurrence in the MS., according to Wise's own note, in line 21 of the same chapter. The *curto* of c. 81, 10 was also, probably, an emendation of Parker's.

[1] See the note to this passage.

[2] Thus *Faroli* for *Caroli*, c. 13, 8; *capti* for *coeti* (i. e. *coetus*), c. 27, 24; *Ine se* for *Mese*, c. 63, 4; *fulconarios* for *falc-*, c. 76, 5. In the latter case the correct reading appears in Parker's transcript (Co), the corrupt one in transcript B. The misreading of *a* as *u*, which is easy in Elizabethan hands, is a most unlikely error in transcribing an eleventh century MS.

[3] Similarly Wise has no note that *genere suo*, c. 83, 4, *lucro*, c. 105, 13, and the alterations and errors of Parker and Camden retained by him, did not occur in the MS.

is below that of the Corpus transcript (§ 28). It is, however, of great service in strengthening the evidence of the transcript in question that certain passages were absent from the MS., and also in occasionally giving corrections from the MS. From it also we are able to distinguish the parts that were in the early hand from those in the later one. But here, again, the evidence is incomplete, for Wise enables us to divide the work between two scribes only, whereas in his description of the MS. he says it was written by several (§ 22).

§ 12. The last edition was that of Henry Petrie in the *Monumenta Historica Britannica*, published in 1848, but prepared many years before. So far as the text is concerned, this edition is merely a reprint of Wise's, so that the errors and alterations of Parker and Camden, and even those of Wise, are retained. The value of the edition lies in the fact that the transcripts and the Annals of St. Neots were collated. The collating, however, was not done in a very trustworthy manner [1], and many discrepancies will be found between the readings given in our apparatus and those cited by Petrie. In every case of difference we have re-collated the passages, so that the reader may rest satisfied that any reading given by Petrie that does not appear in our apparatus, or that varies from our reading, does not really exist. The interpolations are distinguished by the use of square brackets, but, as we have seen (§ 3), the means adopted have been inadequate for the purpose.

§ 13. A translation of the Life was published by Dr. J. A. Giles in *Six Old English Chroniclers*, in Bohn's 'Antiquarian Library,' London, 1848, and another one by Joseph Stevenson, in the *Church Historians of England*, London, 1854, ii. 441 sqq.

[1] It should be noted that in Petrie's collations B refers to the Corpus transcript (Co), and C to the British Museum transcript (B), not, as stated by him (p. 467 note a), *vice versa.*

Still another version is given in *Alfred and the Chroniclers*, by Edward Conybeare, London, 1900, p. 85 sqq.

## 2. DESCRIPTION OF THE LOST MANUSCRIPT.

§ 14. The only MS of the work of which we have any record formed the first tract in a composite volume of MSS. in the Cottonian collection, marked Otho A xii. This volume was almost entirely destroyed in the unfortunate fire in the Cottonian Library on October 23, 1731. The 'Report of the Committee appointed to view the Cottonian Library, published by order of the House of Commons, London, 1732,' marks the first tract of the volume, *Asserius Menevensis de gestis Alfredi Regis, charactere antiquo*, as 'lost, burnt, or intirely spoilt.' Some fragments of the volume survived the fire, and have been restored in modern times. They are now preserved in the British Museum under the old press-mark. No portion of Asser has been found amongst them, and Sir Edward Maunde Thompson informs us that no fragments of the Life exist in the Museum, unless in the form of charred and illegible relics of the fire.

§ 15. Under these circumstances we are dependent upon secondary sources for our knowledge of the MS. Amongst these the facsimile published by Wise naturally ranks first. It was supplied to Wise by James Hill[1], by whom the unsatisfactory collation for Wise's edition was made (§ 11). The facsimile is evidently a very inaccurate one, giving an appearance of irregularity that is alien to the handwriting of the tenth or eleventh century. It is difficult to reconcile this with Wise's statement that the MS. was neatly written (§ 22). So far as one can trust this facsimile, it seems to represent a hand of the early part of the

---

[1] Wise, preface, p. [2]. It is here reproduced.

Domino meo venerabili piissimoque·
omnium brittannie insulae xpiano
rum · rectori · ælfred · anglorum saxo
num · regi · Asser · omnium · servo
rum dei ultimus · mille modam
advota desideriorum · utriusque
vitae · prosperitatem ·

Anno dominicæ
incarnationis · DCCC·XLIX· natus
est ælfred angul saxonum rex in villa
regia quedicitur nuanating nulla paga
que nominatur berrocscire que paga taliter
uocatur aberrocsilua ubibuxus habundan
tissime nasettur cuius genelogia talis serie

*To face p.* xxxii

eleven th century [1]. There is a great variety in the
forms of certain letters in the facsimile, some of which
are no doubt ascribable to careless tracing of the
original. That the scribe of this portion of the MS.
was an Englishman is proved by the fact that he uses
the Anglo-Saxon forms of *f*, *r*, and *d* in *Ælfred*,
line 10. The rest of the facsimile is written in the
modification of the Caroline minuscule employed by
English scribes in writing Latin in the late tenth and
early eleventh centuries [2].

§ 16. We now come to descriptions of the MS. by
scholars who saw it before the Cottonian fire. Parker
gives us very little information regarding it, except that
it was in a very ancient hand (§ 5). It was clearly
his own property [3]. The MS. seems to have been

---

[1] Amongst other traits pointing to such a date may be mentioned the absence of the hyphen as a mark of the division of
words at the ends of the lines in all cases (*Christiano-rum*,
*Saxo-num*, *servo-rum*, *babundan-eissime*, an error in tracing for
*hab-* ?). The hyphen seldom occurs before the eleventh century,
when it came gradually into general use (Wattenbach, *Anleitung
zur lateinischen Palaeographie*, ed. 4, 87). The curling back-
wards of the down-stroke of the *s* in *serie*, last line of facsimile,
occurs in Cott. Charter Augustus, ii. 22, a contemporary text of
1001 (Brit. Museum *Facs*. iv. pl. 12), the hand of which has
several features in common with that in Wise's facsimile.

[2] A Welsh scribe of the ninth or tenth century would have
employed the Hiberno-Saxon hand throughout, and would not
have used it simply for writing English names.

[3] This may be concluded from his preface, and from the
writing and marks made by him in the MS. (§§ 16, 17, 19). It
is also confirmed by a note of Jocelyn's in Cott. Nero C iii 47,
fo. 191 b, of the *Nomina eorum, qui scripserunt historiam gentis
Anglorum, et ubi extant*, printed by Hearne, *Robert of Aves-
bury*, p. 269 sqq. Here we read *Asserius Menevensis. Vide
Baleum*, and a marginal note ' *Habet Mr. Boyer et Stowe, et
Domina Cheke, et Archiep. Cant.* print.' Of these, Stowe's MS.
was, no doubt, the translation mentioned by Bernard, *Catalogi
Librorum Manuscriptorum Angliae*, Oxford, 1697, ii. p. 387,
No. 10,006, in the library of Sir Symond D'Ewes, which was
written in Stowe's hand. Lady Cheke's and Bowyer's copies
were probably transcripts. See, however, p. xxxv, note 1 below.

previously in the hands of John Leland, the antiquary,
who died in 1552. He describes it as 'Asserii Menevensis Historia, qui Alfredi res gestas accurate per-
scripsit,' and as 'Asserii Annales[1].' The passages
quoted by him from it agree very closely with the
text of the Cottonian MS.[2], and in one case his
quotation omits the verb, just as the Cottonian MS.
did[3]. Unfortunately he gives no indication of the

Possibly Jocelyn includes the Annals of St. Neots, which were
then held to be the work of Asser.

[1] *Commentarii de Scriptoribus Britannicis*, ed. Anthony Hall,
Oxford, 1709, pp. 144, 148, 149, 150, 153, 154, 157. By 'Annales'
he does not mean the Annals of St. Neots, often called 'Asser's
Annals' by later writers, but the Life. Leland's enthusiasm
led him to take a higher view of the literary merits of this work
than modern critics have done (p. 157) : 'quod Asserius patroni
sui memoriam, famam, gloriam, modis omnibus cum longissimam
tum clarissimam efficere studens, eius vitam atque adeo facta
illustria omnia libro *Annalium* victuro eleganter, pro rei maie-
state, tanquam rarus Apelles, depinxerit ; ac demum tabulas vel
medio foro spectandas produxerit ; quarum et Marianus Scottus
⟨i. e. Florence of Worcester⟩, venustate totus captus, flores ex
eisdem avidus, veluti stellulas, quibus suam interpolaret historiam,
selegit.' In the notes to his *Cygnea Cantio*, published in 1545,
under 'Alfridus,' he mentions 'Asserius Menevensis,' afterwards
Bishop of Sherborne, as author of the History of Alfred, 'cuius
ego historiam plurimi merito facio, quod Alfrido regi praeceptor
aliquando fuerit, et eius factorum oculatus plane testis' (in
Hearne's edition of Leland's *Itinerary*, ix. p. 32).
[2] In the *Commentarii* he quotes c. 77, 10–24 at p. 144, c. 81,
12–15 at p. 150, c. 102, 17–19 at p. 149, and c. 77, 20–24, with
variations, at p. 150, but more correctly at p. 144. These
passages cannot have been derived by him from the Annals of
St. Neots, which omit them. He refers to c. 106, 32 sqq. at
p. 151, and uses information derived from this chapter in his
notices of Alfred, Asser, Edward the Elder, and Werfrith.
William of Malmesbury's reference to the King's *Enchiridion*
he traces to c. 89, 20 at p. 150, and in like manner he refers
this author's description of Edward as *literatissimus* to Asser
⟨c.75, 21⟩ at p. 153. See § 36, p. lxiii, below. Leland's statement
that Æthelwulf was buried at Steyning, p. 145, is derived from
the Annals of St. Neots (see c. 17).
[3] Cap. 75, 26–31, at p. 157, omitting the verb in line 28.

place where he found the MS.[1]. Mr. Henry Bradshaw asserted that the Cottonian MS. came from
St. Augustine's abbey, Canterbury[2], but he adduced
no authority for the statement, and we have been
unable to find any proof of it. The Life is not mentioned in the list of books in the library at St. Augustine's given by Leland[3], and it does not occur amongst
the historical books in the mediaeval catalogue of this
library[4]. John Bale seems to have had access to
this or some other MS. of the Life, for in his notice
of Asser[5], which, like the rest of his work, is based
upon Leland, he mentions the persecution of Asser
and his kinsman, the bishop of St. Davids, by King

[1] Upon Leland's death in 1552 his MSS. were taken possession of by Sir John Cheke, by order of Edward VI. See the
note of William Burton, the Leicestershire antiquary, at the
end of Hall's edition of the *Scriptores*. Upon Cheke's death
in 1557 the MSS. came into the hands of William Cecil, and
others. According to Jocelyn, Cheke's widow had a MS. of
Asser (see p. xxxiii, note 3, above). As this note seems to have
been written after the Cottonian MS. had come into the possession of Archbishop Parker, it can hardly refer to that MS.,
unless we assume that the Archbishop acquired it from Lady
Cheke and that Jocelyn, his literary secretary, was ignorant of
the identity of Parker's copy with that of Lady Cheke.

[2] *Collected Papers*, p. 485. This learned scholar does not
display his usual accuracy in dealing with the Life, for he refers
here and at p. 467 to the existence of fragments of the Cottonian
MS. See p. cxii, note 3, below.

[3] *Collectanea*, ed. Hearne, iii. p. 7.

[4] Printed by Sir Frederic Madden in *Notes and Queries*,
Second Series, i. 485, and in Edward Edwards, *Memoirs of
Libraries*, 1859, i. 102. Dr. Montague R. James, who is preparing a complete edition of this catalogue, informs us that he
is unable to find any mention of the Life in it. The catalogue
is, however, incomplete. The fourteenth-century catalogue of
the library of Christ Church, Canterbury, contains nothing that
can be identified with the Life (Wanley, *Catalogus* 'praefatio,'
sign. b 2 *verso*; Edwards, *Memoirs*, i. 122 sqq.). Parker
obtained his MSS. from other places besides Canterbury.

[5] *Illustrium Maioris Britanniae Scriptorum . . . Summarium, in quasdam centurias divisum*, Ipswich, 1548, ' Cen-
turia Secunda.'

Hemeid (c. 79, 54), which does not appear in Leland
or in Florence of Worcester. Bale gives no clue to
the *provenance* of the MS., but in the MS. notebook
containing the materials for his *Summarium* he cites
the Life 'ex bibliotheca Ioannis Lelandi [1].' We next
hear of the Life in connexion with the controversy
engendered by the claim made on behalf of Cambridge University to greater antiquity than Oxford
upon the occasion of Elizabeth's visit to it in
1566. John Caius, the Cambridge champion, in his
curiously discursive work on the antiquity of his
university [2], refers to 'Asser seu Asserus, oculatus et
auritus testis, qui ex intimis Alphredi familiaribus
fuit, qui in eius aula vixit, res eius et domesticas et
forenses novit, atque etiam cum doctis regiae familiae
viris consuetudinem habuit, omniaque in vita et in
morte diligenter observavit, ut solent qui historias
veras scribere decreverunt [3].' He refers incidentally
to Asser's account of Alfred's life in Athelney [4], but
as he also cites the vision of St. Neot as from him [5],
it would seem that he has identified the Annals of
St. Neots with Asser. Several of his references occur
in Leland's *De Scriptoribus* [6], from the MS. of which
he may have obtained them, but he clearly knew of
the Life as distinct from the Annals of St. Neots, for
he mentions the relation of the attack upon John the
Old Saxon as occurring in Asser's 'libro de gestis
Alphredi atque etiam in Annalibus [7],' a passage that

---

[1] *Index Britanniae Scriptorum*, ed. R. L. Poole, Oxford, 1902,
p. 35.
[2] *De Antiquitate Cantabrigiensis Academiae, libri duo . . .
Londinensi Authore*. London, 1568. Reprinted by Hearne,
Oxford, 1730.
[3] Page 209, ed. Hearne. He describes Asser as 'Aluredi
sacellanus,' p. 203. Cf. also pp. 205, 218.
[4] Page 223.    [5] Page 204.
[6] Page 118 (Leland, p. 149) ; pp. 212, 218 (Leland, p. 149).
[7] Page 159. Clear evidence that he used the Life and not
the Annals or Florence may be found in his statement that

shows his acquaintance with the titles given by Bale
or Parker to the Life and to the Annals. As Parker
was his literary executor, it is probable that he
derived his knowledge of the Life from Parker's MS.
The Oxford champion, Thomas Caius, who died in
1572, frequently quotes or cites Asser[1], but most of
his quotations are taken from the Annals[2]. He,
however, copied c. 75, 11–21 from the Life[3], for this
passage was omitted by the compiler of the Annals.
It cannot be derived from Florence of Worcester,
since it contains words that Florence did not copy
into his work. We now come to clear and undoubted
references to the MS. The first occurs in a letter,
dated March 31, 16co, from Thomas James, the
first Bodley's librarian, to Thomas Allen[4]. In this
letter James says that he had received Allen's letter
on the last day of December in Cambridge, and
that he had, in consequence, 'sought and sought
again' for the MS. of Asserius Menevensis amongst
the MSS. of Parker's gift in Benet ⟨i. e. Corpus
Christi⟩ College, and elsewhere, but unsuccessfully.
He writes that he had discovered the MS. in
London, in Lord Lumley's library, within the preceding three weeks. His letter is principally concerned with the Camden interpolation (c. 83 b), in

Asser wrote the king's life down to his forty-fifth year (p. 214),
referring to c. 91, 4.

[1] In his animadversions on John Caius, first printed by
Hearne with the work of John Caius.

[2] Pp. 374 (c. 47, 9–12), 408 (c. 92, 5–7), 426 (c. 52, 7–8),
427 (c. 42, 30–35 ; c. 43). There are several other quotations
that may have been taken either from the Life or the Annals,
being passages in which the compiler has introduced no alterations.

[3] Page 423.

[4] James's letter is preserved among Twyne's MSS. in the
Oxford University Archives, iii. 25, and a copy in ii. 75, and
another in Rawlinson MS. D in the Bodleian Library, olim 1290,
nunc 912, fo. 685. See Clarke's edition of Wood's *Life and
Times*, Oxford Historical Society, ii. p. vii ; iv. 198.

which Allen was evidently deeply interested. James identified the Lumley MS. as the one used by Parker from information obtained by him and from the evidence of the volume itself. He describes the MS. as containing notes in red ochre in Parker's hand, with many corrections of errors by the Archbishop's pen, and as an ancient MS. written by at least two hands, the latter part being in a hand that he considered much later than the other one. This later hand, however, used many Anglo-Saxon characters[1]. He notes in the Catalogue that he was then engaged upon, which was published in the same year, that there were two copies of the work in Lord Lumley's library[2]. As he makes no mention of a second MS.

[1] 'I have not only found out a coppie of him (which peradventure you have seene and so hath Mr. Camden likewise elsewhere, yet wowld not answere you), but the very same coppy which I knowe most assuredly the Archebyshop used and you longed to heare of. This booke I sawe, and ⟨it⟩ is to be seene, in the riche and well-furnisht librarie of the right Honourable and right courteous Lord Lumley, with whome I have beene diuerse times, and have from him a coppy of all his manuscripts, which, ere it be long, you shall see. That this booke did belong unto the Archbyshop sometimes, it was told me by the keeper of his librarie, and I fownd it by the Archbyshop's notes of redd oker in diuerse places of the booke, which was usually by him used in all his bookes which he read, as I had seene at Cambridg amonge his bookes there.' He then notices the absence of Camden's interpolation. He proceeds: 'Nevertheles for this copie which the Archebyshop used, thowgh it beare good antiquitie in show, yet I take it to be very faultie; and the Archebyshop hath noted very many escapes ⟨i. e. *lapsus*⟩ with his pen; and besides it was written by two diverse scribes at the least, whereof the later parte of the book, where the poynte in controversie lyeth ⟨c. 83 b⟩, is by much in my opinion the latest, yet hath it many Saxon letters, especially the letters ɼ and *f*, but hereof judge you. The whole booke contayneth pages 107 in the least folio or greater quarto.' He then sets out the dedication, commencement and end of the text (c. 106), which agree exactly with the Cottonian MS.

[2] *Ecloga Oxonio-Cantabrigiensis . . . opera et studio T. I. Novi Collegii in Alma Academia Oxoniensi Socii, Londini,*

in the library in his letter to Allen, in which he recounts the lengthened searches that he had made for MSS. of this work, we may conclude that the second MS. was a transcript. Lumley inherited his library from his father-in-law, Henry, Earl of Arundel, 1511–1580, and at Lumley's death, in 1609, it was sold to King James for the use of Henry, Prince of Wales, and subsequently became part of the Royal Library, now in the British Museum. Hence this transcript may be B (§ 29), which seems to have come from the Royal Library, or Ar (§ 30), which bears the name Arundel upon its first page.

§ 17. In the Lumley Library the MS. was seen by Brian Twyne, who, for controversial purposes, maintains the imperfection of the MS., and doubts whether it was the copy from which Parker printed. He describes it as being marked with red ochre by Parker's own hand, as being imperfect in places, and as filled out with appended pieces of paper in modern handwriting[1]. This marking in red ochre is a well-known characteristic of Parker, and its presence in

1600, lib. ii. 78. In addition to his personal acquaintance with Lumley's library, he received information from Lumley, as appears from his letter to Allen, and from his advice to the reader in his *Ecloga*, ii. § 5.

[1] *Antiquitatis Academiae Oxoniensis Apologia*, Oxford, 1608, p. 144, § 80: 'nisi eum ⟨Parkerum⟩ imperfecto exemplari (quod fortasse in Domini Lumlaei bibliotheca rubra ocra manu propria notatum vidi, mancum tamen et plurimis in locis imperfectum et chartulis appenditiis recenter scriptis suffultum) usum fuisse dicas.' Twyne's MSS. iii. 254 in the University Archives contain a memorandum of his, written shortly after 1630, to inquire 'what is become of the coppy of Asserius that was in the Lord Lumley's library, of which Dr. James writes to Mr. Allen, &c.: because at the ende thereof he saith it set downe at large the foundinge, not the repayringe of the university by Alfred. Mr. Richard James thinkes it is in St. James library.' The passage thus unwarrantably described by Dr. James in his letter of 1600 (see p. xxxviii, note 1, above) seems to be c. 102, 17–19, the nucleus of the mediaeval stories connecting the University of Oxford with Alfred.

the Lumley MS. is, as stated by James, proof of the identity with Parker's MS. It was described as still in the Lumley Library in 1602 by Pits [1].

§ 18. We next hear of the MS. in the possession of Cotton, in whose library it was seen by Archbishop James Ussher, who collated it for his great work, the *Britannicarum Ecclesiarum Antiquitates* [2],

---

[1] *Ioannis Pitsei Relationum Historicarum de rebus Anglicis tomus I*, Paris, 1619, p. 172 : 'Vitam et res gestas Regis Ælfredi Latine. Librum unum. *Anno Dominicae Incarnationis* 849. MS. in bibliotheca Baronis Lunleiani. Extat anno 1602.' From Pits, Bishop Tanner, *Bibliotheca Britannico-Hibernica*, London, 1748, p. 53, copied this reference to the Lumley MS.

[2] *Praefatio*, p. 6 : 'Ac primum, ne quid hic me fugeret, editorum nostrorum historicorum antiquiores quidem, Gildam, Adamnanum, Bedam, Asserium Menevensem, integros, posteriores vero, ubi videbatur opus, cum manuscriptis codicibus diligenter, nec sine fructu, contuli.' Twenty-five years before the publication of his book he wrote to Camden : 'I have been as carefull as I could in viewing the places of authors by me alleged, and, as much as might be, would trust no man's eyes but mine own. Yet in some manuscripts, which were to be had only beyond seas, I have been forced to give credit unto others.' April 28, 1614 (*Opera*, xv. 78). As he spent much time in England, and was frequently borrowing MSS. from the Cottons, we may conclude that he collated the MS. of the present work himself. He refers specifically to the MS. in correcting an error of Camden's (see note to c. 2, 5). His correspondence contains notices of extensive borrowings from the Cottonian collection. Thus on August 4, 1625, Selden asks him for two of Cotton's MSS. of the Old English Chronicle, which he promises to return to him, if he wish (xv. 290). In 1622 Cotton acknowledges the return of eight MSS. from Ussher, who still had others in his hands. Cotton offers to send him whatever MSS. he might wish for (xv. 171). At one time Ussher had in his hands three MSS. of the Chronicle belonging to Cotton (xv. 230). Other notices of borrowings and long-detention of MSS. of Cotton's occur at pp. 274, 283, 386, 428. Some idea of the care with which Ussher worked may be formed from the statement that he used eleven MSS. of Nennius (xvi. 231). In 1624 he borrows from Patrick Young, the keeper of the Prince's Library (xv. 266), a copy of the present work (xv. 270), which seems obviously to be the transcript referred to at xv. 233, and hence is probably our B (§ 29) or Ar (§ 30).

which was given to the world, after many years'
labour upon it, in 1639. The testimony of this great
scholar regarding the MS. is of much greater importance than that of any one else who has left us an
account of the MS., with the solitary exception of
Wanley. Ussher was immeasurably superior in critical
power to the writers whom we are able to cite.
Passing from Parker, Camden, Anthony Wood,
Hearne, and Wise to Ussher gives one the impression
of being suddenly transferred from the critical atmosphere of the later Middle Ages to that of modern
times. He describes the MS. as a copy written in
Anglo-Saxon characters, and dating, if not from
Asser's own time, certainly from a period not far
removed from it[1]. Although the Archbishop has
ascribed too high an antiquity to the handwriting of
the MS., his evidence is valuable as showing how
antique the hand seemed to a very careful and diligent
student of ancient MSS., and one with a special knowledge of O.E. MSS. Unfortunately his collations of
the MS. are not to be found amongst his papers in
Trinity College, Dublin[2]. They would have been of
the greatest importance in constituting the text.

[1] After quoting Twyne's description (§ 17), Ussher states that
the matter added upon inserted pieces of paper is not taken
from any copy of Asser, but from certain annals ⟨those of
St. Neots⟩ that have been wrongly attributed to Asser because
they contained much matter transcribed from him. He protests
against Camden's description *optimum exemplar* of the alleged
Savile MS.: 'quum antiquissimum antigraphum, si non ipsius,
quod omnino videtur, Asserii, certe proximis ab eo temporibus,
characteribus Saxonicis exaratum, adhuc in Cottoniana Bibliotheca conservetur' (*Britannicarum Ecclesiarum Antiquitates,*
Dublin, 1639, c. 11, *Opera,* v. 393). By Saxon characters he
probably meant that it was written in a hand older than the
Norman Conquest, although not in specifically Anglo-Saxon
characters.

[2] Professor Lawlor has been kind enough to examine for me
the two copies of Parker's edition and the three copies of
Camden's in the library of Trinity College, without finding any
*marginalia.*

§ 19. Through the intervention of Ussher Sir John Spelman, who died in 1643, was enabled to inspect the MS. He states that it was, in the opinion of many, the MS. used by Parker, that it was written in a character resembling the Anglo-Saxon, and that it had marks in red ochre, by which, as he says, Parker was wont to note MSS. used by him. He mentions that it contained interpolations in a later hand, among which, however, the Camden interpolation did not occur [1].

§ 20. Anthony Wood, in his *History and Antiquities of the University of Oxford*, published in Latin in 1674, repeats as his own words what Dr. James said in 1600 (§ 16) [2] regarding the correction of the errors in the MS. by Parker 'or else his assistant, Mr. John Josseline,' as he adds, and the later date of the second hand, omitting, however, the mention of the use of Anglo-Saxon characters. We may therefore doubt whether Wood really saw the MS., especially as he refers to a 'paralipomenon written by an old writer, and added thereunto, as Camden and Baleus tell us.' Had he seen the MS. he would have found that

---

[1] *Life of Ælfred the Great*, ed. Hearne, p. 182: 'I . . . have seen an ancient manuscript *Asser. Men⟨evensis⟩* conceived by some to be the very original, by which the archbishop first published that author : and probably enough both for the affinity the character has with the Saxon letters, and also for the lines and marks of red oaker, with which the archbishop was wont to note the manuscripts that he perused. In this manuscript there were the clauses, which in Mr. Camden's edition do immediately precede and follow the clause of the discord ⟨c. 83 b⟩, and they are both in that part of the book, which is of the ancienter and most undoubted hand, whereas other parts are of a later hand and seem supply'd. But I find not in this MS. the clause of the discord, nor any word of the matters therein contained, nor anything at all otherwise than as the archbishop has published.'
[2] This may be seen more clearly in his English text, which was published at Oxford in 1792, i. 45, under the editorship of John Gutch.

this was an addition of Parker's, c. 106 d.   Bale, his
authority, was referring to the Annals of St. Neots,
and it was this work as seen by Leland that Wood
quotes, in a very disingenuous way, against the
antiquity and completeness of Parker's MS. of the
present work.   It is difficult to believe that Wood
could possibly have been guilty of such confusion as
he has made in this passage if his sense of evidence
and logic had not been lulled to sleep by his infatuated
belief in anything that supported the view taken by
him of the excessive antiquity of the University.

§ 21. Thomas Gale in 1691 states most decisively
that the Cottonian MS. was the one used by Parker,
although many had denied that it was [1].

§ 22. Wise in 1722 describes the MS., no doubt
from information derived from James Hill (§ 11), as
an ancient and elegantly written MS., the work of
several scribes, none of whom was well versed in
Latin.   It was not written in O.E. characters, as a
proof of which he refers to the facsimile published
by him [2].   He describes the portion from c. 88, 11 to
the end of c. 98 as being written by a *recentior manus*,
but he gives no hint of its age.   This seems to have
been an eleventh-century hand (§ 24), though Wise
thoughtlessly describes Parker's interpolations, cc.
50 b, c, d, as being also written by a *recentior manus*.
The Parkerian hand he describes elsewhere more

---

[1] *Scriptores Quindecim, i. praefatio*, sign. b *verso*: 'Eam
⟨ vitam Alfridi ⟩ edidit Archiepiscopus Parkerus : codex ipsissimus
quo ille usus est, stat in Bibl. Cottoniana.   Hoc monui, quoniam
id vellent aliqui ita non esse.'   From a note of Hearne's derived
from the papers of Thomas Smith, keeper of the Cottonian
Library, who died in 1710, it would seem that Smith doubted,
despite Gale's statement, whether this was the MS. used by
Parker (*Collections*, iii. 62).

[2] Page 137 : 'Est codex sane vetustus, elegans et bonae notae,
cui describendo plures navarunt operam amanuenses, quorum
tamen nemo linguam Latinam videtur apprime calluisse. . . Et
" characteribus Saxonicis " minime conscriptum esse, ostendit
paginae annexum specimen.'

accurately as *nova manus*[1]. He ascribes c. 106 d to Parker himself.

§ 23. Wise was, however, fortunately able to obtain the judgement of a much greater scholar, Humphry Wanley. The Cottonian collection was well known to Wanley[2], and there was no one who had so minute a knowledge of O.E. manuscripts as he possessed. His accuracy in dating O.E. MSS. is astonishing to modern palaeographers, who, with all the advantages they enjoy for the minute study of handwriting in the shape of accurate photographic facsimiles, seldom find reason to dissent from him[3]. According to Wise, this singularly sagacious scholar assigned the first and earliest hand of the MS. to about the year 1000 or 1001[4]. The limits of age assigned are curiously narrow, but Wanley must have had good reason for

[1] Cap. 70, 3. He notes that a *nova manus* had added 'ergo nec Oxonii' after *lectores boni* in c. 24, 9.

[2] Wanley, besides his work upon this library when compiling his famous *Catalogus*, had been engaged, together with Matthew Hutton and John Anstis, to report upon the Cottonian collection to the Trustees. Harley's copy of this report, in the form of an annotated copy of Smith's catalogue of the library, is preserved in the Bodleian Library (MS. Bodl. Add. D 82). In this Otho A xii is described as *Cod. membr. in 4to, constans foliis* 155.

[3] Dr. G. F. Warner, of the Department of MSS., British Museum, agrees with the high estimate of Wanley's judgement expressed above, and, making allowances for the bad facsimile of the MS., sees nothing in it to conflict with Wanley's ascription of date. It is peculiarly gratifying to find one's conclusions endorsed by a scholar who has so deep a knowledge of O.E. hands as Mr. Warner possesses. Professor Napier informs me that he has seldom found reason to differ from Wanley's statements as to the age of O.E. MSS., which have frequently proved to be wonderfully accurate by philological tests.

[4] Page 137: 'Prior et antiquior huius codicis scriptura (iudicium sequor viri pereruditi, et rei antiquariae accuratissimi indagatoris, Cl. Humfredi Wanleii) circiter annum Domini 1000 vel 1001 exarata fuit.' Wanley, in his *Catalogus*, p. 232 b, published in 1705, refers to the MS. as 'illud Asserii Menevensis exemplar, quo usus est Dn. Matthaeus Parker, Archiep. Cant.'

this precision of statement[1]. In the Cottonian
Library he had at hand a unique collection of O.E.
MSS. for the purposes of comparison, and this consideration adds greatly to the improbability of his
being anything like a century wrong in his dating
of this MS.[2].

§ 24. We may therefore sum up the evidence regarding the MS. at our disposal as follows. It was a small
folio or large quarto volume, containing 107 pages
(p. xxxviii, note 1), and, as it was written in two or
more hands and contained numerous errors of transcription (§§ 16, 17, 20, 22), it was obviously not the autograph of the Welsh author. This is also proved by
the fact that the scribes used Anglo-Saxon characters
(§§ 14, 16, 18), and the English spelling *fas(s)ellus* for
*vassallus* (cc. 53, 3 ; 55, 3). The oldest hand dated
from about the year 1000 or 1001 (§ 23). Of the
second hand the only information we possess is Wise's
description of it as *manus recentior* (§ 22), and James's
statement that it was much later than the other. It,
however, contained Anglo-Saxon characters (p. xxxviii,
note 1). James states that the passages in the
neighbourhood of c. 83 b were in this later hand, but

[1] It is possibly influenced by the Cott. Charter of 1001 cited at
p. xxxiii, note 1, with which Wanley would have an opportunity
of comparing the MS.

[2] Wanley has given a description of his method of fixing
the date of MSS. in the *Philosophical Transactions* for 1705,
pp. 1993–2008. It consisted of careful comparison with hands
the dates of which were known. He states that he 'never entertained any notion, or relied upon any observation, but as
I found it confirmed by the suffrage of concurring circumstances,
and sufficient authority' (p. 1996). He was collecting as early
as 1699 fragments of Latin MSS. for use in dating others
(*Original Letters of Eminent Literary Men*, ed. Ellis, Camden
Society, 1843, p. 275). Compare also what he says in 1697
of the Hatton MS. of the O.E. translation of Gregory's *Pastoral
Care*, which he rightly took to be as old as the time of Alfred,
but wished to compare with the Cottonian MS. as he 'loves two
strings to his bow' (Nichols, *Literary Anecdotes of the
Eighteenth Century*, i. 97).

Sir John Spelman (p. xlii, note 1) was, apparently, unable to distinguish the hand hereabouts from the oldest hand, and Wise makes no note of its being the later one. There is evidence that the chapters in the later hand formed part of the original work in the similarity of style, and in the fact that the older hand or hands resumed, as we may conclude from Wise's silence, after the later hand ceased. The conclusion that the part written in the later hand was part of the original is also supported by the appearance of portions of it in Florence of Worcester, the Annals of St. Neots, and the early part of the work known to us by the name of Simeon of Durham. Three chapters only, cc. 89, 90, 95, have been entirely passed over by these compilers. We have thus evidence that, whatever might have been the age of the later hand, the portion written by it was older than the beginning of the twelfth century. If, as there is reason for believing (§§ 25, 33), the MS. was the one used by Florence of Worcester, it is obvious that the portion in the later hand was an integral part of the work in his time. It must, therefore, have existed then either in the recent hand or in an older one. But, as the recent hand began in the middle of a sentence, it is unlikely that it had replaced an earlier one, and the corresponding portions in Florence agree so closely with it, reproducing even grammatical errors, that we may fairly conclude that in the MS. used by him this portion was written in the later hand. Therefore the later hand cannot have been later in date than the eleventh century.

§ 25. The Cottonian MS. was, as we have seen (§§ 16, 22), described as carelessly written by ignorant scribes, and as containing, in consequence, numerous errors. It is probable that many of these are reproduced in the Co transcript, which has many clerical errors, wrong divisions of words, &c. To the carelessness of the scribes of the MS. may be ascribed the confusions caused by the omissions of verbs[1], and the corrupt passages that have baffled all emendations[2]. It is curious that Florence of Worcester, who seems clearly to have used this MS., has retained a number of these errors. Thus he has *Cætwa*, c. 1, 36, for *Tætwa*[3]; *suppetebat* for *suppeteret*, c. 30, 18; *Fingodwulf* for *Fin, qui fuit Godwulf*[4], c. 1, 21; *Thornsæta*, c. 49, 8, for *Dornsæta*; *sumere debere sciret*, c. 38, 5; *occidit*, c. 49. 21, for *occidentem*; *Orientalem*, c. 67, 10, for *Orientalium*; *cultu*, c. 100, 5, 11, 21, for *curto* (?); and the apparently erroneous *per audacitatem* ... *decipientes*, c. 42, 26, for *paucitatem* ... *despicientes*. The *et legit*, c. 23, 14, is also common to Florence and the MS. Strong evidence that he used the Cottonian MS. is afforded by the error in c. 55, 4, where the scribe's eye has wandered from *pagae* to *paganos*. Florence repeats the error in number in c. 54, 5, and the blunder concerning Pipin, c. 70, 10. He omits with the Cottonian MS. the reference to the armlets of the Danes in c. 49, 15, but he supplies, probably from the Chronicle, the passage omitted from the end of this chapter. He has with the Life eight battles instead of nine in c. 42, 31, but he supplies the account of the battle of Meretun, which should have appeared in c. 40, the omission of which in the Life has been supposed to be the cause of the difference between the number of fights given in the

---

[1] See cc. 24, 3; 74, 7; 74, 47; 75, 28; 91, 26; 105, 14. Whether the omission in c. 18, 3 is to be ascribed to the MS. is doubtful. See p. xlviii, note 4, below. Cf. however p. cxxxi, below.

[2] See cc. 38, 5; 40, 1-2; 75, 6; 76, 16-20; 79, 51; 91, 14; 99, 5-8; 105, 13; 106, 12.

[3] This misreading seems to have arisen from the small *t* of Welsh hands of the ninth and early tenth centuries, in which the top-stroke commenced far to the left of the down-stroke, which is barely crossed, so that confusion with *c* is easy.

[4] On the other hand, Florence has *qui fuit Esla*, c. 1, 16, and *qui fuit* ... *Freothegar*, c. 1, 18, 19, which were omitted in the Cott. MS. and do not appear in the first part of Simeon of Durham.

Chronicle and in the Life, c. 42, 31. He retains *aedificia*, c. 56, 33, which is, apparently, an error for *beneficia*; the active for the passive infinitives[1]; and the *et*, c. 29, 11, for *quae*[2]. The *Stratdutenses*, c. 47, 8, may be a mistaken reading of Parker's of *Stratcludenses*, which is given by Florence. In other cases he corrects the readings, as *Anglorum* for *Saxonum*, c. 21, 7; *rediret* for *dormiret*, c. 67, 9; *elevavit*, c. 56, 29, for *elimavit*; *servando*, c. 20, 4, for *servato*; *ceram* for *coram*, c. 104, 2; *conservare* for *cum servare*, c. 103, 17; *Ecgbrihti* for *Ægbryhta*[3], c. 55, 6; and supplies the missing *defunctus est*[4] of c. 18, 3 and the *et Lundoniam* of c. 4, 4. Florence has a passage at the end of c. 38 that, apparently, did not occur in the MS.[5]. He omits, possibly owing to their obscurity, *cuius numerus*, c. 75, 6, and c. 91, 14–16. In the parts not copied by Florence we have *Eadred*, c. 80, 8, for *Æthered*, c. 80, 22, an error obviously caused by the scribe misunderstanding the latter name as standing for Eadred; *infirmantibus*, c. 25, 8, for *infirmitatibus*; *quod*, c. 69, 3, for *qui*. In c. 26, 1 the scribe wrote *Karolus* for *Ælfredi*. He has confused *indiculus*, c. 79, 38, 40, with *in diluculo*. The *avis*, c. 76, 62, for *apis*, may be due to Parker's transcriber. The MS. seems also to have been used by the author of the first part of the work known to us under the name of

---

[1] *Facere*, c. 14, 5; *scribere*, c. 16, 6; *mandare*, c. 16, 11; *portare*, c. 16, 28; *aedificare*, c. 98, 3; *construere*, c. 92, 7; *pensare*, c. 104, 4. He corrects *appellare*, c. 13, 15, and omits *execrare*, c. 14, 10.

[2] This looks as if the scribe had mistaken a compendium for *quae* as a sign for *et*. The *et* of c. 23, 14, may, therefore, also be a misreading of *qui*.

[3] This, however, may be merely a blunder of Parker's transcriber.

[4] It is possible, despite Wise's statement, that these words really occurred in the MS., and that he ought to have said that *Occidentalium Saxonum* only did not occur.

[5] The words 'Anglice, Latine Anglorum Campus, c. 35, 13, he may have supplied himself.

Simeon of Durham (§ 35), for he writes *Cetwa*, c. 1, 36, *peraudacitatem*, c. 42, 26 ; had evidently the reading *sumere debere sciret*, c. 38, 5, *dormiret*, c. 67, 9, *et legit*, c. 23, 14, *servato*, c. 20, 4, and probably the *aedificia* of c. 56, 33. He makes the obvious correction *Anglorum* in c. 21, 7, and supplies *defunctus est* in c. 18, 3. The other instances are omitted or disguised by him. Most of these errors also appear in the Annals of St. Neots, which has, however, several better readings (§ 34).

§ 26. The scribe of the Cottonian MS. seems to have modernized some of the names in chapter 1. In two other cases we have passages that fit in so badly with the context that we have little hesitation in bracketing them as interpolations. They were, it is evident, made at the time of the writing of this MS. in order to bring the information down to that date. One is the *et, ut credo, usque ad obitum vitae suae* in c. 25, 15, which has not the verb in the future or past tense that is required to make sense. In the other the words *et nunc etiam Sanctus Niot ibidem pausat*, c. 74, 21, are awkwardly inserted after *in qua Sanctus Gueriir quiescit*[1]. This appears in Florence. There is also a curious confusion of present and imperfect tenses in reference to Alfred, which may perhaps be due to the copyist. Thus, c. 106, 46, 49, 50, we read *valeret, si haberet . . . si aliter non habeat*, followed again by imperfects ; in c. 22, 16 *laborat . . . fuit*. C. 91 begins by speaking of the king in the imperfect tense, but the present occurs in line 6, twice in line 7, and again in line 9. In this chapter the verbs referring to the king and his subjects are in seven instances in the imperfect and in fifteen in the present.

---

[1] Dr. Lingard, *History of the Anglo-Saxon Church*, London, 1845, ii. 427-8, ascribes this mention of St. Neot and c. 53, 11-12, which is really due to Parker, to the scribe of the Cottonian MS. There are, however, no grounds for holding that the copyist was a monk of St. Neots (§ 75).

Similarly the customs of the court are mentioned in
c. 100 in the imperfect in five cases, but the present is
used in summing up the administration, line 21. In
c. 106 the imperfect is used fifteen times, but there is
a present reference in *huius temporis*, line 57. The
habits of the king are in the present tense in cc. 22, 16 ;
25, 17 ; 81, 12, 38. There are other instances of the
present in cc. 12, 11, 12, 13 ; 74, 68, 69; 75, 26, 29, 31;
76, 68, 69; 80, 3 ; 93, 4. Cf. *hucusque cotidie*, c. 74, 7;
*adhuc*, c. 91, 50. Imperfects occur cc. 24, 6, 9 ; 25, 3 ;
74, 13, 16 ; 75, 21 ; 76 *passim* ; 77 five times ; 88, 7, 9;
89, 22, 23 ; 92, 3, 5, 7 ; 101, 4, 6, 13 ; 102, 3 *bis*, 9 ;
104 six times ; 105, 6, 8, 10. The theory that these
imperfects are due to a forger who has momentarily
forgotten that he ought not to speak of the king,
in whose reign he professes to be writing, in the past
tense (§ 73), is difficult to reconcile with the numerous
instances in which the imperfect occurs and with the
frequency of the present. A forger would surely have
corrected all or none of the verbs in his draught ;
he would not be likely to issue it to the world with
these contradictions. The view that the imperfects
are due to a transcriber who frequently omits to
change the presents of the copy before him is much
more probable. Thus Florence of Worcester corrects
the present tenses in cc. 91, 6, 7, 9, 47, 69, 70; 100,
21 into imperfects, but retains the presents in c. 12,
11, 13, and the *quorundam hominum relatu audivimus*
of line 15, which was in place in the mouth of a writer
in the time of King Alfred but is ridiculous in that of
Florence. But it is quite possible that the author
used the imperfect although the king was then alive,
just as the Frankish Thegan did (§ 51).

§ 27. To the carelessness of the scribes we may
also assign the singular errors regarding the age of
the king at certain years. These are not present in
Florence and the Annals of St. Neots, as they omit
the dating by the king's age. The king, born in 849,

is in his third year in 851 (c. 3, 2), but in his eleventh in 853 (c. 7, 2), in his seventh in 855 (c. 10, 2), which is correct, in his twelfth in 860 (c. 18, 2), also correct, in his twenty-first correctly in 869 (c. 31, 2). This is repeated in 870 (c. 32, 2), and the king's age is consequently one year too little until 875 (c. 47, 2), where a similar repetition is made, so that there is a mistake of two years in 876 (c. 49, 2). Then, owing to the confusion of the entries of 877 with 878 or to the omission of the former, another year is dropped in 878 (c. 52, 2). Consequently from here until the end of the work the king's age is understated by three years. It has been suggested that these mistakes are proof that the work is spurious (§ 86), but a forger who prided himself upon his rhetorical Latinity would surely have had sufficient knowledge of elementary arithmetic to avoid such glaring contradictions as are here involved. The errors are parallel with those that occur in innumerable chronicles, and must be due to the same cause, the carelessness of the copyist and not of the author. We have therefore emended them in the text. It is possible that the omission of the mention of the battle at Meretun in 871 is due to the carelessness of the scribe[1]. The assign-ment of the events given in the Chronicle under 885 to 884, and the consequent omission of the brief entry for the latter year, have every appearance of being due to a clerical error. The copyist wrote DCCCLXXXIIII and then his eye wandered a line or so lower to DCCCLXXXV, the entries under which date he proceeded to copy (c. 66).

### 3. THE TRANSCRIPTS.

§ 28. The most valuable transcript (Co) is the one preserved in the library of Corpus Christi College, Cambridge, MS. No. 100, forming part of the collection

---

[1] Cf. Pauli, *König Ælfred*, p. 11.

of MSS. bequeathed to the College by Archbishop Parker. The transcript was clearly made for his use, and has at fo. 324 the title *Alfredi Res Gestae* in red chalk in his handwriting. At the top of fo. 325 is the title *Alfredi Res Gestae authore J.*[1] (erased) *Asser*, in the hand of the copyist. The transcript forms part of a folio volume of transcripts on paper made for Parker, in which it follows the transcript of the Annals of St. Neots, and extends from fo. 324 to 361 verso. It and the Annals are in the same hand, a large clerkly one, with large initials and engrossed first words at the commencement of chapters and sections. It appears to be a very close copy made by an indifferent scholar. Many of the mistakes in it probably reproduce those of the MS., and we have therefore noted them in the apparatus. Parker has corrected many errors, and has occasionally altered a word or substituted another for it. It contains occasional marginal abstracts, written in a Parkerian hand. These form part of the marginalia in Parker's edition. The great value of this transcript lies in the fact that it was copied from the Cottonian MS. before the interpolations in the latter were made by Parker[2]. The only ones represented are cc. 50 c, d, which are written on a small piece of inserted paper in the hand that wrote the index at the commencement of the volume. There is a note at the end of c. 50 in the scribe's hand *Deest annus* 877. This is obviously the cause of the interpolated slip, Parker having taken the first chapter from Matthew of Paris and the second, which relates to the same events, from the Annals of St. Neots. At the end of c. 53 is a note *Hic inseritur in alio opere ascripto Asser scriptum quoddam in Vita*

[1] Upon the erroneous ascription of the name John to Asser, see note to c. 106 d.

[2] It has, however, the word *Erigena*, c. 78, 8, which Parker had written in the MS., as we learn from Dr. James's letter of 1600, and *Occidentalium Saxonum*, c. 53, 2.

*Sancti Neoti.* This note is the germ of the most famous of Parker's interpolations in his printed text, the story of Alfred and the cowherd's wife. Collations from this transcript, somewhat inaccurately made, are given by Wise at the end of his 'edition. He describes this transcript as a copy of the Cottonian MS. in his preface. It contains the strange sentence at the commencement of c. 40, which Parker omitted from his edition, although it occurred in the Cottonian MS.

§ 29. The British Museum transcript (B), Cott. MS. Otho A xii*, is a quarto volume on paper in a large, Elizabethan hand, which gradually falls away from a text hand into a cursive one. This is supposed to be the transcript in the Royal Library, No. 577, which Wise mentions, but did not examine. Its origin is obscure. There are no signs of its being used by Parker, and yet it has some of his interpolations. Possibly it was a transcript made for Lord Lumley, whose MSS. came to the Royal Library after his death in 1609 (§ 16). It omits the interpolations cc. 10; 36, 2; 53, 9–10; 53 b; 53 c; 54 b, and, of course, Camden's interpolation, c. 83 b. The interpolations given in it seem all to have been written in the MS.; c. 17 b was clearly added to the MS. as Wise gives collations from it; cc. 50 b, c, d, we are expressly told were written in the MS.; cc. 106 b, 106 c, were probably also added in the MS. as well as 106 d. It would therefore seem that this transcript was made from the MS., and that the copyist reproduced such interpolations as Parker had already inserted in the MS. As c. 54 b is omitted, it would seem that this was written in the MS. after this transcript had been made. Further proof that it was copied from the MS. and not from Parker's printed text is afforded by the absence of the errors of the press, such as *Eowwa*, c. 1, 8, *Faroli*, c. 13, 8. This transcript is very carelessly written, abounding in errors, transpositions of words, blundered forms, omissions, and wrong case and tense endings. These errors have not been corrected by collation with the original. The transcript is followed by a copy of the Latin translation of Alfred's will, which is given in Parker's edition, ending with *mecum tota nobilitas Westsaxoniae*, near the end. There are no marginal abstracts.

§ 30. The Arundel transcript (Ar), in the University Library, Cambridge (Add. 3825), is a late sixteenth-century copy on paper, purchased at the Frere sale in 1896. It bears on the first page 'Arundel,' and was probably the property of the fourteenth Earl of Arundel (§ 16). It is carefully written in a clear, bold hand. The dates are given in Roman numerals, agreeing in this respect with Parker's printed text. It adheres very closely to Parker's text, and reproduces some of his typographical errors. Others, however, are absent, and it has in several respects a close affinity with the British Museum transcript. Thus *Durngueys*, c. 49, 7, seems to be a misreading of the *Durnguers* of B, the *r* being read as *y*; Parker prints *Durngueis*[1]. But as it has all Parker's interpolations[2] and all his marginal abstracts, and his changes in the text, it is evident that his edition must have formed the basis of this copy. Possibly it was made from an early proof, and has thus some variations from the published text.

§ 31. Wise, in his preface, refers to a loan made to him by Roger Gale of a modern transcript of this work, which, he says, seems to be a copy of Parker's edition. This is the transcript preserved in the Library of Trinity College, Cambridge (O 7, 25), a very small octavo volume, written in two or three hands in the latter part of the seventeenth century. It contains, in addition to the text, Parker's preface, the Latin

---

[1] The omission of c. 39, 23–25 by homoeoteleuton also occurs in B.

[2] Except the word *pagae*, c. 55, 4.

version of Alfred's will and of his preface to the translation of Gregory's *Pastoral Care*, which are given at
the end of Parker's edition. It reproduces all Parker's
interpolations. At page 10 is written *Cod. MS. in
Cott. Bibl. Otho A* 12, *forte Cambdeni*, but there are
no signs of collation. The transcript is of no value
for critical purposes. It was presented to the College
by Roger Gale, with other books in the section O, in
1738 [1]. The copy was at one time in the possession
of Thomas Gale, for at page 56 there is a marginal
note (c. 79, 57) *et Novis Antistitem prop⟨osui⟩*, and
this emendation is given by Gale in the preface to his
edition of the Annals of St. Neots. In the same
hand are written (p. 79), at the end of c. 106 *Hic
desinit Codex Cottonianus*, and *peopiscirum* over *gentium*
in c. 13, 29. There is also a note at p. 104 in a
large cursive hand, that the fable concerning Grimbald
(c. 83 b) is not in Camden's exemplar, which the writer
of the note held to be the Cottonian MS. because it
contained notes by him. These notes were, however,
in Parker's hand, not Camden's [2].

§ 32. The copy of the Life mentioned in Dr. Bernard's *Catalogi Librorum Manuscriptorum Angliae*,
&c., Oxford, 1697, 5191, 19, amongst the Junius MSS.
in the Bodleian Library, is merely the printed sheets
of Parker's text.

### 4. EXCERPTS FROM THE WORK IN LATER COMPILERS.

§ 33. The first place amongst the compilers from
this work is, as we have said, held by Florence of

---

[1] M. R. James, *Western MSS. in the Library of Trinity
College*, i. p. vii. This was, no doubt, the 'Asser' that Gale
promises Dr. Charlett, on April 2, 1720, to send for from York-
shire (*Letters written by Eminent Persons in the seventeenth
and eighteenth Centuries . . . from the originals in the Bodleian
Library*, London, 1813, ii. p. 58).

[2] See Wise, p. 163.

Worcester (§ 3). How largely he borrowed from it may be seen by the passages printed in Roman type, which represent the portion of the text supported by his testimony. As he was writing a continuous chronicle, he omitted almost all the references to Asser and very many of the purely biographical details of the king's life. It has hence been maintained that the Life has been fabricated from these passages in Florence (§ 78), but this extreme view is precluded by the evidence as to the age of the MS. of the Life, and also by a dispassionate consideration of Florence's treatment of the text. The omissions are intelligible when we consider the nature of his work. He exercises great licence in transposing parts of the Life, but his reasons are not far to seek. Thus he gives most of the biographical matter relating to Alfred under 871, the year of his accession. He removes the passage relating to Bishop Werferth of Worcester from c. 77 to the year 872, under which he records his consecration. This leads him, naturally enough, to transcribe the greater part of this and the following chapters, which are intimately bound up with the subject that led to the mention of Werferth in the Life. The passage in c. 77, 19, 20, he transfers to the end of the portion that he copies from the next chapter. The reason for this is obvious. In like manner he adds, after the mention of the king's beginning to read and interpret in c. 87, 3, the date of his commencing from c. 89, 14. His transpositions in c. 74, 17, 36, 41, 59, make this confused chapter much clearer. It is unnecessary to multiply instances of his treatment of the text, as they all find explanations in the scope of his work, and his desire to render the information taken from the Life more concise. Purely rhetorical passages he rigorously cuts out, and he frequently omits a word or phrase that is not quite clear in meaning. The readings preserved by him agree so closely with those of the Cottonian MS., that it would seem that he copied

from it, for he repeats most of its errors (§ 25).   He
copies the mistranslation of the Chronicle at cc. 18,
5 ; 83, 6, but he changes the too literal *superius* of
c. 62, 3 to *saepedictus*, and he corrects the *dormiret*,
c. 67, 9, probably by comparison with the Chronicle.
From the latter he has perhaps added the missing
annal for 884, and has corrected in consequence the
date of c. 66.   He also supplies, no doubt from the
Chronicle, the missing annal of 877 (see c. 50, 26).
From the same source or from personal knowledge
he has added *et Lundoniam* in c. 4, 4.   He usually
changes the present tenses to imperfects (§ 26).
Despite his rearrangement of the matter he gives the
conclusion of the Life under 887, under which it
appears in the Life itself.   This alone is a strong
proof that he was copying from the Life[1].   At the
end of c. 38 he has a sentence that does not appear
to have been in the Life.   With the exception of this,
the addition of the *Terente* at c. 49, 6, and the
erroneous date of Æthelred's death (c. 41, 4), he has
no additions that he could not have got from the
Chronicle, or supplied by emendation, or from his
own knowledge.   These exceptions do not seem important enough to cause us to believe that he used
some other MS. than the Cottonian.

§ 34.   The unknown compiler of the Annals of
St. Neots copied very largely from the Life.   As he
has numerous passages that are not in Florence of
Worcester, it is obvious that he did not derive his
matter from him, but from a MS. of the Life.   This MS.,
although agreeing closely with the Cottonian (§ 25),
had more correct readings in cc. 49, 20 ; 55, 4 ; 70, 10,
and, probably, in c. 42, 26.   In c. 48, 2 the Annals
agree with the MSS. of the Chronicle in giving the

---

[1] The view that Florence derived the annalistic part of his
work for the period covered by the Life from hypothetical
Latin annals embodied in the latter and translated by the
compiler of the Chronicle, is shown to be untenable in § 53.

number of the ships as seven, against the six of the Cottonian MS. of the Life, Florence, and the two parts of Simeon of Durham. Similarly, the Annals have *Iglea* in c. 55, 17 with MSS. A, B, and C of the Chronicle, the oldest and best MSS., whereas the Cottonian MS. of the Life had *Æcglea*, which re-appears in Florence, and represents the *Æglea* of MSS. D and E of the Chronicle. In c. 45, 5 the Annals have *Turkesige*, which is mentioned in the Chronicle, and in the second part of Simeon, but is omitted in the Life and in Florence. The Annals also mention the armlets of the Danes in c. 49, 15, which are omitted by the Life and Florence. There is a possibility that all or some of these corrections may have been derived from the copy of the Chronicle used by the compiler. The most remarkable reading in the Annals, one that is peculiar to them, is that of Steyning instead of Winchester as the burial place of King Æthelwulf (c. 17)[1]. As the compiler adhered very closely to his MS., apart from the alterations necessitated by the plan of his work, his evidence is important. It is, therefore, to be regretted that he occasionally abridges the text, and omits most of the merely biographical part.

§ 35. We now come to the work known by the name of Simeon of Durham, a monk of the early part of the twelfth century, whose important work is, like the Life, known through one MS. only. Modern research has shown that Simeon's work consists of two parts, of which the first, which we have distin-guished as SD 1, is of peculiar interest. It represents a compilation that copied the lost Northumbrian Annals from 731, the end of Beda's *Historia Eccle-siastica*, until 801. After that time until 849 the compiler had hardly any material, except the story of Eadburh under 802, which he has taken from the

---

[1] See note to this chapter.

Life (c. 14 sqq.). From 849 to 887 he borrowed very
largely from the Life, and he experiences a scarcity
of material from this time until 951, which seems to
have been the end of the compilation. It was later
continued to 957. As a monk of Durham about the
year 1120 embodied in one volume this work and
another history (SD 2), extending from 848 to 1120[1],
in which the matter derived from the Life is taken
directly from Florence of Worcester, it has been
assumed that the first compilation was older than
the second one, and was probably written about 951.
We may readily grant that SD 1 was an older
compilation, but the evidence that it was drawn
up in the tenth century is, in the absence of a MS.
of that period, necessarily hypothetical. The copy of
the Life used by the compiler of SD 1 had a remarkable resemblance in its errors to the Cottonian MS.
(§ 25), and it had most of the errors in the reckoning
of the king's age. It is probable that the compiler
used this very MS., but a definite conclusion on the
point is rendered difficult by his habit of paraphrasing
the language of the Life. There may also be reflex
influence from Florence of Worcester, owing to the
copying of the latter in SD 2. The remarkable
readings *Mucel Wudu* for *Selwudu*, c. 55, 7, and
*civitas aquae* for *Exae*, c. 49, 23, appear in both
SD 1 and SD 2, and are therefore proof of influence
upon one another. So also are the added *praeceptore
ostendente*, c. 23, 14, and *motus*, c. 56, 18. Similarly
SD 2 must have derived the three verses in c. 1, 26-28
from SD 1 or the MS., as they do not appear in
Florence. But, as a rule, the readings of SD 2 agree
very closely with those of Florence [2].

---

[1] Stubbs, *Roger of Howden*, i. p. xxx. The prefaces of
Hinde's edition of Simeon of Durham for the Surtees Society,
1868, and Mr. Arnold's in the Roll Series may also be consulted.

[2] In c. 56, 29 *elimavit*, which it has with the Corpus transcript, appears to come from the MS. Florence substitutes

§ 36. William of Malmesbury, in his *Gesta Regum Anglorum*, the first edition of which was published in or before 1125, derives most of his matter relating to Alfred from the Life. Bishop Stubbs holds that he borrowed directly from the Life, which he made 'the chief and primary authority' for the section of his work dealing with the reign of Alfred[1]. Since he rewrites the history derived from the Life, as in the case of his other sources[2], we cannot get much assistance from him in verifying readings, or any light upon the MS. used by him. He does not mention the Life amongst his sources, but this may be accounted for by the fact that he mentions only the continuous histories used by him[3], passing over in silence the greater number of writers from whom he borrows matter[4]. It is not, however, certain that he did not use Florence of Worcester instead of the Life, for all the matter embodied by him from the latter may be found in the Worcester writer. This renders Stubbs's conclusion that William was unacquainted with the work of Florence[5] difficult to prove, and there is one passage that tells strongly in favour of the view that he used Florence and not the Life. He states[6] that Alfred's wife Egelswitha bore to him Ethelswida, Edward, and the other children named in the Life (c. 75). In the spelling of William's time Egelswitha and Ethelswida both represent one name, O.E. Æthelswith. The name of Alfred's wife is not given in the Life. Her name was Ealhswith[7], and Malmesbury

*elevavit.* In c. 70, 11 it has a curious agreement with the Annals of St. Neots.

[1] Malmesbury, *Gesta Regum*, ii. p. xxxix.
[2] Ibid. p. xvi.
[3] *Prologus*, vol. i. p. 1.
[4] Stubbs, *l. c.*, ii. p. xv.
[5] *Gesta Regum*, ii. p. cxxxi.
[6] Ibid., c. 121 (p. 129).
[7] She is described as the mother of King Edward in Chronicles B, C, and D under 903, where A merely gives her name. She

has either confused this name with Æthelswith, or
has substituted the latter, a form more familiar to
him.  Nothing is known of a daughter of Alfred
called Æthelswith or Ealhswith, and Malmesbury's
Ethelswida seems to have originated in a misunderstanding by him of Florence's words.  The Worcester
writer in transcribing c. 75, 2 of the Life added the
name of Alfred's wife, his text reading in consequence : ' Nati sunt ergo ei filii et filiae de supradicta
coniuge sua Ealhswitha Egelflæd primogenita, post
quam Eadward,' &c.  Malmesbury has plainly taken
Ealhswitha as a nominative, instead of an ablative, and
has thus ascribed to the king a daughter of the same
name as his wife.  He has added to the confusion
by substituting the name of this imaginary child for
that of Ælfthryth, who married Baldwin of Flanders.
Bishop Stubbs suggests that Æthelswith may have
been one of the children who are recorded in the
Life as dying in their infancy, but he thinks it
is more probable that William meant by this name
Ælfthryth[1].  The latter is mentioned by him, under
the form Elfreda (intended for Elfdreda, an Anglo-
Norman spelling of the name), but he makes her,
like her sister Æthelgeofu, a nun.  This is a violent
attempt of his own to find a place for the imaginary
daughter Æthelswith—Ealhswith, and to account for
Ælfthryth, whom the Life (c. 75, 21) describes as an
unmarried daughter living in her father's court.  We
do not think these errors afford any support for
Stubbs's suggestion that Malmesbury may have ' used
for this part of the story a more complete copy of

is, we may conclude, the Ealhswith whose death is recorded in
all four under 905, and, in error, by B and C also under 902.
She is mentioned, without any description, in Alfred's will
(*Cart. Sax.* ii. 178, 23, 26), and is described as the mother of
Edward the Elder in the Hyde *Liber Vitae*, written *circ.* 1016,
p. 5.

[1] Note to Malmesbury, *Gesta Regum*, p. 129.

Asser than is now extant'[1]. The statement in the
Life, that Alfred had three daughters, is corroborated
by the evidence of his will[2]. Clear proof that
Malmesbury used Florence may be found in his reproduction of part of Florence's encomium of Edward
the Elder[3], the source of which Bishop Stubbs has
not recognized. William used the Appendix to Florence, which Stubbs suggests may be an older compilation[4], but which, if not the work of Florence
himself, has been influenced by him[5]. Other proofs
of the use of Florence may perhaps be found in the
story of King Æthelwulf's diaconate[6], the account
of the rowing of King Edgar upon the Dee by
tributary kings[7], and the narrative of the murder
of Bishop Walchere of Durham[8]. The genealogy

---

[1] Note to Malmesbury, *Gesta Regum*, p. 129.

[2] *Cart. Sax.* ii. 178, 13, 25. This double reference to the
king's three daughters is a fatal objection to Malmesbury's
ascription to him of a fourth, and it precludes any suggestion that the death of Ealhswith, recorded in Chronicles B
and C under 902 and 905, refers to the wife and to a daughter
of Alfred.

[3] *Gesta Regum*, c. 125 (p. 135); Florence, an. 901.

[4] *Gesta Regum*, ii. xxi. He has, for instance, the statement
that King Sigeberht of East Anglia was brother *ex parte matris*
of Eorpweald, c. 97 (p. 97), which is derived from Florence's
appendix. Beda, *Hist. Eccl.* ii. 15; iii. 18 merely states that
Sigeberht was the brother of Eorpweald. There are other
traces of copying from Florence in Malmesbury's account of
Sigeberht.

[5] See, however, p. 110 below. It uses passages from the Life
in the account of Alfred, and adds the name of Alfred's queen,
as Florence has done in the body of his work in copying the
Life. The Scandinavian form of the name of the people of
Götland, *Gouti* = O.N. *Gautar*, O.E. *Gēatas*, is suggestive of
a Worcester origin. See below, p. 170, note 4.

[6] See below, p. c, note 2. This, however, may be an interpolation from Malmesbury. See below, § 41, and p. 108.

[7] See below, p. 108, note 4.

[8] *Gesta Regum*, c. 271 (p. 330); *Gesta Pontificum*, c. 132
(p. 271); Florence, an. 1080.

of Alfred's house given by Malmesbury[1] has names
that occur in Florence, but not in the Cottonian MS.
of the Life. These omissions may, however, have
been supplied either from the Chronicle or from one
of the numerous copies of the West-Saxon royal
pedigree. It is noteworthy that he adds to it matter
taken from Æthelweard. The mention of Alfred's
*Enchiridion* in the Life (c. 89, 20), which is omitted
by Florence, may have been derived by William[2]
from the book itself, which was apparently still extant, as the passage in which it occurs is not taken by
him from the Life, but is of his own composition.
Elsewhere he calls it the King's 'Manualis Liber[3],'
which is the gloss of the Greek word given in the
Life. But as the latter word was fairly well known
and the gloss is the obvious one, it would be unwise
to attach much importance to this agreement with
the Life as against Florence.

§ 37. Giraldus Cambrensis, the brilliant, egotistical,
and inaccurate Welsh writer of the latter part of the
twelfth century, appears to have had access to a copy
of the Life. In his 'Life of St. Ethelbert' (King
Æthelberht of East Anglia) he quoted as from Asser
the account of Eadburh, Offa's daughter (cc. 14, 15),
and also cited Asser, *historicus veraxque relator
gestorum Regis Alfredi*[4], as the authority for the
statement that King Offa commissioned two bishops

---

[1] *Gesta Regum*, c. 116 (p. 120).
[2] Ibid. c. 123 (p. 132).
[3] *Gesta Pontificum*, c. 188 (p. 333).
[4] *Acta Sanctorum*, Maii v, p. 244* note *b*, 245* note *c*; reprinted in *Giraldi Cambrensis Opera*, ed. Brewer, iii. 420, note
*b*, 422; Brompton's Chronicle, in Twysden's *Quindecim Scriptores*, col. 753. Upon Giraldus's Life of Ethelbert Brewer's
Preface, p. xlv, may be consulted. It is not certain that the
quotation given above comes from Giraldus, but it is improbable
that Brompton, who elsewhere displays no first-hand knowledge
of the present work, has added it. Possibly the other reference
to Asser may have been added by the Bollandists.

to inquire into the miracles alleged to have been performed by St. Ethelbert. Nothing of this appears in the Life of Alfred, and it must, unless it be a figment of Giraldus, come from some other work of Asser's. Unfortunately this work of Giraldus has not come down to us, the copy in Cott. MS. Vitellius E vii having disappeared. A copy of this MS. was sent by Dugdale to the Bollandists, but they printed the Life of Ethelbert from the late compilation bearing the name of John Brompton, and gave parallel passages occasionally from Giraldus. It would seem that the Life in Brompton was derived from that of Giraldus. This reference to Asser as the writer of a Life of King Alfred is the only mediaeval one we have met with, and it is noteworthy as coming from a writer who was closely connected with St. Davids, where Asser was brought up (§ 43).

§ 38. Of other twelfth-century compilers little need be said. Alfred of Beverley has much matter from the Life, but it seems to be taken from Simeon of Durham and Florence of Worcester. Ethelred of Rievaulx derives his matter from Florence or SD 2. Bishop Stubbs has remarked that it is not easy to decide whether the compiler of the *Historia post Bedam*, the twelfth-century compilation from which Roger of Howden derived his extracts from the Life, took all his matter direct from Florence or Simeon, or had also a copy of Asser by him at the same time [1]. The author of the St. Albans compilation, the basis of the chronicles of Roger of Wendover and Matthew of Paris, clearly used Florence and Simeon of Durham. Henry of Huntingdon is the only prominent twelfth-century chronicler who takes no matter directly or indirectly from the Life. All the later compilations, such as the *Flores Historiarum*, Ranulph Higden's *Polychronicon*, Richard of Cirencester's

---

[1] *Chronica Rogeri de Hoveden*, i. 35.

*Speculum Historiale*, the Malmesbury *Eulogium*, &c, borrow from Howden, the St. Albans writers, or William of Malmesbury, and not from the Life direct.

## 5. THE AUTHOR. INTERNAL EVIDENCE OF THE TEXT.

§ 39. Apart from the present work little is known of Bishop Asser, who was, according to the dedication, the author. King Alfred mentions him as *Assere, Asserie, minum biscepe* (in the dative case), in his preface to the translation of Gregory's *Pastoral Care*, in the preparation of which he was assisted by him [1]. The form Asserie agrees with the Latinized *Asserius*, which occurs in later writers.   His death as Bishop of Sherborne is recorded in the Chronicle under 910, and in the *Annales Cambriae*, a work closely connected with the diocese of St. Davids, under 908 [2]. It is difficult to say which is the correct year.   The dates in the *Annales* are occasionally a year earlier than those in the Chronicle, placing, for instance, the death of Æthelflæd in 917 against the 918 of the Chronicle, and the death of Alfred in 900 as against 901 in the Chronicle.   Bishop Asser occurs as a witness of charters of Edward the Elder in 900, 902, 903, and 904, but these texts are not free from suspicion [3].   The Wells register preserves a copy of

[1] Ed. Sweet, 6, 21 ; 7, 21.  *Asserie* is the reading of the Cotton MS., *Assere* that of the Hatton MS.  These are both late ninth-century MSS.

[2] This portion of the *Annales* seems to have been composed about 950.  See Mr. Phillimore's excellent article and text in *Y Cymmrodor*, ix. 144.

[3] Pauli, *König Ælfred und seine Stelle in der Geschichte Englands*, Berlin, 1851, p. 6, states that Asser subscribes until 909, but there is no proof of this beyond Kemble's assignment of no. 1087 (*Cart. Sax.* ii. 262, a portion of which is preserved in the early eleventh century *Liber Vitae* of Hyde Abbey, p. 155) to 901-9, the earlier date being fixed by its being witnessed by King Edward and the later by the death of Bishop Denewulf in 909.  The charters in which Bishop Asser occurs as a

a grant by King Edward to Asser, Bishop of Sherborne, of lands in Somerset in exchange for the monastery of Plympton, which is possibly genuine [1]. From the Chronicle we know that he was Bishop of Sherborne, and this is confirmed by the occurrence of his name in the old lists of bishops of that see [2]. The dates of the consecration and death of his predecessor Wulfsige (who appears as Alfsige in Florence's list) are unknown. A Bishop Wulfsige witnesses a charter of 889 in Heming's Worcester chartulary, which we are inclined to think is genuine [3]. He also occurs

witness are in 900, *Cart. Sax.* ii. 235, 22 ; 241, 13 ; 247, 32 ; 249, 41 ; in 901, ib. 232, 36 ; 251, 28 ; in 903, ib. 253, 30 ; in 904, ib. 261, 26 ; 262, 27 ; 269, 11, 31 ; 271, 32 ; 275, 32. It is not certain that any of these texts are genuine, as no contemporary charters of Edward are in existence. The texts cited above come principally from suspicious sources, the Hyde, Winchester, and Wilton chartularies. But the text at 247 is preserved in a copy written about the beginning of the eleventh century, and a portion of that at 262 is preserved, as stated above, in a copy written about 1016. Bishop Asser is alleged to have drawn up a charter the attestation clause of which is preserved in the Athelney chartulary, p. 126, Somersetshire Record Society. It is evidently spurious.

[1] *Cart. Sax.* ii. 268-9. The fact that it is an exchange of a monastery is in favour of its antiquity. Part of its proem agrees with the texts of Æthelwulf's donation, all of which are suspicious. The Bath charter of 1061 (*Codex Diplomaticus*, iv. 150), is clearly modelled upon this grant to Asser, and is probably spurious.

[2] *Reliquiae Antiquae*, ed. Wright and Halliwell, London, 1841-5, ii. 170 (*circ.* 990) ; the Hyde *Liber Vitae*, p. 20 (*c.* 1016) ; Florence of Worcester, ed. Thorpe, i. 237.

[3] *Cart. Sax.* ii. 201, 22. Heming is generally of a high character; but he has included a few spurious charters in his collection, so that his evidence is not quite so valuable as that of the *Textus Roffensis*. In the present charter the language is of the highly rhetorical nature to which we are accustomed in tenth-century charters, and indeed, some of the formulas occur in texts of that period. Cf. 200, 4 sqq. with 531, 2, 5, and the anathema agrees with that at 488, 29 ; 522, 8 ; 531, 26 ; 533, 20 ; 557, 7 ; iii. 26, 33 ; 105, 25. But as portions of formulas of earlier date than this reappear in tenth-century charters, these agree-

as a witness to a spurious charter of 892 [1] and, as
Ulfricus, Wlfricg, to a spurious undated Malmesbury
charter [2].    King Alfred in his will, which may be
dated between 873 and 888 [3], bequeaths a hundred
mancusses each to Bishop Esne, Bishop Wærferth,
'and to him at Sherborne.'    It is possible that Asser
is the bishop meant [4], for he and Wærferth were

ments are capable of being explained as survivals or imitations
of earlier formulas.    Against this may be placed the presence
in this text of earlier features, which are usually absent from
forged texts, such as *in ecclesiasticum ius conscribimus*, 200, 28,
an early phrase, the mention of roboration *propriis manibus
subscripserunt*, one of the most ancient phrases in the O.E.
charters, the exhortation to succeeding generations to observe
the charter, the title *rex Anglorum et Saxonum* (see note to
Dedication of present work), and, generally, the absence in the
body of the charter of ordinary formulas commonly known and
used by forgers.    The charter is drawn up on the model of
Mercian ones, not on West-Saxon lines.

[1] *Cart. Sax.* ii. 209, 18.

[2] Ibid. 210, 19.    Both forms are miscopied for *Wulfsige* owing
to the resemblance of O.E. ſ (*s*) to the later forms of *r*.

[3] Ibid. 178, 33.    The date 880-5 assigned by Kemble, *Cod.
Dipl.* ii. 112, and repeated by Birch, and Earle, *Land Charters*,
p. 144, seems to have no support.    The will was dated by
Manning, *The Will of King Alfred*, Oxford, 1788, p. 14, note *n*,
between the king's accession in 871 and 885, 'when Esne died.'
The latter is an error due to Bishop Godwin's assignment of the
death of Esne, bishop of Hereford, to that year, instead of 787
or 788.    The will, however, is later than 873, the date of the
consecration of Bishop Wærferth of Worcester, and before the
death of Archbishop Æthered of Canterbury, which is recorded
in the Chronicle under 888, in which year also the death of
Æthelwold, a legatee in the will, is recorded.    It is probably
earlier than 884-5 (see note to c. 77, 10).    The king states
that he had made a previous will, since the making of which
the number of his kinsmen had been reduced (*Cart. Sax.* ii.
179, 9).    As the name of Esne does not occur in any of the lists
of bishops of this time, Stubbs has been led to suggest that the
name is an interpolation in the text of the will (*Dict. of Christian
Biography*), the oldest copy of which dates from the early part
of the eleventh century.

[4] Parker in the Latin version of Alfred's will at the end of his
edition of the Life reads *Assero, episcopo de Schireburn*, which

literary assistants of the king, and the bequest is of a large sum. The omission from the will of any mention of Plegmund is, however, difficult to reconcile with this identification of the Bishop of Sherborne[1]. Bishop Esne is otherwise unknown.

§ 40. A later writer, William of Malmesbury, tells us that Asser explained to the king the difficult passages in Boethius' *De Consolatione Philosophiae*, and that the king made his translation from this simplified version[2]. The king in his preface to his version states that he had rendered the work sometimes word for word, sometimes by paraphrase, making no mention of Asser's assistance[3]. Malmesbury's account of Asser's share in the work agrees curiously with the statements in the Life that the author read and interpreted to the king[4]. What grounds Malmesbury may have had for his statement it is now impossible

is repeated by Camden and Wise. But as the first two words are absent from the Latin version in the *Liber de Hyda*, with which Parker's text agrees, it would seem that we have here another of Parker's wanton falsifications of historical texts.

[1] See note to c. 77, 10.

[2] *Gesta Regum*, c. 122 (p. 131) 'Habebat ex Sancto Dewi Asserionem quendam, scientia non ignobili instructum, quem Scireburniae fecit episcopum. Hic sensum librorum Boetii *De Consolatione* ⟨*Philosophiae*⟩ planioribus verbis enodavit, quos rex ipse in Anglicam linguam vertit'; *Gesta Pontificum*, c. 80 (p. 177) 'Asserus, ex Sancto Dewi evocatus, non usquequaque contempnendae scientiae fuit, qui librum Boetii *De Consolatione Philosophiae* planioribus verbis elucidavit, labore illius diebus necessario nostris ridiculo. Sed enim iussu regis factum est, ut levius ab eodem in Anglicum transferretur sermonem.' These words hardly justify the belief that Asser was the author of the Latin commentaries on Boethius used by the king, as pointed out by Dr. Schepss. See Sedgfield's edition of Alfred's version, Oxford, 1899, p. xxxv.

[3] Ed. Sedgfield, p. 1 'Ælfred Kuning wæs wealhstod ðisse bec. . . . Hwilum he sette word be worde, hwilum andgit of andgite' (King Alfred was the translator of this book. . . Sometimes he rendered it word for word, sometimes sense by sense).

[4] cc. 81, 10; 87-89. Cf. also c. 77, 20.

to say.  He was acquainted with the king's handbook [1], but we know too little of the nature of the
contents of this work to affirm or deny the possibility
of its containing information regarding Asser's share
in the learned labours of Alfred.

§ 41. The MSS. of Florence of Worcester contain
under the year 883 the statement that in that year
Swithelm, who, it says, bore Alfred's alms to India,
succeeded to the see of Sherborne upon the death of
Asser.  It is evident that this strange entry has grown
out of the mention in some MSS. of the Chronicle of
the sending of alms by the king to India in 883 by
Sighelm and Æthelstan [2].  The passage is clearly one
of the interpolations in Florence's text derived from
William of Malmesbury [3].  The latter appears to have
identified Sighelm with the Bishop of Sherborne of
that name, *circ.* 926 to 933, and to have inserted him
between Asser and Æthelweard, omitting him from
his real place [4].  The Worcester interpolator seems to
have miswritten the name as Swithelm, to have concluded that Sighelm was bishop at the time of the
alleged mission, and that consequently Asser must
have died before the date of the mission, which he
derived from the Chronicle.  Yet the list of bishops
in the Appendix to Florence has three names between
Asser and Sighelm, and the name of Swithelm does
not appear.  There can be no question of setting up
this evidence against that of the Chronicle and the
*Annales Cambriae,* and we need not hesitate to reject
it with Pauli and Hardy as a blunder [5].

---

[1] See page 153, below.
[2] See below, note to c. 65.
[3] See below, p. 108.
[4] *Gesta Pontificum,* c. 80 (p. 177); *Gesta Regum,* c. 122
(p. 130).  In Richard of Cirencester's *Speculum Historiale,*
ii. 21, Asser himself becomes one of the envoys to India.
[5] *König Ælfred,* p. 6; *Monumenta Historica Britannica,*
p. 78; *Descriptive Catalogue,* i. 552.

§ 42. The name Asser, although not of Celtic origin[1], is met with in Welsh documents, and it is not found in use in England[2]. An Asser witnesses after Cyfeiliog, Bishop of Llandaff, amongst the *clerici* a grant by King Howel ap Rhys[3], who died in 885[4]. Mr. Phillimore suggests to us that this may be the author of the Life, and it is by no means improbable. We find him, apparently, in this district about this year[5]. A little earlier an *Asser filius Marchiud* occurs in the same locality[6]. A *Gulcet filius Asser* is mentioned in the time of William the Conqueror[7], and a grandson of another Asser also appears in the same notice[8]. An *Asser mab Riderch*

[1] The St. Asarius of the calendar of saints seems to have arisen in some way through confusion between St. Macarius and St. Asterius, prelates from Palestine and Arabia who were concerned with the council of Sardica in 347. See Le Quien, *Oriens Christianus*, Paris, 1740, iii. 667 ; *Acta Sanctorum*, Junii iv. 11. It is unlikely that the Welsh name can be derived from these obscure eastern saints.

[2] It must be distinguished from the later English name Asser, which is occasionally found, as e.g. Asser de Prestclive, co. Derby, in the Pipe Roll, 28 Edward I, roll 15. This is an English development from the Old Norse name *Özurr*, adapted into O.E. under the form *Atzur*, which already appears as *Atser* in the eleventh century in Heming's Worcester Chartulary, p. 269. This Atser, a kinsman and chamberlain of Bishop Brihtheah of Worcester, is called *Assere* in the Evesham Chronicle, p. 97, but appears as *Azor* in Domesday, i. 174, col. 1 ; 175, col. 2. Similarly the *Asserus filii Tolrii* (= Toki?) of the Latin version of a deed of 1049-52 preserved in Matthew Paris, *Additamenta*, p. 30 (= Kemble, *Cod. Dipl.* iv. 285, 18), who is probably identical with the Worcestershire landowner last mentioned, clearly bore the O.N. name.

[3] *Liber Landavensis*, ed. Rhys and Evans, Oxford, 1893, p. 236, 29.

[4] *Annales Cambriae.* His death, however, is referred to 894 in the Gwentian Brut (*Archaeologia Cambrensis*, series 3, x, p. 18, quoted in Haddan and Stubbs, *Councils and Ecclesiastical Documents*, i. 207).

[5] See note to c. 79, 33.

[6] *Liber Landavensis*, 223, 21.

[7] Ibid. 276, 18 ; 277, 6.

[8] Ibid. 277, 8.

was living about the same time[1]. Giraldus Cambrensis mentions a canon of St. Davids of this name, a supporter of his[2]. It is possible that the hamlet of Tref Asser, in the parish of Llanwnda, Pembrokeshire, where the author of the Life is said to have been born, really derives its name from this canon.

§ 43. From the Life itself we learn that the author was a relative (*propinquus*) of Nobis, Bishop of St. Davids (c. 79, 57), who died in 873[3], and that he was nurtured, taught, tonsured, and ordained in the western parts of Wales (c. 79, 16). This clearly refers to St. Davids, as it was for that monastery and diocese that he, by the counsel of his colleagues, desired Alfred's protection against the attacks of Hemeid, the King of Dyfed (Pembrokeshire and part of Carmarthenshire), who had expelled Bishop Nobis and the author from it (c. 79, 58). In the latter passage he seems to include himself amongst the bishops (*antistites*). His name appears amongst the Bishops of St. Davids[4], but Bishop Stubbs would explain this as meaning that he was a monk, not bishop, of St. Davids, and that he was Bishop of Sherborne[5]. The author states in his confused way that he was sent for by King Alfred *his temporibus* (c. 79, 1), which is usually taken to mean

---

[1] *Liber Landavensis*, 279, 24.

[2] *De iure et statu Menevensis ecclesiae*, distinctio iv. (*Opera*, iii. 214).

[3] *Annales Cambriae*, ed. Phillimore, *Y Cymmrodor*, ix. 166. Whether this is the same person as Nobis, Bishop of Llandaff, it is impossible to decide. The date of the latter, so far as it can be deduced from the notices in the *Liber Landavensis*, would seem to offer no obstacle to the identification of the two, and the name is a very uncommon one. Some little support for the theory of the identity may perhaps be derived from the occurrence of the name of Asser in the diocese of Llandaff (§ 42), since the author of the Life has described himself as a *propinquus* of Nobis.

[4] *Monumenta Historica Britannica*, p. 77; *Descriptive Catalogue*, ii. 551.

[5] *Registrum Sacrum Anglicanum*, ed. 2, p. 217.

884 [1], the last date mentioned by him in the annalistic portion of the work.  It is however uncertain whether he means that he came to the king in 884, or whether he mentions his visit to the king in connexion with the coming of the other scholars concerned in the revival of learning under the auspices of Alfred.  He expressly states, in c. 73, that he is breaking off from the annalistic portion of his work, and he goes back from there to the king's wedding (c. 74), which occurred in 868 (c. 29), and in c. 77, 10 he mentions the participation of Archbishop Plegmund, whom the king had attracted from Mercia, in Alfred's efforts.  It was not till 890 that Plegmund was made Archbishop, but it is probable that he was with the king some time before he became primate [2].  Bishop Stubbs has remarked that ' Alfred's revival of learning seems distinctly to have begun under Archbishop Plegmund [3],' and he has assigned the arrival of Grimbald, whom the author of the Life mentions in the chapter preceding the account of his own first visit to the king, to 892 or later [4].  Thus if any attention is to be paid to the sequence of the narrative, the author's arrival would have to be placed in 892 or later.  Yet he records that the king began to read and interpret with him in 887 (c. 87 sqq.). We have here a good instance of the confused order in which he writes.  He was conducted to the king at *Denu*, in Sussex [5] (c. 79, 7).  The king desired him

---

[1]  Really 885, the events of that year being merged with those of 884, possibly owing to a scribal error in the Cottonian MS.

[2]  See note to c. 77, 10.

[3]  William of Malmesbury, *Gesta Regum*, ii. p. xlvi.

[4]  Ibid.  See, however, note to c. 78, 4, within.

[5]  Probably East or West Dean, near Seaford.  It is noteworthy that the early thirteenth-century ' Proverbs of Alfred' represent the king as presiding over a meeting of bishops, earls, thanes, and others (a *witena-gemōt*) at Sevorde (ed. Morris, *An Old English Miscellany*, Early English Text Society, p. 102).  These proverbs are seemingly of older date than this text, for Æthelred of Rievaulx says, in his account of Alfred, ' extant parabolae eius plurimum habentes aedificationis, sed et

to remain in his service, but, upon his demurring to
this, suggested that he should remain half of each
year with him, spending the other half in Wales
(ll. 10–23). On his journey homewards to consult his
colleagues he was stricken down with fever *in Wintonia
civitate*, and suffered from it for a year and a week
(line 33). This has usually been taken to refer to
Winchester, and doubts have been thrown upon the
authenticity of a work that could say that the writer
lay ill in the capital [1] for so long a period without the
king's knowledge. Here again it seems to us that
a forger would not have committed such a stupid
blunder as this. The explanation of the passage seems
to be that *Wintonia civitas* is not Winchester but
Caerwent, which was on his way to St. Davids [2].
On his recovery, with the counsel and licence of all
the inmates of St. Davids (*nostri omnes*), he agreed
to the proposed arrangement, in the hope of enlisting
the king's support for St. Davids. He then details
his second visit to the king (c. 81, 9), which was pro-
tracted to eight months, during which he read and
explained to the king such books as he wished (line 10).
With difficulty he obtained leave to return home (line
15), and the king conferred upon him, on Christmas
eve, the monasteries of Congresbury and Banwell, with
other gifts (line 22). At a later time Alfred bestowed
upon him Exeter and its diocese in Saxony and Cornwall (line 30). We may assume that the author then
relinquished his half-yearly sojourn in Wales. Beyond
this he tells us nothing about himself, except the
mention of his assistance to the king in his studies
(c. 88 sqq.). The king, we are told, began to read
and interpret in 887 (c. 87), at Martinmas (c. 89, 14).

venustatis et iocunditatis' (apud Twysden, *Decem Scriptores*,
col. 355).

  [1] It is an anachronism to speak of a capital in the ninth
century.

  [2] See note to this passage.

Beyond this year the chronological portion is not continued, and there are no indications of later dates except the statement that the king suffered from a bodily affliction from his twentieth to his fortieth year and after (c. 74, 9), i. e. after 888 (according to the author's method of reckoning the years), and the statement that the king suffered from illness until his forty-fifth year (c. 74, 63), in which year c. 91, 4, was written. This would fix the date of the composition in 893. The work finishes in an abrupt manner.

§ 44. Throughout the Life the author speaks as a contemporary, and he occasionally cites men from whom he derived his information. The king is quoted as his authority in c. 13, 31 ; and he reports sayings of his in cc. 24, 9 ; 25, 3 ; 76, 41 ; 88, 29 ; 106, 32. With his own eyes he saw that the king always carried about with him his handbook (c. 24, 4 ; cf. 88, 6) and that he was a skilful huntsman (c. 22, 19). He states that he saw Alfred's mother-in-law a few years before her death (c. 29, 9), and that he had seen a 'pagan' boy-monk at Athelney (c. 94, 9). He mentions that certain men had informed him of Abbot John's acquaintance with the art of war (c. 97, 11), and he cites the evidence of men who had been present at the battle of Ashdown (c. 37, 14). The character of King Æthelbald he gives upon the authority of informants (c. 12, 15)[1]. From eye-witnesses he derived the account of Eadburh's begging in the streets of Pavia (c. 15, 24), a city frequented by the English pilgrims on the road to Rome. His knowledge of Berkshire, where the king had large estates, appears in his mention of the abundant growth of box in Berroc wood (c. 1, 4), and in his statement that he had seen the thorn-tree growing on the battle-field of Ashdown (c. 39, 6). The situation of the fortress of Cynuit in Devon is described from personal know-

---

[1] Compare also c. 13, 18.

ledge (c. 54, 13). This would be in his diocese. His description of the position of Wareham (c. 49, 8) is probably also from his own observation[1]. He describes the geographical position of London (c. 4, 4), Surrey (c. 5, 2), Wilton (c. 42, 18), Chippenham (c. 52, 4) Cirencester (c. 57, 5), Fulham (c. 58, 4), Athelney (c. 92, 10), and Rochester (c. 66, 6). In the case of the Isle of Sheppey (c. 3, 7), he states that there was a monastery in it.

§ 45. Of Wales his knowledge seems to have been larger[2]. This is fully in accordance with his character as a Welshman. In c. 80 he mentions the Welsh kings of his time, and, so far as the scanty Welsh records of this time go, he makes no mistake in regard to them. This chapter alone is a very strong argument in favour of the authenticity of the work. It is impossible that an imaginary twelfth-century English forger (§§ 69, 78) could have written this chapter without betraying himself into some grievous error, and it is questionable whether any Welshman of that period could have got together so accurately the names of these ninth-century rulers of Wales. Mr. Bradshaw has already remarked that the Welsh words in the Life 'are of such unmistakeable purity, that it is an absolute impossibility that the work can be a forgery of the twelfth century[3].' Professor Rhys, who has examined the names for us, agrees with this pronouncement. He states that he should date these forms

[1] Possibly also that of Reading (c. 35, 10), and of Shaftesbury (c. 98, 1).

[2] The reference to Offa's Dyke, c. 14, 3, is probably to be ascribed to his local knowledge of Wales, and not to information gleaned by him in England.

[3] *Collected Papers*, Cambridge, 1889, p. 467. The Welsh names used by the author are, in addition to those cited in the next section, *Degui* (c. 79, 52, 56), *Hemeid* (cc. 79, 54; 80, 2), *Nobis* (c. 79, 57), *Demetica regio* (cc. 54, 2 ; 80, 4), *Rotri* (c. 80, 5, 12, 13), *Houil* (line 6), *Ris* (ib.), *Gleguising* (ib.), *Brochmail* (ib.), *Fernmail* (line 7), *Mouric* (ib.), *Guent* (ib.), *Helised* (line 10), *Teudubr* (line 11), *Brecheniauc* (ib.); *Anaraut* (line 13).

between about the middle of the ninth and that of
the tenth century. It therefore seems clear that the
writer of this work, in addition to his accurate knowledge of Welsh history of the ninth century, uses
accurately Welsh of that period. To do this must
surely have been beyond the power of any forger,
more especially an English one, of the twelfth century.
The statement that the Danes came to Devon from
Dyfed (c. 54, 2) is another proof of acquaintance with
events in South Wales.

§ 46. Further evidence of the Welsh origin of the
author may be found in the Welsh names given by
him to places in England. Thus he tells us that
Exeter was called in the British tongue *Cairuuisc*
(c. 49, 23), Cirencester *Cairceri* (c. 57 ,5), Dorchester
*Durngueir* (c. 49, 7). These are the regular Welsh
descendants of the Old Celtic forms recorded in the
Roman names of these cities. Cairceri may have
been derived from the list of cities added to the
*Historia Britonum* (Nennius), but the other two do
not occur in it. In addition he gives us the British
names of Selwood *Coit Maur* (c. 55, 8), and of
Nottingham *Tigguocobauc* (c. 30, 3), which are elsewhere otherwise unknown[1], and he uses Welsh forms
of English river names. Thus the Wiley is the *Guilou*
(c. 42, 19), the Frome is the *Frauu* (c. 49, 6), the Exe
the *Uuisc* (c. 49, 24), the Wiltshire Avon the *Abon*
(c. 52, 5). Of these the first three show specific Welsh
developments in form that are later than the time
when these names were taken over into English. It
would not be difficult for a Welshman to recognize
the Welsh *Abon* in the O.E. *Æfen*, but the variations

---

[1] The explanations of the meaning of local names should
probably also be regarded as a Welsh trait. Giraldus Cambrensis in such phrases as ' Ridhelic, quod Britannice Vadum
Salicis, Anglice vero nunc Wiliford, dicitur ' (*Itinerarium Kambriae, Opera*, vi. 165) curiously resembles the expressions of the
author of the Life.

between the English and Welsh forms of the other
names are too great to be reconciled in this way,
and we must therefore conclude that they were
derived from Celtic-speaking people. It may be
argued that these forms might have come from a
Cornish author[1], but the intimate knowledge of Wales
displayed in the work supports the writer's statement
that he came from Wales. The British name of the
Isle of Thanet *Ruim* (c. 9, 4) may have been derived
from Nennius. It is possible that we have also a
Celtic form in *Cynuit* (c. 54, 6). A clear proof of the
Celtic origin of the writer is afforded by his use of
*dexteralis* for 'south' (cc. 35, 10 ; 79, 4 ; 80, 2), a literal
translation of the Welsh *deheu* 'south, right hand.'
Similarly *sinistralis* for 'northern' (cc. 52, 4 ; 79, 11)
represents the Old Welsh *cled* 'north,' Modern Welsh
*cledd* 'left (hand),' *go-gledd* 'north.' He uses Welsh
spellings of English names in *Geguuis*, O.E. *Gewisse*
(c. 1, 18), *Guihtgara*, O.E. *Wihtgara* (c. 2, 11).

§ 47. It is in accordance with his character as a
Welshman that we find evidence of imperfect knowledge of O.E. grammar. Thus he occasionally mis-
understands the O.E. of the Chronicle[2], and he takes
over O.E. case-endings that are out of place in a Latin
version. He uses O.E. datives singular as nominatives
or accusatives[3], and nominatives as genitives[4] and

[1] Cf. the spurious Glastonbury charter of 682 'iuxta collem,
qui dicitur Brittannica lingua *Cructan*, apud nos *Crycbeorh*'
(*Cart. Sax.* i. 97, 24).
[2] See notes to cc. 18, 5 ; 56, 26 ; 62, 3 ; 66, 13 ; 83, 5. The
error at c. 49, 20 appears to be due to the copyist and not to the
author.
[3] *Aclea*, c. 5, 6 ; *Æcglea*, c. 55, 17 ; *Cippanhamme*, c. 9, 12 ;
*Exanceastre*, cc. 49, 22 ; 52, 3 ; 81, 28 ; *Cirrenceastre*, cc. 57, 4 ;
60, 3 ; *Hrofesceastre*, c. 66, 6. The final -*e* in such forms as
-*scire* (c. 1, 4) ; *Grantebrycge* (c. 47, 11), may possibly be due to
Parker's transcriber (see above, p. xvii, note 2). Æthelweard
similarly uses *Aclea* as nominative (*Mon. Hist. Brit.* 511 D,
514 E).
[4] *Stuf* and *Wihtgar*, c. 2, 6.

ablatives [1]. In the case of the datives plural of the names of people and towns, he treats them as nominatives or accusatives [2]. In one case he substitutes the accusative plural *Basengas* (c. 40, 5) for the dative plural of the Chronicle. Faulty knowledge of O.E. is also responsible for the erroneous translation of *Æsces-dun* as 'mons fraxini' (c. 37, 3).

§ 48. The only hints suggestive of any knowledge of the continent are the mention of the monastery at Condé (c. 65, 6), the description of Charles as *rex Alamannorum* and of his election (c. 70), the situation of the Seine and Paris and the siege of the latter (c. 82), and the statement that Chézy was a *villa regia* (c. 84, 11). The description of the southern portion of the North Sea and the English Channel as the 'marinus sinus, qui inter Antiquos Saxones et Gallos adiacet' (c. 70, 4), which the Chronicle simply calls 'this sea,' is noteworthy in this connexion. The language of the work also shows continental influence (§ 58), and the time of day given for the eclipse in c. 59 seems to be derived from observation in Flanders or North Germany. The author nowhere mentions how he learnt English. If he was acquainted with Old Saxon or Flemish, he would not have experienced much difficulty in understanding English. He refers to German customs in c. 13, 29.

§ 49. The object of the work is referred to upon two occasions only. In the first instance the author states that his principal aim was to put on record as much as he knew of the infancy and boyhood of Alfred (c. 21, 13). In c. 73 he defines his purpose as that of recounting the life, manners, conversation,

---

[1] *Cerdic* and *Cynric*, c. 2, 8.

[2] *Seaxum*, cc. 3, 8, 10; 4, 6, 7; 79, 5. In c. 69, 3 he uses the dat. plural of the Chronicle as a gen. plural. The *Seaxam* of c. 18, 5 seems to be an alteration of Parker's from *Seaxum*. Æthelweard occasionally uses *sætum* and *Defenum* as either indeclinable or as genitives.

and, to some extent, the history of the king. The
variation between the two statements is due to the
confused style of the author (§ 56). He seems to
refer to c. 21 in the *ut promisi* of c. 73, 10, although
there is no promise there or anywhere else [1]. The
work is dedicated to the king. Notwithstanding this
he speaks of England and the English as if he were
addressing his own countrymen. They are *illa gens*
(cc. 1, 17 ; 42, 36 ; 93, 7, 13), their country is *illa regio*
(c. 93, 9), where the pronoun is used as a demonstra-
tive, not as a mere article as it became in the Romanic
languages. Cf. also *eiusdem gentis* (c. 79, 6). The
*nostro more* of c. 54, 9, would seem to refer to the
Welsh. Wessex he calls *Saxonia* (cc. 12, 21, 22 ;
14, 29), which is in accordance with Welsh usages
and not with English. He is more interested in the
spiritual side of life than the secular (c. 16, 12), as one
might expect from his profession.

§ 50. The form chosen by the author for his work
is certainly a remarkable one. He begins abruptly,
after the dedication, by giving the birth and genealogy
of his hero. He then takes up the Chronicle from
that time and renders it into Latin. Into this he
inserts the account of the rising against Æthelwulf
upon his return from Rome (c. 12), which was instigated
by a Bishop of Sherborne, and would therefore possess
some interest for a later bishop of that see. He
then records, on the authority of Alfred, Eadburh's
crimes and death (cc. 13–15) ; next he relates the

---

[1] This seems a more probable explanation of the *ut promisi*
than Lingard's view that it refers to a promise made by the
writer to his brethren at St. Davids (*History and Antiquities of
the Anglo-Saxon Church*, London, 1845, ii. 421). It is possible
that the author sent a copy to St. Davids, where it may have been
seen by Giraldus Cambrensis (§ 37), but it is difficult to believe
that the brethren of St. Davids were sufficiently interested in the
personal history of the king to exact a promise from Asser to
compose a biography of their distant protector. It is hardly
credible that the *ut promisi* can refer to c. 16, 17.

provisions made by Æthelwulf in his will (c. 16).
He then resumes the translation of the Chronicle,
which he abruptly deserts in c. 21 in order to tell us
what he knew of Alfred's childhood (cc. 22-25). The
following ten chapters are derived from the Chronicle,
the translation of which he interrupts in order to
relate what he had learnt about the Battle of Ashdown
(cc. 36-9). He follows the Chronicle from here to
c. 53, adding occasionally somewhat to its matter.
In c. 54 he deals at length with the battle of Cynuit,
which is briefly mentioned, though not by name, in
the Chronicle. That work supplies his material from
here to the end of c. 72, when he states that he now
returns to the object of his work, that is, to give an
account of Alfred's life and manners. He recurs to
the Chronicle at cc. 82-6. The remaining twenty
chapters are biographical, and are not derived from
any source known to us.

§ 51. This curious mixture of chronicle and biography has exposed the work to much adverse
criticism (§§ 62, 76). But even if the work were
unique in character, this arrangement would not condemn it as spurious. It has also been objected that
it is an unparalleled circumstance that the author
wrote the book before the king's death and did not
complete it. A ready parallel for this may be found
in the *Encomium Emmae,* which was written during
her lifetime [1]. A closer parallel exists in the Life of
Ludwig the Pious by Thegan, which was written in
the emperor's lifetime, and was not continued to his
death. This author, like our own, drew up his work
partly on annalistic lines, began with the genealogy

[1] Another parallel is to be found in the Latin verse life of
King Æthelstan quoted by Malmesbury, *Gesta Regum,* c. 132
sqq., which, he tells us, was written during the king's lifetime.
Æthelweard, it may be remembered, carried his Chronicle down
to the death of Edgar in 975, although he lived until 998
(*Crawford Charters,* p. 118).

of the emperor's house, and vaunted the superiority of the younger son over the elder ones (c. 3). He also uses the imperfect and past tenses in speaking of the emperor's figure, habits, &c. (c. 19). Yet this work was undoubtedly written before the death of Louis, and is free from any suspicion of spuriousness. Another Frankish work that may also be cited is the Life of Ludwig by the unknown author described as the 'Astronomer.' This was written after the death of the emperor, and is, like the present work, highly rhetorical. It agrees also with the Life of Alfred in deriving the chronological backbone of the work from the annals, in this case the Frankish imperial annals, which are amplified and, even more than in our author, corrupted and confused. Like the Life of Alfred it gives an account of the childhood of the hero. but this is derived from the monk Adhemar, who was brought up with Ludwig. It is certainly noteworthy that among the scanty list of royal biographies of the ninth century that of Alfred should find two such close parallels in a country so intimately connected with Britain as Frankland. That the author of the Life should have taken these Frankish biographies as his models is by no means improbable, for there are suggestions of an acquaintance with the empire in the few instances of local knowledge given in § 48 ; there is stronger evidence in the language in which the work is written (§ 58) ; and, finally, there is evidence that he was acquainted with the greatest of the Frankish biographies, the Life of Charles the Great by Einhard. In c. 73 he adapts to his own purpose the language of the preface of this famous work[1], and in the following chapters we can perceive some indications that the order of his biographical matter has been influenced by that in Einhard. It is

___

[1] A phrase is also adapted from it in c. 21, 15. Possibly the phrase *eo amplius* is also borrowed (§ 56).

to be regretted that he did not, like Einhard, give us
a description of his hero's appearance. Possibly his
Latinity was unequal to this task, for so good a scholar
as Einhard was compelled to depict the character
and person of the great emperor by means of a patchwork of phrases drawn from Suetonius's life of
Augustus. It may be that this was reserved for
a later part of the work, as in Einhard, where it
comes just before the account of the death of Charles,
and that this was never written. The author of the
Life is much more accurate than Einhard in his
historical details (§ 62).

§ 52. The fact that the Life relates nothing later
than 887, although it was written in 893 (§ 43), and
although the author survived the death of his hero in
899 by nine or ten years, has also brought condemnation upon the work. But, as we have seen, the work
of Thegan, the authenticity of which is unquestioned,
is open to the same objection, and we cannot therefore
attach much weight to it in the present case. It has
been suggested that the author worked from a copy
of the Chronicle that had been brought down to 887
only [1], but it is possible that he omitted the annals
after that year on account of their unimportant nature.
In 893, according to the chronology of the Chronicle,
the Danish attacks upon England recommenced, but
it was not until the next year that anything beyond
the capture of a small fort in Kent is recorded. The
Chronicle seems to be a year in advance of the real
date hereabouts, but if we reduce these dates by one
year there would still remain the possibility that the
author might have written this work in 893 before

---

[1] Thomas Wright, *Biographia Britannica Literaria*, London,
1842, i. 409; Hardy, *Monumenta Historica Britannica*, 78,
note 13; *Descriptive Catalogue*, i. 550; Earle, *Two Saxon
Chronicles*, p. xv ; Ernst Grubitz, *Kritische Untersuchung über
die angelsächsichen Annalen bis zum Jahre* 893, Göttingen, 1868,
pp. 32–3.

the news of the king's laborious and successful campaign reached him in his distant diocese. The years
from 887 to 892 were years of quiet, which is reflected
by the triviality of the entries in the Chronicle. It
is precisely in these peaceful, uneventful years that
the writer's intimacy with the king is placed. The
last few years of Alfred's life were equally quiet,
and a later forger would be at least as likely to place
his imaginary intimacy with the king in those years.
By so doing he would have been able to include in
his work the most brilliant achievements of his hero.
Of the encomiastic nature of the work, whether genuine
or spurious, there can be no doubt. We may therefore recognize in this silence as to the great events
of 893–4 evidence in favour of the authenticity of the
work.

§ 53. It has been suggested by Prof. Pauli that
the Latin annals embedded in this work may reproduce an earlier contemporaneous series of memoranda
written in Latin, and that the Chronicle is translated
from this hypothetical Latin work[1]. Whatever basis

---

[1] *König Ælfred*, p. 6. So also Stubbs, preface to *Roger of
Howden*, i. xc. Cf. Lingard, *History of the Anglo-Saxon
Church*, ii. 423. Stubbs, preface to Malmesbury's *Gesta Regum*,
ii. xxi, cxxviii, suggests that it is 'possible, and even probable,
that there was a Latin version of the Chronicle which formed
the basis of the work of Florence of Worcester and Simeon of
Durham.' Mr. Plummer also expresses his inclination to the
view that the author of the Life and Florence took the annals
for the period covered by the Life from some common source
(*Two Saxon Chronicles Parallel*, ii. lxxxiii, note 4). His reasons
for this view are that ' though Florence is as a rule briefer than
Asser, yet he has here and there phrases which are not in the
latter, e. g. *sui patris rogatu* i. 74 ⟨c. 8, 5⟩, *in sancta . . .
solennitate ib.* 103 ' ⟨c. 87, 3⟩. As c. 87 is not represented at all in
the Chronicle, it is not a part of the hypothetical Latin annals
but of the Life, and the words referred to by Mr. Plummer are
simply taken by Florence from c. 89, 14, and are not derived by
him from any other source or added by him. The only other
ground given is at ii. 97, where Florence has *rediret* instead of
the *dormiret* of the Cottonian MS. of the Life (c. 67, 9). It

there may be for assuming a Latin original behind
the Chronicle at an earlier period [1], there seems to
us to be no reason for doubting that the author of
the Life translated direct from the Chronicle. The
evidences of mistranslations of the O.E. of the latter
work, and the presence of case-endings that can only
be explained as being derived from something written
in O.E. (§ 47), and the phrases *loco funeris dominati
sunt* and *victoriam accipientes* for 'gaining a victory'
are even stronger proofs that an O.E. original lies at
the back of the Latin annals of the present work.
These phrases are too literal translations of O.E.
phrases that are commonly used in the Chronicle [2].
The forms *Iuthitta, Iuthitha* for *Judith* (cc. 11, 11 ;
13, 8 ; 17, 5 ; 70, 7) also point to the use of an O.E.
original. The use of such Welsh expressions as
*sinistralis* for north (§ 46), and the occurrence of the
author's characteristic *suatim utens* (c. 56, 18) may be
explained away as occurring in phrases added by him

would seem that he has in this corrected the Life by the aid of
the Chronicle (§ 33). The *sui patris rogatu* added by him in
c. 8, 5 are hardly sufficient to support the conclusion hinted at
by Mr. Plummer. So far from Florence using an independent
source for these Latin annals, it seems from his reproduction
of the errors in the Cottonian MS. of the Life that he actually
used this very MS. (§ 25 sqq.). The blunder in c. 49, 20,
which Florence has made worse by adding the word *rex*, is
a strong argument in favour of the view that he took his annals
from the Life, and the presence in his text of the British names
of places is further proof of this. The omission of the mention
of Torksey in c. 45 by Florence suggests that he copied from
the Life and not from the Chronicle or its hypothetical Latin
original.

[1] There is, of course, clear evidence of the use in the earlier
part of the Chronicle of the Latin *Recapitulatio* at the end of
Beda's *Historia Ecclesiastica*, but no evidence of the existence
of Latin annals for Alfred's time has ever been produced, and
from the fact of the author of the Life making his own Latin
version from the Chronicle direct we may conclude that he was
ignorant of any such Latin original or version of the Chronicle.

[2] See note to c. 5, 13.

to the Latin annals, but the presence of the Celtic *per gronnosa loca* to render the *on morfæstenum* of the Chronicle (c. 53, 3) cannot be so easily disposed of. Moreover this hypothesis of the existence of Latin annals of this time is faced by the difficulty that the three writers who independently copy these Latin annals into their own chronicles, and who undoubtedly elsewhere copy the Life (§§ 33–5), Florence of Worcester, the compiler of the first part of Simeon of Durham, and the author of the Annals of St. Neots, agree in the version of the Annals only for so long as they have the guidance of the present work. Florence and the Annals of St Neots have independent translations of the Chronicle before and after the time covered by the annalistic part of the Life. The first part of Simeon of Durham has nothing after 801, when the Northumbrian annals ceased, until the period covered by the Life is reached. After the end of the Life the Durham writer suffers from want of material (§ 35), so that it is evident the Latin annals used by him agreed exactly in duration with those in the Life. It is therefore clear that all these three writers derived their Latin annals for this period from the Life. In the case of the Annals of St. Neots all doubt that the compiler copied from the present work is removed by the fact that he stupidly repeats the passages in which the author of the Life states that he was told such and such details by King Alfred, or by men who were present at certain events.

§ 54. The version of the Chronicle used by the author did not agree with any MS. of that work that has come down to us. It had older forms of names than any of the existing MSS. in *Coenred* (c. 1, 13), *Sceapieg* (c. 3, 6). The oldest existing MS. of the Chronicle (A) dates from the very end of the ninth century, the earlier part being apparently written in 891. The Life agrees with this MS. in omitting the king's mission to India in 883, which is awkwardly inserted in the other MSS., and in having no mention of the capture of the raven banner of the Danes in 878. The *Inwari* of c. 54, 1, represents the correct *Inwæres* of A. But the author of the Life did not use this MS., for he has the correct *Caziei* (c. 84, 11) in place of the *Cariei* of A, and the copy used by him differed, as we shall see, from A in other respects. Of all the existing MSS. it bore the closest relationship to the next oldest MSS., namely B and C, which agree so closely with one another that they seem to have been copied from a common original. With them it read 'few' (*féa*) instead of the 'many' (*feala*) of A in c. 2, 9, and it also had *Wihtgara-byrig* (*Guuihtgara-burhg*) with B and C, instead of the incorrect *Wihtgaras-* of A. It also agreed with B and C against A in having the name Creoda in the royal genealogy between Cerdic and Cynric, and in the names Hathra, Bedwig, and Sceaf (c. 1, 15, 37); in the position of c. 6, which is given in A after the account of the battle of Wicganbeorg (c. 3, 5); in the mention of the death of the ealdormen in c. 9, 8, of the siege of the Danes in c. 30, 16, of the name Ceolwulf in c. 46, 16, and of the hostages in c. 49, 12, of Paris in c. 82, 7, and of the Marne twice in c. 84. It agreed with C against A, B, D in omitting Essex in c. 18, 5, but agreed with A, B, D, E in reading *Winburnan* in c. 41, 4 instead of *Scireburnan* in C. The reading *Geata* (c. 1, 22) appears in B only[1]. But it had important differences from B and C. Thus it gives the name of the Hampshire ealdorman in c. 18, 10 as Osric with A, instead of Wulfheard of B and C. In c. 6, the position of which agrees with B, C against A, the number of ships is given as nine with A against the eight of B and C, although the word *comes* seems to agree with the

---

[1] This is so remarkable as to suggest that B has been influenced by the Life. See, however, note to c. 1, 22, p. 160, below.

*ealdorman* from the latter MSS. against the *dux* of A.
It differed from A, B, and C, and agreed with the
later D and E in having *Caziei* in c. 84, 11 instead of
the blundered *Carici* of A, B, C, and in reading
correctly *Sture* in c. 67, 4 for the *Stufe* of A, B, and
C[1]. Finally it differed from all the MSS. in having
correctly *Carlomannus* in c. 68, 1 instead of *Carl*.
It would thus seem that none of the existing four
families of MSS. was copied from a lost original that
agreed exactly with the copy of the Chronicle used
by the author, and the genealogy of the MSS. has to
be carried beyond the lost original of each of the four
groups[2]. The copy used by the author cannot, there-

---

[1] The reading *Æcglea* in c. 55, 17, corresponding to the *Æglea*
of D and E, against the *Iglea* of A, B, and C, is curious. As it
appears as *Ecglea* in Florence, it can hardly be one of Parker's
alterations in the Life. Yet the Annals of St. Neots have *Iglea*,
which appears to have been the reading of the archetype of the
Chronicle. This may represent the true reading of the Life, of
which the compiler seems to have possessed a better copy than
the Cottonian MS. (§ 34). Florence may have corrected his
form by the aid of his copy of the Chronicle, which closely
resembled D (Plummer, *Two of the Saxon Chronicles Parallel*,
ii. p. lxxxiii), but correction by the compiler of the Annals is also
conceivable.

[2] This result differs somewhat from those of other writers.
Ernst Grubitz, in his able *Kritische Untersuchung über die
angelsächsischen Annalen*, Göttingen, 1868, p. 7 sqq., concluded
that the author of the Life used a copy of the C type. Karl
Horst, *Zur Kritik der altenglischen Annalen*, Darmstadt, 1896,
p. 14, stated that it was of the C or D type. The conclusion of
M. Kupferschmidt, *Ueber das Hss.-verhältniss der Winchester
Annalen*, in *Anglia*, xiii. p. 168, that the author used a text
medium between A, G and B, C is more in accord with our own.
Mr. Plummer, ii. p. lxxxiv, note, holds that the copy used was of
the southern type, and probably not 'identical with any of the
existing MSS.' The northern version is, no doubt, later in date
than the time assigned for the composition of the Life (Plummer,
ii. p. lxxi), but this use of the southern version cannot safely be
used as an argument in favour of the authenticity of the Life.
A later southern writer would probably have known only the
southern version.

fore, have been far removed from the archetype of the Chronicle, for the variations represented in the four groups had clearly not yet arisen[1]. This antiquity and accuracy of the copy of the Chronicle used by him is what one would expect from a writer in whose time the Chronicle was, to all appearances, drawn up. Although this ancient copy is not a decisive argument in favour of the authenticity of the work, it certainly places it upon a somewhat higher level than if we had detected proofs of the writer using one of the later and more corrupt copies[2].

§ 55. The author occasionally adds to the annalistic matter derived from the Chronicle. Most of his additions seem to be mere elaborations of the details contained in the Chronicle. But he gives important information regarding the battle of Æscesdun, the site of which he had seen (c. 39, 6); adds the account of

[1] The position of c. 6 in A after the battle of Wicganbeorh (c. 3, 5) is probably to be ascribed to the besetting sin of the scribe of this portion of that MS., that of being misled by homoeoteleuton (cf. Karl Horst, *Zur Kritik der altenglischen Annalen*, Darmstadt, 1896, p. 25 sqq.). In the present case his eye seems to have wandered from the *wæl geslogon* and *sige namon* referring to the battle of Wicganbeorh to the same words in connexion with the battle of Acleah. He then discovered his error, and added 'the heathen army first wintered' (which follows the account of Wicganbeorh in B, C, D, and E), although this passage is out of place after the defeat of the Danes at Sandwich. Then he copies the remainder of the entry relating to this year.

[2] The chronology is naturally that of the Chronicle. There is no indication of the commencement of the year, and the author must have agreed with the year-commencement, whatever it was, used by the compilers of the Chronicle. It would not be a matter of very great importance to him. There is no proof that he commenced the year with the Incarnation, March 25, as Hardy, *Mon. Hist. Brit.*, Introduction, p. 118, note 3, argues. The addition of *ab Incarnatione* does not prove that the year began with that feast, and the years of the Chronicle are reckoned from the Incarnation. Hardy's other ground is that the eclipse of c. 59, ascribed to 879, was that of March 14, 880. The eclipse, however, seems clearly to be that of October 29, 878.

the Danish *vallum* between the Thames and the
Kennet at Reading (c. 35, 9); and the ample details
of the fight at Cynuit (c. 54) which is briefly referred
to, though not by name, in the Chronicle. The scene
of this battle was in Asser's diocese, and the author
states that he had examined the site. He also
supplies the name of the place where the marriage
of Burhred with Alfred's sister was celebrated (c. 9,
12); the name of Alfred's father-in-law and mother-
in-law (c. 29, 5, 7); states that the Danes slain at
Cynuit came from Dyfed (c. 54, 2); mentions the
site of the fortress of the Danes at Rochester, and
that they had brought with them from France the
horses captured by the English (c. 66, 8, 13). As
there are no means of checking these additions to the
Chronicle, their credibility must stand or fall with that
of the Life. In their favour we may urge that there is
nothing improbable in them, and that they mostly relate
to events in a country with which Asser was familiar.
The author states correctly that Archbishop Ceolnoth
was buried at Canterbury (c. 34, 2), and supplies the
time of day when the eclipse in c. 59 occurred. There
is some support for his account of the surrender by
Æthelwulf of the kingdom of Wessex to his son
(c. 12); and his account of the custom of not crowning
the wives of the West-Saxon kings (c. 13, 12), and
of the marriage of Judith to Æthelbald, her step-son
(c. 17, 5), are corroborated by a Frankish chronicle of
the time (§ 90).

§ 56. The style of the work is highly rhetorical, and
gives one the impression that the author thought
more of the display of his powers of composition and
command of recondite words than of the matter conveyed by them. Sometimes, it is true, he shows a
tendency to excessive explanation, but more often his
meaning is obscured by a cloud of verbiage[1]. The

---

[1] In c. 29, 8 'nos ipsi propriis oculorum nostrorum obtutibus
. . . vidimus' is a considerably worse pleonasm than the 'ego

construction of his sentences is occasionally so involved
that they have puzzled the scribes of the Cottonian
MS., who have added to the confusion by omitting
verbs or other important members of the sentences
(§ 25). Confusion is also caused by the author's
unmethodical habit of anticipating events and then
returning suddenly, without due notice, to the theme
from which he has wandered away. In one case he
states that he is narrating events out of their chronological order (c. 74. 41). The aimless wandering to
and fro in this chapter has led to its being frequently
misunderstood, and has in consequence subjected the
work to much misrepresentation. This chapter affords
a good example of the author's ornate style, of his
over-elaboration of details whilst still leaving his
main subject enveloped in a nebulous atmosphere of
words and clauses. This chapter also shows his
tendency to wander off into side issues that considerably perplex his narrative. We have already pointed
out the difficulty of extricating the date of his arrival
from the bewildering arrangement of his materials
(§ 43), and the confused statement of the object of his
work (§ 49). Further instances of these qualities
may be found in cc. 22–25 ; 76 ; 79 ; 81 ; 91 ; 97,
9–19 ; 106. He has a fondness for long words,
which occasionally leads him to do violence to their
meaning, e.g. *velamentum* is used for *velum* (c. 21, 10),
and in many other cases a literal translation of his Latin
would read like nonsense, owing to the perverted
senses in which the words are employed. He evidently
revelled in the long-drawn out metaphors at cc. 76,
62 ; 88, 39 ; 91, 30. Frequently he wanders off into
passages that have the air of sermons (cc. 76, 45 sqq. ;
88, 15 sqq.; 89 ; 90 ; 91, 55 sqq.; 95 ; 96, 20 sqq.).
There are occasional traces of alliteration, especially
at c. 76, 62 sqq. He has a liking for certain phrases,

oculis meis vidi' instanced by Quintilian, viii. 3, § 53. There
are many instances of the parallel defect of macrology.

such as *a primaevo iuventutis suae flore* (cc. 16, 19;
74, 37, 42); *aequali lance* (cc. 37, 6; 99, 25; 104, 6);
*veredicus referens* (cc. 13, 32, 33; 37, 13; cf. 97, 12);
*omnia praesentis vitae studia*, or *curricula*, or *impedimenta*, or *dispendia*, or *temporibus* (cc. 16, 3; 22, 8; 24,
5; 25, 2, 13; 40, 1; 75, 28; 76, 2: cf. cc. 81, 14; 91,
35; 100, 20; 105, 7). Other repetitions will be found
in cc. 21, 15 = 73, 4; 25, 2 = 76, 41; 25, 10 = 91, 10;
25, 3 = 106, 55. He is somewhat given to climax,
strengthening his previous predication by *immo* (cc.
12, 18; 13, 16, 34; 16, 6; 22, 2; 23, 5; 25, 7; 105, 4).
Somewhat similar is the use of *eo amplius* (cc. 22, 12;
74, 10, 63; cf. 91, 4 note; 105, 3).

§ 57. Any argument from the style of the Latinity
is rendered difficult by the entire lack of specimens
of Welsh Latin of this period. From the early part
of the ninth century, when the *Historia Brittonum*
took its present form, no Welsh Latin is known until
we reach the later notices of gifts of the ninth and
tenth centuries in the eleventh-century *Liber Landavensis*. There is also a handful of saints' lives of
uncertain date. But it is noticeable that the vocabulary of the author resembles that of these texts, on
the one hand, and, on the other, that in use in the
chanceries of the English kings in the tenth and
eleventh centuries. In addition to the Celtic Latin *graphium* (c. 11, 4), *gronna* (cc. 92, 9; 97, 25), and perhaps
*gabulum* (c. 89, 11), it has the word *expeditio* for army
(c. 42, 40), and certain archaic Latin words, derived
originally from glossaries or grammatical treatises,
such as *quis = quibus* (c. 88, 42), the adverb *oppido*
(cc. 8, 6; 37, 11), *suatim* [1] (cc. 56, 18; 74, 21; 106, 22),
which also occur in English Latin of this period. In
addition to these it has the word *famen* 'conversa-

---

[1] His fondness for adverbs ending in *-atim* is shared by other
writers of Latin in Western Europe prior to the eleventh or
twelfth century. He has *locupletatim*, c. 98, 9; *densatim*, c. 88,
42; *elucubratim*, cc. 77, 9; 97, 2, and *segregatim*, c. 88, 25.

tion,' 'dialogue' (c. 79, 9), which immediately connects
it with the curious vocabulary of the bewildering
Celtic work known as *Hisperica Famina*[1]. In this
work the high-water mark of pedantic and ostentatious
rhetoric was reached, at the cost of intelligibility.
This Celtic Latinity seems to have been in use in
England from the time of Aldhelm until the Norman
Conquest, when it gave place to the purer and
infinitely more intelligible Latinity derived by the
Normans from their Italian masters[2]. The Life of
Guthlac by Felix, an eighth-century work, is influenced
by this Latinity, which blossoms into extravagances
almost worthy of Aldhelm himself in the hands of
the authors of Æthelstan's charters, which contain
many Hisperic words. In the tenth century many
Englishmen went to the monastery of Fleury, the
great home of this Hesperic Latinity, whither it had
been transplanted from Brittany. It is possible that
this Hisperic Latin of Æthelstan's time may have
been imported from Fleury, but it is likely that the
foreign clerks in Alfred's service may have had a
share in bringing it into favour in England. In view
of the Celtic influences upon the English Latinity

[1] See Bradshaw, *Collected Papers*, p. 464 sqq.; Zimmer,
*Nennius Vindicatus*, Berlin, 1893, p. 291 sqq.; M. Manitius,
*Geschichte der christlich-lateinischen Literatur bis zur Mitte
des achten Jahrhunderts*, Stuttgart, 1891, p. 485. An edition of
this strange production appeared under the care of J. M.
Stowasser at Vienna in the *Dreizehnter Jahresbericht über das
k. k. Franz-Joseph-Gymnasium in Wien*, 1887, and a more
accessible edition is promised by Dr. F. J. H. Jenkinson. Further
fragments of it were published by Professor Zimmer in the
*Nachrichten* of the Royal Society at Göttingen, ' Philos.-histor.
Klasse,' 1895, p. 119 sqq.

[2] The impression made upon a twelfth-century scholar by
it may be gleaned from William of Malmesbury's well-known
criticism of the Latinity of the O.E. royal charters (*Gesta
Pontificum*, c. 196, p. 344), and of Æthelweard (*Gesta Regum*,
prologue, p. 3). Yet Ordericus Vitalis shows that the influence
was not yet dead in Normandy, where at an earlier time Dudo
of St. Quentin was strongly imbued with it.

of the tenth and earlier centuries, and of the agreement in general style and vocabulary, there seems to be good reason for holding that this is such Latin as a Welshman might have written at the latter end of the ninth century.

§ 58. There is another feature that the Latinity of the work has in common with that of the English Latinity of the tenth century, that is the presence of words of Frankish origin. In this, however, the Frankish strain seems to be stronger than in the English charters, and, as we have seen that the author was acquainted with Frankish biographies (§ 51), one is tempted to suggest that he had studied on the continent. He displays some knowledge of it that may have come from personal experience (§ 48), but he says nothing of having studied abroad. The use of the word *Theotiscus* as a collective name for the Germanic peoples (c. 13, 29) is proof that the undoubtedly Welsh author of the work had some contact with Frankland, either directly or through the medium of Frankish teachers or of Bretons who had been influenced by their Frankish neighbours. Brittany was the channel of communication between the Franks and the insular Celts. Celtic influence upon Frankish learning was exercised by the Irish scholars of the eighth and ninth centuries, and it is only natural that we should expect to find a Frankish reaction upon the insular Celts. A significant indication of this influence of the Franks upon the Welsh, exercised, there can be little doubt, through Brittany, is to be found in the fact that Nennius, the only other Welsh writer of this century known to us, embodies in his work the undoubtedly Frankish table of the descent of the Franks, Romans, Britons, &c., from sons of Japheth [1]. The Frankish words in the present work

---

[1] *Historia Brittonum*, c. 17. Upon this folk-table see Müllenhoff, *Deutsche Alterthumskunde*, ii. 329, who thinks that the text of the table, an early sixth-century Frankish compila-

are *fasellus* (cc. 53, 2 ; 55, 3), *satelles* for 'thane' (c. 100, 9), *fiscus* (c. 102, 3), *curtum* (cc. 22, 4 ; 75, 22 ; 81, 10 ; 100, 5, 11, 21), *indiculus* for 'letter' (c. 79, 38, 40), and *castella* in the sense of 'castle' (c. 91, 49). These words are found in use in England, but the author has other Frankish Latin terms that are not met with in England at this time, such as *ministerialis* for 'thane' (c. 76, 31). The form *cambra* =*camera* (cc. 88, 1 ; 91, 21), and *senior* in the sense of 'lord,' 'master' (cc. 13, 2, 19 ; 97, 26), are Frankish Latin words of specifically Romanic origin. *Capellanus* (cc. 77, 13 ; 104, 2, 7) is a term of undoubted Frankish origin, which does not appear to have been introduced into England until after the Norman Conquest.

§ 59. The biblical quotations are derived in two cases (cc. 76, 49 ; 99, 18) from Old Latin versions ; in the remaining cases (cc. 76, 58 ; 89, 9 ; 96, 20 ; 99, 21 ; 101, 12) they may be either from the Vulgate or from Old Latin versions. The use of these pre-Hieronymian versions is noteworthy, for they remained long in use in the Gaulish and Celtic churches[1]. The English,

tion, was taken into Wales by Breton monks. See also Zimmer, *Nennius Vindicatus*, p. 230. In like manner the *Historia Brittonum* derived the tales of the Trojan origin of the Britons from Frankish sources (see Mommsen's edition, p. 116). A proof of this connexion of Welsh scholars with Frankland may be found in the 'Liber de Beneficiis, de raris fabulis,' &c., a ninth-century MS. (Bodl. 572), which Bradshaw, *Collected Papers*, pp. 470, 486, considered to be in 'Welsh handwriting, with tenth-century Cornish glosses.' It represents the monk in the dialogue as answering the question where he had been before by 'Fui antea in Ibernia vel in Britannia vel in Francia nutritus vel fotus fui' (so in MS.). A ninth-century insular Briton who went to Frankland about 840 and became a hermit at Soissons was Mark the Bishop, who is mentioned in Heiric's 'Miracles of St. German' (*Acta Sanctorum*, July 31, p. 272 b). He, however, was educated in Ireland. See further Mommsen, preface to *Historia Brittonum*, p. 120.

[1] See Haddan and Stubbs, *Councils and Ecclesiastical Documents relating to Great Britain and Ireland*, Oxford, 1869, i. 187 ; Samuel Berger, *Histoire de la Vulgate pendant les*

owing to their close intimacy with the church of
Rome, used the Vulgate. The advance of the church
of Rome in Wales and Ireland is marked step by
step by the gradual adoption of the Vulgate. The
fact that the author used an Old Latin version is,
therefore, quite in consonance with his character of
a Welshman writing at the end of the ninth century,
and these quotations are an argument in favour of
the authenticity, though, perhaps, not a conclusive
one. Both the quotations from Old Latin versions
are from very ancient ones. The reading in c. 76, 49
occurs only in the eighth or ninth-century Book of
Armagh and in the ninth-century St. Germain's MS.,
which in the gospels shows Irish influence[1]. The
quotation in c. 99, 18, is also from a very early
version.

§ 60. The only other quotations in the work are
from Sedulius (c. i. 26), St. Gregory's *Regula Pastoralis*
(c. 102, 13), and the hexameter at c. 90, 3, which we
have been unable to trace. It has a Frankish character.
In addition to this the author borrows and adapts,
without mention, a passage from Einhard's Life of
Charles the Great (c. 72) and from Aldhelm (c. 88, 13
and, perhaps, c. 88, 39 sqq., and c. 76, 62). Beda seems
to have been used in c. 4, 5, and Nennius in c. 9, 4.
In c. 103, 3 he quotes as coming from divine scripture
a sentence of St. Augustine, from whom he cannot,
therefore, have taken it direct.

## 6. THE ATTACKS UPON THE AUTHENTICITY OF THE WORK.

§ 61. We have now the unpleasant task of examining
the charges brought against the work. These charges

---

*premiers siècles du Moyen Âge*, Paris, 1893, p. 30 sqq.; Wordsworth and White, *Novum Testamentum Latine*, Oxford, 1889–
98, p. x.

[1] Berger, p. 72.

have been put together with such amazing carelessness, almost every statement of fact being founded upon interpolated matter, upon misunderstandings of the text, or upon unwarrantable assumptions, that we should have preferred to leave them on one side. Historical writers have not cared to examine these charges closely[1], but have satisfied themselves by vague references to the suspicions resting upon the genuineness of the work. This has had the natural result of overshadowing it with a dark cloud of doubt, which has been intensified by the constant citation of its testimony accompanied with reservations as to its authenticity. It is therefore necessary for us to submit these arguments to scrutiny, and for that purpose it is needful to include all of them in our survey. The result is that the dark cloud proves to be at worst nothing more than a thin mist, produced by the author's confusion of thought and language, aided by the blunders of scribes and the wanton alterations of editors.

§ 62. In 1841 Thomas Wright, who about this period was strenuously defending the authenticity of the absurd forgery *De Situ Britanniae*, which Bartram fathered upon Richard of Cirencester, communicated to the Society of Antiquaries a paper in which he threw doubts upon the authenticity of the Life[2]. Rightly recognizing that the chronological portion of the work was little more than a translation of the Chronicle (§§ 50, 53), and that the anecdotes and eulogy of Alfred had been grafted upon it[3], he argues that, if the entries in the Chronicle were contempo-

---

[1] Pauli, *König Ælfred*, passim, and Dr. Lingard, *History of the Anglo-Saxon Church*, ii. 420 sqq., have dealt with a few of them.

[2] *Archaeologia*, xxix. 192–201 ; reprinted in *Essays upon Archaeological Subjects*, London, 1861, i. 172–85, and partly repeated in his *Biographia Britannica Literaria*, London, 1842, i. 409–12.

[3] *Archaeologia*, p. 192 ; *Biographia*, i. 409.

rary, 'it is quite improbable that such a man as Asser
should use them in the way they are used[1].' This
improbability is merely matter of opinion, and it
disappears when we find another ninth-century biographer doing the same thing (§ 51).  Wright then
compares the work to its disadvantage with Einhard's
Life of Charles the Great, remarking that in the
latter we find 'facts told by the biographer with
the vigour and spirit of a man who was active and
interested in them, accompanied with vivid sketches
and clear views of the policy and character of the
great monarch.  When we turn to Asser, we seem to
have a writer who would fain imitate the biographer
of the Frankish emperor, but who only knows the
history of his hero from one bare chronicle, and
depends upon popular traditions for his views of his
personal character[2].'  Similarly we are told that it
appears strange that the Life should have been
written during the lifetime of the king, 'and particularly by a man in the position of Asser,' that
'it is not easy to conceive for what purpose it was
written, or to point out any parallel case,' and that
it is still more difficult to imagine why its author,
who survived the king, did not complete it[3].  It is
maintained that the book 'does not support its own
character; it has the appearance of an unskilful compilation of history and legend[4].'  No evidence is given
in support of this legendary character, and it has no
discernible basis except Parker's interpolation from
the Annals of St. Neots (c. 53 b).  Wright endeavours
to prove that this was part of the Life because the
MS. contained the words 'Et, ut in vita Sancti Neoti
legitur, apud quendam suum vaccarium' (c. 53, 9),
and because there is a second reference to the Life
in c. 74, 21[5].  The former passage is an interpolation

[1] *Archaeologia*, p. 194, note a.          [2] Ibid p. 194.
[3] *Biographia*, p. 408.          [4] Ibid.
[5] *Archaeologia*, p. 195; *Biographia*, p. 410.  At p. 409 of the

of Parker's, and the latter does not refer to a life
of St. Neot at all, and has every mark of being an
early interpolation. For the rest, the character of
Einhard's Life is egregiously overdrawn, and it is
a somewhat unhappy comparison, for if it were not
for external evidence, that work would be more
hopelessly condemned than the present one is by
Wright. It is a medley of phrases culled from
Suetonius, and abounds with chronological errors [1].
An argument that would condemn one biographer
because he has not exactly followed the lines of
another largely resolves itself into a question of
literary feeling and taste, and we may well refuse
to see anything binding in such an argument, more
especially when it is applied to a production of the
ninth century. It is obviously absurd to expect the
author of the present work to describe facts that
happened before he came to Wessex 'with the vigour
and spirit of a man who was active and interested
in them.' On the question of literary feeling it is
enough to quote the remark of Freeman that 'it
seems quite impossible that any forger could have
invented the small touches which bespeak the man
writing from personal knowledge, and that man no
Englishman, but a Briton [2].' The arguments founded

latter work the whole interpolation of c. 53 b is treated as part
of the Life.

[1] See Ranke's well-known characterization of this work in
*Zur Kritik fränkisch-deutscher Reichsannalisten*, in his *Abhandlungen und Versuche*, p. 96 sqq. (*Sämmtliche Werke*, vol. 51);
Wattenbach, *Deutschlands Geschichtsquellen*, i. 153; Ebert,
*Geschichte der Literatur des Mittelalters im Abendlande*, Leipzig, 1880, ii. 96. Ernst Bernheim, *Die Vita Karoli Magni
als Ausgangspunkt zur literarischen Beurtheilung des Histo-
rikers Einhard*, in *Historische Aufsätze dem Andenken an
Georg Waitz gewidmet*, Hanover, 1886, pp. 73-96, has shown
how Einhard's treatment of his subject was dictated by Suetonius,
and that his work of composition consisted of little more than
arranging the phrases of Suetonius so as to suit his purpose.

[2] *Dictionary of National Biography*, i. 161.

upon the fact of the work being written in the king's lifetime, and upon its not being continued until his death—a point that rather tells against the theory that it is a later forgery—will be seen to be of no weight when compared with the parallel instances given in § 51. As almost the whole of the events narrated in the Life happened before the author came to England, it is obvious that he could only obtain a knowledge of them at second hand, and it cannot be seriously maintained that the improbability of his going to the Chronicle for his chronological details is so great that it convicts the work as a forgery. There are grounds for holding that Einhard similarly used the Frankish annals, although many of the events happened during his residence at court[1]. The author was acquainted with Einhard's work (§ 51).

§ 63. Wright argues that the Life is spurious, because, although professing to be written in 893, it borrows from the Chronicle, and 'by the most favourable supposition that has been hazarded on the antiquity of this part of the Chronicle. it was not composed before the beginning of the tenth century, and it is more probable that it is a work of a later period[2].' This would be a fatal argument against the work if the premises were correct. Even in 1841 one must have been in a peculiar frame of mind to believe that the minute entries regarding Alfred's campaigns in the Chronicle were written nearly a century later. Since that time much progress has been made in the study of the Chronicle, the O.E. dialects have been minutely studied and distinguished, and palaeography has become a more exact science. The independent judgement of competent scholars in all three subjects is that we possess in MS. A a copy of the Chronicle that goes back to the time of King

---

[1] Bernheim, p. 82 sqq.
[2] *Archaeologia*, p. 194 ; *Biographia*, p. 409.

Alfred. It is written in archaic West-Saxon that is certainly much older than the middle of the tenth century, and there is no reason for doubting that it is the language of Alfred's time.

§ 64. The next argument is even more baseless. Wright is 'inclined to doubt' the truth of the neglect of Alfred's early education (c. 22, 10) because 'we know that King Ethelwulf was an accomplished scholar, that he had been an ecclesiastic before he came to the throne, that his friends and advisers were ecclesiastics, such as Swithun and Alstan, the former of whom at least was a scholar, that he was a great patron of the clergy and of the Church, that Alfred (his favourite child) was twice carried to Rome before he was six years of age [1].' As Æthelwulf died in Alfred's ninth year, this argument is not of much weight even if the statements upon which it is founded were true. There is no evidence that Æthelwulf was a scholar at all, much less an accomplished one, and the scholarship of Swithun is merely a matter of inference from his office [2]. Against Wright's statements, which are derived from later monkish fabrica-

----

[1] *Archaeologia*, p. 194. Cf. *Biographia*, p. 409, where it is seriously advanced that Alfred's 'mission to Rome is proof that his education was not thus neglected.'

[2] The story that Æthelwulf was educated by Swithun, who subsequently ordained him deacon, comes from the Life of St. Swithun by Goscelin (*Acta Sanctorum*, Julii i, p. 327 A), a professional writer of saints' lives in the eleventh century. This is the source of the statements in Florence of Worcester, i. 68, and William of Malmesbury, *Gesta Pontificum*, ii. c. 75, p. 160. Against this we can place the distinct statement of Landfred, the late tenth-century author of the *Translation of St. Swithun*, that the life and *prisca conversatio* of the saint were unknown because no writing existed (*Acta Sanctorum*, ib. 329 A). There are no details of the saint's life in the verse life ascribed to Wulfstan (MS. Bodl. Auct. F. 2. 14), written between 984 and 1005. How rapidly the story grew may be seen from Henry of Huntingdon, who makes Æthelwulf a bishop of Winchester before he became king.

tions, we have the clear and unquestionable testimony of Alfred himself that, at his accession, he could not find a single priest south of the Humber who could understand the Latin services of the church or could translate a letter from Latin into English [1].

§ 65. Wright next objects that 'the author quotes ⟨c. 13, 31⟩ the oral authority of Alfred in a very ostentatious manner, for the story of Offa's wife ⟨sic⟩ Eadburgha, which must have been familiar to the ears of every inhabitant of Alfred's dominion [2].' This assertion is surely far too sweeping. It was, no doubt, well known that the wife of the king of Wessex was called 'lady' not 'queen,' but that every one outside the court circle knew that this was the result of the poisoning of Beorhtric by Eadburh nearly a century before is a proposition from which we must withhold our assent. Moreover, Alfred's narrative included the continental adventures of Eadburh, which can hardly have been so widely known in Wessex as events that happened at home. The argument assumes that the author is writing for West-Saxons only, and has closed his eyes to people outside Wessex and to posterity [3]. Even if all the details of Eadburh's life had been as fully known in Wessex as Wright maintains, we can scarcely convict the foreign author of forgery because he prefers to vouch the king rather than 'many-tongued fame' for a story for which he could find no written authority [4].

§ 66. On the strength of the interpolated words at the end of c. 53, and of the interpolation from the

---

[1] Preface to translation of Gregory's *Pastoral Care*, ed. Sweet, p. 1.

[2] *Archaeologia*, p. 195 ; *Biographia*, p. 409, to same effect.

[3] Lingard, ii. 426, holds that the author is writing for the monks of St. Davids.

[4] Pauli, *König Ælfred*, p. 11, points out that the *multis habetur incognitum*, with which this story is introduced, is consonant with the foreign origin of the author.

Annals of St. Neots (c. 53 b), and of the reference [1] to St. Neot in c. 74, 21, Wright asserts that the author used a Life of St. Neot. He holds that lives of this saint were not composed until the end of the tenth century, at the time of the felonious transference of the saint's relics from Cornwall to Huntingdonshire in 974 [2]. But as the solitary reference to St. Neot in the Life, apart from Parker's interpolations, speaks of the saint's body as resting in Cornwall with that of St. Gueriir, it is obvious that this passage, whether due to the author or, as we hold, to a tenth-century interpolator, must have been written before the body of St. Neot was carried to Huntingdonshire. The date of the transference was, however, not 974, but about 1000. Before the latter date the fame of St. Neot had wholly eclipsed that of St. Gueriir, so that their burial-place in Cornwall became known as St. Neot, the name it bears to this day. The fact that the author mentions the earlier saint, who was so entirely forgotten that he finds no place in the list of saints and their burial-places in England, which was compiled in the first quarter of the eleventh century [3], is a decided argument in favour of the composition of the work before the middle of the tenth century. For the statement that the author used a Life of St. Neot there is no justification in the text.

§ 67. There is even less basis for the next count in the indictment, that a friend of Alfred's could not have made so much confusion as exists in the chapter (74) containing the reference to SS. Gueriir and Neot. According to Wright this chapter states that, although Alfred was radically cured by St. Neot of the infirmity

---

[1] In the *Biographia*, p. 410, he carelessly asserts that 'there are also other allusions to this life of Neot.'

[2] *Archaeologia*, p. 195; *Biographia*, p. 410.

[3] Liebermann, *Die Heiligen Englands*, Hanover, 1889; the Hyde *Liber Vitae*, Hants Record Society, p. 87 sqq.

from which he suffered from his twentieth to his
fortieth year, he is nevertheless described as still
labouring under it at the time when the book was
written[1]. It is difficult to conceive a forger stupid
enough to make such a blunder, and as a matter
of fact the confusion is due to Wright, not to the
author[2].

§ 68. The next point is that Wright suspects that
the reference to the building of long ships in 877
is an allusion to the ship-building of 897, and that a
contemporary would not have made such a mistake[3].
The author made no such mistake. It is an interpolation of Parker's from Matthew of Paris (c. 50 c).

§ 69. From the author's reference to the *parochia*
or diocese of Exeter (c. 81, 29), Wright concludes
that the work was not fabricated until the end of
the eleventh century, since the see of Crediton was
not transferred to Exeter until the time of Edward
the Confessor, and he states that he was 'not aware
that there was anything in the oldest MS. to contradict
this opinion[4].' The transference to Exeter occurred
in 1050, and we must allow at least half a century
before we can assume that a forger would be likely
to make the mistake of calling Asser bishop of Exeter
in the ninth century. As Sir John Spelman tells us
that this portion of the MS. was in the oldest hand
(§ 19)[5], and this is confirmed by the absence of any note
of Wise to the contrary, it seems that it was written
in the MS. half a century or so before 1050. Again
we have here an argument that really tells in favour
of the work, instead of against it. A forger at the

---

[1] *Archaeologia*, pp. 195-6; *Biographia*, p. 410.
[2] See our note to c. 74, 36. The mistake of Wright's has
been already pointed out by Lingard, ii. 427.
[3] *Archaeologia*, p. 196.
[4] *Archaeologia*, pp. 199-200; *Biographia*, p. 411.
[5] It is possible, however, that by 'the ancienter and more
undoubted hand' he meant merely to distinguish the hands of
the MS. from Parker's interpolated matter.

end of the eleventh century, if he had wished to
ascertain the see of Bishop Asser, would have found
that he was bishop of Sherborne, just as Florence
of Worcester and William of Malmesbury did.  The
obvious source to go to at that period was the widely
circulated list of bishops (§ 39), which would have
speedily shown a reader that there was no continuous
line of bishops at Exeter prior to 1050.

§ 70.  Another argument is a most ill-considered
one.  It is founded upon the 'murder' of John the
Old Saxon by some of his monks (*sic*), which is
narrated in c. 95.  Wright mentions that this story
'appears to have been prevalent at a later period,
as it is alluded to under different forms by historians
of the twelfth century[1].'  The reference is to the
murder of John the Scot at Malmesbury abbey in
William of Malmesbury[2].  Whatever argument is
intended to be founded upon this vanishes at once
when it is seen that William definitely narrates his
story of John the Scot, who is mentioned by him
as distinct from John the Old Saxon.  Wright then
dwells upon the point that the author of the Life
says that the attack upon John the Old Saxon
happened 'some time before,' *quodam tempore* (c. 95,
1 ; c. 96, 1).  This is surely straining the meaning.  He
then adduces the fact that Alfred refers to the slain
abbot as alive in the preface to the *Pastoral Care*,
and that he calls him 'my mass-priest,' and not
'my abbot.'  The latter circumstance does not strike
us as important.  Unfortunately for the rest of the
argument the writer of the Life does not state that
John was slain, but merely wounded, and he commences his narration of this event with a distinct
statement that the plot to murder the abbot mis-
carried (c. 96, 23).  See § 76.

§ 71.  Another objection advanced by Wright is

---

[1] *Archaeologia*, p. 198.
[2] *Gesta Regum*, c. 122 (i. 130, 131).

that the author of the Life does not mention the
king's literary works, more especially his translation
of Gregory's *Pastoral Care*, in which Alfred thanks
Asser for his assistance [1]. Considering the wide circulation of the translation of the *Pastoral Care*, one
can only express surprise that the imaginary forger
at the end of the tenth or eleventh century does not
make any mention of this work. The silence of an
author writing in 893 is more easily explained, for
we have no evidence that the work was then in
existence. Wright argues that it was ' probably ' translated between 890 and 894, but no grounds are given
for this supposition. Our sole means of ascertaining
the date are a consideration of the names of the
bishops to whom the copies of which we have record
were presented by the king. They are Plegmund,
archbishop of Canterbury from 890 to 914, Werfrith,
bishop of Worcester from 873 to 915, Heahstan, whose
death as bishop of London is recorded in the Chronicle
under 898, Swithwulf, bishop of Rochester, who died
in 897 according to the same authority, and a Wulfsige, who may be Asser's predecessor at Sherborne
or the successor of Heahstan at London. Bishop
Stubbs fixes the arrival in the country of Grimbald,
who is also thanked in the preface to the *Pastoral
Care*, as occurring in 892 [2]. Wright alleges that the
' original ' copy of Alfred's version of the *Pastoral
Care*, preserved in the Public Library of Cambridge
University, is addressed to ' Wulfsige, bishop of
Sherborne,' and thinks that this creates a difficulty
in regard to Asser's bishopric [3]. But this is a series
of mistakes. The MS. is not the original, but is
dated by Wanley, quite correctly, as being little
older than the Norman Conquest [4], and it is addressed

---

[1] *Archaeologia*, p. 197.
[2] Malmesbury, *Gesta Pontificum*, ii. xlviii.
[3] *Archaeologia*, p. 199 ; *Biographia*, p. 405, to same effect.
[4] *Catalogus*, p. 153.

simply to 'Wulfsige, bishop.' Wright has derived
the name of the see from Wanley or some other
source, but he might have seen from Archbishop
Parker's text, which he thinks was derived from this
MS., that the bishop's see is not mentioned [1]. The
bishop of Sherborne's copy seems to be represented
by the MS. in Trinity College, Cambridge, but in
this the preface is unfortunately missing. There is
therefore no evidence that the king's version of the
*Pastoral Care* was in existence in 893, the date of the
composition of the Life, and no proof that any other
of the king's literary works had been completed by
that date. Indeed, a date subsequent to the final
discomfiture of the Danes, in the summer of 897,
seems more probable than an earlier date.

§ 72. The next argument is in direct conflict with
the preceding. After blaming the author of the Life
for knowing nothing of the version of the *Pastoral
Care*, Wright states that he is 'inclined to think that
the story concerning Alfred's school for the children
of nobles, where they were to be instructed in the
English and Latin languages ⟨cc. 75, 13 ; 102, 17⟩,
had no other foundation than the words of the king'
in the preface to this very version ! He remarks that
' we have here an indirect recommendation of a certain
mode of instruction, which was to be the result of
the English translations of Latin books, but no indications of any schools having been established for the
purpose [2].' A court school, established apparently
on the model of the Frankish kings, for the sons of
nobles with an infusion of youths of lowlier origin,
which is all that Asser describes, is a very different
thing from the pious wish expressed by the king
that all the youth of free condition who had the
means or faculty (*spēda*) in England should be put

[1] See above, p. xvi, note 2. Lingard, ii. 423, has been misled
by this assertion of Wright's, or by Wanley.

[2] *Archaeologia*, pp. 198-9.

to learning until they could read English, so long
as they are unfit for any other office, and that those
who wished for the sake of promotion to proceed to
learn Latin should do so.   We are unable to see any
argument in this against the present work.

§ 73. This exhausts the arguments brought forward
by Wright, with the exception of his note that the
references to the king are occasionally in the imperfect tense, for the answer to which we may refer to
§§ 26, 51, and that he 'thinks' he 'can sometimes
detect the writer forgetting his assumed character for
a moment, and speaking of things as though he were
living long after the time at which they occurred [1],'
which seems to have no other basis than the use of
the imperfect tense just referred to.   He 'thinks it
impossible that a person would speak of a king of the
country in which he was writing, during his reign,
and in a work addressed to that king, as *rex ille*,' an
expression that 'would rather be used by a person
who was speaking of a king long since dead, and
who would distinguish him from those who came
before and after him [2].'   It might also be used, as it
seems to be in the present work, by a foreign writer,
who similarly speaks of the English as *gens illa*
(§ 49).   'Many of Asser's anecdotes,' we are told, 'are
not only evidently legendary, but they are extremely
puerile.   When we are expecting some remarkable
proof of the great genius of Alfred, this writer tells
us seriously that the pious monarch. . . at length hit
upon the wonderful idea of making horn lanterns [3]'
to protect his time-candles (c. 104).   There is nothing
whatever in this chapter to lead us to expect that
the author is going to give us a remarkable proof
of Alfred's genius.   The mention of the lantern
grows quite naturally out of the subject the author
is treating of, which is not the genius of Alfred, but

---

[1] *Archaeologia*, p. 196.          [2] Ibid. 197.          [3] Ibid.

his rigorous division of the day into twenty-four hours, and the difficulties that he met with and overcame in attaining his object. Then we are told that 'the extraordinary reluctance of Asser to quit Wales, and the extreme anxiety of the king to bring him into England on any terms, are equally difficult to understand[1].' Why, we may ask, in the name of common sense? We find a ready parallel in the case of Charles the Great and Alcuin.

§ 74. The motive of the imaginary forgery Wright would discover in the political needs of the end of the tenth or eleventh century, for he is not clear as to the date of the forgery. He remarks that 'it may have had a political use, either as intended to encourage the Anglo-Saxons in resisting the Danes, or in supporting the English party headed by Earl Godwin against Edward's Norman and French favourites[2].' This is a most lame and impotent conclusion. The conception of a political novel with a purpose is alien to everything we know of English history at either period, and it grossly exaggerates, even for the year 1841, the influence of the democracy in political affairs. Nothing could be better calculated to defeat such an object than the composition of a life of a long dead king in difficult Latin. An appeal to the people would have been made, as it was by Archbishop Wulfstan, by means of homilies written in the vernacular. The work itself does not bear the stamp of a tract intended to fan the languishing flames of patriotism against Danish invaders or foreign favourites of the king. If any object other than its ostensible one could be assigned to it, it would not be that of an appeal to English patriotism written by a foreigner in the learned tongue, but rather that of a forerunner of the *De Instructione Principum*. The purpose of the biography of a great

[1] *Biographia*, p. 408.
[2] *Archaeologia*, p. 200. Cf. *Biographia*, pp. 411–12.

man is in part that of inciting others to follow his example. But in the present work there is no reason to consider that the didactic character is other than incidental, or that it was written with any other purpose than that of celebrating the doings and recording the life of a truly great man.

§ 75. The locality of the imaginary forgery Wright would find at St. Neots, co. Huntingdon, and he assigns the authorship of it to a monk of that house [1]. If we clear away the undoubted interpolations of Parker, we find that the sole reason for connecting the work with St. Neots is the addition—it can hardly be anything but an addition (§ 26)—in c. 74, 20 of the awkward sentence 'et ubi etiam nunc Sanctus Niot ibidem pausat,' and this in reference not to St. Neots in Huntingdonshire but to St. Neot in Cornwall. The author's knowledge is that of Wessex, not of Huntingdonshire (§ 44). If the work be spurious and intended to advertise the powers of any saint, that saint is surely St. Gueriir. The unfortunate interpolation from the Life of St. Neot (c. 53 b) and the fact that later writers mix up St. Neot with the king's victory, just as others introduce St. Cuthbert, cannot by any laws of evidence prove a connexion between the Life and the Huntingdonshire priory. Wright tries to strengthen his case by saying that 'there appeared another edition of the life of Alfred, with the addition of the translation of the entries of the Anglo-Saxon Chronicle previous to Alfred's birth, and a short continuation from the same source. It was printed by Gale, and goes under the name of *Asserii Annales*; but its more proper title is said to be the Chronicle of St. Neots, it having been written there. This circumstance, and the use made of the life of St. Neot, lead me to suggest that the writer of the life of Alfred was a monk of that house [2].' In his

---

[1] *Archaeologia*, p. 201; *Biographia*, p. 411.
[2] *Archaeologia*, pp. 200–201. Cf. *Biographia*, p. 411.

*Biographia Litteraria* he ascribes both works to this monk of St. Neots. The Annals of St. Neots, the work thus referred to, cannot possibly be described as an edition of the Life. It differs in plan, being a chronicle of England from the Roman invasion, and is a *farrago* made up, as may be seen from our introduction to it, from Beda, the Chronicle, the Anglo-Norman Annals, and other sources besides the Life. It is questionable whether the compiler wrote a single line of it himself. That he can have been the author of the Life is impossible by any canons of literary or historic criticism. Such a supposition is excluded by the fact that the compiler of the Annals used the Norman annals, which can hardly have been in existence at the time when the Cottonian MS. of the Life was written, and which were, so far as we know, unknown in England until after the Norman Conquest. Nor is it true that the Annals were composed at St. Neots. They received this title from Leland because he met with the copy of this anonymous work in the monastery library there[1]. In a note added to the translation of Pauli's *Life of King Alfred*[2], Wright argued that it is improbable that the author 'should remain for months suffering from grievous illness in the chief city of the West-Saxons without the knowledge of Alfred.' But the passage referred to (c. 79, 33) does not say clearly that he lay in this city for a year and a week, and the city meant appears to be Caerwent and not Winchester.

§ 76. In 1876–7 Mr. (now Sir) Henry Howorth contributed to the *Athenaeum* a series of articles impugning the authenticity of the Life. These articles are very largely repetitions of Wright's arguments. The non-existent contradictions as to the king's

[1] See the Introduction to this work, p. 98, below.
[2] London, 1852, p. 255, note.

illness[1] (§ 67), the improbability of Æthelwulf's neglect
of Alfred's education[2] (§ 64), the comparison of the
work with Einhard's Life of Charles[3] (§ 62), the
imaginary error about the see of Exeter[4] (§ 69),
the use by the author of a Life of St. Neot[5] (§ 66),
the connexion of the forgery with the monastery
of St. Neots and the Annals[6] (§ 75), and so on
reappear. The conclusions derived from these un-
sound premisses are stated in a much more vehement
manner than Wright's judicial tone. Like Wright,
Howorth holds that the Chronicle is a late tenth-
century compilation[7]. Wright's arguments are occasionally developed with as little success as care.
Thus the argument about the silence as to Alfred's
literary works (§ 71) is repeated, with the addition
that although the Life mentions Bishop Werferth's
translation of Gregory's *Pastoral Care*, it never mentions the king's translation of that work[8]. There
are no grounds for believing that there were two
independent translations of the *Pastoral Care*, and,
as a matter of fact, the author does not refer to
a version of this work, but distinctly to Werferth's
translation of Gregory's *Dialogues*, an entirely different
work, executed, as he says, at the king's desire (c. 77,
6). The unjustifiable identification of the ineffective
attack upon John the Old Saxon by hired ruffians
and the alleged murder of John the Scot by his
pupils at Malmesbury is taken over from Wright
(§ 70), and it is argued that William of Malmesbury, the authority for the murder, is not ' likely to

---

[1] *Athenaeum*, May 27, 1876, pp. 728-9.    [2] Ibid. p. 728.
[3] Ibid. May 27, 1876, p. 728.
[4] Ibid. Sept. 2, 1876, p. 308.
[5] Ibid. May 27, 1876, pp. 728-9.
[6] Ibid. March 25, 1876, p. 426.   The attribution of the Annals
to Asser is erroneously ascribed to the twelfth instead of the
sixteenth century.
[7] Ibid. Sept. 8, 1877, p. 309.
[8] Ibid. Sept. 2, 1876, p. 308.

have been mistaken, as it happened in his own
monastery, and the account of the pseudo-Asser is,
there can be no doubt, of very late composition[1].'
Malmesbury's account has been branded by a distinguished scholar as untruthful[2]. Nothing is known
of John the Scot after 860, and he was probably
dead long before John the Old Saxon came to England. Thus the Life is blamed for not containing
an account that would have at once condemned it as
spurious.

§ 77. Turning to the new matter in Howorth's
articles, the most important point is the statement
that Sir Edward Maunde Thompson had 'examined
the fragments of the MS., which have been rebound,
and he authorized me to say that it is written in two
distinct hands, one of the eleventh and the other of
the twelfth century, and that no portion of it is so
early as the tenth[3].' As we have already stated, not

---

[1] *Athenaeum*, Sept. 2, 1876, p. 309.

[2] Dr. Traube, *Poetae Aevi Carolini*, iii. 522. So also Bishop
Stubbs, who has, by one of his rare lapses, confused Malmesbury's account of John the Scot with that of John the Old
Saxon in the Life, says that it ' was a curious mistake, or worse,
on the part of our author ⟨Malmesbury⟩ to transfer the tragic
history of John's end ⟨sic⟩ from Athelney to Malmesbury.
After confusing him with John Scotus Erigena, it was a light
matter to make him a martyr' (W. Malmesbury, *Gesta Regum*,
ii. p. xlviii). It is curious to notice how frequently the statement in the Life has been misunderstood as recording the
death of John the Old Saxon. In addition to Bishop Stubbs, so
great a scholar as Mabillon has been misled (*Acta Sanctorum
Ordinis Sancti Benedicti*, cent. iv. pars 2, p. 507). Yet he
distinguishes the attack upon John the Old Saxon in the Life
from that upon John the Scot in Malmesbury, remarking that
the latter could hardly have lived until 895 ⟨read 893⟩, that
he is never called priest or monk, and that he could not be
described as experienced in the warlike art (pp. 510, 511). Yet
Christlieb, *Herzog's Real-Encyclopädie*, xiii. 793, was able to
accept Malmesbury's account.

[3] *Athenaeum*, March 25, 1876, p. 426. This seems to have
misled so careful a scholar as Henry Bradshaw, who refers to

a scrap of the MS. has come down to us (§ 14).
Sir E. M. Thompson informs us that he was misled
into making the statement referred to above through
the assumption that the whole of the Cottonian
Otho A xii was in the same handwriting.   The fragments upon which this view of the age of the MS.
was founded have nothing whatever to do with that
of the Life.   The MS. of the latter is distinguished
in Smith's catalogue from the other contents of
Otho A xii as being written *charactere antiquo* [1].
For the age of the MS. of the Life we are thrown
back upon the evidence collected in §§ 14–24, which
shows that one portion of it was in a very early
eleventh-century hand, whilst part of it was in a later
hand.   Howorth identifies the former with the eleventh-
century hand of Thompson's description, and the latter
with the twelfth-century hand.

§ 78.  Misled by this statement as to the preservation
of fragments of the MS., Howorth proceeds to argue
that it was a 'composite one, and actually written in
two different centuries, and probably, therefore, made
up from two different sources [2].'   This conclusion
does not follow if it was, as it seems beyond all doubt
to have been, a copy and not the author's autograph
(§ 24).   Howorth holds that it was the original, the
*fons et origo* [3], a view that it is difficult to reconcile
with the facts set out in § 25.   In consequence of
the preceding statement of Thompson, Howorth is
compelled to admit the existence of a nucleus of the
work in the eleventh century.   This, which is held to
account for the extracts from the Life in Florence of
Worcester, was, we are told, 'manipulated' in the

the non-existent fragments of the MS. of the Life in his
*Collected Papers*, pp. 467, 485.
   [1] *Catalogus Librorum MSS. Bibliothecae Cottoniae*, Oxford,
1696, p. 67.
   [2] *Athenaeum*, March 25, 1876, p. 426.
   [3] Ibid. Sept. 2, 1876, p. 307 ; Aug. 4, 1877, p. 146.

twelfth century by a monk of St. Neots, probably
the author of the Annals of St. Neots[1]. We have
already shown that there are no grounds for connecting
the work with the Huntingdonshire monastery (§ 75).
This eleventh century nucleus is left in much obscurity,
and Howorth argues frequently as if the entire work
had been in the twelfth-century hand. Thus he over-
looks Wise's note that the 'later hand' in the MS.
ceased at the end of c. 98, and assumes that all the
matter after this chapter was in a twelfth-century
hand. He condemns it in unmeasured terms on the
ground that it contains 'a great number of rhetorical
additions,' meaning the portions omitted by Florence
of Worcester (§ 33), which are ascribed to this twelfth-
century 'manipulator' at St. Neots[2]. By a similar
error he is led to maintain that 'the bald sentence'
in c. 79, 1 *de occiduis et ultimis partibus Britanniae
finibus*, to which Florence has prefixed the name
*Asser* instead of the pronoun in the Life, 'was probably all that was contained in the original life,' and
that out of it the manipulator 'has created quite a
long paragraph, in which Asser professes to describe
himself and his first intercourse with Alfred[3].' As,
according to Wise's note, the later hand did not commence until c. 88, 11, there is no justification, even if
Thompson's view about the existence of fragments of
the Life had been right, for this contention. The fact
that Florence alters *omnibus vitae praesentis temporibus*, c. 100, 20, into *omni vitae suae tempore* is
described as 'pregnant' and 'ominous.' We are told
that 'in the one case we have reference to what
took place in Alfred's days; in the other it is "at the
present time[4]."' This is an entire misapprehension.
The phrase in the Life, a favourite one with the

[1] *Athenaeum*, March 25, 1876, p. 426.
[2] Ibid.
[3] Ibid. May 27, 1876, p. 729.
[4] Ibid. March 25, 1876, p. 426.

author (§ 56), does not refer to the 'present time,' but to the 'present life,' that is the life on earth. Even if Howorth's construction could be justified, the legitimate conclusion to be drawn would be that the Life is the older work, and that Florence was, in accordance with the plan of his work (§ 26), changing the time references to the past tense. On the basis of Florence's trivial alteration in this chapter it is boldly stated that 'this is an admitted addition or interpolation of the twelfth century, and we cannot avoid the conclusion that the other similar phrases which are absent from Florence and Simeon were added at the same time[1].' The basis of this sweeping deduction disappears when it is realized that c. 100 was not written in the later hand, and must therefore have been written about a century before the date of Florence's work.

§ 79. Developing Pauli's expression of surprise that Florence of Worcester does not mention Asser among his sources[2], although he 'is not afraid of naming his authorities,' Howorth argues that when Florence wrote 'the work from which he incorporated his facts concerning Alfred made no mention of Asser, and had none of those phrases in it which point to Asser having been its author[3].' This argument collapses when the error in holding that c. 79 was written in the later hand is grasped, and when we consider the evidence pointing to the conclusion that Florence used the Cottonian MS. of the Life (§§ 25, 26, 33). Great stress is laid upon the entry of Asser's death in 883 in the text of Florence[4], but this is a blundered

---

[1] *Athenaeum*, March 25, 1876, p. 426. So also Sept. 2, 1876, p. 309.
[2] *König Ælfred*, p. 6.
[3] *Athenaeum*, March 25, 1876, p. 426.
[4] Ibid. The conclusion drawn from this entry in Florence of Asser's death that 'the work from which he incorporated his facts concerning Alfred made no mention of Asser,' and that the ascription of the work to Asser is 'probably a fabrication of the

interpolation (§ 41). Howorth then adds that Simeon of Durham does not name Asser as an authority, and that, coupled with Florence's silence, 'this concurrence of testimony is overwhelming [1].' We do not attach the slightest importance to this. It was the exception for a mediaeval chronicler to acknowledge his obligations to his predecessors, whom he plagiarized in a manner that seems intolerable to modern ideas. Florence, for instance, mentions only Beda and the English chronicles by name, and yet he uses numerous other sources saints' lives, the Norman Annals, and the present work in some shape or other. It is possibly included in the *fidelium virorum credibilis relatus* [2], if that refers, as it seems to do, to written sources. The argument from the silence of the Durham work is even less weighty. Nor can more be said for that from William of Malmesbury [3], who certainly derived matter from the Life, directly as Bishop Stubbs holds, or, as we think, through Florence of Worcester (§ 36), without mentioning either of them. As he was, in Howorth's words, 'so diligent an historian, and one who knew the materials of Early English history so well,' the fact that he mentions neither the Life nor Florence, although certainly using one or the other extensively, throws into strong relief the extreme danger of arguing from

twelfth century,' is controverted by Wise's facsimile, in which Asser's dedication appears in the very early eleventh-century hand. Moreover, Florence cannot have substituted *Asser* for *ego* of the Life in c. 79, 1 by mere guesswork. The argument that the other passages referring to the author are later in date than Florence is shown to be baseless in § 78.

[1] *Athenaeum*, March 25, 1876, p. 426.    [2] Ed. Thorpe, i. 53.

[3] *Athenaeum*, Sept 2, 1876, p. 307. Malmesbury's silence is advanced as an argument that the Life is a later composition than his own, although Howorth is obliged to allow that some part of it existed in an eleventh-century hand. The weakness of this argument becomes apparent when we see that it would also prove that the work of Florence of Worcester was not in existence in William's time.

the silence of a mediaeval compiler that any given
work was not in existence when he was writing. We
may therefore pass over the argument that the Life
is later than the time of Æthelweard because he does
not refer to it[1]. This writer mentions none of his
sources. We are told that it is 'incredible' that
Æthelweard, 'who devoted himself in his Chronicle to
a special account of Alfred, as bringing before his
relative the glories of their common ancestor, . . . should
have overlooked such a mine of matter as Asser's
Life of the great king[2],' and that he has done so is
held to prove conclusively that the Life was written at
a later date. This is a misrepresentation of Æthelweard's work, which is merely a brief version of the
history of England, with no personal details, drawn
up from the Chronicle, which supplied in abundance
all the material that he needed. It is simply the
fullness of the Chronicle in Alfred's time that causes
that king's reign to occupy so much space in Æthelweard's work. It is a mistake to say that Alfred was
the writer's ancestor, for he distinctly tells us that he
was descended from Alfred's brother Æthelred. This
weak argument from Æthelweard's silence is backed
up by the statement that there is a great probability
that the author of the Life borrowed from Æthelweard[3]. The basis for this is the fact that both
writers use a ship making for a port as a simile for
the author and the object of his work[4]! This argument would equally prove that Cicero also borrowed
from Æthelweard[5]. The interpolated matter from
Matthew of Paris (c. 50 c) Howorth endeavours to
maintain as part of the text on the ground that 'if
we excise it, we leave a gap in the narrative,' and
arguments against the authenticity of the Life are

---

[1] *Athenaeum*, Aug. 4, 1877, p. 146.     [2] Ibid.     [3] Ibid.
[4] Ibid. The parallelism was noted by Pauli, p. 10 note, but
he refrained from the extravagant deduction drawn by Howorth.
[5] See the notes to this passage.

founded upon this chapter[1].   He remarks that Asser
is the only one who makes mention of a sea-fight
upon this occasion[2], when it is not Asser at all but
the much later St. Albans writer who is speaking.
The account of Æthelweard, who is held to be
'by far the best authority for this period[3]'—surely
an extravagant statement even if the Chronicle
was a tenth-century work—is contrasted with this
St. Albans passage to the discredit of the Life, with
which it was first brought into connexion by Archbishop Parker.   Nor is another attempt to prove
that the Life is later in date than Æthelweard more
successful.   The statement that Christmas Day fell
upon Friday in 856 is described, on the authority of
so singularly inaccurate a writer as Dr. Giles, as
a blunder, and is used as an argument that the work
could not be a contemporary production[4].   But there
is no blunder, and the passage is an interpolation

---

[1] *Athenaeum*, Sept. 2, 1876, p. 308.   Dr. Pauli treats this, the
most unjustifiable of all Parker's interpolations, and one that we
can see in the process of being made, much too seriously, as if
it really had some connexion with the Life (*König Ælfred*,
pp. 10, 118 note).   Howorth's objection, based upon the breach
of continuity in the narrative, is not of much weight when
applied to annals, and could be met by retaining the next
chapter, which relates to the same event at Swanwich and
comes from the Annals of St. Neots.   It may, therefore,
possibly have formed part of the MS. of the Life used by the
compiler of the Annals.

[2] From Pauli, p. 119, note 2.

[3] *Athenaeum*, Sept. 2, 1876, p. 308.   No proof of this is
advanced beyond the statement, repeated from Pauli, p. 119,
note 2, that Æthelweard's words sound as if they were a word
for word translation from an O.E. poem, whereas they may be
paralleled by his style elsewhere when he is merely paraphrasing,
as he is also doing in the present case, the words of the Chronicle.
The only other discernible proof is that referred to at p. cxix,
note 3.   Howorth recognizes that the greater part of Æthelweard
is translated from the Chronicle (*Athenaeum*, Aug. 4, 1877,
p. 146).

[4] *Athenaeum*, Sept. 2, 1876, p. 308.

(c. 17 b), as might easily have been discovered. The fact that it is an interpolation of Parker is glossed over at a later time by the remark that we are assured that the passage 'did not exist in the elder recension[1].' But it is nevertheless used as 'pointing the same way' as the ship simile, that is, to borrowing from Æthelweard.

§ 80. A battle in Loch Cuan (Strangford Loch, County Down), we are told was 'undoubtedly the Cynwith ⟨c. 54⟩, in the province of Damnonia, of the old chroniclers, who mistook the Irish Damnonia for Damnonia south of the Bristol Channel, or Devonshire.' The circumstance that the author of the Life places this battle in Devonshire is accordingly advanced as a proof of forgery, as it is 'incredible that a native of South Wales, and a contemporary and close friend of Alfred, could have made such a blunder[2].' It is also astonishing that Æthelweard, who places this battle *in occidentales Anglorum partes*, should have made a similar mistake, especially as Howorth is convinced that this writer's account of Cynuit 'is the most important' one[3]. The Chronicle, which we are told is full of errors and of much less value than the account in Æthelweard and Simeon of Durham[4] (who copies the Life !), also places this fight in Devonshire. There is, however, no blunder in the Life ; the charge is founded upon an impossible identification of two different events. In order to accept this identification we must be prepared to

---

[1] *Athenaeum*, Aug. 4, 1877, p. 146.

[2] Ibid. Jan. 15, 1876, p. 88.

[3] Ibid. March 4, 1876, p. 329. The sole basis for this is that Æthelweard adds the name of the Ealdorman in command, and that by the omission of the *et* between Healfdene and Ingwar, the former is converted into the slain leader of the Danes, who, in the Chronicle and Asser, is described as the brother of Healfdene and Ingwar, and this happens to fit in with the baseless combinations dealt with in this section.

[4] Ibid. March 4, 1876, p. 329.

believe that a battle fought in Devonshire in 878
between Englishmen cooped up in a fort and Danes
was a sea-fight between Norsemen in Strangford
Loch in 877; that the brother of Healfdene and
Ingwar, the slain leader, was Albann = Healfdene himself; and that Odda, the ealdorman of Devonshire
and the leader of the English, according to Æthelweard, was the Irish king Aedh, who was not engaged
in the fight at Strangford Loch! After this it is
a small thing to find that the latter place is on the
east coast of Ireland, whereas Damnonia was on the
west.

§ 81. Howorth maintains that the story of Alfred's
journey to Rome in 853 (c. 8), which is derived from
the Chronicle, is 'surely very doubtful,' and adopts
a suggestion, ascribed to Dr. Pauli[1], that 'the story of
the double journey ⟨cc. 8; 11⟩ has probably arisen
from misplacing the journey of 855.'   He argues that
such a mistake is unlikely to have been made by
a contemporary biographer[2].  But it is not a mistake,
as independent evidence from Rome proves.

§ 82. In connexion with this chapter, Howorth
'questions the probability of Alfred's being consecrated Ethelwulf's successor, as Asser says,' and
inquires if it is 'consistent in any way with Anglo-
Saxon modes of thought that a child of four should
be thus nominated to the exclusion of his elder
brothers[3].'   For this assertion there is no warrant in
the Life, which distinctly states that Æthelwulf left
the kingdom to his two eldest sons (c. 16, 7).

§ 83. Howorth brings forward many arguments
against the famous passage about Alfred and his
mother and the illuminated book[4] (c. 23), but as they
all involve the assumption, which we hold to be base-

---

[1] It is a suggestion intruded without notice in the translation
of Pauli edited by Wright, p. 91, note *.  It does not occur in
the original, p. 69, note 3.

[2] *Athenaeum*, May 27, 1876, p. 728.    [3] Ibid.    [4] Ibid.

less, that this happened in Alfred's twelfth year, it is
not necessary to discuss them.

§ 84. The silence of the Life as to Alfred's mission
to India in 884 is held up as an objection to the
work[1] It really seems to be an argument in its
favour[2].

§ 85. Other sins of omission charged against the
Life of Alfred are that 'we have no details about his
Witenagemots, about the chief laymen at his court,
about his political arrangements, nor about his foreign
policy,' or 'of such romantic events as the voyage of
Othere ⟨sic⟩, about which his master wrote[3].' It is in
favour of the work that it does not contain some of
these things. Reports of proceedings at Witenagemots
outside a legal document would certainly be suspicious
at this date. An account of the king's foreign policy
would have a distinctly modern air. As for Ohthere,
who was a Norseman and not a subject of Alfred, one
fails to see how an account of his voyage could come
into the life of the king, who neither dispatched him
on the voyage nor accompanied him. This argument
is also invalidated by the consideration that we have
no proof that his voyage took place before this work
was written. One looks in vain for the names of
prominent laymen or of ecclesiastics in the court in
the works of Einhard or Thegan.

§ 86. We may now take some points of minor
importance, which are little more than matters of
opinion. Howorth asks, Is the tale of Æthelwulf's
surrender of Wessex to his son (c. 12) 'a probable
one, viewed not from our standpoint, but from that of
the ninth century[4]?' In the light of Frankish history
of the period, we have no hesitation in answering
this query in the affirmative. Moreover, the story

[1] *Athenaeum*, Sept. 2, 1876, p. 308.
[2] See note to c. 65.
[3] *Athenaeum*, Sept. 2, 1876, p. 308.
[4] Ibid. May 27, 1876, p. 728.

finds some corroboration. The *ut credo, usque ad obitum vitae suae* (c. 25, 14) is described as 'most clearly the phrase of an after compiler who has been napping, and has forgotten for the nonce that he should have known nothing of Alfred's death[1].' To us it seems 'most clearly' to be, from its awkward, ungrammatical intrusion into the text, a later interpolation (§ 26). The blunders in regard to the years of Alfred's age (§ 27), together with the non-existent blunder in the interpolated c. 17 b, 9 (§ 79), are adduced as proofs that the work could not have been written by a contemporary of Alfred[2]. The mistakes as to years are so stupid that they can only be ascribed to the copyist (§ 27). The objection to the name of the patriarch of Jerusalem (c. 91, 16) seems to rest upon a clerical error of the copyist of the MS., and we do not see anything 'ominous' in Florence's omission of this passage and of the corrupt clause that precedes it[3] (§§ 25, 33). The *praedandi causa* of c. 67, 3 is branded as giving 'a very improbable' cause for the mission of the king's ships to East Anglia[4],' an enemy's country. With Pauli[5] we see nothing improbable in this. It is seriously advanced against the Life that its author makes the king give *aedificia* to the newly baptized Danes[6] (c. 56, 33). Surely it is beyond the stupidity of any imaginable forger to say that the king rewarded the Danish leader and his men with 'buildings' before they left his kingdom! The word *aedificia* is, as Lappenberg[7] and Pauli[8] have recognized, a scribal error for *beneficia*, as it translates the *fēoh* of the Chronicle.

---

[1] *Athenaeum*, Sept. 2, 1876, p. 307.  
[2] Ibid. p. 308.  
[3] Ibid.  
[4] Ibid.  
[5] *König Ælfred*, p. 145, note 3.  
[6] *Athenaeum*, Sept. 2, 1876, p. 308.  
[7] *Geschichte von England*, i. p. 321, note 2.  
[8] *König Ælfred*, p. 141, note 1.

§ 87. The Life, Howorth tells us, is in the rhetorical passages 'assuredly very much more in the style
of the thirteenth century than of the ninth [1].' The
exact converse is, in our opinion, the truth (§ 57).
One might search in vain in thirteenth-century
English-Latin for anything bearing the peculiar
Celto-Frankish stamp of the Latinity of this work.
Equally wide of the mark is the assertion that it
contains 'certain words which are exceedingly uncommon at the earlier date, and only existed in
obscure quarters, but which became almost household
words at the latter date, such as those referred to by
Dr. Pauli, in his preface, namely the word *vasali*,
the phrase *custos regis, · cambra*, &c. [2].' The word
*vassali* was never a common word in England, and
it was unknown in thirteenth-century legal Latin [3],
and was much more used in the tenth century. As
Florence of Worcester copies it from the Life, it cannot
be later than the date of his death, 1118. Besides,
the word in the Life is *fassellus*, an O.E. spelling that
we should certainly not meet with in thirteenth-
century Latin. *Cambra* appears frequently enough
in the latter period, but always in its classical form
*camera*. *Custos regis* does not occur at all in the
work [4].

§ 88. Finally, Howorth endeavours to prove that

[1] *Athenaeum*, Sept. 2, 1876, p. 309. This seems to be an
exaggeration of Wright's statement that the Life is 'a common-
place specimen of monkish Latin' (*Biographia Britannica
Literaria*, i. 412). Pauli rightly differs from Wright's view,
*König Ælfred*, p. 12.

[2] *Athenaeum*, Sept. 2, 1876, p. 309.

[3] How rare the word was may be seen from the remark
in Pollock and Maitland, *History of English Law*, ed. 1, p. i.
277 that 'Glanville ⟨in the later part of the twelfth century⟩
introduces a very rare word in English legal documents, the
antique word *vassallus*.'

[4] There seems to be a confusion with the *custodes regni* of
Roger of Wendover, i. 363, quoted by Pauli, *König Ælfred*,
p. 155, note 1.

the author was not a Welshman. The grounds for this are that Florence gives, in the manner of the Life, under 908, the British and Saxon names of Chester, and that he states, under dates later than the conclusion of the Life, that certain places are called by such and such *Saxonice* or *in lingua Anglorum*[1]. Howorth claims that these passages 'point as clearly to having been written by a Welshman as the instances quoted from the Vita.' To this we must demur *in toto*. The 908 passage is derived from Beda[2], and the others are not parallel at all, as they do not give the British names. In tenth- and eleventh-century English charters the local names are commonly introduced by periphrastic locutions identical in meaning with *qui dicitur Saxonice*, &c. This trivial contention takes no count of the strong evidence that the author was a Welshman to be found apart from the British names of places given by him (§ 45).

§ 89. The *Times* of March 17, 1898, p. 8, contained an anonymous article against the authenticity of the Life. The arguments are a *réchauffé* of those that we have already dealt with, and the mistake about the existence of the MS. is repeated. The article abounds with errors, misrepresentations, and erroneous assumptions, and the conclusions are pressed home in very violent language. The only novelty about the article is the suggestion that 'some Welshman, perhaps for some political purpose like that of Giraldus Cambrensis, wishing to glorify his nation, and particularly St. David's, seized on this mention of Asser ⟨in Florence of Worcester⟩, compounded a life of Alfred from the Chronicle and Florence of Worcester, together with a life of St. Neot, inserting a few imaginary personal stories to give an air of reality to the narrative, and gave his life to the uncritical world.' This highly improbable theory is supported by a

---

[1] *Athenaeum*, Sept. 2, 1876, p. 309.  [2] *Hist. Eccles.* ii. c. 3.

reference to 'the now admitted forgeries of Ingulph, and of Richard of Cirencester' and the life of St. Grimbald to prove that there is nothing improbable in it.  Ingulph proceeded from the main source of the mediaeval forgeries, the attempt to procure a title for land held by a religious house, and the Life of St. Grimbald belongs to the category of saints' lives, where there was a particular object in view.  Richard of Cirencester, *De Situ Britanniae,* was an antiquarian forgery of the eighteenth century, and cannot possibly be cited as a parallel to a work that goes back at least to the eleventh century.  The passages in cc. 75, 11 ; 102, 17 are unjustifiably described as a reference to 'a public grammar school, presumably at Winchester.'

## 7. SUMMARY.

§ 90.  We have thus examined the charges brought against the Life, and we have not found one dealing with facts that support the view that the work is of later origin than it pretends to be.  Opinions that it ought to have contained certain information cannot in the nature of things command much consideration. We may regret that it does not tell us many things that we would fain know, but the absence of such information cannot fairly be advanced as an argument against it, more especially when we consider the time when it was written and the continental biographies that seem to have been the author's models (§ 51). In the course of a microscopical examination of the work we have failed to discover anything that can be called an anachronism.  There are, it is true, a few features that we cannot justify by contemporary evidence [1], but any conclusion that these things condemn the Life would equally prove that the Cot-

[1] The holding of the office of butler by a great noble, c. 2, 3, and the passages relating to the reviewing of legal sentences by the king, c. 106, are the only ones of any moment.

tonian MS. could not have been written at the time
when it was. The explanation in both cases is that
we possess no records that throw light upon these
usages, and, as they existed at the time of the
writing of the MS. without our having any other
record, they may also have been known in the time
of King Alfred. This absence of anachronism is an
argument in favour of the authenticity of the work.
This argument is strengthened by the presence of
several features that point to its being composed at
least as early as the first half of the tenth century,
and that are, so far as our scanty material enables us
to judge, compatible with an earlier date. These
features are the use of the title *Rex Angul-Saxonum*[1],
the term *Theotiscus* (c. 13, 29), and the mention of
St. Gueriir at the place afterwards known as St. Neot
in Cornwall (c. 74, 20). Agreeing with this date,
although not incompatible with a slightly earlier or
later one, are the evidence of the Welsh forms (§ 46),
the Latinity (§§ 57, 58), the use of an old version of
the scriptures (§ 59), and of an earlier form of the
Chronicle than any that has come down to us (§ 54),
and the reference to the monastery in the Island of
Sheppey (c. 3, 10). The silence of the author regarding literary works that were ascribed to Alfred
in the latter part of the tenth century (c. 77), the
absence of the mythical stories concerning Inguar
and Ubba, which were in circulation in the tenth
century[2], and the silence regarding the numerous
myths that centred round Alfred himself at a slightly
later period, are difficult to reconcile with the view
that the Life is spurious. Similarly the author knows
nothing of the cult that converted King Edmund of
East Anglia into one of the most famous English
saints before the end of the tenth century. To him

[1] See note to Dedication, p. 147 below.
[2] As instanced by Abbo's Life of St. Edmund, and the mystic
raven banner of the Danes (c. 54 b).

he is merely the King of East Anglia (c. 33). A
later forger might be expected to continue the Life
up to the period of Alfred's greatest glory (§ 52) and
up to his death. The information about Wales can
hardly have come from any but a contemporary
writer (§ 45). His statements that Æthelbald married
his father's widow (c. 17), and that it was not cus-
tomary for the wife of the West Saxon king to sit
near her husband or be called queen (c. 13, 12), which
are otherwise unknown in English sources, are corroborated by contemporary Frankish evidence. In like
manner his account of the division of the kingdom
between Æthelwulf and his son (c. 12) finds some
corroboration in the Chronicle. His placing the
coming of Bishop Werferth to Alfred's court before
that of Plegmund (c. 77, 10) is supported by the
evidence of Alfred's will. His mention of seeing a
Danish boy (*paganicae gentis*) in the monastery at
Athelney (c. 94, 10) recalls the statement that Archbishop Oda was the son of a pagan Dane who came
to England in 866 in the army of Inguar and Ubba.
It cannot be a mere coincidence that the author states
that he had seen letters to Alfred from the patriarch
of Jerusalem (c. 91, 16), and that Elias, whose name
is recoverable from the text of the Life by an almost
inevitable emendation, should have written letters to
the rulers of Western Europe at this very time. It
is, of course, within the bounds of possibility that
a writer a century or so later than Alfred's time
might by extreme good luck have avoided all anachronisms, have had access to some lost Welsh
chronicle or records that enabled him to make a list
of the South Welsh princes of Alfred's time, have
been acquainted with Frankish chronicles, and have
seen the letter of the patriarch of Jerusalem. But,
although this is conceivable, it cannot be considered
probable. In addition to this we should have to
hold that the forger had made a lucky guess in sup-

plying the time of the eclipse in c. 59, which cannot have been derived from any Frankish or native chronicle that has come down to us. As the calculation of an eclipse is out of the question at this date, this alone seems a strong proof that the Life is the work of a contemporary of Alfred.

§ 91. The question of motive is an important one in regard to all forgeries. In no respect have the attacks upon the Life broken down more hopelessly than in attempting to find a motive for the hypothetical forger. The greater part of the mediaeval fabrications were concocted with very definite and utilitarian objects, such as to supply the missing details of a saint's life, to magnify the antiquity of a monastery, or to provide legal documents that should support the real or imaginary claims of a religious house to lands, immunities, or prerogatives. Of the deliberate forgery of lives of laymen, except so far as was necessary for the attainment of these objects, there is scarcely a trace. It is even less easy to discover an entirely spurious lay biography The Life was preserved in a MS. that was certainly older than the great age of forgery in England—the period following the Norman Conquest. It is impossible to point to any monastery that could in any way gain by the circulation of the work. St. Davids was far away in Wales, and the statement that Alfred took it under his protection, besides being a very weak appeal to later Welsh princes, is an entirely inadequate reason for writing a book of the nature of the present. There is no specification of the lands or immunities of the house ; there is nothing but a general statement as to incursions upon it. It is still more difficult to believe that the Life was intended to advance the interest of the monasteries founded by Alfred. The only saint mentioned is St. Gueriir, and in this case the testimonial to the power of his intervention is a very imperfect one, differing *toto caelo* from the sweeping curative powers usually ascribed to saints in lives written to magnify their efficacy. When we compare the Life with the mythical British history of Geoffrey of Monmouth, written at a later time and strongly affected by Norman and Breton influences, we cannot help recognizing that the two works stand upon an entirely different plane. The central figure of Geoffrey's fabrications is King Arthur, who had for many centuries been a centre round which a gradually increasing circle of myths had crystallized themselves. There is nothing in the Life of Alfred that makes such amazing calls upon our credulity as does Geoffrey's life of Arthur. By the side of the glittering fictions and glaring improbabilities of the latter, the Life of Alfred displays its hero clothed in the sombre tints of truth.

§ 92. The failure of the attacks upon the authenticity of the Life of Alfred must not, however, be allowed to blind us to the difficulties it presents. Ebert has remarked that it is impossible that it had originally the form in which it has come down to us[1], and Pauli holds that in its present shape it gives rise to grave doubts[2]. He thinks that these doubts would be removed if we possessed a better MS. than the lost Cottonian seems to have been. Both writers are probably influenced in part by the gross interpolations of Parker, and Pauli indeed writes throughout as if there were some reason beyond Parker's ill-judged efforts for regarding these interpolations as having some earlier connexion with the work than the time of Queen Elizabeth. But it is clear that Parker was the first person who brought the interpolated matter into connexion with the Life, and we must judge of the book entirely independently of the falsifications, which have so seriously prejudiced its

[1] *Geschichte der Literatur des Mittelalters im Abendlande*, iii. 250.
[2] *König Ælfred*, p. 4.

good fame. It is to be hoped that future editions of the text will appear free from these mischievous additions, and we regret that it has not been possible to ignore them in the present edition. But when all this foreign matter has been excised, the work still presents some difficulties. Carelessness of transcription may possibly explain those that are merely verbal, but there still remain certain passages that lay the author open to the charge of exaggeration, such as his mention of gold-covered and silver-covered buildings (c. 91, 20), if that be the literal meaning of the passage, and his statement that Alfred might, if he had chosen, have been king before his elder brother Æthelred (c. 42, 6), with whom, it is clear, he was on most intimate terms. The account of Alfred's early illness, of his cure, of his praying for an infirmity that should keep him in the paths of chastity, of the cure of the illness thus acquired at his marriage, and of his being then stricken with a compensatory infirmity immediately afterwards (c. 74) are hard to believe literally[1]. The morbid feelings here ascribed to the king read more like a chapter from a saint's life than a tale that had been told to the author by a man of action and intelligence such as Alfred proved himself to be. That the king did suffer from illness we know from his own testimony, and the mortality table of his house shows that it was not very robust. We may perhaps venture upon the explanation that the author had been misled by his love of rhetoric into greatly exaggerating the bodily sufferings of the king for the purpose of heightening the colours of his picture or of emphasizing the difficulties under which the king performed his life's strenuous work. But in either case the result must be to shake our confidence in his strict veracity. Much may be forgiven to Celtic rhetoric, but one cannot help wondering what

---

[1] Cf. Lappenberg, *Geschichte von England*, i. p. 311.

the 'truth-telling king would have thought of such
exaggerations or misrepresentations. Although the
Life is dedicated to Alfred, he is not otherwise
addressed in it. Lingard [1] has suggested that the
author left the work in an unfinished condition. Its
date of composition was six years only before the
death of the king, and it is conceivable that the
author, busy with the cares of his diocese, laid aside
the incompleted draught upon hearing of the king's
death, an event that would render pointless the dedication to him. The theory that the Cottonian MS.
was copied from an unfinished draught would account
for its strange imperfections, such as the frequent
omissions of verbs in the sentences (§ 25). There
are certain corrupt passages that may be explained
by the theory that the scribes of this MS. have
copied the original readings of the author's draught
as well as those substituted by him during revision [2].
The curiously abrupt ending of the Life favours the
theory that the MS. was incomplete ; but this may
have been an accident peculiar to the Cottonian MS.
It is, however, noticeable that we discover no signs
of the chroniclers who embodied matter from the
Life (§ 33 sqq.) using a copy extending beyond the
point where the Cottonian MS. terminated. On the
whole, we may reasonably conclude that the incomplete nature of the work is not due to the Cottonian
MS. but to the original from which it was copied.

[1] *History of the Anglo-Saxon Church*, iii. 424.
[2] See the notes to cc. 27, 17 ; 38, 5 ; 40, 1-2 ; 99, 5 ; 105, 4 ;
106, 12.

# RECENT WORK ON ASSER'S LIFE OF ALFRED

W. H. STEVENSON did his work so well that the fifty-five years which have elapsed since he published his edition of Asser have brought to light little new material. First in importance is Dr. K. Sisam's note[1] which quotes a passage from a letter of Wanley to Charlett, dated 2 June 1721, which proves the correctness of Stevenson's suggestion that Wanley's precise dating of the first hand in the Cotton MS. of Asser's Life as *c*. A.D. 1000 or 1001 was based on a comparison of it with a surviving charter, Cotton Augustus ii. 22. Wanley writes: 'My authority for adjusting the age of that exemplar is an original charter of King Æþelred, dated A.D. 1001, which as to the hand, agreeth very well with the first part of the Asser, Otho A. 12.' In the same letter Wanley speaks of the several hands in which the Life was written, and pronounces them 'much about the same time.' It should be noted that Wanley in 1721 was a mature and experienced palaeographer, that he was interested in the Asser controversy, and that he had made a special journey to the Cottonian Library to make this comparison, for on 28 March he had written to say that Mr. Wise's query must wait, as he was extremely busy, and had a cold[2]. It is inconceivable that a man of Wanley's skill and experience should have seen a close resemblance to the charter if the manuscript of Asser were actually of a much

---

[1] First published in *Review of English Studies*, vii, 1931, p. 8 n., reprinted in *Studies in the History of Old English Literature*, Oxford, 1953, p. 148 n.
[2] I owe this information to Dr. Sisam.

later date[1], and the fact that there were several hands in the manuscript for him to judge by reduces the risk of wildly inaccurate dating.

In another work[2] Dr. Sisam has shown that the text of the genealogy in cap. 1, as it stood before Stevenson conflated it with the pedigree of Æthelwulf contained in annal 855 of the Anglo-Saxon Chronicle, must represent Asser's text, for it agrees with the versions in C.C.C.C. 183 and Tiberius B v; hence the omission of parts of the 855 genealogy are not to be attributed to the scribe of the Cotton MS. of Asser, as Stevenson supposed. Dr. Sisam notes also that Stevenson overlooked the *Historia Brittonum* as the source of Asser's statement that Geata was venerated as a god.

The only other work dealing with Asser's text is an article by G. H. Wheeler which suggests some emendations of difficult passages[3].

In an interesting article on 'The Literary Form of Asser's "Vita Alfredi"',[4] Marie Schütt shows that the Life is by no means so formless as has hitherto been supposed. Agreeing with Stevenson's remarks on the motive for writing the Life (pp. cviii f. above),

---

[1] Mr. N. R. Ker allows me to quote from a letter to me: 'The facsimile in Wise's edition and Wanley's remarks leave no room for doubt that the manuscript of Asser was, if not very early eleventh century, as Wanley says, certainly eleventh century, and not late eleventh century. But Wanley had the opportunity of comparing the Cotton charter and Otho A xii, and his opinion that the first hand of the Life was very early eleventh century should, I think, carry great weight.' Mr. T. A. M. Bishop concurs with this opinion.

[2] 'Anglo-Saxon Royal Genealogies,' *Proceedings of the British Academy*, xxxix, 1953, pp. 297, 299, 301, 313 f.

[3] 'Textual Emendations to Asser's Life of Alfred,' *English Historical Review*, xlvii, 1932, pp. 86-8.

[4] Ibid. lxxii, 1957, pp. 209-20.

she adds the suggestion that it was intended 'to show to the careful Welshmen what manner of man this was in whom they placed their hopes and to transmit to them his own impression of the great man.' She believes that the work is a draft, but a draft 'which had reached a stage of composition, in which most of the items, though not yet in their final stylistic form, had already been allotted a well-considered place in the work as a whole.' Writing after some of Alfred's great achievements, Asser, who knew Einhard's *Vita Caroli*[1], would have to deal with his *res gestae* as well as with his *vita et conversatio*, and Dr. Schütt offers a convincing explanation of the way the Anglo-Saxon Chronicle, the basis for the *res gestae*, is combined with the biographical sections, Asser's original contribution. Her argument should be read in full, for one cannot do justice to it in small compass. Its main conclusion is to establish the rational trend of Asser's thought, while admitting the presence of 'unskilful transitions, either by elaborate metaphors, or nothing at all.' The influence of the traditional Celtic style of narration has to be reckoned with, beside that of Einhard.

Though Stevenson wrote in the early days of scientific place-name study, his work is so sound in this respect that later scholars disagree little. One can no longer declare categorically, as Stevenson does on p. 235, that 'the use of the genitive was restricted to compounds of which the first member was a personal name,'[2] and so it is possible that Asser was correct in interpreting *Æscesdun* as *mons fraxini*

---

[1] See above, pp. lxxxi, xcv, 294. She points out that conditions were too different for Einhard's work to serve as a model except on points of detail.

[2] See A. H. Smith, *English Place-Name Elements*, i (English Place-Name Society, vol. xxv, 1956), pp. 158 f.

(c. 37). The English Place-Name Society[1] and Dr. Ekwall[2] accept Plummer's identification of *Cynuit* with Countisbury,[3] which Stevenson rejected (p. 265, n. 3); they do not accept the suggestion (p. 319) that *Leonaford* is Landford[4]. There is no reason to reject, as an unlikely interpretation of *Æthelinga-ig*, the *clitonum insula* of the Latin Life of St. Neot, as Stevenson does (p. 259, n. 4), for evidence that estates were set aside for the *æpelingas* occurs in a charter of Ethelred's reign[5]. A few identifications of names not in Asser's text, but in Stevenson's notes, require correction: *Eardulfesleah* (p. 236, n. 4) is Ardley, Oxfordshire[6], and hence the *Cwicelmes hlæw* in its boundaries is a different barrow from the one of this name in the Anglo-Saxon Chronicle, 1006, which is now known as Scutchamer Knob, in East Hendred, Berkshire; the Devon estate of *Liwtun* in Alfred's will is Lifton, not Luton (p. 323, n. 3); Cambridge, not Grantchester, is the *castello . . . nomine Gronte* of Felix's Life of St. Guthlac (p. 331, n. 4).

Similarly, little needs correction in what Stevenson says of the Anglo-Saxon Chronicle. The description of version E as a derivative of A (p. 171) is curious. The true facts concerning the reading here discussed are that not only B and C, but also originally A, read *fea*, but this was altered to *feala* in A by the eleventh-century Canterbury interpolator, to bring it into line with the reading of the archetype of E which he had

[1] *The Place-Names of Devon*, i, 1931, pp. 62 f.

[2] *The Concise Oxford Dictionary of English Place-Names*, s.v. Countisbury.

[3] See also J. J. Alexander, 'Arx Cynuit,' *Devon and Cornwall Notes and Queries*, xvi, 1931, pp. 310–13.

[4] *The Concise Oxford Dictionary of English Place-Names*, s.v. Landford; *The Place-Names of Wiltshire*, p. 386.

[5] Kemble, *Cod. Dipl.* no. 1312.

[6] *The Place-Names of Oxfordshire*, i, pp. 196 f.

before him. Stevenson was writing before M. L. R. Beaven establish the indiction date of 24 September for the commencement of the year in the part of the Anglo-Saxon Chronicle used by Asser[1]. This date explains why Florence of Worcester calculated the day of King Edmund's death for 869, not 870, which puzzled Stevenson (p. 233), and also accounts for the entry of the eclipse of 29 October 878 under annal 879 (pp. 280–6). Stevenson's opinion that Alfred was himself responsible for the statement in annal 853 that the Pope consecrated him king on his visit to Rome (p. 181) has not won general acceptance[2]. A slip in translation appears on p. 198, where Stevenson seems to be taking *be westan wuda* as 'by west-wood' instead of 'west of the wood', while the note to cap. 86 (p. 325), which regards as Asser's addition the statement that the mission to Rome took place in the year the Danes left Paris for Chézy, suggests that he has not noticed that the preceding clause in the annal in the Chronicle contains a relative, and should be rendered: 'And in the same year in which the Danes went up beyond the bridge at Paris...' Asser is only varying the wording of his source. Finally, Asser's rendering of *pritiga sum* as 'thirty' is not necessarily a foreigner's misunderstanding of the idiom (p. 279), for there is evidence that by this date it was losing its precise meaning[3].

In spite of many discoveries in the province of numismatics the coin of Alfred with the regnal title

---

[1] 'The Beginning of the Year in the Alfredian Chronicle,' *English Historical Review*, xxxiii, 1918, pp. 328–42.

[2] See e.g. F. M. Stenton, *Anglo-Saxon England*, p. 683.

[3] e.g. the Alfredian Bede translates *cum duodecim lectis militibus* (*Historia Ecclesiastica*, Bk. iii, c. 1) as *twelfa sum*. Other instances of this usage occur in this work, and also in Alfred's translation of *Orosius*.

REX ANGLO, mentioned on p. 152, remains unique[1]
This appears less remarkable when it is realized that
coins of Alfred with anything more than REX are
extremely rare[2]. In fact, it is only exceptionally that
a fuller title is found until after the reform of 973.
Hence the statement on p. 151 that the regnal title
was invariably 'rex Anglorum' after Æthelstan's
time requires modification. It is true for the period
after 973[3].

In his discussion of Æthelwulf's donation (pp. 186–
91) Stevenson expresses the view that lands granted
as bookland to laymen were normally destined for

[1] Its provenance has been established as the Old Palace at
Croydon by Mr. R. H. M. Dolley, to whom, along with Mr.
C. E. Blunt, I am indebted for all the numismatic information
here given.

[2] An odd die from Alfred's 'Ceolwulf' period has REX A, and
from the same period there occur, each on an odd die, REX S, and
REX SAX, whereas REX SM is found on a single die. In the latter
part of the reign REX S occurs on one die, and REX SAXONUM on
rare coins of Exeter, Winchester, and the Romescot. REX DO,
DORO, is used on Canterbury coins about 890. A single die
from the beginning of the reign reading M–X is to be taken as
an aberration of a die-cutter who was also cutting dies for
Burgred of Mercia.

[3] Apart from two Bath coins at the beginning of his reign
which have REX SAXONUM, Edward the Elder has invariably
RE(X) only; RE(X) is normal throughout Æthelstan's reign,
though REX TO BRI, &c., is common in the latter part of his
reign, and REX BRI occurs on three dies from the Welsh Marches
and REX SAXORUM on an odd die from Mercia; Eadmund uses
RE(X), apart from an odd die from York with REX EB, &c., an
odd die at Chester with REX TO, and a die with REX M which is
probably a privy-mark; Eadred similarly uses RE(X), but REX
ANGLORUM and REX SAXORUM occur on odd dies from Mercia,
while REX I, M, or O are probably privy-marks; Eadwig's coins
supply a unique die from Barnstaple with REX SAXONUM, otherwise only RE(X), while before 973 Edgar normally uses RE(X),
but occasionally REX ANGLORUM, with REX LE and REX TO (BR)
on odd dies at Chester.

ecclesiastical foundations; but that this was not so, at any rate by Alfred's time, is shown by a passage in his will which limits the descent of his booklands to his kindred, with a preference for the male line. Moreover, chapter 41 of his laws, which forbids a man who has inherited bookland to alienate it from his kindred if document or witness shows that such alienation was prohibited either by the men who obtained the bookland or by those who transmitted it, suggests that such a limitation was no new thing in Alfred's reign[1].

Mr. P. Grierson's article,'Grimbald of St. Bertin's,'[2] which carefully examines the sources, English and continental, for the life of this scholar, is particularly important in dating more closely than Stevenson did Asser's visits to Alfred. It shows that Grimbald was still in Flanders in September 885, and came to England in 886 or early in 887, and it suggests February or March 886 as the date of Asser's first visit to Alfred, and March to December 887 as that of his first prolonged stay. Mr. Grierson points out that the attribution to Goscelin of a lost life of Grimbald, which was used by Leland, is erroneous, and that this lost life was based on one, preserved in the medieval breviary of Hyde Abbey, which probably was composed in the second half of the tenth century.

A few points of detail may be mentioned. Dr. R. Vaughan tells me that the list of Parker's gifts to Corpus Christi College, which Stevenson says could not be found (p. xviii, n. 2) has since been found and

---

[1] See also F. M. Stenton, *The Latin Charters of the Anglo-Saxon Period*, Oxford, 1955, pp. 60–65, especially p. 62, where it is pointed out that Alfred's preface to his version of the *Soliloquies of St. Augustine* associates bookland with the idea of permanent possession.

[2] *English Historical Review*, lv, 1940, pp. 529–61.

is now numbered C.C.C.C. 575. A fuller version of the papal letter mentioned on p. 243, n. 3, has since come to light[1], and as it is addressed to the archbishops Ethelred of Canterbury and Wulfred of York it must be assigned to Pope John VIII and dated 873-5. Thus it no longer tells us anything about the English clergy in Rome c. 705, but it is of great interest in showing the papal see still in contact with the English Church at the time when the struggle with the Vikings was at its height. It seems an odd moment to be insisting on a detail like clerical dress.

The identification of Bishop Wulfsige who received a copy of Alfred's translation of the *Cura Pastoralis* with Asser's predecessor at Sherborne, about which Stevenson has reservations (pp. cv, 321 n. 6), is now usually accepted[2], especially since Dr. Sisam has demonstrated his authorship of a verse preface to a copy of Wærferth's translation of Gregory's *Dialogues*[3]. The same author's study of Cynewulf prevents our assigning this poet, as Stevenson does (p. 288 n.), so confidently to eighth-century Northumbria; a Mercian localization and a date as late as the mid ninth century are also possible[4].

The note on Offa's daughters on p. 208 requires correction. Though the Chertsey charter there mentioned may be dubious, it is correct in assigning to Offa a daughter Æthelburg, whom it calls abbess.

[1] V. Wolf von Glanvell, *Die Kanonessammlung des Kardinals Deusdedit*, Paderborn, 1905, i, p. 225; E. Caspar, *Mon. Germ. Hist.: Epist. Karol. Ævi*, v, pp. 293 f. Translated by D. Whitelock, *English Historical Documents* c. 500-1042, p. 811.

[2] e.g. K. Sisam, *Studies in the History of Old English Literature*, p. 145.

[3] Ibid., pp. 201-3, 225-31.

[4] K. Sisam, 'Cynewulf and his Poetry,' ibid. pp. 1-7 (reprinted from *Proceedings of the British Academy*, xviii, 1932).

Alcuin writes to an abbess of this name, suggesting
that she advise her sister to enter a nunnery now her
husband has been killed, and there is little doubt
that this was one of the letters Alcuin wrote after the
murder of Ethelred of Northumbria, and that the sister
in question is Ethelred's widow, Ælfflæd, daughter of
Offa[1]. This Æthelburg is sometimes identified with
the kinswoman of Aldred of the Hwicce to whom he
granted the monastery of Fladbury for her lifetime[2],
though Stevenson is probably right in regarding this
abbess as the daughter of Alfred who occurs in
another document from Worcester.

Finally, it should be noted that the letter of Dunstan assigns to Edward's reign the appointment of
Eadwulf as Bishop of Crediton, with authority in
Cornwall, not to Æthelstan's reign as implied on
p. 322; and that *Beowulf* scholars nowadays would
consider the fact that *Geotena* in l. 445 alliterates
with *g* fatal to Munch's view, quoted on p. 169, n. 1,
that it is an error for *Eotena*.

It remains to add a few paragraphs on the authenticity of Asser's Life of Alfred, for though no arguments against it of any weight have been published
since Stevenson wrote, the matter has been raised
and there are indications that some recent scholars,
without going into the evidence, regard it as an open
question.

One need spend little time in refuting the sugges-

---

[1] *Mon. Germ. Hist.: Epist. Karol. Ævi*, ii, ed. E. Dümmler,
no. 102. The editors of Alcuin's letters consider her to be the
person addressed in nos. 36, 103, 300 under the name
Eugenia.

[2] The identification of the abbess of Fladbury with Offa's
daughter is accepted by W. Levison, *England and the Continent
in the Eighth Century*, p. 251, n. 2.

tion of J. W. Adamson[1] that the Life was forged by
Giraldus Cambrensis, by expanding parts of the
chronicle of Florence of Worcester, and using also
Simeon of Durham and the Anglo-Saxon Chronicle[2].
Even those who do not accept Wanley's views on the
date of the Cottonian manuscript will be disturbed
by the ignoring of the *Annals of St. Neots*, which
survive in a manuscript[3] a generation earlier than
Giraldus, and contain much of the matter claimed by

[1] J. W. Adamson, *The Illiterate Anglo-Saxon*, Cambridge,
1946.
[2] Against any theory that the Life could have been expanded
in this way, it should be noted that, though naturally both
Florence and Simeon suppress the personal references which
are in place only in a contemporary writer, each inadvertently
retains one, which shows that such things were in their source:
Florence, using c. 12, says, with reference to the character of
Æthelbald who died in 860, *sicut quorundam hominum relatu
audivimus*; Simeon quotes from c. 91 the words *de Jerosolima
a bel* (for *ab Elia*) *patriarcha epistolas et dona illi* (*diversa*)
*directa vidimus et legimus*. Florence and Simeon, in the first
part of his *Historia Regum*, are undoubtedly drawing independently on the Life, for each contains words, phrases, and
passages omitted by the other. Both omit as foreign to their
purpose the chapters mainly concerned with Welsh history and
the accounts of Asser's relations with the king.
[3] Trinity College, Cambridge, 770. Mr. T. A. M. Bishop
informs me that the hand of pp. 1–18 is that of a scribe who
appears in several Bury MSS., including New York Pierpont
Morgan 736, facsimile in *New Palaeographical Society*, i,
pp. 113–15, where it is dated second quarter of the twelfth
century, probably before 1135; that the hands of pp. 1–18 and
19–74 associate the MS. with a group of Bury MSS. mediately
and immediately interconnected by the hands of common
scribes; and that the general aspect of their work is first half of
the twelfth century, but rather remote from that of Bury MSS.
of the end of the eleventh century. He says that one of the
scribes appears in MS. Bodl. 297 in genealogies of the kings of
France and dukes of Normandy on p. 72, ending with the
accessions of Louis VI and Henry I; while another wrote
Cotton Charter xxi. 6, *Facsimiles of Royal and other Charters*

Adamson to be his invention. The arguments brought
forward against the authenticity of the Life are mainly
those already answered by Stevenson, whom Adamson cannot have fully understood, since he says he
is 'only half-hearted in repudiating the charge of ro-
mancing brought by some critics against "Asser"'.[1]
He makes no attempt to explain how a late-twelfth-
century writer could have acquired the knowledge of
ninth-century affairs shown by Asser.

Professor Galbraith, in a lecture on 'Historical
Research in Medieval England',[2] while not committing himself to a view that the Life is spurious,
nevertheless implies doubts. Thus he says that it is
'hard to believe that the author really enjoyed the
personal intimacy with the king which he claims.'[3]
This is because Professor Galbraith thinks that an
intimate of the king would have given a different
picture of him; but this is a subjective opinion which
others may not share. A ninth-century Welshman
may well have been interested in aspects of the king's
character other than those which appeal to a modern
historian. Professor Galbraith claims that Stevenson
'has rather silenced than satisfied' critics of Asser[4]
and that 'the strangest book in our medieval library
remains, accepted, if grudgingly, by our best historians because they do not believe historical research had reached the point at which it could have
been fabricated'.[5] Without knowing who are meant
by 'our best historians', one can only say that there

*in the British Museum*, pl. xii. 18, which has been closely dated
to 1140. Stevenson (p. 113) dated the MS. of the *Annals of
St. Neots* early part of the twelfth century.

[1] Op. cit. p. 24.
[2] University of London: Creighton Lecture in History, 1949,
London, 1951.
[3] p. 13.    [4] p. 23.    [5] p. 25.

are many scholars of repute who accept the genuineness of Asser ungrudgingly, and who base their faith
on more than this single argument, strong though it
is. One need not share Professor Galbraith's surprise
that the Life appears to have been unknown to
William of Malmesbury, a fact which he calls 'perhaps the oddest thing about it'.[1] William's collection
of materials was not exhaustive; he had, for example,
fewer versions of the Anglo-Saxon Chronicle at his
disposal than Florence had, and he came across the
Latin poem on King Æthelstan only after a first draft
of his work was completed. All that his ignorance of
Asser suggests is that the work was not widely known
in the twelfth century. It will require stronger evidence
than these implied doubts to refute Stevenson's arguments which show that the work is what it claims
to be.

There is no need to repeat those arguments, but
on some points more can be said. The question of the
*parochia* of Exeter, to which critics of Asser took
exception on the grounds that the see of Exeter was
not established until 1050 (see above, p. ciii), has been
discussed by Dr. Finberg, who interprets the passage
to mean that Asser received the endowments of the
monastery of Exeter while he exercised episcopal
functions in Devon and Cornwall, as a *chorepiscopus*
to the Bishop of Sherborne. He considers that
Wærstan and Putta, whose names are preserved in a
Tawton tradition recorded in *c.* 1580, were successors
of Asser in this office[2].

The only objection of substance which has been
brought against the accuracy of Asser relates to the

[1] p. 23.
[2] H. P. R. Finberg, 'Sherborne, Glastonbury, and the Expan-
sion of Wessex,' *Transactions of the Royal Historical Society*,
5th series, iii, 1953, pp. 115 f.

statements in his last chapter. It is necessary to
consider this in some detail, since Stevenson himself
considered that this chapter 'presents serious difficulties' (p. 342). His first difficulty was that Asser
appeared to be representing the king as receiving
appeals from lower courts. Stevenson held that
Anglo-Saxon law allowed such appeal only when the
courts had failed to do justice, which he interpreted
to refer solely to the failure to reach a decision
within the prescribed time. Æthelstan's second code,
chapter 3, forbids an appeal to the king before justice
has been demanded (in the courts) 'as often as is
required'; the previous sentence in this chapter
shows that the situation primarily envisaged is when
a lord wrongly shields one of his dependants and
thus prevents the plaintiff from securing his rights.
Edgar's third code, chapter 2, similarly allows appeal
to the king only when justice cannot be obtained at
home; but the next clause shows that appeal can be
made, not only when a court has delayed a decision
unduly, but also if the sentence is considered too
heavy[1]. Even if we assume that these later codes
represent the law as it stood in Alfred's day, which is
by no means certain[2], cannot Asser's words about
appeal to the king because of disagreement in the
assemblies of reeves and ealdormen be taken to cover
those cases when justice could not be 'obtained at
home'? Asser may also have in mind, as Stevenson
suggests, the consulting of the king when the parties
in a suit decided to settle it by arbitration rather than

---

[1] III Edgar 2. 1: *Gyf þæt riht to hefig sy, sece siþþan ða
lihtinge to þam cynge.*

[2] One might reasonably argue that these regulations represent
a tightening of the law on this subject, made necessary by the
great increase of legal business after the kings of Wessex had
become kings of England.

by legal process. The document of Edward the Elder's reign referred to in Stevenson's note on p. 342[1] supports Asser's veracity even more than one would gather from this note; for it not only affords an instance of an appeal to the king for his opinion, but the writer's remark: 'And if one wishes to change every judgement (*dom*) which King Alfred gave, when shall we have finished disputing?' strongly confirms Asser's claim that such appeals were common.

The second difficulty which Stevenson found in this chapter seems to me imaginary. He considers that Asser is making a foreigner's mistake in regarding the ealdormen and reeves as judges, whom the king could remove for incompetence or corruption, the real judges being the suitors of the court. It is certainly true that, throughout the Anglo-Saxon period and beyond, examples can be found of decisions made by the whole court[2]; but it is equally true that the Anglo-Saxons used the word *dema* (which is doubtless what Asser is translating as *judex*) of the official in charge of a court, and not of the suitors. This is clear already in chapter 8 of Ine's laws, which begins: 'If anyone asks for justice in the presence of any *scirman* or other *dema*.' It can also be shown that the person presiding over the court was held responsible for the judgements given. Thus the prologue to Edward the Elder's first code declares: 'King Edward commands all the reeves that you judge as just judgements[3] as you can most justly,

[1] It has since been edited by F. E. Harmer, *Select English Historical Documents of the Ninth and Tenth Centuries*, Cambridge, 1914, pp. 30–32, translation pp. 60–63, and translated by D. Whitelock, *English Historical Documents* c. 500–1042, London, 1955, pp. 501–3.

[2] For instances, see F. Liebermann, *Die Gesetze der Angelsachsen*, ii. *Glossar*, s.v. *Urteilfinder*.

[3] *deman swa rihte domas.*

and as it stands in the law-book.' We may compare
Cnut's letter of 1019/20, where he charges all his reeves
'on pain of losing my friendship and all that they
possess and their own lives, that everywhere they
maintain my people justly, and give just judgements.'
The passage quoted above from Edward the Elder's
code surely gives strong support to this chapter of
Asser, for in its insistence on the lawbook, it implies
that the reeve in charge of a court must now be able
to read, or at least have someone to read to him; hence
the need for study mentioned by Asser.

The responsibility of the person presiding comes
out even more clearly in chapter 3 of Edgar's third
code: 'And the judge (*dema*) who pronounces a wrong
judgement on another is to pay to the king 120
shillings as compensation, unless he dare declare on
oath that he knew not how to do it more justly—and
he is always to forfeit his thegnly status (*þegnscipe*),
unless he may redeem it from the king, according as
he will allow him. And the bishop of the diocese is to
exact the compensation on the king's behalf.' Proof
that he erred by ignorance, not through corruption,
thus saves the judge from a heavy fine, but not from
other consequences of his error.

The late Old English treatise known as *Judex* is in
part translated from Isidore, and if it stood alone
might be considered to express an alien conception;
but in view of the laws already cited, it is clear there
is nothing un-English in its use of *dema* as the man
in charge of a court, as in chapter 8, which declares
that no ealdorman is to set foolish or corrupt judges
as his deputies, or in chapter 11, where the wicked
judges who postpone or pervert the judgement out of
avarice, and never bring the suit to an end, are not
the suitors. That a *dema* is a presiding official is clear

also from many non-legal passages: for example, a homily ascribed to Wulfstan admonishes all 'earls and leaders, judges and reeves' never, for bribery or favour, to judge wrong judgements[1].

There does not, therefore, seem to be anything in this chapter of Asser to warrant the suspicion with which it has been regarded. Its claims are supported by a code and a charter both belonging to the reign of Alfred's son. A later forger would probably have included the sheriff among those in charge of assemblies, whereas Asser speaks only of *contiones comitum et praepositorum*, i.e. assemblies of ealdormen and reeves, and has the support of Alfred's laws, which speak of a *folcgemot* of a king's reeve[2], and of a (*folc*)*gemot* of a king's ealdorman[3].

The absence of any reference to Alfred's translations is discussed by Stevenson (pp. civ–cvii), and explained on the assumption that none was completed at the time Asser was writing. It has been objected that this necessitates the compression of Alfred's literary activity into the years 893–9, the first three of which were occupied by heavy campaigning. It must be remembered, however, that Alfred was not working unaided, but had several assistants. Asser himself helped him with the translation of the *Cura Pastoralis* and, according to William of Malmesbury, with *Boethius* also. One might even hazard a guess that his occupation with this work was one of the reasons why Asser never finished his Life of Alfred. But in any case, it is not

---

[1] *undom gedeman*, Napier, *Wulfstan*, p. 267. The passage from Wulfstan's *Institutes of Polity* from which this is taken gives the list: *eorlas and heretogan, and þas woruld-deman, and eac swa gerefan.*

[2] See Alfred 22, 34.

[3] Ibid. 38, 38. 1.

k

altogether safe to argue from Asser's silences. If he
had had a modern writer's sense of arrangement, one
would have expected him to mention in chapter 89
any works he knew undertaken by the king. But
what impressed Asser most was the king's late entry,
after long frustration, into the field of learning, and
he compares it with the late repentance of the thief
on the Cross. He then elaborates this parallel at
length, by comparing Alfred's sufferings and troubles
with those of the repentant thief. Thus he is drawn
away from the topic of the king's studies, and never
returns to it. Whether this was by accident, or
whether he had told us all he knew on this subject,
must remain uncertain[1]. But attention should be
drawn to the verbal parallels between Asser's Life
and the letter Alfred prefaced to his translation of the
*Cura Pastoralis*: *ut antequam aptas humanis artibus
vires haberent* (c. 75) corresponds closely to *ða hwile
ðe hie to nanre oðerre note ne mægen*[2] in a similar context in the letter, while the words *aliquando sensum
ex sensu* (c. 77) are half of the Latin tag which Alfred
translates as *hwilum word be worde, hwilum andgit
of andgiete*[3]. These parallels could indicate that Asser
knew the letter, though they present no difficulty if
this is later than the Life, since Asser may have helped
the king to draft this letter, just as he helped him to

[1] If we could assume that Asser knew of the king's translations, this would explain why he felt that the day on which
Alfred began *divino instinctu legere et interpretari* (c. 87) was
so important that he gave its exact date and a detailed account
of what happened on it. This part gains in significance if Asser
knew that here was the beginning of a great achievement.

[2] The correspondence is closer if one takes *mægen* in its full
sense of 'be strong,' 'have the strength for,' rather than as an
auxiliary.

[3] Compare also *regiae potestatis sollicitudinibus* (c. 25, l. 9)
with *bisgum ðisses kynerices*.

translate the text. But if the Life were a later forgery, we should have to include this letter among the documents used by the forger, and why then should that forger have avoided referring to the work to which it forms the preface ? What conceivable motive could anyone have, if forging a Life of Alfred, for wishing to make it appear to have been composed before the king's literary achievements, and before his last campaigns ? It is hard to see why a forger should have chosen the year 893. If the work is genuine there is nothing odd in Asser, bishop of the *parochia* of Exeter, laying aside his work in a year in which the Danes besieged Exeter, as well as a fort on the north coast of Devon. Why he never returned to it remains an unanswered question.

A great deal of what Asser tells us is supported by other records of the period. Some instances are listed by Stevenson (pp. cxxv–cxxvii), and others mentioned in my previous paragraphs, while the king's readiness to receive foreigners (c. 101) is shown by the various texts cited on p. 301. Asser's remarks about opposition and delay in the building of forts (c. 91) can be illustrated by annal 892 of the Anglo-Saxon Chronicle (a section of this record not used by Asser), for it speaks of a fort as only 'half-made' when the Danes landed. His picture of Alfred reorganizing his court (c. 100) fits in with annal 893, where we read of a similar arrangement with regard to the national levy. The chapter (c. 80) describing how Welsh princes sought alliance with Alfred receives support not only from the presence of Welsh allies with the English forces in annal 893, but also by the statement in the *Annales Cambriae*, 894[1], that Anaraut, the prince of Gwynedd who had, according to Asser, sought

[1] Probably for 895.

Alfred's protection, came 'with the English' to ravage
Ceredigion and Ystrad Tywi. J. E. Lloyd takes these
to be troops lent by Alfred when the Danes raided
Wales in 894[1]. The passage in which Asser tells us
that Alfred distributed one share of his income among
neighbouring monasteries throughout the Saxon kingdom and Mercia (c. 102) should be read in connexion
with the words in Alfred's laws, 'the monastic houses
to which the king's *feorm* belongs'.[2] There remain,
naturally, statements which cannot be checked, statements for which the Life is our only authority. These
constitute no argument against its authenticity, for
they are not intrinsically improbable, and it would be
asking too much to expect to find in the scanty
sources which happen to survive for this period confirmation for everything in the Life. If such could be
found, surely this would be a suspicious circumstance.

Stevenson comments on p. lxxv on the accuracy of
Asser's references to Welsh affairs, and writers on
Welsh history since Stevenson's time share this opinion.
Lloyd, for example, writes: 'The ease with which the
author (Asser) moves in a field in which a later forger
would have infallibly shown his ignorance is a weighty
argument in favour of the authenticity of the work.'[3]
Some recent Welsh writers believe, as does Dr. Schütt[4],
that Asser was writing for his fellow countrymen.
Sir Ifor Williams considers that Asser, in portraying
Alfred rather in the manner of a saint, was wishing
to demonstrate to the clergy in Wales 'how unseemly

[1] *A History of Wales from the Earliest Times to the Edward-
ian Conquest*, London, 1911, 3rd edit. 1939, i, p. 329 f.

[2] Alfred 2. I owe this reference to Sir Frank Stenton.

[3] Op. cit. i, p. 327, n. 28. One may add that K. Jackson, in his
*Language and History in Early Britain*, Edinburgh, 1953, accepts
the Welsh names in Asser as genuine ninth-century forms.

[4] See p. cxxxiv above.

it was for the Welsh princes to ally themselves with the Danish idolators, rather than with that shining Christian, Alfred, who was a pattern of what a king ought to be, as a man, as a Christian, and as a ruler'.[1] He believes that there was in South Wales at that time an opposition party to the policy of submission to Alfred, for which Asser stood, and that this opposition became vocal a generation later in *Armes Prydein*[2]. Without necessarily subscribing to a view that Asser's chief motive was to write political propaganda—for it is still possible to hold that he was mainly actuated by a wish to put on record what he knew of a great man who had honoured him with his friendship—we may note the unquestioning acceptance of the genuineness of the Life. Mrs. N. K. Chadwick also shows how the information given by Asser can be combined with that in other sources[3].

[1] Ifor Williams, *Armes Prydein*, University of Wales Press, 1955, p. xxvi. I owe this reference and the translation above given to Mrs. Rachel Bromwich. Sir Ifor discusses Asser on pp. xxii–xxvi of the above work. He derives the name Asser from Genesis xxx. 13, drawing attention to the number of biblical names adopted by Welshmen of the period. Mrs. Bromwich also informs me that in describing Alfred as rushing into battle *aprino more* Asser may be drawing on the vocabulary of early Welsh poetry, in which *twrch* 'boar' is a conventional metaphor for 'warrior.'

[2] Disapproval of a pro-English policy may account for the contemptuous reference in a Welsh triad to Hyfaidd son of Bleiddig in Deheubarth as one of three kings who were sprung from villeins. This triad is No. 68 in the forthcoming edition, *Trioedd Ynys Prydein*, by R. Bromwich. This reference was unknown to Stevenson. Thomas Jones, in his edition of the Peniarth MS. 20 version of the *Brut y Tywysogyon*, Cardiff, 1952, p. 139, shows that the Himeyd (Asser's Hemeid) of *Annales Cambriae* 892 can be identified with Hyfaidd ap Bleddri of the corresponding annal in the *Brut y Tywysogyon*, and this affords the necessary link with the king mentioned in the triad.

[3] *Studies in the Early British Church*, Cambridge, 1958,

If a later forger composed this Life, he must either have been unbelievably lucky in avoiding anachronisms and in lighting on contemporary conditions, or else have had access to a large number of earlier sources and have gone to great trouble in his use of them[1]. Anyone who would undertake so great a labour in order to deceive must surely have had a compelling motive. The view that the Life is a piece of political propaganda of the tenth or eleventh centuries was disposed of by Stevenson (p. cviii). Until someone produces a convincing motive for so elaborate a deception, and shows how its author collected his material and how he avoided the pitfalls that lie in the path of those who try to reproduce a past age, we need give no further consideration to the view that the Life of Alfred is not the contemporary document it claims to be; and even then, positive evidence of later writing would have to be forthcoming before it could be shown to be spurious.

pp. 83–85. Mrs. Chadwick also suggests (p. 124) that Asser was educated at Llanbadarn Fawr, and only later had an interest in St. David's. Asser's own words (c. 79, ll. 16 f.) are vague as to his place of education.

[1] The difficulty of such a task can be illustrated by comparing a work entitled *The Journal of a Spy in Paris during the Reign of Terror, January to July, 1794*, to which Professor B. Dickins has drawn my attention. This was forged as a joke by Charles Fletcher and took in many persons until A. F. Pollard in a review in *English Historical Review*, xi, 1896, pp. 594–7, exposed it by pointing out inconsistencies and errors. This shows that a writer with the resources of modern libraries at his disposal, and on his mettle to deceive the learned historians of his day, failed to escape detection. A medieval forger would not have to face a scrutiny of this kind, and would see no need to undertake such extensive research work, even if—which is unlikely—he had access to the necessary materials.

# SIGLA.

Quae exscripsit Florentius Wigorniensis litteris rectis, quae vero praetermisit litteris inclinatis excudenda curavimus. Interpolata litteris minoribus impressa sunt.

*Cott* = Codex Cottonianus Otho A xii, qui an. 1731 igne periit (§ 14).

*B* = apographum saeculi sextodecimi, Codex Cotton. Otho A xii* (§ 29).

*Co* = apographum in usum Parkerii factum, Coll. Corporis Christi Cantabrigiae, No. 100 (§ 28).

*Ar* = apographum saeculi sextodecimi, Bibliotheca Universitatis Cantabrigiae, Add. 3825 (§ 30).

## EDITIONES.

*P* = Parkeriana, an. 1574 (§ 4).
*Camd* = Camdeniana, an. 1602–3 (§ 7).
*W* = Wiseana, an. 1722 (§ 11).
*Pet* = Petreana, an. 1848 (§ 12).

## EXPILATORES.

*Flor* = Florentius Wigorniensis (§ 33).
*SN* = Annales, qui dicuntur, Fani Sancti Neoti (§ 34).
*SD* 1 = Simeonis Dunelmensis 'Historiae Regum Anglorum' pars prior (§ 35).
*SD* 2 = Simeonis Dunelmensis 'Historiae Regum Anglorum' pars altera (§ 35).

# ASSERIUS

## DE

# REBUS GESTIS ÆLFREDI

*Domino meo venerabili piissimoque omnium
Brittanniae insulae Christianorum rectori, Ælfred,
Anglorum Saxonum regi, Asser, omnium servorum
Dei ultimus, millemodam ad vota desideriorum
utriusque vitae prosperitatem.*

*Anno Dominicae Incarnationis* DCCCXLIX natus 1
est Ælfred, Angul-Saxonum rex, in villa regia, quae
dicitur Uuanating, in illa paga, quae nominatur
Berrocscire : quae paga taliter vocatur a Berroc
silva, ubi buxus abundantissime nascitur. Cuius 5

---

*Titulum add. W* : Alfredi res gestae authore Asser *Co* (*manu P
scripta*), *P, B    Capita numeris ipse notavi*
*Superscriptio* Brittanniae *imago* : Britanniae *Co B P cett. Edd.*
    1. *Exscripserunt SD* 1 *SD* 2        1 DCCCXLVIII *SD* 2
2 Alfred *B*        Anglorum Saxonum *B*        3 Uuanating *imago*
*P Ar* : Wanating *Co B* : Wanading *Camd W* : Wanetinge *SD* 1
plaga *SD* 2        4 Berrocscire *Ar*        que *imago* : quae *Edd.*
5 abundantissime *B Camd W Pet* : hab- *P Ar* : babundaneissime
(*sic*) *imago*        nascitur *P Ar cett. Edd.* : nasettur (*sic*) *imago*

genealogia tali serie contexitur : Ælfred rex, filius
Æthelwulfi regis; qui fuit Ecgberhti; qui fuit
Ealhmundi; qui fuit Eafa ; qui fuit Eoppa ; qui
fuit Ingild ; Ingild et Ine, ille famosus Occiden-
10 talium rex Saxonum, germani duo fuerunt, qui Ine
Romam perrexit, et ibi vitam praesentem finiens
honorifice, caelestem patriam, cum Christo regnaturus, adiit; qui fuerunt filii Coenred ; qui fuit
Ceoluuald ; qui fuit Cudam ; qui fuit Cuthwine ;
15 qui fuit Ceaulin ; qui fuit Cynric ; qui fuit Creoda ;
qui fuit Cerdic ; qui fuit Elesa ; ⟨qui fuit Esla ;⟩ qui
fuit Geuuis, a quo Britones totam illam gentem
Geguuis nominant; ⟨qui fuit Wig ; qui fuit Freawine ; qui fuit Freothegar ;⟩ qui fuit Brond ; qui fuit
20 Beldeag ; qui fuit Uuoden ; qui fuit Frithowald ;
qui fuit Frealaf ; qui fuit Frithuwulf; qui fuit Finn

6 *post* genealogia *add.* talis *imago Co B P Ar rell. Edd.* 7 Æthelwolfi *B* Ecgberthi *Camd W Pet* : Egberhti *B* 8 Eafae *Flor*
Eoppa *Co B Flor* : Eowwa *Ar Edd.* (*natum ex errore, ut videtur,*
*opcrarum P, litteris p et* ꝑ = *w confusis*) 9 Ingels *Flor* : Ingles
*SD* 2 10 Germani *P Camd W* 13 fuere *Ar* 14 Ceolwald *Flor*
*SD* 2 : Ceolwold *SD* 1 : Ceolwalde *rell.* Cutha *recte Flor* : Cuda
*SD* 1 *SD* 2 Cuderwine *SD* 1 *Edd.* (*ex* Cuðwine *perperam lecto,*
*namque littera* ð *a compendio, quo seculo duodecimo p. C. n.* der,
dre *interdum notabantur, haud facile dinoscas*) 15 Cinric *Co*
*Ar* 16 qui fuit Esla *ex Flor supplevit W, quae exhibet SD* 2 :
*om. Co B P Ar Camd SD* 1 17 Brittones *Co* 18 Gewis
*Flor Ar W* qui fuit Wig . . . Freothegar *ex Flor supplevit W, quae*
*exhibet SD* 2 : *om. Co P Ar Camd SD* 1 20 Beldeag *Flor* (*recte*
Bealdæg, *cf. Chron. Anglo-Sax. ann.* 855): Belde *Co B P Ar cett.*
*Edd. SD* 1 : Bealdeag *SD* 2 Frithowald *Co Flor* : Frithuwald
*SD* 1 : Frithewald *SD* 2 : Frithowalde *rell.* 21 Frithuwulfe *Co*
*Ar* : Frithowulfe *B* : Fritheuulf *SD* 2 : Fridrenwulf (*ex* Friðuwulf
*male lecto ; vide quae ad v.* 14 *adnotavimus*) *SD* 1 Finn, qui fuit
Godwulf *scripsi secutus Chron. Anglo-Sax.* : Fingodwulf(e), Fyn-
*Co P Edd. Ar B* ; *om. SD* 1 : Fingoldwulf *Flor* (*vide infra,* p. 158,

⟨; qui fuit⟩ Godwulf; qui fuit Geata, quem Getam iamdudum pagani pro deo venerabantur. *Cuius Sedulius poeta mentionem facit in Paschali metrico carmine, ita dicens* [a] *:*    25

> *cum sua gentiles studeant figmenta poetae*
> *grandisonis pompare modis, tragicoque boatu*
> *ridiculove Getae seu qualibet arte canendi*
> *saeva nefandarum renovent contagia rerum,*
> *et scelerum monumenta canant, rituque magistro*    30
> *plurima Niliacis tradant mendacia biblis :*
> *cur ego Daviticis assuetus cantibus odas*
> *chordarum resonare decem, sanctoque verenter*
> *stare choro, et placidis caelestia psallere verbis,*
> *clara salutiferi taceam miracula Christi ?*    35

Qui *Geata* fuit Tætuua ; qui fuit Beauu ; qui fuit Sceldwea ; qui fuit Heremod ; qui fuit Itermod ; qui fuit Hathra ; qui fuit Huala ; qui fuit Beduuig ; qui fuit Seth ; qui fuit Noe ; qui fuit Lamech ; qui fuit Mathusalem ; qui fuit Enoch ; ⟨qui fuit Iared ;⟩ 40

---

[a] Paschalis Carminis lib. i. 17 (Opera, *ed. I. Hümer*, Corpus Scriptt. Ecclesiastt. Latinorum, *tom. x. Vindobonae*, 1885).

---

not. 2) *SD* 2        22 Geada *Camd* : Geta *SD* 2        Geatam *Flor* 26–28 *extant in SD* 1 *SD* 2        28 Geta *Hümer*        29 renovant *Co B P Ar Camd*        30 monimenta *Co B P Ar Camd* canunt *Co B P Ar Camd*        magistro *Co B P Ar Camd Hümer* : sinistro '*sic* ⟨*Sedulii*⟩ *Ed. Vienn. Ao.* 1519' *W quod recc. W Pet*        31 tradunt *Co B P*        32 Daviticis *Co P Ar Hümer* : Davidicis *B Camd W Pet*        36 Tætuua *scripsi secutus Chron. Anglo-Sax.* : Caetuua *Co B P Ar Camd W Pet* : Ceatwa *Flor SD* 2 Cetwa *SD* 1        38 Haula *B* : Wala *Flor SD* 1 *SD* 2        Beaduwig *Flor* : Beaduing (*lege* Beaduuig) *SD* 2 : Bedwig *SD* 1        39 Seth *Co B P Ar Camd Flor* : Sem *W Pet SD* 1 *SD* 2 *Legendum tamen* Sceaf (*cf. Chron. Anglo-Sax. ann.* 855)        40 qui fuit Iared *ex Flor supplevit W* : om. *Co B P Ar Camd SD* 1 *SD* 2

B 2

qui fuit Malaleel; qui fuit Cainan; qui fuit Enos;
qui fuit Seth; qui fuit Adam.

**2** *De genealogia matris eius.*

Mater quoque eiusdem Osburh nominabatur,
religiosa nimium femina, nobilis ingenio, nobilis et
genere; quae erat filia Oslac, famosi pincernae
Æthelwulfi regis. Qui Oslac Gothus erat natione;
5 ortus enim erat de Gothis et Iutis, de semine scilicet
Stuf et Wihtgar, duorum fratrum et etiam comitum,
qui, accepta potestate Uuectae insulae ab avunculo
suo Cerdic rege et Cynric filio suo, consobrino
eorum, paucos Britones eiusdem insulae accolas,
10 quos in ea invenire potuerunt, in loco, qui dicitur
Guuihtgaraburhg, occiderunt. Ceteri enim accolae
eiusdem insulae ante aut occisi erant aut exules
aufugerant.

**3** *Anno Dominicae Incarnationis* DCCCLI, *nativitatis autem Ælfredi regis tertio,* Ceorl, Domnaniae
comes, cum Domnaniis contra paganos pugnavit in
loco, qui dicitur Uuicganbeorg, et Christiani victo-
5 riam habuerunt. Et ipso eodem anno primum

---

2 *Exscripserunt totum SD* 2, *partim SD* 1      1 Osburh *Co*:
Osbruh *B*: Osburga *Flor*: Osburgh *rell.*      4 Æthelwolfi *B*      5
Indis *Camd, quod e Cott perperam enotat W, affirmat enim Ussher*
Iutis *in eo extitisse*      6 Wihtgar *Flor SD* 1 *SD* 2: Wihtgur
*Co B*: Wihtzur (*an errore operarum?*) *P Ar Camd W Pet*      8
Cinric *Ar*      9 Brittones *Co*      11 Wihtgaraburg *Flor*: Guuiht
Garaburhg *Co Camd*      13 aufugerunt *Co B P*: fugerant *SD* 2
     3 *Exscripserunt totum SN, partim SD* 1 *SD* 2      2 Karl
*SD* 2: Georl *B*      Dōnania *SN*      3 Domnanus *Co P Camd*:
Domnanis *B*: Dōnanis *SN*      *post* paganos *add.* Normannos sive
Danos *B P Ar Camd* (*ex SN*) Nordimannos (Nordmannos *SN*) sive
Danos      4 Uuicganbeorga *SN*: Wicgambeorg *Camd W Pet*:
Wincanbeorh *SD* 2      6 Scepieg *Co B*: Scheapieg *Camd W Pet*:

hiemaverunt pagani in insula, quae vocatur Sceapieg, quod interpretatur 'insula ovium'; quae sita
est in Tamesi flumine inter East-Seaxum et Cantuarios, sed ad Cantiam propior est quam ad
East-Seaxum; in qua monasterium optimum con- 10
structum est.

Eodem quoque anno magnus paganorum exer- 4
citus cum trecentis et quinquaginta navibus in
ostium Tamesis fluminis venit et Doruberniam, id
est Cantwariorum civitatem, ⟨et Lundoniam⟩ (quae
est sita in aquilonari ripa Tamesis fluminis, in 5
confinio East-Seaxum et Middel-Seaxum, sed
tamen ad East-Seaxum illa civitas cum veritate
pertinet) depopulati sunt, et Beorhtulfum, Merciorum regem, cum omni exercitu suo, qui ad proeliandum contra illos venerat, in fugam verterunt. 10

His ibi ita gestis, praedictus paganorum exer- 5
citus perrexit in Suthrie, quae paga sita est in

---

Sceapeige *SN*     7 quod interpretatur insula ovium *om. SN*
8 Thamesi *B* : Tamensi *SN*    Eastsexum *B*     Centaurios *Camd*
(*errore, ut videtur, operarum*)     9 Cantiam *Co SN Flor* : Cantium
*cett.*    quem *Co*    ad *om. SN*     10 Eastsexum *B*    in qua
... constructum est *om. SN*
    4 *Exscripserunt SN SD* 1 *SD* 2     3 Thamesis *B* : Tamensis
*SD* 1 *SD* 2 : Tamsis *SN*    et Doruberniam ... civitatem *Cott.* (*teste
W*) *Co Flor SD* 1 *SD* 2 : *om. P Camd SN*    Doroborniam ... Cantuariorum *B*     4 et Lundoniam *SN Flor* : *om. Cott.* (*teste W*) *Co
B SD* 1 *SD* 2 : et Londoniam *P Ar Edd.*    *post* Lundoniam *add.*
(*ex SN*) civitatem *P Ar rell.*     quae ... pertinet *om. SD* 1
*SD* 2     5 aquilonali *Flor SN*    Thamesis *B* : Tamensis *SN*
6 Sexum *B SN*    Middle *P W* : Middel *Camd* : Middil *SN* :
Midle *B*    7 Sexum *B*    8 Beortulfum *B*    9 suo *om. B*
    5 *Exscripserunt SD* 1 *SD* 2     1 ita *om. B*     2 Suthrie
*Co* : Suthrye *B* : Suthrigie *SN* : Suthregia *Flor* : Suthrige *SD* 1
*SD* 2 : Suthriae *rell.*

meridiana Tamesis fluminis ripa ab occidentali parte
Cantiae. Et Æthelwulfus, [*Occidentalium*] Saxonum
5 rex, et filius suus Æthelbaldus cum omni exercitu
in loco, qui dicitur Aclea, id est 'in campulo quercus,' diutissime pugnaverunt ; ibique, cum diu acerrime et animose ex utraque parte pugnatum esset,
maxima pars paganae multitudinis funditus deleta
10 et occisa est, ita qualiter nunquam in aliqua regione
in una die, ante nec post, ex eis occisam esse audivimus, et Christiani victoriam honorifice tenuerunt
et loco funeris dominati sunt.

**6**  Eodem quoque anno Æthelstan, [*filius Æthel-
*wulfi regis*], et Ealhere comes magnum paganorum
exercitum in Cantia, in loco, qui dicitur Sandwic,
occiderunt, et ex navibus eorum novem naves cepe-
5 runt ; ceteri per fugam elapsi sunt.

**7**  *Anno Dominicae Incarnationis* DCCCLIII, *nativitatis autem Ælfredi regis quinto.* Burgred, Mer-

---

3 Tamensis *SN*         4 Cantiae *Flor Co B SN*: Cantii *rell.*
Ethelwulfus *Co*: Æthelwolfus *B*: Adheluulfus *SN*    Occidentalium (*ex SN interpolatum*) *B P rell. Edd.*: *om. Cott.* (*teste W*)
*Co SD* 1 *SD* 2 : West *Flor*      5 Adhelbaldus *SN*    *post* exercitu *add.* suo contra praefatum exercitum *SN*      6 Aclea *SN*    id
est . . . quercus *om. SN*     7 accerrime *SN*      9 paganicae *B*    11
occisum *B SN*        13 loci *Co SN*

**6** *Exscripserunt SN SD* 1 (*an.* 852) *SD* 2 (*an.* 852)     1 quo-
que] vero *SN*       Ethelstan *B*: Adhelstan rex *SN*    filius Æthelwulfi regis *om. Cott.* (*teste W*) *Co B SD* 1 *SD* 2 : *exhibent* (*interpolata ex SN*) *P Ar Camd W Pet* (Athelwulfi *P*: Adhelwulfi
*SN*)    2 Ealchére *SN*       paganorum] Nordmannorum *SN*
3 Cantia *Co Flor SN SD* 1 *SD* 2 : Cantio *rell.*      4 et (= æt,
'*apud*') *SD* 1     acceperunt *Cott.* (*teste W*) *Co*      5 ceteris . . .
elapsis *SN*

**7** *Exscripserunt SD* 1 *SD* 2      2 quinto *correxit W* : quinto
*SD* 1 : undecimo *Cott.* (*teste W*) *P Ar Camd*: ijᵒ *Co*: *om. B*

ciorum rex, per nuncios deprecatus est Æthelwulfum,
Occidentalium Saxonum regem, ut ei auxilium
conferret, quo mediterraneos Britones, qui inter ⁊
Merciam et mare occidentale habitant, dominio suo
subdere potuisset, qui contra eum immodice reluctabantur. Nec segnius Æthelwulfus rex, legatione
eius accepta, exercitum movens, Britanniam cum
Burghredo rege adiit, statimque ut ingreditur, 10
gentem illam devastans, dominio Burgredi subdit.
Quo facto, domum revertitur.

Eodem anno Æthelwulfus rex praefatum filium 8
suum Ælfredum, magno nobilium et etiam ignobilium
numero constipatum, honorifice Romam transmisit.
*Quo tempore dominus* Leo Papa [*quartus*] *aposto-*
*licae sedi praeerat, qui praefatum infantem Ælfredum* ⁊
oppido ordinans unxit in regem, et in filium adoptionis sibimet accipiens confirmavit.

Eodem quoque anno Ealhere comes, cum Can- 9
tuariis, et Huda, cum Suthriis, contra paganorum
exercitum in insula, quae dicitur *in* Saxonica *lingua*

---

3 Ethelwulfum *Co* : Æthelwolfum *B*      6 Marciam *Camd W Pet*
domino *Co*      9 eius *om. Co*      10 Burgredo *Co. B* : Burghredi
*Ar Camd*      11 Burghredi *W Pet* : Burghredo *Camd*

8 *Exscripp. SN SD* 1 *SD* 2      1 *post* anno *add.* quoque *B*
Æthelwolfus *B* : Adhelwulfus *SN*      praefatum *om. SN*      2 Alfre-
dum *SN*      4 dompnus *SN*      quartus *om. Cott.* (*teste IV*)
*Co SD* 1 : *exhibent* (*interpolatum ex SN*) *B P Ar Camd W* : *seclusit*
*Pet*      4–5 Quo . . . Ælfredum] Quem Leo Papa, sui patris rogatu
*Flor SD* 2      5 Alfredum *SN*      6 oppido . . . confirmavit]
confirmavit et in filium adoptionis sibimet accepit, et etiam unctus
⟨*sic*⟩ oleo consecravit in regem *SN*

9 *Exscripp. SN SD* 1 (*an.* 854) *SD* 2 (*an.* 854)      1 Aelhere
*Co* : Alchere *SN*      2 Huda] Wada *SD* 1 *SD* 2      Suthreis *B* :
Suthregiis *Flor* : Suthrigiis *SD* 1 : Suthriis *SD* 2      3 quae dicitur
in Saxonica lingua *om. SN SD* 2 : quae Saxonice dicitur *Flor*      in

Tenet, Britannico *autem sermone* Ruim, animose et
5 acriter belligeraverunt, et primitus Christiani victoriam habuerunt, prolongatoque diu proelio ibidem
ex utraque parte plurimi ceciderunt et in aqua
mersi suffocati sunt, et comites illi ambo ibidem
occubuerunt.  Necnon et eodem anno Æthelwulfus,
10 Occidentalium Saxonum rex, post Pascha filiam
suam Burgredo Merciorum regi in villa regia, quae
dicitur Cippanhamme, nuptiis regaliter factis, ad
reginam dedit.

**10**  *Anno Dominicae Incarnationis* DCCCLV, *nati-*
*vitatis autem praefati regis septimo,* [*Eadmundus,*
*Orientalium Anglorum gloriosissimus, coepit regnare VIII.*
*kalend. Ianuarii, id est die natalis Domini, anno aetatis*
5 *suae decimo quarto.  Hoc etiam anno Lotharius, Imperator*
*Romanus, obiit, filius Ludovici Augusti piissimi.  Anno*
*eodem, sub initio Karoli tertii Imperatoris, filii Ludovici*
*secundi*], magnus paganorum exercitus tota hieme
in praefata Scepige insula hiemaverunt.

**11**  Eodem  anno  Æthelwulfus *praefatus venera-*

---

*om. B*    4 Tened *SD* 1 : Thenet *SD* 2    Brittones *Co* : Britannico
autem sermone *om. SN* : Britannice Ruim *Flor*    Ruym *B* : *om.*
*SD* 2    6 diu *om. SN*    7 occiderunt *Co*    9 anno eodem *SN*
Athelwulfus *SN*    10 post Pascha *om. SD* 1 *SD* 2 : *ante* Occiden-
talium *exhibent Co B P Edd. SN*    11 Burchredo *SN*    12
Cyppanhamme *B*    *ante* Cippanhamme *add.* Et (= æt '*apud*')
*SD* 1

10 *Exscripp. SN SD* 1 *SD* 2    1 nativitatis ... septimo *om.*
*SN*    2 praefati *om. B*    *post* septimo *add.* rex *SN*    Ead-
mundus] ' *Abhinc ad* magnus paganorum ⟨*v.* 8⟩ &c. *omnia desunt*
*MS. Cott.' W* : *om. Co B SD* 1 *SD* 2 : *exhibent* (*interpolata*
*ex SN*) *P Ar Camd* : *seclusit Pet*    6 Romanorum *SN*
Hloduuici *SN*    7 sub initio] in initium *SN*    Loduuici *SN*
8 *ante* magnus *add.* eodem anno *SN*    tota hieme] hiemavit *SN*
9 praefata *om. SN*    insula Sceapeige *SN*    hiemaverunt *om SN*
11 *Exscripp. SN SD* 1 *SD* 2    1 *post* Eodem *add.* quoque *SN*

*bilis* rex decimam totius regni sui partem ab omni
regali servitio et tributo liberavit, in sempiternoque
graphio in cruce Christi, pro redemptione animae
suae et antecessorum suorum, uni et trino Deo 5
immolavit. *Eodemque anno* cum magno honore
Romam perrexit, *praefatumque* filium suum Ælfredum iterum in eandem viam secum ducens,
*eo quod illum* plus ceteris *filiis* dil*igebat*, ibique
anno integro remoratus est. Quo peracto, ad 10
patriam suam remeavit, adferens secum Iuthittam,
Karoli, Francorum regis, filiam.

Interea tamen, Æthelwulfo rege ultra mare 12
tantillo tempore immorante, quaedam infamia
contra morem omnium Christianorum in occidentali parte Selwuda orta est. Nam Æthelbaldus
rex, [*Æthelwulfi regis filius,*] et Ealhstan, Scire- 5
burnensis ecclesiae episcopus, Eanwulf quoque
Summurtunensis pagae comes coniurasse referuntur,
ne unquam Æthelwulf rex, a Roma revertens, iterum
in regno reciperetur. Quod inauditum omnibus

---

Adhelwulfus *SN*     praefatus *om. SN*     2 *post* rex *add.* Occidentalium Saxonum *SN*     3 sempiterno *Co B*     4 grafio *Co B*
*P Ar Camd SN*     6 eodem quoque *B SN* : sicque *Flor* : om.
*SD* 1 *SD* 2     7 praefatum *SN*     Aelfredum *SN*     8 eadem
via *SN*     9 eo quod illum] quem *Flor SD* 2     dilexit *Flor*
*SD* 2     ibi *Flor SD* 2     10 remoratus ' *sic MS. Cott.*' *W* : demo-
ratus (*ex SN*) *B P Ar Camd*     11 Iudithtam *SN*
   12 *Exscripsit SN*     1 Æthelwulfo tamen *Co*     Adhelwulfo
*SN*     2 inmorante *Co*     4 Selwudae *Flor* : Salouuda *SN*
Æthelbald *B P Camd* : Adhelbaldus *SN*     5 Æthelwulfi regis
filius *om. Cott.* (*teste W*) *Co* : *exhibent* (*ex SN interpolata*) *B P*
*Ar Camd W* : *secl. Pet*     Æthelwolfi *B* : Adhelwulfi *SN*
Ealchstanus *SN* : Ealhastanus *SD* 1     6 Eamwulfe *Co B*     7
Sumertunensis *B* : Sumurtunensis *SN*     8 Æthelwulfe *Co* :
Æthelwolfe *B* : Adhelwulfus *SN*

10 seculis ante infortunium, episcopo et comiti solummodo perplurimi reputant, ex quorum consilio
hoc factum esse perhibetur.  Multi quoque regali
solummodo insolentiae deputant, quia et ille rex in
hac re et in multis aliis perversitatibus pertinax
15 fuit, sicut quorundam hominum relatu audivimus :
quod et rei sequentis approbavit effectus.  Nam
redeunte eo a Roma, praedictus filius regis Æthelwulfi cum omnibus suis consiliariis, immo insidiariis,
tantum facinus perpetrare tentati sunt, ut regem a
20 regno proprio repellerent : quod nec Deus ita fieri
permisit, nec nobiles totius Saxoniae consenserunt.
Nam, ne irremedicabile Saxoniae periculum, belli-
gerante patre et filio, quin immo tota cum gente
ambobus rebellante, atrocius et crudelius per dies
25 singulos quasi clades intestina augeretur, ineffabili
patris clementia et omnium astipulatione nobilium,
adunatum antea regnum inter patrem et filium divi-
ditur, et orientales plagae patri, occidentales filio e
contrario deputantur.  Ubi enim pater iusto iudicio
30 regnare debuerat, illic iniquus et pertinax filius
regnabat ; nam occidentalis pars Saxoniae semper
orientali principalior est.

**13**    Adveniente igitur Æthelwulfo rege a Roma,

---

10 seculi *SN*    12 regali *om. Ar*    13 *post* ille *add.* Æthelbald
*Co B*    15 sic *SN*    16 regi *Co*    probavit *B*    17 Æthelwulf
*Co* : Æthelwolfe *B* : Adhelwulfi *SN*    18 insiliariis *Flor SN*    19
temptati *Co B Ar SN*    21 Angliae *SN*    22 inremediabile
*Co SN*    *post* irremedicabile *add.* totius *B SN*    Angliae *SN*
23 quinimmo *Ar*    24 rebellantibus *Flor*    28 plagae *Co*
*B P Ar Camd W Pet Flor* : pagae *SN fortasse recte*    e *om. B*
31 Angliae *SN*
    **13** *Exscripsit SN*    1 Adhelwulfo *SN*    4 Adhelbaldum *SN*

tota illa gens, ut dignum erat, in adventu senioris
ita gavisa est, ut, si ille permitteret, pertinacem
filium suum Æthelbaldum cum omnibus suis consiliariis a totius regni sorte expellere vellent. Sed 5
ille, ut diximus, nimia clementia et prudenti consilio
usus, ne ad regni periculum perveniret, ita fieri
noluit; et Iuthitham, Karoli regis filiam, quam a
patre suo acceperat, iuxta se in regali solio [suo.]
sine aliqua suorum nobilium controversia et odio, 10
usque ad obitum vitae suae, contra perversam illius
gentis consuetudinem, sedere imperavit. Gens
namque Occidentalium Saxonum reginam iuxta
regem sedere non patitur, nec etiam reginam appellari, sed regis coniugem, permittit. Quam con- 15
troversiam, immo infamiam, de quadam pertinaci et
malevola eiusdem gentis regina ortam fuisse,
maiores *illius terrae perhibent; quae omnia contraria
seniori suo et omni populo ita peregit, ut non solum
suum proprium odium mereretur, ut a reginali solio 20
proiceretur, sed etiam omnibus suis subsequutricibus
eandem pestiferam tabem post se submitteret.* Pro
*nimia namque illius* reginae malitia omnes accolae
illius terrae coniuraverunt, ut nullum unquam regem

7 proveniret *SN*    8 *ante* et *add.* sed *SN*    Iuthittam *Co B P
Camd* : Iudithtam *SN*    Karoli *Co B Ar* : Faroli *Cott.* (*teste
W*) *P Camd*, 'Fa *pro* Ka' *adn. P Camd*    9 *alterum* suo *om.
Cott.* (*teste W*) *Co B SN*    13 Orientalium *Ar*    14 appellari
*Flor* : appellare *rell.*    15 quae controversia *Flor*    16 infamia
*Flor* : insaniam *B*    17 malivolo *SN*    reginae *B*    orta est
*Flor*    18 maioribus nostris sic attestantibus *Flor*    illius . . ·
seniori *abscissa SN, exhibet editio*    20 meretur et a regali
*Co*    21 subsequatricibus *Cott.* (*teste W*) *Co B P Ar Camd SN*
22 summitteret *SN*    22–7 pro . . . vellet *ad finem capitis subse-
quentis transtulit Flor*    23 nimia namque illius] huiusmodi *Flor*

25 super se *in vita sua* regnare permitterent, qui reginam in regali solio iuxta se sedere imperare
vellet. *Et quia, ut opinor, multis habetur incognitum*
*unde haec perversa et detestabilis consuetudo in*
*Saxonia, ultra morem omnium Theotiscorum, pri-*
30 *mitus orta sit, paulo latius mihi videtur inti-*
*mandum. Quod a domino meo Ælfredo, Angul-*
*saxonum rege veredico, etiam saepe mihi referente,*
*audivi; quod et ille etiam a veredicis multis re-*
*ferentibus, immo ex parte non modica illud factum*
35 *commemorantibus, audierat.*

**14** Fuit in Mercia moderno tempore quidam strenuus *atque universis circa se regibus et regionibus*
*finitimis formidolosus* rex, nomine Offa, *qui vallum*
*magnum inter Britanniam atque Merciam de mari*
5 *usque ad mare fieri imperavit.* Cuius filiam,
nomine Eadburh, Beorhtric Occidentalium Saxonum rex, sibi in coniugium accepit. Quae confestim *accepta regis amicitia et totius pene regni*
*potestate, more paterno* tyrannice vivere *incepit, et*
10 *omnem hominem execrari, quem Beorhtric diligeret,*
*et* omnia odibilia Deo et hominibus facere, *et omnes,*
quos posset, ad regem accusare, et ita *aut* vita aut

---

26 reginali *B SN*      29 Anglia *SN*      Theotiscorum *scripsi*:
Theotiscirum *Cott.* (*teste W*) *Co Camd*: Theothiscirum *B P Ar*:
Theotiscarum *W Pet*: gentium *SN*      *post* Theotiscorum *add.* id
est gentium *B, quae in textum Camd W Pet post* omnium *irre-*
*pserunt ex glossemate* (*ex SN*) *margini P Ar adscripto*      31 Angulo-
*SN*      32 veridico *SN*

14 *Exscripp. SD* 1 (*an.* 802) *SN*      4 Bryttaniam *SN* et *SN*
5 fieri *scripsi*: facere *omnes*      imperabat *B*      filia *B*      6 Eadburh
*Co B Flor*: Eadburga *SN*: Eadburgh *rell.*      Beorchtricus *SN*
7 *post* rex *add.* ut praediximus *Flor*      confestim] mox *Flor*      10

potestate per insidias privare. Et si a rege illud
impetrare non posset, veneno eos necabat; *sicut* de
adolescente quodam regi dilectissimo hoc factum 15
compertum habetur, quem cum ad regem accusare
non posset, veneno eum necavit. De quo veneno
etiam praefatus ille Beorhtric rex inscienter gustasse
aliquid refertur: neque enim illa venenum dare
regi proposuerat, sed puero; sed rex praeoccupavit, 20
inde ambo periere.

Defuncto igitur Beorhtrico rege, cum illa inter **15**
[*Occidentales*] Saxones diutius fieri non posset, ultra
mare navigans, cum innumerabilibus thesauris,
Karolum illum [*magnum et*] famosissimum Francorum regem adiit. Ad quam, cum ante solarium 5
multa regi afferens dona staret, Karolus ait: 'Elige,
Eadburh, quem velis *inter* me et filium meum, qui
mecum in solario isto stat.' At illa, sine delibera-
tione stulte respondens, [*dicens*] ait: 'Si mihi electio
conceditur, filium tuum, in quantum te iunior est, 10
eligo.' *Cui* Karolus respondens et arridens, ait:
'Si me eligeres, haberes filium meum; sed quia

---

hominem omnem *B*　　execrare *Co B P Ar SN*　　Brichtricus *SN*
12 ita] sic *Flor*　　*post* ita *add.* ut *SN*　　14 eum *Ar*　　coepit
necare *Flor*　　15 adholescente *SN*　　16 *post* accusare *add.* vellet
et *SD* 1　　17 eum *om. SN*　　18 Beorthric *B*: Beorhtricus *SN*
19 aliquid *post* rex *v.* 18 habet *B*

　　**15** *Exscripp. SN SD* 1　　1 Beorthrico *B*: Beorchtrico *SN*
illa] regina *Flor*　　2 Occidentales *om. Cott.* (*teste W*) *Co*: *exhibent* (*ex SN interpolatum*) *B P Ar*: *secl. Pet*　　*post* Saxones *add.*
vel Anglos *SN*　　fieri *SN* (ferri *Ed.*): esse *Flor*　　4 magnum
atque (et) famossisimum *om. Cott.* (*teste W*) *Co B Flor SD* 1:
*exhibent* (*ex SN interpolata*) *P Ar Camd W*: *secl. Pet*　　5
quem *P Camd W SN SD* 1　　6 offerens *Flor*　　7 Eadburh *Co B Flor*: Eadburga *SN*: Eadburgh *rell.*　　et] aut *Flor*

filium meum elegisti, nec me nec illum habebis.'
Dedit tamen illi unum magnum sanctimonialium
15 monasterium ; in quo, deposito seculari habitu et
sanctimonialium indumento *as*sumpto, perpaucis
annis abbatissae fungebatur officio. *Sicut enim
irrationabiliter in propria vixisse refertur, ita multo
irrationabilius in aliena gente vivere deprehenditur.*
20 Nam a quodam *suae propriae gentis homine* constu-
prata, *demum palam deprehensa*, de monasterio, imperio Karoli regis, *de*iecta, in paupertate et miseria
leto tenus *vituperabiliter* vitam duxit ; *ita ut ad
ultimum, uno servulo comitata, sicut a multis viden-*
25 *tibus eam audivimus, cotidie mendicans, in Pavia
miserabiliter moreretur.*

16  Vixit ergo Æthelwulfus rex duobus annis postquam a Roma pervenit ; in quibus, inter alia multa
praesentis vitae bona studia, cogitans de suo ad
universitatis viam transitu, ne sui filii post patris
5 obitum indebite inter se disceptarent, hereditariam, *immo commendatoriam*, scribi imperavit epistolam : in qua et regni inter filios *suos, duos scilicet
seniores*, et propriae hereditatis inter filios et filiam
et etiam propinquos, pecuniarum, quae post se

---

8 at] ad *Co B*      9 dicens *om. SN*      11 *post* Karolus *add.*
illi *Flor*      subridens *Flor*      14 ei *Flor*      monialium *SN*
16 monialium *SN*      per paucos annos *SN*      18 rexisse *Ar*
19 inrationabilius *SN*      20 suae propriae gentis homine] laico
*Flor*      construprata *B*      21 dum demum *Co* : demum dum *B*
imperio] iussu *SN*      23 leto *Co SN* : laeto *P* : letho *rell.*   ducit
*SN*      25 quotidie *P Camd W Pet*      26 moriretur *Co Ar SN*

16 *Exscripp. totum SN, partim SD* 1 *SD* 2      1 Ethelwolfus *B* :
Adhelwulfus *SN*      rex *Cott.* (*teste W*) *Co B P Ar W Pet* : *om.*
*Camd*      2 venit *SN* : rediit *Flor*      5 disceptarent *B SD* 1 *Camd* :
discerptarent *Cott.* (*teste W*) *Co P*      6 scribi *scripsi* : scribere *omnes*

superessent, inter animam et filios et etiam nobiles 10
suos, divisionem ordinabiliter literis mandari pro-
curavit. *De qua prudenti consideratione pauca de
pluribus posteris imitanda scribere decrevimus, scilicet, quae ad necessitatem animae maxime pertinere
intelliguntur. Nam cetera, quae ad humanam dis-* 15
*pensationem pertinent, in hoc opusculo inserere necesse
non est, ne fastidium prolixitate legentibus vel etiam
audire desiderantibus procreaverit.* Pro utilitate
namque animae suae, quam a primaevo iuventutis
suae flore in omnibus procurare studuit, per omnem 20
hereditariam terram suam semper in decem manentibus unum pauperem, aut indigenam aut pere-
grinum, cibo, potu et vestimento successoribus suis,
usque ad ultimam diem iudicii, post se pascere
praecepit; ita tamen, si illa terra hominibus et 25
pecoribus habitaretur et deserta non esset. Romae
quoque omni anno *magnam pro anima sua pecuniam,*
*id est* trecentas mancussas, portari praecepit, quae
taliter ibi dividerentur: scilicet centum mancussas
in honorem Sancti Petri, specialiter ad emendum 30
oleum, quo impleantur omnia luminaria illius apo-
stolicae ecclesiae in vespera Paschae, et aequaliter
in galli cantu, et centum mancussas in honorem

---

7 *post* filios *add.* Æthelbaldum et Æthelberhtum *Flor*    duobus *Co*
9 *post* pecuniarum *add.* quoque *SN*    10 inter] propter *SN*    *post*
animam *add.* suam *SN*    11 mandare *Flor Co B P SN*    15-18
Nam . . . procreaverit *om. SN*    15 dispencionem *B*    17 pro
prolixitate *B P Ar*    19 nanque *SN*    21 x^mo *SN*    ma-
nentibus] mensis *SD* 1    23 et *om. Co*    24 ultimum *Co SN*
pasci *SD* 1    25 si] ut *SN*    28 mancossas *Co et hic et*
*vv.* 29, 33, 37 : mancusas *SN et hic et vv.* 29, 33, 37    portari
*SD* 1 : portare *rell.*    quae taliter] qualiter *SN*    29 divide-

Sancti Pauli, eadem condicione, *ad comparandum*
35 *oleum in ecclesia Sancti Pauli Apostoli ad implenda*
*luminaria in vespera Paschae et in galli cantu*,
centum quoque mancussas universali papae apo-
stolico.

**17** Defuncto autem *Æthelwulfo rege* ⟨sepultoque
apud Wintoniam⟩, Æthelbald, filius eius, contra
Dei interdictum et Christianorum dignitatem, necnon et contra omnium paganorum consuetudinem,
5 thorum patris sui ascendens[a], Iuthittam, Karoli,
Francorum regis, filiam, *cum magna ab omnibus*
*audientibus infamia*, in matrimonium duxit, effre-
nisque duobus et dimidio annis Occidentalium
Saxonum post patrem regni gubernacula rexit.

**17 b** [*Anno Dominicae Incarnationis* DCCCLVI *et nativi-*
*tatis Ælfredi octavo, hoc est anno secundo Karoli Impera-*

---

[a] Cf. Levit. xviii. 8; Deut. xxii. 30; xxvii. 20; 1 Cor. v. 1.

---

retur *Co P SN*     30 honore *Co B Flor SN*     32 aecclesiae *Co*
Pasce *Co*     33 honore *Co B Flor SN*     34 condicione] de
causa *Flor*     36 Pasce *Co*
    **17** *Exscripp. SD* 1 *SD* 2         1 Defuncto] Anno DCCCLVII
Adheluulfus, saepe memoratus rex Occidentalium Saxonum, viam
universitatis adiit, ⟨et⟩ quievit in pace, sepultusque est apud Stęningam.
Regnavit Adhelbaldus filius eius post illum duos annos et dimidium,
qui et ipse antea cum patre regnavit annis duobus et dimidio, sed
post patrem contra Deum et Christianorum dignitatem, necnon, &c.
*SN*     *post* rege *add.* illo idibus Ianuarii *Flor*     sepultoque apud
Wintoniam *om. Cott. (teste W) Co SD* 1 : sepultoque apud Stem-
rugam ⟨*leg.* Steningam⟩ *exhibent* (*ex SN interpolata*) *B P Ar*
*Camd*     5 Iudithtam *SN*     7–9 effrenis . . . rexit *om. SN*
    **17 b** *Interpolatum ex SN: om. Cott.* (*teste W*) *Co SD* 1 *SD* 2
*Quamquam* ' *totam hanc clausulam deesse MS. Cott.*' *dicit W, quae-*
*dam tamen ex ea adnotat* (*vv.* 2, 4): *hinc colligas eam interpolatam*
*fuisse* ' *manu recentiori* ' (*cf. cc.* 50 *b c d*, 54 *b*)     1 Dominicae
Incarnationis *om. SN* : Domini *P*     et *om. B* : et nativitatis Ælfredi
octavo *om. SN* : nativitatis autem *B*     2 *post* Ælfredi *add.* regis

*toris tertii, anno vero regni Æthelwulfi, Occidentalium*
*Saxonum regis, decimo octavo, Hunberchtus, Orientalium*
*Anglorum antistes, unxit oleo consecravitque in regem Ead-* 5
*mundum gloriosissimum, cum gaudio magno et honore*
*maximo, in villa regia, quae dicitur Burua, in qua tunc*
*temporis regalis sedes erat, anno aetatis suae decimo quinto,*
*sexta feria, luna vicesima quarta, die natalis Domini.*]

   *Anno Dominicae Incarnationis* DCCCLX, *nati-* 18
*vitatis autem Ælfredi regis duodecimo,* Æthelbald,
[*Occidentalium Saxonum*] ⟨rex, defunctus est⟩, et
in Scireburnan sepultus, et Æthelberht, frater suus,
Cantiam et Suthrigam, Suth-Seaxam quoque suo 5
dominio, ut iustum erat, subiunxit. In cuius diebus
magnus paganorum exercitus, de mari adveniens,
Wintoniam civitatem hostiliter invadens depopu-
latus est. Cui, cum ad naves cum ingenti praeda
reverterentur, Osric, Hamtunensium comes, cum 10
suis, et Æthelwulf comes, cum Bearrocensibus, viriliter obviaverunt, consertoque proelio *oppido* pagani
passim trucidantur, et, cum diutius resistere non

---

*B*    octavo] decimo *Cott.* (*teste W*) *B P Ar Camd*    3 Adheluulfus
*SN*    4 Hunberchtus *SN*: Nunberctus *Cott.* (*teste W*) *B P Camd*:
Nunberchus *Ar*    7 Burna *SN*: Burya *B*    in qua] quia *SN*
  18 *Exscripp. SN SD* 1 *SD* 2    1 Dominicae Incarnationis
*om. SN*    nativitatis . . . duodecimo *om. SN*    2 Aelfridi *Co*
regis] clitonis *SD* 1    Adhelbaldus *SN*    3 Occidentalium
Saxonum rex *om. Cott.* (*teste W*) *Co B SD* 1 *SD* 2 : *exhibent* (*ex
SN interpolata*) *P Ar Camd: secl. Pet*    defunctus est *om. Cott.*
*teste W*)    4 Scireburnam *B* : Scireburna *SN*: Scireburmam *in*
Scireburnia *correctum Co*: Schireburnam *Ar*    Ethelberht *B* :
Adhelbrictus *SN*    5 Cantiam *SN Flor SD* 1 : Cantiam *ex*
Cantium *correctum Co* : Cantium *B P Ar Edd*    Suthrigiam *SN*:
Suthregiam *Flor SD* 2    Seaxum *B SN*    6 *post* subiunxit *add.*
regnavitque annis quinque *SN*    10 Osricus *SN*    Hamptu-
nensium *Ar*    11 Æthelwulfe *B*: Adheluulfus *SN*    12 *post*
proelio *add.* longe ab omni *SN*    13 diu *SN*

C

possent, muliebriter fugam arripiunt, et Christiani
15 loco funeris dominati sunt.

19  Æthelberht itaque, quinque annis regno pacifice et amabiliter atque honorabiliter gubernato.
cum magno suorum dolore, universitatis viam adiit,
et in Scireburnan iuxta fratrem suum honorabiliter
5 sepultus requiescit.

20  *Anno Dominicae Incarnationis* DCCCLXIV pagani
hiemaverunt in insula Tanet, et firmum foedus
cum Cantuariis pepigerunt.  Quibus Cantuarii
pecuniam pro foedere serva*to* reddere promi-
5 serunt.  Interea tamen, vulpino more pagani, noctu
clam castris erumpentes, foedere disrupto et pro-
missionem pecuniae spernentes (sciebant enim
maiorem pecuniam se furtiva praeda quam pace
adepturos), totam orientalem Cantiae plagam de-
10 populati sunt.

21  *Anno Dominicae Incarnationis* DCCCLXVI, *na-*
*tivitatis autem Ælfredi regis decimo octavo,*
Æthelred, Æthelberhti regis frater, Occidentalium

---

19 *Exscripp.* SN (*ante* Æthelred *an.* 866 *cap.* 21 *v.* 3), *SD* 1
*SD* 2        1 Adhelberchtus, rex Occidentalium Saxonum, frater
Adhelbaldi *SN*        2 amicabiliter *SN*        3 viam *om. Co*
4 Scireburna *SN*: Scireburnam *B*: Schireburnam *Ar*        honorifice
*Flor*

20 *Exscripp. SN SD* 1 *SD* 2        1 *post* pagani *add.* Nordmanni
sive Dani *SN*        2 Tenet *B*: Tened *SD* 1: Thenet *SD* 2
4 servando *Flor SD* 2        6 dirupto *Flor SD* 1 *SD* 2        promissione *Co*        8 maiorem pecuniam se *om. B*        9 Cantiae
*Cott.* (*teste W*) *Co B SN Flor SD* 1 *SD* 2: Cantii *P rell.*

21 *Exscripp. inde ab initio usque ad* factus est *v.* 9 *SN SD* 1
*SD* 2        1 Anno . . . octavo] Eodem vero anno *SN*
3 Æthelred] Alfred *B*: Adherędus *SN*: Æthelfred *Ar*        Ethel-
berhti *Co*: Æthelberti *Camd* (*errore, ut videtur, operarum*), *quod*

Saxonum regni gubernacula suscepit. *Et* eodem
anno magna paganorum classis de Danubia 5
Britanniam advenit, *et* in regno Orientalium
Saxonum, quod Saxonice 'East-Engle' dicitur,
hiemavit, ibique ille exercitus maxima ex parte
equester factus est. *Sed, ut more navigantium
loquar, ne diutius navim undis et velamentis con-* 10
*cedentes, et a terra longius enavigantes longum cir-*
*cumferamur inter tantas bellorum clades et annorum*
*enumerationes, ad id, quod nos maxime ad hoc opus*
*incitavit, nobis redeundum esse censeo, scilicet ali-*
*quantulum, quantum meae cognitioni innotuit*, de 15
infantilibus et puerilibus *domini mei venerabilis*
*Ælfredi, Angulsaxonum regis*, moribus hoc in loco
breviter inserendum esse existimo.

*Nam, cum* communi et ingenti patris sui et **22**
matris amore supra omnes fratres suos, immo ab
omnibus, nimium diligeretur, et in regio semper
curto inseparabiliter nutriretur, accrescente infantili
et puerili aetate, forma ceteris *suis* fratribus de- 5
centior videbatur, vultuque et verbis atque moribus
gratiosior. *Cui ab incunabulis ante omnia et cum*

---

*receperunt W Pet* : frater ipsius Adhelberchti regis *SN*      4 *post*
Saxonum *add. (ex c.* 19) quinque annos *P Ar Camd, quae defuisse*
*in Cott. adnotavit W*      5 magnus *B*      de Danubia *om. SN* :
Danubio *Camd W Pet*      6 Angliam *SN*      7 Anglorum *Flor*
*SN SD* 1 *SD* 2      quod . . . dicitur *om. SN*      9–18 Sed . . .
existimo *om. SN*      15 de infantilibus] *quae inde ab his verbis*
*usque ad finem cap.* 24 *leguntur, ea post* suscepit *cap.* 42 *v.* 5 *ex-*
*hibet Flor*      18 existimamus *Flor*
   **22** *Exscripp. partim SD* 1 *SD* 2      1 *post* communi *add.*
itaque *Flor*      3 diligebatur *Flor*      4 curro *Co, alterum* r
*in erasura* : *om. SD* 1 *SD* 2      nutriebatur *Flor*      5 ceteris]
cunctis *Flor*      6 atque] et *Co* : ac *Ar*

C 2

*omnibus praesentis vitae studiis, sapientiae deside-*
*rium cum nobilitate generis, nobilis mentis ingenium*
10 *supplevit*; sed, proh dolor! *indigna* suorum parentum et nutritorum incuria usque ad duodecimum
aetatis annum, *aut eo amplius*, illiteratus permansit.
*Sed* Saxonica poemata die noctuque solers auditor,
relatu aliorum saepissime audiens, docibilis memo-
15 riter retinebat. In omni venatoria arte *industrius*
*venator incessabiliter laborat non in vanum; nam*
incomparabilis omnibus peritia et felicitate *in illa*
*arte*, sicut et in ceteris omnibus Dei donis, fuit, *sicut*
*et nos saepissime vidimus.*

**23** Cum ergo quodam die mater sua sibi et fratribus suis quendam Saxonicum poematicae artis
librum, quem in manu habebat, ostenderet, ait:
'Quisquis vestrum discere citius istum codicem
5 possit, dabo illi illum.' Qua voce, immo divina
inspiratione, instinctus ⟨Ælfredus⟩, et pulchritudine
principalis litterae illius libri illectus, ita matri respondens, *et fratres suos aetate, quamvis non gratia,*
*seniores anticipans,* inquit: 'Verene dabis istum
10 librum uni ex nobis, scilicet illi, qui citissime intelligere et recitare *eum* ante te possit?' Ad haec
illa, arridens *et gaudens atque affirmans*: 'Dabo,'
infit, 'illi.' Tunc ille statim tollens librum de
manu sua, magistrum adiit et legit. Quo lecto,
15 matri retulit et recitavit.

---

3 sapiens *B*      10 parentum suorum *B*      13 *post* Saxonica
*add.* tamen *Flor*      17 pueritia *B*

**23** *Exscripserunt SD* 1 *SD* 2      3, haberet *B*      5 poterit *Flor*
6 instructus *B*      Ælfredus *ex Flor addidi*      13 infit *lineola*
*subducta deletum, supra-scripto* inquit *Co* : inquit *B*      14 *post*

Post haec cursum diurnum, *id est celebrationes* **24**
*horarum, ac deinde* psalmos quosdam et orationes
multas ⟨didicit⟩; quos in uno libro congregatos in
sinu suo die noctuque, *sicut ipsi vidimus, secum
inseparabiliter*, orationis gratia, inter omnia prae- 5
sentis vitae curricula ubique circumducebat. Sed,
proh dolor! quod maxime desiderabat, liberalem
scilicet artem, desiderio suo non suppetebat, eo
quod, *ut loquebatur*, illo tempore lectores boni in
toto regno Occidentalium Saxonum non erant.     10

*Quod maximum inter omnia praesentis vitae* **25**
*suae impedimenta et dispendia crebris querelis et
intimis cordis sui suspiriis fieri affirmabat: id est,
eo quod illo tempore, quando aetatem et licentiam
atque suppetentiam discendi habebat, magistros non* 5
*habuerat; quando vero et aetate erat provectior et
incessabilius die noctuque, immo omnibus istius insulae medicis incognitis infirmitatibus, internisque
atque externis regiae potestatis sollicitudinibus, necnon et paganorum terra marique infestationibus* 10
*occupatus, immo etiam perturbatus, magistros et
scriptores aliquantula ex parte habebat, legere ut non
poterat. Sed tamen inter praesentis vitae impedi-*

---

magistrum *add.* statim *B*     *post* legit *add.* praeceptore ostendente
*SD* 1 *SD* 2
  **24** *Exscripserunt partim SD* 1 *SD* 2     **3** didicit *Flor*: *om.*
*rell.*   quae *Flor*   congregatus *Co*: congregata *Flor*   **5** in-
seperabiliter *B*     **7** literalem *B*     **8** scilicet *om. B*     suo
*om. B*     **9** lectores boni] grammatici *Flor*     **10** *post* erant
*add. ex cap.* 74, vv. 41–64 cum autem in primo . . . fatigavit *Flor*
  **25** **2** suae *om. B*     et *om. Co B*     **7** incessabilibus *B P Ar*
**8** infirmitatibus *B*: infirmantibus *Co Ar Edd.*: 'forte infirmitatibus' *W*     internisque atque] internisque at *Co*: iterumque
ac *B*     **11** occipatus *Co*     perturbatos *Co Edd.*     **12** ut] et *Co B*

*menta ab infantia usque ad praesentem diem* [*et, ut*
15 *credo, usque ad obitum vitae suae*] *in eodem insatura-*
*bili desiderio, sicut nec ante destituit, ita nec etiam*
*adhuc inhiare desinit.*

26    *Anno Dominicae Incarnationis* DCCCLXVII, *nati-*
*vitatis Ælfredi praefati regis decimo nono*, praedictus paganorum exercitus de Orientalibus Anglis
ad Eboracum civitatem migravit, quae in aquilonali
5 ripa Humbrensis fluminis sita est.

27    Eo tempore maxima inter Northanhymbros discordia diabolico instinctu orta fuerat, sicut semper
populo, qui odium incurrerit *Dei*, evenire solet.
Nam Northanhymbri eo tempore, ut diximus,
5 legitimum regem suum, Osbyrht nomine, regno ex-
pulerant, et tyrannum quendam, Ælla nomine, non
de regali prosapia progenitum, super regni apicem
constituerant. Sed, advenientibus paganis, consilio
divino et optimatum adminiculo, pro communi
10 utilitate, discordia illa aliquantulum sedata, Osbyrht
et Ælla, adunatis viribus congregatoque exercitu,
Eboracum oppidum adeunt. Quibus advenientibus,

---

14–15 et . . . suae *seclusi*    16 destitit *B*    17 adhuc] nec *Co*
    26 *Exscripp.* *SN SD* 1 *SD* 2    2 Ælfredi] ' *MS. Cott. habuit*
Karoli, *sed deletur*' *W*    4 Eboracam *SN*    aquilonali *Co*
*Flor SN SD* 1 *SD* 2 : aquilonari *B Ar Edd.*    5 Humbrensis
*Co B Ar* ' *Sic MS. Cott.*, Humbsensis *Edd. P et Camd*' *W* (*mani-*
*festo errore operarum ex similitudine litterarum* ſ *et* p *orto*) :
Humbrae *Flor*
    27 *Exscripp.* *SN SD* ſ *SD* 2    1 Northamhymbros *B* :
Nordanhymbros *SN*    2 orta *om. B*    4 Northamhymbri *B* :
Nordanhymbri *SN*    4 eo *om. B Edd. praeter Pet*    5 ligi-
timum *Co*    Osbyrth *Co* : Osbirht *B* : Osbriht *Flor* : Osbrichtum
*SN*    6 Ella *Co*    7 prosapie *Co*    10 illi *B*    Osbriht
*Flor* : Osbrichtum *SN*    11 Ella *B*    congregato *SN*

pagani confestim fugam arripiunt, et intra urbis
moenia se defendere procurant. Quorum fugam et
pavorem Christiani cernentes, etiam intra urbis 15
moenia eos persequi et murum frangere instituunt;
quod et fecerunt. Non enim tunc adhuc illa civitas
firmos et stabilitos muros illis temporibus habebat.
Cumque Christiani murum, ut proposuerant, fregis-
sent, et eorum magna pars in civitatem simul cum 20
paganis intrasset, pagani, dolore et necessitate
compulsi, super eos atrociter irrumpunt, caedunt,
fugant, prosternunt intus et extra. Illic maxima ex
parte omnes Northanhymbrensium coetus, occisis
duobus regibus, deleti occubuerunt. Reliqui 25
vero, qui evaserunt, pacem cum paganis pepigerunt.

Eodem anno Ealhstan, episcopus Scireburnensis **28**
*ecclesiae, viam universitatis adiens, postquam episco-*
*patum per quinquaginta annos honorabiliter rexerat,*
*in pace in* Scireburnan sepultus est.

*Anno Dominicae Incarnationis* DCCCLXVIII, *nati-* **29**
*vitatis Ælfredi regis vigesimo, idem ipse praefatus*

---

16 menia *SN*      21 intrassent *Flor*      22 erumpunt *B*      23
prosternan *B*      24 Northanhimbrensium *Ar* : Nordanhym-
brensium *SN*: Northanhymbrenses *B*      coetus *ex Flor corr. W* :
*om. B* : coeti *Co Flor* (*ed. Thorpe*) : capti *Cott* (*teste W*) *P Ar
Camd SN*: caesi *SD* 2      occisis duobus regibus *om. B*      25
*post* regibus *exhibent* (*ex SN interpolata*) cum multis nobilibus *P
Ar Camd*: *om. Cott.* (*teste W*) *Co B*      delete *Co* : ibi *SN*
   **28** *Exscripp. SN SD* 1 *SD* 2      1 Ealchstanus *SN*      Scy-
reburnensis *SN*      2-4 ecclesiae . . . sepultus est] quinquagesimo
sui episcopatus anno obiit, et Scireburne sepelitur *Flor*      4 Scyre-
burnan *SN*
   **29** *Exscripp. SN SD* 1 *SD* 2      1 *post* nativitatis *add.* autem
*B*      2 *post* vigesimo *exhibent* (*ex SN interpolata*) fames valida

*ac* venerabilis Ælfred rex, secundarii tamen tunc
ordine fretus, uxorem de Mercia, nobilem scilicet
5 genere, filiam Æthelredi, Gainorum comitis, qui
cognominabatur Mucill, subarravit et duxit. Cuius
feminae mater Eadburh nominabatur, de regali
genere Merciorum regis; *quam nos ipsi propriis*
*oculorum nostrorum obtutibus non paucis ante obitum*
10 *suum annis frequenter vidimus,* venerabilis scilicet
femina, ⟨quae⟩ per multos annos post obitum viri
sui castissima vidua leto tenus permansit.

30　　Eodem anno praedictus paganorum exercitus
Northanhymbros relinquens, in Merciam venit, et
Snotengaham adiit (quod Britannice ‘Tigguoco-
bauc’ interpretatur, Latine autem ‘speluncarum
5 domus’), et in eodem loco eodem anno hiemaverunt.
Quibus illic advenientibus, confestim Burhred,

---

erat *B P Ar*: *om. Cott.* (*teste W*) *Co*　　idem ipse *Cott.* (*teste W*)
*Co*: *om. B P Ar Camd W Pet*　　*post* ipse *praebent* (*ex SN inter-*
*polatum*) Tunc *P B Ar Camd W Pet*　　praefatus] *anno eodem SN*
3 ac *om. B SN*　Ælfredus *SN*　5 Adhelredi *SN*　Grainorum
*B*: Gainorem *SN*　quae *B*　6 Mucil *Flor Camd*: *in marg.*
*adnotant P Ar* eo quod erat corpore magnus (*ex SD* 1 Mucel eo
quod erat corpore magnus et prudentia grandaevus), *quae in textum*
*Camd irrepserunt*　subarravit *Cott.* (*teste W*) *Co Flor SN*: expetivit *B P Ar Camd W Pet*　cuius] *ab inde usque ad finem*
*capitis om. SN*　7 Eadburgh *B Ar*　9 optutibus *Co*:
intutibus *B*　11 quae *scripsi*: et *omnes*　viri] patris *Flor*
12 leto *scripsi*: loeto *Co*: letho *B P Ar Edd.*

30 *Exscripserunt SN SD* 1 *SD* 2　　1 *post* eodem *add.* vero
*SN*　　2 Northamhymbros *B*: Northanhimbros *Ar*: Nordanhymbros *SN*　in Merciam venit et *om. B*　3 Snotengaham
*Co B P Ar SN*: Scnotengaham *Camd* (*errore operarum*), *quod*
*recc. W Pet*: Snotingaham *Flor*　adiit] venit *B*　quod] *ab inde*
*usque ad* domus *om. SN*　Tiguo- *B SD* 1　5 et in eodem loco
eodem anno hiemaverunt] ibidemque hiemavit *SN*　eodem loco]
illo loco *Flor*　6 Quibus . . . confestim *om. SN*　Burrhred

Merciorum rex, et omnes eiusdem gentis optimates
nuncios ad Æthered, Occidentalium Saxonum
regem, et Ælfred, fratrem, dirigunt, suppliciter ob-
secrantes, ut illi illis auxiliarentur, quo possent 10
contra praefatum pugnare exercitum. Quod et
facile impetraverunt. Nam illi fratres, non segnius
promissione, congregato ex omni parte ⟨regni⟩
sui immenso exercitu, Merciam adeunt, et usque
ad Snotengaham, bellum unanimiter quaerentes, 15
perveniunt. Cumque pagani, tuitione arcis muniti,
bellum dare negarent et Christianis frangere murum
non suppeter̃et, pace inter Mercios et paganos
facta, duo illi fratres Æthered et Ælfred cum suis
cohortibus domum reversi sunt. 20

Anno *Dominicae Incarnationis* DCCCLXIX, *nativi-* 31
*tatis autem Ælfredi regis vigesimo primo*, praefatus
paganorum exercitus iterum ad Northanhymbros
equitans Eboracum civitatem adiit, et ibi anno
integro mansit. 5

Anno *Dominicae Incarnationis* DCCCLXX, *nativi-* 32

---

*B* : Burchredus *SN*    8 Æthelred *B* : Æthelredum *B*    9 *post*
et *add.* ad *SN*    Ælfrẹdum *SN*    *post* fratrem *add.* eius confestim *SN*    10 illi illis] sibi *Flor*    possunt *W*    12 perpetraverunt *Co*    *inde a* Nam *usque ad* perveniunt (v. 16) *om. SN*
13 regni *add. W*    15 Scnotengaham *Camd W Pet* : Snotingaham *Flor*    18 suppeteret *scripsi* : suppetebat *omnes*    19 *post*
facta *add.* est *SN, omissis quae inde usque ad finem capitis sequuntur*
Æthelred *B*    et Ælfred *supplevit* (*ex Flor*) *W*

31 *Exscripp. totum SD* 1 *SD* 2, *partim SN*    2 *post* primo
*praebent* (*ex SN⁻interpolata*) *B P Ar Camd W* fames magna
et mortalitas hominum et pestis animalium et, *quae om. Cott.*
(*teste W*) *Co Flor* : *seclusit Pet*    3 Northamhymbros *B* :
Northanhimbros *Ar* : Nordanhimbros *SN*    4 Eboracam *Co*
*SN SD* 2

32 *Exscripp. SN SD* 1 *SD* 2    2 secundo *correxi* : primo

*tatis autem Ælfredi regis vigesimo secundo*, supra
memoratus paganorum exercitus per Merciam in
Orientales Anglos transivit, et ibi in loco, qui
5 dicitur Theodford, hiemavit.

33   *Eodem anno Eadmund, Orientalium Anglorum
rex, contra ipsum exercitum atrociter pugnavit. Sed,
proh dolor! paganis nimium gloriantibus, ipso cum
magna suorum parte ibidem occiso, inimici loco
5 funeris dominati sunt, et totam illam regionem suo
dominio subdiderunt.*

34   Eodem anno Ceolnoth, archiepiscopus Doroberniae, *viam universitatis adiens*, in eadem civitate
in pace sepultus est.

35   Anno *Dominicae Incarnationis* DCCCLXXI, *nativitatis autem Ælfredi regis vigesimo tertio*, exosae
memoriae paganorum exercitus Orientales Anglos

---

*Cott.* (*teste W*) *Co B P Ar Edd. SD* 1      3 *pro* memoratus paganorum exercitus *substituit* (*ex cap. subseq.*) Sed proh dolor! pagani
nimium gloriantes *SN*      Mercios *B*      *post* Merciam *add.* item *SN*
4 Orientalem Angliam *B*      transierunt *SN*      5 Theodforda
*SN*      hiemaverunt *SN*
    **33** *Exscripsit primum locum SD* 1   *Substituit Flor* Eodem
anno sanctissimus et gloriosissimus Orientalium Anglorum rex
Eadmundus, ut in sua legitur Passione, ab Inguaro rege paganissimo,
Indictione II, xii. kal. Decembris, die Dominico, martyrizatus est,
*quae exscripsit SD* 2.   *Haec temporis computatio quadrat in an.*
869, *quo dies Dominica incidit in a. d.* 12 *Kal. Dec.*      2 pugnavit
atrociter *B*      3 pagani nimium gloriantes per Merciam (*ex cap.*
32 *usque ad finem*) *SN*      ipse *Cott.* (*teste W*) *B P Ar Camd:*
ipso *Co rell.*      4 ibidem *om. B*      occisa *Cott.* (*teste W*) *Ar*
    **34** *Exscripp. SN SD* 1 *SD* 2      1 Eodem anno] quo etiam
anno *Flor*      *post* eodem *add.* quoque *SN*      *post* anno *add.*
domnus *SN*      Ceolnothus *SN*      *post* Doroberniae *add.* antistes
*Co B P Ar Edd.*: antistes civitatis *SD* 1      2 viam universitatis
adiens] defunctus *Flor SD* 2      adeuns *B*
    **35** *Exscripp. SN SD* 1 *SD* 2      2 tertio *correxit W*: secundo

deserens et regnum Occidentalium Saxonum adiens,
venit ad villam regiam, quae dicitur Rædigam, in 5
meridiana Tamesis fluminis ripa sitam, in illa paga,
quae dicitur Bearrocscire ; tertioque adventus sui
*ibidem* die ⟨duo⟩ comites eorum cum magna illius
parte in praedam equitaverunt, aliis vallum inter
duo flumina Tamesen et Cynetan a dextrali parte 10
eiusdem regiae villae facientibus. Quibus Æthelwulf, Bearroccensis pagae comes, cum suis *sodalibus*
in loco, qui dicitur Englafeld ⟨Anglice, Latine
Anglorum Campus⟩, obviavit, et animose ex utraque
parte *ibidem* pugnatum est. Cumque ibi diu utrique 15
resisterent, altero paganorum comite occiso, et
maxima exercitus parte deleta, ceterisque fuga
elapsis, Christiani victoriam accipientes, loco funeris
dominati sunt.

His ibi ita gestis, post quatuor dies Æthered, 36
rex et Ælfred, frater eius, adunatis viribus congregatoque exercitu, Rædigum adierunt. Cumque

---

*Cott. (teste W ) Co B P Ar Camd SD* 1     5 Redigan *B* : Redigam
*Ar* : Readingum *Flor* : Rędinga *SN* : et ( = æt '*apud*') Redingum
*SD* 1     6 Thamesis *B* : Tamensis *SN*     *post* Tamesis *add.*
flumensis *Cott. (teste W )* Co B Ar P Camd          plaga *SD* 1
7 Bearrocschire *Ar* : Bearrocscyre *SN*     8 duo *ex Flor addidi*
9 aequitaverunt *Co*     10 Tamesen *Co P Ar Flor* : Tam̄sē *SN* :
Tamesem *SD* 2 : Thamesin *B* : Tamesin *Camd W Pet*     Cyne-
tam *W Pet* : Cinetam *B* : Kynetam *SN*     dextra *Flor SD* 2
11 villae regiae *B*     Æthelwolfe *B* : Adheluulfus *SN*     12
Berrocensis *Co* : Beorroccensis *SN*     13 Englofeld *Camd*
Anglice . . . campus *ex Flor addidi*     14 et] ubi *Flor*     15
ibidem *om. Flor*

36 *Exscripp. SN SD* 1 *SD* 2     1 Æthelred *Co B* : Adherędus *SN*     2 *post* rex *add.* (*ex SN*) Occidentalium Saxonum *P*
*Ar Camd, quae om. Cott. (teste W )* Co B rell.     Aelfrędus *SN*
adunatis *om. B*     3 Rædigum *Co* : Redigum *B SD* 1 : Redigam

usque ad portam arcis pervenissent, caedendo et
5 prosternendo quoscunque de paganis extra arcem
invenissent, pagani non segnius certabant, lupino
more, totis portis erumpentes, totis viribus bellum
perquirunt. Ibique diu et atrociter ex utraque
parte dimicatum est, sed, proh dolor! Christianis
10 demum terga vertentibus, pagani, victoriam accipientes, loco funeris dominati sunt, ibique Æthelwulfus praefatus comes inter ceteros occubuit.

37    Quo dolore et verecundia Christiani commoti.
iterum post quatuor dies contra praefatum exercitum in loco, qui dicitur Æscesdun, quod Latine
'mons fraxini' interpretatur, totis viribus et plena
5 voluntate ad proelium prodeunt. Sed pagani, in
duas se turmas dividentes, aequali ⟨*lance*⟩ testudines
parant—habebant enim tunc duos reges et multos
comites—concedentes mediam partem exercitus
duobus regibus et alteram omnibus comitibus.
10 Quod Christiani cernentes, et etiam ipsi exercitum
in duas turmas *oppido* dividentes, testudines non
segnius construunt. Sed Ælfred citius et promptius
cum suis, *sicut ab his, qui viderunt, veredicis*
*referentibus audivimus*, ad locum proelii advenit :

*Ar* : Readingum *Flor SN* : Rædigam *P rell. Edd.*    4 portum *B*
6 certabant lupino] cretabolino (*ex* certabant lupino *conflatum*) *SN*
7 totis portis erumpentes *om. S*    8 *an* perquirentes ?    9 *post*
sed *exhibent* (*ex SN interpolatum*) heu *P Ar Camd W* : *seclus.*
*Pet* : *om. Cott.* (*teste W*) *Co B*    11 Adheluulfus *SN*
    37 *Exscripp. SN SD* 1 *SD* 2    3 Ascisduñ *B* : Escendun
*SD* 2    4 viribus *om. SN*    5 bellum *B*    6 lance *om. Co* :
lancea *B*    testudinis *Co B* : testudine bellum *Flor*    8 exercitus
*om. B*    10 etiam et *SN*    11 oppido *Cott.* (*teste W*) *Co* :
*om. Flor* : similiter *SN B P Ar Edd.*    testudinem haud *B*
12 Aelfrędus *SN*    14 referentibus *om. B*    venit *Flor*

nimirum erat enim adhuc frater suus Æthered rex 15
in tentorio in oratione positus, audiens missam, et
nimium affirmans se inde *vivum* non discessurum
antequam sacerdos missam finiret, et divinum pro
humano nolle deserere servitium; et ita fecit.
Quae regis Christiani fides multum apud Do- 20
minum valuit, sicut in sequentibus apertius declara-
bitur.

Decreverant ergo Christiani, ut Æthered rex 38
cum suis copiis contra duos paganos reges sumeret
proelium, Ælfred vero, suus frater, cum suis cohortibus contra omnes paganorum duces belli sortem
† sumere debere sciret. Quibus ita firmiter ab 5
utraque parte dispositis, cum rex in oratione diutius
moraretur et pagani parati ad locum certaminis
citius advenissent, Ælfred, tunc secundarius, cum
diutius hostiles acies ferre non posset, nisi aut bello
retrorsum recederet, aut contra hostiles copias ante 10
fratris adventum in bellum prorumperet, demum
viriliter aprino more Christianas copias contra
hostiles exercitus, ut ante proposuerat, *tamen*
quamvis rex adhuc non venerat, dirigens, divino
fretus consilio et adiutorio fultus, testudine ordi- 15

---

15 adhuc] tunc *Flor SD* 2        suus frater *SN*        Æthelred *Co B* :
Ætherędus *SN*        17 vivum] de vita *Cott.* (*teste W* ) *Co*        de-
cessurum *B*        20 Deum *Co SN*        21 aptius *Flor*

    38 *Exscripp. totum SN SD* 2, *partim SD* 1        1 Decreverunt
*Flor*        Æthelred *Co B* : Adherędus *SN*        rex] ' *sic MS Cott.*
Sex *edd. P et C*[*amd*]' *W* (*errore operarum, cf. c.* 26, *v.* 5 *adnot.*)
3 Ælfrædus *SN*        suus] sus *Co*        *post* frater *add.* tres *Cott.*
(*teste W* ) *Co* (*an ex* frater *ortum* ?)        8 Aelfrędus *SN*
10 cederet *B Flor SD* 2        11–13 demum . . . proposuerat *om. SN*
13 exercitus] turmas *B*        proposuerant *Co B Flor SD* 2 *Pet*
14 *post* venerat *add.* copias *SN*        15 consilio] auxilio *SN*

nabiliter condensata, confestim contra hostes
vexilla movet. ⟨Tandem rex Æthered, finitis
quibus occupatus erat orationibus, advenit, et, in-
vocato magni mundi principe, mox se certamini
20 dedit.⟩
39 Sed hoc in loco nescientibus intimandum est,
quod ille locus certaminis belligerantibus inaequalis
erat ; nam p⁓gani editiorem locum praeoccu-
paverant, Christiani ab inferiori loco aciem diri-
5 gebant. Erat quoque in eodem loco unica spinosa
arbor, brevis admodum, *quam nos ipsi nostris propriis oculis vidimus,* circa quam *ergo* hostiles inter
se acies, cum ingenti omnium clamore, illi perperam
agentes, isti pro vita et dilectis atque patria pugna-
10 turi, hostiliter conveniunt. Cumque aliquandiu
animose et nimium atrociter hinc inde utrique
pugnarent, pagani divino iudicio Christianorum
impetum diutius non ferentes, maxima suarum
*copiarum* parte occisa, opprobriosam fugam cepere ;
15 quo in loco alter de duobus paganorum regibus et
quinque comites occisi occubuerunt, et multa millia
paganae partis in eodem loco, et insuper per totam
campestrem Æscesdun latitudinem ubique dispersa,
*longe lateque* occisa corruerunt. Cecidit ergo
20 Bægscecg rex et Sidroc ille senex comes et Sidroc

17-20 Tandem . . . dedit *ex Flor addidi*

39 *Exscripp. totum SN SD* 2, *partim SD* 1          1 in *om. SN*
3 ẹditiorem *SN*          praeoccupaverunt *Flor*          5 una *Flor*
13 suorum *B Flor*          14 copiarum *om. B*          15 quod *Co*
17 paganae partis] illorum *Flor* : paganae gentis *SN*          18
Æscesdun *Flor* : Etscesdun *SD* 1 : Æscendun *Co Edd.* : Æscends-
down *B* : Ascendum *Ar* : *om. SN*          *post* dispersa *add.* et *Flor*
19 occisi *SN*          corruerunt] cubuerunt *B*          *post* ergo *add.* illic *SN*

iunior comes, et Osbern comes, et Fræna comes,
et Hareld comes, et totus paganorum exercitus in
fugam usque ad noctem et etiam usque ad diem
sequentem, quousque ad arcem qui evaserant pervenerunt, versus est, *quos Christiani usque ad noctem* 25
*persecuti sunt* [*et*] *ubique prosternentes.*

† *Quibus cum talia praesentis vitae dispendia alieni-* 40
*genis perperam quaerentibus non sufficerent.* His
ibi gestis, iterum post quatuordecim dies Æthered
rex una cum fratre suo Ælfred, adunatis viribus
contra paganos pugnaturi, Basengas adierunt. 5
Quibus *hinc inde* hostiliter convenientibus, et diu
resistentibus, pagani victoriam accipientes, *loco*
*funeris dominati sunt. Quo proelio peracto, de*
*ultramarinis partibus alius paganorum exercitus*
*societati se adiunxit.* 10

*Et* eodem anno post Pascha Æthered rex *prae-* 41
*fatus,* regno quinque annis per multas tribulationes

---

*Flor SD* 2      20 Bægscecg *Co* : Beagstecg *B* : Beagscecg *Ar* :
Bagsecg *Flor* : Beagsecg *SN* : Bægsceg *Edd.*      21 Obsbern *Camd*
(*errore operarum, ut videtur*), *quod recc. W Pet* : Osbearnus *SN*
Frena *B Ar* : Freano *SN*      22 Harald *Flor* : Haroldus *SN*      23
*post* fugam *exhibet* (*ex v.* 25) versus est *SN*      *quae inter* noctem *et*
persecuti *v.* 26 *intercedunt, ea om.* B Ar, *quorum librariorum
oculi a* noctem *v.* 23 *ad* noctem *v.* 25 *aberraverunt*      26 persecuti *SN B* : persequuti *Co Edd.*
   40 *Exscripp. totum SN, partim SD* 1 SD 2      1 Quibus ...
sufficerent *Cott.* (*teste W*) *Co* : om. B P Ar *Camd SN* : *e textu
reiecc. W Pet*      2 *post* his *add.* ita *B*      3 *post* ibi *add.*
ita *SN*      Æthelred *Co B* : Adheredus *SN*      4 Aelfrędo *SN*
5 pugnaturus *Flor SD* 2      adiit *Flor SD* 2      6 *post* hinc *add.*
vel *SN*      7 resistentibus] simul certantibus *Flor*      victoriam
accipientes] victoria potiuntur *Flor SD* 2      *post* accipientes *add.*
et *SN*      8 peracta *Co*      9 partibus alius *om. Co*
   41 *Exscripp. SN SD* 2      1 Æthelred *Co* : Adhereadus *SN*

strenue atque honorabiliter cum bona fama gubernato, viam universitatis adiens, in Winburnan
5 *monasterio* sepultus, adventum Domini et primam
cum iustis resurrectionem expectat [a].

42 *Eodem anno* Ælfred supra memoratus, qui usque
ad id temporis, viventibus fratribus suis, secundarius
fuerat, totius regni gubernacula, divino concedente
nutu, cum summa omnium illius regni accolarum
5 voluntate, confestim fratre defuncto suscepit. *Quod*
*etiam vivente praedicto fratre suo, si dignaretur*
*accipere, facillime cum consensu omnium potuerat*
*invenire, nempe quia et sapientia et cunctis moribus*
*bonis cunctos fratres suos praecellebat, et insuper eo*
10 *quod nimium bellicosus et victor prope in omnibus*
*bellis erat.* Cumque regnare prope quasi invitus
uno mense impleto coeperat—nimirum enim non
putabat se, nisi divino fultum auxilio, tantam
paganorum unquam posse solum sufferre austeri-
15 tatem, quin etiam viventibus suis fratribus, cum
magna multorum detrimenta sustinuisset—contra

[a] Luc. xiv. 14.

---

4 adeuns *B*      *post* adiens *add.* ix. kal. Maii *Flor*      Wynburnan
*B* : Winburnam *Co W Pet*      5 *post* sepultus *add.* est, ubi *Flor*
primamque *Flor*

42 *Exscripp. totum SN, paululum SD* 1 *SD* 2      1 Alfrędus *SN*
*post* Ælfred *add.* saepe *SN*      5 volutate *SN*      *post* suscepit *add.*
*partem cap.* 21 *et capita* 22, 23, 24 *Flor, ut ad cap.* 21 *v.* 15 *adnotavi*
6 praedicto *om. SN*      7 cum *om. SN*      poterat *SN*      8 bonis
moribus *B*      11 regnaret *SN*      prope *om. SN*      12 *post* mense
*add.* non iam *SN*      coeperat ... nisi *om. SN*      13 *post* putabat
*add.* in *Co P Ar Camd W Pet, quod ortum esse ex* nisi *sequenti*
*suspicor*      se *om. B*      nisi *B Flor* : *om. rell. SN*      fultum
*Flor* : fultus *Co B P Ar Edd. SN*      13–16 tantam . . . sustinuisset *om. SN*      14 solum *Flor* : solus *Co B P Ar rell.*

universum paganorum exercitum in monte, qui
dicitur Wiltun, qui est in meridiana ripa fluminis
Guilou, de quo flumine tota illa paga nominatur,
cum paucis et nimium inaequali numero acerrime 20
belligeravit, et cum hinc inde utrique hostiliter et
animose non parva diei parte pugnarent, pagani ad
integrum suum periculum propriis suis conspectibus
cernentes, et hostium infestationem diutius non
ferentes, terga in fugam verterunt.   Sed, proh 25
dolor ! peraudacitatem persequentium decipientes,
iterum in proelium prodeunt, et victoriam capientes,
loco funeris dominati sunt.  Nec hoc cuiquam
mirabile videatur, quod Christiani parvum in proelio
numerum habebant : erant enim Saxones maxima 30
ex parte in *eodem* uno anno octo contra paganos
proeliis populariter attriti, in quibus octo proeliis
unus rex paganorum et novem duces cum innumeris
cohortibus occisi periere, exceptis cotidianis et
nocturnis irruptionibus innumerabilibus, quas ⟨rex⟩ 35
Ælfred *saepe memoratus* et singuli duces illius gentis
cum suis et etiam perplures ministri regis contra
paganos infatigabiliter *studiose* exercebant.   In
quibus frequentissimis irruptionibus quot millia
paganae expeditionis occisa perierunt, nisi soli Deo, 40

---

16 multorum *Cott.* (*teste W*) *Co B Ar* : *om. Camd*      17 monte]
loco *SN*      18 Wylton *B*      19 Guylou *B* : Wili *SN*      22
non] cum *Ar*      26 peraudacitatem persequentium decipientes
*Co B P Ar Edd.* : peraudaciam p. decipientes *Flor* : paucitatem
persequentium despicientes *SN*      29 quod] quem (*perperam*
quoniam *Ed.*) *SN*      *post* Christiani *add.* tam *SN*      30 *post*
Saxones *add.* vel Angli *SN*      34 cottidianis *SN* : quotidianis *rell.*      35 rex *ex Flor addidi*      36 Aelfredus *SN*
37 et *om. SN*

incognitum est; exceptis his, qui in octo *supra memoratis* proeliis trucidati sunt.

43 Eodem quoque anno Saxones cum iisdem paganis, ea condicione, ut ab eis discederent, pacem pepigerunt; quod et impleverunt.

44 Anno *Dominicae Incarnationis* DCCCLXXII, *nativitatis autem Ælfredi regis vigesimo quarto*, praefatus paganorum exercitus Lundoniam adiit, et ibi hyemavit, cum quo Mercii pacem pepigerunt.

45 Anno *Dominicae Incarnationis* DCCCLXXIII, *nativitatis autem Ælfredi regis vigesimo quinto*, saepe memoratus exercitus Lundoniam deserens, in Northanhymbrorum regionem perrexit, et ibi hye-
5 mavit in paga, quae dicitur Lindesig; cum quo iterum Mercii pacem pepigerunt.

46 Anno *Dominicae Incarnationis* DCCCLXXIV, *nativitatis autem Ælfredi regis vigesimo sexto*, supra memoratus saepe exercitus Lindissig deserens,

---

41 supra memoratis] praedictis *Flor*

**43** *Exscripp. SN SD* 1      1 *post* anno *add.* Occidentales *SN* hisdem *Co SN*: eisdem *B*

**44** *Exscripp. SN SD* 1 *SD* 2      1 dominicae *om. Camd* 2 autem Ælfredi *om. B*   quarto *correxit W*: tertio *Cott.* (*teste W*) *Co B P Ar SD* 1 *rell.*   3 Lundoniam *Co SN Flor*: Londoniam *rell.*

**45** *Exscripp. SN SD* 1 *SD* 2      2 quinto *corr. W*: quarto *Cott.* (*teste W*) *Co B P Ar SD* 1 *rell.*   saepe *om. SN*   3 *post* memoratus *add.* paganorum *SN*   Lundoniam *Co SN Flor*: Londoniam *rell.*   4 Northanhimbrorum *Co*: Nordanhymbrorum *SN*   5 paga quae] loco qui *SN*   Lindesig] Turkesige *SN*: *post* Lindesig *add.* apud Torchasiam *SD* 2   cum] in *Co*

**46** *Exscripp. totum SN, partim SD* 1 *SD* 2      1 DCCCLXXIII *SN*   2 sexto *corr. W*: quinto *Cott.* (*teste W*) *Co B P Ar Camd SD* 1   supra memoratus saepe] saepe dictus paganorum *SN* 3 Lindissi *Co SD* 1: Lindessi *B*: Lindissem provinciam *SD* 2:

Merciam adiit, et hyemavit in loco, qui dicitur
Hreopedune. Burghredum quoque Merciorum 5
regem regnum suum deserere et ultra mare exire
et Romam adire contra voluntatem suam coegit,
vigesimo secundo regni sui anno; qui, postquam
Romam adierat, non diu vivens, ibi defunctus est,
et in Schola Saxonum in ecclesia Sanctae Mariae 10
honorifice sepultus, adventum Domini et primam
cum iustis resurrectionem expectat. Pagani *quoque*
post eius expulsionem totum Merciorum regnum
suo dominio subdiderunt, quod tamen miserabili
condicione cuidam insipienti ministro ⟨regis⟩ (cuius 15
nomen erat Ceolwulf) eodem pacto custodiendum
commendaverunt, ut qualicunque die illud vellent
habere iterum, pacifice illis assignaret. Quibus in
eadem condicione obsides dedit et iuravit, nullo
modo se voluntati eorum contradicere velle, sed 20
oboediens in omnibus esse.

Anno *Dominicae Incarnationis* DCCCLXXV, *nati-* 47
*vitatis autem Ælfredi regis vigesimo septimo*, supra
memoratus saepe exercitus Hreopedune deserens,

---

Lindisig *SN*    5 Hreopedun *SN*    Burhgredum *Co* : Burgredum
*B* : Burhtredus *SD* 2 : Burhredum *Flor* : Burgoredum *SN*    9 ibi
defunctus est *Co SN*: ‘*Sic Flor* Ibidem functus est *in ceteris*’ *W, quae
exhibet Ar* : ibidem defunctus est *B*    10 scola *SN*    post
Saxonum *add.* sive Anglorum *SN*    13 eius] cuius *Co Flor SN*
15 regis *Flor* : om. *Cot.* (*teste W*): *praebent* (*ex SN interpolatum*) *P
Ar Camd W* : *secl. Pet*    cuius *Co B Ar SN Flor* : eius *P Edd.*
16 Ceolwulfe *Co* : Ceodwulf *B* : Seolwulf *Ar* : Ceoluulfus *SN*    17
commendarunt *B*    illud *om. Flor*    18 habere] nostre *Co* (*ex
compendio* h̄re *male pro* n̄re *lecto*)    pacifice illis assignaret] id sibi
pacifice resignaret *Flor*    Quibus in eadem *om. SN, exhibet tamen
Ed.*    19 *post* iuravit *add. ex v. seq.* se *B*    21 esset *SN*
    47 *Exscripp. SN SD* 1 *SD* 2    2 septimo *corr. W* : sexto
*Cott.* (*teste W*) *Co B P Ar Camd SD* 1    supra *om. SN*    3 *post*

in duas se divisit turmas : cuius altera pars cum
5 Healftene in regionem Northanhymbrorum perrexit, et ibi hiemavit iuxta flumen, quod dicitur
Tine, et totam Northanhymbrorum regionem suo
subdidit dominio, necnon et Pictos et Stratclut-
tenses depopulati sunt. Altera quoque pars cum
10 Gothrum et Osscytil et Anvind, tribus paganorum
regibus, ad locum, qui dicitur Grantebrycge, pervenit, et ibi hiemavit.

**48**    Eodem anno Ælfred rex navali proelio in mare
contra sex naves paganorum belligeravit, et unam
ex eis cepit, ceteris per fugam elapsis.

**49**    Anno *Dominicae Incarnationis* DCCCLXXVI, *nati-*
*vitatis autem Ælfredi regis vigesimo octavo*, saepe
memoratus paganorum exercitus noctu de Grantebrycge exiens, castellum, quod dicitur Werham,
5 intravit ; quod monasterium sanctimonialium inter

---

memoratus *add.* paganorum *SN*        5 Healstene *B* : Half-
dene *Flor* : Halfdena *SN* : Healfene *Camd* (*errore operarum*)
Northanhimbrorum *Co* : Nordanhymbrorum *SN*        7 Tyne *B*
Northanhimbrorum *Co* : Nordanhymbrorum *SN*        8 Stratclut-
tenses *scripsi secutus Flor* : Stratduttenses *Co B P Ar rell. Edd.* :
Stretcluttenses *SD* 1 : Strecledenses *SN* (*cf.* Stræcled, Strecled
*Chron. Anglo-Sax eodem in anno*)        10 Guthrum *Flor SD* 2 :
Gutthrum *SD* 1 : Guthram *SN*        Ossityl *B* : Oscytel *Flor SD* 1 :
Oskitel *SD* 2 : Oscitill *Ar* : Osketellus (*sic*) *SN* (Osketello *Ed.*)
Anvind *scripsi auctore Chron. Anglo-Sax.* : Amund *Co B P Ar*
*rell. Edd. Flor SD* 1 *SD* 2 : Anandus (*sic*) *SN* (Anando *Ed.*)
11 Grantebrycque *B* : Grantebricge *Ar SN*
    **48** *Exscripp. SN SD* 1 *SD* 2        1 Aelfredus *SN*        mari *B*
2 sex] VII *SN*
    **49** *Exscripp. totum SN, partim SD* 1 *SD* 2        2 octavo
*corr. W* : sex Cott. (*teste W*) *Co B P Ar Camd* : septimo *SD* 1
saepe memoratus *om. SN*        3 nocte clam *SN*        Grantebrycq;
*B* : Grantebricge *P Ar*        4 Wærham *SN*        5 quod] ubi

duo flumina Frauu ⟨et Terente⟩ et in paga, quae
dicitur *Britannice Durngueir*, Saxonice *autem*
Thornsæta, tutissimo terrarum situ situm est, nisi
ab occidentali parte tantummodo, ubi contigua
terra est.  Cum quo exercitu Ælfred rex foedus 10
firmiter ea condicione, ut ab eo discederent, pepigit :
cui ille exercitus electos obsides, quantos ⟨ipse⟩
*solus* nominavit, sine ulla controversia dedit, necnon
*et* sacramentum in omnibus reliquiis, quibus ille rex
maxime post Deum confidebat, iuravit, (in quibus 15
nec alicui genti prius iurare voluit) citissime de
regno suo se exiturum *esse*.  Sed, more suo, solita
fallacia utens, et obsides et iuramentum atque
fidem promissam non custodiens, nocte quadam,
foedere disrupto, omnes equites, quos habebat, occi- 20
dit, versusque inde [*Domnaniam*] *ad* alium locum,
qui dicitur Saxonice Exanceastre, *Britannice autem*

---

*Flor*   quod . . . terra est (*v.* 10) *om. SN*      6 et Terente *ex*
*Flor add. W*      7 Durngueir *scripsi auctore Co* : Durnguers *B* :
Durngueys *Ar* : Durngueis *P Camd W Pet*      8 Thornesæta *B*
9 solummodo *B*      10 exercitu *om. SN*    Aelfrędus *SN*    *post*
rex *add.* Occidentalium Saxonum *SN*      11 *post* firmiter *add.*
et *Flor*    ea *om. Co B*    pepigit *post* firmiter *praebet SN*
12 ipse *ex Flor addidi*    13 solus *om. Flor*    14 et *om. B*    15
Dominum *P Ar Edd.*    *post* quibus *exhibent* (*ex SN interpolata*)
et super armillam, super (supra *SN*) quam *P Ar Camd* (= on
þam halgan beage *cet. Chron. Anglo-Sax.*): *om. Cott.* (*teste W*) *Co
B Flor SD* 1 *SD* 2      16 *post* voluit *add.* ut *SN*      17 se
*om. B*    esse *om. Co*      20 *post* quos *add.* rex *Flor W* : *om.
Cott.* (*teste W*) *Co B P Ar Camd SN SD* 1 *SD* 2      occidit]
occidentem *SN*      21 versus in *SN* (indeque versus *Ed.*)    inde]
mare *B*    Domnaniam *om. Co Flor, quod interpolatum* (*ex
SN*) *a P suspicor*    ad] *om. B Flor*    alium *om. B P Ar
Camd SN* : *exhib. Cott.* (*teste W*) *rell.*    locum *om. Co*    22
Anglice *SN*    Exanceastre *Co B Flor.* : Exanceastre *SD* 1 *SD* 2 :
Eaxanceastre *P Ar Camd W Pet* : Exanceastra *SN*    Britannice

*Cairuuisc,* Latine *quoque* civitas ⟨Exae, quae⟩ in
orientali ripa fluminis *Uuisc* sita est, prope mare
25 meridianum, quod interluit Galliam Britanniamque,
inopinate direxit, *et ibi hyemavit.*

50     Eodem quoque anno Halfdene, rex *illius partis*
Northanhymbrorum, *totam* regionem sibimet et
suis divisit, et illam cum suo exercitu coluit.

50 b    [*Eodem anno* Rollo cum suis Normanniam penetravit. *Idem*
*Normannorum dux Rollo cum in antiqua Britannia sive*
*Anglia hyemaret, militaribus fretus copiis, quadam nocte*
*fruitur visione mox futurae certitudinis. De hoc Rollone*
5 *vide plura in Annalibus.*]

50 c    [*Anno* DCCCLXXVII, *pagani, instante tempore autumnali,*

---

. . . Exae *om. SN*      23 Cairwysc *B* : Caruuist *Ar*    Exae, quae
*ex Flor add. W* : aquae *alia manu in rasura, omissis* quae . . .
hyemavit, *SD* 1, *SD* 2      *post* quae *add.* civitas *SN*     24
Uuisc] eiusdem *Flor* : Exa *SN*      25 quod] quia *Cott. (teste W)*
*Co B P Ar Camd*      quod . . . direxit *om. SN*      Brittanniamque
*Co*     26 direxit] adiit, quem, collecto exercitu, rex Ælfredus est
insecutus; sed quia civitatem iam intraverat, illum assequi non
poterat. Veruntamen quot et quantos voluit obsides ab eis extorsit,
firmumque cum eis foedus pepigit; quod illi tempore non modico
bene custodierunt, ibidemque hiemaverunt *Flor (cf. Chron. Anglo-*
*Sax. ann* 877).    et ibi] ibique *SN*

     50 *Exscripp. SN SD* 2     1 quoque] paganus *Flor*     Hal-
dene *Co B* : Halfdena *SN*     *post* partis *add.* quae in *Co SN* : quae
*B*    2 Northanhimbrorum *Co Ar* : Northamhymbrorum *B* : Nordanhymbris erat *SN*    totam *om. Co B*     3 colunt *Co SN*

     50 b *Interpolatum (ex SN) in B P Ar Camd.* ' *Sectionem hanc et*
*duas proxime sequentes omittit vetus MS. Cott.; inseruit tamen (locis*
*non suis) recentior manus' W* : om. *Co, in quo adnotatur aequali*
*manu* ' *Deest annus* 877 '     1 *post* penetravit *add.* xv. kal. Dec.
*Flor SN SD* 2     4 *post* certitudinis *somnium Rollonis refert SN*
De . . . Annalibus ⟨*id est SN*⟩ *sunt profecto adnotatio P, quam recc.*
*Ar Camd W; seclusit Pet*

     50 c *Ex Matthaei Paris* ' *Chronicis Maioribus' tom.* i. *p.* 409
(*sive ex anonymi eius descriptoris* ' *Floribus Historiae*' i. 450)
*interpolatum. In Cott. scriptum fuisse* ' *manu recentiori' testatur*

*partim in Exeanceastre residebant et pars Merciam praeda-*
*tura recessit. Crescebat insuper diebus singulis perversorum*
*numerus, adeo quidem, ut si triginta ex eis millia una die*
*necarentur, alii succedebant numero duplicato. Tunc rex* 5
*Ælfredus iussit cymbas et galeas, id est longas naves, fabri-*
*cari per regnum, ut navali proelio hostibus adventantibus*
*obviaret, impositisque piratis in illis vias maris custodiendas*
*commisit. Ipse vero Eaxancestre, ubi pagani hyemabant,*
*properans, illis inclusis, civitatem obsedit. Nautis quoque* 10
*suis mandavit, ut in parte freti vitale hostibus subsidium*
*denegarent. Occurrerunt autem nautis suis centum et*
*viginti naves armatis militibus oneratae, qui in auxilium*
*suorum concivium advenerunt; quas, cum paganis militibus*
*ministri regis cognovissent repletas, ad arma prosiliunt et* 15
*viriliter barbaras nationes invadunt. Pagani vero, qui iam*
*fere per mensem inter fluctus pelagi naufragium pertulissent,*
*inutiliter proelium reddiderunt; unde in momento agminibus*
*eorum laceratis, in loco, qui dicitur Suanewic, undis submersi*
*omnes pariter perierunt.]* 20

[*Eodem anno exercitus paganorum Werham deserens,* **50 d**

---

*W (vide c. 50 b), in quo fuit 'notula' (teste W) 'Haec forsan*
*ex alio exemplari'; in Co scriptum aequali manu in schedula*
*inserta; in textum recepp. B Ar P Camd W; secl. Pet* 1
post anno *add.* Dominicae Incarnationis Co       pagani] Nefandi
paganorum acervus *Paris Flores*       2 Exanceastre *B Ar*:
Exonia *Paris Flores*       resedit *Paris Flores*       post pars *add.* eius
*Paris Flores*       Marciam Co       praedaturam *B P*       6 Alfredus
*Co*       cymbas] cyulas Co *Paris Flores*       7 advenientibus *B*
9 Exeanceastream *Co*: Exancestre *B Ar*: Exonia *Paris Flores*
post hyemabant *add.* hostiliter *Paris Flores*       12 post denegarent
*add.* cumque nautae ex praecepto regis illuc summopere properarent
*Paris Flores*       autem nautis suis *om. Paris Flores*       13 arma-
torum militum *Paris Flores*       millibus *Ar*       qui] quae omnes
*Paris Flores*       16 vero] quoque *Paris Flores*       19 Suanewic
*correxi auctore Paris*: Gnavewic Co *Ar P Edd.*: Gravewic dicitur
ordine inverso *B*       20 perierunt *om. B*

50 d *Interpolatum (ex SN) in Cott. (vide cap. 50 b) Co in schedula*
*(vide cap. 50 c), B P Ar Camd W: seclusit Pet. In Cott. adscripta*
*fuisse in fine* Ex Annalibus Asserii *testatur W*       1 Eodem

*partim equitando, partim navigando, cum pervenerunt ad
locum, qui Suanavine dicitur, perierunt centum et viginti
e navibus : equestrem vero exercitum rex Ælfred insequebatur*
5 *tunc, quousque venit ad Exanceastriam. Ibi accepit obsides
et iuramentum ab eo, ut cito discederent.*]

**51** *Ipso anno, mense Augusto, ille exercitus perrexit
in Merciam, et illam regionem Merciorum partim
dedit Ceolwulfo, cuidam insipienti regis ministro,
partim inter se divisit.*

**52** Anno *Dominicae Incarnationis* DCCCLXXVIII,
*nativitatis autem Ælfredi regis trigesimo,* supra
memoratus saepe exercitus Eaxeancestre deserens,
Cippanham, villam regiam, quae est sita in sinistrali
5 parte Wiltunscire, *in orientali ripa fluminis, quod
Britannice dicitur Abon,* adiit, et ibi hyemavit. Et
multos eiusdem gentis ultra mare compulit hostiliter et penuria atque pavore navigare, et maxima
ex parte omnes illius regionis habitatores suo sub-
10 diderunt dominio.

---

anno] Anno DCCCLXXVII item *SN*        2 *post* navigando
*add.* sed *SN*        pervenissent *B*        3 Suanevyne *B* : Swanawic
*recte SN*        4 Ælfredus *B Ar*        insequens *SN*        5 tunc
*om. SN*        6 discederet *B P Ar* : discederent *Camd W* : discessurus erat *SN*

  **51** *Exscripp. SN: om. Co*        2 Merciorum regionem *B*        3 Ceolwulfo *Co B Ar* : Cleolwulfo *P (errore operarum) quod recc. Camd
W Pet (margine correx. Pet)*  `quidam *SN*

  **52** *Exscripp. totum SN, partim (an* 877) *SD* 1 *SD* 2        2
trigesimo *corr. W* : vicesimo septimo *Cott. (teste W) Co B P Ar
Camd* : v. octavo *SD* 1  supra... deserens] magnus paganorum exercitus Danorum sive Nordmannorum post Theophaniam latenter *SN*
3 ex Eanceastre *Co* : Exancestre *B* : Exeancestre *Ar*        4 Cyppanham
*B*        refiam *(errore operarum) P Ar*        5 Wiltanscire *B* : pagae
Wyltunensis *SN*        quod . . . dicitur *om. SN*        6 Adbon *SN*
adiit *om. SN*        7 *post* eiusdem *add.* Occidentalium Saxonum *SN*
hostili vi *SN*        8 et] et pro *SN* (ut pro *Ed.*)        navigare]
navigarent et abdicarent se in oceano *SN*        9 regiones *B*

Eodem tempore Ælfred *saepe supra memoratus* **53**
*rex*, cum paucis suis nobilibus et etiam cum quibusdam *militibus* et fasellis, per sylvestria et gronnosa
Summurtunensis pagae loca in magna tribulatione
inquietam vitam ducebat.   Nihil enim habebat quo 5
uteretur, nisi quod a paganis et etiam a Christianis,
qui se paganorum subdiderant dominio, frequentibus
irruptionibus aut clam aut etiam palam subtraheret.
[*Et, ut in vita Sancti Neoti patris legitur,* ⟨*diu latebat*⟩
*apud quendam suum vaccarium.*]                                      10

[*Contigit autem die quodam, ut rustica, uxor videlicet* **53 b**
*illius vaccarii, pararet ad coquendum panes, et ille rex*
*sedens sic circa focum praeparavit sibi arcum et sagittas*
*et alia bellorum instrumenta.   Cum vero panes ad ignem*
*positos ardentes aspexit illa infelix mulier, festinanter* 5
⟨*cu*⟩*currit et amovit eos, increpans regem invictissimum,*
*et dicens: 'Heus homo*

   *urere, quos cernis, panes gyrare moraris,*
   *cum nimium gaudes hos manducare calentes!'*
*Mulier illa infausta minime putabat illum esse regem* 10

---

**53** *Exscripp. totum SN, partim SD* 1 *SD* 2           1 Ælfred
*om. B* : Alfr̨edus *SN*      supra *om. B*        2 *post* rex *add.* Occidentalium Saxonum (*ex SN interpolata*) Co B P Ar Edd., *quae*
*defuisse in Cott. adnot. W*      alterum cum *om. B*        3 militibus
*om. Co*      et *om. Co B*      fasellis *Co Flor* : vacellis *B* : vasellis *P*
*Ar* : vasallis *Camd W Pet* : vasallis *SN*        4 Sumertunensis *B* :
Sumur- *SN*      pagae] fagae *P*      *post* tribulatione *add.* et angustia
*SN*      5 inquietus *Flor*      6 et] vel *Flor*      a *om. B*      7 sub-
diti erant *SN*      8 *ad* subtraheret *in Co adscriptum est* Hic
inseritur in alio opere ascripto Asser scriptum quoddam ⟨*scilicet cap.*
*53b*⟩ in Vita Sancti Neoti      9 et . . . vaccarium *om. Co B* :
*interpolata* (*ex SN*) *in P Ar rell. Edd. De Cott. nihil adnotavit W*
diu latebat *ex SN addidi*

**53 b** *Interpolatum* (*ex SN*) *in P Ar Camd W* : *secl. Pet* : *om.*
*Cott.* (*teste W*) *Co B*      1 quadam *Camd SN*      3 circa]
contra *SN*      6 cucurrit *scripsi* : currit *Co B P Ar Edd. SN*

*Ælfredum, qui tot bella gessit contra paganos, tantasque
victorias accepit de eis.*]

**53 c** [*Non solum autem eidem glorioso regi victorias de inimicis
et prosperitatem in adversis conferre Dominus dignatus est,
verum etiam ab hostibus fatigari, adversitatibus affligi,
despectu suorum deprimi, multotiens eum idem benignus
5 Dominus permisit, ut sciret, quoniam 'unus est omnium
dominus, cui curvatur omne genu, cuius in manu corda sunt
regum, Qui ponit de sede potentes et exaltat humiles'* ᵃ, Qui
suos fideles in summa prosperitate positos flagellis adversitatum vult aliquando tangi : ut depressi de Dei misericordia
10 non desperent, et exaltati de honore non superbiant, sed etiam
sciant cui debent omnia, quae habent. Quam siquidem adversitatem praefato regi illatam non immerito ei evenisse
credimus, quia in primo tempore regni sui, cum adhuc
iuvenis erat, animoque iuvenili detentus fuerat, homines sui
15 regni sibique subiecti, qui ad eum venerant et pro necessitatibus suis eum requisierant et qui depressi potestatibus
erant, suum auxilium ac patrocinium implorabant. Ille vero
noluit eos audire, nec aliquod auxilium ⟨eis⟩ impendebat, sed
omnino eos nihili pendebat. Quod beatissimus vir Neotus
20 adhuc vivens in carne, qui erat cognatus suus, intimo corde
doluit, maximamque adversitatem ob hoc ei venturam spiritu
prophetico plenus praedixerat. Sed ille et piissimam viri
Dei correptionem parvi pendebat, et verissimam eius pro-
phetiam non recipiebat. Quia igitur quicquid ab homine
25 peccatur, aut hic aut in futuro, necesse est ut quolibet modo
puniatur, noluit verus et pius iudex illam regis insipientiam
esse impunitam in hoc seculo, quatenus illi parceret in districto iudicio. Quare ergo idem saepedictus Ælfredus in*

---

ᵃ Ephes. iv. 6; Isa. xlv. 23; Prov. xxi. 1; Luc. i. 52.

---

11 Alfredum *SN*

53 c *Interpolatum (ex SN) in P Ar Camd W : seclus. Pet : om.
Cott. (teste W) Co B*     11 quae *om. SN (quod tacitus supplevit
Ed.)*     14 iuvenis *SN* (invenis *Ed. operarum errore*)     animo *SN*
18 voluit *P*     eis *ex SN addidi*          22 praedixit *SN*
27 parcerent *Ar*          28 Alfredus *Camd* : Alfredus *SN*

*tantam miseriam saepius incidit, ut nemo subiectorum suorum*
*sciret ubi esset vel quo devenisset.*]                    30

Eodem anno frater Inwari et Healfdene cum **54**
viginti et tribus navibus de Demetica regione, in qua
hyemaverat, post multas ibi Christianorum strages
factas, ad Domnaniam enavigavit, et ibi a ministris
regis cum mille *et* ducentis infelici exitu perperam 5
agens occisus est ante arcem Cynuit ; quia in eadem
arce multi ministri regis cum suis se concluserant
confugii causa. Sed cum pagani arcem imparatam
atque omnino immunitam, nisi quod moenia nostro
more erecta solummodo haberet, cernerent,—non 10
enim effringere moliebantur, quia *et* ille locus situ
terrarum tutissimus est ab omni parte, nisi ab
orientali, *sicut nos ipsi vidimus,*—obsidere eam
coeperunt, putantes homines illos manum cito
daturos fame et siti et obsessione coactos, quia 15
nulla aqua illi arci contigua est. Quod non ita,
ut putabant, evenit. Nam Christiani, antequam
talem penuriam omnino subire paterentur, divinitus

---

30 *post* devenisset *add. SN* Verumtamen in maximis necessitatibus
ac periculis ei posito Beatus Neotus saepe apparuit, consolans eum
ac praedicens illum (eum *Ed. tacite*) bene superaturum omnia mala
sibi instantia.

54 *Exscripp. totum SN, partim SD* 1 *SD* 2       1 Inwari
*Co B* : Inguar *SD* 1 *SD* 2 : Hynguari *rell.*    Healfdene *Co P Ar*
*SN*: Halsdene *B* : Healfdenae *Camd rell. Edd.*       3 ibi *om. Ar*
4 Damnaniam *B*     5 et *om. SN SD* 2      in felici *Co* : in faelici
*B*       6 Cynwyt *B* : Cynwith *SD* 1 *SD* 2       8 refugii *SD* 2
Sed] verum *Flor*       imperatam *B*      9 omnino *om. B*      10
erecti *SN* (*quod tacitus correxit Ed.*)     13 sicut] ut *B*      sicut
nos ipsi vidimus *om. SN*       15 obsessione *Cott.* (*teste W*) *Co*
*Flor SN* (obsidione *Ed.*): obsidione *B Ar P Edd.*       16 illi
arci] ei *Ar* : ille arce *SN*       *post* arci *add.* erat *Ar*       est
*om. Ar*       17 anteaquam *B*       18 subire] ferre *B*

instigati, multo melius iudicantes aut mortem aut
20 victoriam mereri, diluculo super paganos ex improviso irrumpunt, et a primo tempore hostes hostiliter
cum rege suo maxima ex parte, paucis ad naves
per fugam elapsis, prosternunt.

**54 b** [*Ibique acceperunt spolia non minima. In quo etiam
acceperunt illud vexillum, quod Reafan nominant. Dicunt
enim quod tres sorores Hinguari et Hubbae, filiae videlicet
Lodebrochi, illud vexillum texuerunt, et totum paraverunt
5 illud uno meridiano tempore. Dicunt etiam, quod in omni
bello ubi praecederet idem signum, si victoriam adepturi
essent, appareret in medio signi quasi corvus vivens volitans :
sin vero vincendi in futuro fuissent, penderet directe nihil
movens. Et hoc saepe probatum est.*]

**55** Eodem anno post Pascha Ælfred rex cum paucis
[*adiutoribus*] fecit arcem in loco, qui dicitur Æthelingaeg, et de ipsa arce semper cum [*nobilibus*] fassellis
Summurtunensis ⟨*pagae*⟩ *contra* paganos infatigabi-

---

21 a primo] '*Sic Flor* Aprino *Edd. P et C*[*amd*]' *W, nihil de Cott.
enotato* : aprino *B Ar* : prima hora *omisso* tempore *SN*
**54 b** *Interpolatum* (*ex SN*) *in P Ar Camd W* : *secl. Pet* : *om.
Cott.* (*teste W*) *Co B. In Cott. interpolatum fuisse ex eo apparet,
quod W inde adnotavit* Reafau v. 2  2 Reafan *SN* (Reafun *perperam
Ed.*) *W Pet* : Reafau *Cott.* (*teste W*) *P Ar Camd*  3 Hinguari *P
Ar* : Hungari *Camd* (*errore, ut videtur, operarum*) *W Pet* : Hynguari
*SN* (Hinguari *perperam Ed.*)    Hubbae *SN* (Aubbae *Ed. perpe-
ram*) : Habbe *P Ar* : Habbae *Camd W Pet*    6 signum] regnum
*Ar*    8 sin] si *SN*

**55** *Exscripp. totum SN, partim SD* 1 *SD* 2    1 Ælfredus *B* :
Alfrędus *SN*    2 adiutoribus *om. Cott.* (*teste W*) *Co* : *exhibb.* (*ex
SN interpolatum*) *Co B P Ar Camd* : *secl. Pet*    Ethelingaag *B* :
Æthelingaeig *SN*: Ethelingalge *SD* 1 : *SD* 2    3 nobilibus
*om. Co* : *exhibb.* (*ex SN interpolatum*) *B P Ar Camd W Pet*
fassellis *Cott.* (*teste W*) *Co Flor* : vascellis *B* : vassellis *P Ar* : vasallis
*SN Camd W Pet*    4 Sumertunensis *B* : Sumur- *SN* : Sumurtunen-
sibus *Flor*    pagae *om. Cott.* (*teste W*) *Co B Flor Ar* : *exhibb.* (*ex SN
interpolatum*) *P Camd W Pet*    contra *om. Cott.* (*teste W*) *Co*

liter rebellavit. Iterumque in septima hebdomada 5
post Pascha ad Petram Ægbryhta, quae est in orientali parte saltus, qui dicitur Seluudu, Latine autem
'sylva magna,' *Britannice 'Coit Maur,'* equitavit ;
ibique obviaverunt illi omnes accolae Summurtunensis *pagae et* Wiltunensis, *omnes accolae* Hamtu- 10
nensis pagae, qui non ultra mare pro metu paganorum navigaverant ; visoque rege, sicut dignum erat,
quasi redivivum post tantas tribulationes recipientes,
immenso repleti sunt gaudio, *et* ibi castra metati
sunt una nocte. Diluculo sequenti *illucescente*, rex 15
inde castra commovens, venit ad locum, qui dicitur
Æcglea, et ibi una nocte castra metatus est.

Inde sequenti mane *illucescente* vexilla com- **56**
movens ad locum, qui dicitur Ethandun, venit, et
contra universum paganorum exercitum cum densa
testudine atrociter belligerans, animoseque diu
persistens, divino nutu, tandem victoria potitus, 5

---

5 debellavit *Flor* 6 Aegbrihta *Co Ar* : Eghritha B : Ecgbrihti
*Flor* : Egcbrichti *SN* : Ecgberti *SD* 1 *SD* 2 7 *post* qui *add.* Anglico
eloquio *SN* Saluudu *SN* : Mucel-pudu (*ex* -wudu *scripto litteris
Anglo-Sax.* pudu *perperam intellecto*) *SD* 1 (-purlu *Edd.*) *SD* 2
(-pudu *Edd.*) 8 Britannice Coit Maur *om. SN* Coit Mapur (*ex*
Mawur *scripto Anglo-Saxonice* Mapur *ortum*) *SD* 1 *SD* 2 (Coitmawr
*Edd.*) 9 *post* illi *add.* eii *B* omnes *om. B* Sumertunensis *B* :
Summurtunensis . . . accolae *om. SN* 11 propter metum *SN*
12 navigarent *SN* : aufugerant *B* 14 ibique *SN* 16 inde
*Cott.* (*teste W*) *Co B W Pet SN* : in *P Ar Camd* 17 Ecglea
*B Flor* : Iglea *SN* *post* castra metatus est *Alfredi somnium
de Sancto Neoto narrat SN*

56 *Exscripp. totum SN, partim SD* 1 *SD* 2 1 Inde
*post* movens (*v.* 2) *exhibet SN* sequenti *om. SN* mane]
die *Flor* vixilla *Co B* 2 Eððandun *SD* 1 : Eðdandun *SD* 2
(Edderandun *Edd.* ð *pro* der *male lecto*) venit *post* exercitum (*v.* 3)
*exhibet SN* et] ubi *Flor* 5 tantem *SN* (*quod tacitus*

paganos maxima caede prostravit, et fugientes
usque ad arcem *percuticns* persecutus est, et omnia,
quae extra arcem invenit, homines scilicet et equos
et pecora, confestim caedens homines, surripuit, et
10 ante portas paganicae arcis cum omni exercitu suo
viriliter castra metatus est. Cumque ibi per quatuordecim dies remoraretur, pagani fame, frigore, timore,
et ad extremum desperatione perterriti, pacem ea
condicione petierunt, ut rex nominatos obsides,
15 quantos vellet, ab eis acciperet, et ille nullum eis
daret, ita tamen qualiter nunquam cum aliquo
pacem ante pepigerant. Quorum legatione audita
rex suatim *utens*, misericordia motus, nominatos,
quantos voluit, obsides ab eis accepit. Quibus
20 acceptis, pagani insuper iuraverunt se citissime de
suo regno exituros, necnon *et* Godrum, rex eorum,
Christianitatem subire et baptismum sub manu
Ælfredi regis accipere promisit. Quae omnia ille
et sui, ut promiserant, impleverunt. Nam post
25 hebdomadas ⟨*tres*⟩ Godrum, paganorum rex, cum
triginta electissimis de exercitu suo viris, ad Ælfred
regem prope Æthelingaeg in loco, qui dicitur Alre,

*emendavit Ed.*) *post* potitus *add.* et *Flor* 6 et fugientes]
fugientes vero *Flor* 12 moraretur *Flor* *post* timore *add.*
perterriti *SN* 13 perterriti] percussi *SN* 16 tamen] vero
*SN* *post* cum *add.* alio *SN* *post* aliquo *add.* rege vel principe
*SN* 18 suatim utens *Co SN*: suatim *Flor* (*Codd.* suapte *Edd.*)
*SD* 1 *SD* 2: sua ipsius *B P Ar Edd. De Cott. nihil adnotat W*
*post* utens *add.* consilium *SN* 21 Guthrum *Flor*: Gythram *SN*:
Gutthrum *SD* 1, *SD* 2 23 Alfrędi *SN* 25 tres *addidi auctore*
*Chron. Anglo-Sax.*: *om. Cott. Co B Ar Edd. SN* (tres *tacitus*
*add. Ed.*): septem *ex Flor supplevit W* Guthrum *Flor*: Guthram
*SN* (Gythram *Ed.*): Guderun *SD* 1 26 electissimus *P*
Alfrędum *SN* 27 Æthelinga ege *Co SN Flor*: Ethelingaag *B*

pervenit. Quem *Ælfred* rex in filium adoptionis sibi suscipiens, de fonte sacro baptismatis elevavit. Cuius chrismatis solutio octavo die in villa regia, 30 quae dicitur Wædmor, fuit. Qui, postquam baptizatus fuit, duodecim noctibus cum rege mansit. Cui rex cum suis omnibus multa et optima beneficia largiter dedit.

*Anno Dominicae Incarnationis* DCCCLXXIX, *nati-* 57 *vitatis autem Ælfredi regis trigesimo primo*, praefatus paganorum exercitus de Cippanhamme, ut promiserat, consurgens, Cirrenceastre adiit, *quae Britannice Cairceri nominatur*, quae est in meridiana 5 parte Huicciorum, ibique per unum annum mansit.

Eodem anno magnus paganorum exercitus de 58 ultramarinis partibus navigans in Tamesin fluvium venit, et adunatus est superiori exercitui, sed tamen hyemavit in loco, qui dicitur Fullonham, iuxta flumen Tamesin. 5

---

Aalr *Co Flor W*: Aarl *SD* 2: Autre *B* 28 Alfredus *SN* 29 sacri *Flor* elevavit *B Edd. SN*: elimavit *Co Flor SD* 2 31 Weadmor *Flor*: Wedmor *SD Ar*: Wedmore *SN* 33 omnibus] nobilibus *B* beneficia *scripsi*: aedificia *Co B Ar Edd.*

57 *Exscripp. totum SN SD* 1, *partim SD* 2 2 Ælfred *B* trigesimo primo *correx. W*: vigesimo octavo *Cott. (teste W) Co B Ar P Camd SD* 1 3 Cyppanhamme *B* 4 promiserant *B post* promiserat *add.* egressus *SD* 1, *inde pergens ad* ad Orientales *c.* 60 *v.* 4 Cyrrenceastre *B*: Cyrenceastram *SN* quae *Co B SD* 1: qui *Co B P Ar cett.* quae . . . nominatur *om. SN* 5 Brittanice *Co post* Britannice *add.* eloquio *SD* 1 6 Huuictiorum *B post* Huicciorum *add.* sita *SN*

58 *Exscripp. SN SD* 1 *SD* 2 1 *ante* Eodem *add.* et *SN* 2 *post* partibus *add.* venit *SN* Tamesin *scripsi*: Thamensem *Cott. (teste W)*: Tamensen *Co*: Tamesem *B*: Tamesem *Flor*: Taṁsē *SN*: Tamensi fluvio *SD* 1 *SD* 2: Thamesim *P Ar*: Thamesin *Camd W Pet*: Tæmese *vel* Tæmesan (*acc. sing. Anglo-Saxonice*) *scriptum fuisse suspicor* 4 Fullanham *Flor SN* 5 Tamesin

**59** Eodem anno eclipsis solis inter nonam et vesperam, sed propius ad nonam, facta est.

**60** *Anno Dominicae Incarnationis* DCCCLXXX, *nativitatis autem Ælfredi regis trigesimo secundo*, saepe memoratus paganorum exercitus Cirrenceastre deserens, ad Orientales Anglos perrexit, ipsamque
5 regionem dividens coepit inhabitare.

**61** Eodem anno exercitus paganorum, qui in Fullonham hiemaverat, Britannicam insulam deserens, iterum ultra mare navigans, ad Orientalem Franciam perrexit, et per unum annum in loco, qui dicitur
5 Gendi, mansit.

**62** *Anno Dominicae Incarnationis* DCCCLXXXI, *nativitatis autem Ælfredi regis trigesimo tertio*, *praefatus* exercitus superius in Franciam perrexit. Contra quem Franci pugnaverunt, et,
5 finito proelio, pagani, equis inventis, equites facti sunt.

---

*scripsi* : Thamensis *Co P* : Thamesis *Ar* : Thamensem *B* : Tamense
*Flor* : Tam̃sis *SN* : Thamesin *Camd W Pet*
**59** *Exscripp. SN SD* 1 *SD* 2    1 vespernam *Camd*    2 ad
*om. SN*
**60** *Exscripp. SN SD* 1 *SD* 2    2 trigesimo secundo *corr.*
*W* : vigesimo nono *Cott.* (*teste W*) *Co B P Ar Camd SD* 1
3 paganorum *om. Co B*    Cyrenceastre *SN*
**61** *Exscripp. SN SD* 1 *SD* 2    1 paganorum exercitus *SN*
Fulanhamme *Co* : Fullanham *Flor* : Fullanhamme *SN*    2
Brittanicam *Co*    Britannicam insulam] Angliam *SN*    5 Gendi
*Cott.* (*teste W*) *Co* : Gendi, id est Gent *Flor* : Gaent *P Ar Camd*
*W Pet SN* : Gaynt *B* : Gant *SD* 2
**62** *Exscrip. SN*; *fusius eadem reddunt, multis additis, SD* 1
*SD* 2    2 trigesimo tertio *corr. W* : trigesimo *Cott.* (*teste*
*W*) *Co B Ar P Camd SD* 1    3 *post* exercitus *add.* paganorum
*Flor*    superius] saepedictus *Flor*    5 pagani] pani *SN*
(*quod tacitus correxit Ed.*)

*Anno Dominicae Incarnationis* DCCCLXXXII, *nati-* **63**
*vitatis autem Ælfredi regis trigesimo quarto*, praefatus exercitus suas naves per flumen, quod dicitur
Mese, sursum tanto longe in Franciam pertraxit, et
ibi uno anno hyemavit. 5

Et eodem anno Ælfred, *Angulsaxonum* rex, navali **64**
proelio contra paganicas naves in mare congressus
est ; ex quibus duas cepit naves, occisis omnibus,
qui in eis erant. Duarumque aliarum navium duo
principes, cum omnibus suis sociis, valde proelio et 5
vulneribus fatigati, depositis armis, curvo poplite, et
supplicibus precibus, dederunt se regi.

*Anno Dominicae Incarnationis* DCCCLXXXIII, *na-* **65**
*tivitatis autem regis Ælfredi trigesimo quinto*, praefatus exercitus naves suas per flumen, *quod dicitur*
Scald, contra flumen navigans, ad monasterium
sanctimonialium, quod dicitur Cundoth, traxit, et 5
ibi anno uno mansit.

*Anno Dominicae Incarnationis* DCCCLXXXIV, *na-* **66**
*tivitatis autem Ælfredi regis trigesimo sexto, prae-*

---

**63** *Exscripp. SD* 1 *SD* 2    2 trigesimo quarto *corr. W* :
trigesimo primo *Cott.* (*teste W*) *Co B P Ar Camd SD* 1    4
Mese *Co SD* 1 *SD* 2 : Ine se *Cott.* (*teste W*) *Ar P Camd* : Inese *B* :
*in* Mese *corr. W auctore Flor*

  **64** *Exscripp. SD* 1 *SD* 2    4 duo *om. B*    5 utilde *Co*

  **65** *Exscripp. totum SD* 1, *partim SD* 2    2 trigesimo quinto
*corr. W* : trigesimo secundo *Cott.* (*teste W*) *Co B P Ar Camd*
*SD* 1    4 Scaldad *Flor*    5 Cundoth *scripsi secutus Chron.*
*Anglo-Sax. et SD* 1 : Cundath *Flor* : Cundoht *Co B. P Ar Camd*
*W Pet*    6 permansit *B*

  **66** *Exscripp. totum SN SD* 1, *partim* ( *post cap.* 71 *transpositum*)
*SD* 2    1 DCCCLXXXIV] DCCCLXXXV *Flor SD* 2 *SN Chron.*
*Anglo-Sax.* nativitatis . . . sexto *om. Co B* : *exhibet SD* 1 *alia manu*
2 trigesimo sexto *corr. W* : trigesimo tertio *Cott.* (*teste W*) *SD* 1 :
trigesimo quarto *P Ar Camd*    *post* praefatus *add.* paganorum

*fatus* exercitus in duas se turmas divisit: una etenim
*turma* in Orientalem Franciam perrexit, et altera
5 ad Britanniam veniens, Cantiam adiit, civitatemque.
quae Hrofesceastre Saxonice dicitur, in orientali
ripa fluminis Medwæg sitam, obsedit. Ante huius
portam pagani castellum sibimet firmum subito
fabricaverunt; nec tamen illam civitatem expugnare
10 potuerunt, quia cives illi se viriliter defenderunt.
quousque Ælfred rex, cum magno exercitu adiu-
torium illis conferens, supervenit. Et tunc pagani,
relicta arce sua, et omnibus equis, quos de Francia
secum adduxerant, derelictis, maxima parte necnon
15 captivorum suorum *in arce* dimissa, adveniente
subito rege, ad naves suas confestim confugiunt, et
Saxones statim derelictos a paganis captivos et
equos diripiunt. Pagani itaque, magna necessitate
compulsi, eadem aestate iterum Franciam adierunt.

**67** Eodem anno Ælfred, Angulsaxonum rex, classem
suam de Cantia, plenam bellatoribus, in Orientales
Anglos dirigens, praedandi causa, transmisit. Cum-

---

*Flor* praefatus] paganorum *SN* 3 se *B Flor SN*: *om. Co*
*P Ar Camd W Pet* 4 alteri *Co* *post* altera *add.* vero turma
*Flor* 5 Britanniam] Angliam *SN* Cantiam *Co Flor SN*
*SD* 1 *SD* 2 : Cantium *rell.* 6 Rofesceastre *B* : Hrofesceaster
*Flor* : Hrofesceastra *SN* Saxonice *om. SN* 7 Medweg *Ar* :
Medweag *Flor* : Medouuege *SN* 8 sibimet *SN*: ibimet *P Ar
Camd W Pet* : ibimet *Co B* (*post* pagani): *om. Flor* 9 fabri-
caverant *B* nec ... potuerunt] sed tamen non potuerunt ex-
pugnare civitatem *SN* 11 Aelfredus *SN* 12 collaturus
*Flor* supervenit *post* rex (*v.* 11) *praebet SN* Et tunc pagani]
pagani vero *SN* 13 aequis *Co* 14 parte *om. Co* nec-
non] et *SN* 15 in] pro *Co* 16 confestim *om. B* et
Saxones] At Angli *SN* 17 diripiunt captivos et equos a
paganis derelictos *SN* 18 aequos *Co*
**67** *Exscripsit SD* 1 ; *eadem aliis verbis narrat SD* 2 2 Cantia

que ad ostium Sture fluminis advenissent, confestim
tredecim naves paganorum, paratae ad bellum, 5
obviaverunt eis, initoque navali proelio, hinc inde
acriter pugnantes, pagani omnes occisi et omnes
naves cum omni pecunia eorum captae sunt. Cumque inde victrix regia classis *dorm*iret, pagani, qui
[*ad*] Orientalium Anglorum regionem habitabant, 10
congregatis undecunque navibus, eidem regiae
classi in ostio *eiusdem* fluminis in mari obviaverunt, consertoque navali proelio, pagani victoriam
habuerunt.

Eodem quoque anno Carlomannum, Francorum 68
Occidentalium regem, aprorum venationem agen-
tem, singularis congressione horrendo dente dilacerans miserabili funere percussit. Cuius frater
Hlothuuicus superiori anno defunctus est ; qui et 5
ipse erat etiam Francorum rex : ipsi etenim ambo
filii Hlothuuici regis Francorum erant. Qui *etiam*

---

*Co B Flor SD* 1 : Cantio *rell.* Orientalem Angliam *B* 4 Sture
*Co Ar* : Sturae *rell.* venissent *Flor* 5 sexdecim *Flor Chron.*
*Anglo-Sax.* ad bellum paratae *B* 6 *post* hinc *add.* et *Flor*
9 dormiret *Cott.* (*teste W* ), *Co B P rell.* : rediret *Flor* : consertoque
navali proelio 〈*ex versu* 13〉 cum Anglis ubi dormiebant somno
inerti *SD* 1 pagani *om. B* qui *om. Cott.* 〈*teste W*〉 *Co* 10 Orientalium *scripsi* : Orientalem *omnes* Angolrum *Co* inhabitabant *Flor*
68 *Exscripp. SN SD* 2 1 eodem quoque anno *om. Flor*
Carlomannum *Cott.* (*teste W* ) : Carlmannum *Co* : Caorlmannum *B* :
Carolomannum *P rell.* : Karlomannum *Flor SN* 3 singularis
(*Gallice 'sanglier'*) *post* dente *Flor* : singulari *Co B P Ar Edd.*
*SN SD* 2 *post* dente *praebent* aper (*ex glossemate, quod alia*
*manus supra versum scripsit, in SN interpolatum*) *P* (*errore opera-*
*rum* arer), *Ar B Camd SD* 2 *W Pet* : defuisse *Cott.* testatur *W* post
dilacerans *add.* ferus *Flor* : *om. Co B P Ar Camd rell. SN SD* 2
5 Hlothuinicus *B* : Luduwicus *Flor* : Hloduicus *SN* superiori]
tertio *Flor* *post* anno *add.* ante *Flor* 7 Hlothuinci *B* :

*Hlothuuicus* supra memorato anno, quo eclipsis solis
facta est, defunctus est ; ipse quoque Hlothuuicus
10 filius Karoli Francorum regis erat, cuius filiam
Iuthittam Æthelwulfus, Occidentalium Saxonum
rex, ad reginam sibi paterna voluntate suscepit.

**69** Eodem quoque anno magnus paganorum exercitus de Germania in regionem Antiquorum Saxonum, *quae Saxonice dicitur Eald Seaxum*, supervenit. Contra quos, adunatis viribus, iidem Saxones
5 et Frisones bis in uno illo anno viriliter pugna-
vere. In quibus duobus bellis Christiani, divina
opitulante misericordia, victoriam habuere.

**70** Eodem quoque anno Carolus, Alamannorum rex,
Occidentalium Francorum regnum et omnia regna,
quae sunt inter mare Tyrrhenum *et* illum marinum
sinum, qui inter Antiquos Saxones et Gallos ad-
5 iacet, voluntario omnium consensu accepit, absque
Armoricano regno. Qui Karolus Hlothuuici regis

---

Luduwici *Flor* : Hloduuici *SN*      *post* regis *add*. Occidentalium
*SN*      8 Hlothuincus *Co B* : Hloduuicus *SN*      aeclipsis *Co*      9
Ludowicus *Flor* : Hloduuicus *SN*      10 Karoli *Co B Flor SN* :
Caroli *P rell*.      11 Iudditam *C* : Iudittham *B* : Iudittam *SN*
12 sibi] sub *SN* (sibi *tacitus emendavit Ed*.)      paterna] pari *Co B*
*SN* (*om. Ed*.)

69 *Exscripp. totum SD* 1, *partim SD* 2      1 eodem] praesenti *Flor*      3 quae *scripsi* : quod *Co B P Ar Camd W Pet*
Saxum *Co*      5 bis *scripsi auctoribus Flor et Chron. Anglo-Sax*.:
ibi *Co B* : ibidem *P Ar Camd W Pet*

70 *Exscripp. SN SD* 2      1 quoque] insuper *Flor* : *om. SN*
Carolus *Co* : Farlus *B P Ar Camd W Pet* : Karolus *Flor SN*
Alamannorum *Flor SN* : Alemannorum *SD* 2 : Almannorum *rell*.
3 'Tyrrhenum *per novam manum in MS. Cott*.' *W* : Terrenum *Co*
*B P Ar Camd W Pet Flor* : Tirrenum *SD* 2 : Trenum (*in* Tirrenum
*emendatum alia manu*) *SN* (Tyrrhenum *tacitus emend. Ed*)      maris
*SN*      6 *post* Armoricano *habent* (*ex glossemate* i. Britannia

filius fuit; ipse vero Hlothuuicus germanus Karoli
regis Francorum, patris Iuthittae, reginae prae-
dictae, *erat*: qui *etiam* duo germani fuerunt filii
Hlothuuici; Hlothuuic vero ille filius *Caroli* ⟨*anti-* 10
*qui, qui etiam fuit filius*⟩ Pipini.

Eodem anno *beatae memoriae* Marinus papa *uni-* 71
*versitatis viam migravit. Qui* Scholam Saxonum
in Roma morantium, pro amore et deprecatione
Ælfredi, Angulsaxonum regis, ab omni tributo et
telonio benigne liberavit. Qui etiam multa dona 5
praedicto regi illa vice transmisit: inter quae

---

Minori, *quod alia manus scripsit supra versum iu SN, interpolata*)
id est, Minori Britannia *B P Ar Camd W*: *seclusit Pet*: *om. Cott.*
(*teste W*) *Co supra* regno *scripsit* id est Lidwicii *alia manus in
N, ex* butan Lidwiccium *Chron. Anglo-Sax.* (= ' *absque Aremori-
canis*') *orta* (*quae male emendavit in* Lidwicus *similitudine viri
nominis* Lodouicus *deceptus, omissis* id est, *Ed.*) Karolus
*Co Flor SD* 2 *SN*: Farlus *B Ar P Camd rell. Edd. post*
Karolus *add.* filius *Co B P Ar Camd, quamquam* filius *versu se-
quenti retinent* Lodouici *Co B*: Luduwici *Flor*: Hlodwici *SN*:
Lodowici *SD* 2 7 Lodouicus *B*: Luduwicus *Flor*: Hloduuicus
*SN*: Lodowicus *SD* 2 Karoli *Co B Ar Flor SN*: Caroli *P rell.
Edd.* 8 *post* patris *praebent* videlicet (*ex SN interpolatum*) *P Ar
Camd W Pet*: *om. Co B Flor SD* 2 Iudittae *Co SN*: Iuditthae *B*:
Inditte *Ar* reginae *om. Co B Flor* 9 erat *om. Co B Flor*
etiam *om. Co B Flor* 10 Lodovici *Co B*: Loduuici *SN*:
Luduwici *Flor* Lodovic *Co B*: Luduwicus *Flor*: Hloduuicus *SN*
filius Caroli antiqui, qui etiam fuit filius Pipini *restitui secutus
Chron. Anglo-Sax.*: filius Pipini sive Caroli *Cott.* (*teste W*): filius
Pippini *Co Flor*: filius Karoli magni et antiqui atque sapientissimi,
qui etiam fuit filius Pipini *exhibent* (*ex SN interpolata*) *B P Camd
W*: *seclusit Pet*; *quae praebet Ar omissis* atque sapientissimi:
filius fuit Caroli magni illius famosi atque sapientissimi, qui fuit
filius Pipini regis *SD* 2

71 *Exscripp. SN SD* 1 *SD* 2 2 Scolam Anglorum *SN*
3 morantium] consistentem *SN* 4 Occidentalium Saxonum *SN*
*post* et *add.* talento *B P Ar Camd W Pet, quod errore inter
scribendum ex* telonio *sequenti ortum suspicor* 5 tolono *Co*:

dedit etiam non parvam illius sanctissimae *ac venerabilissimae* crucis partem, in qua Dominus noster Iesus Christus pro *universali* hominum

10 salute pependit.

**72**    Eodem quoque anno *ille* paganorum exercitus, *qui* in Oriental*ibus* Anglis habitavit, pacem, *quam* cum Ælfredo rege pepigerat, opprobriose fregit.

**73**   *Igitur, ut ad id, unde digressus sum, redeam, ne diuturna enavigatione portum optatae quietis omittere cogar, aliquantulum, quantum notitiae meae innotuerit, de vita et moribus et aequa conversatione,*

5 *atque, ex parte non modica, res gestas domini mei Ælfredi, Angulsaxonum regis, postquam praefatam ac venerabilem de Merciorum nobilium genere coniugem duxerit, Deo annuente, succinctim ac breviter, ne qua prolixitate narrandi nova quaeque fastidientium*

10 *animos offendam, ut promisi, expedire procurabo.*

**74**   *Cum ergo nuptias honorabiliter in Mercia factas, inter innumerabiles utriusque sexus populos, sollemniter celebraret, post diuturna die noctuque convivia, subito et immenso atque omnibus medicis incognito*

5 *confestim coram omni populo correptus est dolore. Incognitum enim erat omnibus, qui tunc aderant, et etiam hucusque cotidie cernentibus—quod, proh dolor! pessimum est, tantam diuturnitatem a vigesimo aetatis suae anno usque quadragesimum, et*

10 *eo amplius, annum per tanta annorum curricula*

---

telone *Flor SD* 2    5–6 qui . . . inter quae *om. B*    7 dedit *om. SN*    etiam] ei *Flor*    ac venerabilissimae *om. SN*
   **73** 2 navigatione *B*    quetis *Co*    10 promissi *C*
   **74** 2 sollemniter *Co* : solemniter *rell.*    7 et *om. B*    etetim *pro* et etiam *Co*    cotidie *Co* : quotidie *rell.*    *pro in* proh

*incessanter protelasse—unde talis dolor oriebatur.
Multi namque favore ⟨sic⟩ et fascinatione circum-
stantis populi hoc factum esse autumabant; alii
diaboli quadam invidia, qui semper bonis invidus
existat; alii inusitato quodam genere febris; alii* 15
*ficum existimabant, quod genus infestissimi doloris
etiam ab infantia habuit.* Sed quodam tempore,
divino nutu, *antea,* cum Cornubiam venandi causa
adiret, et ad quandam ecclesiam orandi causa
divertisset, in qua Sanctus Gueriir requiescit [*et nunc* 20
etiam Sanctus Niot ibidem pausat], *suatim utens
—erat enim sedulus sanctorum locorum visitator
etiam ab infantia, orandi et elecmosynam dandi
gratia—*diu in oratione tacita prostratus, *ita* Domini
misericordiam deprecabatur, quatenus *omnipotens* 25
*Deus* pro sua immensa clementia stimulos praesentis et infestantis infirmitatis aliqua qualicunque
leviori infirmitate mutaret, ea tamen condicione,
ut corporaliter exterius illa infirmitas non appareret, ne inutilis et despectus esset. *Timebat enim* 30
*lepram aut caecitatem, vel aliquem talem dolorem,
qui homines tam cito et inutiles et despectos suo*

---

*mutatum Co* 14 diabolica *Cott. (teste W) Co B P Ar Camd*
15 quo- *ad finem versus scriptum,* dam *ad initium sequentis negli-
genter omisso Co* 16 existimabant *B* : existimant *Co P Ar Camd
W Pet* 17 *ante* Sed *inseruit* cum in primaevo (*v.* 41) . . .
desperabat (*v.* 59) *Flor ann.* 871 20 Gueijr *B* : Gueryr *Camd
W Pet* 20–21 et . . . pausat *seclusi* 21 etiam] etiā *Co, quod
pro* etenim *compendio scripto perperam intellexit Pet* : etiam *post*
sanctum *exhibet Flor* Niot *Cott. (teste W) Co Flor* : Niotus *B* :
Neotus *rell.* suatim utens *ex Co reposui* : sublevatus est *B P Ar
Camd W Pet* 24 Dei *Flor* 25 quatinus *Co* 26 inmensa
*Co* 28 ea] et *Co* 29 illa] ea *B* 30 despectus] deprecatus
*Ar* enim *Co B* : *om. rell.* 32 *prius* et *om. B* suos *Co*

*adventu efficiunt.* Oratione autem finita, coeptum
iter arripuit, et non multo post tempore, ut in
35 oratione deprecatus fuerat, se ab illo dolore medi-
catum esse divinitus sensit, ita ut funditus eradicaretur, *quamvis et hunc dolorem in primaevo iuven-*
*tutis suae flore devota oratione et frequenti Deo*
*supplicatione pius supplex nactus fuerat. Nam, ut*
40 *de benevola mentis suae devotione Deo succinctim ac*
*breviter, quamvis praeposterato ordine, loquar,* cum
in primaevo iuventutis suae flore, *antequam pro-*
*priam coniugem duceret,* mentem suam *propriam* in
Dei mandatis stabilire vellet, et se a carnali desi-
45 derio abstinere non posse cerneret, offensam Dei
incurrere, si aliquid contrarium voluntati illius
perageret ⟨*metuens*⟩, saepissime, galli cantu et matu-
tinis horis clam consurgens, ecclesias et reliquias
sanctorum orandi causa visitabat; ibique diu pro-
50 stratus orabat, quo Deus Omnipotens, propter suam
misericordiam, mentem illius amore suae servitutis
*multo robustius* per aliquam infirmitatem, quam
posset sustinere, non tamen quo eum indignum et
inutilem in mundanis rebus faceret, *ad se penitus*
55 *convertens* corroboraret. Cumque hoc saepius
magna mentis devotione ageret, post aliquantulum
intervallum *praefatum* fici dolorem Dei munere
incurrit, in quo, diu et aegre per multos annos
*la*borans, se, etiam de vita, desperabat, *quousque,*

---

36 divinitus *post* dolore *praebet B*      *Ab* eradicaretur *pergit Flor ad*
Sed (*v.* 60)      41 cum ... desperabat (*v.* 59) *ante* Sed (*v.* 17)
*posuit Flor*      43 duceret] haberet *B Flor*      44 *post* stabilire
*add.* ut *Co*      45 *post* cerneret *add.* ne *Flor*      46 incurreret
*Flor*      47 metuens *om. Cott.* (*teste W*) *Co*      59 laborans

*oratione facta, a se penitus eum amovit.*   Sed, proh 60
dolor!  eo amoto, alius infestior in nuptiis, *ut
diximus,* eum arripuit, qui a vigesimo aetatis suae
anno usque ad quadragesimum quintum eum die
noctuque incessabiliter fatigavit ; *sed, si aliquando
Dei misericordia unius diei aut noctis vel etiam* 65
*unius horae intervallo illa infirmitas seposita fuerat,
timor tamen ac tremor illius execrabilis doloris
unquam eum non deserit, sed quasi inutilem eum,
ut ei videtur, in divinis et humanis rebus propemodum effecit.*                                    70

Nati sunt ergo ei filii et filiae de supradicta 75
coniuge sua [*scilicet*] Æthelflæd primogenita, post
quam Eadwerd, deinde Æthelgeofu, postea Ælfthryth, deinde Æthelweard natus est, *exceptis his,
qui in infantia morte praeveniente praeoccupati* 5
*sunt;* † *cuius numerus est* † Æthelflæd, adveniente

---

*Cott. (teste W ) B P Ar Camd*: roborans *Co Flor W Pet*      60
pro *in* proh *mutatum Co*      61 eo] et *Co*      63 *post* quintum
*add. Flor* et eo amplius (*cf. v.* 10 *et cap.* 91 *v.* 4)      eum *om.*
*Co*: illum *Flor*      68 eum *om. B*

   **75** *Exscripp. SD* 1 *partim, paululum SD* 2 (*ann.* 871)      2 *post*
sua *add.* Ealhswytha *Flor*: Elſswitha *SD* 2      scilicet *P Ar Camd
W Pet*: sed *Co*: videlicet *B*      Æthelflæd *scripsi*: Æthelfled *Co B
Ar*: Æthelflœd *P rell. Edd.*: Ægelflæd *Flor*      post quam]
postea *B*      3 Eadward *Flor*      Ethelgeouu *Co*: Ethelgouu *B* :
Æthelgeovu *Flor*      Elfthryght *B*: Ælfthrith *Ar*      4 Ethel-
werd *B*: Æthelward *Flor*      6 cuius numerus est *Co, locus non-
dum sanatus* : de quorum numero *B* : de quorum numero est *P Ar
Camd W Pet. Obadiah Walker, apud Ioannem Spelman, in* ' *Vita
Ælfredi,' Oxonii,* 1678, *pag.* 173, *not. b, lacunam, quam post* est
*statuit, coniecit supplendam esse cum* Edmundum, *quem Alfredi
filium natu maximum finxit Thomas Rudborne, auctor mendax
' Historiae Maioris Wintoniensis,' lib. iii. cap.* 6 (*apud* Wharton,
' *Anglia Sacra,' tom.* i. *pag.* 207). *Quem secuti sunt Tyrrell,
' History of England,'* 1700, *tom.* i. *pag.* 311, *et W.    Legendum esse*

matrimonii tempore, Eadredo, Merciorum comiti,
matrimonio copulata est; Æthelgeofu *quoque*
monasticae vitae regulis, devota Deo virginitate,
10 subiuncta et consecrata, divinum subiit servitium;
Æthelweard, omnibus iunior, *ludis* literariae
disciplinae, divino consilio et admirabili regis
providentia, *cum* omnibus pene totius regionis
nobilibus *infantibus* et etiam multis ignobilibus,
15 sub diligenti magistrorum cura traditus est. *In
qua schola utriusque linguae libri, Latinae scilicet
et Saxonicae, assidue legebantur, scriptioni quoque
vacabant, ita,* ut antequam aptas humanis artibus
vires haberent, *venatoriae scilicet et ceteris artibus,*
20 *quae nobilibus conveniunt,* in liberalibus artibus *stu-
diosi et ingeniosi* viderentur. Eadwerd et Ælfthryth
semper in curto regio nutriti *cum magna nutritorum
et nutricum diligentia, immo cum magno omnium
amore, et ad omnes indigenas et alienigenas humili-*
25 *tate, affabilitate et etiam lenitate, et cum magna patris
subiectione huc usque perseverant. Nec etiam illi* sine

---

de quorum numero Æthelflæd *coniecit Pet. Expectares potius
numerum eorum,* ' *qui in infantia* ' *mortui sunt*     Æthelflæd
*scripsi*: Æthelfled *Co*: Ethelfled *B*: Æthelfled *Ar*: Æthelflœd *P
rell. Edd.*     7 Eadredo *Co B P Ar Camd W Pet SD* 1 : Ætheredo
*Flor*     8 Ethelgeofu *B*     9 Deo *om. Ar*     virginitate *om. B*     10
coniuncta *Co B*     servitium subiit *B*     11 Ethelwerd *B* : Æthelward *Flor*     ludis *Cott.* (*teste W*) *SD* 1 : ludi *Co B Ar P Camd*
litterariae *Co*     12 regis] patris *B*     13 cum omnibus] et
omnes *Flor*     14 nobiles *Flor*     multis *om. Co B* : multi
ignobiles *Flor*     15 traditi sunt *Flor*     16 scholae *B*
Latine *P*     17 legebantur assidue *B*     21 viderentur] in-
struerentur *Flor*     Eadward *Flor*     Elfthright *B* : Ælfthrith *Ar*
22 curia regis *SD* 1     24 et alienigenas *om. Co B*     humilitate *Co B* : humiliata *Ar P rell. Edd.*     25 affabilitate
*om. Co B*     levitate *B*     26 nec etiam illi] non *Flor*

liberali disciplina inter cetera praesentis vitae studia,
*quae nobilibus conveniunt, otiose et incuriose ⟨vivere⟩*
*permittuntur, nam et* psalmos et Saxonicos libros
et maxime Saxonica carmina studiose didicere, *et* 30
*frequentissime libris utuntur.*

Interea tamen rex, inter bella et praesentis vitae 76
frequentia impedimenta, necnon paganorum infesta-
tiones et cotidianas corporis infirmitates, *et* regni
gubernacula regere, *et* omnem venandi artem agere,
aurifices et artifices suos omnes *et* falconarios *et* 5
accipitrarios canicularios quoque docere, *et* aedificia
supra omnem antecessorum suorum consuetudinem
venerabiliora et pretiosiora nova sua machinatione
facere, *et* Saxonicos libros recitare, et maxime carmina Saxonica memoriter discere, aliis imperare, 10
*et* solus assidue pro viribus *studiosissime* non desinebat. *Divina quoque ministeria* et missam *scilicet*
cotidie audire, psalmos quosdam et orationes *et*
horas diurnas et nocturnas celebrare, et ecclesias
nocturno tempore, *ut diximus*, orandi causa clam a 15
suis adire solebat et frequentabat. Eleemosynarum
quoque *studio et largitati indigenis et advenis*
*omnium gentium, ac maxima et incomparabili*
*contra omnes homines* affabilitate atque iocundi-

---

28 vivere *addidi*     30 studiose *om. Co*

76 1 Interea tamen] At *Flor*     *post* rex *add.* Ælfredus *Flor*
*post* et *add.* frequentissima *B omisso* frequentia *v.* 2     3 cotidianas *Co* : quotidianas *rell.*     5 falconarios *Co Flor* : fulconarios
*Cott. (teste W) P Camd Ar* : fulconarinarios *B*     8 precisiora
*Camd (errore, ut videtur, operarum)*     12 et *om. B*     13 cotidie
*Co* : quotidie *rell.*     et] ac *B*     14 divinas *Camd (errore, ut*
*videtur, operarum)*     15 a *om. Co*     16 elemosynarum *Co*
17 *post* quoque *add.* dator largissimus *Flor*     19 contra]
erga *B*     affabilitate atque iocunditate] omnium affabilissimus et

20 tate, *et* ignotarum rerum investigationi solerter *se*
† *iungebat.* Franci autem multi, Frisones, Galli,
pagani, Britones, et Scotti, Armorici sponte se suo
dominio subdiderant, nobiles scilicet et ignobiles ;
quos omnes, sicut suam propriam gentem, secundum
25 suam dignitatem regebat, diligebat, honorabat,
pecunia et potestate ditabat. *Divinam quoque*
*scripturam a recitantibus indigenis, aut etiam, si casu*
*quodam aliunde adveniret, cum alienigenis pariter*
*preces audire sedulus et sollicitus solebat.* Episcopos
30 quoque suos et omnem ecclesiasticum ordinem,
comites ac nobiles suos, ministeriales etiam et
omnes familiares admirabili amore diligebat. Filios
quoque eorum, qui in regali familia nutriebantur,
non minus propriis diligens, omnibus bonis moribus
35 instituere et literis imbuere solus die noctuque inter
cetera non desinebat. *Sed quasi nullam in his omni-*
*bus consolationem haberet, et nullam aliam intrinsecus*
*et extrinsecus perturbationem pateretur, ita tamen*
*cotidiana et nocturna anxius tristitia ad Dominum*
40 *et ad omnes, qui sibi familiari dilectione adsciti*
*forent, querelaretur et assiduo gemebat suspirio, eo*
*quod Deus Omnipotens eum expertem divinae sapien-*
*tiae et liberalium artium fecisset: in hoc pium et*

---

iucundissimus *Flor*  20 investigator *Flor*  solertissimus
*Flor*  de se nugebat *Co B*  22 Brittones *Co*  Scotti
*Co* : Scoti *rell.*  26 *post* potestate *add.* quoque *B*  27 a
*om. B*  28 cum *om. Co*  pariter] per inter *Co*  29 scedulus
*Co*  sollicitus *Co B* : solicitus *rell.*  30 aeeclesiasticum *Co*
35 litteris *Co*  nocteque *Co*  37 et] aut *B*  38 pateretur
perturbationem *B*  39 cotidiana *Co* : quotidiana *rell.*  Deum
*Co B*  40 dilectioni *Co B*  41 querelaretur *Co B Ar P* :
querelabatur *correx. Camd tacitus, quod recc. W Pet*  assidue *Co B*
42 Deus . . . expertem *post* artium *posuit B*  43 pium *om. B*

*opinatissimum atque opulentissimum Salomonem*
*Hebraeorum regem aequiparans, qui primitus, de-* 45
*specta omni praesenti gloria et divitiis, sapientiam a*
*Deo deposcit, et etiam utramque invenit, sapientiam*
*scilicet et praesentem gloriam, sicut scriptum est,*
*'Quaerite ergo primum regnum Dei et iustitiam*
*eius, et haec omnia praestabuntur vobis* ᵃ.' *Sed* 50
*Deus, Qui est semper inspector internarum mentium,*
*meditationum et omnium bonarum voluntatum insti-*
*gator, necnon etiam, ut habeantur bona desiderata,*
*largissimus administrator, neque enim unquam ali-*
*quem bene velle instigaret, nisi et hoc, quod bene et* 55
*iuste quisque habere desiderat, largiter administraret,*
*instigavit mentem eius interius, non extrinsecus:*
*sicut scriptum est, 'Audiam, quid loquatur in me*
*dominus Deus* ᵇ.' *Coadiutores bonae meditationis*
*suae, qui eum in desiderata sapientia adiuvare* 60
*possent, quo ad concupita perveniret, quandocunque*
*posset, acquireret; qui subinde—velut apis pruden-*
*tissima, quae primo mane caris e cellulis consurgens*
*aestivo tempore, per incerta aeris itinera cursum*
*veloci volatu dirigens, super multiplices ac diversos* 65
*herbarum, holerum, fruticum flosculos descendit, pro-*
*batque quid maxime placuerit atque domum reportat*
*—mentis oculos longum dirigit, quaerens extrinsecus*

---

ᵃ Matt. vi. 33 (Versio Antiqua).     ᵇ Ps. lxxxv. 8.

---

44 oppulent- *Co*     45 Ebreorum *Co*     47 depossit *Co*     49
primum *om. Co*     53 etiam *om. B*     54 administer *B*     aliquem unquam *B*     55 *primum* et *om. B*     57 incitavit *B*
59 Deus] meus *B Ar*     quo adiutores *Co B*     62 apis *scripsi*:
avis *Co B P Ar Camd W Pet*     63 caris *Co* : charis *rell.*     66
holerum *Co P Ar Camd* : olerum *B W Pet*     *post* holerum *add.*
et *B*     futicum *Co*     68 longe *B*

*quod intrinsecus non habebat, id est in proprio*
70 *regno suo.*

77 *At tunc Deus quaedam solatia regiae benevolentiae,*
*tam benevolam et iustissimam querelam illius diutius*
*non ferens, veluti quaedam luminaria, transmisit*
Werfrithum, *scilicet* Wigernensis ecclesiae epi-
5 scopum, in divina *scilicet* scriptura *bene* eruditum,
qui, imperio regis, libros Dialogorum Gregorii
papae *et Petri sui discipuli* de Latinitate primus
in Saxonicam linguam, *aliquando sensum ex sensu*
*ponens,* elucabratim et elegantissime interpretatus
10 est ; deinde Plegmundum, Mercium genere, Doro-
bernensis ecclesiae archiepiscopum, venerabilem
scilicet virum, sapientia praeditum ; Æthelstan
quoque et Werwulfum; sacerdotes *et capellanos,*
Mercios genere, eruditos. *Quos quatuor Ælfred*
15 rex de Mercia ad se advocaverat, et multis hono-
ribus et potestatibus extulit *in regno Occidentalium*
*Saxonum, exceptis his, quae Plegmundus archiepi-*
*scopus et Werfrithus episcopus in Mercia habebant.*
Quorum omnium doctrina et sapientia regis indesi-

---

69 haberet *B*

77 *Exscripp. Flor (ann.* 872), *paululum SD* 1    2 beni-
volam *Co*    4 Wuerfrithum *Co P* : Puerfrithum *Ar* (P = p,
*littera Anglo-Sax. qua* w *notabatur*) : Werfrithus *Flor*    Wigorn-
ensis *Ar*    aecclesiae *Co*    5 divinis *Flor*    scripturis *Flor*
bene *om. B*    eruditum] doctissimus *Flor*    6 libros *om. B*
9 interpretatus est] transtulit *Flor*    10 Deinde] Hunc eundem
et processu temporis *Flor*    Doroburnensis *B*    11 archiepiscopus *Ar*    12 tethelstun *Co* : Æthelwulfum *B* (*perperam*
Ethelwulphum *Pet*)    13 sarerdotes *Ar*    14 eruditos] quam
optime literis instructos *Flor*    15 vocavit *Flor*    17 Plegi-
mundus *Co*    18 Werfrythus *B*    19 Quorum ... implebatur

nenter desiderium crescebat et implebatur. *Nam* 20
*die noctuque, quandocunque aliquam licentiam ha-*
*beret, libros ante se recitare talibus imperabat—non*
*enim unquam sine aliquo eorum se esse pateretur—*
*quapropter pene* omnium librorum notitiam habebat,
*quamvis per se ipsum aliquid adhuc de libris intelligerc* 25
*non posset. Non enim adhuc aliquid legere inceperat.*

*Sed, cum adhuc nec in hoc quoque regalis avaṛitia,* **78**
*sed tamen laudabilis, grata esset,* legatos ultra mare
ad Galliam *magistros acquirere* direxit, indeque
advocavit Grimbaldum, sacerdotem et monachum,
venerabilem *videlicet* virum, cantatorem optimum, 5
*et omni modo* ecclesiasticis disciplinis et in divina
scriptura eruditissimum, et omnibus bonis moribus
ornatum ; Iohannem quoque, aeque presbyterum et
monachum, acerrimi ingenii virum, *et in omnibus*
*disciplinis literatoriae artis eruditissimum, et in* 10
*multis aliis artibus artificiosum. Quorum doctrina*
*regis ingenium multum dilatatum est, et eos magna*
*potestate ditavit et honoravit.*

*His temporibus ego quoque a rege advocatus* de **79**
occiduis et ultimis Britanniae finibus *ad Saxoniam*
*adveni, cumque per multa terrarum spatia illum*

---

ad finem capitis sequentis transtulit *Flor*    21 quandocunque . . .
talibus *om. Ar*    23 unquam *om. B*    24 omnium pene *B*
pene] ut in brevi *Flor*    haberet *Flor*    25 *post* libris *praeb*
non *Co, sed deletum*    26 non *om. Co*

78 2 tamen *om. B*    *post* legatos *add.* etiam *Flor*    3 magistros]
legatos *B*    direxit *Cott.* (*teste W*) *Co B W Pet* : dixerit *P Ar*
*Camd*    4 advocarit *Camd* (*errore forsitan operarum*) *quod recepp.*
*W Pet*    *post* advocavit *add.* Sanctum *Flor*    8 *post* Iohannem *add.*
Erigena *Co*    aeque *om. B.*    9 *post* virum *add.* Asserum etiam,
*deinde* (*ex cap.* 79, *vv.* 1, 55) de occiduis et ultimis Britanniae
finibus e monasterio Sancti Dewi *Flor*

*adire proposueram, usque ad regionem Dexteralium*
5 *Saxonum, quae Saxonice Suth-Seaxum appellatur,*
*ductoribus eiusdem gentis comitantibus, perveni.*
*Ibique illum in villa regia, quae dicitur Dene,*
*primitus vidi. Cumque ab eo benigne susceptus*
*fuissem, inter cetera sententiarum nostrarum famina,*
10 *me obnixe rogabat, ut devoverem me suo servitio et*
*familiaris ei essem, et omnia, quae in sinistrali et*
*occidentali Sabrinae parte habebam, pro eo relin-*
*querem: quae etiam maiori mihi remuneratione*
*reddere pollicebatur. Quod et faceret. Respondi*
15 *ego 'Me talia incaute et temerarie promittere non*
*posse. Iniustum enim mihi videbatur, illa tam*
*sancta loca, in quibus nutritus et doctus ac coronatus*
*fueram, atque ad ultimum ordinatus, pro aliquo*
*terreno honore et potestate derelinquere, nisi coactus*
20 *et compulsus.' Ad quod ille ait: 'Si nec tibi hoc*
*suppetat subire, saltem dimidiam partem servitii*
*tui mihi accommoda, ita ut per sex menses mecum*
*fueris et tantundem in Britannia.' Ad quod ego*
*taliter respondi 'Nec hoc suaviter et temerarie*
25 *sine consilio meorum posse promittere.' At vero,*
*cum illum meum servitium, sed nesciebam quare,*
*desiderare cognoscerem, promisi, me iterum ad eum*
*post sex menses, sospite vita, reversurum, cum tali*
*responso, quod mihi et meis utile ac sibi placabile*
30 *esset. Cumque hoc sibi responsum videretur proba-*

---

**79** 4 audire *B*     13 quae *scripsi*: quod *omnes*     15 temerarie
et incaute *B*     16 videtur *B*     17 et] ac *B*     ac] et *B*     19
*post* derelinquere *add.* volui *Co*     nisi *om. Co*     *post* nisi *add.* aut
*B*     *post* coactus *add.* aut expulsus *Co B*     20 et compulsus *om. Co*
21 saltim *Co*     23 Brittania *Co*     26 sed] at *B*     30 sibi hoc *Co Ar*

*bile, dato revertendi pignore statuto tempore, quarto
die ab eo equitantes ad patriam remeavimus. Sed,
cum ab eo discesseramus, in Wintonia civitate febris
infesta me arripuit; in qua sedule per duodecim
menses et una hebdomada die noctuque sine aliqua* 35
*vitae spe laboravi. Cumque statuto tempore ad cum,
sicut promiseràm, non pervenissem, transmisit ad
me indiculos, qui me ad eum equitare festinarent, et
causam remorationis perquirerent. Sed, cum equitare
ad eum non possem, alium transmisi ad eum in-* 40
*diculum, qui remorationis meae causam illi pate-
faceret et, si de illa infirmitate resipiscere possem,
me velle implere quae promiseram, renunciaret.
Discedente igitur infirmitate, ex consilio et licentia
nostrorum omnium, pro utilitate illius sancti loci et* 45
*omnium in eo habitantium, regi, ut promiseram, eius
servitio me devovi ea condicione, ut per sex menses
omni anno cum eo commanerem, aut, si simul possem,
sex menses protelare, aut etiam per vices, ut tribus
mensibus in Britannia, ut  tribus  in  Saxonia* 50
*commanerem, et illa adiuvaretur per* † *rudimenta
Sancti Degui in omni causa, tamen pro viribus.
Sperabant enim  nostri, minores  tribulationes et
iniurias ex parte Hemeid regis sustinere,—qui saepe
depraedabatur  illud* monasterium  et  parochiam 55

---

35 unam hebdomadam *B*      38 indiculos *corr. W* : indiluculos *Cott.*
(*teste W*) *P Ar Camd* : in diluculos *Co* : in diluculo *B*      40 indiculum *corr. W* : indiluculum *Cott.* (*teste W*) *Ar P Camd* : in
diluculum *Co* : in diluculo *B*      44 Descendente *Co*      46 in-
habitantium *B*      regi *om. B* : regem *Co*      *post* promiseram *add.*
in *Co B*      50 Brittania *Co*      Britannia . . . Saxonia *ordine
inverso B*      ut *Cott.* (*teste W*) *Co rell.* : *om. B* : et *coniecit W*
52 Degui] digni *B*

Sancti Degui, *aliquando expulsione illorum antis-*
*titum, qui in eo praeessent, sicut et Nobis archi-*
*episcopum, propinquum meum, et me expulit aliquando*
*sub ipsis,—si ego ad notitiam et amicitiam illius regis*
60 *qualicunque pacto pervenirem.*

80    *Illo enim tempore et multo ante omnes regiones*
*dexteralis Britanniae partis ad Ælfred regem per-*
*tinebant et adhuc pertinent: Hemeid scilicet, cum*
*omnibus habitatoribus Demeticae regionis, sex filiorum*
5 *Rotri vi compulsus, regali se subdiderat imperio;*
*Houil quoque filius Ris, rex Gleguising, et Brochmail*
*atque Fernmail filii Mouric, reges Guent, vi et tyran-*
*nide Eadred, comitis, et Merciorum compulsi, suapte*
*eundem expetivere regem, ut dominium et defen-*
10 *sionem ab eo pro inimicis suis haberent. Helised*
*quoque filius Teudubr, rex Brecheniauc, eorundem*
*filiorum Rotri vi coactus, dominium regis praefati*
*suapte requisivit. Anaraut quoque filius Rotri, cum*
*suis fratribus, ad postremum amicitiam Northan-*
15 *hymbrorum deserens, de qua nullum bonum nisi*

---

56 Digni *B* : Dewi *Flor* (*v. c.* 78, 9)    57 et Nobis *scripsi* : et
nobis *Co* : ex nobis *Cott.* (*teste W*) *B Ar P Camd* : et Novis *emend.*
*Galeus, Praef. ad XV Scriptores, quae rec. W* : ex *ortum e com-*
*pendio pro* et *male lecto coniecit Pet, equidem natum ex emendatione*
*P in Cott. scripta suspicor*    59 ad *om. Co*
  80 2 dexteriales *Co*    Brittaniae *Co*    4 *post* regionis *add.*
et *Cott.* (*teste W*) *Co B Ar P Camd*    5 Rotricum pulsus *per-*
*peram pro* Rotri ⟨vi⟩ compulsus *Co*  6 Hovel *Co B*    Gleguisinge
*Co*    7 Fernmail *Co Ar P* : Fernemail *B* : Fernail *Camd W Pet,*
*quod ex errore operarum editionis Camd ortum censeo*    regis *B*
8 Eudred *Co* : Endred *B*    11 Teudubr *Cott.* (*teste W*) *Co* :
Teudyr *B P rell. Edd.* : Teudir *Ar*    Brecheniauc *scripsi* : Breche-
niane *Cott.* (*teste W*) : Bracheinauc *Co* : Brachoniae *B* : Brechoniae
*P Ar Camd W Pet*    12 Rotrivi *Co*    vi] sextus *B*    praefati
regis *B*    13 requirunt *Ar*    14 Northamhymbrorum *B*

*damnum habuerat, amicitiam regis studiose requirens*
*ad praesentiam illius advenit, cumque a rege hono-*
*rifice receptus esset, et ad manum episcopi in filium*
*confirmationis acceptus, maximisque donis ditatus,*
*se regis dominio cum omnibus suis eadem condicione* 20
*subdidit, ut in omnibus regiae voluntati sic oboediens*
*esset, sicut Æthered cum Merciis.*

*Nec in vanum illi omnes regis amicitiam acquisi-* 81
*verunt. Nam, qui desideraverunt potestatem ter-*
*renam augere, invenerunt; qui pecuniam, pecuniam;*
*qui familiaritatem, familiaritatem; qui utramque,*
*utramque. Omnes autem habuerunt amorem et* 5
*tutelam ac defensionem ab omni parte, qua rex*
*seipsum cum suis omnibus defendere potuit. Cum*
*igitur ad eum advenissem in villa regia, quae dicitur*
*Leonaford, honorabiliter ab eo susceptus sum, et cum*
*eo illa vice octo mensibus in curto mansi, in quibus* 10
*recitavi illi libros quoscunque ille vellet, et quos ad*
*manum haberemus. Nam haec est propria et usita-*
*tissima illius consuetudo die noctuque, inter omnia*
*alia mentis et corporis impedimenta, aut per se ipsum*
*libros recitare, aut aliis recitantibus audire. Cumque* 15
*ab eo frequenter licentiam revertendi quaererem et*
*nullo modo impetrare possem, tandem cum et licentiam*
*omnino exposcere statuissem, diluculo vigiliae Natalis*
*Domini advocatus ad eum, tradidit mihi duas epi-*
*stolas, in quibus erat multiplex supputatio omnium* 20

---

17 pervenit *B*      19 didatus *Co*      20 se *B*: *om. rell.*
22 Œthelred *Co*: Ethelred *B*      Mercis *B*
81 1 reges *B*      adquiverunt *Co*      3 pecunia *Camd*      4 qui
*om. Ar*      5 habuerunt amorem *ordine inverso B*: habuer
tamorem *P errore operarum*: habuerunt *om. Co*      7 cum suis
seipsum cum omnibus suis *B*      14 alia] illa *Ar*      18 statuissem]

*rerum, quae erant in duobus monasteriis, quae
Saxonice cognominantur Cungresbyri et Banuwille,
et mihi eodem die tradidit illa duo monasteria cum
omnibus, quae in eis erant, et sericum pallium valde*
25 *pretiosum et onus viri fortis de incenso, adiciens his
verbis ' non ideo dedisse parva illa, quod sequenti
tempore nollet dare maiora.' Nam sequentis temporis
successu ex improviso dedit mihi Exanceastre, cum
omni parochia, quae ad se pertinebat, in Saxonia et*
30 *in Cornubia, exceptis cotidianis donis innumerabilibus in omni genere terrestri divitiae, quae hoc in
loco percensere longum est, ne fastidium legentibus
procreent. Sed nullus existimet, pro vana aliqua
gloria aut adulatione aut maioris honoris quaerendi*
35 *gratia, me talia hoc in loco dona commemorasse :
quod coram Deo nec ideo fecisse testor, sed ut nescientibus propalarem, quam profusus in largitate
ille sit. Tunc confestim dedit mihi licentiam equi-
tandi ad illa duo monasteria omnibus bonis referta,*
40 *et inde ad propria revertendi.*

**82** *Anno Dominicae Incarnationis* DCCCLXXXVI, *nativitatis autem Ælfredi trigesimo octavo,* saepe
memoratus exercitus *regionem fugiens* iterum *et* in

---

divisissem *Co* 21 duabus *Co* monasteriis duobus *B* 22
Cungresbyri *Co*: Amgresbyri *rell., quod ex* Cun- *pro* Am- *in Co
neglegenter lecto ortum esse censeo* Banuwylle *Co* 23 duo
illa *B* 25 adijciens *Co B* 26 ideo non *B* 30 cotidianis *Co*: quotidianis *rell.* 31 divitiae *Cott.* (*teste W*) *Co*:
copiae *B Ar P cett. Edd.* 32 recensere *B* 33 aliqua vana *Co*
aliqua *om. B* 34 adolatione *Co* 37 protelarem *B*
 82 *Exscripp. partim SD* 1 *SD* 2 2 octavo *corr. W*: quinto
*Cott.* (*teste W*) *Co B Ar P Camd SD* 1 3 *post* exercitus *add.*
paganorum, Orientali Francia derelicta *Flor post* regionem *exci-
disse videntur* Orientalium Francorum fugit iterumque *Co* et

Occidentalium Francorum regionem venit, *naves suas intrans* in flumen, quod Signe dicitur, *sursum* 5 contra longe navigans Parisiam civitatem adiit, et ibi hiemavit, *et castra metatus est in utraque parte fluminis prope ad pontem, ut transitum pontis civibus prohiberet—quia illa civitas in medio fluminis sita est in insula parva*—obseditque *illam* civitatem 10 anno illo integro. Sed, Deo misericorditer favente *et civibus viriliter se defendentibus*, munitionem irrumpere non potuit.

Eodem anno Ælfred, Angulsaxonum rex, post **83** incendia urbium stragesque populorum, Lundoniam civitatem honorifice restauravit et habitabilem fecit ; quam [*genero suo*] Ætheredo, Merciorum comiti, commendavit servandam. Ad quem regem omnes 5 Angli et Saxones, qui prius ubique dispersi fuerant aut cum paganis sub captivitate erant, voluntarie converterunt, et suo dominio se subdiderunt.

---

*om. Co*    5 intrans *scripsi secutus Flor* (*cf. cap.* 84, *vv.* 13, 14): intus *Cott.* (*teste W*) *Co* (*subest fortasse error pro* intrans, *quod compendio scriptum* (intᵃns) *facile cum* intus *confundi potest*): dirigens *B Ar P Camd W Pet* in ostium fluminis *Flor* Signe] Sequana *Flor* post dicitur *add.* intrans *Flor* 6 Parisium *SD* 1 7 in utraque parte *scripsi*: utraquam partem *Co*: Intra quam partem *rell.* 10 obseditque *Co*: obsedit *rell.* illam *om. Co*: quam *Flor*

**83** *Exscripp. SN SD* 1 *SD* 2 1 Ælfredus *B*: Alfredus *SN* Anglorum *SD* 1: Occidentalium Saxonum *SN*: Anglo- *Flor* 2 Lundoniam *Flor SN*: Londoniam *rell.* 4 genero suo *om. Co, quae idcirco seclusi; in B P Ar Camd W Pet interpolata* (*ex SN*) *arbitror. De Cott. nihil adnotat W* Adherędo *SN* 6 *post* Angli *add.* Merci, Cantuarii, Australes et Occidentales *SN* ibique *Co* 7 conpaganis *Co* sub] sine *Cott.* (*teste W*) *Co Flor SD* 2 8 converterunt] venerunt *Flor*: reverterunt *SN*

**83 b** [Eodem anno exorta est pessima ac teterrima Oxoniae discordia
inter Grymboldum doctissimosque illos viros, quos secum illuc
adduxit, et veteres illos scholasticos, quos ibidem invenisset, qui eius
adventu leges, modos, ac praelegendi formulas ab eodem Grymboldo
5 institutas omni ex parte amplecti recusabant. Per tres annos haud
magna fuerat inter eos dissensio, occultum tamen fuit odium, quod
summa cum atrocitate postea erupit, ipsa erat luce clarius. Quod
ut sedaret rex ille invictissimus Ælfredus, de dissidio eo nuntio et
querimonia Grymboldi certior factus, Oxoniam se contulit, ut finem
10 modumque huic controversiae imponeret, qui et ipse summos labores
hausit, causas et querelas utrinque illatas audiendo. Caput autem
huius contentionis in hoc erat positum : veteres illi scholastici con-
tendebant, antequam Grymboldus Oxoniam devenisset, literas illic
passim floruisse, etiamsi scholares tunc temporis numero erant
15 pauciores quam priscis temporibus, plerisque nimirum saevitia ac
tyrannide paganorum expulsis. Quinetiam probabant et ostendebant,
idque indubitato veterum annalium testimonio, illius loci ordines ac
instituta a nonnullis piis et eruditis hominibus fuisse sancita, ut
a Divo Gilda, Melkino, Nennio, Kentigerno, et aliis, qui omnes
20 literis illic consenuerunt, omnia ibidem felici pace et concordia
administrantes, ac Divum quoque Germanum Oxoniam advenisse,
annique dimidium illic esse moratum, quo tempore per Britanniam
iter fecit adversus Pelagianorum haereses concionaturus, ordines et
instituta supra mirum in modum comprobavit. Rex ille inaudita
25 humilitate utramque partem accuratissime exaudivit, eos piis ac
salutaribus monitis etiam atque etiam hortans, ut mutuam inter se
coniunctionem et concordiam tuerentur. Itaque hoc animo discessit
rex, quosque ex utraque parte consilio suo esse obtemperaturos et
instituta sua amplexuros. At Grymboldus, haec iniquo animo
30 ferens, statim ad monasterium Wintoniense ab Ælfredo recens fun-
datum proficiscebatur, deinde tumbam Wintoniam transferri curavit,
in qua proposuerat post huius vitae curriculum ossa sua reponenda,
in testudine, quae erat facta subter cancellum ecclesiae Divi Petri in
Oxonia. Quam quidem ecclesiam idem Grymboldus extruxerat ab
35 ipso fundamento de saxo summa cura perpolito.]

---

**83 b** *Interpolavit Camd* (*vide quae in prolegomenis* §§ 8–10 *de
hoc loco egimus*). *Locum defuisse in Cott. testatur W*     16
probabant . . . annalium *om. Camd in 'Britannia' ed.* 1600     19
Nemrio *Camd :* Ninnio '*Britannia*'     24 supra] *forte* supradicta *W*   •   29 *post* amplexuros *add.* sperans '*Britannia*'

*Anno Dominicae Incarnationis* DCCCLXXXVII, *na-* **84**
*tivitatis autem Ælfredi regis trigesimo nono*, supra
memoratus paganorum exercitus Parisiam civitatem
derelinquens incolumem, eo quod aliter proficere
sibimet non poterat, classem suam *sub illo ponte* 5
*sursum* contra Signe longe remigando, tam diu
direxit, donec ad ostium fluminis, quod Materne
nominatur, pervenisset; tunc Sigonam deserentes
in ostium Materne divertunt, contra quod diu ac
longe navigantes, demum non sine labore usque ad 10
locum, qui dicitur Caziei, id est villa regia, pervenerunt. In quo loco hiemaverunt integro anno.
Sequenti anno in ostium fluminis, quod dicitur
Iona, intraverunt, non sine magno regionis damno,
et illic remorati sunt anno uno. 15

Eodem anno Carolus, Francorum rex, viam uni- **85**
versitatis adiit; sed Earnulf, filius fratris sui, sexta,
antequam defunctus esset, hebdomada, illum regno
expulerat. Quo statim defuncto, quinque reges
ordinati sunt, et regnum in quinque partibus con- 5
scissum est, sed tamen principalis sedes regni ad

---

**84** *Exscripp. partim SD* 1 *SD* 2     1 nativitas *Co*     2 nono
*corr. W* : sexto *Cott.* (*teste W*) *Co B Ar P Camd SD* 1     supra
memoratus] praedictus *Flor*     6 Sigene *Co* : Sequanam *Flor*
7 donec] quoad *B*     hostium *Co P et hic et alibi*     Materne *Flor* :
Materre *Co Ar P Camd W Pet SD* 1 : Matterre *B*     8 Sequanam
*Flor*     9 Materne *Flor* : Materrae *Co B Ar P Camd W Pet*
10 usque *om. B·*     11 Caciei *B·* : Cazei *SD* 1

**85** *Exscripp. totum SN, paululum SD* 2     1 Carolus *Co* :
Karolus *B Flor SN SD* 2 : Farlus *P Ar Camd W Pet*     Francorum
rex] Imperator *SN*     universae carnis *Flor*     2 Earnulfe *Co* :
Earnulfus *B·*: Arnulfus *SN*     3 fuisset *B*     ebdomada *Co*
5 partes *Flor*     concessum *Co* : concisum *B* : divisum *Flor*

Earnulf iuste et merito provenit, nisi solummodo
quod in patruum suum indigne peccavit. Ceteri
*quoque* quatuor reges fidelitatem et oboedientiam
10 Earnulfo, sicut dignum erat, promiserunt: nullus
enim illorum quatuor regum hereditarius illius
regni erat in paterna parte, nisi Earnulf solus.
Quinque itaque reges confestim, Karolo moriente,
ordinati sunt, sed imperium penes Earnulf remansit.
15 Talis ergo illius regni divisio fuit: *nam* Earnulf
orientales regiones Hreni fluminis, Hrothuulf quoque
internam partem regni accepit, Oda etiam occidentale regnum, Beorngar et Witha Langobardiam,
nec non et illas regiones, quae in illa parte montis
20 sunt. Nec tamen tanta et talia regna inter se
pacifice servaverunt. Nam bis pleno proelio inter se
belligeravere, et illa regna persaepe devastaverunt
invicem, et unusquisque alterum expulit de regno.

**86** Eodem quoque anno, *quo ille exercitus Parisiam
civitatem deserens Caziei adiit,* Æthelhelm, comes
Wiltunensium, Ælfredi regis et Saxonum eleemosynam Romam duxit.

---

7 Arnulfum *SN*    iusto *SN*    solummodo quod *ordine inverso B*
11 eorum *B*    12 Arnulfus *SN*    13 igitur *B*    Karolo
*Co B Flor SN* : Farlo *Ar P Camd W Pet*    14 ordinati] consecrati
*SN*    Earnulfum *B* : Arnulfum *SN*    15 divisio fuit *B SN P Ar
Camd W Pet* : om. *Cott.* (*teste W*) : dinam (*pro* divisio fuit nam)
*Co* : extitit divisio *Flor*    Arnulfus *SN*    16 Hrenis *Co* : Hrénis
(s *partim erasum*) *SN*    Rodulfus *SN*    17 Otto *SN*    etetim
*Ar*    18 Beoragar *B* : Berengarius *SN*    Wido *SN*    Langobardiam *SN* : Longobardiam *B Flor* : Languobardiam *rell.*    19
regiones] partes *Flor*    20 pacifice inter se *B*    21 servaverunt]
tenuerunt *B*    23 expulere *Flor*
   **86** *Exscripsit SD* 2    2 Cazei *Co B*    3 Wiltunnensium
*Co*    elemosynam *Co* : eleemosynas *Flor*    et *reiciendum suspicatus est W, ego tamen retinui auctore Chron. Anglo-Sax.*

*Eodem* quoque anno saepe memoratus Ælfred, 87
Angulsaxonum rex, divino instinctu legere et interpretari simul uno eodemque die primitus inchoavit.
*Sed, ut apertius ignorantibus pateat, causam huius*
*tardae inchoationis expedire curabo.* 5

*Nam cum quodam die ambo in regia cambra* 88
*resideremus, undecunque, sicut solito, colloquia*
*habentes, ex quodam quoddam testimonium libro illi*
*evenit ut recitarem. Quod cum intentus utrisque*
*auribus audisset et intima mente sollicite perscruta-* 5
*retur, subito ostendens libellum, quem in sinum suum*
*sedulo portabat, in quo diurnus cursus et psalmi*
*quidam atque orationes quaedam, quas ille in iuven-*
*tute sua legerat, scripti habebantur, imperavit, quod*
*illud testimonium in eodem libello literis mandarem.* 10
*Quod ego audiens et ingeniosam benevolentiam illius*
*ex parte, atque etiam tam devotam erga studium*
*divinae sapientiae voluntatem eius cognoscens, im-*
*mensas Omnipotenti Deo grates, extensis ad aethera*
*volis, tacitus quamvis, persolvi, Qui tantam erga* 15
*studium sapientiae devotionem in regio corde in-*
*seruerat. Sed, cum nullum locum vacuum in eodem*
*libello reperirem, in quo tale testimonium scribere*

---

**87** *Exscripsit partim SN*   2 instincto *W Pet* : instinctu *rell.*
interpretare *Co B*   3 *post* inchoavit *add.* in sancta videlicet Beati
Martini Turonensis episcopi solennitate (*ex cap.* 89, *v.* 14) *Flor*
**88** 2 collo quia *Co*   5 solicite *B*   6 sinu suo *B*
7 sedulo *om. B*   diurni *B*   8 quaedam] quasdam *Co*
9 scripti habebantur *om. Co*   quod *scripsi* : quo *omnes*
10 litteris *Co*   11 ingeniosam] '*Ab hoc loco usque ad* locupletatim
ditavit ⟨*ad finem cap.* 98⟩ *manum recentiorem exhibet Cod. Cott.*'
*W Cf. cap.* 98, *v.* 9 *not.*   12 etiam *om. Co*   13 divinae *om.*
*Co B*   sapientiae studium *B*   inmensas *Co*   14 gratias *B*
18 repperirem *Co*   20 aliquantis pedis tuli *Co*   eligans *Co*

*possem—erat enim omnino multis ex causis refertus*
20 *—aliquantisper distuli, et maxime quia tam elegans*
*regis ingenium ad maiorem divinorum testimoniorum*
*scientiam provocare studebam. Cui, cum me, ut*
*quanto citius illud scriberem, urgeret, inquam:*
*'placetne tibi, quod illud testimonium in aliqua*
25 *foliuncula segregatim scribam? Incognitum est*
*enim, si aliquando aliquod taliter aut plura reperi-*
*amus, quae tibi placuerint, testimonia; quod si in-*
*opinate evenerit, segregasse gaudebimus.' Quod ille*
*audiens, 'ratum esse consilium' inquit. Quod ego*
30 *audiens et gaudens festinus quaternionem promptum*
*paravi, in cuius principio illud non iniussus scripsi,*
*ac in illa eadem die non minus quam tria alia sibi*
*placabilia testimonia, illo imperante, in eodem quater-*
*nione, ut praedixeram, scripsi. Ac deinde cotidie inter*
35 *nos sermocinando, ad haec investigando aliis inventis*
*aeque placabilibus testimoniis, quaternio ille refertus*
*succrevit, nec immerito, sicut scriptum est 'super mo-*
*dicum fundamentum aedificat iustus et paulatim ad*
*maiora defluit,' velut apis fertilissima longe lateque*
40 *gronnios interrogando discurrens, multimodos divinae*
*scripturae flosculos inhianter et incessabiliter congre-*
*gavit, quis praecordii sui cellulas densatim replevit.*

---

23 urgebam *Co* 24 *post* placetne *add.* illud *sed lineola sub-*
*ducta deletum Co* 26 repperiamus *Co*: reperiemus *B* 27 pla-
cuerunt *B* 28 segregarsse *Ar* 30 festinans *B* promptum
*scripsi*: promptam *omnes* 32 in illa *correx. W*: nulla *Cott.*
(*teste W*) *Co rell.*: om. *B* eodem *B* 33 eodem *scripsi*:
eadem *omnes* 34 deinde *om. Co* cotidie *Co*: quotidie *rell.*
35 vos *Co* haec] et *Co* 36 ille refertus *scripsi*: illa referta
*omnes* 37 succretavit *Co* inmerito *Co* 40 interrogogando
*Co* multimodis *Co* 42 quis *Co*: quibus *B*: queis *rell.*

*Nam primo illo testimonio scripto, confestim legere* **89**
*et in Saxonica lingua interpretari, atque inde per-*
*plures instituere studuit, ac veluti de illo felici latrone*
*cautum est, Dominum Iesum Christum, Dominum su-*
*um, immoque omnium, iuxta se in venerabili sanctae* **5**
*Crucis patibulo pendentem cognoscente; quo subnixis*
*precibus, inclinatis solummodo corporalibus oculis,*
*quia aliter non poterat, erat enim totus confixus*
*clavis, submissa voce clamaret: 'Memento mei, cum*
*veneris in regnum tuum, Christe* [a] *,' qui Christianae* 10
*fidei rudimenta in gabulo primitus inchoavit discere.*
*Hic aut aliter, quamvis dissimili modo, in regia*
*potestate sanctae rudimenta scripturae, divinitus in-*
*stinctus, praesumpsit incipere* in venerabili Martini
solemnitate. † *Quos flosculos undecunque collectos a* 15
*quibuslibet magistris discere et in corpore unius*
*libelli, mixtim quamvis, sicut tunc suppetebat, redi-*
*gere, usque adeo protelavit quousque propemodum ad*
*magnitudinem unius psalterii perveniret. Quem*
*enchiridion suum, id est manualem librum, nominari* 20
*voluit, eo quod ad manum illum die noctuque soler-*
*tissime habebat; in quo non mediocre, sicut tunc*
*aiebat, habebat solatium.*

*Sed, sicut a quodam sapiente iamdudum scri-* 90
*ptum est*

*invigilant animi, quibus est pia cura regendi,*

_____

[a] Luc. xxiii. 42.

_____

**89** *Scriptum fuisse 'manu recentiori' in Cott. testatur W (cap.* 88,
*v.* 11)   2 lingua Saxonica *B*   inde *om. B*   5 omnium] hominum *Co*   9 summissa *Co*   12 aut] autem *B*   13 sanctae *Co*
*B* : S. *P* : sacrae *rell.*   14 *post* venerabili *add.* Sancti *Co B*   17
supputabat *B*   19 Quem *B* : quam *rell.*   20 inchiridion *Ar*
 **90** *Scriptum fuisse ' manu recentiori' in Cott. testatur W (cap.*

*magnopere invigilandum mihi censeo in eo, quod*
5 *ante aliquam, quamvis dissimili modo, similitudinem*
*inter illum felicem latronem et regem composuerim :*
*namque patibulum exosum est unicuique, ubicunque*
*male habet. Sed quid faciat, si non possit se inde*
*eripere aut etiam effugere, vel qualicunque arte*
10 *causam suam meliorare ibidem commorando? Debet*
*ergo, velit, nolit, cum moerore et tristitia sufferre,*
*quod patitur.*

**91** Erat itaque rex, ille multis tribulationum clavis
confossus, quamvis in regia potestate constitutus ;
nam a vigesimo aetatis anno usque ad quadragesimum quintum annum, *quem nunc agit*, gra-
5 vissima incogniti doloris infestatione incessanter
fatigatur, ita ut ne unius quidem horae securitatem
habeat, qua aut illam infirmitatem non sustineat
aut sub illius formidine lugubriter *prope* constitutus
non desperet. Praeterea assiduis exterarum gen-
10 tium infestationibus, quas sedulo terra marique sine
ullius quieti temporis intervallo sustinebat, *non sine*
*materia* inquietabatur. Quid loquar de frequentibus
contra paganos expeditionibus et bellis et incessabilibus regni gubernaculis? † *De cotidiana natio-*

---

88, *v.* 11)   1 sic ut *Camd W Pet*   4 mihi *om. B*   senseo *Co*
6 faelicem *B*   7 unicuique *om. B*   *post* unicuique *add.* esse
*Co*   10 commemorando *B Ar*   11 velit, nolit *om. B*
  **91** *Scriptum fuisse 'manu recentiori' in Cott. testatur W*
(*cap.* 88, *v.* 11) *Partim exscripsit, partim aliis verbis exhibet*
*SD* 1   4 annum *om. B   post* annum *add.* et eo amplius *Flor*
(*cf. cc.* 22, 12 ; 74, 10, 63)   6 fatigatur *Co BP Ar W Pet* :
fatigatus *Camd* : fatigabatur *Flor*   7 haberet *Flor*   quo *Co B*
*P Ar Flor*   aut] ut *B*   sustineret *Flor*   9 desperaret *Flor*
13 et . . . et] de . . . de *Flor*   14 cotidiana *Co* : quotidiana *rell.*

*num, quae in Tyrreno mari usque ultimum Hiberniae* 15
*finem habitant? Nam etiam de Hierosolyma ab El⟨ia⟩*
*patriarcha epistolas et dona illi directas vidimus et*
*legimus.* De civitatibus et urbibus renovandis et
aliis, ubi nunquam ante fuerant, construendis? ⟨De⟩
aedificiis aureis et argenteis incomparabiliter, illo 20
edocente, fabricatis? De aulis et cambris regalibus,
lapideis et ligneis suo iussu mirabiliter constructis?
De villis regalibus lapideis antiqua positione motatis
et in decentioribus locis regali imperio decentissime
constructis?   † *Qui maxima, excepto illo dolore, per-* 25
*turbatione et controversia suorum, qui nullum aut*
*parvum voluntarie pro communi regni necessitate*
*vellent subire laborem.   Sed tamen ille* solus divino
fultus adminiculo susceptum semel regni guberna-
culum, *veluti gubernator praecipuus, navem suam* 30
*multis opibus refertam ad desideratum ac tutum*
*patriae suae portum, quamvis cunctis propemodum*
*lassis suis nautis, perducere contendit, haud aliter*
titubare ac vacillare, quamvis inter fluctivagos ac
multimodos praesentis vitae turbines, non sinebat. 35

---

*post* cotidiana *coniecit* legatione *W p.* 173, *ego opinor mendum*
*in* cotidiana *latere*      15 quae in] *om. B* : aut *Co*      Tyrreno
*emend. W* : Cyrreno *Co P Ar Camd* : eyrreno *B.*      Hiberniae
*Co B* : Hyberniae *rell.* : Hyberiae *coni. W p.* 173      16 Hiero-
solymae *B* : Hierosolima *Ar*      ab Elia *scripsi* : a Bel *SD* 1 : Abel
*rell.*      17 patriarcha *Co B SD* 1 : patriarchae *rell.*      19
De *ex Flor supplevit W*      23 motatis *Cott.* (*teste W*) *Co B P*
*Ar Camd* : mutatis *ex Flor correx. W Pet*      25 Quid *Co B*      27
voluntariae *Co*      28 *post* divino *add.* sane *Flor*      31 ac tutum *om. B*
tutum] tuum *Co*      33 lassis suis] lassiscentibus *Co*      nautis suis *B*
perducere *Co B Ar P Camd* : producere *W Pet*      34 flucti-
vagas *Co B Ar P Flor*      35 multimodas *Co B Ar P Flor*

Nam assidue suos episcopos et comites ac nobilis-
simos, sibique dilectissimos suos ministros, *necnon*
et praepositos, *quibus post Dominum et regem omnis*
*totius regni potestas, sicut dignum, subdita videtur*,
40 leniter docendo, *adulando*, hortando, imperando, ad
ultimum inoboedientes, post longam patientiam,
acrius castigando, vulgarem stultitiam et pertina-
ciam omni modo abominando, ad suam voluntatem
et ad communem totius regni utilitatem sapientis-
45 sime usurpabat et annectebat. At si inter *haec*
regalia exhortamenta propter pigritiam populi im-
perata non implentur, aut tarde incepta tempore
necessitatis ad utilitatem exercentium minus finita
non provenirent, ut de castellis ab eo imperatis
50 adhuc non inceptis loquar, aut nimium tarde inceptis ad perfectum finem non perductis, et
hostiles copiae terra marique irrumperent, *aut, ut*
*saepe evenit, utraque parte*, tunc contradictores im-
perialium diffinitionum *inani poenitentia pene exina-*
55 *niti verecundabantur. Inanem enim poenitentiam*
*scriptura teste nomino, qua homines innumerabiles*
*nimio detrimento pluribus insidiis perpetratis saepe*
*perculsi dolent. Sed quamvis per* † *hanc rem, heu, proh*

---

36 et *om. Flor*    37 sibique dilectissimos *om. Co*    38 pro-
positos *B*    quibus] quorundam *Cott.* (*teste W*): quorum decimo *Co B, quae ab* quorum dน̄io (*videlicet* dominio) *profecta reor*
40 laeniter *B*    *post* docendo *add.* monendo *B*    adolando *Co*    *post*
imperando *add.* vel *B*    43 omı̄no *B*    45 usurpabat et
annectebat] attrahebat *Flor*    At si *Flor*: Ac si *Co*: et si *B Ar P*
*Camd W Pet*    46 exortamenta *Co*    47 implerentur *Flor*
49 pervenirent *Flor*    51 deductis *B*    et *Co Flor*: quod
*rell.*    53 contra ductores *B*    54 penetet *Co*    exaniniti *B*
57 insiliis *Co*    58 hanc rem heu *B P Ar Camd W Pet* (*ex*
*emendatione P, ut videtur*): hac reecheu *Co*    pro *in* proh

*dolor! eulogii miserabiliter contristentur, et per-*
*ditis eorum patribus, coniugibus, liberis, ministris,* 60
*servis, ancillis, operibus, et omni supellectili flebiliter*
*commoveantur, quid detestabilis iuvat poenitentia,*
*quando nec occisis suis propinquis succurrere valent,*
*nec captivos suos a captivitate exosa redimere, nec*
*etiam interdum sibimet, qui evaserint, adiuvare* 65
*valent, quoniam propriam unde sustentent vitam non*
*habent.* Sera *igitur* poenitentia *nimium* attriti *poeni-*
*tent, et* regalia ⟨se⟩ praecepta incuriose despexisse
dolent, et regalem sapientiam *totis vocibus* collau-
dant, *et* quod ante refutaverunt, totis viribus implere 70
promittunt, *id est de arcibus construendis et ceteris*
*communibus communis regni utilitatibus.*

De *voto quoque et proposito excellentissimae medi-* **92**
*tationis suae, quam semper inter prospera et adversa*
*sua nullo modo praetermittere poterat, praetereundum*
*esse hoc in loco utiliter non existimo. Nam, cum de*
*necessitate animae suae solito cogitaret,* inter cetera 5
*diuturna et nocturna* bona, *quibus assidue et maxime*
*studebat,* duo monasteria construi imperavit : unum
monachorum in loco, qui dicitur Æthelingaeg, *quod*

---

*mutatum Co* 59 miserabiliter *om. B* 60 eorum] enim *Co*
61 ancellis *Ar* opibus *B* 63 occurrere *B* 64 redimere]
liberare *B* 65 evaserunt *Co B* 68 se *ex Flor addidi post*
praecepta *add.* nimium *B* dispexisse *Co* 69 doluere *Flor*
sapientiam *om. B* collaudantes *Flor* 71 promisere *Flor*
92 *Scriptum fuit ' manu recentiori' in Cott. (vide cap. 88, v.* 11)
*Exscripp. totum SN (ann.* 900), *partim SD* 1 *(ann.* 887), *SD* 2
*(ann.* 888) 1 De . . . existimo *(v.* 4) *om. SN* 2 semper *Cott.*
*(teste W) Co :* om. *B Ar P Camd* 3 *post* sua *add.* tomnitens,
*in* committens *correctum, Co* 5 *post* cetera *add.* quae rex idem
gessit *Flor* 6 diuturna et nocturna *om. SN* 7 construi
*scripsi :* construere *omnes* 8 Æthelingaege *Co :* Ethelingaag

*permaxima gronna paludosissima et intransmea-*
10 *bili et aquis undique circumcingitur, ad quod nullo*
*modo aliquis accedere potest nisi cauticis, aut etiam*
*per unum pontem, qui inter duas* [*alias*] *arces operosa*
*protelatione constructus est : in cuius pontis occiden-*
*tali limite arx munitissima praefati regis imperio*
15 *pulcherrima operatione consita est ; in quo mona-*
*sterio* diversi generis monachos *undique congregavit*
*et in eodem collocavit.*

93  *Nam primitus, quia nullum de sua propria gente*
*nobilem ac liberum hominem, nisi infantes, qui nihil*
*boni eligere nec mali respuere pro teneritudine in-*
*validae aetatis adhuc possunt, qui monasticam volun-*
5 *tarie vellet subire vitam, habebat ; nimirum quia*
*per multa retroacta annorum curricula monasticae*
*vitae desiderium ab illa tota gente, nec non et a*
*multis aliis gentibus, funditus desierat, quamvis per-*

---

B : Æthelingaeige *SN*     *post* Æthelingaeg *add.* ubi *Flor*     *post*
Æthelingaeige *add.* in quo constituit Iohannem abbatem, religio-
sum virum, de genere Antiquorum Saxonum, quia nullum de sua
*etc.* (*cc.* 93, 1 ; 94, 1) *SN omissis* quod . . . collocavit     9 permaxima *scripsi* : per maxima *omnes*     gronna *B* : gronnia *rell.*
intransmeabili *Co Ar P Camd* : intransmeabilis *B* : intransmea-
bilia *W Pet*     10 et ' *forte deesset* ' *W*     11 cauticis *Cott.*
(*ut videtur*) *Co B Ar P Camd* : nauticis *aut* navaticis *coniec. W* :
cauticis *pro* caudicis *scriptum puto*     15 pulcherima *Co*     16
diversis *Flor*     monachos] monachis coadunatis, primitus Iohannem, presbyterum et monachum, genere Eald Saxonum, abbatem
constituit (*ex cap.* 94, *v.* 1) *Flor, inde pergens ad cap.* 98     undi-
cunque *B*
    **93** *Scriptum fuit ' manu recentiori ' in Cott.* (*vide cap.* 88, *v.* 11)
*Exscripsit SN ann.* 900     1 Nam primitus *om. SN*     qui *B*
*post* nullum *add.* potuit invenire (*sic*) *SN*     2 ac] vel *SN*
3 *post* teneritudine *add.* et *SN*     invalida *SN*     4 aetate *SN*
adhuc possunt *om. SN*     voluntariae *Co*     5 habebat . . .

*plurima adhuc monasteria in illa regione constructa*
*permaneant, nullo tamen regulam illius vitae ordina-* 10
*biliter tenente, nescio quare, aut pro alienigenarum*
*infestationibus, qui saepissime terra marique hosti-*
*liter irrumpunt, aut etiam pro nimia illius gentis*
*in omni genere divitiarum abundantia, propter quam*
*multo magis id genus despectae monasticae vitae fieri* 15
*existimo; ideo diversi generis monachos in eodem*
*monasterio congregare studuit.*

Primitus Iohannem, presbyterum ⟨et⟩ monachum, **94**
*scilicet* Eald-saxonum genere, abbatem constituit;
*deinde ultramarinos presbyteros quosdam et dia-*
*conos. Ex quibus, cum nec adhuc tantum numerum,*
*quantum vellet, haberet, comparavit etiam quam-* 5
*plurimos eiusdem gentis Gallicae, ex quibus quosdam*
*infantes in eodem monasterio edoceri imperavit, et*
*subsequenti tempore ad monachicum habitum sub-*
*levari. In quo etiam monasterio unum paganicae*
*gentis edoctum in monachico habitu degentem, iuvenem* 10
*admodum, vidimus, non ultimum scilicet eorum.*

*Facinus quoque in eodem monasterio quodam* **95**
*tempore perpetratum muti taciturnitate silentii ob-*
*livioni ⟨non⟩ traderem, quamvis indignum facinus*

---

existimo (*v.* 16) *om. SN*      qui *Co B*      12 qui *scripsi*: quae
*omnes*     se piissime *Co*      hostiliter terra marique *B*      **14**
habundantia *Co*      15 multo magis *om. B*      17 congregate *Co*
   94 *In Cott. scriptum fuit ' manu recentiori' (vide cap.* 88, *v.* 11).
*Clausulam primam exscripp. Flor (vide c.* 92, 16 *not.) SD* 2 *SN*
(*vide c.* 92, 8 *not.*)      1 et *ex Flor addidi*      7 in *om. Co B*
8 ad] et *Co*     monachorum *B*      10 monastico *B*
   95 *Scriptum fuit ' manu recentiori' in Cott. (vide cap.* 88, *v.* 11)
1 quodam *om. B*      2 tempore *om. B*      3 non *addidi*      tradere
*Co*     fac non (*perperam pro* facinus) *suprascripto* factu *manu*
*correct. Co, unde* factu non *male adnotat Pet*

STEVENSON                  G

*est, quia per totam scripturam impiorum turpia facta*
5 *inter venerabilia iustorum, sicut zizania et lolium*
*in tritici segetibus, interseminantur : bona scilicet ut*
*laudentur, sequantur, aequiparentur, sectatores quo-*
*que eorum omni honore venerabili digni habeantur;*
*mala vero ⟨ut⟩ vituperentur, execrentur, et ut*
10 *omnino effugiantur, imitatores quoque eorum omni*
*odio et despectione ac vindicta corripiantur.*

**96** *Nam quodam tempore, cum instinctu diabolico qui-*
*dam sacerdos et diaconus, Gallici genere, ex praefatis*
*monachis, invidia quadam* [*latenti*] *excitati contra*
*suum abbatem praefatum Iohannem, nimium latenter*
5 *in tantum amaricati sunt, ut Iudaico more dominum*
*suum dolo circumvenirent et proderent. Nam duos*
*eiusdem gentis Gallicae servulos praemio conductos*
*ita fraudulenter docuerunt, ut nocturno tempore, cum*
*omnes delectabili corporis quiete graviter dormirent,*
10 *patefactam armati intrarent ecclesiam; quam post*
*se iterum solito more clauderent et unicum abbatis*
*adventum in ea absconditi praestolarentur. Cum-*
*que solus solito ⟨more⟩ orandi causa ecclesiam*

---

5 venerabilia *Co B P Ar* : venerabiliora *Camd W Pet*     zizannia
*Co*     lilium *Co*     7 sequentur *Co B* (*ante* laudentur)     aequi-
perentur *P*     8 abeantur *Co*     9 *prius* ut *addidi*
    **96** *Scriptum fuit 'manu recentiori' in Cott. (vide cap.* 88, *v.* 11).
*Exscripsit SN*     2 diaconus et sacerdos *B*     diaconos *Co*
generis *B*     3 latenti *om. SN quod ex* latenter *versu se-*
*quenti errore inter scribendum profectum esse suspicatus, seclusi*
4 Ioannem *B*     7 Gallicae gentis *B P Ar SN*     servulos] ministros
*B*     8 ita fraudulenter docuerunt *om. SN*     cum . . . patefactam *om. SN*     9 graviter *om. B*     11 clauderent *scripsi*
*secutus SN* : claudent *Co* : claudebant *B P Ar Camd W Pet*     uni
cum *Co*     12 abscondi *Co* : absconsi *SN*     praesularentur *Co*
13 solita *B*     more *ex SN addidi*

*latenter intraret, et ante sanctum altare flexis ad*
*terram genubus se inclinaret, hostiliter irruentes* 15
*in eum, tunc eum ibidem occiderent. Cuius corpus*
*exanime inde trahentes ante ostium cuiusdam mere-*
*tricis, quasi illic occisus esset in meretricando, iacta-*
*rent. Quod etiam machinaverunt, crimen crimini*
*addentes, sicut dictum est: 'Et erit novissimus error* 20
*peior priore* ª.' *Sed divina misericordia, quae semper*
*innocentibus solet subvenire, impiam impiorum medi-*
*tationem maxima ex parte frustrata est, quo non per*
*omnia evenirent, sicut proposuerant.*

*Omni itaque mala doctrina a malis doctoribus* 97
*malis auditoribus elucubratim exposita et condicta,*
*nocte adveniente atque suppetenti, et impunitate pro-*
*missa, latrunculi duo armati in ecclesia ⟨se⟩ conclu-*
*serunt, adventum abbatis praestolantes. Cumque* 5
*media nocte Iohannes solito ⟨more⟩ furtim, nemine*
*sciente, orandi gratia ecclesiam intrasset et flexis*
*genibus ante altare incurvaret, tunc duo illi latrun-*

ª Matt. xxvii. 64.

---

15 seipsum *B*      16 *post prius* eum *add.* et *SN*      alterum eum
*om. Co SN*: eum tunc *B*      occiderent *ex Co SN reposui*: occidere
conarentur *W Pet*: o. conabantur *B Ar P Camd*      17 examine
*errore operarum SN Ed.*      exinde *B*      hostium *in* ostium
*mutatum Co*      20 error *om. Co*      22 meditationum *Co SN* (*quod*
*correxit Ed. tacitus*)      24 eveniret *Co*: evenirent *post* proposuerant *B*
97 *Scriptum fuit 'manu recentiori' in Cott.* (*vide cap.* 88, *v.* 11).
*Exscripsit SN*      1 omnis *compendio scriptum B*      mala *om. B*
3 atque . . . promissa *om. SN*      suppetentia *Co*: suppetentiam *B*
in punitate *Co*      4 latrunculi duo armati *ex SN reposui*: latrun-
culos duos armatos *rell.*      aecclesia *Co*: ecclesiam *B*      se *ex*
*SN addidi*      5 abbas *SN*      6 Ioannes *B*      more *ex SN addidi*
furtim *om. SN*      7 aecclesiam *Co*      8 genibus *B Ar SN*:
genubus *rell.*      curvaret, *suprascripto* incurvaret *manu corr. Co*:
curvaretur *B*: oraret *SN*      illi duo *B SN*      latrunculi] nequis-

*culi ex improviso dispoliatis gladiis in eum irrumpunt*
10 *et crudelibus afficiunt vulneribus. Sed ille ut solito*
*ac semper acris ingenio et, ut audivimus de eo a*
*quibusdam referentibus, bellicosae artis non expers,*
*si in meliori disciplina non studeret, statim ut*
*sonitus latronum audivit, priusquam videret, in-*
15 *surgens acriter in eos, antequam vulneratur, et voci-*
*ferans, quantum poterat reluctabatur, inclamitans*
*daemones esse et non homines; non enim aliter*
*sciebat, quia nec hoc homines ausos esse existimabat.*
*Vulneratus est tamen antequam sui advenirent. Sui*
20 *ergo hoc rumore expergefacti et etiam, audito dae-*
*monum nomine, perterriti utrique et inexpertes, et*
*etiam illi, Iudaico more, domini sui proditores, hinc*
*inde ad ecclesiae ostia concurrunt, sed antequam*
*advenirent, latrunculi praecipiti cursu ad proxi-*
25 *mantia sibi gronnae latibula, semivivum abbatem*
*relinquentes, confugiunt. Monachi vero seniorem*
*suum semivivum colligentes, cum gemitu et moerore*
*domum reportaverunt, sed nec etiam illi dolosi minus*
*lachrymabantur innocentibus. Sed Dei misericordia*

---

simi *SN*    9 in ex proviso *Co*    dispoliatis *ex `Co B SN reposui* :
evaginatis *rell.*    10 officiunt *Co*    ut solito . . . vulneratur et
(*v.* 15) *om. SN*    11 ac] hac *Co* : huc *B*    *post* et *add.* etiam
*Co B*    13 in] non *B*    non *om. B*    destuderet *Co*    14
sonitum *B*    15 anteaquam *B*    vulneraretur *Co B*    17 et
*om. B*    non . . . sciebat *om. SN*    *post* enim *add.* hoc *B*
aliqualiter *B*    18 esse *om. B*    19 *post* advenirent *add.* usque
ad mortem *SN*    Sui . . . advenirent (*v.* 24) *om. SN*    20 hoc
rumore] quorum more *Co*    atque *B*    21 *an* utique?
23 aecclesiae *Co*    hostia *Co B*    anteaquam *B*    24 proxi-
mantia sibi gronnae *om. SN*    25 *post* latibula *add.* paludis
*SN*    27 semivivum colligentes *om. SN*    28 sed . . .
redeamus (*v.* 34) *om. SN*    dolosi *om. B*    29 lacrimabantur *Co*

*tantum facinus impunitum fieri non permittente,* 30
*latrunculi, qui hoc perpetraverunt, omnes tanti*
*sceleris persuasores capti ligatique per varia tor-*
*menta morte turpissima periere.* His ita relatis, ad
incepta redeamus.

Aliud quoque monasterium iuxta orientalem 98
portam Sceftesburg, habitationi sanctimonialium
habile, idem *praefatus* rex aedificari imperavit;
in quo propriam filiam *suam* Æthelgeofu, devotam
Deo virginem, abbatissam constituit, *cum qua etiam* 5
*aliae multae nobiles moniales in monastica vita Deo*
*servientes in eodem monasterio habitant.* Quae duo
monasteria terrarum possessionibus et omnibus
divitiis locupletatim ditavit.

*His ita diffinitis, solito suo more intra semetipsum* 99
*cogitabat, quid adhuc addere potuisset, quod plus*
*placeret ad piam meditationem; non inaniter in-*
*cepta, utiliter inventa, utilius servata est. Nam*
*iamdudum in lege scriptum audierat, † Dominum* 5
*decimam sibi multipliciter redditurum promisisse*
*atque fideliter servasse, decimamque sibi multipliciter*
*redditurum fuisse.* Hoc exemplo instigatus et ante-

---

32 perswasores *Co* : perpetratores *B*     33 itaque *B*

**98** *Scriptum fuit ' manu recentiori' in Cott.* (*vide v.* 9 *et cap.* 88,
*v.* 11). *Exscripp. totum SN, partim SD* 1 *SD* 2     2 Sceftes-
burge *Co* : Scestesburgae *B* : Sceaphtesburgh *SN*     habitationi *Co*
*B Flor SN* : habitationem *P Ar Camd W Pet*     monialium *SN*
3 habile *Co Flor SN* : habitabile *B P Ar Camd W Pet*     praefatus
*om. SN*     aedificari *scripsi* : aedificare *omnes*     4 Ethelgeofu
*Ar* : Æthelgeovam *SN*     6 sanctimoniales *SN*     7 habitant
... monasteria *om. SN*     8 positionibus *Co B P Camd*     9 locu-
pletatum *SN*     ditavit] ' *Hic desinit manus recentior Cod. Cott.*' *W*

**99** *Paululum exscripsit SD* 1     1 itaque *B*     6 reddituram
*Co*     7 servisse *Co*     8 reddituram *Co*

*cessorum morem volens transcendere, dimidiam ser-*
10 *vitii sui partem, diurni scilicet et nocturni temporis,*
*nec non* etiam dimidiam partem omnium divitiarum,
quae annualiter ad eum cum iustitia *moderanter*
acquisitae pervenire consueverant, Deo devote et
fideliter *toto cordis affectu pius meditator* se daturum
15 spopondit ; quod *et quantum potest humana discretio*
*discernere et servare, subtiliter ac* sapienter adimplere
studuit. *Sed ut solito suo more cautus evitaret,*
*quod in alio divinae scripturae loco cautum est :* ' *Si*
*recte offeras, recte autem non dividas, peccas*[a],' *quod*
20 *Deo libenter devoverat quomodo recte dividere posset,*
*cogitavit, et, ut dixit Salomon,* ' *Cor regis in manu*
*Domini*[b],' *id est consilium ;* consilio divinitus invento omnium uniuscuiusque anni censuum succes-
sum bifarie primitus ministros suos dividere aequali
25 lance imperavit.

100    His ita divisis, partem primam *secularibus negotiis*
*pertinere addixit, quam etiam* in tribus partibus
sequestrari praecepit, *cuius* primam *divisionis partem*
*suis bellatoribus* annualiter largiebatur, *item* suis
5 ministris nobilibus, qui in curto regio vicissim com-
morabantur, in pluribus ministrantes ministeriis.
*Ita enim ordinabiliter agebatur regalis familiaritas*
*tribus omni tempore vicissitudinibus :* in tribus

    [a] Gen. iv. 7 (Versio Antiqua).          [b] Prov. xxi. 1.

---

11 necnon] Ad haec *Flor*      dimidiam etiam *B*      13 acquesitae
*Co P*      15-16 et . . . ac] mentis alacritate *Flor*      22 *ante*
consilio *add.* Denique *Flor*      23 omnem *compendio scriptum B*
24 ministros] magistros *Camd*
    100 *Paululum exscripsit SD* 1      2 tres portiones *Flor*      3
cuius] quarum *Flor*      4 item] id est *Co B*      5 cultu *Co*
*Flor : om. SD* 1

namque cohortibus praefati regis satellites pruden-
tissime dividebantur, *ita* ut prima cohors uno mense 10
in curto regio die noctuque administrans commo-
raretur, menseque finito et adveniente alia cohorte,
prima domum redibat, et ibi duobus, propriis
quivis necessitatibus studens, commorabatur mensibus. Secunda itaque cohors mense peracto, ad- 15
veniente tertia, domum redibat, ut ibi duobus com-
moraretur mensibus. Sed et illa, finito unius mensis
ministerio et adveniente prima cohorte, domum
redibat, ibidem commoratura duobus mensibus. *Et*
hoc ordine omnibus vitae *praesentis* temporibus 20
talium vicissitudinum in regali curto rotatur ad-
ministratio.

*Talibus itaque primam de tribus praedictis partibus* 101
*partem, unicuique tamen secundum propriam digni-*
*tatem et etiam secundum proprium ministerium,*
*largiebatur ;* secundam autem operatoribus, quos
ex multis gentibus collectos et comparatos prope- 5
modum innumerabiles habebat, in omni terreno
aedificio edoctos : tertiam autem *eiusdem partem*
advenis ex omni gente ad eum *ad*venientibus longe
propeque positis et pecuniam ab illo exigentibus,
etiam et non exigentibus, *unicuique secundum pro-* 10

---

10 ita] adeo *Flor*   11 cultu *Co Flor*   commemoraretur *Co*   13 *post*
duobus *add.* (*ex v.* 14) mensibus *B*   14 quivis] suis *Co B* : quis *Flor*
studens *om. B*   mensibus *om. B*   19 duobus mensibus commoratura
*Co* : duobus comm. m. *B*   20 omni *Flor*   *post* vitae *add.* suae *Flor*
tempore *Flor*   21 cultu *Cott.* (*teste W*) *Co Flor*   rotabatur *Flor*
   101 *Paululum exscripsit SD* 1    4 secundum *Co*   autem]
vero partem *Flor*   5 collecto, set *Co*   et] etiam *Co B* : vel
etiam *Flor*   propemodum *om. B*   6 *post* innumerabiles *add.*
prope *B*   7 *an* artificio ?   9 propeque] lateque *B*

*priam dignitatem*, mirabili dispensatione *laudabiliter et, sicut scriptum est ' Hilarem datorem diligit Deus* [a],' hilariter impendebat.

102 Secundam *vero* partem omnium divitiarum suarum, quae annualiter ad eum ex omni censu perveniebant *et in fisco reputabantur, sicut iam paulo ante commemoravimus, plena voluntate Deo devovit,* 5 *et* in quatuor partibus aequis *etiam* curiose suos ministros *illam* dividere imperavit, ea condicione, ut prima pars *illius divisionis* pauperibus uniuscuiusque gentis, qui ad eum veniebant, discretissime erogaretur. *Memorabat etiam in hoc, quantum* 10 *humana discretio custodire poterat, illius sancti papae Gregorii observandam esse sententiam, qua discretam mentionem dividendae eleemosynae ita dicens agebat: ' Nec parvum cui multum, nec multum cui parvum, nec nihil cui aliquid, nec aliquid cui nihil* [b].' Secundam 15 *autem* duobus monasteriis, quae ipse fieri imperaverat, et servientibus in his Deo, *de quibus paulo ante latius disseruimus*; tertiam scholae, quam ex multis suae *propriae* gentis nobilibus et etiam pueris

---

[a] 2 Cor. ix. 7.
[b] S. Gregorii *Regula Pastoralis*, iii. cap. 20 : ' Unde et necesse est, ut sollicite perpendant, ne commissa indigne distribuant ; ne quaedam quibus nulla, ne nulla quibus quaedam, ne multa quibus pauca, ne pauca praebeant quibus impendere multa debuerunt.' Cf. Isidori Hispalensis ' Sententiarum ' lib. iv, cap. 48, §§ 5, 6.

---

12 scriptum] dictum *Co*
102 1 Secundum *Co* vero] autem *Flor* 4 *post* ante *add.* reputavimus *sed lineola subducta deletum B* 5 partes aequales *Flor* equis *Co B* : *om. P Ar Camd W Pet* etiam *om. Co B* 12 elemosynae *Co* 13 *prius* nec] ne *Co B P* : nec *Camd W Pet* 14 nihil *deletum Co* cui aliquid *om. Co* Secundum *Co* 15 imperavit *Co* 17 deseruimus *Co* 18 propriae suae *B* et etiam pueris *om. B P Ar Camd W Pet* *post* pueris *add.* et etiam

ignobilibus studiosissime congregaverat ; quartam
circum finitimis in omni Saxonia et Mercia mona- 20
steriis, et etiam quibusdam annis per vices in
Britannia et Cornubia, Gallia, Armorica, Northanhymbris, et *aliquando etiam* in Hybernia, ecclesiis
*et servis Dei inhabitantibus*, secundum possibili-
tatem suam, *aut ante* distribuit, *aut sequenti tempore* 25
*erogare proposuit, vita sibi et prosperitate salva.*

His ita ordinabiliter ab eo*dem rege* dispositis, 103
*memor illius divinae scripturae sententiae, qua*
*dicitur : ' Qui vult eleemosynam dare, a semet ipso*
*debet incipere* [a] *,' etiam quid a proprio corporis sui et*
*mentis servitio Deo offerret, prudenter excogitavit* ; 5
*nam non minus de hac re quam de externis divinis*
*Deo offerre proposuit, quin etiam* dimidiam partem
servitii mentis et corporis, in quantum infirmitas *et*
possibilitas atque suppetentia permitteret, diurno
scilicet ac nocturno tempore, *suapte* totisque viribus 10
se redditurum Deo spopondit. *Sed quia distantiam*
*nocturnarum horarum omnino propter tenebras, et*
*diurnarum propter densitatem saepissime pluviarum*
*et nubium aequaliter dignoscere non poterat*, excogi-
tare coepit, qua ratione *fixa et sine ulla haesitatione* 15

[a] S. Augustini *Enchiridion de Fide*, c. 20 : ' Qui enim vult ordinate
dare eleemosynam, a se ipso debet incipere.'

---

*Co*      19 ignobilibus *om. B*      22 Cornubia et Britannia *B*
Northanhymbris *B* : Northimbris *Co* : Northymbris *Ar P rell.*
*Edd.* : Northymbria *Flor*      25 distribuere *B Ar*      26 prosperitate ' *Sic Ed. P :* posteritate *Ed. Camd* ' *W*      salva
*om. Co*

   **103** 1 ordinabiliter *B* (*post* rege) *Flor* : ordinaliter *Co P Ar Camd*
*W Pet*      8 servitii mentis] servi timentis *Co*      mentis *om. B*
12 omnino *post* tenebras *B*      *post* tenebras *add.* equaliter (*ex v.* 14)
sepissime (*ex v.* 13) *Co*      et *om. Co*      14 et *om. Co*      aequaliter

*hunc* promissum voti sui tenorem leto tenus in-
commutabiliter, *Dei fretus misericordia*, conservare
posset.

104 *His aliquandiu excogitatis*, tandem, invento utili
et discreto consilio, *suos capellanos* ceram offerre
*sufficienter imperavit, quam adductam* ad denarios
pensari in bilibri praecepit ; cumque tanta cera
5 mensurata fuisset, quae septuaginta duos denarios
pensaret, sex candelas, unamquamque aequa lance,
inde capellanos facere iussit, ut unaquaeque candela
duodecim uncias pollicis in se signatas in longitudine
haberet. Itaque hac reperta ratione, sex illae
10 candelae per viginti quatuor horas die nocteque
sine defectu coram sanctis multorum *electorum Dei*
reliquiis, quae semper *eum* ubique comitabantur,
ardentes *lucescebant. Sed cum aliquando per diem
integrum et noctem ad eandem illam horam, qua
15 anteriori vespera accensae fuerant, candelae ardendo
lucescere non poterant, nimirum ventorum violentia
inflante, quae aliquando per ecclesiarum ostia et
fenestrarum, maceriarum quoque atque tabularum,
vel frequentes parietum rimulas, nec non et tento-
20 riorum tenuitates, die noctuque sine intermissione*

---

om. *Co* (*cf. v.* 12)    dinoscere *Co Camd* : discernere *B*    *post*
poterat *add.* Unde *Flor*    17 conservare *Flor* : cum servare *Co*
(*compendio* con *pro* cum *lecto, id quod saepe fit*) : servare *rell.*
   104 2 ceram *ex Flor correxit W* : coram *Cott.* (*teste W*) *Co B Ar*
*P Camd* : sibi ceram sufficientem offerret *Flor*    4 pensari
*scripsi* : pensare *omnes*    bilibri] trutina *Flor*    tantum cerae
admensurata *B*    6 pensare *Co*    7 capellanis *Flor*    iussit]
mandavit ita *Flor*    10 noctuque *B Flor*    11 sanctis *om. Flor*
electorum Dei] sanctorum *Flor*    12 eum *om. B* : cum eo *Co*
comitabant *Co*    13 ardenter *B* : ardebant *Flor omisso* lucescebant
14 et] ac *B*    17 hostia *Co Ar*    18 atque] et *B*    19 fre-

*flabat, exardescere citius plus debito ante eandem*
*horam finiendo cursum suum cogebantur, excogitavit,*
*unde talem ventorum sufflationem prohibere potuisset,*
*consilioque artificiose atque sapienter invento, later-*
*nam ex lignis et bovinis cornibus pulcherrime con-* 25
*struere imperavit. Bovina namque cornua alba ac in*
*una tenuiter dolabris erasa non minus vitreo vasculo*
*elucent. Quae itaque laterna mirabiliter ex lignis et*
*cornibus, ut ante diximus, facta, noctuque candela in*
*eam missa, exterius ut interius tam lucida ardebat,* 30
*nullis ventorum flaminibus impedita, quia valvam ad*
*ostium illius laternae ex cornibus idem fieri im-*
*peraverat. Hoc itaque machinamento ita facto, sex*
*candelae, unaquaeque post alteram, per viginti quatuor*
*horas sine intermissione nihil citius, nihil tardius* 35
*lucescebant. Quibus extinctis, aliae incendebantur.*

*His ita ordinabiliter per omnia digestis, dimidiam,* **105**
*sicut Deo devoverat, servitii sui partem custodire*
*cupiens, et eo amplius augere, in quantum possibilitas*
*aut suppetentia, immo etiam infirmitas, permitteret,*
*taediosus examinandae in iudiciis veritatis arbiter* 5
*existebat, et in hoc maxime propter pauperum curam,*

quenter *Co B*        tentoriarum *Co B*        22 horam] coram *Co*
finiendo *post* suum *exhibet B*        24 atque] et *B*        laternam *W*
*Pet* : lanternam *Co B P Ar Camd*        26 ac in] iacij *Co* : et in *B*
27 erasa] crassa *ex* erassa *emendatum Co*        28 laterna *W Pet* :
lanterna *Co B P Ar Camd*        lingnis *Co*        29 cornubus *B*        30
eam] eandem *B*        32 hostium *Co*        laternae *W Pet* : lanternae
*Co B P Ar Camd*        35 sitius *Co*
    **105** *Exscripsit partim SN (ann.* 900)        1–8 His . . . regno]
Erat enim ille rex fortissimus defensor sanctarum Dei ecclesiarum,
clementissimus consolator orphanorum et viduarum, largissimus distributor eleemosinarum in toto regno illo *etc. SN*        2 voverat *B*
4 permitteret] *vide p.* 341 *infra*        5 in examinandis *B*        6 *post*
curam *add.* solverunt *Cott.* (*teste W*) *Co*

*quibus die noctuque inter cetera praesentis vitae debita*
*mirabiliter incumbebat. Nam in toto illo regno*
*praeter illum solum pauperes aut nullos aut etiam*
10 *paucissimos habebant adiutores; nimirum quia etiam*
*pene omnes illius regionis potentes et nobiles ad secu-*
*laria magis quam ad divina mentem declinaverant*
*negotia: magis enim unusquisque* † *speciali etiam in*
*secularibus negotiis, quam communi.*

106 *Studebat ⟨is⟩ quoque in iudiciis etiam propter nobi-*
*lium et ignobilium suorum utilitatem, qui saepissime*
*in contionibus comitum et praepositorum pertina-*
*cissime inter se dissentiebant, ita ut pene nullus*
5 *eorum, quicquid a comitibus et praepositis iudicatum*
*fuisset, verum esse concederet. Qua pertinaci dissen-*
*sione obstinatissime compulsi, regis subire iudicium*
*singuli subarabant, quod et confestim ab utraque*
*parte implere festinabant. Sed tamen ille, qui in*
10 *sua parte aliquam de illa causa iniustitiam fieri*
*cognosceret, ad talis iudicis iudicium, contra volun-*
*tatem tamen, quamvis per vim* † *lege et stipulatione*
*venire coactus esset, voluntarie nolebat accedere.*
*Sciebat enim ibidem nihil ex sua malitia confestim*
15 *posse delitescere; nimirum* erat namque rex ille
in exequendis iudiciis, sicut in ceteris aliis omni-

---

7 diu *B*      9 etiam *om. SN*      13 magis . . . communi *om.*
*SN*      etiam *Cott.* (*teste W*) *Co* : lucro *rell.*      14 *post* communi
*add.* inhiabat *B P Ar Camd W Pet, quod om. Cott.* (*teste W*) *Co*
106 *Exscripsit partim SN*      1 Studebat . . . nimirum
(*v.* 15) *om. SN*      is *om. Cott.* (*teste W*) *Co*      etiam *om. B*      2
*post* et *add.* etiam *B*      utilitate *B, quod pro* utilitates *legit Pet*
4 nullius *B*      5 indicatum *Co*      fuisset iudicatum *B*      8
sub arrabant *Co*      9-10 implere . . . parte *om. Ar*      12 legis
astipulatione *B*      15 nimirum *Cott.* (*teste W*) *Co* : nec mirum *rell.*
namque] praeterea *Flor*      ille] idem *Flor*      16 ceteris *om. B*

bus rebus, discretissimus indagator. Nam omnia
pene totius suae regionis iudicia, quae in absentia
sua fiebant, sagaciter investigabat, qualia fierent,
iusta aut etiam iniusta, aut *vero* si aliquam in 20
illis iudiciis iniquitatem intelligere posset, leniter
*utens suatim* illos ipsos iudices, aut per se ipsum
aut per alios suos fideles quoslibet interrogabat,
quare tam nequiter iudicassent, utrum per igno-
rantiam aut propter aliam quamlibet malevo- 25
lentiam, id est utrum pro aliquorum amore vel
timore aut *aliorum* odio aut etiam pro alicuius
pecuniae cupiditate. Denique si illi iudices pro-
fiterentur propterea se talia ita iudicasse, eo quod
nihil rectius de his rebus scire poterant, tunc ille, 30
discrete et moderanter illorum imperitiam et insipientiam redarguens, aiebat, ita inquiens : 'Nimium
admiror vestram hanc insolentiam, eo quod, Dei
dono et meo, sapientium ministerium et gradus
usurpastis, sapientiae autem studium et operam 35
neglexistis. Quapropter aut terrenarum potestatum
ministeria, quae habetis, illico dimittatis, aut sapientiae studiis multo devotius † docere ut studeatis,

---

aliis *om. Ar*      18 suae totius *B*      20 etiam *om. SN*      in-
iuste *SN* (*quod correxit Ed. tacitus*)      aut etiam iniusta *om. SN*
vero *om. SN*      21 iudiciis illis *B*      laeniter *B*      leniter ...
iudices *om. SN*      22 utens suatim *ex Co reposui* : advocatos *B*
*P Ar Camd W Pet*      ipsum *om. B*      24 tam *Cott.* (*teste W*)
*Flor* : ita *B P Ar Camd SN* : ita tam *Co W Pet*      25 *post*
propter *add.* aliquam *B*      aliam *om. SN*      quamlibet *om. B*
26 id est utrum] vel *SN*      28 paecuniae *B*      29 eo *om. SN*
30 poterant] nossent *SN*      31 moderate *SN*      32 dicens *SN*
nimirum *B*      33 hanc vestrum *B*      34 meum *Co*      38
docere *om. Co* : de ceteris *SN*      ut *om. SN*      docere ut studeatis
impero] quam hactenus insistere, mando studeatis *Flor*

impero.' Quibus auditis verbis, perterriti ⟨ac⟩ veluti
40 pro maxima vindicta correcti, comites et praepositi
ad aequitatis discendae studium totis viribus se
vertere nitebantur, ita ut mirum in modum illiterati
ab infantia comites pene omnes, praepositi ac
ministri literatoriae arti studerent, malentes in-
45 suetam disciplinam *quam* laboriose discere, quam
potestatum ministeria dimittere. *Sed* si aliquis
litteralibus studiis aut pro senio vel etiam pro nimia
inusitati ingenii tarditate proficere non valeret, suum,
si haberet, filium, aut etiam aliquem propinquum
50 suum, vel etiam, si aliter non habeat, suum proprium
hominem, liberum vel servum, quem ad lectionem
longe ante promoverat, libros ante se die nocteque,
quandocunque *unquam* ullam haberet licentiam,
Saxonicos imperabat recitare. *Et* suspirantes
55 nimium intima mente dolebant, eo quod in iuventute
sua talibus studiis non studuerant, felices arbitrantes

---

39 ac *ex Flor addidi*    41 se vertere] revertere *B*    42 *post* modum
*add.* illi *SN* (*ex* illiterati *sequenti ortum*)    illiteratos *Co*    43
praepositos *Co*    ac] et *B*    44 ministros *Co*    litteratoriae *Co*
malentes] magis *SN*    45 quam *om. SN*    *post* discere *add.*
volentes *SN*    47 litteralibus *Co SN*: literalibus *B P Ar Flor*:
liberalibus *Camd W Pet*    vel etiam pro *Cott.* (*teste W*) *Co B P
Ar Flor*: vel etiam *SN*: aut *Camd W Pet*    49 filium *post*
valeret (*v.* 48) *habet SN*    etiam aliquem *om. SN*    50
suum *om. SN*    aliter si *B*: taliter *Ar*: alium *SN*    haberet *Flor SN*    52 sese *B*    noctuque *B Flor*: et nocte
*SN*    53 unquam *om. SN*    54 Anglicos *SN*    *post*
recitare *add.* in quibus, iussu regis praefati, fuerunt scripta iusta
iudicia inter potentes et inpotentes, et alia multa utilia tam cleri
quam plebi *omissis quae sequuntur SN*    Et] Ipsi vero senes
nimium suspirantes *Flor*    suspirantes (*ex Cott. ut videtur*) *W
Flor*: suspirans *Co B P Ar Camd*    55 dolebant (*ex Cott. ut
videtur*) *W Flor*: dolebat *Co B P Ar Camd*    56 studuerant

huius temporis iuvenes, qui liberalibus artibus
feliciter erudiri poterant, se vero infelices existi-
mantes, qui nec hoc in iuventute didicerant, nec
etiam in senectute, quamvis inhianter desiderarent, 60
poterant discere. *Sed hanc senum iuvenumque in
discendis literis solertiam ad praefati regis notitiam
explicavimus.*

[*Anno Dominicae* 900, *Ælfredus veridicus, vir in bello* 106 b
*per omnia strenuissimus, rex Occidentalium Saxonum nobi-
lissimus, prudens vero et religiosus atque sapientissimus, hoc
anno, postquam regnasset viginti et novem annis et dimidio
super totam Angliam, praeter illas partes, quae subditae* 5
*erant Dacis, cum magno suorum dolore viam universitatis
adiit, die septimo kalend. Novemb., anno regni sui vigesimo
nono et dimidio, anno vero aetatis suae quinquagesimo primo,
Indictione quarta. Qui apud Wintoniam civitatem regalem
decenter et regali honore est sepultus in ecclesia Sancti Petri,* 10
*Apostolorum principis. Mausoleum quoque ipsius constat
factum de marmore porphyrio pretiosissimo.*]

[*De cuius regimine laborioso hos versus proloqui dignum* 106 c
  duxi :

  *Nobilitas innata tib:, probitatis honorem,
  armipotens Ælfrede, dedit, probitasque laborem,
  perpetuumque labor nomen; cui mixta dolori*          5

---

(*ex Cott. ut videtur*) W *Flor* : studuerat *Co B P Ar Camd*
faelices *B*      57 qui] in *Co*      58 faeliciter *B*      eruditi *B*
infaelices *B*      59 hoc nec *Co*      62 literis] libris *B*      63
explicavimus] '*Hic desinit Codex Cott.*' *W* : *desinit etiam Co*

106 b *Interpolatum ex SN, praeter* postquam . . . Dacis (*vv.*
4-6), *quae ex Henrici Huntingdon* '*Historia Anglorum,*' *lib. v.
cap.* 13, *hauriuntur, in B P Ar Camd ; secl.* W *Pet*      1 viridicus
*P Camd*      2 Orientales *B*      3 et *om. B* : atque *SN*
4 novem] octo *H. Hunt*      dimidium *B P Camd*      9 quarta]
tertia *SN*      Wyntoniam *B*      regale in *B*      11 Mausolaeum *B*
106 c *Interpolatum ex Hen. Huntingdon loco laud. in B P Ar
Camd ; secl.* W *Pet. Auctoris nomen in margine exhibent P Ar
Camd*      5 nominem *compendio scriptum B*

gaudia semper erant, spes semper mixta timori.
si modo victor eras, ad crastina bella pavebas.
si modo victus eras, ad crastina bella parabas.
cui vestes sudori iugi, cui sica cruore
10    tincta iugi, quantum sit onus regnare, probarunt.
non fuit immensi quisquam per climata mundi
cui tot in adversis vel respirare liceret.
nec tamen aut ferro contritus ponere ferrum,
aut gladio potuit vitae finisse labores.
15    iam post transactos vitae regnique dolores,
Christus ei sit vera quies sceptrumque perenne.]

106 d   [Hic Iohannes Asser, episcopus quondam Scireburnensis,
scripsit Ælfredi res gestas, et annales Britanniae.  Huius
Asseri annalibus vetustus quidam author paralipomenon
addidit, et eum obiisse scribit anno Domini 909.]

---

8 ad] et B     9 fica B     10 tincta] iuncta B     opus B
106 d Interpolatum in B P Ar Camd; secl. W Pet. 'Hanc
notulam ⟨in Cott.⟩ addidit Reverendiss. Archiep. Parkerus' (W),
quam ex Balaei 'Scriptoribus,' cent. Sec. contexuerat (cf. p. 98, not. 3,
p. 115 infra)     1 quondam om. Camd

# APPENDIX

## THE ANNALS OF ST. NEOTS

§ 1. Character of the work, p. 97.    § 2. Origin of Name, p. 98.
§ 3. Probably an East-Anglian compilation, p. 100.    § 4. Date of
compilation, p. 102.    § 5. Use of Frankish sources, p. 103.    § 6.
English sources, p. 104.    §§ 7, 8. Version of O.E. Chronicle employed, p. 105.    §§ 9–11. Relations with Florence of Worcester,
p. 107.    § 12. Compiler does not use William of Malmesbury or
Geoffrey of Monmouth, p. 111.    § 13. Use of the work by later
compilers, p. 111.    §§ 14–16. Description of unique MS., p. 113.
§ 17. Early transcripts, p. 114.    § 18. Previous edition, p. 115.

§ 1. THE compilation known since the time of Leland [1]
by this name has been so long and closely connected
with the Life of Alfred, owing to Archbishop Parker's
unfortunate conclusion that it embodied a fuller text of
the latter work than that contained in the Cottonian MS.,
and to his consequent interpolations from it [2], that we
have found it necessary to print it along with the Life.
In doing so we have omitted the passages drawn from
the Life and from other well-known sources, indicating
merely the beginning and ending of each extract.  These
extracts and the translations from the Old English
Chronicle constitute by far the greater part of the work [3].

[1] See below, p. 98, note 3.
[2] See above, p. xix.
[3] Of the matter whose sources we have been unable to trace, the
most important is the vision of Rollo given under 870 (see below,
§ 5, p. 103); the famous story of Alfred and the cowherd's wife
and the appearances of St. Neot to Alfred, given under 878, which
are professedly taken from a life of that saint (see below, p. 256);
the account of the miraculous raven-banner of the Danes under the
same year (see below, p. 265); the passages relating to St. Edmund
(see below, p. 99); the mention of the place of burial of Guthrum,
the Danish King of East Anglia (see below, p. 100); the notice of

The compiler's office was restricted to changing a word here and there, omitting a clause or word, and substituting *Angli* for *Saxones*, *Anglia* for *Saxonia*, and *Nordmanni* for *Dani*, proceedings that stamp the work as a post-Conquest production. He commences his work abruptly by an extract from Beda without explaining the object of his work. A lack of literary feeling on the part of the compiler is revealed throughout the compilation. He displays so little intelligence in piecing together his extracts that he transcribes passages in which the authors of the matter conveyed by him refer to themselves or their times, and, as he does not mention the sources whence he derived the passages, he thus makes himself the witness of events that happened many centuries before his birth[1]. The absence of thought thus exhibited renders it difficult to believe that he was the author of the passages for which we have been unable to find sponsors. Possibly, however, he may have translated into Latin the extracts from the Chronicle, as his version differs from those of Florence of Worcester, Henry of Huntingdon, and other compilers from the Chronicle[2].

§ 2. Nothing is known of the compiler or of the date or place of the compilation. Leland met with a copy of the work at the priory of St. Neots, in Huntingdonshire, and hence bestowed upon it the title *Chronicon Fani Sancti Neoti*[3]. This has no other merit beyond that of

---

the murder of St. Æthelberht, King of East Angʹia under 794 (see below, p. 110); and the eulogy on Alfred under 900. The blunder about King Ceolwulf under 731 seems to be deduced from the Chronicle (see below, § 7, p. 107).

[1] Thus he repeats 'senior monasterii nostri' under 651, by which Beda meant his own monastery of Jarrow-on-Tyne. Under 741 he similarly repeats 'nos autem illos vidimus, qui usque ad nostram aetatem duraverunt, qui huic rei interfuerunt et nobis viva voce sunt testati,' referring to events of that year. From the Life he copies 'quod a domino meo audivi,' c. 13, 32; 'quam nos ipsi propriis nostris oculis vidimus,' c. 39, 6; 'sicut ab his, qui viderunt . . . audivimus,' c. 37, 13.

[2] See below, p. 105, note 1.

[3] *Commentarii de Scriptoribus Britannicis*, ed. Anthony Hall, Oxford, 1709, p. 152, in reference to the date of Alfred's death 'quod quanquam ex multis abunde liqueat autoribus, illustrissime tamen ex eo libello, qui Asserii annales in epitomen redegit. Nos

distinguishing this anonymous chronicle, for there is
nothing to connect it specially with the Huntingdonshire
monastery beyond the long extract from the Life of
St. Neot.   It would be rash to conclude from this that
the compiler was a member of the monastery of St. Neots,
although access to a Life of this saint might be easier
there or in its vicinity.   It is not, however, St. Neot but
St. Edmund who receives the greatest attention.   The
work embodies not only long extracts from Abbo's
'Passion of St. Edmund,' but contains notices of the
commencement of Edmund's reign in 855, of his consecration as king in the following year, and of his death in
870, containing much information peculiar to itself.   The
extract from the Life of St. Neot may perhaps be due to
the compiler's singular passion for visions, such as the
appearance of St. Neot to Alfred.   Thus he transcribes at
length the vision of Furseus from Beda under 651, that
of Charles Martel under 741, of Charles III ('the Fat')
under 886, and of Rollo under 876.   Three of these are
visions of punishment in a future state, but the dream of
the Norman leader is of much the same nature as that
of Alfred.

igitur, quoniam apud fanum Neoti in vetus exemplar nuper incidimus,
ipsa tam bonae fidei autoris verba subiciemus,' quoting the passage
from the Annals under 900.   Extracts from the work are given in his
*Collectanea*, ii. 190 (ed. Hearne, vol. iii. p. 214), where he describes
it as 'Chronicon Fani Sancti Neoti, incerto autore.'   Hearne notes
that Leland wrote at first ' Ex libro annalium autoris incerti nominis,
sed quem constat familiarem fuisse Alfredo, sive Aluredo, regi,
literatorum omnium Maecenati'; with 'Asserionis' interlined over
'autoris incerti' in a darker ink, but in Leland's hand.   These words
Leland afterwards cancelled.   The priory of St. Neots was surrendered
to the King on December 21, 1539 (*Monasticon*, iii. 465 a), and the
MS. was probably carried off about this date by Leland, whose
search among monastic libraries, &c., ceased before 1545 (*Dict. Nat.
Biography*, xxxiii. 14).   It is curious that Bale makes no mention of
these annals in his notebook (*Index Britanniae Scriptorum*, ed. R. L.
Poole, Oxford, 1902), which contains so many references to works in
Leland's 'bibliotheca.'   But in the *Illustrium Maioris Britanniae
Scriptorum Summarium*, Ipswich, 1548, fo. 65, Bale adds to his
notice of Asser's Life of Alfred ' Author quidam vetustus et doctus
Paralepomena ⟨sic⟩, opus tersum et spectabile, huius historiarum
libro postea annexuit, ut saepe Lelandus notat in antiquarum doctio-
num syllabo' (i. e. his work *De Scriptoribus Britannicis*).

§ 3. The references to St. Edmund's predecessors on the throne of East Anglia are, although few in number, more at home in a work proceeding from the great East Anglian monastery bearing his name than in one composed in the Huntingdonshire priory. In the latter the interest would be historically with the kings of Mercia, who are ignored by the compiler. Thus he omits the whole of c. 7 of the Life, which relates to the latter kingdom. He devotes considerable attention to the succession of the kings of Wessex, but this may be ascribed to the feeling that they demanded notice in a work dealing with the history of England as a whole, since they represented the line from which the sole kings of England sprang. The substitution of *Wili* as the name of the Wiltshire river Wiley for the Celtic *Gwilou* of the Life, c. 42, 19, which is elsewhere transcribed so slavishly, is the only passage suggestive of a knowledge of Wessex. This alone is insufficient evidence upon which to claim a West Saxon origin for the work[1]. The mention of King Guthrum's burial at Hadleigh under 890, which is known only from this compilation, is further evidence of interest in East Anglia. It might, it is true, have been derived from an East Anglian addition to the copy of the Chronicle, or of the translation of the Chronicle, used by the compiler. But, if we accept this supposition, we must admit that acquaintance with a copy containing East Anglian additions is more natural in a compiler working in an East Anglian monastery than in a Mercian or West Saxon one. When the erroneous identification of *Sceobyrig* (Shoebury, co. Essex) with Sudbury (co. Suffolk) was written by a second hand in the twelfth century between the lines in the entry for 893, the MS. must have been accessible to some one with a local knowledge of East Anglia. The fact that the monastery

---

[1] The mention of the regnal year of Ceadwealla of Wessex under 685, the foundation of Glastonbury under 726, and the description of Alfred's tomb at Winchester under 900 may be explained without adopting the hypothesis of West Saxon origin. The statement that the abbot Cenwulf who fell in 904 was abbot of Peterborough is suggestive of an interest in that monastery. The death of the founder of that monastery is excerpted under 705.

of St. Edmunds possessed a copy of the Norman Annals [1],
from which the compiler borrowed so largely, does not,
in view of the wide distribution of these annals in English
monasteries in the twelfth century [2], afford a very strong
argument for referring the compilation of the work to an
inmate of Bury St. Edmunds.   It was, however, known
to the monks of Bury, for the late twelfth century copy
of Florence of Worcester that belonged to the East
Anglian monastery [3] contains several additions that
seem to have been copied directly from the present
work and not immediately from the sources [4].   This
MS. also contains a marginal addition of *utens* to complete the curious phrase of the author of the Life *suatim
utens* in c. 56, 18, which would seem to have been
taken directly from a MS. of the Life or from the

---

[1] In addition to the use of these annals in the construction of the
twelfth-century *Annales Sancti Edmundi*, published by Liebermann,
*Ungedruckte anglo-normannische Geschichtsquellen*, Strassburg, 1879,
pp. 107 sqq., the St. Edmund's copy of Florence of Worcester (Bodleian
MS. 297) affords evidence of the use of these annals in the East
Anglian monastery.   Besides numerous additions from the Annals of
St. Neot (see below, note 4), it has several marginal notes taken
from the Norman Annals that do not occur in the Annals of St. Neots,
while many of the extracts in the latter work do not appear in this
MS.   The notices in the *Annales S. Edmundi* derived from the
Norman Annals occasionally differ in dates and in other respects
from those in the present work.   But most of the variations may be
due to errors in transcription.

[2] See Liebermann, *l. c.*, p. 31.        [3] See note 1 above.

[4] Thus under 734 it introduces the letter of Cuthbert relating the
last moments and death of Beda in the same way as the present work ;
it has the account of the punishment of Charles Martel given in the
present work under 741 ; the anointing of St. Edmund as King under
856 ; the minute details of the date of St. Edmund's death and other
passages added to the matter derived from Abbo's *Passio Sancti
Edmundi* under 770 ; the notice of the length of reign and the burial
of Guthrum at Hadleigh, exactly as in the present work under 890,
which it continues in the words of Florence of Worcester ' Hic in
Orientali Anglia cum suis habitavit,' &c., instead of the corresponding
sentence in the present work ; and the passage under 912 translated
from the Chronicle is reproduced in the same words, whereas it
appears more correctly in a different form in Florence under 913 and
914.   The Bury MS. then proceeds with the two extracts from the
Norman Annals given in the present work, but completes the last
one by copying the remainder of the entry from the Norman Annals.
See also p. 252, below, note to c. 49, 24.

present work, since Florence omits the participle.  The
evidence of the possession by St. Edmunds of copies
of the Norman Annals, of the Life of Alfred, and of
the present work are in favour of the composition of
the latter within its walls, for the two former and the
Chronicle and Beda supplied almost the whole of the
matter copied out by the compiler.  On the other hand,
we have the difficulty that the later compiler of the
*Annales Sancti Edmundi* makes no use of the present
compilation, taking his matter relating to English history
before the Norman Conquest from the work of Ralph de
Diceto, and from Roger of Wendover, or rather the
St. Albans compilation embodied by him.  The latter
compilation borrowed from the present work, for the
passages common to the two are inserted in exactly the
same manner as in the present work [1].

§ 4.  The date of the compilation is as uncertain as the
place of origin.  It is not continued beyond the year 914,
and is evidently incomplete.  The use of Norman sources
is proof that it is later in date than the Norman Conquest,
while the evidence of the unique MS. of the work limits
its date to the early part of the twelfth century.  It is
probably later than the year 1104, the date of the
completion of Hariulf's chronicle of the monastery of
St. Riquier in Ponthieu (*Chronicon Centulense*) from
which was derived, in all probability, the account of the
vision of Charles III under 886.  This work was written
in 1088, but the author continued it to 1104 [2], and it is

---

[1] Thus it inserts into matter derived from Abbo's *Passio Sancti
Edmundi* the clause giving the date of his death under 870 in the
present work, commencing ' Passus est,' but omitting the reference to
the reigns of the emperor and of the King of Wessex (Wendover,
i. 314; Matthew Paris, *Chronica Maiora*, i. 400).  It gives under
897 the description of Rollo's dream (Wendover, i. 364; Paris, i. 433,
434) as in the present work under 870, with a few insignificant alterations.  For the account of Alfred's alleged encounter with the cowherd's wife and his vision of St. Neot it goes to a life of St. Neot
differing from that used by the compiler of the present work, but
quoting the same verses.  See p. 257, below.

[2] See the edition by Ferdinand Lot, Paris, 1894, p. xvii, in the
excellent *Collection de textes pour servir à l'étude et à l'enseigne-
ment de l'histoire*.  Hariulf states that his work was a continuation
of an earlier one by Saxovalus (p. 283).  M. Lot remarks that

possible that the vision may have been in circulation even earlier in an independent form.

§ 5. In addition to this vision, the compiler borrowed from the Frankish Annals under 883, and from the record of the synod of Cérizy in 741 under 858. His most important continental source was the Norman Annals. The original of these annals has not been preserved, but the copy used by the compiler agreed very closely with the version preserved by the monastery of St. Évroul at Ouche in Normandy[1]. The Norman Annals were introduced into England after the Norman Conquest, and were widely circulated in the south of the country. They form the basis of several monastic chronicles, notably of those of Bury St. Edmunds[2], a twelfth-century compilation of later date than the present work. The vision of Rollo given under 876 differs from those described by Dudo of St. Quentin and later Norman writers, and is evidently of late date. It is possibly derived from some lost life of Archbishop Franco of Rheims, by whom Rollo was baptized, as here stated. Its Rouen origin is clear.

William of Malmesbury, who copies from Hariulf this vision and other matter, may have derived these materials from a common source, a MS. of St. Wandrille (Fontenelle) in Picardy (p. lv, note 2 ; cf. p. xxii, note 7).

[1] Hence we have quoted them as *Annales Uticenses*. They are printed in the appendix to Le Prevost's and Delisle's edition of the history of Ordericus Vitalis, Paris, 1838–1855, v. 139 sqq. Upon the various texts of these annals, which had a wide circulation in Normandy and on the Continent, see Delisle, in the fifth volume of Ordericus Vitalis, p. lxviii; Ludwig Theopold, *Kritische Untersuchungen über die Quellen zur angelsächsischen Geschichte des achten Jahrhunderts*, Lemgo, 1872, pp. 84 sqq. ; and the excellent account of Liebermann, *Ungedruckte anglo-normannische Geschichtsquellen*, p. 31 sqq., and in *Neues Archiv der Gesellschaft für ältere deutsche Geschichtskunde*, iv. 26. Liebermann remarks that all the English copies of these annals seem to descend from the Rouen version, of which the Ouche Annals appear to be a faithful copy. The Rouen entries do not appear in the present work, but the close agreements with the Ouche annals, which are based upon the Rouen recension, make it probable that the compiler of the present work had before him a MS. of the Rouen recension. This latter was made late in the eleventh century, the Rouen entries being continued down to circ. 1085. See Holder-Egger's history of the Norman Annals in Pertz, *Mon. Germ. Hist.*, 'Scriptores,' tom. xxvi, p. 489.

[2] See above, p. 101, note 1.

From Frankish sources was also derived the notice of the death of Charles the Bald, which is entered wrongly under 879.

§ 6. The English sources used in the compilation are Beda's *Historia Ecclesiastica*, the Chronicle, the Life of Alfred, Abbo of Fleury's 'Passion of St. Edmund,' a life of St. Æthelberht, King of East Anglia, and a life of St. Neot. The text of the latter has not come down to us, but the verses quoted from it occur in a twelfth-century MS. life of this saint[1]. The compiler makes extensive use of the Life of Alfred, embodying nearly the whole of it. He omits the passages relating to the author, the interpretations of local names, and, like Florence, *anno Dominicae Incarnationis* and the note of Alfred's age under each year. With these exceptions, he fortunately transcribed the Life very accurately. The MS. used by him agreed closely with the lost Cottonian MS.[2], and his evidence is of value as supporting readings of the latter recorded in the transcripts that have been entirely obliterated in the editions. Thus he has preserved in c. 97, 9 the reading *dispoliatis*, which occurs in transcripts Co and B. Parker substituted *evaginatis*, which is tacitly repeated by the other editors. Similarly his *suatim utens* in c. 56, 18 is supported by the occurrence of this strange expression elsewhere in the Life and by Florence's *suatim*, but is obscured by Parker's emendation *sua ipsius*, a reading repeated by the later editors without a word about any variation from the MS. The copy used by the compiler had *dormiret* in c. 67, 9, which Florence emended into *rediret*. The compiler, not understanding the adverb *oppido*, c. 18, 12, added *longe ab omni*, where Florence and the Durham compilers omitted it altogether. In c. 37, 11 he substituted *similiter* for this adverb. Occasionally he has manifestly superior readings to those of the Cottonian MS. of the Life[2], so that it is probable that he used a better MS. In these cases, as there are no such difficulties as that presented by *oppido*, we see no reason for thinking that he has deserted the readings of the copy before him.

---

[1] See below, p. 256.
[2] See above, p. xlix, § 25 ; p. lvii, § 34 ; p. 254, note 3, below.

The reading *Turkesige* for the *Lindesig* of the Life, c. 45, 5, suggests that the copy of the Life used by the compiler differed from the Cottonian MS., each of them omitting one of these two names, both of which occur in Chronicles A, B, and C.

§ 7. Historically the greatest interest in the compilation centres round the matter taken from the O.E. Chronicle. The chronology in the eighth century differs from that of the existing MSS. of the Chronicle, and, as it is demonstrably more accurate, Theopold has concluded that the compiler used a copy of this work more correct than any that has come down to us[1]. That the copy from which the Latin was translated was an ancient one is proved by the reproduction of the old spelling *Koenuualh* in 642 and 672, where the existing copies have the later form *Cen-*[2]. In like manner the early form *Oisc* occurs under 455, as in Beda, for which the extant MSS. of the Chronicle have wrongly substituted *Æsc*, which

---

[1] *Kritische Untersuchungen*, pp. 53, 85. He rightly concludes with Grubitz that these Latin annals are not a relic of the hypothetical Latin original of the Chronicle. See above, p. lxxxiii, § 53. That the Latin translation in the present work is of late date is proved by the rendering of the O.N. *hold* in the Chronicle under 904 by 'baro,' a Frankish term that was unknown in England before the coming of the Normans. The use of the accusative *Ludecan* in the Chronicle in 825 as a nominative in the corresponding entry under 827 proves that the Latin version is derived from one written in O.E. and that the translator's knowledge of O.E. was somewhat imperfect. This is also proved by the annal of 903, where Æthelwald is described as a brother of King Alfred, although correctly called a 'patruelis' of King Edward under 900 with the Chronicle. The error under 903 has evidently arisen from a mistranslation of the same passage in the Chronicle, owing to the translator referring the pronoun *his* to Alfred and rendering *fædran sunu* as though it were *fæder sunu*, 'father's son.' The former word *fædera* is the O.E. cognate (apart from a declensional change) of Latin *patruus*, Greek πάτρως, 'paternal uncle,' and the confusion with *fæder* could only have arisen at a late time, when the full endings of the O.E. were becoming blurred and when the suffixless genitive *fæder* was being replaced by one with the *-es* ending. The translation can therefore not have been made much before the date that we have assigned for the compilation of the present work, and may possibly be due to the compiler. The suggestion that this Latin version of the Chronicle was used by the compiler of the Annals of Lund is shown to be baseless at p. 112, below.

[2] See note to c. 1, 13, p. 160, below.

was more intelligible to the copyists.   The type of MS.
represented in the compilation agreed with MS. A in
assigning six years for the reign of Ceol under 591,
against the five years of MSS. B and C.   But this may
be derived from a copy of the regnal table, and not from
the Chronicle.   Apart from this it seems to have had no
agreements with A against the other MSS.¹  It was most
nearly related to B and C.   Thus under 528 Cynric is
assigned a reign of twenty-seven years with them and F,
against twenty-six in A and E, but this, again, may be
due to a copy of the regnal table.   With B, C, and D it
states under 900 that Æthelwold was elected king by
the Northumbrians, which does not appear in A, and it
supports the reading *Byrhtnoð*, *Beorhtnoð* of B, C, D
in this year against the *Beornoð*² of A under 905 by
*Brichtnoth* under 904.   It, however, differs from B and
agrees with C, D, E and F in assigning the commencement of Cuthred's reign to 740, against the 741
of A and B, and again in placing Ine's journey to Rome
in 726 instead of 728 with A and B.   Under 842 it has
correctly *Quantauuic*, corresponding to the *Cwantawic*
of A and B under 839, where C has blundered the name
into *Cantwarabirig*, followed by *Cantwic* in D, E, and
*Cwantuwic* in G.   With B, C, D, E it mentions the
capture of the Raven-banner of the Danes in 878, which
is missing in A and in the Life.   On the other hand it
agrees with the two latter in having no mention of
Alfred's mission to India, which appears in B, C, D,
E, and F under 883.   It would therefore seem that, as
with the Life, the MS. of the Chronicle used by the
compiler was nearer to the original than any extant
copy.   With the late MSS. E and F it agrees in recording the commencement of the reign of Æthelberht of
Kent under 565, and in mentioning the length of his
reign.   The seven years assigned to Ceolwulf under 731
may be due to a clerical error.   Under 709 the title *rex*
is added to Offa, who was King of East Anglia.   This

¹ Mr. Plummer, *Two Saxon Chronicles parallel*, ii. ciii, note 6,
holds that up to 892 it was nearest to A.
² Upon the confusion of these names see Napier and Stevenson,
*Crawford Charters*, p. 85, note 4.

does not occur in Beda or the Chronicle, and seems to be another East Anglian trait. The compiler has committed a singular error under 731 in stating that Ceolwulf, the ex-king of Northumbria, became bishop of Lindisfarne. He has clearly confused his name with that of Cynewulf, whose succession to the bishopric is recorded, with the tonsuring of King Ceolwulf, under 737 in D, E, and F.

§ 8. From the numerous omissions of entries in the Chronicle, Sir Thomas Hardy has concluded that the compiler used an imperfect copy of the Chronicle. But it is probable that he did not embody all the matter in the copy before him. The few entries given by him under the reign of Edward the Elder are suggestive of an eclectic use of the Chronicle, rather than of imperfections in the copy of the latter. In a similar manner he omits much of the contents of the Norman Annals. For the latter part of the reign of Alfred and for that of Edward the variations in arrangement of the material seem to suggest that the Chronicle at the back of the Latin version differed widely from the existing copies. But this may be due to rearrangement of the material by the translator. Such rearrangement is apparent in the entry under 910, which is noticeable for containing the name of the battle of Wodnesfeld, which occurs in Æthelweard and in Florence, but is omitted in Chronicles A, B, C, D, where the battle is recorded under 911 without the name of the site. The name of the Danish leader Eagellus does not appear in the Chronicle or in the other sources.

§ 9. The relationship of the Annals to the work bearing the name of Florence of Worcester is somewhat obscure. Florence commenced his work before 1095[1], and died in 1118, and his autograph has not been preserved. The four twelfth-century MSS. of his work are copied from an edition that contained a continuation to

---

[1] Ordericus Vitalis, iii. c. 15, states that John (by whom he means Florence) of Worcester commenced his work by the order of Bishop Wulfstan (ed. Le Prevost, ii. 159), who died in 1095. This passage was written before 1124. See Delisle, vol. v, p. xlvi.

1131[1], which in the MS. at Corpus Christi College, Oxford, reaches down to 1141. This MS., which is held to be the best, has several additions from William of Malmesbury that are absent from the other MSS. What is more remarkable is that the notices of the deaths and successions of bishops are added in a different coloured ink and, apparently, a different hand at the ends of lines, and have thus the appearance of interpolations. In the same manner passages from Asser are continued, although in many cases the sentences were complete without such continuations. These additions concerning the bishops and from Asser appear in all the other MSS. The blundered entry that places Asser's death in 883 shows how untrustworthy these entries may be[2]. As it seems clear that the text of Florence had been tampered with in other respects between his death and 1131, it is difficult to resist the suspicion that these notes about bishops were additions in the margin made after his death[3]. They occur almost without exception at the end of paragraphs, which is exactly the position that would be occupied by marginal additions when embodied in the text of a copy. The fact that three out of the four MSS. have these suspected additions embodied in the text is not a conclusive argument that they formed part of Florence's work, for the text common to all four MSS. embodies passages derived from William of Malmesbury[4]. These must have been added after

---

[1] Corpus Christi College, Oxford; Lambeth MS. no. 42; Corpus Christi College, Cambridge, no. 92; and Bodley MS. no. 297.

[2] Further examples of the inaccuracy of these notes about the succession of bishops may be found in Theopold, p. 95.

[3] Theopold speaks unreservedly of these notices as being due to an interpolator. He has been misled by the remarks of Hardy in the *Monumenta Historica Britannica*, p. 86, into regarding the notices of the bishops, which occur in all four of the early MSS., as being as clearly interpolations as the passages from Malmesbury that occur only in the Corpus Christi, Oxford, MS.

[4] Thus 'the story of Denewulf, which follows a notice of his succession, one of the suspicious entries regarding the succession of bishops, is from Malmesbury, *Gesta Pontificum*, § 75, p. 162, with unimportant changes, and that about Bishop Byrnstan under 932 is from the same source, § 75, p. 163. The passage regarding St. Wistan under 850 and in the Appendix, p. 267, ed. Thorpe, seems also, from

the death of Florence, for Malmesbury's *Gesta Pontifi-cum* was not completed until 1125[1], and his *Gesta Regum* is little, if at all, earlier in date[2]. The suggestion that Malmesbury may have copied from Florence is precluded by his custom of recasting, instead of copying, matter derived from other writers, except in the case of documents. Interpolation in the Middle Ages was easy and almost inevitable, for copyists commonly embodied in the text they were transcribing marginal additions that did not clash very violently with the text.

§ 10. The compiler of the Annals of St. Neots was clearly not acquainted with Florence's work. The translation of the passages from the Chronicle given by him varies from that of Florence, and his excerpts from the Life of Alfred were made independently of those in Florence, including many words and passages that are omitted by the Worcester writer. The additions and corrections of the Life in Florence are unknown to him[3]. Apart from some agreements arising from both using the Chronicle, and some partial agreements in giving regnal years, which both may have derived independently from regnal tables, the only agreement between the Annals and the body of Florence's work noticed by us is the application of the title 'venerabilis' to Beda under 734, the statement under 827 that King Ludeca of Mercia

the agreement in phraseology, to be taken from the *Gesta Regum*, § 212, p. 263, repeated in *Gesta Pontificum*, § 161, pp. 297–8. Under 973, in the narrative of the rowing of King Edgar upon the Dee by tributary rulers, the remark assigned to Edgar agrees verbatim with that in the *Gesta Regum*, § 148, p. 165. But this may be a case of borrowing by Malmesbury from Florence, or possibly from a common original, as suggested by Stubbs. See the present writer in the *English Historical Review*, xiii, p. 505, note 5. The passage at the end of the annal for 827 regarding St. Swithun is derived from Goscelin's life of this saint (*Acta Sanctorum*, July, vol. i, p. 327 a), and is probably also an interpolation, as it agrees so closely in character with those derived from Malmesbury. The same remark applies to the passages from Abbo of Fleury's *Passio S. Edmundi* at the end of the annals for 859 and 870.

[1] *Gesta Pontificum*, § 278, p. 442.
[2] Stubbs, introduction to *Gesta Regum*, i. xix.
[3] Thus he omits the date of the death of King Æthelred, which Florence added to c. 41, and the notice of the battle of Merantun after c. 40.

was trying to avenge the death of his predecessor when he met his death, and the entry under 876 of the words 'Rollo cum suis Normanniam penetravit, xv. kal. Decembris.' This is derived from the Norman Annals, and therefore forms more naturally a part of the present work than of that of Florence, who, apart from this passage, shows no signs of acquaintance with these Annals. In Florence the words are added at the end of the entry for the year, and have thus the position that would be occupied by an interpolation. The notice of St. Edmund derived from Abbo's 'Passion' of that saint given in Florence under 859 is represented in the present work under 870 by the transcription of Abbo's words at length. But although there are no clear proofs of the use of Florence by the compiler to be derived from the body of Florence's work, there are three agreements with the Appendix to the Worcester writer's work. Thus the account of the death of King Sigebert of East Anglia in 651 agrees with the Appendix[1] in the addition of certain words to Beda ; under 794 the words 'innocenter sub pacis foedere occisus est ab Offa, rege Merciorum perfidissimo' occur in the Appendix[2], without the last word, which would hardly be applied by a Worcester writer to King Offa, the greatest name in the list of benefactors of that monastery[3]. The statement under 654 'Anna rex . . . a Penda, rege Merciorum, occisus' also occurs in the Appendix[4], but the agreement in this case may be accidental. It would seem that in the 794 passage the Annals of St. Neots have preserved a fuller reading than the Appendix. Thus the only agreement of importance is in the passage about King Sigebert. This is difficult to explain. If the compiler borrowed from the Appendix, it is curious that his debt should be so exceedingly small, and the same objection applies to the theory of borrowing by the Appendix from the Annals. Bishop Stubbs has suggested that the Appendix to Florence is an older compilation, and that it is con-

---

[1] Ed. Thorpe, p. 143.  [2] Ibid. p. 262.

[3] In this case both writers may be borrowing from a lost life of St. Æthelberht. See p. 208, note 3 below.

[4] Ed. Thorpe, p. 261.

nected with the lists of bishops and kings[1], the original
of which goes back to the ninth century. This theory
might explain the agreements between the wording of
the Appendix and the Annals of St. Neots, but there
are difficulties in the way of its acceptance. In the early
MSS. of Florence the sketches of the history of the
various kingdoms, in which these agreements occur, are
written in the margins of the pages containing the lists
of bishops and kings. These lists were current a century
or so before Florence's death without any traces of such
marginal histories, which would therefore seem to be of
later date. The sketches occasionally agree in wording
with the body of Florence's work[2], but they give several
passages from Beda at greater length than Florence does.

§ 11. The Annals share with Florence the error in
giving the length of Alfred's reign as twenty-nine and
a half years[3], but it is clearly not borrowed from him,
for the king's death is correctly referred to 7 kal.
November (October 26) against the 5 kal. November
(October 28) of Florence, and the year is given as 900,
whereas Florence follows the Chronicle in assigning it
to 901.

§ 12. The compiler shows no sign of acquaintance
with the works of William of Malmesbury. This and
his ignorance of the chronicle portion of the work of
Florence of Worcester are arguments in favour of composition very early in the twelfth century. The marvellous
history of Geoffrey of Monmouth, completed in 1147,
is unknown to the compiler. It is a work that would
have appealed strongly to his tastes.

§ 13. The Annals of St. Neots had, possibly owing
to their stopping at so early a date as 914, a very small
circulation. The somewhat later St. Albans compilation

---

[1] See above, p. lxii.

[2] In addition to the instances given at p. lxii, note 5, above, there
is the agreement in the wording of the passage about St. Wistan,
which may, however, be a later interpolation. See above, p. 108,
note 4.

[3] For the origin of the error see the present writer's article on the
date of King Alfred's death in the *English Historical Review*, xiii,
p. 71.

made use of them, and thus handed down to later
writers some of their contents[1]. The dream of Rollo
given in the Annals under 876 appears also in John of
Tynemouth's *Historia Aurea,* a late fourteenth century
production[2], and in Polydore Vergil[3], and in the compilation known by the name of John Brompton[4], but
seems in all these cases to have been taken from one of
the St. Albans writers. There are no grounds for holding that the Annals or the Latin version of the Chronicle
imbedded in them formed part of the sources of the
Swedish twelfth-century compilation now known as the
*Annales Lundenses*[5].

---

[1] See above, note 1, p. 102.

[2] MS. Bodl. 240, p. 314, the Bury St. Edmunds copy, written in
1377.

[3] *Anglica Historia,* lib. v (Basle edition, 1570, p. 102; Leyden
edition, 1651, p. 134).

[4] Printed by Twysden, *Decem Scriptores,* col. 810.

[5] Lappenberg, *Geschichte von England,* i. 329, note 2, drew attention
to the citations by Adam of Bremen in his *Gesta Hammaburgensis
Ecclesiae Pontificum,* i. c. 41; ii. c. 22, from unknown *Gesta
Anglorum.* See also Lappenberg, i. 392, note 2 ; Pauli, *Forschungen
zur deutschen Geschichte,* xii, p. 143, note 5, and in Pertz, *Scriptores,*
xiii. 102. They seem to be taken from the Northumbrian Annals.
Waitz in his edition of the *Annales Lundenses* in the *Nordalbingische
Studien,* Kiel, 1850, v. 5, remarked the presence in them of a number
of entries relating to early times that had come from England. The
English entries were referred by Prümers to the O. E. Chronicle, and
Theopold, *Kritische Untersuchungen,* pp. 53, note 2, 86, note 2, laid
emphasis upon the agreements in the wording of certain entries in
the Lund Annals and the Annals of St. Neots, and was inclined to
regard the latter as the vehicle by which the English and Frankish
entries reached the north of Europe. The entries relating to England
that he particularly drew attention to, those of 604 and 642, are taken
into the Annals of St. Neots and into the Lund Annals in the words
of Beda's *Recapitulatio* at the end of his *Historia Ecclesiastica,* and
the Lund Annals for 166, 189, 430, 449, 567, 601, 642, 655, 668 are
derived from the same source. The Lund entry for 407 is made up
from Beda's chronicle (in the *De sex huius saeculi aetatibus*) and
the *Recapitulatio.* As the compiler mentions under 725 and 730
that Beda wrote his *calendarium* and martyrology and his ' Historia
Anglorum,' and as he elsewhere uses his chronicle, it is obvious that
the agreements in wording between the Lund Annals and the Annals
of St. Neots prove only that both used Beda s works. The greater
part of the matter derived from Beda in the Lund Annals does not
appear in the Annals of St. Neots. The late entries in Chronicle E,
which have formed the basis of the claim that the Chronicle was used

§ 14. One MS. only of this work is known. It is preserved in the library of Trinity College, Cambridge, under the press mark R 7, 28, and was presented to the College by Thomas Neville, Dean of Canterbury, who was Master of the College from 1593 to 1615 [1]. Dr. M. R. James states that the MS. formerly belonged to Archbishop Parker [2]. It is paged in red pencil (partly cut away by the binder), and under 909 is a note in a Parkerian hand against the record of Asser's death 'Ergo aut non est As⟨s⟩er Annalium horum auctor aut non totius operis.' The MS. is on vellum, and now measures $6\frac{3}{8}$ inches by $4\frac{1}{2}$ inches, and has suffered much from an early binder's knife, so that the first line of p. 36 is entirely pared away [3], and the twelfth century marginalia are cut into. At the head of the first page a Parkerian hand (perhaps that of Parker himself) has written 'Annales Io. Asser, Epi. Wigorn.' (sic), which has also suffered from the binder's knife. The Annals occupy the first seventy-four pages of the volume, which is a composite one, including other works having no connexion with them. A considerable portion of the last page is left blank, so that the work appears to be complete.

§ 15. The handwriting of the MS. is of the early part of the twelfth century, and the capitals are written in blue, red, green, and violet. From pages 1 to 18 it is written in a neat and well-formed hand in brown ink,

by the compiler of the Lund Annals, are, on the other hand, English translations of entries in the Norman annals that appear in their original Latin form in the Lund Annals. Waitz, in his edition of these Swedish annals (in Pertz, *Mon. Germ. Hist.*, 'Scriptores,' xxix, pp. 185 sqq.), has concluded that the entries relating to England had already been added to the Rouen form of the Norman Annals before the latter came to the hands of the Swedish compiler. There are no proofs of this, however. Waitz would also ascribe the addition of the Irish annals that appear in the Lund work to the same earlier redactor.

[1] M. R. James, *The Western MSS. in the Library of Trinity College, Cambridge*, 1900-1, ii. 239.

[2] Ibid.

[3] It is supplied at the foot of p. 35 in a Parkerian hand, so that the damage to the margins is not due to the binder who affixed the present binding, which is considerably later than Parker's time.

after which a second and somewhat rougher hand commences. This second hand employs a darker ink, and is
more sparing than the first in the use of capitals, although
it frequently writes personal names in small capitals.
A third and more compressed hand appears towards
the end, which may, however, be that of the second
scribe. Throughout the entire work *ę* is used for *ae*
and *oe*, although *ae*, *æ* and *e* are also used. The English
*hér, hér, hér*, derived from Abbo's *Passio S. Edmundi*,
at p. 48, *Ycanhó* under 654, and *Áclea* from the Life
of Alfred, c. 5, 6, have accents, and the marginal additions written by the first hand under 527 and 579 are
referred to their places in the text by *þ*, the OE. sign
for 'that.' This suggests that the scribe was an Englishman, but Norman spellings occur, such as *Medouuege*
in a passage from the Life, c. 66, 7, the *Adhel-* forms
of names in *Æthel-*, and in the representation of OE.
*ð* by *d*. There are what may possibly be traces of
English influences in some of the letters, but it is hardly
yet possible to separate definitely the OE. and French
elements in the composite hands used at this time.

§ 16. A later twelfth or early thirteenth century hand
has added several interlinear and marginal glosses and
marginal notes. There are also traces of marginal notes,
some of which have been pared away by the binder,
in an early sixteenth century hand, and of others in
a somewhat later hand, which may be that of Parker
or one of his secretaries. The earlier sixteenth century
hand seems to be that of John Leland, for Parker's
transcript, which was clearly taken from this MS., states
that the original had notes in Leland's hand. At p. 73
the Parkerian hand has written after 'tam cleri quam
plebis' in the passage under 900 before the notice of the
anointment of Edward the words 'Hactenus Asserius,'
which marks the end of the extracts from the Life.

§ 17. A transcript made for the use of Parker is preserved among his MSS. at Corpus Christi College,
Cambridge, no. 100, fol. 261–319. It is in the same
hand as the copy of the Life, which it precedes[1]. On

---

[1] See Introduction, p. lii, above.

the first page is the title 'Annales Britanniae, authore I. Asser, cum paralipomenis alterius scriptoris,' and at the end is a note, in a small hand, ' Hic liber transcriptus e quodam vetustissimo codice, notato in margine manu Iohannis Leilandi.' To this is added in a cramped hand, ' Asserius Menevensis scriba scripsit Ælfridi res gestas et annales Britannię : huius Asserii annalibus vetustus quidam auctor paralipomenon addidit. Hęc Balęus,' founded upon the wording of Bale quoted above[1]. Extracts from the work in the hand of John Joscelyn, Parker's literary secretary, are preserved in the British Museum, Cottonian MS. Vitellius E xiv, fol. 148 (olim 158) sqq.[2], with the title ' Annales Asserii Menevensis ab anno Christi 596 ad annum 914[3].' It commences with the year 596 (=597) 'anno 147⁰ ex quo Horsus et Hengistus fratres venerunt in Angliam.' Fol. 163 (olim 170) verso has the final note after the annal for 914 ' Finis historiae Asserii Scire⟨burnensis⟩[4].'

§ 18. The work was printed from the Trinity College MS. at Oxford in 1691 by Thomas Gale in his *Quindecim Scriptores*, i. 141–175. This is somewhat carelessly edited, containing silent alterations of errors in the original, with numerous misprints, and occasional blunders such as *tumidi* for *Tuidi* in the 705 passage from Beda (p. 149), *tertius* for *territus* in the annal for 876 (p. 167). In the passage derived from the Life, c. 49, 20, Gale has falsified the text by comparison with the printed text of Asser or Florence, or perhaps with Parker's transcript of the present work. In the latter the reading of the MS. ' occidentem versus in Domnaniam ' is altered to ' occidit versusque inde Domnaniam,' the erroneous

---

[1] See p. 99, note.

[2] See Introduction, p. xxviii, note 4. above.

[3] In the early seventeenth-century table of contents at fol. 2, which seems to have been written after the volume had come into the possession of Cotton, the work is entered as ' Annales Asserii Menevensis, ab anno Christi 596 ad annum 914, ex antiquo manuscripto codice in bibliotheca Collegii Sancti ⟨sic⟩ Trinitatis, Cantabrigiae, per Iohannem Gosselinum exscriptae ' (sic).

[4] A transcript in the hand of William Lambarde is preserved in the Bibliothèque Nationale, at Paris, according to Hardy, *Catalogue of Materials*, i. 557.

reading in the Life and Florence. Gale added to this
passage, without warning the reader, *rex* from Florence
of Worcester, a serious falsification of the text for which
he could not allege the authority, such as it was, of
Parker or Camden.   In the copy of c. 46, 18 of the Life
Gale has inserted without notice the words 'Quibus
in eadem' from the Life, and 'tres' in c. 56, 25, and
he has altered the 'Liduicii' of c. 70, 6 into 'Lidwicus,'
under the impression that it was a personal name, in an
interlinear note that he has, as in other cases, absorbed
into his text.   In like manner he corrected the *Sarepte*,
derived from the Ouche Annals under 746, into *Soracte*.

# CHRONICON

## FANI SANCTI NEOTI

### SIVE

## ANNALES, QUI DICUNTUR, ASSERII

Igitur *Brittannia Romanis usque ad Gaium Iulium Caesarem inaccessa atque incognita fuit . . . bellorum tumultibus undique est circumventus et conflictatus est ⟨ex Bedae 'Hist. Ecclesiast.' i. 2⟩.*

*Anno autem ab urbe condita* DCCXCVII⟨1⟩ Claudius 5 imperator *. . . capta et subversa sunt ⟨ex eadem cap. 3⟩.*

*Anno ab Incarnatione Domini centesimo quinquagesimo sexto . . . in pace servabant ⟨ex eadem c. 4⟩.*

Anno ab Incarnatione Domini CLXXXVIIII *. . . regno potitus est ⟨ex eadem c. 5⟩.* 10

Anno Dominicae Incarnationis CCXLVI⟨1⟩ *Philippus imperat, primus Christianus imperator ⟨ex Annalibus Uticensibus⟩.*

Anno Domini CCLXXXVI *Diocletianus et Maximinianus ⟨ex eisdem ann. 285⟩.* Hoc tempore *Sanctus* martyr 15 *Albanus passus est ⟨ex Bedae 'H. E.' i. 7⟩.*

Anno Incarnationis Christi CCCX, hoc est *anno ab urbe condita* MLXI, *Constantinus*, filius Constantii et Helenae, gloriosae reginae, *imperat ⟨ex Annal. Utic.⟩.*

*Codex unicus titulo caret. Vide supra, pagg.* 98, 113, §§ 2, 14.
*Utic. = Annales Uticenses (vide pag.* 103, § 5, *supra).*

Anno CCCLXV⟨I⟩ *Hilarius Pict⟨avensis⟩* episcopus *obiit ⟨ex eisdem⟩.*

⟨CC⟩CLXIX. *Hoc ⟨tempore Med⟩iolano Sanctus ⟨Ambros⟩ius episcopus ordinatur ⟨ex Annal. Utic. ann.* 368⟩.

5 ⟨CC⟩CLXXV. *Am⟨brosium per⟩fida obsidio⟨ne vexav⟩it, nec priusquam ⟨prolatis b⟩eatorum Gerva⟨sii et Prota⟩sii martyr⟨um⟩, Deo ⟨revelan⟩te, reliquiis in⟨corrup⟩tis nefanda ⟨coepta d⟩eseruit ⟨ex eisdem⟩.*

Anno Dominicae ⟨Incarnationis⟩ CCCLXXIX *Theodo-*
10 *sius* imperat ⟨*ex eisdem*⟩.

Anno Christi CCCXCV *Archadius* imperat ⟨*ex eisdem*⟩.

Anno Domini CCCCVIII *Honorius* imperat ⟨*ex eisdem*⟩.

*Anno* Dominicae ⟨Incarnationis⟩ CCCCIX *Roma a Gothis fracta ; ex quo tempore Romani in Brittannia*
15 *regnare cessarunt* ⟨*ex Bedae '* H. E.' v. 24; cf. i. 11⟩.

Anno Christi CCCCX. *Hoc tempore inventio corporis Sancti Stephani primi martyris et sociorum eius ⟨ex Annal. Utic.⟩.*

Anno Dominicae ⟨Incarnationis⟩ CCCCXII *Sanct*us
20 *Martin*us *Turonensis archiepiscop*us transiit ⟨*ex eisdem*⟩.

Anno Dominicae ⟨Incarnationis⟩ CCCCXXI Sanctus *Hieronimus* migravit ad Dominum ⟨*ex eisdem an.* 420⟩.

Anno Dominicae ⟨Incarnationis⟩ CCCCXXIII *Theodosius filius Archadii* imperat ⟨*ex eisdem*⟩.

25 Anno Dominicae ⟨Incarnationis⟩ CCCCXXIV Hoc tempore Sanctus *Augustinus* obiit ⟨*ex eisdem an.* 423⟩.

Anno Dominicae ⟨Incarnationis⟩ CCCCXXV *Huius temporis aetate extitit exordium regum Francorum. Primus Faramundus ⟨ex eisdem⟩.*

30 Anno Christi CCCCXXX *Clodio secundus rex Francorum ⟨ex eisdem⟩.*

---

3–8. *in margine scripta eadem manu. Quae abscissa sunt, et hic et alibi supplevimus.*

Anno Domini ccccxxxvii *Meroveus tertius rex Francorum* ⟨*ex eisdem*⟩.

*Anno* Domini ccccxlix *Marcianus cum Valentiniano imperium suscipiens* vii *annis tenuit, quorum tempore Angli a Brytonibus accersiti Bryttanniam adierunt* ⟨*ex* 5 *Bedae* '*H. E.*' v. 24 ; cf. i. 15⟩.

Anno Christi ccccl *Child*ericus quartus rex Francorum ⟨*ex Ann. Utic.*⟩.

Anno ccccLv bellum apud Cantiam in loco, qui dicitur Aegelesthrep, contra Bryttones et regem Brit- 10 tonum Guirthegirnum, in quo cecidit Horsa.  Et frater eius Hencgistus règnum suscepit cum filio Oisc apud Cantuarios ⟨*ex Chron. Anglo-Sax.*⟩.  Eo tempore, anno ccccLxxiii, *Clodoveus* quintus rex Francorum ⟨*ex Ann. Utic.*⟩. 15

Anno ccccLxxxviii Oisc filius Hencgisti coepit regnare super Cantuarios, et regnavit xxiiii annis ⟨*ex Chron. Anglo-Sax.*⟩.

*Anno* eodem Sanctus *Remigius baptizavit Clodoveum reg*em Francorum primum Christianum ⟨*ex Ann. Utic.*⟩. 20

Anno ccccxcii *Theodericus* rex Francorum ⟨*ex eisdem*⟩.

*Anno* ccccxcv *venere in Brittanniam duo duces, videlicet Cęrdic et Kynricus, filius eius, cum* v. *navibus, in loco, qui dicitur Cęrdices ora, et statim die eodem pugna-* 25 *verunt cum Bryttonibus,* et acceperunt victoriam ⟨*ex Chron. Anglo-Sax.*⟩.

Anno dix *Sanctus Benedictus* claruit ⟨*ex Ann. Utic.*⟩.

*Anno* dxx⟨vii⟩ *Theodebal⟨dus⟩* I. *anno ; cu⟨i suc-*

---

7. Childebertus *Utic. In margine scripsit prima manus* Anno Christi cccclxxxiii Clodoveus, quintus rex Francorum, *quae postea delevit.  Vide infra, vers.* 14.

14. *supra* Clodoveus *scripsit alia manus* I.

27. *in margine scripta.*

*cessit Clo⟩tharius ; post q⟨uem iiii. filii⟩ eius Haribertus
⟨Parisius⟩, Guntrann⟨us Aureliano⟩, Hilpericus Su⟨es-
sionis, Sige⟩bertus Metti⟨s⟩ ⟨ex eisdem⟩.*

Anno DXXVIII. *Hoc tempore Dionisius in urbe Roma*
5 *Paschalem* cyclum *composuit. Tunc Priscianus profunda
grammaticae rimatur ⟨ex eisdem ann. 527⟩.*

*Tum Arator, subdiaconus Romanae aecclesiae, poeta cla-
ruit ⟨ex eisdem ann. 530⟩.*

DXIX Regnavit Cẹrdic rex primus Occidentalium Sax-
10 onum annos XV ⟨*cf. Chron. Anglo-Sax. an.* 534⟩.

DXXXIIII ⟨K⟩ynricus annos XXVII ⟨*ex eisdem*⟩.

*Hoc tempore Sigebertus, rex Francorum, occisus est fraude
Hilperici, germani sui, cum quo bellum inierat, regnumque
eius Childebertus, filius eius adhuc puerulus, cum Bruni-*
15 *childe matre regendum suscepit ⟨ex Ann. Utic. an. 556⟩.*

DLX Ceaulin ann. XVII ⟨*ex Chron. Anglo-Sax.*?⟩. Hoc
tempore, id est *anno* Dominicae Incarnationis DLXV,
*Columba presbyter de Scottia venit Brittanniam ad
docendum Pictos, et in insula Hii mon⟨asterium⟩ fecit*
20 ⟨*ex Bedae* 'H. E.' v. 24 ; *cf.* iii. 4⟩.

Anno eodem Æthelbrihtus, rex Cantuariorum, regnum
optinuit, et gubernavit annis LIII ⟨*ex Chron. Anglo-
Sax.*?⟩.

Anno DLXX⟨XV *Chil* ⟩debertus, rex Fr⟨ancorum⟩ ⟨ex
25 Annal.Utic.⟩.

Anno DLXXIX *Chilperi⟨cus, rex Francorum⟩ ⟨ex Ann.
Utic.⟩.*

DXCI Ceol ann. VI ⟨*ex Chron. Anglo-Sax.*⟩. Huius
regis tempore, id est, anno Dominicae Incarnationis
30 ⟨DCXVI⟩, Sanctus *Papa Gregorius misit Brittanniam*

---

5. circulum *Utic.*                    6. rimatus est *Utic.*
9. DXIX *in margine.*                  11. DXXXIIII *in margine.*
16. DLX *in margine.*                  19. ducendum *Cod.*
24. *in margine scripta eadem manu.*   28. DXCI *in margine.*

*Augustinum cum monachis, qui verbum Dei genti Anglo-*
*rum evangelizarent* ⟨*ex Bedae ' H. E.'* v. 24; *cf.* i. 23⟩.

Anno DLXXX—.

⟨DX⟩CVII Ceoluulfus ann. XIIII. Eodem anno Dominicae Incarnationis DXCVII *venere Brittanniam prae-* 5
*fati doctores, qui fuit annus plus minus* CL *adventus An-*
*glorum in Brittanniam* ⟨*ex Bedae ' H. E.'* v. 24; *cf.* i. 25⟩.

*Anno* Dominicae Incarnationis DCI *misit* sanctus *papa*
*Gregorius pallium Bryttanniam Augustino iam facto epi-*
*scopo, et plures verbi ministros, in quibus et Paulinum* ⟨*ex* 10
*eadem ; cf.* i. 29⟩.

*Anno* DCIIII *Orientales Saxones fidem Christi percipiunt*
*sub rege Sęberchto et antistite Mellito* ⟨*ex eadem ; cf.* ii. 3⟩.

Anno Incarnationis Christi DCV *sanctus Papa Gregorius*
*obiit* ⟨*ex Annal. Utic. et Bedae ' H. E.'* v. 24; *cf.* ii. 1⟩. 15

⟨DCX⟩I *Kynegylsus,* rex *Occidentalium Saxonum* primus
Christianus, *regnavit annis* XXXI ⟨*ex Chron. Anglo-Sax.*⟩
*Baptizatus est apud Dorcacęstram a* Sancto *Byrino*
*episcopo, suscepitque eum* de sacro fonte Sanctus *Os-*
*uualdus,* Nordanimbrorum rex, *anno Christi* DCXXXV ⟨*ex* 20
*Chron. Anglo-Sax.*⟩.

*Anno Christi* DCXVI Sanctus *Æthelbryhtus, rex Can-*
*tuariorum,* migravit ad Christum ⟨*ex Chron. Anglo-Sax.*⟩,
quem Sanctus Augustinus episcopus baptizavit primum
⟨*cf. Bedae ' H. E.'* i. 26⟩. 25

Anno DCXXXV—.

*Anno* DCXX *Dagobertus, rex* Franc⟨orum⟩ ⟨*ex Ann.*
*Utic.*⟩.

Anno DLXXX—.

1. gentem *Cod.*
3. *in margine scripta eadem manu.*
4. DX *abscissa.* 6. *post* minus *addidit* annus *Cod.*
16. ⟨ ⟩I *in margine.*
20. anno Christi DCXXXV *in margine.*
26. *errore hic addita.*

DCXXXIII ⟨Ed⟩uuinus, Nordan⟨himb⟩rorum rex, occisus ⟨*ex Chron. Anglo-Sax.*⟩. Anno eodem ⟨*Flodo*⟩*veus*
cepit reg⟨nare⟩, *filius Dagoberti* ⟨*ex Annal. Utic.*⟩.

Anno Christi DCXXXIIII Sanctus *Byrinus episcopus*
5 praedicavit ⟨*apud*⟩ *Occidentales Saxones* ⟨*ex Chron.
Anglo-Sax.*⟩.

Anno Christi DCXXXVI praedicavit *apud Orientales
Anglos* Sanctus *Felix episcopus* ⟨*ex eisdem*⟩.

Anno Christi DCXLII *Koenuualch* regnavit XXXI *annis*
10 ⟨*ex Chron. Anglo-Sax.*⟩.

Anno primo regni sui *occisus est* Sanctus rex *Osuualdus*
⟨*Bedae 'H. E.'* v. 24; *cf.* iii. 9⟩.

Et anno Domini DCXLIIII Sanctus episcopus *Paulinus,
quondam Eboraci* archipraesul, *sed tunc Rofensis antistes,*
15 *migravit ad Dominum* ⟨*ex Bedae 'H. E.'* v. 24; *cf.* iii.
14⟩.

Anno DCLI Sanctus *Osuuinus,* Nordanhymbrorum
rex, fraudulenter *occisus, et* sanctus antistes *Aidanus
defunctus est* ⟨*Bedae 'H. E.'* v. 24; *cf.* iii. 14⟩.

20 His temporibus *Sigeberht*us, rex Orientalium Anglorum,
*dum adhuc regni infulas teneret* ⟨*ex Bedae 'H. E.'* iii. 19
usque ad finem*⟩.

Hoc tempore *Sigebercht*us, rex *Orientalium Anglorum,
pro amore regni caelestis, relicto regno et cognato suo*
25 *Ecgrico commendato, in monasterio, quod sibi fecerat,
monachus factus est.* Et *multo post tempore contra
regem Merciorum Pendan, ad confirmandum militem, invitus in certamen ductus, suae professionis non inmemor,
dum nisi virgam tantum in manum habere voluit, occisus*
30 *est, una cum rege Ecgrico.* Quorum regni successor factus
est Anna, filius Eni fratris Reduualdi* ⟨*ex Flor. Wig.
append.* 1, 261?; *cf. Bedae 'H. E.'* iii. 18⟩.

---

1. *in margine scripta eadem manu.*

Anno Christi Incarnationis DCLIIII *Anna, rex Orientalium Anglorum, a Penda, rege Merciorum, occisus est, et* Sanctus *Botulfus* abbas *fabricavit monasterium apud Ycanhó* ⟨*ex Chron. Anglo-Sax. et Bedae* ' *H. E.*' iii. 18⟩.

Anno DCLV *Penda periit, et Merci facti sunt Chri-* 5 *stiani* ⟨*ex Bedae* ' *H. E.*' v. 24; *cf.* iii. 24⟩. Anni ab initio mundi usque huc V̄DCCCL ⟨*ex Chron. Anglo-Sax.*⟩.

Anno Domini DCLIX *Clotharius* rex Francorum ⟨*ex Annal. Utic.*⟩.

Anno Christi DCLXIIII *eclypsis facta. Ceadda et Wil-* 10 *fridus Nordanhymbrorum ordinantur episcopi* ⟨*ex Bedae* ' *H. E.*' v. 24; *cf.* iii. 26–28, iv. 1⟩, et anno eodem Sanctus *Deusdedit* archiepiscopus *transiit* ⟨*ex Chron. Anglo-Sax.; cf. Bedae* ' *H. E.*' iv. 1⟩.

Anno Dominicae Incarnationis DCLXV⟨III⟩ *Sanctus* 15 *Theodorus ordinatur* archi*episcopus* ⟨*ex Bedae* ' *H. E.*' v. 24; *cf.* iv. 1⟩.

Anno Domini DCLXX *Osuiu*us, *rex Nordanhymbrorum, obiit* ⟨*ex Bedae* ' *H. E.*' v. 24; *cf.* iv. 5⟩.

Anno DCLXXII *Sexburch, regina* ipsius *Koenuualchi,* 20 *regnavit annum unum* ⟨*ex Chron. Anglo-Sax.*⟩.

Anno Incarnationis DCLXXIII *Sancta* virgo Christi *Ætheldritha* regina *coepit aedificare monasterium apud Elig* ⟨*ex Chron. Anglo-Sax.*⟩.

Anno DCLXXIV *Aescuuine* annis II. regnavit ⟨*ex* 25 *eisdem*⟩.

Anno Christi DCLXXVI *Kentuuine* regnavit annis IX. ⟨*ex eisdem*⟩.

Anno Christi Incarnationis DCLXXVII *Sanctus Audoenus* episcopus *migravi*t *ad Dominum* ⟨*ex Annal. Utic.*⟩. 30

Anno Dominicae Incarnationis DCLXXVIII *cometa apparuit.* Sanctus *Wilfridus* episcopus *a sede sua* ex-

---

2. regem *Cod.*

*pulsus est ab Ecgfrido rege, et pro eo Bosa, Eata, et Eadhead consecrati antistites* ⟨*ex Bedae 'H. E.'* v. 24 ; *cf.* iv. 12, v. 19⟩.

Anno Incarnationis Christi DCLXXIX *Sancta* regina
5 et virgo Christi *Ætheldrytha* migravit ad Dominum ⟨*ex Chron. Anglo-Sax. ; cf. Bedae 'H. E.'* iv. 19⟩. Et anno eodem reges extiterunt Francorum *Theodericus et Childericus* ⟨*ex Annal. Utic.*⟩.

Anno Christi DCLXXX Sancta *Hilda abbatissa obiit*
10 apud *Streanesheala* ⟨*ex Bedae 'H. E.'* v. 24 ; *cf.* iv. 23⟩.

Anno DCLXXXII *mortuo Childerico, regnavit Theodericus* ⟨*ex Annal. Utic.*⟩.

Anno primo Ceaduuallae, id est, anno Dominicae Incarnationis DCLXXXV, *Ecgfridus, rex Nordanhymbrorum,*
15 *occisus est* a Pictis ⟨*ex Bedae 'H. E.'* v. 24 ; *cf.* iv. 26⟩.
Hoc tempore Sanctus antistes Cuthberhtus multis virtutibus claruit ⟨*ex Bedae 'H. E.' passim*⟩.

Anno Dominicae Incarnationis DCLXXXVII—
*Pippinus primus maior domus efficitur* ⟨*ex Annal.*
20 *Utic.*⟩.

*Anno regni Aldfridi* regis Nordanhymbrorum *tertio, Ceaduualla, rex Occidentalium Saxonum* . . . ⟨*ex Bedae 'H. E.'* v. 7 *usque ad finem, versibus praetermissis*⟩.

*Anno post hunc, quo Ceaduualla Romae defunctus est,*
25 *proximo, id est* DCXC ⟨*ex eiusdem* v. 8 *usque ad* Doruvernensium sunt corpora deposita⟩.

Anno DCXCVIII *Clodoveus* rex Francorum ⟨*ex Annal. Utic.*⟩.

Anno DCC *Childebertus, frater Clodovei* ⟨*ex eisdem*⟩.
30 Anno Dominicae Incarnationis DCCIII Sanctus *Hedda* episcopus transiit ⟨*ex Chron. Anglo-Sax.*⟩.

18. *post* DCLXXXVII *duo versus erasi sunt.*

Anno Dominicae Incarnationis DCCIIII *Athelrędus,* rex *Merciorum, factu*s est *monachus,* commisitque *regnum Coenrędo* cognato suo ⟨*ex Bedae ' H. E.'* v. 24 ; *cf.* v. 19⟩.

*Fuit autem temporibus* huius *Keonrædi, qui post Athel- rędum regnavit* ⟨*ex Bedae ' H. E.'* v. 13, *omissis ad finem* 5 *capitis* 'Hanc historiam . . . narrandam esse putavi.'⟩.

Anno Dominicae Incarnationis DCCV *obiit Sexuulfus episcopus* ⟨*ex Chron. Anglo-Sax.*⟩, fundator *monasterii* apud *Medeshamstede* ⟨*ex Bedae ' H. E.'* iv. 6⟩, quod Burh vocatur.                                                                      10

Anno eodem *obiit Aldfridus* monachus, olim *rex Nordanhymbrorum* ⟨*ex Chron. Anglo-Sax.; cf. Bedae ' H. E.'* v. 24⟩.

Huius regis tempore *erat* quidam *paterfamilias in regione Nordanhymbrorum* ⟨*ex Bedae ' H. E.' v.* 12 *usque* 15 *ad finem*⟩.

Anno DCCIX Sanctus *Aldhelmus episcopus transiit* ⟨*ex Chron. Anglo-Sax.*⟩.

Anno eodem *rex Merciorum Kenredus* cum rege *Orientalium Saxonum Offa perrexit ad Romam. Ibi* 20 ambo *attonsi monachi* ef*fecti,* atque ibi migraverunt ad Dominum ⟨*ex Bedae ' H. E.'* v. 19⟩.

Anno DCCXIIII *Sanctus Guthlacus* anachorita *transiit* ⟨*ex Chron. Anglo-Sax.*⟩.

Anno DCCXVI *Dagobertus* secundus rex Francorum 25 ⟨*ex Annal. Utic.*⟩.

Anno DCCXVII *Karolus* Martellus, *filius Pipini* primi, *maior domus fit* regis Francorum Dagoberti secundi ⟨*ex eisdem*⟩.

Anno DCCXX *mortuo Dagoberto, Franci Danihelem* 30 *clericum* in *regem levaverunt,* atque Chilpericum nun- cupaverunt ⟨*ex eisdem*⟩.

Anno DCCXXVI. Hoc anno Ine, *rex Occidentalium Saxonum,* XXXVIII anno regni sui, ⟨post⟩ monasterium constructum atque dedicatum apud Glastoniam, regnum reliquit, *Romam perrexit, et ibi vitam praesentem honorifice finiens, caelestem patriam cum Christo regnaturus adiit* ⟨*ex Asser cap.* I *et Chron. Anglo-Sax.*⟩. Cui successit

5 in regnum Æthelherdus, regnavitque annis XIIII ⟨*ex Chron. Anglo-Sax.*⟩.

Anno DCCXXIX *cometa apparu*it et Sanctus *Egbrychtus transiit* ⟨*ex Bedae* ' *H. E.*' v. 24 ; *cf.* v. 23⟩.

Anno DCCXXXI Ceoluulfus, rex Nordanhymbrorum,
10 coepit regnare, et regnavit annis VII, ad quem Venerabilis Beda scripsit Hystoriam Anglorum. Qui post, relicto imperio, monachus factus, Lindisfarnensium extitit episcopus. ⟨*Vide supra, pag.* 107, § 7⟩

*Anno* DCCXXXIV *luna sanguineo rubore perfusa, quasi*
15 *hora integra,* II. *kalendarum Februaria*rum *circa gallicantum, dehinc nigredine subsequente, ad lucem propriam reversa* est ⟨*ex Bedae continuatione*⟩. Eodem anno migraverunt ad Dominum Sanctus *Tatuuinus* archiepiscopus Doroberniae, et Sanctus *Beda* venerabilis pres-
20 byter ⟨*ex Chron. Anglo-Sax.*⟩.

Incipit epilogium de obitu beati atque eximii doctoris Bedae, qui Giruuinensis monasterii presbyter extitit, doctorque praecipuus. *Dilectissimo in Christo collectori Cuthuuino Cuthbertus condiscipulus in Deo aeternam*
25 *salutem. Munusculum, quod misisti . . . sed brevitatem sermonis ineruditio linguae facit* ⟨*ex Cuthberti epistola de obitu Bedae*⟩.

Anno DCCXL *Cuthred rex* regnavit *ann.* XVI ⟨*ex Chron. Anglo-Sax.*⟩.
30 Anno DCCXLI *Karolo* Martello *defuncto,* filii eius *Karolomannus et Pippinus maioratum domus adipiscuntur* ⟨*ex Ann. Utic.*⟩.

*Karolus princeps, Pipini regis pater, qui primus inter omnes Francorum reges ac principes res ecclesiarum ab eis*

*separavit atque divisit . . . nobis viva voce sunt testati, qui viderunt et audierunt* ⟨*ex epistola Synodi Carisiacensis ad Hludowicum, regem Germaniae, directa, anno* 858, *apud Boretii et Krause* 'Capitularia Regum Francorum' = 'Mon. Hist. Germaniae,' *Legum sect.* II, *tom. ii.* 432, 31⟩. 5

Anno DCCXLVI *Karolomannus Romam perrexit, et monachus effectus est in Mont*e *Sarepte, ubi ecclesiam in honore Sancti Silvestri construxit, et inde* ad montem *Cassinum monasterium Sancti Benedicti transiit* ⟨*ex Ann. Utic.*⟩. 10

Anno DCCLII *Pipinus rex efficitur* ⟨*ex eisdem*⟩.

Anno DCCLVII *Sigebrychtus* regnavit annum unum ⟨*ex Chron. Anglo-Sax. ann.* 754⟩. Anno eodem *Parisius Pipinus, rex* Francorum, cum filiis eius *Karol*o et *Karolom*anno *et filia Sigila, benedictus est a Sancto Ste-* 15 *phano papa inter sacra missarum solennia, praecipiente Sancto Petro et Sancto Paulo et Sancto Dionisio* ⟨*ex Ann. Utic. ann.* 756⟩.

Anno DCCLVII *Kyneuulfus* regnavit ann. XXIX ⟨*ex Chron. Sax. an.* 755?⟩. 20

Anno DCCLXIII *hiemps illa maxima* ⟨*ex Ann. Utic.*⟩.

Anno DCCLXVIII *Pipinus, rex* Francorum, *obiit* ⟨*ex eisdem*⟩.

Anno DCCLXIX *initium regni Karoli* Magni, *regis* Francorum ⟨*ex eisdem*⟩. 25

Anno DCCLXXI *Karolomannus, frater Karoli* magni, *obiit* II *Non. Decembris* ⟨*ex eisdem*⟩.

Anno DCCLXXIIII *Karolus* magnus *Romam vadit. Inde reversus, Papiam cepit cum rege Desiderio, captis civitatibus et direptis univers*ae *Italiae* ⟨*ex eisdem*⟩. 30

Anno DCCLXXVI *conversio Saxonum* ⟨*ex eisdem*⟩.

---

7. Soracte *tacitus emendavit Galeus.*
30. universis *Utic.*

Anno DCCLXXVIII *Karolus* magnus *in Hispanias
intravit, Pampiloniam urbem destruxit, apud Caesar
Augustam exercitum suum coniunxit, et, acceptis obsidibus,
subiugatisque Saracenis, per Narbonam et Wasconiam*
5 *Franciam redit* ⟨*ex eisdem*⟩.

Anno DCCLXXX *Saxonia capta est* ⟨*ex eisdem*⟩.

Anno DCCLXXXIII *Witichingis cum sociis in* A⟨*n*⟩-
*tiniaco baptizati partem* regioni *contulerunt* ⟨*ex eisdem*⟩.

Anno DCCLXXXVI Brichtricus, rex Occidentalium
10 Saxonum, regnavit annis XVI ⟨*ex Chron. Anglo-Sax.*⟩.
Anno primo regni ipsius Franci *signum crucis in vestibus*
⟨*ex Ann. Utic.*⟩.

Anno DCCLXXXVII *ite*⟨*ru*⟩*m Karolus Romam perrexit, deinde ad Sanctum Benedictum et Capuam* ⟨*ex*
15 *eisdem an.* 786⟩.

Anno DCCLXXXVIII *Karolus per Alemanniam venit
ad fines Bauuariae* ⟨*ex eisdem*⟩.

Anno DCCLXXXIX. *Hoc anno Brychtricus* rex *accepit
Eadburgam, filiam Offae* regis Merciorum, in matri-
20 monium ⟨*ex Chron. Anglo-Sax. an.* 787⟩. Et eo etiam
tempore *primum* III *naves Normannorum* applicuerunt
in insula, quae dicitur Portland ⟨*ex Chron. Anglo-Sax.*⟩.

Anno DCCXC *Tassilio dux venit in Franciam, et
Bauuaria capta est* ⟨*ex Ann. Utic.*⟩.

25 Anno DCCXCII *Karolus pergit in Sclavos, qui dicuntur
Wilti* ⟨*ex eisdem*⟩.

Anno DCCXCIII *Karolus Hungrorum regnum vastat*
⟨*ex eisdem*⟩.

Anno DCCXCIIII Sanctus Æthelbrihtus, Orientalium
30 Anglorum rex, *innocenter sub pacis foedere occisus est*

---

5. in Hispanias intravit *post* redit *exhibet Utic.*
8. regni sui *Utic.*
21. *supra* Normannorum *scripsit alia manus* id est Danorum.
26. Vulti *Utic.*

*ab Offa, rege Merciorum* perfidissimo. ⟨*Cf. Flor. Wig.
App.* i. 262 ; *Chron. Anglo-Sax. an.* 792.⟩

Anno DCCXCVI *Adrianus papa obiit* ⟨*ex Chron. Anglo-
Sax.*⟩.

Eodem anno Offa, perfidus rex Merciorum, *obiit*, anno 5
XXXIX regni sui, regnavitque Ecgfridus, filius ipsius, post
illum diebus centum quadraginta uno ⟨*ex Chron. Anglo-
Sax. ann.* 755, 795⟩.

Anno DCCXCIX Sanctus *Leo Papa* a Romańis de *sede
sua* est *expulsus,* et *oculis evulsis ac lingua praecisa,* sed, 10
*Deo iuvante, visum recep*it et *loquelam, sed et sedem
propriam* ⟨*ex Chron. Anglo-Sax. an.* 797⟩.

Anno DCCC *Dominus Karolus* magnus, *rex* Francorum, *imperator factus est, et a Romanis appellatus est
Augustus, qui illos, qui Leonem Papam dehonestaverant,* 15
*morte dampnavit, sed precibus* Sancti *papae, morte indulta,
exilio retrusit. Ipse enim papa Leo Imperatorem eum
sacraverat* ⟨*ex Ann. Utic.*⟩.

Anno DCCCII *Ecgbrychtus, rex Occidentalium Saxonum,* regnavit annis XXXVII. mensibus VII ⟨*ex Chron.* 20
*Anglo-Sax.*⟩.

*Anno* DCCCXIIII *Karolus* magnus *imperator, dum
Aquisgrani hiemaret, anno aetatis circiter* LXXI, *regni
autem* XLVII, *subactaeque Italiae* XLIII, *ex quo vero Imperator et Augustus appellatus est anno* XIIII, v. *kal.* 25
*Februarii rebus humanis excessit* ⟨*ex Annalibus Regni
Francorum*⟩. *Initium regni Loduuici, filii ipsius Karoli
magni* ⟨*ex Ann. Utic.*⟩.

Anno DCCCXV *Berneardus, rex Langobardorum,* nepos
Karoli Imperatoris, *excaecatus mor*itur ⟨*ex eisdem*⟩. 30

Anno DCCCXVI Dompnus *papa Leo* migravit ad Dominum ⟨*ex Chron. Anglo-Sax.*⟩.

Anno DCCCXXII *fames valida* ⟨*ex Ann. Utic.*⟩.

16. sanctae *Cod.*            17. detrusit *Utic.*

Anno DCCCXXIII *in territorio Tullensi iuxta Com-*
*merciacum villam puella quaedam, annorum circiter* XII,
*post sacram communionem, quam in Pascha de sacerdotis*
*manu sumendo perceperat, primo pane, deinde aliis omnibus*
5 *cibis et potibus abstinendo, in tantum ieiunasse perhibetur,*
*ut, nulla penitus corporis alimenta percipiens, sine omni*
*victus desiderio plenum triennium compleverit. Coepit*
*autem ieiunare,* ut diximus, *anno Domini* DCCCXXIII, *et*
*anno* Domini DCCCXXV, *circa Novembris mensis initium,*
10 *peracto ieiunio, escam sumere ac more ceterorum mortalium*
*vivere coepit* ⟨*ex Annal. Francorum an.* 825⟩.

Eodem anno *natus est Karolus* rex gloriosus Francorum, *filius Loduuici* Imperatoris et Iudith imperatricis,
apud *Franconoford,* id⟨*ib*⟩*us Iunii. In quo palacio novo*
15 *illo anno imperator hiemavit, et a Paschali papa in die*
*Paschae Romae coronatus et imperator est appellatus* ⟨*ex*
*Annal. Utic.*⟩.

Anno DCCCXXV Beornulfus, rex Merciorum, in bello
occiditur ab Orientalibus Anglis ⟨*ex Chron. Anglo-Sax.*
20 *an.* 823⟩.

Anno DCCCXXVII *Ludecan, Merciorum* rex, dum suum
praedecessorem atque propinquum ulcisci vellet, ab
eisdem East Anglis occiditur, et v. *comites cum eo* ⟨*ex*
*Chron. Anglo-Sax. ; cf. Flor. Wig. an.* 825⟩.

25 Anno DCCCXXXI. *In isto anno dereliquerunt Loduui-*
*cum, et elegerunt Lotharium* ⟨*ex Ann. Utic.*⟩.

Anno DCCCXXXIII *redditum est Loduuico regnum* ⟨*ex*
*eisdem*⟩.

Anno DCCCXXXIX mortuo *Ecgbrychto* rege nobili, re-
30 gnavit *Adheluulfus,* rex Occidentalium Saxonum filius
pro eo, regnavitque annos XVIII et dimidium ⟨*ex Chron.*
*Anglo-Sax.*⟩.

4. sumenda *Cod.*  5. cybis *Cod.*
25. *scilicet* Franci.

Anno DCCCXL *Loduuicus Imperator obiit* XII *kal. Iulii* ⟨*ex Ann. Utic.*⟩.

Anno DCCCXLI *bellum inter tres fratres, scilicet Loduuicum, Lotharium, et Karolum, filios Lodwici imperatoris, haud procul ab urbe Autisiodorensium, in quo Chris-* 5 *tianus ut*erque *populus mutua se caede prostravit.* VII *kal. Iulii divis*um est *reg*num ⟨*ex Ann. Utic.*⟩.

Anno DCCCXLII *translatio Sancti Audoeni episcopi, quando Normani vastaverunt Rothomagum et succenderunt monasterium illius, idus Maii* ⟨*ex eisdem*⟩.  Ipso 10 anno bellum contra paganos apud *Lundoniam,* et item apud *Quantauuic,* et rursum apud *Hrofescestram* ⟨*ex Chron. Anglo-Sax. an.* 839⟩.

Anno DCCCLI *venerunt Normanni in Sequanam* ⟨*ex Ann. Utic.*⟩. 15

Eodem anno *Ceorl, Domnaniae comes . . . propior est quam ad East Seaxum* ⟨*ex Asser c.* 3, *vv.* 2–9⟩.

*Eodem quoque anno* ⟨*ex eiusdem c.* 4 *usque ad finem; deinde sequuntur cc.* 5, 6, 8, 9⟩.

Anno DCCCLV rex Eadmundus, Orientalium Anglo- 20 rum gloriosissimus, coepit regnare VIII kal. Ianuarii, id est die Natalis Domini, anno aetatis suae XIIII.

Hoc etiam anno *Lotharius, Imperator* Romanorum, *obiit, filius Hloduuici* Augusti piissimi ⟨*ex Ann. Utic.*⟩.

Anno eodem initium regni Karoli Imperatoris, filius 25 Loduuici secundi.

Eodem anno *magnus paganorum exercitus hiemavit in insula Sceapeige* ⟨*ex Asser c.* 10 *usque ad finem capitis* 16⟩.

Anno DCCCLVI, hoc est anno secundo Karoli Imperatoris tertii, anno vero regni Adheluulfi, Occiden- 30 talium Saxonum regis, XVIII, Hunberchtus, Orientalium Anglorum antistes, unxit oleo consecravitque in regem Eadmundum gloriosissimum, cum gaudio magno et

6. utrinque *Utic.*

honore maximo, in villa regia, quae dicitur Burna, quia
tunc temporis regalis sedes erat, anno aetatis suae XV.
sexta feria, luna XXIIII, die Natalis Domini.

Anno DCCCLVII Adheluulfus, saepe memoratus rex
5 Occidentalium Saxonum, viam universitatis adiit, ⟨et⟩
quievit in pace, sepultusque est apud Stęningam. Regnavit Adhelbaldus, filius eius, post illum duos annos et
dimidium, qui et ipse antea cum patre regnavit annis
duobus et dimidio ; sed post patrem *contra De*um *et*
10 *Christianorum dignitatem, necnon et . . . in matrimonium*
*duxit* ⟨*ex Asser c.* 17, *vv.* 2–7⟩.

Anno DCCCLIX Hoc *anno coepit gelare* II *kal. Decem-*
*bris et finivit Non. Aprilis* ⟨*ex Ann. Utic.*⟩.

Anno DCCCLX *Adhelbald*us, *Occidentalium Saxonum*
15 *rex* ⟨*ex Asser c.* 18 *et usque ad finem c.* 20⟩.

Anno DCCCLXV *venerunt Normanni* in Franciam,
*medio Iulii* ⟨*ex Ann. Utic.*⟩.

Anno DCCCLXVI *Adhelbercht*us, rex Occidentalium
Saxonum, frater Adhelbaldi, *quinque annis* ⟨*ex Asser*
20 *c.* 19 *usque ad finem*⟩. Eodem vero anno *Adherędus,*
*frater* ipsius *Adhelberchti* regis, *Occidentalium Saxonum*
*regni gubernacula* ⟨*ex Asser c.* 21 *usque* factus est *v.* 9⟩.

Anno DCCCLXVII *praedictus paganorum exercitus* ⟨*ex*
*Asser c.* 26 *usque ad finem ; sequuntur cc.* 26, 27⟩.

25 Anno DCCCLXVIII *fames valida* ⟨*ex Ann. Utic.*⟩.

Anno eodem *Aelfrędus venerabilis rex secundarii . . .*
*subarravit et duxit* ⟨*ex Asser c.* 29⟩.

Eodem vero *anno . . . pax inter Mercios et paganos*
*facta* est ⟨*ex Asser c.* 30, *vv.* 1–19⟩.

30 Anno DCCCLXIX *item fames* magna *et mortalitas*
*hominum et pestis animalium* ⟨*ex Ann. Utic.*⟩.

Eodem anno *praefatus paganorum* ⟨*ex Asser c.* 31
*usque ad finem*⟩.

Anno Dominicae Incarnationis DCCCLXX Sanctissi-

mus *Deoque acceptus* rex Orientalium Anglorum *Ead-*
*mundus,* ex *Antiquorum Saxonum nobili prosapia* ⟨*ex*
*Abbonis Floriacensis Passione S. Eadmundi, c.* 3, *deinde*
*sequuntur c.* 4 *et c.* 5 *usque ad* ' *in exterminium adducere*
*totius fines Brittanniae.*' *Deinde*⟩ '*Praedicti iniqui duces* 5
*Hinguar et Hubba*' ⟨*ex eadem usque ad* '*coram maternis*
*obtutibus*'⟩. *Cumque iam multitudine . . . in exercitu*
*contraheret minus* ⟨*ex eadem, c.* 6⟩. *Dirigit* impius Hinguar dux ad Sanctum Eadmundum, *accito uno ex com-*
*militionibus, qui exploret . . . iudicaberis et regno* ⟨*ex* 10
*eadem, c.* 7⟩. *Quo audito, rex sanctissimus alto cordis*
*dolore ingemuit, et directo nuntio ait:* '*Omnipotens rerum*
*arbiter . . . subdere collo iugo nisi divino servitio*' ⟨*ex*
*eadem, c.* 8⟩. *Et ait ad eum, qui de condicione regni*
*locuturus ab impiissimo Hinguar fuerat missus . . .* '*re-* 15
*sponsa perfer quantocius*' ⟨*ex eadem, c.* 9⟩. *Sanctus vir*
et rex Eadmundus *vix verba compleverat* ⟨*ex eadem,*
*c.* 10 *usque ad finem capitis*⟩. *Talique exitu* ⟨*ex eadem,*
*c.* 11 *usque ad finem capitis*⟩. *Quidam* autem Christianae
*religionis delitescendo interfuit* praedicto *horribili specta-* 20
*culo, quem subtractum* ⟨*ex eadem, cap.* 12 *usque ad finem*
*capitis*⟩. *Quod ut factum est, . . . ut increparet pro-*
*phetae insipientiam* ⟨*ex eadem, c.* 13⟩. Haec magnalia
Christus suo concessit martyri primum, et multa post
alia contulit et confert adhuc, Qui vivit in secula secu- 25
lorum. Passus est autem Sanctus Eadmundus, Orientalium Anglorum rex gloriosissimus, XII. kal. Decembris,
anno Christi Incarnationis DCCCLXX, Indictione tertia,
secunda feria, luna XXII, anno aetatis suae XXIX, anno
vero regni sui XVI, et anno etiam XV imperii Karoli 30
tertii Augusti, filii Lodovici Secundi. Hoc est autem
anno quinto Adherędi regis Occidentalium Saxonum.

---

26. Passus est autem Sanctus Edmundus *supra versum scripta.*
31. *post* Secundi *scripsit supra versum alia manus* Augusti.

Sancto rege sic martyrizato, *proh dolor ! pagani nimium gloriant*es ⟨*ex Asser c.* 33⟩, *per Merciam* ⟨*ex eadem, c.* 32 *usque ad finem*⟩, *et totam illam regionem suo dominio subdiderunt* ⟨*ex eadem, c.* 33⟩, eo quod omnes fortiores et
5 nobiliores eiusdem gentis una cum Sancto rege, sive ante beatum regem crudeliter occubuerunt. *Eodem . . . sepultus est* ⟨*ex Asser c.* 34 ; *deinde sequuntur cc.* 35, 36, 37, 38, 39⟩. *His ibi gestis* ⟨*ex c.* 40 *usque ad finem. Sequuntur cc.* 41–50⟩.
10 *Rollo cum suis anno eodem Normanniam penetravit,* xv. *kal. Decembris* ⟨*ex Ann. Utic.*⟩. Idem Normannorum dux Rol⟨lo⟩ cum in antiqua Brytannia sive Anglia hiemaret, militaribus fretus copiis, quadam nocte fruitur visione mox futurae certitudinis. Visum enim est sibi
15 dormienti, supra se et exercitum suum subito exsurrexisse examen apum, suoque stridore avolare versus occidentem per maris medium, terramque petentes insidere gregatim in frondibus diversarum arborum, moxque omnem circa regionem quasi advenientibus congratulantem, aspersam
20 coloribus variorum florum. Evigilans itaque industrius dux, secum primo visionem tractat, eiusque significantiam sapienter ad requiem cursus sui suorumque in eisdem partibus, ubi apes viderat requievisse, coniectat. Pulchreque in hanc spem confortatur, quod tota illa regio
25 subitis floribus induebatur. Erat enim hoc quasi quaedam divinae pietatis evocatio, ut ex Dei munere adepta terra illa mox in Christi floreret titulo, variisque virtutum floribus in vera religione sua suorumque ornaretur successio. Advocatis ergo suis, strenuus dux edocet som-
30 nium, illucque totius classis iubet parari cursum. Aspirat quoque prospere divina miseratio, tum necessario venti spiraculo, tum maris et caeli habitu iocundissimo subeunt

12. *supra* Brytannia *scripsit alia manus* id est Anglia.
27. florerent *Cod.*

Sequanae hostium, optatoque cursu perveniunt ad ipsam
metropolim Rothomagum, fiuntque rebellantium inter-
nicies, dedentium vero se et eorum societati confaven-
tium defensio et requies. . Amore ergo pacis, potissimum
autem proelii taedio, allecto Francorum rege, impellente- 5
que hinc gratia illinc violentia, facta est tota regio illa
ducis suorumque Normannorum dominica, ut eam scilicet suis usibus possiderent et in regis Francorum fideli-
tate eam sibi recognoscerent et deservirent. Suscepta
itaque tota monarchia illa, redit inclitus dux Rotho- 10
magum, destructum eius relevat murum, reparat pro-
pugnacula, fossaque et turribus eius ambit moenia.
Interea frequentius accersito ad colloquium suum eius
archiepiscopo Francone, venerabil⟨is⟩ vitae viro, divinae
religionis instruitur documento et super talibus paulatim 15
coepit delectari, interius inspirante Spiritu Sancto.
Abluitur tandem, eodem pontificante, divinae regenera-
tionis sacramento in agnitionem Dei, eiusque exemplo
omnis exercitus eius eodem modo Christo regeneratus
in albis candescit fidei.      Insistit deinde Christianae 20
fidei amator gloriosus dux in combustis ecclesiis et
monasteriis reparandis in Christi honore, sanctorumque
corporibus referendis, quae sua suorumque hostili ablata
fuerant formidine, relataque ad sua ampliori relocavit
cultu et reverentia ; summo enim studio usus est et dili- 25
gentia circa sanctorum reliquias devotius recondendas,
adhibitis in eorum famulitio clericis vel monachis, prout
didicerat quosque fuisse in singulis sanctorum locis.
Terras etiam non solum eas, quae ex antiquo eis ad-
iacebant, verum plures superaddidit, ut eos intercessores 30
haberet apud Deum, Qui eos sibi sanctificavit. Omnibus
itaque recte curatis, verus Christicola, ut pius pater,
omnibus pie praefuit.
     Ipso anno *Hloduuicus rex*, filius Lodwici imperatoris,

*obiit. Ite⟨ru⟩m* ipso anno *Karolus Italiam ingreditur,
et eandem terram per aliam viam Karlomannus intravit.
Inde Karolus territus fugit, et in eodem itinere mortuus
⟨est. Ex Ann. Utic.⟩.*

5 Anno DCCCLXXVII item exercitus paganorum Węrham
deserens, partim equitando, partim navigando, sed cum
pervenerunt ad locum, qui dicitur Suanauuic, perierunt
CXX e navibus. Equestrem vero exercitum rex Alfredus
insequens quousque venit ad Exancęstram, ibi accepit
10 obsides et iuramentum ab eo, ut cito discessurus erat
⟨*ex Chron. Anglo-Sax.*⟩. *Ipso anno* ⟨*ex Asser c. 51
usque ad finem*⟩.

Anno DCCCLXXVIII magnus paganorum *exercitus* Danorum sive Nordmannorum post Theophaniam latenter
15 *Cippanham, villam regiam* ⟨*ex Asser c. 52 usque ad finem.
Sequitur c. 53*⟩. Et, ut in vita Sancti patris Neoti legitur,
diu latebat apud quendam suum vaccarium.

Contigit autem die quadam, ut rustica, uxor videlicet
illius vaccarii, pararet ad coquendum panes, et ille rex
20 sedens sic contra focum praeparavit sibi arcum et sagittas
et alia bellorum instrumenta. Cum vero panes ad ignem
positos ardentes aspexit illa infelix mulier, festinanter
⟨cu⟩currit et amovit eos, increpans regem invictissimum,
et dicens : '*Heus homo*
25     *urere, quos cernis, panes gyrare moraris,*
       *cum nimium gaudes hos manducare calentes?*'

Mulier illa infausta minime putabat illum esse regem
Alfredum, qui tot bella gessit contra paganos, tantasque
victorias accepit de eis.

30 Non solum autem eidem glorioso regi victorias de
inimicis et prosperitatem in adversis conferre Dominus

---

3. tertius *Galeus perperam.*
9. insequens *ex* insequente *factum Cod.*
25. girare *Cod.*

dignatus est, verum etiam ab hostibus fatigari, adversitatibus affligi, despectu suorum deprimi multotiens eum
idem benignus Dominus permisit, ut sciret, quoniam
'unus est omnium dominus, cui curvatur omne genu,
cuius in manu corda sunt regum, Qui ponit de sede 5
potentes et exaltat humiles[a],' Qui suos fideles in summa
prosperitate positos flagellis adversitatum vult aliquando
tangi : ut depressi de Dei misericordia non desperent,
et exaltati de honore non superbiant, sed etiam sciant
cui debent omnia, ⟨quae⟩ habent.  Quam siquidem 10
adversitatem praefato regi illatam non inmerito ei evenisse credimus, quia in primo tempore regni sui, cum
adhuc iuvenis erat, animoque iuvenili detentus fuerat,
homines sui regni sibique subiecti, qui ad eum venerant
et pro necessitatibus suis eum requisierant et qui depressi 15
potestatibus erant, suum auxilium ac patrocinium implorabant.  Ille vero noluit eos audire, nec aliquod
auxilium eis impendebat, sed omnino eos nihili pendebat.
Quod beatissimus vir Neotus adhuc vivens in carne, qui
erat cognatus suus, intimo corde doluit, maximamque 20
adversitatem ob hoc ei venturam spiritu prophetico
plenus praedixerat.  Sed ille et piissimam viri Dei correptionem parvi pendebat, et veris⟨s⟩imam eius prophe-
tiam non recipiebat.  Quia igitur quicquid ab homine
peccatur, aut hic aut in futuro necesse est ut quolibet 25
modo puniatur, noluit verus et pius iudex illam regis
insipientiam esse impunitam in hoc seculo, quatenus illi
parceret in districto iudicio.  Quare ergo idem saepedictus Alfredus in tantam miseriam saepius incidit, ut
nemo subiectorum suorum sciret ubi esset vel quo de- 30
venisset.

Verumtamen in maximis necessitatibus ac periculis
ei posito Beatus Neotus saepe apparuit, consolans eum

[a] Ephes. iv. 6 ; Isa. xlv. 23 ; Prov. xxi. 1 ; Luc. i. 52.

ac praedicens illum bene superaturum omnia mala sibi instantia.

*Eodem anno . . . ⟨ex Asser c. 54 usque ad finem⟩.* Ibique acceperunt spolia non minima. In quo etiam
5 acceperunt illud vexillum, quod Reafan nominant ⟨*ex Chron. Anglo-Sax.*⟩. Dicunt enim, quod tres sorores Hynguari et Hubbae, filiae videlicet Lodebrochi, illud vexillum texuerunt, et totum paraverunt illud uno meridiano tempore. Dicunt etiam, quod in omni bello ubi
10 praecederet idem signum, si victoriam adepturi essent, appareret in medio signi quasi corvus vivens volitans ; si vero vincendi in futuro fuissent, penderet directe nihil movens. Et hoc saepe probatum est.

*Anno eodem post Pascha ⟨ex Asser c. 55 usque ad*
15 *finem⟩.* Nocte illa, cum se sopori dedisset, apparuit ei quaedam effigies in speciem Sancti Neoti, quondam eius familiaris amici et propinqui, ammonuitque, ut omnem terrorem et metum barbarorum abiceret, ne in desperationem incideret propter multitudinem eorum, quia
20 Dominus in crastinam visitaturus esset eum et plebem suam, et quia propter arrogantiam suam, quam habuit in iuventute, omnia illa adversa sibi sustinenda fuissent. Et adiecit: 'Cras praecedam tota die ante vexilla tua, ut securius dimices contra hostes tuos, nihil timens, et
25 scias, quia Dominus Omnipotens pugnat pro te et pro populo tuo.' Statimque rex sompno excitus letissimus effectus est de angelica visione.

*Mane illucescente vexilla commovens inde ⟨ex Asser c. 56 usque ad finem⟩.*
30 *Anno* DCCCLXXIX, *Indictione* XII, *Non. Octobris, praecellentissimus Imperator Karolus sanctae recordationis, insignisque memoriae temporalem finiens cursum, feliciter, ut credimus, ad gaudia migravit aeterna. Hic siquidem*

15. soporem *Cod.*     17. amicus et propinquus *Cod.*

*fuit serenissimi Augusti Hludovici filius, ac nepos glorio-*
*sissimi Caesaris eiusdem nominis Karoli* ⟨' *ex libro quodam*
*abbatiae S. Farae Meldensis,*' Pertz, *M. H. G.* ' *Scriptt.*'
iii. 367⟩.

*Eodem anno ęclypsis solis inter nonam et vesperam, sed* 5
*propius nonam facta est* ⟨*ex Asser c.* 59⟩. Ipsoque anno
obiit Hlodovicus, rex Occidentalium Francorum, frater
Iudittae, reginae Adhelwlfi, regis Anglorum ⟨*ex Chron.*
*Anglo-Sax. an.* 885 ; *cf. an.* 879⟩.

Eodem vero anno *praefatus paganorum exercitus* ⟨*ex* 10
*Asser c.* 57 *usque ad finem ; sequitur deinde c.* 58⟩.

*Loduuicus, rex Saxonum, adhuc fratre suo Karlomanno*
*vivente, Bauuariam ingreditur* ⟨*ex Ann. Utic.*⟩.

Anno DCCCLXXX *saepe memoratus paganorum exer-*
*citus* ⟨*ex Asser c.* 60 *usque ad finem ; sequitur deinde c.* 61⟩. 15

Anno DCCCLXXXI *initium belli Francorum contra paga-*
*nos* ⟨*ex Ann. Utic. an.* 879⟩, *finito*que *proelio pa*⟨*ga*⟩*ni,*
*equis inventis, equites facti sunt* ⟨*ex Asser c.* 62⟩.

Anno DCCCLXXXII *Loduuico, filio Loduuici regis,*
*primum exeunte ad pugnam, Deoque donante, potiti sunt* 20
*victoria, et pars innumerabilis eorum maxima cecidit* ⟨*ex*
*Ann. Utic. an.* 879⟩.

Anno DCCCLXXXIIII *sedes Normannorum in Dius-*
*burg* ⟨*ex eisdem*⟩.

Anno DCCCLXXXV Paganorum *exercitus divisit se in* 25
*duas turmas* ⟨*ex Asser c.* 66 *usque ad finem*⟩.

*Eodem*que *anno Karlomannum* ⟨*ex Asser c.* 68 *usque*
*ad finem*⟩.

*Anno eodem Karolus* ⟨*ex eiusdem c.* 70 *usque ad finem*⟩.

*Eodem anno beatae memoriae Marinus* ⟨*ex eiusdem c.* 71 30
*usque ad finem*⟩.

Anno DCCCLXXXVI Alfredus, rex Occidentalium Saxo-

---

21. victoria *scripsi* : victoriam *Utic. Cod.*

num, *post incendia urbium* ⟨*ex Asser c.* 83 *usque ad finem*⟩.

Karolus Tertius Imperator, filius Hloduuici, regis Noricorum sive Baioariorum, hoc tempore vidit visionem,
5 quam ita ut hic constat scriptam referebat, dicens : ' Ego Karolus, gratuito Dei dono' ⟨*ex Hariulfi Chron. Centulensi*, iii. 21 ; *extat etiam apud Will. Malmesbur.* ' *Gesta Regum*,' ii. 111⟩.

Anno DCCCLXXXVII *Karolus* Imperator *viam uni-*
10 *versitatis adiit* ⟨*ex Asser c.* 85 *usque ad finem*⟩.

Anno DCCCXC obiit *Guthram, rex* paganorum, *qui et Athelstanus nomen in baptismo suscepit.* Qui primus apud *Orientales Anglos* regnavit post passionem sancti regis Eadmundi, ipsamque regionem divisit, *coluit*, atque
15 primus *inhabitavit* ⟨*ex Chron. Anglo-Sax.*⟩. Mortuus est itaque anno XIIII postquam baptismum suscepit, mausoleatusque in villa regia, quae vocatur Headleaga, apud Orientales Anglos.

Anno DCCCXCI *cometae apparuerunt post Pascha circa*
20 *Rogationes* ⟨*ex Chron. Anglo-Sax. an.* 892⟩.

Anno DCCCXCII *magnus* paganorum *exercitus venit de orientali regno* Francorum *usque ad Bononniam*, indeque *cum* CCCL *navibus in ostium Limene* fluminis, et ibi non longe a flumine in loco, qui dicitur *Apuldran*,
25 *fec*erunt *castellum* firmissimum. Quod Limene flumen currit de silva magna, quae vocata est *Andreadesuueald*, quae silva habet spatium *in longitudine ab oriente in occidente*⟨*m*⟩ *milliaria* CXX *et eo amplius, et in latitudine* XXX ⟨*ex Chron. Anglo-Sax. an.* 893⟩.

30 Eodem anno *Hastengus* venit cum LXXX *navibus in ostium Tamensis* fluminis *fecit*que sibi firmissimum oppidum apud Middeltunam in australi ripa Tamensis. Non multo post fecit aliud in aquilonali

5. scriptum *Cod.*          33. alium *Cod.*

parte Tamensis in loco, qui dicitur *Beamfleot* ⟨*ex eisdem
an.* 894⟩.

Anno DCCCXCIII *initium regis Karoli pueri ; huius
miles Hagano.*   Eodem anno *capta est civitas Ebroacensis*
a Nordmannis, *sed episcopus, Sebar nomine, Deo auctore,* 5
*evasit* ⟨*ex Ann. Utic.*⟩.

Hoc etiam anno Alfredus, rex Occidentalium Saxonum,
pugnavit contra Nordmannos in loco, qui dicitur *Fearn-
hamme ; qui eos* occidit et regem eorum sauciavit atque
*fugavit,* necnon et *spolia* multa eis *diripuit, transieruntque* 10
*Tamensis flumen* coacti, ad East Seaxam profecti sunt,
sed tamen multi in Tamense perierunt.   *Rex* vero
Alfredus, ut *audivit, quod* magna pars paganorum exercitus, quae inde fugata est, perrexit per mare navigans
usque ad *Exanceastram,* qui statim equestrem atque 15
pedestrem secum illo adducens exercitum, contra eos
atrociter pugnans, illosque ibidem devicit, stravit atque
fugavit.   Interea ex praecepto regis Alfredi Adhered,
comes Merciorum, una *cum civibus ˙ Lundoniae* et aliis
innumeris bellatoribus prudentissimis, venit usque *Beam-* 20
*fleotam, munitionemque* paganorum obsedit, *fregit,* atque
innumera spolia ibidem *accepit* in auro et argento, equis
et vestibus.   In quibus etiam et *uxor Hastengi cum
duobus filiis* ad Lundoniam est adducta.   Et ante regem
Alfredum praesentata ; *quos* rex statim *iussit reddi,* eo 25
quia filii *sui unus erat filiolus* regis Alfredi, *alter Adheredi
comitis.*   Cum autem Hastengus iterum venit *Beam-
fleatam,* reparavit ibidem *castellum,* quod fractum fuerat.
Deinde perrexit ad *Sceobyrig, et ibi construxit munitionem*
validissimam, adiunctusque est ei *exercitus* ille, qui 30
apud Apuldran sedit, necnon et *ab Orientalibus Anglis
et a Nordanhymbris* non minima sed maxima multitudo,
qui simul properantes sursum trans *Tamensem* fluvium

29. *supra* Sceobyrig *scripsit alia manus* id est Sudbiri.

depraedantes quousque pervenerunt ad *ripam Sabrinae*
fluminis, et ibi apud *Buttingatunam* munitissimum *oppi-*
*dum* fecerunt, sed mox *Adheredus, comes* Merciorum, *cum*
*comitibus Eathelmo et Eathelmnotho* ⟨*sic*⟩, necnon et
5 cum *aliis* fidelibus regis, *obsed*it oppidum ex omni parte,
quousque paganis defecit omnis victus, sic ut *carnes*
*equorum suorum comederent,* ac demum *fame* coacti *pro-*
*cedunt ad* bellum contra eos, qui ex *orientali parte ob-*
*sidionis* erant. Ceciderunt ibidem multi ex utraque
10 parte, tamen, Deo auxiliante, *Christiani victoria sunt*
*potiti,* Dani vero in fugam sunt versi. Item ad *East*
*Seaxum* redierunt, unde venerunt ⟨*ex eisdem*⟩.

Anno DCCCXCIV praefatus exercitus paganorum hiemavit *in insula,* quae vocata est *Mereseige* ⟨*ex eisdem an.*
15 895⟩.

Anno DCCCXCV Hastengus cum exercitibus sibi ad-
haerentibus, *tertio anno postquam venerunt in ostium*
Tamensis et in ostium *Limene* fluminis, *mare transivit*
*sine lucro* et sine honore ; sed multis *perditis* ex sociis
20 suis, applicuit in ostium *Sequanae* fluminis ⟨*ex eisdem*
*ann.* 896⟩.

Anno DCCCXCVIII *Arnulfus Imperator obiit, et Lod-*
*uuicus* filius eius *in regem elevatur.* Eodem anno *Rollo*
*cum exercitu suo Carnotensem civitatem obsedit, sed epi-*
25 *scopus eiusdem urbis Walthelmus nomine, vir religiosis-*
*simus, Richardum, Burgundiae ducem, et Ebalum, Picta-*
*vensium comitem, in suo auxilio provocans, tunicam*
*Sanctae Mariae Virginis in manibus ferens, Rollonem*
*ducem, Divino nutu, fugavit, et civitatem liberavit* ⟨*ex Ann.*
30 *Utic.*⟩.

⟨A⟩nno DCCCC Alfredus veridicus, vir in bello per
omnia strenuissimus, rex Occidentalium Saxonum nobi-
lissimus, prudens vero et religiosus atque sapientissimus,
hoc anno cum magno suorum dolore viam universitatis

adiit, die VII kal. Novembris, anno regni sui XXIX et
dimidio, anno vero aetatis suae LI, Indictione III.   Qui
apud Wintoniam civitatem regalem decenter et regali
honore est sepultus in ecclesia Sancti Petri, Apostolorum
principis.   Mausoleum quoque ipsius constat factum de 5
marmore porfirio pretiosissimo.

*Nam inter cetera bona . . . Aethelingaeige ⟨ex Asser
c. 92 vv. 4–8⟩, in quo constituit Iohannem abbatem, reli-*
*giosum virum, de genere Antiquorum Saxonum ⟨ex*
*eiusdem c. 94, v. 1⟩, quia nullum potuit invenire de sua* 10
*propria gente . . . monasticam . . . vitam ⟨ex eiusdem*
*c. 93, vv. 1–5⟩; ideo diversi . . . studuit ⟨ex eodem,*
*vv. 16–17⟩.*

*Nam quodam tempore ⟨ex eiusdem c. 96 usque ad finem,*
*sequitur deinde c. 97 usque ad domum reportaverunt* 15
*v. 28⟩. Aliud quoque monasterium ⟨ex eiusdem c. 98*
*usque ad finem⟩.*   Erat enim ille rex fortissimus defensor
sanctarum Dei aecclesiarum, clementissimus consolator
orphanorum et viduarum, largissimus distributor elemo-
sinarum.   *Nam in toto illo regno praeter illum . . .* 20
*declinaverunt negotia ⟨ex Asser c. 105, vv. 9–13⟩. Erat*
*namque rex . . . imperabat recitare ⟨ex c. 106, vv. 15–54⟩,*
in quibus, iussu regis praefati, fuerunt scripta iusta iudicia
inter potentes et inpotentes, et alia multa utilia tam cleri
quam plebis.
                                                         25
⟨A⟩nno eodem Eaduuardus, filius ipsius regis Aelfrẹdi,
unctus est in regem, regnavitque annis XXVI.   Hoc
etiam anno *Adheluuoldus, patruelis* regis Eaduuardi,
discessit ab eo, perrexitque ad *exercitum* paganorum, qui
occupaverat gentes *Nordanhymb*rorum, statimque totus 30
exercitus elegit eum ad regem ⟨*ex Chron. Anglo-Sax.*⟩.

Anno DCCCCII Sanctus *Grimbaldus sacerdos* transiit.
Et *Adhulfus comes, frater Alchsuuithae* reginae, *obiit* ⟨*ex*
*eisdem, ann.* 903⟩.

Anno DCCCCIII *Adheluuoldus*, rex Danorum, frater ⟨*sic*⟩ regis Aelfrędi, venit cum classe magna ad *East Seaxam* ⟨*ex eisdem ann.* 904⟩.

Anno DCCCCIIII *Adheluuoldus*, rex paganorum, adduxit
5 magnum *exerci*tum ab East Seaxa et ab Orientalibus Anglis per totam *Merciam depraedantem* et occidentem, *quousque pervenit ad Criccaladam, ibique transiit Tamensem* et ubique circa *Bradenam* maxima spolia *diripuit, indeque reversus est.* Rex vero *Eaduuardus, quam citius*
10 *potuit, congregavit exercitum* Christianorum, et *perrex*it usque *inter Fossas* et usque *Husam* flumen, et *depraedavit terram eorum usque ad paludes boreales.* Cum autem rex expectavit ibidem *exercitum* eius de *Cantia*, subito supervenit Adheluuoldus, rex Danorum, cum tota
15 paganorum gente, qui confestim contra hostes vexilla erexerunt, consertoque proelio hinc et inde atrociter pugnantes, ceciderunt multi ex utraque parte. Ex parte autem Christianorum *Sigeuulfus* et *Sigehelmus comes* et *Æduuoldus* praeses et *Kenuulfus, abbas* de Burch, et
20 *Sigeberchtus, filius Sigeuulfi*, et *Eadwoldus, filius Accan, et multi alii* ex *nobil*ibus Anglorum. Ex *parte* vero Nordmannorum *ceciderunt Eochricus* et *Athelwoldus, reg*es eorum, et *Brichtsin*us, *filius* Bricht*nothi clitonis*, et *Hysopa* et *Oskytellus barones et multi plures*, quorum
25 numerus nemo scit, sed tamen, proh dolor! *pagani loco funeris dominati sunt.* Eodem etiam anno *Alchsuuyth*a regina, mater regis Eadwardi, *decessit* ⟨*ex eisdem ann.* 905⟩.

Anno DCCCCIX *A*⟨*s*⟩*ser, episcopus Scireburnensis, obiit, et Frithestanus suscepit episcopatum Uuintoniae* ⟨*ex eisdem*
30 *ann.* 910⟩.

Anno DCCCCX bellum apud Wodnesfeldam, in quo ceciderunt *Eouuilsus* et *Healfdena, reges* paganorum, et *Ochter et Scurfa comites*, et *Othulf*us et *Bensingu*s et

---

11. flumen *scripsi* : fluminis *Cod.*

*Anolafus niger* et *Thurfridus* et *Osfridus* et *Godefridus* et alius *Godefridus* et Eagellus et *Agamundus*, primates paganorum, et multi alii innumerabiles quasi arena maris ⟨*ex eisdem ann.* 911⟩.

Anno DCCCCXI *Loduuicus* Imperator, *filius Arnulfi* 5 Imperatoris, *obiit*, et *Burchardus* dux *occiditur. Conradus, filius Conradi, in regem elevatur* ⟨*ex Ann. Utic.*⟩.

Ipso anno *Aetheredus, comes* Merciorum, *obiit.* Et *Eaduuardus* rex *suscepit Lundoniam et Oxenafordam, cum omnibus eis adiacentibus* ⟨*ex Chron. Anglo-Sax.* 10 *ann.* 911, 912⟩.

Anno DCCCCXII *Eaduuardus rex iussit aedificari urbem aquilonalem apud Heortfordam, inter* flumina, quae nuncupata sunt *Memeran et Beneficeam et Lygeam, circa festivitatem Sancti Martini.* Circa quoque *festivitatem* 15 *Sancti Iohannis Baptistae* praecepit construi *urbem* apud *Wittham.* Item ipso anno apud Heortfordam in *australi parte Lygean* fluminis ⟨*ex eisdem ann.* 913⟩.

*Hoc* etiam *anno baptizavit Franco*, archiepiscopus Rotomagensis, *Rollonem* ducem Nordmannorum ⟨*ex* 20 *Ann. Utic.*⟩.

Anno DCCCCXIIII *facta est pax inter Karolum*, regem Francorum, *et Rollonem*, ducem Northmannorum ⟨*ex Ann. Utic.*⟩.

1. *supra* Godefridus *scripsit alia manus* id est Gutheferth.
6. dux] rex *Utic.*
12. aedificare *Cod.*
16. construere *Cod.*

# NOTES

**Dedication.** This was written in the Cottonian MS. in capital letters, as shown by Wise's facsimile. The description of Alfred as 'ruler of all the Christians of the island of Britain' is somewhat surprising, for there is no proof of any subjection to him of the people of Northumbria beyond the mention of their taking oaths to him in 893 (894 according to the chronology of the Chronicle) or of Scotland. But it must be borne in mind that the latter was not comprised under the dominion of the kings who bore the rank of *Bret-walda* or *Bryten-w(e)alda*, a title ascribed to Alfred's grandfather in the Chronicle under 827[1]. It is possible that the description here applied to Alfred may have been influenced by this title, for *rector* is the natural translation of *wealda*. According to cap. 80 most, if not the whole, of Wales was under Alfred's supremacy. The Chronicle says under 901 that he was king of all England, except the parts that were under Danish government (that is, East Anglia, north-east Mercia, and Northumberland). The remainder of Mercia seems to have been in some sort of dependency upon him, after the death of its last king, under the rule of his son-in-law Æthelred[2]. Rulership over the whole island of Britain is

[1] It is noteworthy in this connexion that the Chronicle calls Ecgbyrht *Bryten-walda* or *Bret-walda* as soon as his rule reached the Humber. The agreement with the Northumbrians is related afterwards, and the reduction of the North Welsh is narrated in the following year.

[2] The statement in this work, cap. 80, 22, that Æthelred was subordinate to Alfred, harmonizes with the evidence of the charters of Æthelred and Æthelflæd, his wife, which are allowed or witnessed by Alfred; *Cart. Sax.* ii. 166, 173, 200, 222 (all from later copies). Cf. also p. 279, which is either spurious or interpolated. It is possible that this superiority of Alfred was the ground upon which Edward the Elder took the direct government of Mercia into his own hands upon Æthelflæd's death. According to the Appendix to Florence of Worcester (ed. Thorpe, i. 267), Alfred acquired the portion of Mercia that Ceolwulf ruled over (see c. 51). The part under Æthelred's power may have been identical with Ceolwulf's dominion. Its boundaries were defined and possibly changed by Alfred's agreement with Guthrum.

asserted in the titles of Æthelstan[1] and the succeeding
kings, but as it is not, as in the present case, restricted
to Christians[2], it does not seem that the description here
given to Alfred is an imitation of the imperial styles of the
tenth century. Possibly it is to be referred to c. 83, 6, in
which we are told that all the Angles and Saxons who had
been hitherto dispersed or under captivity to the Danes
turned to Alfred and submitted to his rule[3]. This was in
886, and it is possible that Alfred adopted about this time

---

[1] Æthelstan is described as 'rex Anglorum et aeque totius Bryttanniae
curagulus' ( = 'curam agens') in a contemporary charter of 939 (*Cart. Sax.*
ii. 447), and in other charters of which the originals are not preserved,
occasionally with slight modifications (ibid. ii. 412, 414, 415, 417, 418,
420, 421, 439, 457, 459, 462); and as 'rex Anglorum per Omnipatrantis
dexteram totius Britanniae regni solio sublimatus' in contemporary
charters of 930 and 934 (ibid. ii. 403; iii. 681, *Crawford Charters*, no. iv,
p. 6), and in a charter of 932 (*Cart. Sax.* ii. 390), which is preserved in a
somewhat later tenth-century copy, and in texts derived from chartularies
(ibid. ii. 349, 357, 363, 378, 383, 385, 392, 394, 406, 407, 423, 425, 426,
465). On some of his coins he is 'rex totius Brit(anniae).' The later
kings usually describe themselves as kings of Albion or Britannia and of
all the surrounding peoples, or as having acquired the empire of the whole
of Albion. In the O.E. version of a charter of 934 Æthelstan is twice
described as 'Ongol Saxna cyning ond Brytæn walda,' representing the
Latin 'rex et rector totius huius Britanniae insulae' (*Cart. Sax.* ii. 410).
This is a title of the later kings, and is not found in any genuine charter
of Æthelstan's (see p. 150, note 3, below), and the charter is open to
grave suspicions on other grounds.

[2] Æthelstan, under the impossible date of 850, is called 'rex Angul
Sexna et Norþhymbra imperator, paganorum gubernator, Brittanno-
rumque propugnator' (*Cart. Sax.* ii. 466). This title is applied, with
occasional modifications, to Eadred (ibid. iii. 28, 37, 41, 73, 687) and
Eadwig (ibid. iii. 114), and even to Æthelred (*Cod. Dipl.* vi. 166). These
texts, which are all derived from chartularies, form a related group, which
is distinguished by peculiarity of composition from all other O.E. charters, with the exception of a charter of Eadred of 946. In this Edmund is
said to have governed 'regimina regnorum Angulsaxna et Norþhymbra,
paganorum, Brettonumque' (*Cart. Sax.* ii. 576). The original of this
was at Worcester in 1649, according to Dugdale's list (in Wanley's
*Catalogus*, 1705, p. 299, no. 49). It was printed by Wanley, p. 302,
because it was 'formae minus usitatae,' without saying that the writing
was of later date, although the differently shaped crosses in the subscrip-
tions mentioned by him suggest a post-Norman scribe.

[3] This, however, seems to be a mistranslation of the Chronicle under
886, which states that all the English who were not under captivity to
the Danes submitted to him ('him all Angelcyn to-cirde þæt buton
Deniscra manna hæftniede was').

the style 'rex Angul-Saxonum,' by which he is described in
the present work[1], or the equivalent 'Anglorum Saxonum
rex,' as in this dedication.　He was then the only English
king in the country, and the style of his predecessors 'rex
Occidentalium Saxonum[2],' or simply 'Saxonum rex,' as correctly used in this work[3], might be exchanged for one that
should include the Angles, whose importance was so great
that Alfred himself calls his own language *Englisc*, not
*Seaxisc*.　The compound *Angul-Saxo* first occurs on the
continent[4], and was used to distinguish the English Saxons
from the Old Saxons.　It came into use in England in or
shortly after Alfred's time, and was employed to describe
the political union of the Angles and Saxons.　Its appearance in the present work may possibly be due to the
Frankish element discernible in its Latinity[5].　The style 'rex
Angulsaxonum' was used by Edward the Elder, if we may
place any trust in the charters ascribed to him[6], and by

---

[1] See cc. 1, 2 ; 13, 31 ; 21, 17 ; 64, 1 ; 67, 1 ; 71, 4 ; 73, 6 ; 83, 1 ; 87, 1.

[2] His father's title was 'rex Occidentalium seu (*or* necnon et) Cantuariorum' (the latter title used in Kentish charters), as we learn from
original charters of his (*Cart. Sax.* ii. 17, 30, 33), and the same style
was used by Æthelberht and Æthelred his sons (ibid. ii. 113, 19 ; 115, 11 ;
129, 1), which are also contemporary texts.　See also 86, 10 ; 107, 30 ;
132, 2.

[3] Æthelwulf is 'Saxonum rex' in c. 5, 4, but 'Occidentalium Saxonum
rex' in cc. 7, 4 ; 9, 10 ; 68, 11.　The latter title is applied to Æthelred in
30, 8.　Cf. also cc. 17, 9 : 21, 4.

[4] It occurs in the form *Engel-saxo* in the Life of Alcuin, written
between 823 and 829, in Pertz, *Scriptores*, xv. 193 ; Jaffé, *Monumenta
Alcuiniana*, p. 25.　There are similar instances of the composition
of two ethnic names in O.E. ; see Theodor Storch, *Angelsächsische
Nominalcomposita*, Strassburg, 1886, p. 7.　There is, however, no reason
to refer the form *Angul*, as Storch does, to Latin influences, since it
occurs in other O.E. compounds, such as *Angul-cyn*, &c.　*Angul-Seaxe* is
exceedingly rare in works composed in O.E.　Apart from the late translations of charters, it seems to occur only in the curious mixture of O. E.
and Latin in the poetical introduction to Aldhelm, in the tenth-century
copy in the library of Corpus Christi College, Cambridge, no. 326, in
the lines ' Ealdhelm, æþele sceop, etiam fuit ipselos ⟨ὑψηλός⟩ on aðel
Angelsexna ⟨*corrected to* Angol-⟩, byscop on Bretene'; Napier, *Old
English Glosses*, Oxford, 1900, p. xiv.

[5] See Introduction, § 58, p. xciii.

[6] No charter of Edward is preserved in an original form, and the
majority of the texts ascribed to him come from the Winchester and
Hyde chartularies, and the remainder from chartularies of little better
character.

Æthelstan in the early part of his reign[1], and occasionally by his successors until the time of Eadwig[2]. It is applied to Edgar in a charter that is obviously spurious[3]. Its non-occurrence elsewhere amongst the great number of charters bearing Edgar's name shows that it did not survive in use after his accession. Its sporadic occurrence in eleventh-century charters[4] is therefore to be assigned to the antiquarian uses of older formulas in the chanceries of that time, by which they are characterized. In most of the examples of late date it is combined with other titles, and is merely part of the rhetorical embroidery of the charters.

[1] He is described as 'Angel-Saxonum Denorumque gloriosissimus rex' in an undated demise by the monks of Hyde (*Cart. Sax.* ii. 326, a tenth-century copy), and in charters of 926 in later copies (ibid. ii. 333, 335), and in a spurious or much corrupted charter of 930 in the Abingdon chartulary (ibid. ii. 346). In the dubious Winchester charter of 934, referred to at p. 148, note 1, he is 'Angul-Saxonum necnon et totius Brittanniae rex' (ibid. ii. 410). Little weight can be placed upon the statement in the Appendix to Florence of Worcester (ed. Thorpe), p. 271, that Æthelstan 'monarchiam primus Anglo-Saxonum obtinuit.'

[2] Edmund is described as 'rex Anglo-Saxonum' or 'rex Anglo-Saxona' (= O.E. gen. pl. *Seax⟨e⟩na*) in two Glastonbury charters of 940 (*Cart. Sax.* ii. 472, 473), the former of which is most probably spurious, and the latter belongs to the curious group of charters mentioned at p. 148, note 2. Both formulas are alien to the genuine charters of this king. Eadmund is 'rex et rector Angul-Sæxna' in another charter of the latter class (ibid. ii. 505). In the strange Worcester charter of 946 (ibid. ii. 577), belonging to the same class (see p. 148, note 2), Eadred is said to govern 'sceptra diadematum Angulsaxna cum Norþhymbris et paganorum cum Brettonibus.' Eadwig calls himself 'Angul-Saxonum basileus,' &c., in a contemporary charter of 956 (ibid. iii. 143). Cf. also ibid. iii. 107, 141, 145, 166, 238, from the Abingdon and Winchester chartularies, and therefore open to doubt.

[3] *Cart. Sax.* iii. 446, from the Winchester chartulary. The formulas of this charter are unknown except in a charter assigned to Eadwig (ibid. iii. 155). Both are dated 956.

[4] Æthelred subscribes in 1001 (a contemporary charter) as 'rex et rector Angul-Sexna' (*Cod. Dipl.* iii. 317), and is called 'Angul-Saxonum rex' in a doubtful text dated 1005 in the Eynsham register (ibid. iii. 340). Edward the Confessor is described as 'Angul-Saxonum rex' in a contemporary (?) charter of 1044 (ibid. iv. 79), and, with the addition of 'aeque totius Albionis rex,' another piece of antiquarianism, in a contemporary (?) charter of 1049 (ibid. iv. 115). He is 'basileus totius gentis Anglo-Saxonum' in a text from the Abingdon chartulary in 1050 (ibid. iv. 123), and 'Angul-Saxonum rex' in a suspicious Bath charter of 1061 (ibid. iv. 150). See Introduction, p. lxvi, note 3, and p. 192, note 4, below, concerning these antiquarian survivals.

It was clearly an intermediate stage between 'rex Occidentalium Saxonum' and 'rex Anglorum,' which latter was adopted
by Æthelstan when he became really king of all England,
and which continued to be the official style of the kings
long after the Norman Conquest. The real title of the
kings is to be discovered not in the highly rhetorical styles
ascribed to them in the bodies of the charters, but in the
subscription clauses. In the vast majority of cases from
Æthelstan onwards the king is described in such clauses as
'rex (*or occasionally* basileus) Anglorum.' The evidence of
the coins is to the same effect. Æthelstan is 'rex Saxorum'
(*sic*), the style of the early part of his reign, or 'rex totius
Britanniae' on his coins. After his time the royal title is
invariably 'rex Anglorum.' We may therefore conclude
that the employment of the title 'rex Angul-Saxonum' in
the present work is evidence that it was composed not
later than the middle of the tenth century. Whether this
title was employed by Alfred at the date assigned for the
compilation we are unable to decide, for there is no contemporary charter of his in existence. In his literary
works he describes himself simply as 'Alfred the king,' and
in his will, which was written between 873 and 888 [1], and
is preserved in an eleventh-century copy, as 'king of
the West-Saxons.' It is true that he is called 'Anglorum
Saxonum rex' or 'Angul-Saxonum rex' in several charters,
but the texts are derived from chartularies of such indifferent
repute that little confidence can be reposed in them [2]. But
that he did change his title from 'rex Occidentalium Saxonum' is proved by the existence of a unique coin, on which

---

[1] See Introduction, p. lxvii, note 3.

[2] He is 'rex Anglorum et Saxonum' in a Worceste charter of 889
(*Cart. Sax.* ii. 200, 201), concerning which see above, p. lxvi, note 3; and
'rex Anglorum,' &c., in a spurious Chertsey charter (ibid. ii. 203); 'Anglorum Saxonum rex' in a Glastonbury charter of 891 (ibid. ii. 204), and in
an Abingdon charter of 892–901 (ibid. ii. 224); 'Angul-Saxonum rex' in
a spurious or interpolated Winchester charter (ibid. ii. 205), in a spurious
Wilton charter of 892 (ibid. ii. 209), and in a Malmesbury charter (ibid.
ii. 210). His title is 'rex Saxonum' in 880 in a charter from the *Textus
Roffensis*, the most trustworthy chartulary containing O.E. charters in
existence (ibid. ii. 168), and in a Winchester charter of 882 (ibid.
ii. 171), and in a post-Conquest forgery (ibid. ii. 212). The title also
occurs in a charter at Canterbury (ibid. ii. 219), which, from the evidence
of the language, must be considerably later than Alfred's time.

he is described as 'rex Anglo'[1].' Whether this represents 'Anglorum,' 'Anglorum Saxonum,' or 'Anglo-Saxonum,' it is impossible to decide, but it certainly adds greatly to the probability that he might have been described as 'Angul-Saxonum rex' in his lifetime, and we cannot therefore condemn the present work because this title is applied to him. Moreover, allowance must also be made in such a work for the use of titles that did not form the official style, if such existed, of the king. As examples we may cite the inscription, apparently contemporary, in the gospel of Mæil Brith Mac Durnan recording its presentation to Canterbury by 'Aethelstanus, Anglosæxana rex et rector[2],' a style not found in his genuine charters[3], and his description as 'Angel-Saxonum Denorumque gloriosissimus rex' in the Hyde demise referred to above[4].

1. This chapter is derived from the West-Saxon royal pedigree, a copy of which occurs in the Chronicle under 855. To this the author has added the mention of Alfred's birth and the place of his birth, the derivation of Berkshire from Berroc wood, the statements as to the abundant growth of box in the latter, that the Britons called the West Saxons *Geguuis*, and that the pagans formerly worshipped Geata as a god, and the quotation from Sedulius.

1, 1. The date of Alfred's birth may have been derived from the West-Saxon regnal table and genealogy, which states that he was twenty-three years of age at his accession, which the Chronicle records under 871 (872 in C). A copy of this regnal table is prefixed to the Parker MS. of the Chronicle, and another copy was, perhaps, prefixed to Chron. B, if the detached leaf in Cott. Tiberius A iii, fo. 178 really formed part of it[5]. An early fragment of it, containing the passage about Alfred's age, is printed in Sweet's *Oldest English Texts*, p. 179. This is slightly older than the Parker MS. of the Chronicle. The table also

---

[1] Figured in *Montague Sale Catalogue*, no. 545; British Museum *Catalogue of Anglo-Saxon Coins*, ii. p. 34, type 4.

[2] See the facsimile in Westwood, *Palaeographia Sacra Pictoria*, 'Gospel of Mæil Brith Mac Durnan,' p. 9.

[3] The texts in which this title is applied to him (*Cart. Sax.* ii. 347, 396, 408) are spurious.

[4] See above, p. 150, note 1.

[5] See Plummer, *Two Saxon Chronicles Parallel*, ii. lxxxix.

occurs in the Cambridge University Library MS. of the
translation of Beda's *Ecclesiastical History* ascribed to
Alfred[1], and an eleventh-century version of it has been
printed by Professor Napier[2] from the British Museum
Add. MS. 34, 652. In the latter the king's age is given as
twenty-two. It has been suggested that this table was
drawn up by Alfred[3], and it is somewhat remarkable that it
should be found in connexion with the Chronicle and the
translation of Beda, with both of which he seems to have
been concerned. It also occurred in his lost *Handboc*, for
William of Malmsbury refers his readers to Alfred's *Liber
Manualis*, which was seemingly still extant, to prove that Centwine was 'arctissima necessitudine consanguineus' of Ine[4].
Centwine does not occur in the West Saxon royal pedigree
copied into the Chronicle under 855, as that deals only
with the lineal ancestors of Alfred, and it therefore seems
clear that Malmsbury met with this table in the king's
*Handboc*. Upon the genealogy see p. 157, below.

[1] Printed in Miller's edition, Early English Text Society, i. 486, and
in Professor Schipper's edition, Leipzig, 1899, p. 703. The seventeenth-
century editor of the O.E. version of Beda, Abraham Wheloc, states
that the table occurred in more than one O.E. version of Beda. Cf.
Schipper, p. 743.

[2] *Modern Language Notes*, xii. 106, Baltimore, 1897.

[3] By Wheloc in 1643. Cf. also Grubitz, *Kritische Untersuchung
über die angelsächsischen Annalen*, Göttingen, 1868, p. 23 ; Karl Horst,
*Zur Kritik der altenglischen Annalen*, Darmstadt, 1896, p. 13. But the
table is probably considerably older than Alfred's time, for the name
*Celm* clearly represents the Northumbrian *Celin*, *Caelin*, which Beda,
*Hist. Eccl.* ii. 5, says was in West Saxon *Ceaulin*. i. e. *Ceawlin*. Sweet's
text and the Cambridge one also preserve an eighth-century orthography
in *Eaba, Eabing*. See Napier, p. 110. Another fact pointing to an older
origin is the mention of Creoda as king of Wessex between Cerdic and
Cynric. See below, p. 157 sqq. Bishop Stubbs (Will. of Malmsbury, *Gesta
Regum*, ii. p. xxii, note 2) states that Hardy had disposed of the attribution of this list to Alfred, because the earliest list known to him was of
the time of Edward the Martyr. Hardy, however, mentions that it
occurs in the Parker MS. of the Chronicle, which is much older than
St. Edward's time.

[4] *Gesta Pontificum*, lib. v, sec. 188, p. 333: 'Qui enim legit Manualem
Librum regis Elfredi, repperiet Kenten ⟨ = Centwine⟩, Beati Aldhelmi
patrem, non fuisse regis Inae germanum, sed arctissima necessitudine
consanguineum.' The genealogy at the end of Florence of Worcester,
ed. Thorpe, i. 272, cites the *Dicta regis Elfredi* to prove that Cenfus
was king of Wessex (674), whereas the Chronicle says that Æscwine,
his son, succeeded.

**1, 2 villa regia,** also cc.9, 12 ; 35, 5 ; 52, 4 ; 56, 30 ; 79, 7 ; 81, 9 ; applied to Chézy at 84, 11. Although these terms were used to describe a village on the royal demesne in Frankish Latin [1], the occurrence in the present work need not be ascribed to Frankish influence, for *villa regia* was used by Beda [2], and the *villa regia* seems therefore to be merely the *cyninges-tun* of Alfred's laws [3]. At c. 91, 23 stone buildings are called *villae regiae*.

**1, 3 Uuanating.**—The birth of Alfred at Wantage rests solely upon the authority of this work. This village was in the possession of Alfred, and was bequeathed by him to Ealhswith (his wife) [4]. It occurs again in Eadred's will [5], so that it would seem to have been an ancient possession of Alfred's house, which held much land in the vicinity. It is probably in this connexion that the Chronicle mentions under 647-8 that King Cenwealh of Wessex gave 'three thousands' [6] of land about Æscesdun (the Berkshire Downs)

---

[1] Waitz, *Deutsche Verfassungsgeschichte*, ed. 3, ii. part 1, p. 181, note 5; part 2, p. 191; Richard Schröder, *Lehrbuch der deutschen Rechtsgeschichte*, ed. 3, p. 194; Ducange, *s. vv.*

[2] Beda, *Hist. Eccl.* ii. 9, 14 bis, 16; iii. c. 17, 22.

[3] Ed. Liebermann, 1, 2, vol. i, 48; ed. Schmid, p. 68. The terms *villa regia, regalis* or *vicus regalis*, are not unknown in the charters. See *Cart. Sax.* i. 220, 36; 271, 23; 380, 11; 382, 27; 409, 30; 447, 10; 486, 23; 497, 25; 504, 4; 528, 30; 573, 15; 581, 30; 585, 11; &c.

[4] See his will in *Cart. Sax.* ii. 178. Concerning Ealhswith see Introduction, p. lx, note 7.

[5] *Cart. Sax.* iii. 75, 24.

[6] If this means three thousand hides, as Mr. Plummer holds (p. 23), the area conveyed would be more than that of Berkshire at the time of Domesday, which Professor Maitland works out at 2,473 hides (*Domesday Book and Beyond*, p. 505). It seems, therefore, improbable that hides are meant, and the omission of hides is still more improbable in the case of the *hund þusenda landes* of Beowulf, line 2995, referred to by Mr. Plummer. This is more than the entire numbers of hides and carucates in Domesday for the whole of England, except Northumberland, Durham, Westmoreland, Cumberland, and part of Lancashire. See Maitland, p. 507. Moreover the passage from *Beowulf* reads ' hund þusenda landes ond locenra beaga,' ' a hundred thousands of land and locked arm-rings,' so that the sum was made up in land and in currency, and *þusend* applies as much to the latter as to the former. The ' thirty thousands' paid by the men of Kent in 694, according to the Chronicle, for killing the West Saxon (joint-king?) Mul, seem to have been sceattas (Kemble, *Saxons in England*, i. 283; Schmid, *Die Gesetze der Angelsachsen*, pp. 594, 675; Seebohm, *Tribal Custom in Anglo-Saxon Law*, p. 444). A contemporary Kentish charter of 805-9 was made ' pro con-

to his kinsman Cuthred.   According to the regnal table [1], Ine
and Ingeld, from the latter of whom Alfred was descended,
had a sister Cuthburh, and she is mentioned in the Chronicle
in 718 as queen of Bernicia and abbess of Wimborne.   As
we have here proof of the use of the name-stem *Cūð* in
Alfred's family, it is probable that Cuthred was closely
connected with it, and that Alfred's extensive Berkshire
estates may represent this gift of 647–8.

**1, 3 paga**, 'shire, district.'   This form is peculiar to the
present work, in which it occurs in cc. 5, 2 ; 12, 7 ; 35, 6 ;
42, 19 ; 45, 5 ; 49, 6 ; 53, 4 ; 55, 4, 10, 11.   That this was
the reading of the original seems to be shown by the fact
that Florence of Worcester and the compiler of the Annals
of St. Neots agree in copying the word in this form.   It
has possibly arisen from a confusion of *pagus* and *plaga* [2].
*Pagus* was employed in Frankish Latin to describe a district
corresponding to an English shire, and the use of *paga* may
be ascribed to Frankish influence.   *Pagus* for shire occurs
in spurious O. E. charters [3].

**1, 4 Berroc silva**.   This wood is mentioned by name
as late as 1199 in a charter of confirmation by John to the
nuns of Fontévrault of the possessions of the nunnery of

petenti pecunia, id est tria milia denariorum' (Brit. Mus. *Facs.*, ii. pl. 7 ;
*Cart. Sax.* i. 445, 6), and another Kentish charter, also contemporary,
written *circ.* 850, refers to the payment of 'ten thousands' (Brit. Mus.
*Facs.*, ii. pl. 19 ; *Cart. Sax.* i. 561, 4).   See also *Cart. Sax.* i. 575, 23 ;
576, 7, 8.   The foundation charter of Gloucester has preserved a trace
of very ancient origin in the corrupted 'cum uno suleaura ⟨*for* anulo
aureo ?⟩, in quo fuit xxx. milia' (*Cart. Sax.* i. 95, 20, where Mr. Hart's
impossible suggestion that this is an error for *sulinga*, a purely Kentish
land measure, is noted).   The denomination had gone out of use before
the latter part of the tenth century, for Æthelweard converts Mul's
wergeld into 30,000 *solidi* of 16*d.* each (*Mon. Hist. Brit.* p. 506 E),
that is 2000*l.*   In a similar way the scribes of Chron. B and C inserted
the word 'hides' in this passage.

[1] See note to c. 1, 1, p. 152, above.
[2] The *pagae* of the Annals of St. Neots in c. 12, 28, where the others
have *plagae*, may represent the reading of the original.
[3] The spurious St. Denis charters of 790 and 795 apply *pagus* to
Sussex (*Cart. Sax.* i. 351, 10 ; 361, 23).   These are Frankish forgeries.   See
the writer's remarks in *English Historical Review*, vi. 736 sqq.   Other
instances are 895 *Cart. Sax.* ii. 205, 2 'in paga (*sic*), qui dicitur Dorset';
212, 28 'in pago Suthfolchi' (upon this charter see p. 201, note 4,
below); 900–3 ibid. ii. 247, 22 ; 257, 20 'in pago, qui dicitur Hamtun,'
the former being an early eleventh-century forgery.

Amesbury[1], which had been granted to them in 1179 by Henry II upon the expulsion of the nuns[2]. After the mention of Letcombe (co. Berks) the charter proceeds 'et de redditu nemoris de Barroc xx. sol. et decimam pasnagii tam den⟨arum⟩[3] quam porcorum, et quot porcos ibi habere voluerint quietos de pasnagio, et centum porcos in Chet⟨Chute Forest, co. Wilts⟩ quietos de pasnagio.' Guest[4] thinks that the Barroc Wood originally included Windsor Forest, but that by the date given above it had shrunk down to the

---

[1] *Rotuli Chartarum*, p. 14 a. John's charter is merely a repetition of that of Henry II. The latter is recited in the Inspeximus charters of Edward II, enrolled on the Charter Roll of his tenth year, membrane 10, no. 16, and of Edward III, enrolled on the Charter Roll of his seventeenth year, mem. 12, no. 16. The spelling in both enrolments is *Berroch'* (where *ch* has the Anglo-Norman value of *k*). The date of the charter of Henry II is fixed by the mention of the making of the confirmation in 1179, a date that is repeated in John's charter.

[2] Round, *Calendar of Documents in France*, p. 378.

[3] This word is printed in the *Monasticon* from the *Cartae Antiquae*, an authority inferior to the Charter Rolls, as *denariorum*. But it is clearly a Latinization of O.E. *den*⟨*n*⟩, 'valley,' which was used to express 'a woody valley, or place, yielding both covert and feeding for cattel, especially swine' (Lambarde, *Roman Ports of Kent*, Oxford, 1693, p. 108). The more usual word in O.E. charters is *den-bera*, which is explained as 'pascua porcorum' in a contemporary charter of 863 (*Cart. Sax.* ii. 116, 7; Ordnance Survey *Facsimiles of Anglo-Saxon Charters*, i. pl. 10) or *den-berende*, translated by Thorn in the fourteenth century as 'dennas glandes portantes' (Twysden, *Decem Scriptores*, col. 1776). *Den* (neut.) also occurs in O.E. in this sense (*Cart. Sax.* i. 553, 12; ii. 114, 22, Brit. Museum *Facsimiles of Ancient Charters*, ii. pl. 36; *Cart. Sax.* ii. 585, 12; Brit. Mus. *Facsimiles*, iii. pl. 13; *Cod. Dipl.* iii. 227, 31; Ordn. Survey *Facs.* iii. 33), and is Latinized as *dena* in Domesday Book, i. 2, col. 2; 14 b; 30 b, col. 1; 56 b, col. 2, the last one being a Berkshire entry. The word was unfamiliar to John's chancery clerks, for in the case of the enrolment of his charter to St. Peter's, Ghent (*Rot. Chart.* 184 a), 'decimis de Andredewal'' represent the more correct *dennis* of the charters of Henry I and II (*Cartae Antiquae*, T. 8), which are repeated almost word for word. In the forged charter of Edward the Confessor to Ghent the word is represented by *vallis* (*Cod. Dipl.* iv. 81). As this archaic *den'* in John's charter to the nuns of Fontévrault is derived from the confirmation of Henry II, and as the latter is a repetition of some older charter, it is possible that Barroc Wood may not have been generally known by that name so late as John's time. But the charter is a welcome confirmation of the mention in the present work of the existence of a wood called Berroc. The statement of Green, *Making of England*, p. 96, that Bearruc meant 'box,' rests upon a mistranslation of the passage in the Life.

[4] *Origines Celticae*, ii. 152.

valley of the Kennet. He bases his conclusion upon this charter, giving an erroneous reference to the *Monasticon*, iv. 102 (for ii. 336). The charter mentions Kintbury, Challow, Fawley, South Fawley, 'Rotlea' (Temple Rothley, co. Leicester?), Letcombe, and then Barroc Wood. If any conclusion could be safely drawn from the wording of the charter, it would be that Barroc Wood was near Letcombe Basset rather than in the valley of the Kennet. Kintbury, Challow, and Fawley were in the possession of the nuns of Amesbury at the time of Domesday[1]. Challow and Fawley are close to Wantage. Francis Wise, the editor of Asser, claimed that Berroc Wood was identical with Boxgrove, in Sulham, near Reading. He tells us that 'the last remains of Boxgrove were grubbed up not above two years ago' (i. e. in 1736), and the memory of the growth of box in Tilehurst was still current in his time[2]. Gough, in his edition of Camden's *Britannia*, has accepted this identification, but there is little to support it, since the growth of box was not restricted to this part of the county. It is recorded, for instance, in the name of *Boxford*, formerly *Box-ora*, between Newbury and Fawley.

1, 6 **genealogia**. This is derived, not from the West-Saxon regnal table referred to in the note to line 1, but from the genealogy of Æthelwulf, Alfred's father, which is entered in the Chronicle under 855. This deals only with the lineal ancestors of Æthelwulf, not with all the kings of Wessex, as the regnal table does, and it does not give the duration of the reigns. The descent of Æthelwulf also occurs in the regnal table, but therein it is only deduced from Cerdic, not from Woden, Geat, and Adam, as in the 855 pedigree. The copy of the genealogy used by the author of the present work agreed with the text in Chron. B, C, and D, and with the Sweet, Cambridge, and Tiberius A. iii texts of the regnal table against Chron. A, the copy of the regnal table prefixed to it, and Napier's text of the regnal table, in making Creoda the son of Cerdic and the father of Cynric. In the latter group Cynric is made the son of Cerdic. It seems clear that

---

[1] Vol. i, p. 60 a.
[2] *A Letter to Dr. Mead concerning some Antiquities in Berkshire*, Oxford, 1738, p. 41.

Creoda occurred in the archetype of the regnal list and, from the agreement of Chron. B, C, and D, in the archetype of the Chron., a position long and erroneously assigned to A. Creoda is also mentioned in the late tenth-century pedigree of Alfred's house in Tiberius B v[1], and in the list in the *Textus Roffensis*[2], which are copied from a common archetype[3]. That Creoda was in the original of the pedigree and regnal table is proved by the fact that

---

[1] Printed by Wright in *Reliquiae Antiquae*, 1841–5, ii. 171, and in part by Pauli, *Neues Archiv der Gesellschaft für ältere deutsche Geschichtskunde*, v. 637. This is a copy, with continuations, of the ninth-century royal genealogies and list of bishops in Sweet, *Oldest English Texts*, p. 167 sqq., a copy of which was used by the compiler of the *Historia Brittonum* (Nennius). The West Saxon genealogy has been added in Wright's text.

[2] Ed. Hearne, Oxford, 1720, p. 61. This text has been influenced by the Life, for it substitutes *Eata* for the *Eat* of Wright's list on the authority of the *Geata* of the Life. This is proved by the presence of another West Saxon royal genealogy in Old English in the *Textus*, pp. 59–60, which has *Geata*, ' whom the heathens worshipped as God,' a statement derived from the Life, c. 1, 22. It also repeats from the Life, c. 1, 17, that ' the Britons called the land Gewis ' from Gewis (see p. 163, below). The West Saxon genealogy given by Ordericus Vitalis, *Historia Ecclesiastica*, ed. Le Prevost, vol. iii. p. 161, was probably derived by him from the present work or from Florence of Worcester, for it has the form Geata, the passage ' quem Geatam iamdudum pagani pro Deo venerabantur,' the form *Cetuua*, and the conflate *Fingoldwulf* for *Fin, qui fuit Godwulf*. This conflation occurred in the Cottonian MS. of the Life, in Florence, and in Simeon of Durham, part 1. The editions of Florence exhibit *Fin, qui fuit Godwulf*, the reading of the Corpus Christi College, Cambridge, MS., but the Corpus Christi College, Oxford, the Bodleian, and the Lambeth MSS. have *Fingoldwulf*. M. Delisle has identified Orderic's source with the original of a MS. at Avranches, written about 1205, which formerly belonged to Orderic's monastery of Saint-Évroult, Ouche (Le Prevost's edition, vol. v. p. li). This copy agrees with Orderic's text, and has, in the parts not copied by him, the names added by Florence to the Life in c. 1, 18, 19. It has also the remark that the Britons call the West Saxon *Gewis*. It has some additions derived from the O.E. Chronicle. As Ordericus visited Worcester and saw there Florence's work, the O.E. genealogies in which he specially mentions (lib. iii. vol. ii. pp. 160–1), it is probable that his text of the genealogy of the West Saxon house was copied from Florence by him during his visit, and that the Avranches MS. is a transcript of his copy.

[3] The original was written in the reign of Edgar, as both texts say that Edward, Edmund, and Æthelred, the Æthelings, are sons of Edgar. Edmund, an illegitimate son, died, according to Malmesbury, *Gesta Regum*, c. 159, five years before his father's death, which occurred in 975.

the retention of his name is necessary for the alliteration,
which is then complete from Cerdic downwards, and is
only broken in the 855 text in the continuation to Sceaf
by the latter name and by those of Woden and Sceldwea [1].
But Creoda's name is omitted in all the complete versions
of the regnal table at the commencement, and it would
seem that he was omitted in the copy used by the compiler
of the Chronicle, for Cynric is referred to as the son of
Cerdic under 495, 534, 597, 674, 685, 688. The last four
are portions of the West-Saxon pedigree, and omit Creoda
in all the MSS. The author of the present work thus
contradicts himself within a few lines, for he makes Cynric
the son of Creoda in c. 1, 15, and of Cynric in c. 2, 8. Possibly
the detection of this discrepancy is the reason why Creoda
has been omitted from the 855 pedigree in Chron. A. It
is noteworthy that the copy of the regnal table prefixed to
the latter similarly omits Ceawlin from the list of kings,
although he is mentioned in the Chron. In later copies
the Northumbrian form of his name Celin [2] has in consequence been identified with Ceolwulf, and the two have
been merged. It seems, as the editor has already suggested [3],
that there has been a similar confusion or conflation of the
names Creoda and Cerdic. The consequent omission of
Creoda has introduced complications into the regnal tables
and the Chronicle. The regnal tables say that Cerdic
and Cynric conquered Wessex six years after their arrival,
which is dated 494, and that Cerdic reigned sixteen years.
The Chronicle, on the other hand, says that he and Cynric
began to reign in 519, and that he died in 534. Cynric
then reigned alone twenty-six years, the succession of
Ceawlin being ascribed to 560. This discrepancy may be
reconciled by assuming that Cerdic reigned from 500 to
516, Creoda from 516 to 534, and Cynric from the latter
date until 560. This would assign to Creoda a reign of
eighteen years. The seventeen years assigned for Cynric's
reign in the regnal table prefixed to A, against the twenty-
six in Tiberius A. iii and, by implication, in the body of

---

[1] R. Henning, *Sceaf und die westsächsische Stammtafel*, in *Zeitschrift
für deutsches Altertum*, Berlin, 1897, xli. 168.
[2] See above, p. 153, note 3.
[3] *English Historical Review*, xiv. 40.

the Chronicle, may, perhaps, have arisen from a confusion
of the seventeen or eighteen years of Creoda with the
twenty-six of Cynric. There is a similar confusion between
the duration of the reign of Ceawlin and Ceolwulf consequent upon their conflation.

1, 13 **Coenred.** This preserves an older form of the
name than any MS. of the Chronicle under 855. MS. A,
however, has *Coen-* under 685, 704, 716. The representation of the *i-umlaut* of *o* by *oe* (*Coen* < *Coin* < *Cōni-*) is very
rare in the MSS. of Alfred's time [1], and must, therefore, have
been copied by the author from some old MS. On the
other hand the work has a later form than A in *Freothe-*,
line 19, against the *Frithu-* of A [2], which is preserved in
lines 20, 21. The introduction of the late tenth-century
form *Freothe-* in line 19 is, no doubt, to be assigned to the
scribe of the Cott. MS., who has inadvertently written the
form of his own time, in which the *brechung* of *i* before
*u* to *eo* and the reduction of unaccented *u* to *e* had already
occurred. The late eleventh-century confusion of *æ* and *ea* [3]
represented by the form *Beldeag* for *Beldæg*, line 20, probably comes from Florence of Worcester, the Cott. MS.
having, if we may trust the collations and editors, *Belde.*

1, 22 **Geata, Getam.** The way in which the author
accommodates the O.E. *Gēat* to the *Geta* of his quotation,
with which it has no connexion, is worthy of note. The
weak form *Gēata* seems to be due entirely to this attempt
at reconcilement. It occurs as *Geata* and *Eata* in the two
genealogies in the *Textus Roffensis* [4], both of which show
proofs of being influenced by the Life. It also appears in
MS. B of the Chronicle, which is somewhat older in date
than the Cottonian MS. of the Life. In this case the

---

[1] P. J. Cosijn, *Altwestsächsische Grammatik*, Haag, 1888, i. § 79,
p. 96.

[2] Ibid. i. § 29, p. 52, where, by an oversight, some later forms are
given from MS. B of the Chronicle.

[3] Napier, *Old English Glosses*, p. xxvii. § 1, 1.

[4] See above, p. 158, note 2. The older copy in Tiberius B. v (see
above, p. 158, note 1) has *Eating, Eat,* which is probably an error
that has arisen from a rubricator's failure to insert the initial letters. It
may, however, be a late form of *Geating, Geat.* See Sievers, *Angelsächs.
Grammatik*, ed. 3, § 212, note 2.

addition of the final *a* to the name may be a clerical error
due to the surrounding names ending with that letter, more
especially as the other MSS. of the Chronicle prove by their
agreement that *Geat* was the reading of the archetype.
Florence of Worcester writes *Geata* in the Northumbrian
royal pedigree under 547, where MSS. B and C of the
Chronicle have merely the patronymic *Geating*, the *Gioting*
of the ninth-century text[1]. Florence probably wrote *Geata*
under the influence of the Life. It also appears in the
Avranches MS., which is probably based upon Florence[2].

**1, 18 Geguuis** = O.E. *Gewis*. The Welsh spelling of
*guu*, *gw* for *w* occurs in *Gwilou*, the river Wiley, O.E.
*Wilig*, and in *Guuihtgaraburhg*, c. 2, 11, although *w* is more
usually used in English names. *Gu* is naturally used in
Welsh names, *Degui* (St. David), c. 79, 52, 56; *Gleguising*,
c. 80, 6; *Guent*, c. 80, 7; and *Durngueir* (from Dornovaria),
c. 49, 7. The Welsh form of the river-name *Exe*, O E. *\*Esce*,
*Exe*, is spelt *Uuisc* in c. 49, 24. Possibly the scribe of the
Cottonian MS. may have corrected the orthography of
some of these and of other English names into O.E.
spelling. The meaning of the present passage is probably
that the West Saxons, who even in Beda's time had ceased
to be called *Gewisse*[3], were still known to the Britons by
this name. It is applied to the English in the *Annales
Cambriae* in the form *Giuoys*[4], and in the later *Brut y
Tywyssogion* as *Iwys*[5]. The latter form shows that the
name was of English origin and not Celtic, for the O.E. *g*
was a spirant, and hence could be written *i* when followed

---

[1] Sweet, *Oldest English Texts*, p. 171, line 110. This form disconnects
the name from the O. N. *Gautr*. This text preserves several early eighth-
century forms. See Sievers, in *Anglia*, xiii. 19, note 1.

[2] See above, p. 158, note 2.

[3] *Historica Ecclesiastica*, iii. 7: 'gens Occidentalium Saxonum, qui
antiquitus Geuissae vocabantur.' The West Saxons are called *Gewissi*
in ii. 5; iv. 15, 16; v. 19. It was used as an antiquarian revival in
the royal titles of the kings of the tenth century. See further upon the
name the present editor's note in the *English Historical Review*, xiv. 36,
note 15.

[4] Under the year 900 in the tenth-century version printed by Mr. Egerton
Phillimore, in *Y Cymmrodor*, ix. 167.

[5] Ed. Rhys and Evans, *Red Book of Hergest*, p. 260: *Alvryt urenhin
Iwys* (Alfred, king of Iwys).

by a palatal vowel, as in this case, whereas later Welsh *g* was a stop (like *g* in English *God*) in such a position. The spelling *Iewisse* occurs in the late tenth-century record of the synod alleged to have been held by Edward the Elder in consequence of the letter of Pope Formosus in 905[1]. There is a pedigree in O.E. from Adam to Edward the Confessor in the *Textus Roffensis*, in which it is asserted that the Britons called the land of the English *Gewis* ('ða wæs Gewis, of ðam Brittas clypedan ðæt land Gewis') from Gewis[2]. In the fictions of Geoffrey of Monmouth, in which names of localities are personified with a facility worthy of the Greeks, the Gewisse are converted into Geuuissa, printed Genuissa[3], the daughter of Claudius, just as the Mercians are converted into *Marcia*, to whom the Mercian laws are ascribed. The *Wissei* and *Gewissei* are made to do duty for the names of the Britons inhabiting Wessex before the arrival of the Saxons[4]. The ultimate source of Geoffrey's knowledge of this ancient name of the West-Saxons may be the present work or Beda, but the perversion is his own.

**1, 24 Sedulius.** That the ensuing quotation was present in the original work is proved by the presence of the first three lines, followed by *et cetera*, in the northern compilation handed down to us by Simeon of Durham. From Simeon these three lines were taken by the twelfth-century author of the St. Albans compilation that forms the nucleus of the chronicles of Roger of Wendover and Matthew of Paris[5]. But in these works they are transferred to Offa under 758, whose pedigree from Woden to Adam agreed with the one here given. Sedulius was, from his religious subjects, a very favourite poet in Western Europe. Beda and Aldhelm make frequent references to him in their grammatical works, and he was well known to Alcuin

---

[1] *Cart. Sax.* ii. 276, 277; Warren, *Leofric's Missal*, Oxford, 1883, p. 1 b.

[2] Ed. Hearne, p. 60. This is, however, derived from the present work. See above, p. 158, note 2.

[3] *Historia Britonum*, iv. c. 14, 15.

[4] Lib. vi. c. 6; lib. vii. c. 4; lib. viii. c. 10.

[5] Wendover, i. 235; Paris, i. 342. It is repeated from Paris in the work known as the *Flores Historiarum*, i. 383, the earlier part of which is really a copy of Paris.

and to the Carolingian poets. See the index of writers
who quote or imitate him given at the end of Huemer's
edition, to which the present work should be added. The
passage here quoted appears, rearranged so as to suit the
requirements of metrical prose, in the prologue to the Life
of St. Eloy[1]. The commencement of the first hymn of
Sedulius is quoted in the late tenth-century Life of St.
Oswald[2]. Sedulius is mentioned amongst the authors in
the library at York by Alcuin[3]. Leland met with a copy of
the *Carmen Paschale* at Sherborne[4]. Sedulius is referred to
in a poem wrongly attributed to Alcuin, but which seems
to be by Æthilwald, a contemporary Northumbrian (?)
writer[5]. In the present work the passage has been misunderstood, for the reference is to the slave Geta, who
appears in Terence, and not to the god Gēat. The
meaning was clear to Aldhelm, who quotes this line in his
letter to Acircius[6].

**2.** This chapter is derived principally from the Chron.
(see note to line 6), but the mention of Alfred's mother, of
her father Oslac, and of their descent from Stuf and Wihtgar
are additions. The descent here ascribed to Alfred is
possibly the reason why Stuf and Wihtgar are mentioned
in the Chron. under 530 and 534.

**2, 3 Oslac, pincerna.** An Oslac occurs as a witness to
a contemporary charter of Æthelberht in 858[7], but his rank

---

[1] D'Achéry, *Spicilegium*, ed. Baluze, ii. 76, quoted by E. Norden,
*Die antike Kunstprosa*, Leipzig, 1898, p. 759. Norden was not aware
of this borrowing from Sedulius.

[2] Ed. Raine, *Historians of the Church of York*, i. 458.

[3] *Carmen de Pontificibus Ecclesiae Eboracensis*, 1549, ibid. i. 395;
ed. Dümmler, *Poetae Latini Aevi Carolini*, i. 204.

[4] *Collectanea*, iii. 255, ed. Hearne, iv. 150.

[5] Dümmler, *Epistolae Merowingici et Karolini Aevi*, i. 243; cf.
Henry Bradley, *English Historical Review*, xv. 291. The poem is
printed in Giles's edition of Aldhelm's works, p. 108.

[6] Angelus Maius, *Auctores Classici*, Rome, 1833, v. 574; *Aldelmi
Opera*, ed. Giles, p. 307.

[7] Brit. Mus. *Facs.* ii. pl. 33, *Cart. Sax.* ii. 101. The Osric, ealdorman of Hampshire, mentioned in c. 18, 10, was probably a kinsman of
Alfred's mother. The occurrence of an *Os-* name in a great Hampshire
family, such as the ealdorman's must have been, is a strong confirmation of the information given in the Life concerning Oslac and his
family. Alfred mentions in his will a kinsman named Osferth (*Cart.*

is not defined.   There is nothing but this passage to
support Kemble's statement that the office of *pincerna* ' was
one of the highest dignity, and was held by nobles of the
loftiest birth and greatest consideration [1].'   The instances
of this title in the charters, which have been collected by
Kemble [2], are derived, with one exception, from chartularies
of indifferent repute, and there is not one of them that is
free from suspicion.   The excepted   charter   is one of
Uhtred, king of the Hwiccii, dated 756, in the third year
of Offa's reign, with the attestation ' Duddan pincerni ' (gen.
sing.) [3].   Kemble has branded this text as spurious, but,
apart from the strange errors in date, there is nothing in it
to cast doubt upon its authenticity.   The *pincerna* was an
officer of somewhat subordinate importance in the Frankish
court [4], and this mention of Oslac, a man of most noble
descent, and therefore not a noble by service, as fulfilling
the office of butler raises suspicions of the ascription of
later Frankish or English customs to Æthelwulf's court.   But
against this may be urged the fact that there is an equally great
difficulty about the mention of a great nobleman holding
this office at the time when the burnt Cottonian MS. of this
work was written.   The word *pincerna* occurs in the O.E.
glossaries, and must have been familiar through its occurrence in the Hieronymian translation of the Bible.   The

*Sax.* ii. 178, 20), to whom he leaves lands in Sussex.   He was probably a member of the Hampshire family.   See p. 217, below.

[1] *Saxons in England*, ii. 111.

[2] To Kemble's instances may be added that of ' Wigheard pincerna '
in 809 (*Cart. Sax.* i. 458, 5, a late copy).

[3] *Cart. Sax.* i. 325, 13.   The real date of the charter must be 777–779,
as it is witnessed by Bishop Tilhere (of Worcester) and by Bishop
Berhthun (of Lichfield).   This Dudda is, no doubt, the person of that
name in a charter of Uhtred's brother Ealdred, dated 781 (ib. 332, 18).
In the first-mentioned charter, he witnesses after the *principes* and *praefecti*.   The originals of both these charters, which were seen at Worcester
by Dugdale in 1643 (Wanley, *Catalogus*, p. 300, Nos. 83, 92), and are
mentioned by Wanley amongst the charters in the possession of Lord
Somers (ib. p. 301, Nos. 2, 4), had disappeared from the latter collection
by 1722, when Smith printed them at the end of his edition of Beda's
*History*, pp. 765, 767.   From Wanley's silence, we may conclude that
these charters presented no palaeographical peculiarities to arouse the
doubts of this accomplished judge of O.E. hands.

[4] H. Brunner, *Deutsche Rechtsgeschichte*, ii. 102, § 71; Richard
Schröder, *Lehrbuch der deutschen Rechtsgeschichte*, ed. 3, p. 139.

absence of evidence that great nobles held such originally menial offices about the king[1] does not justify us in rejecting this passage as the work of a later forger. The possibility that nobles did hold such offices at this time is deducible from the occurrence of 'Eastmund pedesecus' in the contemporary charter of Æthelberht cited above, where he witnesses next to the dux Æthelmod and before Oslac. We can hardly be wrong in identifying Eastmund with the minister of the same name who witnesses a contemporary charter of 862 and 863, and with the *dux* of the same name in a contemporary charter of 867 and 868[2]. At and for some time after this period the *duces* seem to have been drawn exclusively from the great nobles. *Pedisequus, pedisecus* occurs occasionally in the earlier charters as the name of an important official, to judge by the position of his signature, and it is evident that the word is used in a special sense, and not in the general sense of servant or attendant, which it bears in classical Latin[3]. Kemble was unable to define his duties otherwise than by suggesting that he was the king's messenger, an unlikely suggestion that would dissever his office at once from that of Hunferth, who 'sat at the feet' of the king in *Beowulf*, and who was evidently an important person in the court. The title disappears from the later charters, and in copies of early ones is occasionally misunderstood or perverted. As the disappearance of the *pedisecus* from the list of witnesses precedes the time when the lay officers of the court are mentioned with specific official titles, it is probable that his functions may have been divided amongst several officers, and that his acting as *pincerna* was the one that most struck the author of this work.

---

[1] Beda, iv. c. 3, tells us that Ouini, who accompanied Æthelthryth into Northumbria, was ' primus ministrorum et princeps domus,' to her, but his rank is uncertain.

[2] An earlier instance seems to occur in the case of Æðelheah, who is described in a charter of 812 as *ped' sec'* (Ordn. Survey *Facs.* i. pl. 6, Canterbury, contemporary ; *Cart. Sax.* i. 478, 8), and in a ninth-century copy of a charter of 814 as *dux* (Brit. Mus. *Facs.* ii. pl. 14; *Cart. Sax.* i. 481, 9).

[3] The fem. *pedissequa* is used by Florence, an. 1051 (ed. Thorpe, i. 207), in the classical sense, but his usages are no criteria as to the meanings in the ninth century in England.

**2, 5 Gothis et Iutis.** The second of these names was misprinted, probably by an emendation of the German printer, as *Indis* in Camden's edition, although given correctly as *Iutis* in Parker's edition. It is a proof of the carelessness with which the collation of the Cottonian MS. was done for Wise's edition, that it is stated in his apparatus that the MS. read *Indis*[1]. In addition to the evidence of Parker's text and of the transcripts that the MS. had *Iutis*, we have the much higher authority of Archbishop Ussher, who states categorically that it had this reading[2].

The author of the present work probably intended to convey that the *Iuti* or *Iutae* were the same people as the Goths. Similarly, William of Malmesbury states that *Anglia Vetus* lies between the Saxons and Goths[3], evidently on the basis of the well-known passage in Beda[4]. Such a con-

---

[1] Wise's error has, no doubt, arisen from a fruitful cause of wrong statements as to the reading of MSS. in critical apparatus, namely, the overlooking during collation of a variant reading in a MS., and then the statement, made when drawing up the apparatus, that the particular MS. has the reading of the text used as the basis of the collation. To avoid such mistakes, constant reference is required to the MS.

[2] *Britannicarum Ecclesiarum Antiquitates*, c. 12 (*Opera*, ed. Elrington, Dublin, 1847, v. 446): "'de Gothis et Iutis." Ita enim ex autographo legendum est ; non, ut in Francofurtensi editione vitiossissime habetur, Indis.' At the same time he drew attention to the current misreading in the editions of his time of Beda's *Iutae* as *Vitae* (through *iutae* being read *uitae*), a form that still misleads local writers and others to connect the name of these people with the Isle of Wight, which was known as *Vectis* long before their appearance upon the scene. The endeavour to connect the names of the island and of the people is as old as the thirteenth century, for the Claudius MS. C 9, of Malmesbury's *Gesta Regum*, c. 5, calls the people *Wichti* instead of *Iuti*, as in the other MSS.

[3] *Gesta Regum*, p. 121, § 116. There is what appears to be an earlier confusion of the Iuti with the Goths in the words ascribed to Belisarius by Procopius, *De Bello Gothico*, ii. c. 6, ed. Comparetti, ii. p. 44: ἡμεῖς δὲ Γότθοις Βρεττανίαν ὅλην συγχωροῦμεν ἔχειν . . . 'Ρωμαίων κατήκοον τὸ ἀνέκαθεν γεγενημένην. As he elsewhere—iv. c. 20 (iii. p. 146)—calls the inhabitants of 'Brittia' Ἀγγίλοι τε καὶ Φρίσσονες καὶ οἱ τῇ νήσῳ ὁμώνυμοι Βρίττωνες, it is possible that the Iuti, who seem to have been clearly a Frisian tribe, may be meant by the Γότθοι, but it is more probable that the latter word is used as a general name for any Germanic invaders of the empire.

[4] *Hist. Eccl.* i. c. 15. The *Anglia Vetus* suggests that the immediate source was Æthelweard (*Mon. Hist. Britt.* p. 502 D). In this case William's *Gothi* have originated from Æthelweard's *Gioti* (see p. 170, below), not from Beda's *Iutae*.

fusion could hardly be made by an Englishman in the time
of King Alfred, and this mention of the Goths, whose name
is correctly given by Alfred as Gotan [1] (without the erroneous
*th* of the classical forms), is, no doubt, to be ascribed to
the foreign origin of the author, who has been led by learned
associations to connect two unrelated ethnic names.   There
is no trace of the people of Kent calling themselves *Iuti* or
*Iutae*, except the passage in Beda, and it is clear that they
early abandoned this name in favour of *Cantware*, ' dwellers
in Kent.'  Their kinsmen in the Isle of Wight and in Hampshire have left hardly any more trace of their ethnic denomination.   The *Iutae*, *Iuti* are not mentioned in the
Chron., except in the late interpolation common to MSS.
A and E under 449, which is undoubtedly derived from
Beda.   This writer must be also the source whence the
author of the present work derived the form of the name.
The evidence of philology proves that he cannot have
derived it from any contemporary form.   Beda latinizes
the name as *Iuti*, *Iutae*, but it must have been in Germanic
an *i*-stem, like so many other Germanic and O.E. ethnic
and tribal names, for West-Germanic *iu* can only be explained
as arising from an original *eu* followed in the next syllable
by an *i*, which modified the *eu* into *iu* [2].  Beda's form may
represent an original \**Juti-z* (i. e. \* *Yuti-z*) or \**Euti-z*.  If
the former be the correct form, there can be no question
of connecting the name with the Jutes of Jutland, for in
Old Norse the semi-vowel must have disappeared before
the following *u* [3], as, for example, in the case of O.N. *ok*

---

[1] In the translation of Orosius, ed. Sweet, 16, 18; 48, 14, 19; 276, 4, 14,
21; 288, 19; 290, 19, 25, 32; 292, 12; 294, 17; 296, 7, 10; 298, 3; translation of Boethius, ed. Sedgfield, 3, 1; 7, 1; (metra 1) 151, 5, 9; 152,
23, 38.   The same form also occurs in the translation of Beda ascribed
to Alfred, ed. Schipper, 30, line 591, and in Bishop Werferth's translation
of Gregory's *Dialogues*, 10, 24; 14, 15; 66, 6, 15; 185, 26; 187, 13;
194, 16.

[2] Sievers, in Paul, Braune, and Sievers *Beiträge zur Geschichte der
deutschen Sprache und Literatur*, xviii. 411.

[3] It was pointed out as early as 1848 by Munch, *Samlede Afhand-
linger*, Christiania, 1873, i. 433, that the O. N. form *Jótar* (*Iótar*) might
descend from an original \**Iut-* (i. e. \**Euti-*) or \**Jiut-* (i. e. \**Jeuti-*),
but not from a \**Jut-*, and that, if from the second, the initial *j* would
be preserved in O. E. as *g*.  It is probable that Beda would have so
represented it, for he writes *Giudi urbs*, *Hist. Eccl.* i. 12 (cf. the *Iudan-*

from an older *juk*, from a Germanic *jugom*, cognate with
Greek ζυγόν, Latin *iugum*, O.E. *geoc*, New English *yoke*.
The evidence, however, points to \**Euti-z* as the true form.
A letter of Theodebert to Justinian, written between 534
and 547, mentions the *Saxonibus Euciis* amongst the people
subject to his rule[1], and it is a fair conclusion that this
represents *Eutii*, and that it is a continental reference, the
only one known, to Beda's *Iuti*, *Iutae*. The O.N. name of
the people of Jutland, *Iōtar*, might be connected with either
form[2], but the Danish form of their name, *Jyder*, points to
*Jeuti-*[3]. In the Anglian dialects the name *Iuti* would yield
regularly *Iote*, *Eote*. The latter form occurs in the O.E.
version of Beda, iv. 16, in the compound *Eota-land*, but this
may be merely a modernization of Beda's form. In West-
Saxon the *iu* would be according to rule smoothed to *ie*,
and therefore *Iete* would have been the form of Alfred's
time. By the end of the tenth century the West-Saxon *ie*
had become *ȳ*, and we may therefore recognize this people
in the *Ytum*, dat. pl., in the lay of Widsith, line 26, and
also in the *Ytene*, which Florence of Worcester records as
the name of the New Forest[4]. That this was equivalent to
'provincia Iutarum' may be inferred from his using this latter
term (the *Iutae* of which must have been copied from Beda)
in another passage that also relates to the death of William
Rufus[5]. One MS. of the translation of Beda really renders
Beda's *Iutarum* by *Ytena*[6], of which the nom. pl. would be
\* *Ȳte*. This should clinch the matter, unless this form can
be regarded as due to an erroneous identification of the
district of Ytene (i. e. *Ytena*, gen. pl.) with the ethnic name.

*byrig* of Chron. D, an. 952), and *Giuli* (*De Temporum Ratione*, c. xv),
Gothic *jiuleis*, our *Yule*, where the text preserves an eighth-century
Northumbrian form.

[1] *Monumenta Germaniae Historica*, 'Epistolae Merowingici et Karolini Aevi,' i. 133.

[2] Ten Brink, *Beowulf*, 204. This was previously recognized by
Munch, l. c.

[3] According to a communication of Professor Möller, cited by
Kossina, *Indogermanische Forschungen*, vii. 293.

[4] An. 1100 (ed. Thorpe, ii. 45): 'in Nova Foresta, quae lingua Anglorum Ytene nuncupatur.'

[5] Appendix (ed. Thorpe, i. 276): 'in provincia Iutarum, in Nova
Foresta.' Concerning this Appendix see above, p. 110.

[6] The Corpus MS., book iv. 16 (ed. Schipper, 426, line 2,146).

This does not seem very probable. Finally, these Iuti seem
to be referred to in their continental home as *Eotena*, gen.
pl., *Eotenum*, dat. pl., in Beowulf[1], a variant form of the name
that probably corresponds to the *Euthiönes* represented in
the fifth century by the nom. sing. *Euthio* of Venantius
Fortunatus[2].

It has been the misfortune of this obscure German race
to bear a name that was liable to confusion with that of
other tribes. Confusion with the name of the Goths might
be produced in the early stages of O.E. through the pronunciation, which seems to have obtained, of the O.E. *g*
when followed by a guttural vowel as a voiced spirant (as in
Dutch), and not, as in later times, as a stop (as in our *God*).
The date of the change to the latter is not known, and we
cannot therefore be certain as to the pronunciation in the
ninth century. The fact that Jutland is called Gotland in
Alfred's account of Ohthere's voyage[3], is an apparent justification of the confusion of the names of the Iuti and Goths
by the author of the present work. But this is weakened by
the fact that this portion is missing in the contemporary
Lauderdale MS.[4], and by the possibility that Jutland was
at that time known to the Norsemen as Gotland, or rather
\**Hreið-Gota-land*[5]. Confusion of the Iuti of Beda with the

---

[1] Lines 903, 1,073, 1,089, 1,142, 1,146. Their king Fin is described
as king of the Frisians in *Widsith*, line 27, and his people are called by
this name in *Beowulf*. The *Geotena* of *Beowulf*, 445, is usually regarded
as an error for *Gēatena*, but it may represent *Eotena*, as Munch, l. c.,
has suggested.

[2] Just as the Frisians are called both *Frisii* and *Frisiones* by Latin
writers, and the Saxons are in O.E. both *Seaxe* (*i*-stem) and *Seaxan*
(an *on*-stem).

[3] Translation of *Orosius*, 19, 28. 20.

[4] Munch, p. 434, suggests that the king or the scribe has erred, for in
the account of Wulfstan's voyage in *Orosius*, 20, 3, the island of Gutland,
off the coast of Sweden, is also called ' Gotland.'

[5] *Reiðgotaland* is given by Snorre and the Hervarar Saga as the old
name of Jutland, and is also said to have been the old name of Denmark.
The name occurs in the dat. pl. *Hraiþkutum* on the famous early tenth-
century runic inscription at Rök, in East Götland, and Bugge, *Anti-
qvarisk Tidskrift for Sverige*, part v, p. 35, interprets the name as
referring to the inhabitants of Götland (in O.N. the *Gautar*). Heinzel
has maintained that the uncertainty as to the position of the Hreiðgotar
(the *Hreðgotan* of Beowulf) arises from confused recollections of the East
Gothic kingdom of Eormanric, and claims that the memory of the latter

Jutes of Jutland, when the Danish settlements in England
made the English acquainted with the latter folk, was facili-
tated by the development in some O.E. dialects of a semi-
vowel before an initial *eo*, so that *Eotas* became *Geotas* [1].
This seems to be the origin of Æthelweard's identification
of the Danish Jutes, whom he calls *Gioti*, with the earlier
settlers in England [2], for his information was clearly derived
from a Danish source. There was another northern people
with whom the name of the *Iuti* was confused in England at
this time. This was the Γαυτοί of Procopius [3], O.N. *Gautar*,
whose name is recorded in the Swedish province of Götland
and in the name of Göteborg (Gothenburg). This name, by
the action of well-known phonological laws, became in O.E.
*Gēatas* [4]. The Iuti of Beda are called by this name in the
O.E. translation [5]. A great Scandinavian scholar has, indeed,
tried, but unsuccessfully, to identify the Iuti with the Gautar,
and has confused the latter with still another northern folk [6],
whose name is preserved in the isle of Gutland, and who
were really, at all events in name, Goths (O.N. *Gotnar*,
sing. *Goti* = O.E. \**Gota*).

**2, 6 Stuf et Wihtgar.** This is derived from the entries

---

is enshrined in the Czeck name for Austria, *Rakusy*, derived through
\**Hradagoza* from Goth. \**Hraþgutans* ( *Ueber die Ostgotische Heldensage*,
in the *Sitzungsberichte d. k. Akad. d. Wissensch., Phil.-Histor. Klasse*,
cxix. iii. 15 sqq., Vienna, 1889). The forms and meaning of *Hreðgotan*,
&c., have been dealt with by Bugge, in Paul, Braune, and Sievers'
*Beiträge*, xxiv. 445.

[1] Sievers, *Angels. Grammatik*, ed. 3, 21, anm. 2.
[2] *Monumenta Historica Britannica*, 502 D.
[3] *De Bello Gotico*, ii. c. 15 (ed. Comparetti, ii. 101).
[4] The Appendix to Florence of Worcester, ed. Thorpe, i. 270, calls
them *Gouti*, but this must be derived from a Scandinavian source, O.N.
*au* being usually represented by *ou* in O.E. This is another proof of
the Danish influence in Florence, to which attention has been called in
the *Crawford Charters*, p. 144.
[5] Book i. 15, ed. Schipper, p. 41.
[6] Bugge, in Paul and Braune's *Beiträge*, xii. 1 sqq. The passage
cited at p. 6 note, from the Laws of Edward the Confessor, that the
' Guti et Saxones Germanie, cum veniunt, debent protegi sicut coniurati
fratres et cives regni,' is really a later antiquarian interpolation, and
refers, not to the Jutes of Jutland, but to the inhabitants of the island of
Gutland, a great centre of trade with England. Cf. Liebermann, *Über
die Leges Anglorum saeculo XIII ineunte Londoniis collectae*, Halle,
1894, pp. 26, 52.

in the Chron. under 530, 'Her Cerdic ond Cynric genamon Wihte ealond, ond ofslogon fea(la) men on Wihtgara byrig' ('in this year Cerdic and Cynric captured the Isle of Wight, and slew many men in Wihtgara-burh)' and 534, 'hie ⟨Cerdic and Cynric⟩ saldon hiera tuæm nefum Stufe ond Wihtgare Wiht ealand' ('they delivered the Isle of Wight to Stuf and Wihtgar, their two *nefan*'). The final clause about the previous slaying or flight of the other inhabitants of the isle has, no doubt, been added by the author, and is based merely upon the necessity of accounting for the conquest of the island when only a few of its inhabitants had been killed. The MS. of the Chron. used by the author agreed with MSS. B and C in reading *fēa*, 'few,' instead of *feala*, 'many,' as in A and its derivative E. It is difficult to say which was the reading of the archetype, for there are irregularities about both forms [1]. The *nefan* of the second passage has been carelessly rendered 'nephews' by modern translators of the Chron., and has hence drawn suspicions upon this annal that are philologically unjustified. It is difficult to conceive a forger so stupid as to say that Stuf and Wihtgar were 'nephews' of Cerdic and Cynric, who are described immediately before as father and son. The author of the present work calls Cerdic the *avunculus* and Cynric the *consobrinus* of Stuf and Wihtgar. That Stuf and Wihtgar were grandsons of Cerdic and sons of a sister of Cynric is probably what this annal intended to convey, and would convey, to an Englishman of the ninth century. O.E. was rich in collective names of relationship that have no representatives in modern English, such as *āþum-swerian*, 'father-in-law and son-in-law,' *suhter-gefædera*, 'paternal uncle and nephew,' and *nefan* is used in a somewhat similar way in the annal of 534. *Nefa* is the O.E. representative of a widely diffused Indo-Germanic word, Sanskrit *nápāt-*, Greek ἀνεψιός from

---

[1] *Fēa*, a contraction of *feawe*, is poetical and non-West Saxon; Cosijn, *Altwestsächsische Grammatik*, ii. p. 62 ; Sievers, *Angelsächsische Grammatik*, ed. 3, § 301, an. 1. The latter thinks this form may occur in early West Saxon, an opinion probably based upon the present instance. The *feala* of this passage is the only example of the spelling in early West Saxon noted by Cosijn, i. p. 38, the normal form being *fela*. Mr. H. C. Chadwick, *Studies in Old English*, p. 136, holds that *fēa* is correct, and that it represents the neuter plural. See Sievers, *Angelsächs. Grammatik*, ed. 3, § 301, 1.

\*ἀ-νεπτυjος[1] (and, probably, νέποδες), Latin *nepos*, &c.[2], that has, like many others of these relationship names, meanings that vary widely. The original meaning of this word was, apparently, 'descendant,' which was specialized as 'grandson.' But it could also be applied to collateral descendants from a common ancestor, and hence obtained the meaning of 'nephew,' especially a sister's son. Both meanings, 'grandson' and 'nephew,' are recorded in Germanic and in O.E. Thus in *Beowulf* it signifies 'grandson' and 'sister's son'[3]. The latter is the prevailing meaning when applied to nephews, and, if we assign this sense to it in the annal of 533, we are at once reminded of an ancient German family custom that attracted the attention of Tacitus—the intimate, almost fatherly, connexion between a man and his sister's son[4]. But although there is a savour of antiquity about this participation of a sister's sons, we cannot use it as a decisive argument in favour of the antiquity of the annal, for it may be an accidental coincidence. Professor Gummere has shown how widely this relationship between a man and his sister's son is recorded in the later English ballads, and notices that it was going out of use at the time of the composition of *Beowulf*, which, however, preserves distinct traces of the custom[5].

**2, 11 Guuihtgaraburhg.** The spelling *-burhg* is probably to be ascribed to the modernizing tendencies of Parker's transcriber. In the Chron. the dat. sing. *byrig* is used. The *gw* for *w* is a Welsh spelling; see note

---

[1] See Delbrück, *Die indogermanischen Verwandtschaftsnamen*, in *Abhandlungen der philol.-hist. Classe der k. sächsischen Gesellschaft der Wissenschaften*, 1889, xi. p. 509, who cites the Gothic *niþjis*, συγγενής, sb. = Indogerm. \**neptios*, p. 496.

[2] For further examples see Brugmann, *Grundriss der vergleichenden Grammatik der indogermanischen Sprachen*, ed. 2, i. 508; O. Schrader, *Reallexikon der indogermanischen Altertumskunde*, Strassburg, 1901, p. 182, s. v. 'Enkel.'

[3] In 882 *Fitela* is *nefa* to his *eam*, 'maternal uncle,' a sense still preserved in some of the Dialects (see Professor Wright's *English Dialect Dictionary*, s. vv. 'eam,' 'neam').

[4] *Germania*, 20, 4: 'Sororum filiis idem apud avunculum qui apud patrem honor.' See upon this passage Müllenhoff's exhaustive note in *Deutsche Altertumskunde*, iv. 318 sqq., Berlin, 1900; H. Brunner, *Deutsche Rechtsgeschichte*, i. 82.

[5] See his article on 'the Sister's Son' in *An English Miscellany, presented to Dr. Furnivall*, Oxford, 1901, pp. 133 sqq.

to c. 1, 18. The personal name *Wiht-gār*, from which this compound is derived, is, however, spelt in the English fashion. It is noticeable that the version of the Chron. before the author had the form *Wihtgara-*, the archaic gen. sing. of *gār*[1], which had already fallen into desuetude by the time of the writing of the Parker MS. of the Chron., for the scribe substitutes *Wihtgaras* for *Wihtgares*, the later gen. sing., under 530, preserving the correct *Wihtgara* under 544. The MS. of the Chron. used by Florence had, like Chron. B, C, the correct *Wihtgara* under both dates. Under the latter date Florence explains the name as meaning ‘civitas Wihtgari[2],’ which is possibly derived from some older source, for in his time the name could not be explained in this way without violence to grammar. *Wihtgara-burh*, which has been erroneously regarded as meaning ‘the fortress of the men of Wight,’ the *Wiht-ware* or *Wiht-waran*[3], has been identified since the time of Camden with Carisbrooke. But it is not easy to derive the latter name from *Wihtgara-burh* or *Wihtgares-burh*, for such a derivation assumes the loss of the chief-stressed first member of the compound and the survival of the weak-stressed second member. In other cases of names

[1] That is, as was first pointed out by Professor Cosijn, in *Taalkundige Bijdrage*, Haarlem, 1878, ii. 272, *gāra* is the gen. sing. of an old *u*-stem, and *gāru*, ‘spear,’ is recorded in the Erfurt Glossary, in the compound *aet-garu* = later *æt-gār* (ed. Sweet, *Oldest English Texts*, 440). See Professor Sievers, in *Beiträge zur Geschichte der deutschen Sprache und Literatur*, ix. 273; and the present writer in the *English Historical Review*, xiv. 37. The Epinal and Corpus glossaries, however, read *aetgaeru*, 440. See upon these forms Chadwick, *Studies in Old English*, p. 156.

[2] From Florence, the twelfth-century author of the St. Albans compilation embodied by Roger of Wendover, ed. Coxe, i. 284, and Matthew Paris, *Chronica Maiora*, i. 380, have borrowed this gloss and inserted it in their reproduction of the present chapter. Hence it obtained a wide circulation in the thirteenth and following centuries.

[3] No such change of *g* to *w* is known in O.E., which either retains the *w* at the beginning of the second member of a compound, or, in rare cases, omits it owing to its absorption, through weakness of stress, in the following vowel. It is always retained in the rather numerous instances of the composition of *-waru*, *-ware*, &c., and in the fem. personal names compounded with *-waru*. On the *Wihtgara* of the Tribal Hidage (*Cart. Sax.* i. 414) see the writer's note in the *English Historical Review*, xiv. 37, note 19.

compounded with *Wiht*, the first member has, according
to rule, survived, although sometimes found shortened
owing to the length of the composition[1]. In the case
of White Lackington, co. Somerset, from * *Wihtlācing-tun*
('Wihtlāc's town')[2], the *wight* resulting from *wiht* has,
owing to the preservation of the original strong stress,
been identified with the adjective 'white,' and accordingly
released from the compound within a century or so of
the present time. But if a similar process had occurred
in the case of *Wihtgara-burh*, we should still be faced
by the difficulty that the *g* of the resultant *Gara-burh* or
*Gares-burh* has become irregularly *c*, and, what presents
much greater difficulty, that the *burh* or *byrig* has changed
into *brook*. Carisbrooke is not mentioned by name in
Domesday, but we have forms of the name about the
same date that show beyond doubt that the name is
a compound of *brook* and not of *burh*[3]. A confusion of
the two words is out of question at so early a date, and
we must therefore relegate *Wihtgara-burh* to the category
of unidentified places in early O.E. history. Nothing
is known of the British stronghold to which this name is
proleptically applied in the Chron. under 530, and there
is now no village in the Isle of Wight with the suffix
*-borough* or *-bury*. The name *Newport* is obviously contrasted with some older 'port' or town, the memory of
which has died. But this need not be *Wihtgara-burh*,
which is never mentioned after the record of Wihtgar's
burial in it. Whether the mention of his burial at this
place in the Chron. is founded upon a local name then

---

[1] e.g. *Wiht-lac(h)es-ford*, now Wixford, co. Warwick (*Cart. Sax.*
iii. 321), *Wihtlaxford*, 1286-7, *Inquisitiones post Mortem*, i. 94 b;
*Wihtrices-hamme* (*Cod. Dip.* iv. 37), now Wittersham, co. Kent;
* *Wihtheringas, Wihttringes* (*Cart. Sax.* i. 99, spurious), now Wittering,
co. Sussex.

[2] *Domesday Book*, i. 94 b, col. 1, *Wislageton*, for * *Wistlageton* (*st*
being the Norman representation of O.E. *ht*, with which it probably
agreed in pronunciation), *Wyslagentona, Exon Domesday*, 412; 1316
*Whightlakinton, Nomina Villarum*, p. 378 a.

[3] 1070-2 *Gallia Christiana*, xi. Instrum. p. 125, *Caresbroc*; 1132-3,
*Caresbroc, Monasticon*, v. 317 a, by *Inspeximus* of Richard II; *Kares-
broc, temp.* Hen. II; ib. 319 a; 1154-5 *Caresbroch*, vi. 1092 (= Round,
*Calendar of Documents preserved in France*, p. 135); 1225, 1226
*Car(r)ebroc, Rot. Litt. Clausarum*, pp. 35 b, 50 b, 100 b.

in existence, or whether *Wihtgara-burh* was merely derived
from tradition or song, it is impossible to decide.

3. This chapter is derived from the Chron., with the
addition that Ceorl was *Domnaniae comes*, a natural deduction from the entry in the Chronicle, the description of
the site of the Isle of Sheppey and the mention of the
monastery in it. MS. A of the Chron. inserts after the
account of the fight at Wicganbeorg the passage represented
by c. 6, which here occupies the position that it has in
MSS. B, C, D, E. The author of the present work has
substituted by mistake the name of Sheppey for that of
Thanet, as in B, C, D, E ; the name is omitted in A and F.
The word *ærest*, here rendered correctly *primum*, is found
only in A, B and C. In consequence of this substitution of
Sheppey for Thanet the author has been compelled to
omit the equivalent adverb in c. 10, where the Chron. has
it. The form *Sceap-ieg* preserves the Old West-Saxon form
*ieg* in use in Alfred's time, and is older than the forms
in the Chron. It would, however, be hazardous to found
any argument as to the antiquity of the present work upon
this form, for it may have been copied from a lost MS. of
the Chron. that preserved the old orthography. See Introduction, § 54, p. lxxxv.

3, 2 **Ceorl.** This is clearly the *Ceorlus princeps* who
attests a contemporary charter of King Æthelwulf at Dorchester, co. Dorset, in 848 [1].

3, 4 **Uicganbeorg**, 'Wicga's Hill' or 'tumulus.' This
is usually identified with the coast village of Wembury,
co. Devon, in consequence of a suggestion of Bishop
Gibson [2]. But the philological objections to this identification are fatal. *Wicgan-* could not develop into *Wem-*,
and *-beorg* could not become *-bury*. Although *beorge*, the
dat. sing. of *beorh*, *beorg*, frequently produces *-borough* in
composition in modern forms, through the Middle English
*ber(e)we*, it is not permissible to reverse this and say that
the dat. sing. *byrig* of *burh*, 'borough, fort,' can become
*-borough*. As a matter of fact Wembury appears as early

---

[1] British Mus. *Facs.* ii. pl. 30, *Cart. Sax.* ii. 35, 7.
[2] *Chronicum Anglosaxonicum*, Oxford, 1692, 'Nominum locorum
explicatio,' p. 49.

as the twelfth century as *Wenbiria* [1], and therefore cannot possibly be derived from *Wicgan-beorg*. The regular descendant of the latter would be *Wigborough*, or, in Devonshire, *Wiggaborough* (cf. *Wiggaton*, parish of Ottery St. Mary). There is a Wigborough, in the parish of South Petherton, co. Somerset, some five miles from the boundary of Devonshire [2], and it is possible that this is the place referred to in this annal, although it is not in Devon, for the *fyrd* is occasionally found fighting outside its county. Mr. J. B. Davidson identified *Wicgan-beorg* with Weekaborough or Wickaborough, in the parish of Berry Pomeroy, co. Devon [3], but the modern forms suggest a derivation from O.E. *wíc*, which frequently appears as *week* in local names in the west country, Hants, &c.

**3, 10 monasterium.** This is Minster in Sheppey, founded by St. Sexburh in the seventh century [4]. This monastery disappeared during the Danish ravages, but the fact that the present work speaks of it as still existing affords us no criterion as to the age of the compilation, for the date of the destruction is unknown. The writer of the Kentish saints' lives, which were composed shortly before 1000, speaks of the monastery as being still in existence, possibly through copying an early original [5]. The

[1] It is copied as *Weybiria* in an Inspeximus of a charter of Henry I, 1133–1139, probably from an original *Wenbiria* (*Rot. Chart.* 2 Edw. III, mem. 13, no. 46, where the *y* is slurred; *Monasticon*, vi. 53 a), and as *Wenbiria* in a charter of Henry II in the same Inspeximus, which is assigned to 1158 by Eyton, *Court, Household, and Itinerary of Henry II*, p. 34.

[2] It occurs in 1225 as *Wiggeberg* (Somerset Pleas, ed. Chadwyck-Healey, Somersetshire Record Society, p. 49); *c.* 1230 as *Wigberghe*, *Wigeberhe* (*Inquisit. post Mortem*, Hen. III, *temp. Incerto*, no. 123); in 1242-3 as *Wyggebergh* (Som. Pleas, p. 320); in 1270 as *Wiggeber'*, *Wygheberghe* (*Inq. post Mortem*, 55 Hen. III, no. 12) and in 1327 as *Wygebeare, Wigebere* (*Inq. post Mortem*, 1 Edw. III, no. 35, second numbers), and as *Wigeberga, Wigebergh* in the *Testa de Nevill*, pp. 162 b, 170 b. Eyton identifies the *Winche-berie* of the *Domesday Survey*, i. 98 b, col. 1, *Winchin-beria* of the *Exon Domesday*, p. 442, with *Wigborough*. As the identification seems to be correct, the forms must be corruptly copied for *Wichenberge* or *Wighinberge*.

[3] See Plummer, *Two Saxon Chronicles*, ii. 77.

[4] See the Kentish Saints' Lives (ed. Liebermann, *Die Heiligen Englands*, Hannover, 1889, i. 18) and the foundation legend printed in Cockayne's *Leechdoms*, iii. 430, from an early eleventh-century MS.

[5] Cf. Liebermann, l. c. p. viii.

Danes were in Sheppey in 1016 (Chron.), and the destruction of the monastery may have occurred about that time.
That in Thanet was destroyed in 988, according to a much
later Canterbury authority, which records the capture of
its abbess in 1011 and the removal of St. Mildred's body
thence to Canterbury in 1030[1].

**4.** This chapter is derived from the Chron., to which
the author has added the description of the site of London
and the explanation that Dorubernia is 'Cantwariorum
civitas.' which is necessitated by his use of the Latin name
of Canterbury instead of the *Cantwaraburh* of the Chron.
It is noteworthy that he retains the *w* of the English
spelling in his *Cantwariorum*. He has also added 'qui
ad proeliandum contra illos venerat' in line 10, which is a
sufficiently obvious deduction from the words of the Chron.
The Cottonian MS. clearly agreed with MSS. D, E, F of
the Chron. in omitting the mention of the capture of
London, but the name of this city occurs in Florence and
the Annals of St. Neots. It may, however, have been
added in both cases from the Chron.

**4, 4 Lundoniam . . . pertinet.** This seems to be based
upon Beda, *H. E.* c. ii. 3 'provincia Orientalium Saxonum, qui
Tamense fluvio dirimuntur a Cantia . . . quorum metropolis
Lundonia civitas est, super ripam praefati fluminis posita.'

**4, 8 depopulati sunt.** A somewhat free rendering of
the *brǣcon* of the Chron., which has the sense of ' captured,
took by storm.'

**5.** This chapter is based upon the Chron., to which the
author has added the description of the situation of Surrey,
the explanation of the names of Aclea, and the description
of the obstinate nature of the fighting, the latter of which
may be merely the product of his rhetoric. The passage,
' maxima pars paganae multitudinis funditus deleta et occisa
est, ita qualiter nunquam in aliqua regione in una die,
ante nec post, ex eis occisam esse audivimus,' curiously mis-
translates the Chron., which has ' þær þæt mæste wæl geslogon
on hæþnum herige þe we secgan hierdon oþ þisne andweardan
dæg' = 'they inflicted the greatest slaughter upon the heathen
army that we have heard tell of up to the present day[2].'

---

[1] Thomas Thorne, in Twysden, *Decem Scriptores*, coll. 1780, 1781, 1783.
[2] Gregory of Tours, ix. 25, copied by Paul the Deacon, iii. 29, uses

**5, 6 Aclea.** The author has taken over from the
Chron. the dat. *-lēa*, which he uses as a nom. instead of
*lēah.* The place is usually identified with Ockley, co.
Surrey, but numerous mediaeval forms of the latter are
written *Ockelee, Okkele* [1], which, with the modern form,
point to an O.E. *\*Occan-lēah.* It seems to be the *Hoclei*
of Domesday Book, i. 35 b, col. 2, which can hardly be
derived from O.E. *āc,* for the change of O.E. *ā* to *o* had
not occurred by the time of the Survey, which accordingly
writes *Aclei* for O.E. *Acleage* (dat. sing.) in other counties.
Stubbs [2] quotes ' be suðan Wudigan gæte at Aclee on West-
Sæxum' from the Durham Ritual, a note written in 970 [3].
Mr. Plummer suggests that Newdigate, near Ockley, represents *Wudigan gæt* [4]. Formally, however, it descends from
O.E. *\*Niwedan-geate* [5], a form that could not be confused
with a name derived from *Wudiga.* The place referred to
in the Durham Ritual appears to be Woodyates, co. Dorset,
which is on a Roman road. Close by it is a place called
Oakley.

**5, 13 loco funeris dominati sunt.** This is a too
literal translation of the O.E. ' wælstowe gew(e)ald ahton,'

a curiously similar expression regarding the slaughter of the Franks by
the Lombards in 588, ' tantaque ibi fuit strages de Francorum exercitu,
ut olim similis non recolatur.'

[1] See *Surrey Fines,* published by the Surrey Archaeological Soc.,
p. 8 *Ockel(eye),* 1213–4; pp. 34, 48, 68 *Ockele(ye),* 1253–4, 1271–2,
1303–4, 1309–10; *Okkele, Ockle, Testa de Nevill,* 219 a, 220 b. See
also British Museum *Index to Charters and Rolls.* The forms *Okele(ge),*
*Okele(ye),* which occur as early as 1219–20 (*Surrey Fines,* pp. 11, 32,
47), do not connect the name with *oak,* and the modern form does not
favour such derivation. Gough, in his edition of Camden, calls the
village *Oakley,* and Aubrey spells it *Okeley.* It is noticeable that Æthelweard places the battle in Surrey (*illic*), ' near the wood called Aclea.'
The Chronicle does not state that the battle was in Surrey.

[2] Haddan and Stubbs, *Councils,* iii. 439.

[3] Liebermann, *Archiv für das Studium der neueren Sprachen,* vol. civ,
p. 122.

[4] *Two Saxon Chronicles Parallel,* ii. 78. It may be questioned
whether a writer in the tenth century would describe a place in Surrey
as lying in Wessex.

[5] The form was well preserved as late as 1317–8, when it is spelt
*Nywedegate* (*Inq. post Mortem,* 11 Edw. II, no. 50). It occurs in the
Pipe Roll for 1219–20 (4 Hen. III, ro. 3) as *Newedegat',* and is clearly
derived from the past participle of the verb *nīwian,* ' to make new,
restore.'

which is thus rendered at c. 18, 15. In the present instance, however, the Chron. has *sige namon*, literally 'took (the) victory,' which may be represented by the 'victoriam honorifice tenuerunt.' The author has, in like manner, substituted a translation of the former for the latter O.E. expression at c. 33, 4. Both phrases are represented in 'victoriam accipientes, loco funeris dominati sunt,' cc. 35, 18; 36, 11; 40, 7, where the Chron. has only 'wælstowe gewald ahton.' Similarly *sige namon* is rendered 'victoriam capientes, loco funeris dominati sunt' at c. 42, 27. It would seem from these additional words that the author felt that there was a doubt about the meaning of the literal version of the O.E. The occurrence of 'loco funeris dominati sunt' is proof conclusive that the annalistic portion of the present work is a translation from an O.E. original, which can only have been the Chron. See Introduction, § 53. It is surprising that a Welshman should have used this literal translation of an O.E. phrase, for, as we are informed by Professor Rhys, no such expression is recorded in Welsh.

**6.** From the Chron. See note to c. 3, above, as to agreement between the position of this chapter with MSS. B, C, D, E of the Chron. against A. The present work has 'nine' ships with A, D, E, F, whereas B and C have 'eight.' In A, D, E, and G Ealhere is described as *dux* ; the *comes* of the present text seems to represent the *ealdorman* recorded in B and C.

**7.** From the Chron. It is from the fuller account given in MSS. A, B, C, G, not from the abridgement in D and E ; in F it is missing. The author has added the description of the position of the 'Mediterranei Britones' (=the *Norþ Walas* of the Chron.), the amplification 'qui contra eum immodice reluctabantur,' the mention of Burhred being in Æthelwulf's company, the statements that Æthelwulf devastated the insurgents' country (*gentem*), and that he then returned home. All these are easy deductions from the language of the Chron. In line 9 the author uses *Britannia* for the *Norþ Walas* (that is the people, not the land) of the Chron.

**7, 8 segnius.** This seems to have been rather a favourite word with the author. See cc. 30, 12 ; 37, 6 ; 37, 12.

**8.** From the Chron. The author has added the mention

of Alfred's retinue. A letter from the pope to Alfred's father, regarding the ceremony at Rome, has been fortunately preserved for us in a twelfth-century collection of papal letters, now in the British Museum[1]. In it the pope describes Alfred as his *spiritalis filius*, and states that he had invested him with the insignia of a Roman consul. Bishop Stubbs has suggested that this was regarded ' by the English a few years later, and perhaps by Alfred himself, as an anticipation of coronation, and the unction, which might be that of confirmation, as that of royal consecration[2].' The words used by the author of the present work agree with those of the author of the *Annales Francorum* in describing the ceremony at Rome in 781, when Karloman and Ludwig, the sons of Charles the Great, were *uncti in reges* by the pope[3]. Later writers regarded this as a coronation[4], and it is recorded that these boys were nominal kings under their father. It is noteworthy that the pope addresses Charles after this ceremony as *spiritalis compater*[5], which coincides with Leo's description of Alfred as his *spiritalis filius*. It is

[1] Add. MS. 8873, fo. 168, from which it was printed by Paul Ewald in his description of this collection in the *Neues Archiv der Gesellschaft für ältere deutsche Geschichtskunde*, v. 389. The letter is as follows: *Edeluulfo, regi Anglorum* ⟨marginal direction for rubricator⟩. '⟨F⟩ilium vestrum Erfred, quem hoc in tempore ad Sanctorum Apostolorum limina destinare curastis, benigne suscepimus, et, quasi spiritalem filium consulatus cingulo ⟨cinguli *emend.* Ewald⟩ honore vestimentisque, ut mos est Romanis consulibus, decoravimus, eo quod in nostris se tradidit manibus.' The letter is printed in the *Epistolae Karolini Aevi*, iii. p. 602.

[2] Preface to Malmesbury, *Gesta Regum*, ii. xliii.

[3] *Annales Regni Francorum*, an. 781, ed. F. Kurze, Hanover, 1895, p. 56: ' ibi baptizatus est domnus Pippinus ⟨that is Karloman⟩ . . ab Adriano papa, . . et duo filii supradicti domni Caroli regis magni uncti sunt in regem ⟨reges *v. l.*⟩ a supradicto pontifice, hi sunt domnus Pippinus rex in Italiam et domnus Hludowicus rex in Aquitaniam.' Carte, *History of England*, i. 293. suggests that ' this precedent seems to have engaged Ethelwolf to take the like step in regard to Alfred.' But the action of the pope seems to have been spontaneous.

[4] *Vita Hludowici Imperatoris* (Pertz, *Scriptores*, ii. 607): ' benedictione regnaturo congrua et regali insignitus est diademate per manus Adriani venerandi antistitis.' Similarly the recension of the *Annales* ascribed to Einhart describes the ceremony as a coronation. See Abel, *Jahrbücher des fränkischen Reiches unter Karl dem Grossen*, i. 313.

[5] Abel, *Jahrbücher*, l. c.

possible that the confirmation of Alfred at Rome, if confirmation it was, came to be regarded as his hallowing
to kingship owing to the influence of the Frankish clerks
in his court, who connected it, perhaps not entirely
without justification, with the anointing of the sons of
Charles. The latter were at the time younger than Alfred.
The writer of the present work describes Alfred as an
*infans*, a term that is more consonant with his being then
in his fourth year than in his eleventh, the obviously
corrupt reading of the Cottonian MS. The evidence
that Alfred was born in 849 is too strong to be set
aside in favour of an earlier date, as Bishop Stubbs
suggests[1].

It is, however, noticeable that the two proceedings referred to in the pope's letter are kept distinct in the entry
in the Chron., which tells us that the Pope Leo ' hallowed
Alfred to king and took him as bishop's son.' This is
duly rendered in the present chapter by 'unxit in regem,
et in filium adoptionis sibimet accipiens confirmavit.' It
would therefore seem that it was the ceremony of creation
as consul that was misunderstood by Alfred or by the
writer of this entry in the Chron. as a coronation as king.
This entry cannot well have been written until after Alfred's
accession to the throne in 871, and it is possible that he
regarded his coronation in England as the consummation
of the ceremony at Rome. In any case it is difficult to
reject the theory that we can detect his influence in this
strange entry. Notwithstanding this annal the Chron.
records the continuation of his father's reign and the accessions of his three brothers before him. There are no
grounds for believing that he became king of any portion
of the West Saxon realm in consequence of the ceremony
at Rome[2], for his tender years and the claims of his elder
brothers must have precluded such an arrangement. It is
therefore clear that the statement that he was hallowed
as king by the pope is a misapprehension. Alfred was, no
doubt, crowned solemnly upon his accession. What purports to be his coronation oath is preserved in the chartu-

[1] Preface to Malmesbury, l. c.  See above, p. 152, note to c. 1, 1.
[2] Cf. Carte, *History of England*, i. 289.

lary of Athelney[1], a monastery that owed its foundation to
him. It is in the usual form of the ancient coronation
oath used by Dunstan at the crowning of Æthelred the
Unready[2]. The same form was used at that of Edgar[3], and
if the Athelney record may be trusted, we can bridge over
much of the distance between Dunstan and the formula
in the Pontifical of Archbishop Ecgberht of York[4]. The
statements derived from compilations embodying the words
of the Life regarding the ceremony at Rome were eagerly
seized upon by later monkish writers who were anxious to
magnify the power of the papacy. The record was considered too strong for the monks of Westminster, who
supported their claim that the kings of England were
always crowned in the abbey by a series of the most
impudent forgeries[5], and they were compelled to admit
that Alfred was not crowned in the abbey. They, however,
pretended that the very crown with which he was crowned
at Rome was brought to England by him, and was preserved among the regalia in the abbey. A 'crown of King
Alfred' was found among the regalia at the time of the
Commonwealth. It was seen by Sir John Spelman shortly
before the Parliament melted it down with the remainder
of the regalia. He described it as being 'of very ancient
work, with flowers adorned with stones of a somewhat
plain setting[6].' There can be little doubt that this was

[1] Published in a translation by the Somersetshire Record Society,
1899, p. 126.
[2] Printed by Stubbs, *Memorials of St. Dunstan*, p. 355.
[3] *Vita Oswaldi*, c. iv, in Raine, *Historians of the Church of York*,
i. 437.
[4] Printed by Maskell, *Monumenta Ritualia Anglicana*, ed. 2, ii. 84;
Stubbs, *Select Charters*, ed. 3, p. 62. See also his *Constitutional
History*, Library ed., i. 173. The name of Maskell may be added
to those who have been misled by the interpolations in the Life of
Alfred (see Introduction, p. xiii, above). The interpolated chapter,
17 b, is described by him as 'a very important account, by a contemporary, of the coronation of Edmund, king of the East Angles'
(ii. xxix), whereas it comes from the Annals of St. Neots.
[5] Such, for instance, as the spurious charter of Edgar, printed in the
*Crawford Charters*, no. VI., *Cart. Sax.* iii. 549, wherein it is stated
untruly that Westminster 'locus etiam consecrationis regum antiquitus
erat.'
[6] *Life of King Ælfred*, p. 201.

the crown of Edward the Confessor of the earlier records, and its ascription to Alfred, who is depicted on his coins as wearing a diadem, not a crown, is subsequent to the attempt made by William de Sudbury, a fourteenth-century monk of Westminster, to prove that the abbey still preserved the regalia brought by Alfred from Rome [1].

The confusion of the ceremony of creation as consul with that of hallowing as king was probably due to the magnificence of the costume of the consul. There was some resemblance between the two ceremonies, both involving the girding with a sword. This we learn from the pope's letter to Æthelwulf and from the contemporary account of the crowning of the future Emperor Ludwig II as king of Lombardy by Pope Sergius at Rome in 844 [2]. There were probably other resemblances, more especially in costume. Stubbs has suggested that the consular 'pretexta' was mistaken by Alfred and his suite for a regal garment [3], but it is probable that the consular costume had progressed much in splendour under Byzantine influence. Possibly among other changes the purple cloak, which the consuls wore only when celebrating triumphs [4], had become a more usual portion of the costume, for the dignity being at this time entirely honorary, the state garments would be the ones most likely to survive. We have, unfortunately, no descriptions of the costume of the Roman consuls at this time, the consular diptychs having gone out of use when the office ceased to be a real one [5] (apart from its

---

[1] See the text reproduced in Richard of Cirencester's *Speculum Historiale*, ii. p. 27 sqq.

[2] *Liber Pontificalis*, ed. Duchesne, ii. 89: 'Tunc almificus pontifex manibus suis ipsum Hludovicum, Imperatoris filium, oleo sancto perunguens, regali ac pretiosissima coronavit corona, regemque Langobardorum perfecit. Cui regalem tribuens gladium illique subcingere iussit.' Prudentius of Troyes, *Annales Bertiniani*, ed. Waitz, p. 30: 'Hlodowicum pontifex Romanus unctione in regem consecratum cingulo decoravit.' Cf. Dümmler, *Geschichte des ostfränkischen Reiches*, ed. 2, i. pp. 250-1.

[3] Introduction to Malmesbury, *Gesta Regum*, ii. p. xliii, note 2.

[4] Mommsen, *Römisches Staatsrecht*, i. pp. 332, 346; ii. part 1, p. 83. According to Dionysius of Halicarnassus, lib. iii. c. 62, § 2, the consuls used also the crown in triumphs, so that they were costumed as kings.

[5] See Ducange, *Dissertatio de Imperatorum Constantinopolitanorum Numismatibus*, at the end of his *Glossarium Latinitatis*; Daremberg and Saglio, *Dictionnaire des antiquités grecques et romaines*, i.

union with the office of emperor). Even the meaning of the honorary office conferred upon Alfred by the pope is doubtful. The pope's letter proves the correctness of Gregorovius's suggestion that the popes assumed the right, after the severance of Rome from the rule of the emperor at Constantinople, of granting the honorary dignity of consul[1]. By Leo's time the title had become a somewhat common one in Rome, being borne by notaries and even merchants[2]. It was not, therefore, a very high dignity that Leo conferred upon Alfred, being little more than a brevet of Roman nobility, unless he had in his mind some recollections of the former importance of the office of consul. A century earlier Pope Gregory III had offered to Charles Martel the dignity of Roman consul in order to induce him to protect him against the Lombards[3]. In this case consul has the older sense, and meant the transference to Charles of the emperor's power over Rome. Alfred in his version of Orosius renders the *consul* of his original correctly by *ealdorman*, so that he cannot have confused the office with that of king, and have concluded that his creation as consul was equivalent to being invested with regal rank. It is somewhat curious that Alfred conferred upon his grandson Æthelstan a scarlet cloak, a gemmed belt, and a Saxon sword with a golden sheath[4]. It would

1474 sqq.; Prof. Westwood, *Gentleman's Magazine*, ccxv. 143. The figures of consuls in the diptychs wear no sword, but are shown with richly embroidered gowns and sceptres. The girding referred to in Leo's letter means, no doubt, girding with a sword, and is therefore a sign of change in the costume of the consuls.

[1] *Geschichte der Stadt Rom im Mittelalter*, ed. 4, Leipzig, 1886-96, ii. 419.

[2] Ibid. Cf. however, iii. 346.

[3] Continuator of *Fredegar*, c. 22 (110), ed. Krusch, *Mon. Hist. German.*, 'Scriptores Rerum Merovingicarum,' ii. 179. Cf. Theodor Breysig, *Jahrbücher des fränkischen Reiches* (*Die Zeit Karl Martells*), Leipzig, 1869, p. 97.

[4] Malmesbury, *Gesta Regum*, c. 133, vol. i. p. 145, relates, on the authority of an old Latin poem celebrating the deeds of Æthelstan, that Alfred made him a knight prematurely, 'donatum chlamyde coccinea, gemmato baltheo, ense Saxonico cum vagina aurea.' Stubbs (ibid. p. 145, note 2; ii. p. lxii.) is doubtful as to the date of the work cited by Malmesbury, but as the latter states that it was composed during Æthelstan's lifetime (c. 132), it must have contained a dedication or apostrophe to that king. The explanation of this ceremony as that of

perhaps be too rash to suggest that these were the very ornaments that Alfred received from the pope, but we may, perhaps, venture upon the suggestion that Alfred was led to confer these things upon the young Æthelstan, who was then about the same age as he himself was when he received the consular vestments from the pope, by pleasant recollections of the ceremony at Rome. The coincidence is at any rate striking.

It is worthy of note that a reference to Alfred's visit to Rome occurs in the O.E. version of St. Augustine's *Soliloquies*, where, in a disquisition on the difference between knowledge gained by seeing a thing or being told of it, he says that it seems to him that he knows who built Rome and that he knows many other things that happened before his time, but, he adds, he does not know who built Rome because he had himself seen it [1].

Æthelwulf was in communication with Rome some years before this time, for Prudentius of Troyes mentions the presence at the Frankish court of the envoys of the English king, who brought with them an account of a vision of a priest in England, in which he is charged with a threat of punishment to mankind unless they amend their evil ways. They also sought permission for the English king to pass through Frankland on his way to Rome [2].

**9.** From the Chron., with the addition of the British

conferring knighthood obviously comes from Malmesbury. Doubts have been expressed as to whether Æthelstan was born before Alfred's death, but as Malmesbury states, evidently on the authority of this poem, that Æthelstan was thirty years old at his accession, it would seem, as this occurred in 924, that he must have been about five years old at the time of Alfred's death.

[1] *King Alfred's Old English Version of St. Augustine's Soliloquies*, ed. H. L. Hargrove, 'Yale Studies in English,' New York, 1902, p. 69, 23 : ' Me þincð nu þæt ic wite hwa Romeburh timbrode, and æac feala oðra þinga þe ær urum dagum geweordon wæs, þa ic ne mæg æalla ariman. Nat ic no þi hwa Rome⟨burh⟩ timbrede þe ⟨ = þy⟩ ic self hyt gesawe.'

[2] *Annales Bertiniani*, an. 839 : 'Verum post sanctum Pascha imperatori in Francia repedanti rex Anglorum legatos misit, postulans per Franciam pergendi Romam orationis gratia transitum sibi ab imperatore tribui, monens etiam curam subiectorum sibi erga animarum salutem solicitius impendendam, quoniam visio cuidam apud illos ostensa non minimum animos eorum terruerat. Cuius seriem visionis imperatori mittere studuit.'

name of Thanet, the statement that the marriage of Burhred took place at Chippenham, and a few minor elaborations of the words of the Chron. The statement that the Christians were at first victorious occurs only in MSS. A, B, C, and G, whilst A omits the record of the slaying of the two ealdormen. MSS. D and E omit the date of Burhred's wedding.

**9, 4 Britannico autem sermone Ruim.** This is, no doubt, derived from the *Historia Britonum* (Nennius) 'insulam, quae in lingua eorum ⟨Saxonum⟩ vocatur Tanet, Britannico sermone Ruoihm[1].' Lappenberg[2] cites Thorne's notice of a charter of 694[3] as proof that this name was still in use at that date, but as it does not occur in the text of the charter that has come down to us[4], it must be regarded as a borrowing from the present work. Thanet is not an English name, but a British one. It is recorded as Tanatus in Solinus[5], from whom it has been copied by Isidore of Seville as Thanatos[6], under the influence of the Greek θάνατος, an association that may have given rise to the strange story in Procopius of the ferrying of the dead over from Gaul to Britain.

**10.** From the Chron. See note to cap. 3 upon treatment of original.

**11.** From the Chronicle, with the addition of the statements that Alfred accompanied his father to Rome, that his father loved him better than his other sons, and of Judith's name. The latter occurs in the Chronicle under 885.

**11, 2 decimam totius regni partem.** Few things in our early history have led to so much discussion as the famous 'Donation' of Æthelwulf. Selden saw in it the institution of tithes and the grant of glebe lands, a view

---

[1] Mommsen, *Monumenta Germaniae Historica*, 'Chronica Minora,' iii. 171.

[2] *Geschichte von England*, i. 66, note 3.

[3] Apud Twysden, *Quindecim Scriptores*, col. 2234.

[4] *Cart. Sax.* i. 122.

[5] *Collectanea Rerum Memorabilium*, ed. Mommsen, Berlin, 1864, c. 22, § 8. Solinus was a third- or fourth-century compiler, and the source of his reference to Thanet seems to have been a lost chorography (Mommsen, p. xviii).

[6] *Etymologiarum* lib. xiv. c. 6, § 3.

that was challenged by Carte. The theory that the
king made a grant to the Church of tithes was controverted by Kemble[1], and Bishop Stubbs has truly
remarked that Æthelwulf could not have made such
a grant because the tithe 'was not his to bestow[2].' The
learned bishop has collected the charters purporting to
relate to this grant of Æthelwulf[3]. The majority of them
are drawn up in one form, a somewhat obscure one, in
which he has recognized presumptive evidence of their
genuineness[4]. These uniform texts come from chartularies of the lowest possible character, such as those of
Winchester, Malmesbury, Glastonbury, and Hyde, and the
formulas are not those of Æthelwulf's authentic charters, including phrases that are used in charters of later times. Of
these uniform texts one only is preserved in what purports
to be the original form[5], but it is written by a scribe who
was not an Englishman in an imitative hand, which may

---

[1] *Saxons in England*, ii. 481–90.

[2] Haddan and Stubbs, *Councils*, iii. 637.

[3] Ibid. iii. 638 sqq.

[4] This form appears in the copies from Winchester (*Cart. Sax.*
ii. 62), Malmesbury (ibid. ii. 66), Glastonbury (ibid. ii. 68), Abingdon
(ibid. ii. 67), and in a charter of unknown origin (ibid. ii. 64;
see below, page 188, note 1). Portions of the same form occur in
charters from Malmesbury (ibid. ii. 83, and, with the date 844, ibid.
ii. 26), from Crowland (ibid. ii. 85), and from Roger of Wendover
in general terms (ibid. ii. 85). The two Winchester charters (ibid. ii.
73, 75) differ in style and object, but reproduce the dating clause of the
preceding form. They also contain the very late story that Æthelwulf
was *nutritus* in that monastery (see Introduction, page c, note 2), which
is fatal to their authenticity. The dating clause occurs in a fragment
of an early tenth-century copy of a charter of Æthelwulf, where the
*palatium* of the texts previously cited is more naturally *villa regia*
(Brit. Mus. *Facs.* iv. pl. 9; *Cart. Sax.* ii. 82, 3). Another Winchester
charter purports to have been made by Æthelwulf, ' quando decimam
partem terrarum per omne regnum meum sanctis ecclesiis dare decrevi '
(ibid. 78, 8), but, from its formulas, it is obviously spurious. The
O.E. version of this grant (ibid. 79) seems to be founded upon the words
of the Chron. in reference to Æthelwulf's donation. The O.E. charter
from Winchester referring to this donation (ibid. 96) is an obvious
forgery. See p. 246, note 3, below. The proems of the uniform texts
are derived from late tenth-century formulas, while the mention of the
singing of psalms, &c., does not appear to have any connexion with
the ordinary ' book ' of this time, and indeed is out of place in the context.

[5] Brit. Mus. *Facs.* ii. pl. 32; *Cart. Sax.* ii. 64.

have been copied from a somewhat older (spurious) original. It appears to date from the eleventh century [1]. Apart from these uniform texts stands one that is preserved in the *Textus Roffensis*, a chartulary of the highest character. It contains ancient Kentish formulas, and seems to be genuine [2]. By it the king grants to a minister of his certain lands 'pro decimatione agrorum, quam, Deo donante, caeteris ministris meis facere decrevi,' with power to bequeath it to whomsoever he wished, but with no expressed exemption from royal dues or services. There is preserved a contemporary charter of Æthelwulf, dated 855, but with an error in the indiction, by which he grants land to a minister of his 'pro expiatione piaculorum meorum et absolutione ⟨'obsol-' MS.⟩ criminum meorum,' with like power of disposition, but with exemption 'ab omni servitute regali intus et foris, magnis et modicis, notis et ignotis [3].' If the date of this is really 855, as it seems to be, it must relate to the 'Donation.' These exemptions from worldly services were peculiar to land given for religious purposes [4], and the reference to the expiation of the king's sins and the absolution for his crimes can only be explained by the theory that the land was granted with an understood reversion to a house of religion. Very many of the genuine charters are grants to laymen with exemptions from services and with power to bequeath to whomsoever they wished. The 'book' by which the grant was made to the laymen was frequently handed over with the land, sometimes, as in the case of the charter in the *Textus Roffensis*, with an endorsement from the original grantee testifying the grant to the particular monastery. The majority of the early charters made to laymen that have been preserved came into the hands of ecclesiastical or monastic foundations, and a very large proportion of them imply, by their

---

[1] Dr. Warner, who has kindly examined the original for us, is inclined to date it nearer 1100 than 1000. He remarks that the scribe was evidently puzzled by the O.E. ꝑ (= *r*), which in several instances he copied as *n*, afterwards lengthening the lower limb. This is not an error that an English copyist would be likely to make.

[2] *Cart. Sax.* ii. 86. The reference to the journey to Rome, in the dating clause, is, however, suspicious. See below, page 193, note 4.

[3] Brit. Mus. *Facs.* ii. pl. 31; *Cart. Sax.* ii. 61.

[4] Maitland, *Domesday and Beyond*, p. 271.

reference to the need of almsgiving or of making gifts for the service of God, that they were made with an understood reversion to religious uses. In many cases the land granted to the layman seems to have been at the time of the making of the charter his own property, and the charter is really a dedication of the possessions to religious uses. In a famous case Æthelwulf books, with the consent of the *Witan*, land to himself, free from royal and other services [1]. The exemption from royal services is meaningless if he intended to keep the land in his own possession. That he did not so intend is proved by the proem, in which the duty of almsgiving is inculcated. King Alfred in his will bequeaths to Winchester abbey certain 'bookland' on the conditions that his father had specified in his will [2], which has not been preserved. The power of bequeathing the land freely was the most essential feature of the book from the legal point of view. Without the grant of such power the land would descend automatically to the kindred, and it is this interference with the ordinary law of descent that caused so much solemnity to be employed in drawing up the 'book,' which is invariably in the form of a gift from the king with the consent, expressed or implied, of the *Witan*. A powerful man might sometimes be able to obtain such a grant for himself, but the cases seem to have been exceedingly rare. The next most essential feature of the 'book,' the exemption of the land conveyed by it from all secular duties except the so-called *trinoda necessitas*, was distinctly a feature of land devoted, or intended to be devoted, to religious uses. Whether any legal object was obtained by interposing one or more lives between the making of the book and the entry of the religious house upon the possession of the land does not appear. But as many grants are made to bishops and abbots for the uses of their houses without the intermediary of any laymen, it would seem that land could be conveyed immediately to religious institutions. It is improbable that in all these cases the land dealt with was the private property of the bishop or abbot, although it clearly was in some instances.

---

[1] Brit. Mus. *Facs.* ii. pl. 30 ; *Cart. Sax.* ii. 33.
[2] *Cart. Sax.* ii. 178, 4.

It would therefore appear that when the king booked land of his own to a thane or other layman with reversion after the death of the grantee, the object was to reward him and at the same time to devote the land to the service of God.

From the Rochester charter it would seem that this was exactly what Æthelwulf did in that particular instance, and that the whole of the *decimatio* of his lands was made in the first place to his thanes. Such a distribution might be described in the words of the Chronicle, 'gebocude Æþel-wulf cyning teoþan dæl his londes ofer eall his rice Gode to lofe and himselfum to ecere hælo' ('King Æthelwulf booked a tenth part of his land throughout his kingdom to the praise of God and for his eternal health'). The author of the Life has overlooked the restriction of the grant to the king's own lands. It is hardly possible to reconcile with the words of the Chronicle Kemble's explanation, which Stubbs hesitatingly accepted[1], that Æthelwulf 're-leased from all payments, except the inevitable three, a tenth part of the folklands or unenfranchised lands, whether in the tenancy of the Church or of his thanes,' and that in the tenth so released he 'annihilated the royal rights, *regnum* or *imperium*[2].' The latter turns upon a highly strained rendering of the *regno* of the Life[3]. This is merely a rendering of the *rice* of the Chron., which was never employed in the artificial sense assumed by Kemble. We now know that folc-land could not be in the possession of the Church. Kemble placed second the grant of a tenth of Æthelwulf's 'private estates' to various thanes or clerical establishments, and thirdly 'the charge upon every ten hides of his own land of a poor man in food and clothing[4],' which rests upon the evidence of Roger of Wendover and Matthew of Paris. He has not noticed that their informa-tion is derived from the Life in its account of Æthel-wulf's will (c. 16, 18). Similarly Stubbs quotes William of Malmesbury for this statement[5], without recognizing its

---

[1] Haddan and Stubbs, *Councils*, iii. p. 637.

[2] *Saxons in England*, ii. p. 489.

[3] And upon the grant of exemption from royal tribute in the spurious charters in *Cart. Sax.* ii. pp. 83, 84, 85.

[4] *Saxons in England*, pp. 485, 489.

[5] Haddan and Stubbs, *Councils*, iii. 646.

source in the present work. This testamentary disposition must be kept distinct from the question of the Donation [1], for it did not take effect until some three years after the making of the latter. If Æthelwulf had any political purpose in making grants to his thanes on the eve of his departure for Rome, his object was imperfectly obtained if the story of the rebellion of his son and many of his subjects told in the next chapter is true.

**11, 3 in sempiterno graphio,** ' in everlasting alms or inheritance.' It is noticeable, in connexion with the Welsh origin of the author of the Life, that this phrase occurs in the early Welsh Life of St. Carantoc: ' et postulavit rex ⟨ Arthurus ⟩, ut reciperet Carrum in sempiterno graphyo [2].' The word *graphium* was adopted into Welsh as *greif*, and occurs in early inscriptions with the meaning of land secured by deed as private inheritance [3]. With it may be compared the ' in sempiterna consecratione' or 'servitute' of the Welsh charters preserved in the *Liber Landavensis* [4]. In the present case it seems to be the author's pedantic rendering of the ' in sempiternam hereditatem' of King Æthelwulf's charters [5]. Possibly the author may have seen some of

---

[1] It is confused with the Donation in a spurious Hyde charter of 901 (*Cart. Sax.* ii. 248, 15), which is influenced by the group of uniform charters relating to the Donation mentioned at page 187, note 4, above. The Donation itself is referred to in a forged Winchester charter (ibid. iii. 403, 28).

[2] Rees, *Lives of Cambro-British Saints*, p. 99; *Acta Sanctorum*, Maii tom. iii. p. 586 F.

[3] See Professor Rhys's reading of the inscription at Merthyr Mawr, in Glamorgan, published in the *Archaeologia Cambrensis*, 1899, p. 156. Cf. also the early Welsh deeds printed by Seebohm, *The Tribal System in Wales*, pp. 211, 212, 217, 219.

[4] Ed. Rhys and Evans, pp. 76, 129, 190, 195, 200, 221, 236, 239. Cf. ' in perpetua consecratione,' p. 198.

[5] *Circ.* 840, *Cart. Sax.* ii. 156, 16, a blundered eleventh-century copy; 841, ibid. ii. 12, 13 (*Textus Roffensis*); 845, Brit. Mus. *Facs.* ii. pl. 29; *Cart. Sax.* ii. 30, 16 (contemporary); 850, *Cart. Sax.* ii. 47, 4, and xvii. 15 (late copies). The phrase occurs in private charters of Æthelwulf's time, and in royal charters of his predecessors and successors, *Cart. Sax.* i. 517, 7; 530, 38; 552, 6; 586, 8; ii. 29, 11; 113, 27; 115, 14; 129, 10; 132, 21; 133, 18; 158, 17; 201, 30, &c. Elsewhere it is represented by ' in perpetuam hereditatem,' ' in aeternam hereditatem,' ' in perpetuae possessionis hereditatem,' ' in libertatem hereditariam,' and ' in sempiternam elemosinam,' &c.

the genuine deeds connected with the Donation, or have known that the royal charters usually contained this definition[1] of the estate in the land conveyed by them. Although γραφεῖον was used in early ecclesiastical Greek in the sense of 'scripture,' 'Holy Scripture[2],' the development in sense of *graphium* from 'writing style' through 'written deed' to 'property held by written deed,' 'an estate in land conferred by written deed,' seems to be due to Celtic Latinity. It is found in what purports to be a grant by a Cornish (?) 'count' in the Athelney chartulary[3] in the time of King Æthelstan, whereby Lanlovern is granted 'in diocesim sempiternam,' an obvious mistake due to the scribe of the chartulary, which has disappeared, or to the eighteenth-century copyist, for 'in graphium sempiternum.' This latter phrase is found in English charters of the middle of the tenth century with the meaning of 'Book of Life[4],' and in texts of doubtful authenticity with the same meaning as it has in the Life[5]. The words of a grant of 900 : 'confirmata est in sempiterno graphio in cruce Christi pro redemptione piaculorum Aðelwlfi regis[6],'

---

[1] It is represented by 'in perpetuam libertatem' and 'in perpetuam hereditatem' in the Winchester text (*Cart. Sax.* i. 63, 27), and the late eleventh-century one, at 65, 20, but is absent from the other texts, unless 'in libertatem ponamus' in some of them be a corrupt rendering of it.

[2] E. A. Sophocles, *Greek Lexicon of the Roman and Byzantine Periods.*

[3] Published in a translated form by the Somersetshire Record Society, vol. xiv. p. 156.

[4] A.D. 940, Ordnance Survey *Facsimiles*, ii., Winchester College, pl. 3; *Cart. Sax.* ii. 469, 2 (contemporary ; A.D. 947, Brit. Mus. *Facs.* iii. pl. 13; *Cart. Sax.* ii. 586, 11 (contemporary). It also occurs in texts, derived from later chartularies, between 941 and 949 (*Cart. Sax.* ii. 500, 10; 504, 11; 531, 38; 535, 17; 586, 12; 590, 26; iii. 191, 28) in one of 1002 (*Cod. Dipl.* vi. 143, 31), and in another of 1019 (ibid. iv. 8, 2). These latter, if genuine, must be ascribed to the use of old formulas in the chanceries of Æthelred and Cnut. See above, p. 150.

[5] In the formula 'Hoc (autem) eulogiae fructuosum ⟨*vv. ll.* futurorum, fructuorum⟩ munusculum in sempiterno graphio cum signaculo sanctae crucis maneat quamdiu,' &c., A.D. 937, *Cart. Sax.* ii. 421, 9, Wilton; A.D. 949, ibid. iii. 31, 25, Glastonbury; A.D. 946-951, ibid. 46, 25, Abingdon. A spurious Winchester charter of 904 is granted 'perpetualiter in sempiterno graphio in cruce Christi' (ibid. ii. 273, 19).

[6] *Cart. Sax.* ii. 238, 23 ; altered to 'cum superno chirographo' in the spurious text at 239, 28. Cf. also the variant in a Shaftesbury charter

so closely resemble the 'in sempiterno graphio in cruce
Christi pro redemptione animae suae' (to wit, Æthelwulf)
of the Life that one is tempted to suspect that the author
of this charter derived the phrase from the present work.
The charter is so obviously spurious that it cannot be
adduced as evidence that the Life is older than the date
borne by the charter. The fact, however, that 'sempiternum graphium' was employed in the early part of the
tenth century in the English royal chancery, which was
then strongly influenced by Franco-Celtic Latinity[1], is one
that lends countenance to the view that the Life is at least
as old as that period.

**11, 7 Romam perrexit.** This second visit of Alfred to
Rome is known only from the present work. Freeman
has suggested that Alfred stayed in Rome from 853, the
date of his first visit (c. 8), until the arrival of his father in
856[2]. But this is not compatible with the statement of
this work or with the evidence of a Rochester charter
dated 855, which is witnessed by Alfred. This is preserved in a ninth-century copy, possibly contemporary[3],
and is supported by another Rochester charter in the
*Textus Roffensis*, which seems also to be genuine[4]. There
is nothing improbable in the statement that Æthelwulf
took his youngest son with him, the son whom he had sent

---

of 935, 'in sempiterno graphio cum signaculo sanctae crucis' (ibid. ii.
414, 23), a fragment of the formula mentioned in the preceding note.
This chartulary also contains a grant of King Edmund, in which
'perpetua graphii custodia' and 'graphio' are applied to the protecting
deed (ibid. ii. 502, 14, 28). These charters are, however, of a suspicious
nature. An Abingdon charter of 944 replaces 'graphio sempiterno' by
'stilo perhenni' (ibid. ii. 556, 18). This charter preserves a reminiscence
of the latter phrase in 'cum syngrapho agiae crucis,' p. 557, 3, which
also occurs in a Wilton text of 940 (ibid. ii. 482, 24), and in a Winchester
one of 943 (ibid. 529, 10).

[1] *Graphia* is used in the sense of 'writing,' 'scripture,' by Mico of
St. Richer, an early ninth-century Frankish poet (*Poetae Latini Aevi
Carolini*, ed Dümmler, iii. 295, 6; 301, 7; 302, 9).

[2] *Dictionary of National Biography*, i. 154.

[3] Brit. Mus. *Facs.* ii. pl. 31; *Cart. Sax.* ii. 62, 4. There is an error
in the indiction, which appears as the first instead of the third, so that
the charter may possibly belong to 853.

[4] *Cart. Sax.* ii. 87, 5, dated 855, 'quando ultra mare perrexi' (of
Æthelwulf). With the exception of this unusual form of dating, there
is nothing suspicious diplomatically about the charter. See p. 188, above.

to the Eternal City two years earlier. The arrival of Æthelwulf at the court of Charles the Bold in 855 on his way to
Rome is recorded by Prudentius, bishop of Troyes, who
died in 861[1], and the visit of the West Saxon king to Rome
is entered in the contemporary Life of Pope Benedict III,
855–858, in the *Liber Pontificalis*, which contains a list of
his rich gifts[2]. The statement in Lappenberg[3] that Æthelwulf restored the Saxon School at Rome, rests upon the
authority of William of Malmesbury[4], who probably invented this statement[5].

**11, 11 Iuthittam.** At this time Judith cannot have
been more than thirteen years of age[6]. But such early
marriages were not uncommon among the Franks. Hilde-
gard, the wife of Charles the Great, was married to him at
the age of thirteen, according to her epitaph[7]. Hathui,
abbess of Gernrode, was married before 959 at the same
age to Sigifrid, son of the Markgraf Gero[8]. By the Lom-

---

[1] *Annales Bertiniani*, ed. Waitz, 1883, p. 45 : ' Karlus etiam
Edilvulfum, rege⟨m⟩ Anglorum Saxonum, Romam properantem, honorifice suscipit, omni regio habitu donat, et usque ad regni sui terminos
cum obsequiis rege dignis deduci facit.'

[2] Ed. Duchesne, ii. 148 : ' Huius temporibus rex Saxorum, ... nomine,
causa orationis veniens, relictis omnibus suis rebus et regnum proprium
suum amisit, Roma⟨m⟩ properans ad limina apostolorum Petri et Pauli
cum multitudine populi. Et optulit dona Beato Petro apostolo, corona⟨m⟩
ex auro purissimo, pens⟨antem⟩ lib⟨ras⟩ iiii.; baucas ⟨ = vasa⟩ ex auro
purissimo ii, pens. lib.— ; spata⟨m⟩ i. cum auro purissimo ligata⟨m⟩;
item imagines ii. minores ex auro purissimo ; gabathe ⟨ = candelabra⟩
Saxisce de argento exaurate iiii.; saraca⟨m⟩ ⟨ = tunicam⟩ de olovero
⟨ = holoporphuro⟩ cum chrisoclavo ⟨ = auroclavo⟩ i.; camisa⟨m⟩
alba⟨m⟩ sigillata⟨m⟩ olosyrica ⟨ = holoserica⟩; vela maiora de fundato
⟨ = cloth of gold?⟩ ii. Et ipse rex Saxorum, postulante sanctissimo
domno papa, ut facias ⟨sic⟩ roga⟨m⟩ ⟨ = donativum⟩ in ecclesia Beati
Petri apostoli publica⟨m⟩, de pondere aurum vel argentum librarum
ad episcopos, presbiteros, diaconos et universo clero et optimatibus
Romani⟨s⟩ tribuit aurum ; ad populum vero minutum argentum. Et
postmodum, finita causa orationis, reversus est ad proprium regnum
suum. Et post paucos dies vitam finivit, et perrexit ad Dominum.'

[3] *Geschichte von England*, i. p. 295, whence it has been adopted in
*Dict. of Nat. Biography*, xviii. p. 42.

[4] *Gesta Regum*, c. 109.

[5] See p. 245, below.

[6] Lappenberg, *Geschichte von England*, i. 295; Dümmler, *Geschichte
des ostfränkischen Reiches*, ed. 2, i. 416.

[7] Dümmler, *Poetae Latini Aevi Carolini*, i. 58.

[8] Thietmar of Merseburg's *Chronicon*, ed. Kurze, Hanover, 1889,

bard, Swabian, and Frisian laws twelve years of age was defined as the marriageable age for a girl[1]. It has been frequently stated that this marriage was an act of senile folly on the part of Æthelwulf, but there is no evidence that he was more than a middle-aged man at this time. He appears as king of Kent in a Rochester charter dated 823[2], but the date is clearly wrong. The Chron. records under 823 that he was sent into Kent with Bishop Ealhstan (of Sherborne) and Ealdorman Wulfheard, and that they drove King Bealdred out. As the Chron. hereabouts is two years behind in its chronology[3], the date must be corrected to 825. ' Æthelwulf may have been at this time some years under twenty-one, for the public life of a king's son began very early in the ninth century, and he may have been a few years under fifty at the time of his marriage with Judith.

**12.** This chapter is due to the author. The account of the conspiracy against Æthelwulf during his absence and of his surrendering Wessex to his rebellious son, which rests wholly upon the authority of the Life, has been advanced as an argument against its authenticity[4]. But there are indications in the Chronicle and in the O.E. regnal lists that Æthelbeald was king of Wessex during his father's life for a period closely corresponding to that deducible from the Life. The Chronicle states under 855 that Æthelwulf went to Rome in that year, stayed there twelve months, returned home and died 'two years after he came from the Franks.' His wedding with the daughter of Charles the Bald occurred on October 1, 856[5]. Thus his death is fixed as occurring

---

viii. c. 3, p. 195. Dümmler, *Kaiser Otto der Grosse*, Leipzig, 1876, p. 5, states that the marriageable age of a girl was considered to be fourteen or fifteen.

[1] Karl Weinhold, *Die deutschen Frauen im Mittelalter*, ed. 2, Vienna, 1882, i. p. 294.

[2] *Cart. Sax.* i. 550, 24, from the copy in the *Textus Roffensis.*

[3] Grubitz, *Kritische Untersuchung über die angelsächischen Annalen*, p. 14; Theopold, *Kritische Untersuchungen über die Quellen zur angelsächsischen Geschichte des achten Jahrhunderts*, p. 54 sqq.

[4] See Introduction, § 86, page cxxi, above. Plummer, *Two Saxon Chronicles Parallel*, ii. 81, thinks that the account 'sounds very mythical.'

[5] See below, p. 200, note 2.

late in 858[1]. His son Æthelbeald died in 860, according to the Chronicle, which nevertheless assigns to him a reign of five years. This would throw back the commencement of his reign to 855, the year in which Æthelwulf left England[2]. The present work states that Æthelbeald reigned two and a half years (c. 17, 7). The Annals of St. Neots, on the basis of this and of the five years assigned to him by the Chronicle, the genealogies, and the regnal table, say that he reigned jointly with his father two and a half years and the like period alone. The Chronicle, however, mentions his accession to the rule of Wessex at his father's death, which probably means that he then became sole or undoubted king. The discrepancy between the five years and the two and a half assigned for his reign over Wessex cannot be explained away by the suggestion that he was an under-king of Kent or some other portion of his father's realm during his father's life, for in no other case is the period spent as under-king reckoned as part of the reign as king of Wessex. The conclusion therefore seems unavoidable that Æthelbeald ruled over Wessex during his father's life and with his father's assent. Some report of this quarrel between Æthelwulf and Æthelbeald seems to have reached Rome, for the author of the account of his visit to Rome in the *Liber Pontificalis*[3] states that Æthelwulf lost his own realm, but does not state that he was deprived altogether of kingly dignity. Upon Æthelwulf's death his son Æthelberht succeeded to the kingdoms of Kent, Surrey, Sussex and Essex, which we may conclude

[1] Florence of Worcester states that he died on January 13, which is cited by Green, *Conquest of England*, p. 85, as from Prudentius of Troyes. One MS. reads *Junii* instead of *Januarii*, which does not agree with the statement of the Chronicle, unless the two years of the latter are used loosely because he returned in 856 and died in 858. Prudentius records his death in the latter year. Florence's date must be received with doubt, in view of his error as to the date of King Æthelred's death (see note to c. 41, 4, p. 240, below).

[2] Æthelwulf left England early in that year, as Stubbs, *Councils*, iii. 612, note *e*, has concluded from the position of the entry of his arrival in Prudentius. If he spent twelve months in Rome, as the Chronicle says, he must have reached there before June, 855, for in the July of the following year he was affianced to Judith, according to Prudentius (see below, page 200, note 2).

[3] See above, page 194, note 2.

were the portions of the West Saxon kingdom under Æthelwulf's immediate rule.   It is plain that the author of the
Life conceived Æthelwulf as still king of Wessex, although
the rule of that kingdom had been handed over to Æthelbeald, for the crowning of Judith is regarded as that of
a queen of Wessex (c. 13, 8). and Æthelwulf is made to
divide his kingdom between his two eldest sons (c. 16, 7)
by his will.   The compiler of the Chronicle was under the
necessity of mentioning Æthelbeald's succession as sole
king of Wessex at his father's death, and he seems to have
solved the difficulty by the crude method of recording his
accession to the throne after his father's death and by
assigning to him the full length of his reign, instead of
deducting the portion that overlapped that of his father's.

Carte has suggested that the marriage with Judith was the
cause of the rebellion of Æthelbeald, who imagined that
there was some design of leaving the crown to her children [1].
In this case it must have been the espousal, not the marriage,
that drove him into rebellion.   From July, 856, the date of
the former ceremony, to the end of 858, when Æthelwulf
died, is, roughly speaking, two and a half years.   Thus the
time agrees very closely.   It is probable that Æthelbeald
was left as regent during his father's lengthy absence from
England, and that the taste of power may have tempted
him into rebellion independently of the marriage with
Judith, or that may have been the deciding consideration
that induced him to take the step.   Freeman has suggested
that the hallowing of Alfred as king at Rome may have
contributed [2].   But the ceremony at Rome, which we now
know was not a coronation of Alfred as king, occurred two
years before Æthelwulf's departure, and three years before
Æthelbeald's unfilial act, and the true nature of the pope's
action must have been known to the latter long before his
outbreak.

**12, 3 in occidentali parte Selwuda.**  Note the retention of the O.E. gen. sg. *wuda*.   This description of the
land constituting Somerset, Devon, and Cornwall seems to
be a ninth-century or early tenth-century one.   In the

[1] *History of England,* i. 295  So Lappenberg, *Geschichte von
England,* i. 296.
[2] *Dictionary of National Biography,* i. 154.

Chron. under 709 Aldhelm's bishopric of Sherborne is described in MSS. A, C, D, E, F as 'be westan wuda,' which B represents by 'be westan Selewuda.' It would seem that 'West Wood' was the older name of the belt of woodland forming the eastern boundary line of the diocese, and that, at a later time, Selwood was substituted for it. In 878 in the Chron. Selwood [1] is mentioned as the dividing line, and again in 894. After this date we do not meet with any references to Selwood as forming an important boundary, although Æthelweard tells us that Aldhelm's bishopric was commonly called *Sealuudscir* [2]. The forest of Selwood had shrunk still more by the time of the perambulation of 1298 [3], when it occupied a small portion of the eastern boundary of Somerset about Frome.

**12, 5 Ealhstan.** It is noteworthy that the author speaks in c. 28 of Bishop Ealhstan's 'honourable' discharge of his office, in spite of the blame dealt out to him in the present chapter for his political action [4]. Florence of Worcester has avoided the contradiction by simply following the Chronicle, which does not qualify Ealhstan's tenure of the bishopric.

**12, 6 Eanwulf, Summurtunensis pagae comes.** This is the Ealdorman Eanulf who is recorded in Chron. A, B, C, and G under 845 as the leader of the Somersetshire men at the defeat of the Danes at the mouth of the Parrot, with the aid of Bishop Ealhstan, with whom we find him connected in the present chapter. In Chron. D, E, and F the ealdorman's name appears as Earnulf, but this is plainly a corruption, for an 'Eanulfus prin-

---

[1] MS. E has *Wealwudu*. Professor Earle regards this as a real name which he connects with *Wealh*, 'Welshman' (*Two Saxon Chronicles Parallel*, p. 306). But the MS. authority is so late and bad that it is probably to be ascribed to a miscopying of the *Sealwyda* of MS. A, possibly under the influence of *be Westan-wuda*.

[2] *Monumenta Historica Britannica*, 507 A.

[3] Hearne, *Adam de Domerham*, i. 185; Collinson, *History of Somerset*, iii. 56; Phelps, *Modern Somerset*, i. 45.

[4] This inconsistency, if it is one (see below, p. 227), has been pointed out in the singularly virulent tract entitled *The Impertinence and Imposture of Modern Antiquaries Displayed . . . by Philalethes Rusticus* (William Asplin, M.A., vicar of Banbury), published in 1739 or 1740 in answer to *A Letter to Dr. Mead concerning some Antiquities in Berkshire* (by Francis Wise, B.D.), Oxford, 1738, p. 19.

ceps' (a title applied to the great ealdormen) witnesses
the record of the proceedings of the Council of Kingston
in 838[1], in company with King Æthelwulf. This is, no
doubt, the ealdorman of Somerset. He appears to be the
'dux Eanwulf' who witnesses charters of King Ecgberht
relating to Kent in 833[2] and 838[3], and of King Æthelwulf
relating to the same county[4]. The Glastonbury chartulary
contains what purports to be a grant to 'Eanulphus princeps' of land in Somerset in 842[5]. The name of Eanwulf
appears, as a *dux*, among the witnesses of several of the
dubious texts relating to Æthelwulf's Donation[6], and in
other charters derived from later copies[7], most of which
are of a suspicious nature. According to a dubious Winchester charter he was a benefactor to that abbey, and was
the grandfather of Ealdorman Ordlaf[8]. An 'Eanwulf dux'
appears in Mercian charters about the same time, but he
is probably another person[9].

**12, 15 audivimus.** The author frequently uses the
plural pronoun in reference to himself. In c. 21 he uses

---

[1] Brit. Mus. *Facs.* i. pl. 17; *Cart. Sax.* i. 590, 11.

[2] Brit. Mus. *Facs.* i. pl. 16; *Cart. Sax.* i. 574, 28. The charter,
which is preserved in a tenth-century imitative copy, is genuine, despite
the error in copying the date as 773.

[3] Brit. Mus. *Facs.* iv. pl. 8; *Cart. Sax.* i. 585, 10, a late tenth-century
copy.

[4] A.D. 859, Brit. Mus. *Facs.* ii. pl. 34; *Cart. Sax.* ii. 102, 20, contemporary; A.D. 860-2, Brit. Mus. *Facs.* ii. pl. 38; *Cart. Sax.* ii. 108,
22, an eleventh-century copy, with the date 790. He also appears with
Æthelwulf among the witnesses to a charter dated 873 (Ordnance Survey
*Facs.* iii. pl. 19; *Cart. Sax.* ii. 154, 22). This is in a ninth-century
hand, the work of a scribe ignorant of Latin. He seems to have copied
twice over the list of witnesses of some charter of King Æthelwulf that
served as a model for this. Hence the second 'Eanulf dux' in line 32.

[5] *Cart. Sax.* ii. 13, 20.

[6] Ibid. ii. 28, 11; 64, 9; 65, 34; 67, 19; 70, 6.

[7] Ibid. ii. 22, 5; 45, 23; 73, 7; 74, 38; 77, 30; 79, 16; 80, 15;
94, 34.

[8] Ibid. ii. 234, 35.

[9] A.D. 864, *Cart. Sax.* ii. 120, 26; A.D. 860-865, ibid. ii. 123, 20,
spurious. He is probably the Eanwulf who witnesses a contemporary
charter of 836 (Brit. Mus. *Facs.* ii. pl. 24; *Cart. Sax.* i. 582, 37) and
an Abingdon charter of 852 (*Cart. Sax.* ii. 60, 18), perhaps also a
Worcester charter of 875 (ibid. ii. 161, 24). This is more probably the
king's thane to whom a grant was made in 872 by Werferth, bishop of
Worcester (ibid. ii. 149, 14).

the singular and the plural indiscriminately. Usually, however, he speaks in the singular when relating his own experiences. This use of the 'pluralis urbanitatis,' which became common in later mediaeval writings, is not incompatible with the age of the author. It is used by John Scotus at a slightly earlier date[1]. Einhard speaks in the singular, as does Beda, Aldhelm, Nennius, and Felix of Croyland.

**13.** This chapter is due solely to the author, with the exception of the mention at the commencement of the joy of Æthelwulf's people at his return, which is derived from the Chron. under 855. The Chron. does not, however, say that they were prepared to eject his son if he had wished.

**13, 9 iuxta se in regali solio.** The statement that the wife of the king of Wessex was not allowed to sit on the throne by her husband's side or to be called queen is known only from this passage in insular sources. But its accuracy is confirmed by the contemporary evidence of Prudentius of Troyes[2]. It was probably a knowledge of this usage that caused Charles the Bald to have his daughter crowned before she left for England[3]. Lappenberg's attempt to bring this custom into connexion with some hypothetical law of the West Saxons resembling the Salic Law[4] is difficult to reconcile with the record of the Chronicle that Sexburh ruled Wessex for a year after her husband's death in 672. The title of *regina* was applied to the wives of the kings of Mercia until the end of that

---

[1] See, for example, the quotation from him given below, p. 219, note 1.

[2] *Annales Bertiniani*, an. 856, ed. Waitz, p. 47: 'Edilvulf, rex Occidentalium Anglorum, Roma rediens, Iudith, filiam Karli regis, mense Iulio desponsatam, kalendis Octobribus in Vermaria ⟨Verberie on the Oise, near Senlis⟩ palatio in matrimonium accipit, et eam, Ingmaro, Durocortori Remorum episcopo, benedicente, imposito capiti eius diademate, reginae nomine insignit, quod sibi suaeque genti eatenus fuerat insuetum; patratoque regiis apparatibus utrimque atque muneribus matrimonio, cum ea Brittaniam, regni sui dicionem, navigio repetit.'

[3] The service used upon this occasion has been printed by Sirmond, from a Liége MS. that has now disappeared, in his edition of Hincmar's works, and thence by Boretius and Krause, *Mon. Hist. Germ.*, 'Capitularia Regum Francorum,' ii. 425. It is entitled 'Benedictio super reginam, quam Edelulfus rex accepit in uxorem.'

[4] *Geschichte von England*, i. 330.

kingdom, and Alfred's sister Æthelswith, the widow of
Burhred of Mercia, is called *cwēn* in the Chron. under 888.
The wives of the kings of Northumbria and of Kent were
known as *reginae*. This use of the name in the other
English kingdoms is a *prima facie* argument that it was
also used in Wessex. Whether it was employed prior to
Eadburh's crime we are unable to prove, owing to the lack
of early West Saxon records. Eadburh herself witnesses
with this title in a Malmesbury[1] and an Abingdon charter[2],
but both are open to grave suspicions. Frithogyth, the
wife of King Æthelheard of Wessex, is called *regina* in
two charters dated 729 and 737 in the Glastonbury chartulary[3], but again we can put no trust in the evidence. It
is, however, noticeable that she is called *cwēn* in the Chron.
under 737. There is no trace of the use of *regina* in ninth-
century West Saxon charters after the time of Eadburh[4],
and the author of the Life speaks as if the custom of not
calling the king's wife 'queen' still continued despite the
coronation of Judith and the fact that Æthelwulf placed her
by his side on the throne[5]. The widow of King Edmund

[1] *Cart. Sax.* i. 387, 5, dated 796.
[2] Ibid. i. 391, 18, dated 801.
[3] Ibid. i. 213, 25; 214, 24; 228, 10, 16.
[4] The Rochester charter witnessed by 'Elwytha regina' (i.e. Ealhswith) in 895 (*Cart. Sax.* ii. 214, 10) is a clumsy twelfth-century forgery,
which has been already condemned on palaeographical grounds by
Hickes, *Dissertatio Epistolaris*, p. 66. It is witnessed by a bishop
(*minister!*) of Norwich, whereas the East Anglian see was not transferred thither until the time of William the Conqueror, and the forger
has made a similar blunder in regard to Chichester. As this charter is
not included in the *Textus Roffensis*, it must have been fabricated after
the compilation of that chartulary. It relates to a grant in Suffolk,
which was not under Alfred's government in 895. It has the 'Volo
et praecipio' of the Anglo-Norman writ-charter, and has clearly been
made up after the date of the *Textus* by a forger who made use of the
Life of Alfred, from which he derives 'Etheldredus, Ganniorum dux'
(c. 29, 5), and also his 'Eaddredus comes' (c. 80, 8), without noticing
that the latter was a mistake for Æthelred, who also appears as a witness,
and that the former is mentioned as dead (c. 29, 11) before the date of
the composition of the Life, which was in 893. An unknown *Wulfðryd
regina* witnesses a charter of King Æthelred in 868 in the Winchester
chartulary (*Cart. Sax.* ii. 135, 38). It comes from a highly suspicious
source.
[5] He, however, calls her *regina* in c. 68, 12, which renders the *cuēn*
of the Chron.

is called *cwēn* in Chron. D under 946, but this may be
a later addition[1]. So far as we can judge by the evidence
of the charters, the title did not come into use again until
the reign of Edgar, when it is applied to his wife Ælfthryth
in several charters[2]. She is, however, frequently described
as the 'king's wife' (*coniux, laterana,* or *conlaterana*)[3], the
title ascribed to the consort of the West Saxon king in
line 15. It is probable therefore that Robertson's conclusion that this title was reintroduced by this ambitious
and unscrupulous woman is correct[4]. Although later royal
consorts are described by this title[5], and there is a coronation service for the queen dating at least as far back as
Æthelred's time[6], the king's wife continued to be known
in English as 'Lady.' The development of O.E. *cwēn* from
'woman' to 'king's wife' is obscure, but it does not seem
to have been affected by this curious West Saxon usage.

**13, 29 Theotiscorum.** The use of *Theotisci* as a collective name for the Germanic races is clearly due to
Frankish influences. The term arose in the eighth century
amongst the Franks, and was applied at first to the Germanic languages to distinguish them from Latin and
Romance. Its earliest appearance is in a document
relating to England in 786[7], and in form it is O.E. or Low

---

[1] She is called simply *matrona* in a grant to her by King Edgar, her
stepson (Brit. Mus. *Facs.* iii. pl. 25, contemporary; *Cart. Sax.* iii. 312,
5). See *Crawford Charters,* p. 87, note 1.

[2] *Cart. Sax.* iii. 624, 27; 629, 15; 637, 7; 646, 38. These are
authentic texts. It is also applied to her in charters of doubtful
authenticity (ibid. iii. 381, 20; 497, 15; 502, 32; 520, 26; 559, 15;
599, 30; 623, 21; 652, 2; *Monasticon Anglicanum,* ii. 324 b; *Cod.
Dipl.* iii. 176, 31; 324, 15).

[3] *Cart. Sax.* iii. 464, 14, contemporary (?); 393, 21; 433, 31; 466,
22; 591, 5; 596, 21, all more or less suspicious. She is called 'the
king's wife' in the O.E. text at iii. 162, 9, which may be genuine.

[4] *Historical Essays,* p. 168.

[5] For instance, Cnut's wife Ælfgifu in the drawing in the Hyde
*Liber Vitae* representing the royal couple.

[6] Maskell, *Monumenta Ritualia Anglicana,* ii. p. 53.

[7] The report of the papal legates George, cardinal-bishop of Ostia,
and Theophylactus, bishop of Todi, of their mission to England, printed
by Dümmler, *Epistolae Aevi Carolini,* ii. 20, from a Wulfenbüttel
tenth-century codex. In the corrupt text derived from the Magdeburg
centuriators in Haddan and Stubbs, *Councils,* iii. 460, and, in part,
*Cart. Sax.* i. 348 (where it is wrongly dated 787), the word is replaced

German [1], the O.H.G. form corresponding to O.E. *þeodisc* being *diutisk*, whence *Deutsch* has descended. It occurs in 788 in the Lorsch Annals in a passage that Brunner regards as taken from a legal instrument of that year [2]. The transference of the adj. from the language to the speakers of the language was inevitable, and the division of the Carolingian empire between the sons of Ludwig the Pious by the treaty of Verdun in 843 raised it to the dignity of a national name. It was firmly established in consequence of the treaty of Meersen in 870, which had the result of connecting all the German-speaking people of the empire, with the exception of the Flemish portion of Neustria, with the East Frankish kingdom [3]. Up to the death of Ludwig the Pious the word is used exclusively of the language, and

by *Teutonice*, probably by the centuriators. Professor Dove, *Das älteste Zeugniss für den Namen Deutsch*, in the *Sitzungsberichte d. philosoph.- philolog. u. d. historisch. Classe* of the Bavarian Academy, 1895, p. 230, thinks that the word is due to the Frankish abbot Wigbod, who accompanied the legates by order of Charles, and rejects the view that the word is an addition of the tenth-century copyist.

[1] Dove, *Bemerkungen zur Geschichte des deutschen Volksnamens*, in the Bavarian Academy's *Sitzungsberichte*, 1893, i. 237, suggests that the term is due to Boniface (Wynfrith) and his English companions. So also in his 1895 article, p. 234. An English example occurs, apparently, in a contemporary charter of Æthelwulf, dated 843 (Ordn. Survey *Facs*. iii. Stowe, pl. 17 ; *Cart. Sax.* ii. 18, 16) : ' unus ⟨*sic*⟩ singularis silva . . . quem ⟨*sic*⟩ nos Theodoice "snad" nominamus.' This cannot be a personal name, as it is considered to be in the British Museum *Catalogue of the Stowe MSS.* i. 700, where it is emended to the impossible *Theodo[r]ice*. It is, no doubt, intended for *Theodisce*. Although this charter is written in O.E. handwriting, it would seem to have been draughted by a Frank, for the unmistakably Old High German spellings *Alahhere* and *Walahhere* occur amongst the witnesses. These names appear on the attached slip in the O.E. spellings as *Alhhere* and *Wealhhere*. We cannot be far wrong in ascribing this Frankish influence and the use of *Theodisce* to Felix, the Frankish secretary of Æthelwulf, who is referred to at p. 225, below. The form *Walah-here* (evidently from this charter) is cited by Bülbring, *Altenglisches Elementarbuch*, § 447, as containing an O.E. parasitic vowel, and Chadwick, *Studies in Old English*, p. 178, note, similarly explains the *Ualach-* forms of the Namur MS. of Beda's *Historia Ecclesiastica*. This was written by continental scribes, and the forms are therefore due to Frankish influence. These appear to be the only instances of *a* as a parasitic vowel in O.E., and its non-occurrence elsewhere supports our explanation of its origin.

[2] *Deutsche Rechtsgeschichte*, i. 30, note 4.

[3] Waitz, *Deutsche Verfassungsgeschichte*, ed. 2, v. pp. 8, 132 ; Richard Schröder, *Lehrbuch der deutschen Rechtsgeschichte*, ed. 3, p. 384 sq.

this is the prevailing use for another century after that time. But it was applied to the race early enough for a contemporary of Alfred to have become acquainted with it abroad. Thus Walafrid Strabo, writing about 840, contrasts the *Theodisci* with the *Latini*, and in 843 an Italian record speaks of 'vassi domnici tam Teutisci quam Langobardi[1].' The Annals of Fulda in 876 substitute for it *Theuthonica* under antiquarian and classical influences, and it was, after a long struggle, superseded by *Teutonicus* in the eleventh century[2]. The use of *Theodiscus* would be naturally preferred by a Low German writer, and the more classical *Teutonicus* by one who was not a German. The occurrence of the former in the present work may therefore be considered as an argument in favour of its composition at some date earlier than the date of the Cottonian MS. (*circ.* 1000).

**14.** This chapter is due to the author. It contains the earliest record of the great boundary dyke between England and Wales, the relics of which still bear the name of the great Mercian ruler. In Welsh it is known as *Clawdd Offa*, and the English name appears to be a modern translation of this. The O.E. genitive of *Offa* was *Offan*, and a compound of this with *dic* would have come down to us as *Ofdyke* or *Offingdyke*. If the name was not a compound, we should have had something like *Off's Dyke*, for the final vowel would have disappeared during the Middle English period, unless it was retained by learned influence. The erection of the dyke is ascribed by Giraldus Cambrensis in the twelfth century to Offa[3]. The Germanic peoples were acquainted with such boundary ditches. Tacitus mentions the *latus agger* erected by the Angrivarii to divide their territory from that of the Cherusci[4]. The famous Danne-

---

[1] Waitz, v. p. 9, note 1.

[2] Waitz, v. 8, note 2; p. 132, note 4; Dove, *Bemerkungen*, p. 202.

[3] *Descriptio Cambriae*, ii. c. 7 (*Opera*, vol. vi, p. 217): 'Sicut et Offa suo in tempore; qui et fossa finali, in longum extensa, Britones ab Anglis exclusit.' It is also mentioned in an insertion in the later *Brut y Tywysogion* (*Monumenta Historica Britannica*, p. 843; ed. Ab Ithel. p. 8, Rolls Series). This mention does not occur in the older text in the *Red Book of Hergest*, ed. Rhys and Evans, Oxford, 1890. Cf. Rhys and Brynmor-Jones, *The Welsh People*, p. 141.

[4] *Annalium* ii. c. 19: 'Silvas quoque profunda palus ambibat, nisi

virke was a similar boundary erected shortly after Alfred's
time to form the southern boundary of Denmark.

**14, 6 Eadburh.** The marriage of Eadburh to Beorhtric,
king of Wessex, is recorded in the Chronicle under 787
(= 789[1]). It is an event that would possess a special
interest for Alfred, for it meant the subjection of Wessex to
the great Mercian ruler, and also the exile of Alfred's grandfather Ecgberht. The statement that Eadburh commenced
to live after the tyrannical manner of her father is, as we see
from the agreement of the transcripts and the Annals of
St. Neots, a part of the Life, and not, as has been suggested[2],
a later interpolation. Heinsch has remarked with justice
that such a story in the mouths of the West Saxons would
assume a somewhat biased colouring, owing to their dislike
of the Mercians[3].

**14, 15 adolescente quodam.** Lappenberg states that
the victim of Eadburh was a young ealdorman named Worr,
whose high birth and amiability of character had gained
him an influence over Beorhtric that she resented[4]. This
is not justified by the evidence at our disposal. The Life
does not mention the name of the favourite, but as it calls
him *adolescens* and *puer*, it is clear that he cannot be the
Ealdorman Worr, whose death is recorded in the same
annal as that of Beorhtric in the Chronicle under 800. It
is this collocation, which may be accidental, that has caused
Lappenberg to identify Worr with the object of Eadburh's
hatred. Worr was probably a West Saxon ealdorman, and
his name occurs as *princeps* among the witnesses to two

---

quod latus unum Angrivarii lato aggere extulerant, quo a Cheruscis
dirimerentur.' Müllenhoff, *Deutsche Altertumskunde*, iv. p. 423, identifies the remains of this dyke.

[1] The latter is the date in the Annals of St. Neots (above, p. 128),
which has here, as in other cases, preserved the original date of the
Chronicle (see above, p. 105).

[2] Joseph Heinsch, *Die Reiche der Angelsachsen zur Zeit Karls des
Grossen*, Breslau, 1875, p. 102. His reason is that Florence omits the
reference to her father's tyranny, but this is, no doubt, to be explained by
the reverence felt for him at Worcester as a great benefactor. Cf. above,
p. 110.

[3] Heinsch, *loc. laud.*

[4] *Geschichte von England*, i. 268. Heinsch, p. 101, repeats the
identification without comment.

charters of Beorhtric [1]. As these, however, come from the Abingdon chartulary, and are otherwise suspicious, we cannot attach much weight to their evidence.

**15.** This chapter is due entirely to the author. Although it is possible that the story of Eadburh may have been slightly 'improved' in transmission, it is probably true in its main outlines. It has no connexion with the Life of Alfred, and is introduced merely to explain the dislike of the West Saxons for the title of queen. We do not recognize anything in it that would suggest that it is the work of a later forger, and we see no reason for branding it as entirely legendary [2]. Alfred's family might be expected to have an interest in the fate of the daughter of Offa, whose marriage with Beorhtric excluded his grandfather Ecgberht from the throne. The emperor's jest, although somewhat brutal, is mild in comparison with some of those ascribed to him on the later and somewhat dubious authority of the monk of St. Gall. Charles was probably acquainted with Eadburh by name, for she would seem to have been the daughter of Offa whose hand he demanded for his son Charles. The latter was alive at the time to which this story must be referred, and may well have been the son here mentioned. This demand for the hand of Offa's daughter is recorded in the Lives of the Abbots of Fontenelle, which were written between 834 and 845 [3]. In it we read that Gervold, who became abbot in 787-8, was a friend of Offa's, that he had been sent to him by Charles on several missions, and was finally dispatched to him in connexion with the quarrel that arose between the two monarchs in consequence of Offa's asking for the hand of Bertha, Charles's daughter, for his son, as a condition for his assent [4]. From the work it does not appear whether this

---

[1] *Cart. Sax.* i. 360, 16; 391, 21.

[2] As Heinsch, p. 103, has done.

[3] *Gesta Abbatum Fontanellensium*, ed. Löwenfeld, Hanover, 1886, p. 5.

[4] Ibid. c. 16, p. 46: 'Hic nempe Gervoldus super regni negotia procurator constituitur per multos annos, per diversos portus ac civitates exigens tributa atque vectigalia, maxime in Quentawich (Wicquinghem, at the mouth of the Canche, Pas-de-Calais). Unde Offae, regi Anglorum sive Merciorum potentissimo, in amicitiis valde cognoscitur adiunctus. Extant adhuc epistolae ab eo ad illum, id est Gervoldum, directae,

last mission occurred before Gervold became abbot, but it
was evidently about the time of his appointment, for Alcuin
writes in 790 that he may have to go on an embassy in
connexion with the closing of the ports of Charles's
dominions to the English[1], which we know from the
Fontenelle book was Charles's reply to Offa's demand.
The marriage of Eadburh with Beorhtric is recorded in the
Chronicle under 787, which we may correct to 789[2], as
the dates hereabouts are two years in arrear of the real
ones. Another daughter of Offa, named Ælflæd, was
married to Æthelred of Northumbria in 792[3], and was
therefore presumably younger than Eadburh. Considering
the early age at which princesses were then married[4], it is
probable that she was not of marriageable age at the time of
Eadburh's union with Beorhtric and of Charles's demand.
It was possibly this dispute that caused Charles to receive
Ecgberht, a proceeding that would, no doubt, still further
embitter the relations between the Frankish monarch and
the powerful ruler over the Mercians. Gervold's mission

quibus se amicum ac familiarem illius carissimum fore pronuntiat.
Nam multis vicibus ipse per se iussione invictissimi regis Caroli ad
praefatum regem Offam legationibus functus est. Novissime vero
propter filiam eiusdem regis, quam in coniugium expostulabat Carolus
iunior; sed illo hoc non acquiescente, nisi Berta, filia Magni Karoli, eius
filio nuptui traderetur, aliquantulum potentissimus rex commotus, praecepit, ut nemo de Brittania insula ac gente Anglorum mercimonii causa
litus Oceani maris attingeret in Gallia.'
   [1] *Epistolae Karolini Aevi*, ed. Dümmler, ii. 32; Jaffé, *Monumenta
Alcuiniana*, ep. 14, p. 167: 'Sed nescio quid de nobis venturum fiet.
Aliquid enim dissensionis, diabolico fomento inflammante, nuper inter
regem Karolum et regem Offan exortum est, ita ut utrimque navigatio
interdicta negotiantibus cessat. Sunt qui dicunt nos pro pace esse in
illas partes mittendos.' Alcuin writes from England in 790 while
engaged upon this mission (ibid. p. 35; Jaffé, ep. 17, p. 173), which was
not immediately crowned with success. Another letter referring to
peace has been assigned to 790 by Jaffé, but Dümmler relegates it to the
period between 793, the year of Alcuin's return to the continent, whence
he writes this letter, and 796, the date of Offa's death (ibid. p. 125;
Jaffé, ep. 15, p. 169). The negotiations are dealt with by Heinsch,
p. 54 sqq.
   [2] The Annals of St. Neots have preserved the correct date (see above,
page 205, note 1).
   [3] The contemporary Northumbrian Chronicle, as preserved in the
first part of Simeon of Durham (see above, p. lviii, § 35).
   [4] See note to c. 11, 11, p. 194, above.

was evidently a failure, for it was necessary to send Alcuin, who succeeded in restoring friendship between the two kings. The Life of Æthelberht, king of East Anglia, who was slain by Offa in 794[1], states that a daughter of Offa's, named Althrida or Alfrida (i. e. Ælfthryth), was affianced to Æthelberht, and that after his death she retired to Croyland[2]. Nothing, however, is known of her historically[3], and, if she ever existed, she must, from the date of Æthelberht's death, have been younger than Eadburh and Ælflæd. How little credence can be given to this Life of Æthelberht may be seen from the fact that it calls Althrida the sole daughter of Offa.

**15, 24 sicut a multis videntibus eam audivimus.**
This is not impossible, although it is somewhat surprising to find a man writing in 893 thus refer to a woman who was married in 789. Assuming that Eadburh was fifteen at that time, she would be eighty in 854, so that men of

---

[1] *Annals of St. Neots*, p. 128, above.

[2] *Acta Sanctorum*, Maii tom. v, pp. 243* F, 244* E; *Giraldi Cambrensis Opera*, ed. Brewer, iii. 419; Richard of Cirencester, ed. Mayor, i. 286.

[3] The Appendix to Florence of Worcester, ed. Thorpe, p. 266, states that Cynethryth bore to Offa two daughters, Eadburh, who married King Beorhtric of Wessex, and Ælfthryth, 'quae virgo permansit,' making no mention of the undoubtedly historic Ælflæd. It is evident that this passage is founded upon the Life, c. 14, 5, and upon a Life of St. Æthelberht (see above, p. 110, note 3). The Chertsey chartulary contains what purports to be a confirmation by King Offa of the lands of that monastery, made for himself, his queen Cynethryth, Ecgfrith, his son, and his daughters Ethelburga the abbess, Æthelfleda, Edburga, and Æthelswitha, or Æthelfthitha (*Cart. Sax.* i. 349, 31). This is dated 787, and has been suspected by Stubbs, *Councils,* iii. 463. We have no proof of the grant of general confirmations until long after this date, and we have little doubt that the charter is a post-Conquest forgery. Ælflæd, who witnesses as Æthelfleda, has been clearly derived from the work of Simeon of Durham, and the forger seems to have taken his mention of the synod of Acleah from Richard of Hexham, the continuator of Simeon's work, under 788. See the quotation in Haddan and Stubbs, *Councils,* iii. 464. Eadburh is, of course, derived from the Life of Alfred by means, probably, of Simeon. The date is that of her marriage in the Chronicle. Æthelswitha or Æthelfthitha is clearly the Althrida of the Life of St Æthelberht, the Ælfthryth of Florence. The Abbess Æthelburh, described in this charter as a daughter of Offa, was really the daughter of an Ælfred (*Cart. Sax.* i. 305, 14, a genuine charter preserved by Heming), and a kinswoman of Aldred, sub-regulus of the Hwicce (ibid. 331, 23).

sixty might well have mentioned their reminiscences to the author between 887 and 893[1]. In 853 Alfred himself had been sent to Rome (c. 8), and young men in his train might have heard the history of Eadburh from older men, have seen her in Pavia or elsewhere on the journey to Rome, and have conveyed the information to the author. But in this case we might have expected him to vouch Alfred, whose attention would, no doubt, have been drawn to the ex-queen of Wessex. It was probably at Alfred's court where the writer met the men who had seen Eadburh, although we cannot exclude the possibility of his meeting men who had looked upon her before he came to Alfred. He may have met these men either in Wales or in Frankland, where the fate of Eadburh would be well known.

**15, 25 in Pavia . . . moreretur.** Pavia was on the road to Rome, and was hence frequented by English pilgrims on their journey to the latter[2]. In the itinerary of Archbishop Sigeric to Rome in 990 its name seems to have been blundered[3]. In the tenth century Bishop Theodred in his will bequeaths a white mass cope that he had bought at Pavia[4]. With this story of Eadburh's begging in that city we may compare the statement of St. Boniface, written about 747, as to the presence of English prostitutes or adulteresses in the cities of Lombardy, Frankland, or Gaul[5]. At the date of this letter the Lombards still spoke their native Germanic tongue, and it is probable that as late as Eadburh's time it was still the predominant speech in Lombardy[6]. It was a tongue whose relationship to Old English would facilitate its acquisition by natives of England.

**16.** This chapter is due to the author, with the exception

---

[1] The remarks of Stubbs, William of Malmesbury, *Gesta Regum*, i. p. xviii, upon the length of time that may be covered by the memory of two men are suggestive.

[2] Alfred's sister, Queen Æthelswith, was buried there in 888, according to the Chronicle.

[3] Printed by Stubbs, *Memorials of Dunstan*, p. 391 sqq.

[4] *Cart. Sax.* iii. 211, 8, from a fourteenth-century copy (see note to c. 33, p. 232, below).

[5] Dümmler, *Epistolae Karolini Aevi*, i. 355; Haddan and Stubbs, *Councils*, iii. 381.

[6] See W. Bruckner, *Die Sprache der Langobarden*, Strassburg, 1895, p. 12 sqq.

of the statement that Æthelwulf reigned two years after his return from Rome, which is derived from the Chronicle.

**16, 5 hereditariam . . . epistolam.** The following details are clearly taken from Æthelwulf's will. Bishop Stubbs has suggested that the author saw this will[1], which has not been preserved. That there was such an instrument is proved by Alfred's will[2], wherein he states that he produced 'Aþulfes cinges yrfe gewrit' ('King Æthelwulf's will,' literally 'writing concerning his inheritance'). The references to it, however, relate only to the disposition of the king's lands among his sons. This agrees with what is said in line 7 of the present chapter.

**16, 20 per omnem . . . terram . . . in decem manentibus unum pauperem.** This provision is referred to in a charter in the Hyde chartulary, dated 901, in which King Edward states that he makes the grant for the food of the monks of Newminster 'ex decimatione, quam avi mei decimaverunt ex eorum propriis terris istius regni ministris suis aliquibus . . . et pascendis pauperibus tradiderunt, ea ratione, ut in multis locis est scriptum[3].' It is difficult to feel any confidence in the authenticity of this text.

**16, 26 Romae . . . magnam pro anima sua pecuniam.** Nothing is recorded of these gifts of Æthelwulf to Rome in the *Liber Pontificalis*, unless they are referred to in the statement that during the time of Pope Nicholas (858–867) certain Englishmen came to Rome and placed in the chapel of St. Gregory in St. Peter's a *tabula* of silver, the weight of which is not given[4]. It is difficult to reconcile

---

[1] William of Malmesbury, *Gesta Regum*, ii. p. 40.

[2] *Cart. Sax.* ii. 177, 9.

[3] Ibid. ii. 248, 12.

[4] *Liber Pontificalis*, ed. Duchesne, ii. 161, 32 : 'Huius igitur tempore, cum multi ad sanctitatis eius nomen accurrerent, quidam de Anglorum gente Romam venerunt, qui in oratorio Beati Gregorii Papae et Confessoris Christi, infra sacram principis Apostolorum edem constructo, unam tabulam argenteam posuerunt, habentem lib. . . .' The absence of any reference to Æthelwulf's bequest in this work may be due to the change of style in the compilation. After the commencement of the account of Nicholas, a new writer appears, who pays little attention to recording gifts, but is more interested in political events. Father Duchesne would identify him with the librarian Anastasius, to whom the authorship of the early part of the *Liber Pontificalis* used to be assigned (ii. pp. v, vi).

this with the statements in the Life. Such bequests to
Rome as are described in the Life would be quite in
accordance with Æthelwulf's religious character. On his
visit to Rome he bestowed very rich gifts [1]. He could hardly
charge his heirs for ever with payment of three hundred
mancusses yearly, as the Life seems to state, for his interest
in the estates of his family was only a life one [2].

**16**, 30. This gift of Æthelwulf's to St. Peter's, Rome, is
mentioned in a Rochester charter of Alfred, bearing date
895, but this is a fabrication based, directly or indirectly,
upon the present work [3].

**16**, 37 **universali papae.** The use of this title came in
about the end of the seventh century [4]. It was in common
use in the ninth century [5], but as it was employed in the

---

[1] See above, page 194, note 2.

[2] Malmesbury, *Gesta Regum*, c. 109, ascribes to Æthelwulf the grant
of the *tributum* to St. Peter that the English still paid in his time to
the pope, referring to Peter's Pence (*Rom-feoh*, *Rom-pening*, *Heorð-
pening*), evidently identifying the present passage with that mysterious
impost. A similar attempt has been made by Paul Fabre, *Étude sur le
Liber Censuum*, Paris, 1892, p. 132, who connects with it the mentions
in the Chron. of the dispatch to Rome of the alms of the king and
of the West Saxons in the time of Alfred and Edward the Elder.
Dr. Jensen, *Transactions of the Royal Historical Society*, xv, pp. 180,
182, brings Æthelwulf's alms into relationship with Peter's Pence,
which in later times amounted to 299 marks yearly, by substituting
tacitly 'mark' for 'mancus' in the present passage, thus multiplying
the sum by four. It is noteworthy that Offa is alleged to have promised
to send 365 mancusses yearly to Rome for the maintenance of the poor
and of lights. This appears from a letter of Leo III to Offa's successor
Cenwulf, written about 787 (Haddan and Stubbs, *Councils*, iii. p. 525 ;
Jaffé, *Monumenta Alcuiniana*, p. 363; Jaffé-Wattenbach, *Regesta Pontificum Romanorum*, no. 2494). Dr. Liebermann accepts the origin of
Peter's Pence in this grant of Offa, and also describes Malmesbury's
reference to Æthelwulf as a confirmation of the grant by the latter king
(*Ueber die Leges Edwardi Confessoris*, Halle, 1896, p. 55). Pope
Alexander II (1066-73) writes to William the Conqueror that the
English used to send a yearly pension to Rome, part of which went
to the pope and part to the Schola Anglorum (Jaffé-Wattenbach,
no. 4757).

[3] *Cart. Sax.* ii. 212, 24. See above, page 201, note 4.

[4] See J. Friedrich, *Die Constantinische Schenkung*, Nördlingen,
1889, p. 108 sqq. ; *Registrum Gregorii Magni*, ed. Ewald and Hartmann, i. 321.

[5] It is occasionally used in the *Liber Pontificalis* in the ninth century,
but as the lives in the following century are not by contemporary writers,

Imperial chancery after that time, we cannot claim that its appearance in the Life limits the compilation of the latter to the ninth century. We have, however, been unable to find an English instance later than the present one.

**17.** This chapter is due to the author. The marriage of Æthelbeald to his father's widow, which is known only in English sources from the Life or from its derivatives, is recorded by Prudentius of Troyes, a contemporary Frankish chronicler[1]. This confirmation is an important argument in favour of the authenticity of the present work. It is noticeable that the author assigns two and a half years as the duration of Æthelbeald's reign over Wessex, whereas the Chronicle, the regnal tables, and royal genealogies ascribe to him a reign of five years. It is evident that half of the latter term must have been during the time of Æthelwulf[2], as stated in the Annals of St. Neots, no doubt on the authority of the present chapter. The statement that Æthelbeald was compelled to separate from Judith, although accepted by some writers[3], is unsupported by any competent testimony[4], and does not harmonize with the

no definite conclusion can be drawn from their evidence. In 963 Otto the Great addresses John XII as 'summus pontifex et universalis papa' (Liudprand, *Historia Ottonis*, ed. Pertz, p. 172) and the Emperor Henry I applies the same titles to Benedict VIII (Hardouin, *Concilia*, vi. col. 799). For another imperial use of the title, see the emperor's advocate's argument calling the pope 'universalis pontifex' in *Monumenta Germaniae Historica*, 'Libelli de Lite Imperatorum et Pontificum saeculis xi. et xii. conscripti,' i. 78, 36 (cf. ii. 672, 2).

[1] *Annales Bertiniani*, an. 858, p. 49 : 'Edilvulf, Rex Occidentalium Saxonum, moritur; relictam eius, Iudit reginam, Adalboldus, filius eius, uxorem ducit.'

[2] See note to c. 12, page 195, above.

[3] Lappenberg, *Geschichte von England*, i. p. 297, who has misled Dümmler, *Geschichte des ostfränkischen Reiches*, ed. 2, ii. p. 37.

[4] The authorities are the twelfth-century St. Albans compilation (in Roger of Wendover, ed. Coxe, i. p. 295; Matthew of Paris, *Chronica Maiora*, i. p. 387; *Flores Historiarum*, i. p. 427), where it is entered under 859, and the work of Thomas Rudborne, *Annales Ecclesiae Wintoniensis* (in Wharton, *Anglia Sacra*, i. p. 204), a fifteenth-century compilation of no value for early times. Rudborne, who is sometimes critical (see the present writer in the *English Historical Review*, xvii. p. 630), seems to have derived this information from the unknown work of Gerard of Cornwall, *De Gestis Regum Westsaxonum*, a late writer who embodied many figments in his work (see *English Historical Review*, xvii. p. 630, note 17). This story makes the separation proceed

contemporary Frankish account of her leaving England upon
Æthelbeald's death, wherein she is described as his relict[1].

**17,** 2. The statement in the Annals of St. Neots that
King Æthelwulf was buried at Steyning is otherwise unknown. The Cottonian MS. of the Life contained no
mention of the place of his sepulture, and Florence of
Worcester has clearly derived his 'apud Wintoniam' from
the Chron. As the Annals of St. Neots elsewhere transcribes the Life so carefully, it is probable that this reading
is derived from the MS. of that work used by the compiler
of the Annals. In that case we should have to conclude
that the Cottonian MS. was not the one from which the
compiler derived his extracts from the Life. There are other
grounds for this view[2]. Steyning was the property of King
Alfred, who bequeathed it to his nephew Æthelwold[3]. It
seems to have come into royal hands again after Æthelwold's unsuccessful rebellion against Edward the Elder,
and was granted by Edward the Confessor to the abbey of
Fécamp[4], and hence became an alien priory. In the list
of the burial-places of English saints, which dates in its present form from the early part of the eleventh century, it is
stated that St. Cuthmann is buried at Steyning[5]. Of him
nothing is really known, although a life of him exists[6]. It

from the gentle remonstrances of St. Swithun, which is no doubt a
Winchester invention. Cf. Introduction, p. c, note 2, above.

[1] Hincmar, *Annales Bertiniani*, ed. Waitz, p. 56 : 'filia eius ⟨*scil.*
Karoli⟩ Iudith, relicta scilicet Ædelboldi, Regis Anglorum, quae,
possessionibus venditis, quas in Anglorum regno optinuerat, ad patrem
rediit et in Silvanectis civitatem debito reginae honore . . . servabatur.'
This is entered under **862**, the date of her elopement with Baldwin of
Flanders.

[2] See Introduction, § 34, p. lvii, above.

[3] *Cart. Sax.* ii. 178, 20.

[4] *Cod. Dipl.* iv. p. 229, from the *Cartae Antiquae*, EE. no. 1, in the
Public Record Office, a late twelfth- or very early thirteenth-century copy.

[5] *Die Heiligen Englands*, ed. Liebermann, ii. 48, p. 19 ; *Liber Vitae*
of Hyde, 94, 2.

[6] *Acta Sanctorum*, Februarii tom. ii. pp. 197-9. The suggestion at
p. 197 B that he lived at the end of the ninth or beginning of the tenth
century rests upon the erroneous suppositions that Steyning was granted
by the English to Fécamp after the Norman Conquest, that it was in
Normandy, and that consequently St. Cuthmann must have migrated
from England to Normandy. This migration could not be placed
before the conversion of the Normans to Christianity. It is to be

is evidently of late date and has been written to order, and the author had no materials. We may even doubt whether he had any legendary evidence before him. If some sort of religious establishment existed at Steyning in Æthelwulf's time, it is not improbable that he should be buried there. The Chron., however, records his burial at Winchester, so that, if he was originally interred at Steyning, his body must have been transferred by Alfred to Winchester, after 893, the date of the composition of the Life. Alfred's body was in like manner transferred from Old Minster, Winchester, to New Minster by Edward, his son[1], and afterwards to Hyde, when the New Minster was removed thither.

**17, 5 thorum patris sui ascendens.** According to Beda King Eadbald of Kent married his father's widow, a proceeding that the historian describes as ' fornicatione . . . qualem nec inter gentes auditam apostolus testatur[2].' Possibly the author of the Life was acquainted with this passage, but whether he drew his description of such a marriage as unknown among pagans from Beda or from the text referred to by him, it is certainly wrong. The step taken by the Kentish king was part of the reaction against Christianity that marked his accession. The prohibition of such marriages was one of the restrictions introduced among the Germans by Christian influence[3]. The legality of marriage with a step-mother was one of the questions submitted to Gregory by Augustine as a result of his experience in England[4]. The question had arisen some years before the accession of Eadbald. It is difficult to believe that this heathen institution of marriage with a step-mother can have been the cause of Æthelbeald's marriage with Judith, as Weinhold suggests[5]. The custom existed in

regretted that this suggestion has been reproduced in the uncritical notice of this saint in the *Dictionary of Christian Biography*, i. 731.

[1] *Liber Vitae* of Hyde, 5, 19; 6, 17.

[2] *Hist. Eccl.* ii. c. 5.

[3] Edgar Loening, *Geschichte des deutschen Kirchenrechtes*, Strassburg, 1878, ii. p. 562; Weinhold, *Die deutschen Frauen im Mittelalter*, i. 359 sqq.

[4] Beda, *Hist. Eccl.* i. c. 27, question 5; Haddan and Stubbs, *Councils*, iii. p. 20. Hartmann, in the *Registrum Gregorii Magni*, ii. p. 332, decides in favour of the authenticity of these questions and answers.

[5] *Die deutschen Frauen*, i. p. 360. If it was, as he suggests, a

Scotland until the twelfth century, when Queen Margaret is said to have procured its suppression[1]. There is an instance of it in Wales as late as the ninth century[2]. Procopius records that Hermigisl, king of the Warni, on his death-bed commanded his son to espouse his step-mother[3]. The custom was also known among the Lithuanians[4], and, indeed, seems to have widely spread among pagans.

**17 b, 7 Burua.** This is an error of Parker or his printer for *Burna*, as in the Annals of St. Neots, whence this interpolation was taken. In the mythical *Liber de Infantia Sancti Eadmundi* by Geoffrey de Fontibus, written between 1148–1156, the coronation of Edmund is fixed at 'villa Burum,' which is described as lying on the boundary of Essex and Suffolk on the river Stour[5]. This is the modern Bures St. Mary, co. Suffolk, which appears in Domesday as *Bure*[6]. The variations in form represent obviously the gradual supersession of the O.E. dative plural by the nominative plural. The Domesday form, if it may be trusted, represents the dative singular. The form in the Annals of St. Neots must therefore be miswritten for *Buran*, a form of the dative plural. There are several agreements as to events between these annals and the work of Geoffrey, but the borrowing seems to have been on the part of the latter, who professes to have compiled his work from matter that had been told to him and from materials that he had met with in reading[7].

**18.** From the Chronicle. The author of the Life has, however, made a curious confusion in stating that, upon Æthelbeald's death, Æthelberht joined to his realm Kent,

---

political institution, it must have gone out of use before Beda's time, to judge by his language. Robertson, *Historical Essays*, p. lxvii, attempts to explain the custom as arising from 'the desire of preventing the joint property from passing beyond the limits of the mæg.'

[1] Haddan and Stubbs, *Councils*, ii. p. 158, § 5.
[2] *Liber Landavensis*, p. 189.
[3] *De Bello Gothico*, iv. c. 20. This was for political reasons.
[4] Schrader, *Reallexikon der indogermanischen Altertumskunde*, p. 910.
[5] Ed. Arnold, *Memorials of St. Edmund's Abbey*, i. 101. One MS. reads 'villa de Bures.'
[6] Vol. ii. p. 392.
[7] *Memorials of St. Edmund's Abbey*, i. 93, 'quaedam ab aliis mihi tradita, quaedam viva lectione cognita.'

Surrey, and Sussex, for, according to the Chron., he succeeded to these kingdoms and to that of Essex upon his
father's death, and the author of the Life states that Æthelbeald was king of Wessex until his death (c. 17). He
should have stated that Æthelberht added Wessex to his
dominions upon Æthelbeald's death, or, as the Chronicle
puts it, succeeded 'to all the kingdom.' The author's error
has probably arisen from the passage at the end of the
annal for 855 in the Chronicle, which is separated from
that of 860 by nothing but the numerals of the years 856,
859. This annal for 855 states that Æthelbeald succeeded
to Wessex, and Æthelberht to Kent, Essex, Surrey, and
Sussex. Chron. C omits from this list the name of Essex,
just as the author of the Life does in the present chapter,
but this seems to be a mere coincidence of no importance,
since Essex occurs in the other MSS., and was, therefore,
no doubt present in the archetype and in the copy before
the author.

**18, 10 Osric, Hamtunensium comes.** The name of
the ealdorman is so given in Chron. A, D, E and G, but
appears as Wulfheard in B and C. An Ealdorman Wulfheard is recorded as fighting the Danes at Southampton in
the Chron. under 837, which records his death in the same
year. The reading 'Osric' appears to be the correct one
in the annal for 860, for an 'Osric princeps' witnesses
a contemporary charter of King Æthelwulf in 847[1]. He
also witnesses several of the suspicious charters relating to
that king's Donation[2], and some other doubtful texts[3].

---

[1] Brit. Mus. *Facs.* ii. pl. 30; *Cart. Sax.* ii. 34, 41. He is, no doubt,
the *Oric dux* of a Rochester charter of 860-2, wrongly dated 790 by
the copyist (*Cart Sax.* ii. 108, 23), since *Oric*, an impossible O.E.
name, must be miswritten for *Osric* or *Ordric*. In another Rochester
charter of 850 his name is miscopied *Orric*, owing to the frequent misreading of the O.E. *s* as *r* (ibid. ii. 48, 27). He also occurs with other
witnesses of about this date in the strange eleventh-century charter dated
874 (*Cart. Sax.* ii. 157, 14).

[2] *Cart. Sax.* ii. 28, 10; 65, 35; 67, 18.

[3] Ibid. ii. 71, 18; 99, 31, both from the Winchester chartulary. The
latter in the invocation, movent clause, and anathema shows influence
of the deeds relating to the Donation, whilst the former uses the same
formulas as the spurious charter of King Ine in the same chartulary
(*Cart. Sax.* i. 148), including an immunity clause derived from King

It is worthy of note that this Hampshire ealdorman bears a name beginning with the stem *Os-*, which occurs in the name of Alfred's mother *Os-burh* and of her father *Os-lac*[1].

**18, 14 muliebriter** is an addition of the author. It is possibly a reminiscence of Nennius[2].

**19.** Based upon the Chronicle under 860. The description of Æthelberht as reigning 'pacifice et amabiliter atque honorabiliter' is a translation of the words of the Chronicle : 'he hit heold on godre geþuærnesse ond on micelre sibsumnesse.' One is tempted to believe that this characterization of the reign is due to the kind remembrances in Alfred's mind.

**20.** From the Chronicle, with expansions. It appears under 865 in Chron. A, B, D, E, but under 866 in C. It is probable that the Cottonian MS. of the Life had 865, for these events are mentioned after the death of Æthelberht, who is assigned a five years' reign and whose accession is placed in 860. The date 864 is probably due to Parker's transcriber. A scribe in the eleventh century would have represented the numeral by iiii, not by iv. The compiler of the Annals of St. Neots refers this chapter to 864 also.

**20, 4 servato.** As this reading occurs in all the texts except Florence of Worcester and SD 2, which transcribes him, it is evident that his *servando*, although a preferable reading, is an emendation of his own.

**21.** The first part is derived from the Chronicle, omitting the mention of the making of peace between the Danes and the East Angles, and adding that the former came 'de Danubia.'

**21, 5 Danubia.** If this reading existed in the original work, it must be explained as arising from an erroneous connexion of the names of the Danes with the Danube. The Danes were in possession of the mouths of the Rhine some few years before this date[3], but it is improbable that

---

Edgar's chancery. The Shaftesbury charter witnessed by *Osric dux* in 860 (*Cart. Sax.* ii. 106, 24) is a suspicious text.

[1] See above, p. 163, note 5.

[2] *Historia Britonum*, ed. Mommsen, p. 188 : 'et barbari victi sunt, et ille victor fuit, et ipsi in fugam versi usque ad ciulas suas mersi sunt in eas muliebriter intrantes.'

[3] See Dümmler, *Geschichte des ostfränkischen Reiches*, ed. 2, ii. p. 48 ; Steenstrup, *Normannerne*, ii. p. 177.

the author has confused the names of the two great rivers.
The Danes probably came to England from the mouths of
the Rhine on this occasion[1].

**21, 9 ut more navigantium loquar.** The comparison
of the author's work and its object to a ship making for port
occurs again in c. 73, 2, 'ne diuturna enavigatione portum
optatae quietis omittere cogar.' Cf. also c. 91, 30. With
c. 73, 2 may be compared the words of Cicero, 'nam et
quum prospero flatu eius ⟨scil. fortunae⟩ utimur, ad exitus
pervehimur optatos[2].' The allegory is used by St. Jerome,
'ad portum explanationum . . . pervenire poterimus[3],' and,
again, 'si me ad optatos portus aestus attulerit, gubernator
putabar infirmior[4].' The figure was a common classical
one. Quintilian, who gives it as an example of allegory[5],
employs it himself in his epistle dedicatory[6]. It was equally
popular with the writers of the early Middle Ages. The
eighth-century Felix of Croyland makes use of it[7], and it
occurs in the same century in the poems of Fortunatus[8].
An instance almost contemporary with Asser may be quoted
from John Scotus[9]. It is, therefore, evident that the argu-

---

[1] Steenstrup, ii. p. 178, who refers to the peace enjoyed for a few
years after 864 by the lands about the Rhine mouth. It is impossible
to attach much weight to his other argument, which is the occurrence
about this time of *Scaldingi* in England as a name for the Danes, and
the connexion of this name, with Lappenberg, *Geschichte von England*,
i. p. 212, with the name of the river Scheldt, *Scaldis*. This denomination occurs only in the late tenth century *Historia de Sancto Cuthberto*,
and relates to much earlier events (Simeon of Durham's works, ed.
Arnold, i. pp. 200, 202). It is much more probably a somewhat corrupted form of *Skioldungar*, the *Scyldingas* of Beowulf, the name of the
royal race of the Danes and, by extension, of the Danes themselves.

[2] *De Officiis*, 2, 6, 19.

[3] *Commentariorum* lib. xiv, prolog.

[4] Epistola xvii, *ad Innocentium* (Benedictine edition of his works,
iv. 2, col. 23). Cf. also Ep. i, *ad Rufinum* (ibid. iv. 2, col. 2); Ep. v,
*ad Heliodorum* (ibid. iv. 2, col. 11); *Comment. in Abdiam prophetam*,
c. 1, praef. (ibid. iii. p. 1455); *Comment. in Zachariam* (ibid. iii.
p. 1706).

[5] *Institutiones Oratoriae*, lib. viii. c. 6, § 44.

[6] 'Permittamus vela ventis et oram solventibus bene precemur.'

[7] *Vita S. Guthlaci*, ed. Birch, Wisbech, 1881, p. 2.

[8] Polycarp Leyser, *Historia Poetarum et Poematum Medii Aevi*,
Halae, Magdeburgi, 1721, p. 165, lxiii. § 4.

[9] *De Praedestinatione*, praef.: 'nos vero e diverso inter undosum veli-
volumque pelagus imperii senioris nostri, Domini videlicet gloriosissimi

ment that the author of the Life derived the allegory from
the late tenth century Æthelweard[1], and that the Life is
later in date than his work[2], has no validity[3].

**21,** 15 **quantum meae cognitioni innotuit.** Cf. c. 73,
3. Suggested by a phrase of Einhard in the passage quoted
in the note to the latter chapter.

**22,** 4 **curto,** 'court.' The use of this word in reference
to the king's palace is one of the proofs of Frankish influence
discernible in the Life[4]. The form is somewhat unusual[5],
but the reading given in the text is supported by Florence
of Worcester, and the *curto* of c. 75, 22 is also reproduced
by him. It is clear that this was the reading of the Cottonian MS. of the Life. Florence agrees with the Corpus
transcript in reading *cultu* (for *curto*) in c. 100, 5, 11, 21,
the reading in the last instance being noted by Wise as that
of the Cottonian MS. This curious form, which seems to
be due to an error on the part of the scribe of the Cottonian
MS., is another proof that Florence used that MS. The
author of the first part of the chronicle bearing the name of
Simeon of Durham substitutes *curia* for *curto* in c. 75, 22,
and the word does not appear in his extracts from the other

Caroli, quasi quaedam navicula diversis fluctibus agitati, quandoque
tamen in portu serenitatis eius stabilitanda occupati, vix aliquando ad
vestigia sapientiae intuenda brevissimo temporis sinimur intervallo' (ap.
Migne, *Patrologiae Cursus Completus*, cxxii, col. 355).

[1] *Mon. Hist. Brit.* p. 514 A : 'veluti advecta navis per gurgites
undarum longinqua spatia, tenet iam portum, quae diligenti tramite
explorarat, ita et nos, quasi more nautarum, ingredimur.'

[2] See Introduction, p. cxvii, above.

[3] Other examples of the use of this figure may be found in the eleventh-
century Life of St. John of Beverley, in Raine's *Historians of the Church
of York*, i. p. 240, and Heming's preface to the Worcester chartulary,
written at the end of that century, ed. Hearne, p. 258. It is unnecessary
to cite more instances, but reference may be made to Dante's use of the
simile in *Purgatorio*, i. 2 ; *Paradiso*, ii. 1.

[4] See Introduction, § 58, p. xciv. above. Numerous Frankish examples of its use in this sense may be found in Ducange's *Glossarium
Mediae et Infimae Latinitatis* under ' Cortis.'

[5] It seems to occur in a Worcester charter of 816 in 'duobus in curtis'
(*Cart. Sax.* i. 498, 2), unless this is due to confusion between the ablative plural terminations of the second and third declensions, of which
there are several instances in Mercian charters of this period. The
original of this charter, which is clearly genuine, was in existence in
Hickes's time, who printed it (*Thesaurus*, i. 173).

chapters [1]. None of the passages occur in the Annals of St. Neots, so that we have no evidence as to the reading in the MS. used by the compiler of that work.

The more usual form *curtis* was used, in the sense of 'enclosure,' 'estate,' before the date of the present work, by English writers. The occurrence of this form in Beda's *Chronica* [2] is due to his excerpting the Roman *Liber Pontificalis*. It occurs in a charter of King Swæbhard of Kent, dated 676, in the chartulary of St. Augustine's, Canterbury [3], which, from the formulas, seems to be genuine, and in another Kentish charter a little later in date from the same chartulary [4], which also seems to be genuine. It is also found in a Wiltshire charter of 778, which is preserved in an early, if not contemporary, copy [5], and it is used in a ninth-century text bearing the name of Archbishop Wulfred of Canterbury [6], who died in 832. There are other instances in charters of later date [7]. Abbo of Fleury explains the name O.E. of Bury St. Edmunds, ' Beodricesweorð,' as meaning ' Bedrici curtis [8].'

**22, 10 parentum et nutritorum incuria.** This sharing of the blame for the neglect of Alfred's education prior to his twelfth year between his *parentes* and *nutritores* agrees with the view that his mother died before his father's second

---

[1] The second part of this chronicle, which is founded upon Florence of Worcester (see Introduction, § 35, p. lix, above), abbreviates the passages in which the word occurs so much that it is not represented in the abstracts in any of the instances.

[2] Edited by Mommsen, *Monumenta Germaniae Historica*, ' Chronica Minora,' iii. p. 317, 17.

[3] *Cart. Sax.* i. 67, 12. Cf. also p. 70, 10.

[4] Ibid. i. 107, 30, where it is spelt *cortem*.

[5] Brit. Mus. *Facs.* ii. pl. 3; *Cart. Sax.* i. 314, 28.

[6] Brit. Mus. *Facs.* ii. pl. 17; *Cart. Sax.* i. 523, 23.

[7] *Cart. Sax.* ii. 200, 22, 36, a Worcester charter dated 889 relating to London, which may be genuine (see Introduction, p. lxvi, note 3, and p. 151, note 2, above). In a Wilton charter of 988 it renders O.E. *haga* a ' haw' or enclosed dwelling in a town (*Cod. Dipl.* iii. 239, 29), and it has this meaning in the Worcester text just cited and in a dubious Chertsey charter relating to London (ibid. iii. 354, 17, 21, 27) between 1006 and 1012, and in a Worcester grant made between 1046 and 1060 (ibid. iv. 138, 19). The form *curta* occurs, in the same sense, in a Worcester demise made between 972 and 992 (ibid. iii. 258, 21).

[8] *Passio Sancti Edmundi*, c. 14, ed. Arnold, *Memorials of St. Edmund's Abbey*, i. 19.

marriage in 856[1]. His father died in 858, in Alfred's ninth or tenth year.

**23.** This famous chapter, which is due entirely to the author, has been one of the main causes for the doubts thrown upon the authenticity or veracity of the Life. It has been frequently interpreted as saying that Alfred read the book[2], a view for which there is some warrant in line 14. But it is obvious that the verb *legit* must either refer to the master[3], or must have some other meaning than 'read[4].' This conclusion holds good whether the work be genuine or spurious, for we cannot conceive a forger so stupid as to tell us that an unlettered boy could take a book from his mother, go out of the room to a master, and return forthwith able to read it[5]. This is clearly not what the author intended to convey. He tells us that the mother promised to give the book to the son who should learn it the most speedily, and that Alfred hereupon inquired whether she would really give it to him who should most quickly understand it and recite it before her. The author was therefore obviously referring to learning the contents of the book by rote[6]. By taking the passage in this sense we avoid any contradiction

---

[1] See note to next chapter.

[2] Lappenberg, *Geschichte von England*, i. p. 311; Stubbs, in William of Malmesbury's *Gesta Regum*, ii. pp. xli–xliii; Freeman, *Dict. of National Biography*, i. p. 154.

[3] Green, *Conquest of England*, p. 100, states without qualification that Alfred 'sought a master who repeated it ⟨the book⟩ to him till the boy's memory enabled him to recite its poems by heart.' This is a somewhat free rendering of the 'adiit et legit' of this chapter. It is possible that the *et* in this sentence may be a misreading by the copyist of a compendium for *qui*, for a similar substitution of *et* for *quae* seems to occur in c. 29, 11. See above, p. xlviii, note 2.

[4] It is not until 887 that the author records that Alfred began 'legere et interpretari simul' (c. 87, 2). Cf. c. 89, 1. Previously the author read aloud (*recitare*) to him (cc. 81, 11, 15; 88, 4), and others performed the like office for him (cc. 76, 9, 27; 77, 22). Cf. the use of *recitare* in c. 106, 54. The *legebantur* of c. 75, 17, if it is faithfully reproduced from the original, seems to refer to reading aloud by the teacher.

[5] The author tells us that Alfred was unable to understand a book by himself until after the arrival of Plegmund, Werfrith, and the other Mercian scholars at his court, 'non enim adhuc aliquid legere inceperat' (c. 77, 26). This was before he began 'legere et interpretari simul' in 887. See preceding note.

[6] So Pauli has rightly concluded (*König Ælfred*, p. 68).

of the author's statement a few lines previously that Alfred
remained ignorant of letters until and after his twelfth year
(c. 22, 11). Unfortunately this latter passage has been taken
as defining the time when the incident related in this chapter
occurred[1]. This is largely an outcome of the view that the
present chapter means that Alfred read the book. This
ascription of the incident to his twelfth year or later leads
to very grave difficulties. It is most natural to refer the
term *mater* to Alfred's mother Osburh, not to his step-
mother Judith. Alfred would complete his twelfth year in
861 or 862, and as he is said to have remained illiterate
until after his twelfth year, this episode cannot, if it be brought
into connexion with c. 22, 11, be placed earlier than 862.
The author records the marriage of Æthelwulf, Alfred's father,
with Judith in 856 (cc. 11, 10; 13, 8). He can hardly have
been so thoughtless as to tell the story of the book of poems
a few pages later under the impression that Alfred was still
under the kindly care of Osburh in 862. Indeed, in c. 22, 11
Alfred is under the care of *nutritores*, not his parents, before
this date. In order to fit the story into Alfred's twelfth or
thirteenth year, Lappenberg has taken the violent course of
describing Osburh as the cast-off wife of Æthelwulf, and he
has found several supporters[2]. There is not the slightest
evidence that Æthelwulf treated her in this brutal way, and
his well-known religious character renders the supposition
that he did so a very unlikely one. The alternative view
that *mater* must refer to Judith, does not mend matters.

---

[1] Lappenberg, i. p. 311 ; Stubbs, *loc. laud.*; Freeman, *Dict. of National
Biography*, i. 154, who says unreservedly that the story is placed in
Alfred's twelfth year by Asser.

[2] *Geschichte von England*, i. pp. 294, 311. Dr. Giles, *The Life and
Times of Alfred the Great*, London, 1848, p. 82, suggested that Osburh
was then living in retirement, like the Empress Josephine. Cf. also
Wright, *Biographia Britannica Literaria*, London, 1842, i. p. 385.
As a result of placing this story in Alfred's twelfth year and of his own
theory that Alfred remained in Rome from 853 to 856 (see above, p. 193),
Freeman was ' driven, however unwillingly, to suppose that Osburh,
the mother of Æthelwulf's children, was put away to make room for '
Judith, and that she survived her husband (*Dict. of National Biography*,
i. p. 154). There is no evidence for this view. See below, p. 224,
note 3. Mr. Hunt also ascribes the story of the book to Osburh, and
consequently adopts the view that she was cast aside by Æthelwulf (*Dict.
of National Biography*, xviii. p. 42 ; xlii. p. 305).

Bishop Stubbs has laid stress upon the improbability of
this light Frankish princess interesting herself in Old
English poems [1]. In addition to the difficulty raised by her
marriage with Æthelbeald, Alfred's brother, between the
death of his father in 858 and Æthelbeald's death in 860,
it is extremely doubtful whether she was in England in
Alfred's twelfth or thirteenth year. She is recorded to have
returned to France upon the death of Æthelbeald [2]. In
862 she eloped from Senlis, where she had been living
some little time, with Baldwin of Flanders [3]. So serious
are the difficulties raised by the view that the events in this
chapter relate to Alfred's twelfth or thirteenth year, that
Stubbs proposed to obviate them by assigning Alfred's
birth to an earlier date than 849, the year given in the Life,
because the Cottonian MS. of the latter described 853 as
the eleventh year of his life (c. 7, 2) [4]. But this is one of
several blunders in the numbering of his years, and it is
disproved by the more general reckoning of his age from
849 [5]. The statement that he was born in that year is
supported by the evidence of the West Saxon royal
genealogies, two copies of which go back to Alfred's time [6].
Another objection to placing the story of the book in
Alfred's thirteenth year is that his brothers were then
grown up [7]. Bishop Clifford attempts to explain the statement that Alfred remained illiterate until his twelfth year,

[1] Preface to William of Malmesbury's *Gesta Regum*, ii. p. xlii.

[2] Hincmar, *Annales Bertiniani*, ed. Waitz, p. 56. The *Genealogia
Comitum Flandrensium*, in Martene and Durand, *Thesaurus Novus
Anecdotorum*, Paris, 1717, col. 379, cited by Stubbs, in Malmesbury's
*Gesta Regum*, ii. p. xliii, note 4, is a mere echo of Hincmar's words,
with the exception of the statement that Æthelbeald died in the same
year in which he was married to Judith. The only charter witnessed by
Judith is one of Æthelbeald's in 860 in the Shaftesbury chartulary (*Cart.
Sax.* ii. 106, 24). It is a very doubtful text.

[3] Hincmar, *loc. laud.* Baldwin was banned for this on November 3,
862, at the meeting of Charles the Bald, Ludwig, and Lothaire at
Savonnière (Boretius and Kruse, *Capitularia Regum Francorum*, ii.
p. 160, § 5).

[4] Malmesbury, *Gesta Regum*, ii. pp. xli–xlii.

[5] See Introduction, § 27, p. l, above.

[6] See above, p. 152, note to c. 1, 1.

[7] Giles, *Life of Alfred the Great*, p. 83, accepted by Howorth,
*Athenaeum*, May 27, 1876, p. 728; Freeman, *Dict. Nat. Biography*, i.
p. 154.

as meaning that, although he could read Saxon books, he was unable to read Latin MSS., which, he wrongly alleges, were written in a different hand to the Saxon one, and abounded in contractions [1].

These various difficulties have arisen from hastily reading the Life, and are due to the author's bad arrangement of his material and to his obscurity of style. As the author tells us explicitly that he is turning aside from the chronological order so that he may relate something of Alfred's life as an infant and as a boy (c. 21, 12), there is no justification for referring the events related in this chapter to 866, the last date mentioned by the author (c. 21) before deserting the chronological sequence. The mention of Alfred's infancy cannot be reconciled with either the year 862 or 866. The author then tells us that Alfred remained ignorant of letters until his twelfth year and after (c. 22, 10), but that he had learned many Saxon poems from the recital of others (c. 22, 13). It is evident that the present chapter should follow this last statement, for it is clearly given as an example of his powers of memory in learning the poems of his race. Unfortunately the author has interposed an account of Alfred's skill as a huntsman, which he considered as part of his education [2], at the end of c. 22. There is no reason why the story related in the present chapter should not be assigned to some time earlier than Alfred's departure for Rome with his father in 855 (c. 11), when Alfred would be in his sixth or seventh year [3]. The date of Osburh's death is not recorded [4], and she may have

---

[1] *Athenaeum*, June 24, 1876, p. 859. His arguments are of a most fanciful nature. He attempts to explain the *duodecimum* of c. 22, 11 as a wrong extension of *duodevimum*, an abbreviation that he supposes may have represented *duodevicesimum*, because 866, Alfred's eighteenth year, is the latest preceding date (c. 21, 2).

[2] Cf. c. 75, 19.

[3] Freeman's assertion that 'in no case could we put the story before the return of Æthelwulf in 856' (*Dict. of National Biography*, i. p. 154) has no basis beyond his theory that Alfred stayed in Rome from 853 until the arrival and return of his father in 856. This view conflicts with the statement in the Life, c. 11, 8, and seems to be quite baseless. See p. 193, and p. 222, note 2, above.

[4] The statement in Malmesbury, *Gesta Regum*, c. 121 (vol. i. p. 125), *Gesta Pontificum*, c. 130 (p. 269) that Alfred's mother was with him when St. Cuthbert is alleged to have appeared to him in Athelney (in

been alive at the time when her husband set out upon this journey. There is nothing improbable in the statement that a clever boy, whose keen intellect cannot but have been sharpened by his visit to Rome in 853, learned by heart a book of poems in his fifth or sixth year[1].

**24, 3 in uno libro congregatos.** This book is again described, in almost the same terms, in c. 88, 6.

**24, 9 lectores boni in toto regno . . . non erant.** This lack of teachers is supported by Alfred's statement, in the preface to the translation of Gregory's *Pastoral Care*, that at his accession he could not think of a single scholar south of the Thames. He states that learning had so gone out of use in England that there were (apparently at the time of his accession) very few south of the Humber who could understand in English their (Latin) service-books or who could translate a Latin letter into English, and he expresses his belief that there were not many beyond the Humber possessed of these powers[2]. His father Æthelwulf, however, had a Frankish secretary of the name of Felix, who is described by Lupus of Ferrières, in a letter to Æthelwulf, as one 'qui epistolarum vestrarum officio fungebatur[3].' The date of this letter is unknown, but it is later than 847 and probably prior to Æthelwulf's marriage with Judith in 856[4]. There are traces of Frankish influence in this king's charters[5], which may be due to Felix.

---

878, not 872, as stated by Stubbs, in the introduction to the *Gesta Regum*, ii. p. xlii) is, as Stubbs has recognized, worthless as evidence. It is derived from one of the stories that claimed the merit of the king's victories as due to the interposition of a particular saint.

[1] Pauli, *König Ælfred*, p. 67, would ascribe the incident of the book to 853, and suggests the presence of Alfred's sister, who was married to Burhred of Mercia in that year, which was also the year of Alfred's visit to Rome. The Life, however, makes no mention of her presence, and its silence is an argument in its favour.

[2] 'Swæ clæne hio wæs oðfeallenu on Angelcynne ðæt swiðe feawa wæron behionan Humbre ðe hiora ðeninga cuðen understondan on Englisc oððe furðum an ærendgewrit of Lædene on Englisc areccean ; ond ic wene ðætte noht monige begiondan Humbre næren. Swæ feawa hiora wæron ðæt ic furðum anne anlepne ne mæg geðencan be suðan Temese, ða ða ic to rice feng.'

[3] Ed. Dümmler, *Epistolae Aevi Karolini*, iv. p. 22. It is reprinted from Baluze's text by Haddan and Stubbs, *Councils*, iii. p. 648.

[4] So Dümmler concludes, p. 22, note 2.

[5] See above, p. 203, note 1.

Nothing whatever is known of Felix beyond this reference
of Lupus to him and a letter from Lupus addressed to him
begging him to use his influence in obtaining from Æthelwulf the lead for which Lupus had written to him[1]. Felix
seems to have left Æthelwulf's service before these letters
were written, and may have returned to the continent
before Alfred's birth. In any case the presence of this
educated Frank at Æthelwulf's court is no argument against
the truth of the statement in the Life that there were no
good teachers in Wessex, more especially when that assertion is supported by the testimony of Alfred himself.

**25, 8 incognitis infirmitatibus.** Cf. c. 74, 4.

**26.** From the Chronicle, with the addition of the reference to the situation of York north of the Humber, but
omitting the statement in the Chronicle that the Danish
army 'for . . . ofer Humbre muþan to Eoforwic ceastre'
(' went over the mouth of the Humber to York ').

**27.** From the Chron. with a few unimportant expansions.

**27, 4 ut diximus.** This seems to relate to *eo tempore*,
not to the Northumbrians, for there is no previous mention
of them.

**27, 17 Non enim tunc adhuc . . . firmos . . . muros . . .
habebat.** This is the only addition of any importance to
the Chron. It is introduced to explain the ease with which
the Northumbrians breached the walls (' þa ceastre bræcon,'
' they stormed the caster,' are the words of the Chron.).
If the author had seen the remains of the Roman fortifica-
tions at York, he could hardly have penned this sentence
without some qualification. From his language it might
be thought that he was writing at a time when York had
strong walls, but his *tunc*, *adhuc*, and *illis temporibus* are
as loosely employed as they are pleonastic[2]. This sentence
does not suggest that he had seen York, which was under
Danish government the whole of the time of Asser's sojourn
at Alfred's court.

[1] *Epp. Aevi Karolini*, iv. p. 23; Haddan and Stubbs, iii. p. 649.
In this letter Lupus states that he became acquainted with Felix in the
monastery of Faremoutiers-en-Brie (Seine-et-Marne, France) some years
earlier.

[2] Or have we here traces of the retention by the copyist of readings
in the author's draught that were intended to be cancelled? Cf. Introduction, p. cxxxi.

**28.** From the Chronicle, which, however, has nothing
corresponding to the adverb *honorabiliter*, which conflicts
somewhat with the account of the bishop's plotting against
Æthelwulf given in c. 12. May we not recognize in this
addition the hand of a successor of Ealhstan, perhaps
grateful to this strong politician for his government of the
see? Bishop Stubbs has suggested that the record of
the length of Ealhstan's episcopate, which also appears in the
Chronicle, may have come originally from Asser, and that
writing from memory he may have made a mistake of ten
years[1]. The latter suggestion is induced by the mention
of an 'Alfstanus, electus in episcopum Scireburnenis' in
a charter of Ecgberht's in the Winchester chartulary dated
924, an error for 824, and in the twenty-third year of
Ecgberht's reign[2]. The charter comes from a chartulary of
the most untrustworthy character, which contains several
spurious grants from this king, and it is impossible to feel
much confidence in its testimony.

**29.** The information contained in this chapter is known
only from the present work.

**29, 3 secundarii tunc ordine fretus.** The title of
*secundarius* is applied to Alfred in cc. 38, 8; 42, 2. It is
otherwise unknown in English sources. Freeman has suggested that it means *subregulus*[3], but it seems rather to
mean viceroy or almost joint-king[4]. It agrees with the
prominent part that Alfred plays in the Chronicle during
his brother's reign.

**29, 5 Æthelredi, Gainorum comitis, qui cognomina-
batur Mucill.** From the use of the imperfect tense we
may conclude that Æthelred died before the compilation
of the Life. Hence we may safely reject the Rochester
charter of 895, which is witnessed by 'Ætheldredus, Ganniorum comes[5].' It is a clumsy twelfth-century forgery,
based upon the information contained in the Life[6]. Apart
from this we have no mention of the district or people

[1] Haddan and Stubbs, *Councils*, iii., p. 595.
[2] *Cart. Sax.* i. p. 516, 10.
[3] *Dict. of National Biography*, i. p. 154.
[4] So Lappenberg, *Geschichte von England*, i. p. 309.
[5] *Cart. Sax.* ii. p. 214, 9.
[6] See above, p. 201, note 4.

under Æthelred's rule. The name has been long connected with Gainsborough, in Lincolnshire, but this is one of the unscientific identifications that modern historians such as Lappenberg, Freeman, and Kemble have accepted from the older writers. As there was no genitive plural in -s in Old English, it is certain that Gainsborough cannot be derived from the Gaini, and that town was not in Mercia, but in Lindsey[1]. It is difficult to explain *Gaini* as an O.E. form, and it is probable that the name is corrupt. The district ruled over by Æthelred was probably, like the districts of the later Mercian ealdormen, an older kingdom that had become merged in that of Mercia. Unfortunately we do not know all the Mercian divisions ruled over by ealdormen before the introduction of the shire system. In the latter part of the tenth century and in the early part of the eleventh we have records of ealdormen of the Hwicce (an old kingdom corresponding to Gloucestershire and Worcestershire and, apparently, a part of Oxfordshire) and of the Magesætan (older form Magonsætan), in Herefordshire. In the Appendix to Florence of Worcester the list of the bishops of Hereford is headed ' Hecana,' with a subtitle ' Nomina praesulum Magesetensium sive Herefordensium[2].' The only other record of the former name (which seems to be a weak genitive plural, representing a nominative plural *Hecan*) is the statement in the same work that Mereweald, the son of King Penda, was king of the

[1] See letters of Henry Bradley in the *Academy*, June 2, 1894, p. 457, and of the writer, June 30, 1894, p. 536.
[2] Ed. Thorpe, i. p. 238. This list corresponds to the early ninth-century list, so far as that extends, in the Cottonian MS. Vespasian B vi., printed in Sweet, *Oldest English Texts*, p. 169. Unfortunately the heading of this list is partly illegible, so that we can read only ' Nomina episcoporum Uest . r . . .' (where the *r* may belong to *westor*, an old form of *west* that occurs in early compounds). A later copy of this list with continuation is printed from Cott. MS. Tiberius B v. by Wright, *Reliquiae Antiquae*, ii. p. 170, with the additional name of Bishop Eadwulf (*circ.* 825–827). In the lists of other bishops in this MS. names appear that are lacking in the Vespasian text, so that it cannot have been copied from that MS. It must, however, have been transcribed from a very early MS. The name of the see of ' Hecana' is left blank by the copyist, either because he could not read the MS. before him, or because he did not understand the name. The name of the see is also lacking in other copies of the list (*Monumenta Hist. Brit.* p. 621).

Westan Hecani[1]. The Hecani would thus seem to be
another name for the Magesætan, a fact that may explain
the statement in the Appendix that Worcester was the
ancient metropolis of the Hwiccii or Magesetenses[2]. Of
all the Mercian divisions known to us, that of the Hecani
is the only one that has any similarity in name to Gaini[3].

But although we may not be able to identify the district
ruled over by Æthelred, we have some confirmation of
his existence in the appearance of a 'Mucel dux' as a
witness to Mercian charters between 814 and 866 or 868[4],

[1] Ed. Thorpe, i. p. 265. The interlined 'Hecana quae nunc Hereford dicitur' in the dubious foundation charter of Winchcombe Abbey
(*Cart. Sax.* i. 473, 1) has, like most of the other interlineations of the
names of episcopal sees, been taken from the Appendix to Florence of
Worcester, i. p. 238.

[2] Perhaps the unrecorded East Hecani occupied land that formed
part of the diocese of Worcester. The statement that the Hwicce and
the Magesætan were identical conflicts with what we know of their history.

[3] The presence of the form Westan Hecani in the Appendix precludes
a suggestion that might otherwise have seemed plausible, viz. that the
*He* of *Hecana* has arisen from some conflation with the initial of
Hereford.

[4] He occurs in contemporary charters of 815 (Ordnance Survey *Facs.*
iii. pl. 12; *Cart. Sax.* i. 492, 21); 823 (Brit. Mus. *Facs.* ii. pl. 16;
*Cart. Sax.* i. 512, 13); 824 (Ordn. Survey *Facs.* iii. pl. 14; *Cart. Sax.*
i. 518, 28, written *Mucael*); 825 (Brit. Mus. *Facs.* ii. pl. 18; Ordn.
Survey *Facs.* iii. pl. 15; *Cart. Sax.* i. 532, 6); 836 (Brit. Mus. *Facs.* ii.
pl. 24; *Cart. Sax.* i. 582, 31, written *Mucoel*); 840 (*Cart. Sax.* ii. 3, 26);
*circ.* 848 (Ordn. Survey *Facs.* i. pl. 8; *Cart. Sax.* ii. 35, 24). He
occurs in a charter of 814, written in a somewhat later hand (Brit.
Mus. *Facs.* ii. pl. 14; *Cart. Sax.* i. 481, 10), and in the following
texts derived from chartularies, most of which are free from doubt:
814 (*Cart. Sax.* i. 489, 3); 816 (ibid. i. 495, 29; 498, 24); 824 (ibid. i.
521, 4); 825 (ibid. i. 537, 2); *circ.* 840 (ibid. ii. 2, 19); 840 (ibid.
ii. 5, 19); 841 (ibid. 7, 21; 12, 3); 843-4 (ibid. ii. 20, 29); 845 (ibid.
ii. 33, 6); 855 (ibid. ii. 89, 11; 90, 22; 91, 31); 857 (ibid. ii. 95, 30);
864 (ibid. ii. 120, 25); 866 (ibid. ii. 126, 35), and he witnesses the
following Mercian charters, which are of doubtful authenticity: 848
(ibid. 37, 7; 39, 25, called *princeps*); 852 (ibid. ii. 58, 24; 60, 15, called
*p(rinceps)*); 868 (ibid. ii. 140, 9). A second 'Mucel dux' witnesses
the charters of 836 (ibid. i. 582, 39); 840 (ibid. ii. 5, 21); 845
(ibid. ii. 33, 12); *circ.* 848 (ibid. ii. 35, 27); 848 (ibid. ii. 39, 32).
'Mucel dux' witnesses a West Saxon charter of 868, which comes from
the Winchester chartulary and is open to suspicion (ibid. ii. 136, 2).
He also witnesses a charter of King Æthelred of Wessex about this
time, which has been ascribed to King Edgar (ibid. iii. 488, 31). It is
a blundered St. Paul's charter that seems to have derived some of the

and of a second *dux* of the same name between 836 and 848. The appearance of two names is probably due to the presence of father and son, in which case we may conclude that the signatures between 848 and 868 belong to the son. He may well have been Alfred's father-in-law. That he should witness under his second name is not unlikely, for we find a Mercian *princeps* called Brorda and Hildegils, according to the contemporary Northumbrian Annals[1], who witnesses Offa's charters as *Brorda*. The name *Mucel* has been frequently explained erroneously as meaning 'big,' on the strength of the interpolation of Parker's marginal gloss to that effect in Camden's text of the Life, which gloss was founded upon one in the first part of Simeon of Durham, into which it must have been obtruded late in the twelfth century. An 'Æthelred dux' witnesses West Saxon charters of 862 and 863[2] in addition to Æthelred, the son of King Æthelwulf, but whether he was the future father-in-law of Alfred is doubtful.

**29, 6 subarravit,** formed from *sub* and *arrha*[3], represents literally the English verb *wed*, which refers to the giving of security upon the engagement of marriage. *Subarrare*, which is used by Aldhelm in the same sense, is glossed by *beweddian* in Napier's *Old English Glosses*.

**30.** From the Chronicle, with the explanation of the name of Nottingham and of its British and Latin interpretation, and a few expansions. MS. A of the Chron. omits the reference to the siege through overlooking the sentence 'ond hie hine inne besæton' ('and they besieged them therein').

**30, 3 Snotengaham ... quod Britannice 'Tigguoco-bauc' interpretatur, Latine autem 'speluncarum domus.'** There is either a corruption or an obscurity in

witnesses from a genuine charter of about 868 (see the present writer's letter in the *Academy*, June 30, 1894, pp. 536–7).

[1] As preserved in Simeon of Durham, part 1, under 799 (ed. Arnold, ii. p. 62).

[2] *Cart. Sax.* ii. 108, 29 ; 114, 35 ; 116, 28. Of these texts the two latter are preserved in contemporary writings, while the former exists in an eleventh-century copy, and is clearly genuine, despite the error in date, which appears as 790.

[3] Cf. the Latin glossary in Mai, *Classicorum Auctorum ... tom. VIII*, p. 19. This verb is also used in c. 106, 8.

expression here, for *Snotengaham* does not mean 'house of
caves,' no such word as *snoting* or *snoteng*, 'cave,' being
known in Old English. Moreover, the suffixes *-ing*, *-ung*,
*-eng*[1] are not found in any of the Germanic dialects with
any function corresponding to such a formation. The
name is a patronymic or possessive from a personal name
*Snot*[2], probably connected with the adj. *snotor*, 'wise.' The
Old Welsh *Tigguocobauc* does, however, mean 'dwelling of
caves' (literally 'cavy house'), being a compound of *tig*
(Modern Welsh *tŷ*), 'house,' and *guocobauc* (Modern Welsh
*gogofawg*), an adjective derived from *gogof*, 'cave.' Whatever was the source from which the author derived the
name, it is certainly applicable to Nottingham, which has
long been famous for the houses excavated out of the soft
sandstone upon which it stands. Possibly his information
about the cave-dwellings there came from Alfred. There
is no record in Welsh of any town bearing the name of
Tigguocobauc, and *tŷ* is not applied to towns or villages.

**31.** From the Chronicle.

**32.** From the Chronicle.

**33.** From the Chron. The *winter* of the original is
correctly rendered *eodem anno*. It is noticeable that there
is no reference to Edmund as a saint and martyr by reason
of his death while fighting against the heathen Danes. This
is, we think, an argument in favour of the authenticity of
the Life. If it had been composed at the latter end of the
tenth century, the author could hardly have failed to know
of Edmund as something beyond an East Anglian ruler.
The cult was of rapid growth, for East Anglian coins in-
scribed 'Sc. Eadmund' are in existence that were struck
by the men who acted as moneyers for Guthrum-Athelstan,
the Danish king of East Anglia, whose death is recorded
in the Chron. under 891. Many of these coins come from

---

[1] The form *-eng* occurs in ninth- and early tenth-century writings. As
*Snotengaham* is the form in MS. A of the Chron., and evidently of the
archetype, it was, no doubt, copied from the version of the Chron. used
by the author. It cannot therefore be safely adduced as a proof that the
Life was composed in Alfred's time.

[2] Cf. Förstemann, *Altdeutsches Namenbuch*, ed. 2, vol. i. col. 1352.
A survival of the O.E. personal name *Snotta* occurs as a surname in
the case of Peter *Snotte* in 1279 (*Calendar of Close Rolls*, p. 570).

the great Cuerdale find [1], which is dated 905 at the latest.
The monastery of St. Edmunds is referred to in the will of
Bishop Theodred of London, 926–951, which is preserved
in later copies proceeding from the monastery at Bury [2].
It seems, however, to be genuine. Owing, no doubt,
largely to the monastic revival, the fame of Edmund so
increased shortly after Theodred's time that the monks of
Bury were able to induce Abbo of Fleury to write a life
of him [3]. This was between 985 and 988 [4]. Apart from
the doubtful and, in some cases, incredible, traditions preserved by Abbo, nothing is known of this king beyond the
brief entry in the Chron. that records his defeat and death
at the hands of the Danes in 870. Ælfric rendered into
English the work of Abbo within a few years of its publication, and it appears in his *Lives of Saints* under
November 20. By the eleventh century Edmund had become one of the most popular of English saints. Florence
of Worcester felt it necessary to supply more information
regarding him, and accordingly replaces the passage in the
present work by information taken from Abbo's work,
while the compiler of the Annals of St. Neots transcribes
Abbo at considerable length. In the passage substituted
by Florence that writer has, in accordance with his usual
practice, calculated the day of the week upon which the
calendar day fell. These calculations are of no more value
than if they had been made at the present day, and they
cannot be cited to prove that the year is correctly given
because they agree with it. The day of Edmund's death
was, no doubt, taken by Florence from a calendar [5]. It is

[1] See British Museum *Catalogue of Anglo-Saxon Coins*, i. p. xxix.
[2] *Cart. Sax.* iii. 210, 21.
[3] It is printed in the *Memorials of St. Edmund's Abbey*, ed. by
Thomas Arnold, in the Rolls Series, i. p. 1 sqq.
[4] See Abbo's letter to Dunstan, printed by Stubbs, *Memorials of
St. Dunstan*, p. 378. This agrees with the information given by
Ælfric, *Lives of Saints*, ed. Skeat, ii. p. 314.
[5] It is entered, for example, under November 20 in the eleventh-
century calendars in Cott. MS. Vitellius A xviii, printed in Hampson,
*Medii Aevi Calendarium*, i. p. 432, and Titus D xxvii, Ælfsin's
Winchester calendar, printed by Hampson, i. p. 445. Upon the latter
see Birch, *Transactions of the Royal Society of Literature*, 1878, p. 495,
reproduced in the Hyde *Liber Vitae*, p. 269 sqq. Probably Florence's
source was the Worcester calendar preserved in the Bodleian Library

curious that he should have calculated the day for 869, while recording the event under 870.

**34.** From the Chronicle, with the addition that Archbishop Ceolnoth was buried at Canterbury. Chronicle D has, by a curious blunder, subjoined the words *to Rome* to the *gefōr* of the other MSS., thus converting the entry of Ceolnoth's death into a record of a journey to Rome. The statement of the Life that Ceolnoth was buried at Canterbury is supported by the evidence of Gervase of Canterbury in his treatise on the burning and rebuilding of Canterbury Cathedral, written about 1185, in which he describes the site of the archbishop's tomb[1].

**35.** From the Chronicle, with the addition of the description of Reading as a *villa regia* and its situation, and the statement that part of the Danish army constructed a *vallum* between the Thames and the Kennet at Reading, the explanation of the name Englafeld, and a few expansions. The version of the Chronicle agreed with B, C, D and E in recording the death of the second Danish *eorl* (whose name is given in them). The scribe of A has omitted this passage.

**35, 9 in praedam equitaverunt.** This renders the *ridon upp* of the Chron., and would therefore seem to be the meaning of this phrase in O.E. From the Chron. it appears that it was these raiding earls whom Æthelwulf defeated at Englefield, and this is probably what the author intended to convey, the other detachments of the Danes remaining at Reading to construct the entrenchment.

**35, 10 dextrali parte,** 'on the southern side.' This is a latinization of the Old Welsh *i parth dehou* (Modern Welsh *deheu*), where *deheu*, Irish *dess* (from an Indo-Germanic *\*deksuo-*, Gothic *taihswa*, cognate with Greek δεξι(ϝ)ός,

---

(Hatton MS. 113, formerly Junius 99; Piper, *Die Kalendarien und Martyrologien der Angelsachsen*, Berlin, 1862, p. 69), which contains an entry ' Sci. Eadmundi regis et mart'' under Nov. 20. This MS. was at Worcester in the time of Florence's patron Bishop Wulfstan (see above, p. 107, note 1), and contains notes concerning the bishop and his parents.

[1] Ed. Stubbs, *Historical Works of Gervase of Canterbury*, Rolls Series, i. 11. So also his ' Actus Pontificum Cantuariensis Ecclesiae,' ib. ii. 349.

Latin *dexter*)[1], means both 'right hand' and 'south.' It occurs again in c. 79, 4. In like manner *sinistralis* is used for 'north' in cc. 52, 4; 79, 11. It is a translation of the Old Welsh *i parth cled*, or *i parth guocled* (Modern Welsh *gledd, gogledd*, Irish *clé, fochla*), which means both 'north' and 'left hand[2],' and is cognate with the Gothic *hleiduma*[3], 'left hand,' from the root *klei-*, 'lean' (Greek κλίνω, Latin *acclinare*, &c.). This usage of speaking of the south as the 'right hand' and the north as the 'left hand' is of Indo-Germanic origin[4], but there are no traces of it in the Germanic dialects. The use of it in the present work must therefore be ascribed to the Celtic author. In like manner *parth deheu* is represented by *pars dextralis, pars dextera* in the early Welsh charters in the *Liber Landavensis*[5], meaning Deheubarth or South Wales.

**36.** From the Chronicle. The mention of the Danish fort and the description of the fighting round it are additions to the account given by the Chronicle.

**37.** From the Chron., with the addition of the explanation of the name of Æscesdun, the story of Æthelred's piety, and a few minor details. The Chron. states that the Danes were in two bodies, one commanded by the two kings, whose names are given, and the other by the earls, and that Æthelred fought the former, Alfred the latter. This is represented by the commencement of the next chapter. The *mediam* of line 8 of the present chapter is probably a scribal error for *unam* or *primam*, for it is difficult to understand it as it stands, and it does not correspond with what is stated in the Chron.

**37, 3 Æscesdun, quod Latine 'mons fraxini' interpretatur.** This interpretation of *Æscesdun* is erroneous. It is not a mistake that an Englishman in the ninth century would be likely to make. Although *Æsces* is the

---

[1] Stokes, *Urkeltischer Sprachschatz*, p. 145, in Fick's *Vergleichendes Wörterbuch der indogermanischen Sprachen*, ed. 4.

[2] Zeuss-Ebel, *Grammatica Celtica*, p. 617; Stokes, p. 101.

[3] C. C. Uhlenbeck, *Kurzgefasstes etymologisches Wörterbuch der gotischen Sprache*, Amsterdam, 1896, p. 75.

[4] Zeuss-Ebel, p. 57, note *; Schrader, *Reallexikon der indogermanischen Altertumskunde*, p. 370.

[5] Ed. Rhys and Evans, 69, 4; 71, 16; 161, 1; 162, 4; 165, 15; 169, 23; 192, 20; 212, 12; 223, 21; 230, 13, 24; 237, 25.

genitive singular of *æsc*, 'ash-tree,' it is not true that
*Æsces-dun* means the 'ash-tree-down,' for in O.E. such
compounds were primary ones, that is, they were compounded with the stem and not an inflected form of the
stem. The use of the genitive was restricted to compounds
of which the first member was a personal name, as it must
be in the present case, or in some cases the name of an
animal or bird. A compound of the tree-name and down
must have been *Æsc-dun*, and the genitive singular would
be as unusual as in such modern compounds as 'ash-
wood.'

Many attempts have been made to identify the site of
this battle[1], but it is impossible to do more than connect
it with *Æsces-dun* in Berkshire. The name still exists in
Ashdown Park, in the manor of Ashbury, at the western
end of the Berkshire Downs[2], and this has been advanced
as the site of the battle. But it is evident that Æscesdun
was also applied to the Downs at Compton Beauchamp to
the east of this[3], and also to the Downs east of *Cwichelmes-*

---

[1] Bishop Kennet's endeavour to connect it with Ashendon, co. Bucks
(*Parochial Antiquities*, Oxford, 1695, p. 35) which finds some support
in the blundered form *Æscendun* in c. 39, 18, is open to the objection,
in addition to others, that Buckinghamshire was not in Wessex, but in
Mercia. Bishop Gibson identified Æscesdun with Aston, near Wallingford, a more suitable site, but not bearing a corresponding name, since
it represents an O.E. *\*Ēast-tun*, as has been pointed out by Francis
Wise (*A Letter to Dr. Mead concerning some antiquities in Berkshire*,
Oxford, 1738, p. 20).

[2] This Ashdown was formerly the property of Glastonbury Abbey.
The chartulary of that monastery has two charters relating to it. One
is a grant by Æthelwulf of Wessex in 840, the formulas of which agree
with genuine charters of this king. In this the name has been modernized
by the scribe of the chartulary to *Aisshedoune*, a form that could not
well occur before the thirteenth century (*Cart. Sax.* ii. 6, 7). The other
purports to be a grant by King Eadred in 947 to an Ealdorman Edrigus
(a misreading of *Edsigus* for *Eadsige*) of land at *Aysshedoune* (ibid.
ii. 593, 15). A note in the chartulary states that the manor 'nunc
vocatur Aysshebury.' Green, *Conquest of England*, p. 103, seems to
regard this Ashdown as the site of the battle. A camp near Ashdown
Park has acquired the name of 'Alfred's Castle,' under which it appears
in the old Ordnance Survey. The name is an obvious antiquarian
figment.

[3] A charter in the Abingdon chartulary dated 955 contains a grant of
land ' in loco, qui dicitur æt Cumtune, iuxta montem, qui dicitur Æsces
Dune' (*Cart. Sax.* iii. 69, 22). As it mentions ' Welandes smiððe,' the

*hlæw.* This appears from the Chron. under 1006, which
records that the Danes from Cholsey proceeded 'andlang
Æscesdune' ('along Æsces-dun') to *Cwichelmes-hlæw.*
Under 648 we read in the Chron. that King Cenwealh
of Wessex granted to Cuthred, the son of Cwichelm, 'three
thousands[1]' of land 'be Æscesdune,' that is 'by or along
Æscesdun.' Taken in connexion with this grant it is
natural to suppose that it was Cuthred's father whose name
is preserved in Cwichelmes-hlæw[2]. But as his baptism is
recorded in the Chron. under 636, it is unlikely that he
would be buried in heathen fashion under a barrow. It is
more probably the pagan King Cwichelm of Wessex whose
death is entered in the Chron. under 593, who is meant[3].
This barrow is still in existence[4]; it is situate on the edge
of the Downs in the parish of East Hendred, and its name
has become corrupted to Scutchamfly Barrow[5], under

well-known Wayland Smith's Cave, this charter cannot relate to
Compton, near Ilsley, as it has been said to do. The spurious will
of Hean, alleged to have been the first abbot of Abingdon, in the same
chartulary, contains a gift of land ' in Escesdune,' but no details of its
position appear (*Cart. Sax.* i. 49, 12).

[1] Concerning this expression, see above, p. 154, note 6.

[2] Wise, *loc. laud.* p. 20; Lysons, *Magna Britannia*, 1806, i. p. 161;
Earle, *Two of the Saxon Chronicles Parallel*, p. 284.

[3] The St. Albans compilation (in Roger of Wendover, ed. Coxe,
i. p. 126; Matthew of Paris, *Chronica Maiora*, i. p. 274) adds, under
626, to the matter derived from Beda, *H. E.* ii. c. 9, that Edwin of
Northumbria, ' Quichelmum vero in loco, qui lingua Anglorum " Qui-
chelmeshlawe " usque hodie dicitur, interemit, et in testimonium victoriae
nomen loco dedit, et sic cum triumpho ad patriam remeavit.' The source
of this is unknown, and it is probably an invention of the compiler.

[4] A shire-moot is recorded as meeting at *Cwicelmes-hlæw* in a contemporary O.E. document, which may be dated between 990 and 994
(British Mus. *Facs.* iii. pl. 37; *Cod. Dipl.* iii. 292, 26), and it is mentioned in an Abingdon charter of 995 in the boundaries of a place
called ' Eardulfes Leah' (ibid. vi. 129, 21), possibly another form of the
name of Ardington.

[5] It appears on Saxton's map in 1579 as Cuckhamsley Hill. Wise,
*Letter to Dr. Mead*, p. 19, says, 'it is called by the neighbouring people
*Cuchinslow*, and *Scuchamere*,' to which he adds in *Further Observations upon the White Horse and other Antiquities in Berkshire*, Oxford,
1742, p. 9, the form *Scuchinslow*. The latter is the source of the
modern form. In Nichols's *Bibliotheca Topographica Britannica*, 1790,
iv. p. 26, a writer in 1759 with local knowledge describes it as ' Cuckhamsley Hill, commonly called Scutchamore Hill.' It appears under
the former name in Lysons's map in 1806.

which it appears on the old Ordnance map. The land granted to Cuthred, or at any rate some of it, came into the possession of Alfred, and we have ventured to connect that fact with this grant to Cuthred[1]. In 661 the Chron. records that King Cenwealh of Wessex 'harried' Wulfhere of Mercia 'as far as Æscesdun[2].' Here, again, the name can hardly be used of a solitary hill, but must apply to a range, as it clearly does in the case of the grant of 648. Francis Wise, writing in 1738, states that the shepherds still called the Downs 'Ashdown[3],' and he rightly concluded that Æscesdun was 'a district or country rather than a town[4].' But he endeavoured to restrict the name to 'that ridge of hills from Letcombe, and thereabouts, going to Wiltshire,' a proceeding that led him to reject the identification of Cwichelmes-hlæw, and to imagine that it was 'some town in North Wiltshire or Gloucestershire.' This restriction of Æscesdun was the result of his theory that the battle was fought under the White Horse under Uffington Castle, an idea that has been widely accepted[5]. He mentions no local traditions in support of the identification, so that it is evident that the suggestion was new. Otherwise there would have been a crop of 'local traditions,' which are almost invariably artificial productions stimulated by the identifications of antiquaries, to support the location of the battle on this site. Previous to Wise's time the White Horse had been connected with Hengist and Horsa, another antiquarian figment based upon the imaginary white-horse ensign or arms of the Jutes.

The charter cited above relating to Compton Beauchamp has been carelessly assigned to Compton, near Ilsley, by Joseph Stevenson, and he has cited it as proving that the battle took place in that parish[6]. This suggestion was

[1] See p. 154, note to c. 1, 3, above.
[2] The reading *oþ* of MS. A seems to be more correct than the *on* of B and C.
[3] *A Letter to Dr. Mead*, p. 22.
[4] Ibid. p. 20.
[5] He thought the White Horse might be a memorial of the victory (ibid. p. 23).
[6] *Chronicon Monasterii de Abingdon*, ii. p. 510, note 6, by which Mr. Plummer, *Two of the Saxon Chronicles Parallel*, ii. p. 87, has been misled.

made by Lysons[1], who recognized Æsces-dun in the
Domesday manor of *Assedone*, where it is placed in the
Hundred of Nachededorne[2], which is now included in the
Hundred of Compton. Lysons stated that this manor was
in or near the parish of Ashampstead. The Domesday
name of the Hundred represents an O.E. '*æt Nacodan
þorne' ('at the naked thorn'), and it is tempting to identify
this bare or leafless thorn with the 'unica spinosa arbor' of
the Life (c. 39, 5). The spelling *Assedone* in Domesday
might represent *Æsces-dun*, since in such positions the
scribes of the Survey frequently omit the *s* of the genitive.
It might equally stand for an O.E. *\*Æscan-dun* (from the
personal name *Æsca*), since the weak-accented *-an* in such
compounds is very commonly given as *-e* in the Survey.
We have proof that it is in this case in a contemporary
charter written within a very few years of the accession of
Henry II in 1154. By this Robert de Bachepuz (whose
family name is preserved in Kingston Bagpuize near the
Berkshire Downs) grants to his son John his land in *Conton*
(Compton) and *Aissendene*[3]. This latter form shows that
the second member of the compound was not, as appears
from Domesday, *dūn*, but *denu*, 'valley,' so that the O.E. form
of the name must have been *\*æt Æscan-dene*. It occurs in
1345 as *Assheden'*[4], in 1428 as *Ashedene*[5], and in 1494 as
*Assheden, Asshedeyn*[6]. This name can therefore no longer
be brought into connexion with *Æsces-dun*.

**38.** With the exception of the first clause, concerning
which see the note to preceding chapter, the matter in this
chapter rests solely upon the authority of the author.

**38, 5 sumere debere sciret.** The corruption here
has probably arisen from the scribe of the Cottonian MS.
copying the original wording as well as the alterations in the
author's draught[7]. As the word *sumeret* occurs in line 2,
it is likely that the writer would substitute another word for

[1] *Magna Britannia*, i. p. 161.
[2] Vol. i. p. 60, col. 2.
[3] British Museum, Add. Charter 21,172.
[4] *Inquisitiones post Mortem*, 19 Ed. III, no. 32, first number.
[5] *Feudal Aids*, i. p. 66.
[6] *Calendar of Inquisitions post Mortem and other analogous Documents*, Henry VII, i. pp. 400, 401, no. 934.
[7] See Introduction, p. cxxxi, above.

*sumere* in this line. Possibly he wrote *sumere deberet*, and altered these words to *subiret*, for which purpose he added *iret* and underdotted for deletion *mere de*, and the scribe has overlooked these marks of deletion. It is noteworthy that Alfred of Beverley reads *subiret* in his extract from this chapter[1], but this is merely an alteration of his own[2]. *Experiretur* might also be suggested, but, although the *sciret* might represent part of this word, it is difficult to account for the corruption of the rest of it into the reading of the Cottonian MS.

**39.** This chapter is due to the author. The account of the result of the battle and the names of the slain Danes agree with the Chronicle, whence they are, no doubt, derived.

**39,** 24 **arcem.** This fortress or camp is not mentioned in the Chron. It probably means Reading, for the author of the Life has described the elaborate defences raised there by the Danes (c. 35, 9), and they evidently fled in the direction of Reading, for we next meet with them at Basing (c. 40, 5)[3]. This addition seems therefore to proceed from what the author had heard on the site of the battle of Ashdown. His addition of 'et etiam usque ad diem sequentem,' in line 23 of the present chapter, may be founded upon information gleaned in the locality.

**40.** From the Chron. It is curious that the text, as it has come down to us, omits all mention of the battle of Meretun, which resulted in a victory for the Danes, although fortune favoured the English for the greater part of the day. The omission of this battle, if due to the author, has probably been caused by his hastily taking the 'ond þæs ymb ii. monaþ gefeaht Æþered cyning wiþ þone here æt Meretune' as the commencement of the entry relating to the battle of Basing, which is in the same words, with the exception of the difference of time and place. The author

---

[1] *Aluredi Beverlacensis Annales*, ed. Hearne, Oxford, 1716, p. 103.

[2] It is certain that he derived his matter hereabouts not from the Life, but from Florence of Worcester, for he has the clause 'tandem rex . . . certamini dedit' at the end of c. 39, which occurs only in Florence.

[3] The Danes remained at Reading for some time after this, for MSS. B, C, D and E of the Chron. record that the newly arrived Danes joined those at Reading after the battle of Meretun. See note to c. 40.

reproduces in the last clause of this chapter the entry in the Chron. following the account of the battle of Meretun, omitting, however, with Chron. A, the statement that the newly arrived Danes, who he says came from beyond sea, joined the others at Reading, which is recorded in B, C, D and E. M. Kupferschmidt connects this omission of the battle of Meretun with the mention of eight battles in c. 42, 31, against the nine of the Chron.[1] But as the Chron. does not specify the site of two of these battles, or give any other information about them, it is improbable that the difference in number in the Life is due to intentional alteration[2].

**40, 1–2 Quibus ... sufficerent.** This strange sentence, which Parker quietly omitted, may best be explained by the theory that the copyist of the Cottonian MS. has reproduced a reading that occurred in the MS. before him, and that it represents a sentence in the author's draught that was intended, owing to change of construction, to be omitted[3].

**41.** From the Chronicle, with the addition of the characterization of Æthelred's reign.

**41, 4 viam universitatis adiens.** Florence of Worcester adds the date of the death of Æthelred, 9 kal. May (April 23), and this date has been adopted by historians[4]. But although it agrees with the statement of the Chronicle that the king died after Easter, 871, in which year Easter fell on April 15, we cannot attach much weight to it. It is the date of the death of Æthelred the Unready, as given in the Chronicle under 1016. It would therefore seem that Florence has wrongly referred the day of this king's death, which he probably found in some calendar, to the earlier Æthelred. Æthelred's death is entered, for example, in Ælfsin's eleventh century calendar (Cottonian MS. Titus D xxvii)[5], a Winchester (Newminster) compilation, and has

---

[1] *Ueber das HSS.-verhältniss der Winchester Annalen,* in *Englische Studien,* xiii. p. 168.

[2] See Introduction, p. xlvii, above.

[3] See Introduction, p. cxxxi, above.

[4] Lappenberg, *Geschichte von England,* i. 308 ; Pauli, *König Ælfred,* p. 105, note 3; *Dictionary of National Biography,* xviii. 27; Green, *Conquest of England,* p. 104, note; Ramsay, *Foundations of England,* i. 244.

[5] Printed by R. T. Hampson, *Medii Aevi Kalendarium,* 1841, i. 438, and by Birch in the *Transactions of the Royal Society of Literature.*

been rightly connected with Æthelred the Unready by
Ferdinand Piper[1].

**42.** This is a paraphrase of the Chronicle, with amplifications. The author is responsible for the statement that
Alfred might have been king instead of his brother. In his
confused manner he states as the grounds for this assertion
that Alfred excelled all his brothers in wisdom, although at
the time he is referring to all his brothers except Æthelred
were dead.

**42,** 18 **fluminis Guilou.** This is a Welsh form of the
name of the Wiley, which must have come from some Welsh-
speaking people in the vicinity of that river[2]. It represents
a Welsh development from an older *Wilavia*, the English
development from which produced *Wilig*[3]. A Welsh form
of the name of another river of like origin appears to be
recorded in the 'fluvium, qui ⟨*sic*⟩ dicitur Weluue,' which is
mentioned in a grant to the monastery at Wells in 766[4],
and in the *Welewe-stoc* of a spurious Bath charter, with the
impossible date 984[5]. This latter is Wellow, co. Somerset,
which probably derived its name from the affluent of the
Avon upon which it is situated. There is a 'Pays de
*Gwelou*' in the Domnonée (Dumnonia) of Britanny, which
Loth has compared with the *Guilou* of the Life[6]. It is
called in Latin 'pagus Velaviensis.'

**42,** 26 **peraudacitatem persequentium decipientes.**
The reading of the Annals of St. Neots, 'paucitatem persequentium despicientes,' seems preferable, and probably
represents what the original said, for the Chron. tells us
that Alfred had with him only a small force, and that he
pursued the Danes for a long time. This is duly repro-

---

xi. p. 497, and in the appendix to the Hyde *Liber Vitae*, Hampshire
Record Society, 1892, p. 270.

[1] *Die Kalendarien und Martyrologien der Angelsachsen*, Berlin, 1862,
p. 104, note.

[2] See below, p. 248, note to c. 49, 6.

[3] This form occurs frequently in texts derived from the Wilton,
Winchester, and Shaftesbury chartularies. As a non-English name it
is almost invariably used as an indeclinable substantive.

[4] *Cart. Sax.* i. 283, 20, 30, possibly genuine.

[5] *Codex Diplom.* iii. 204, 5.

[6] *L'émigration bretonne en Armorique, par J. Loth*, Rennes, 1883,
p. 191.

duced in this chapter (lines 20, 30). This reading of the
Annals of St. Neots is one of several features that suggest
that the compiler of that work used a better text of the Life
than the Cottonian MS.[1]

**42, 31 octo ... proeliis.** The Chron. mentions nine.
See note to c. 40.

**42, 36 singuli duces.** This represents the 'anlipig
aldormon' of MS. A of the Chron., which adjective does
not appear in the other MSS. It was plainly in the copy
used by the author of the Life, and must have been part
of the archetype of the Chron. The reading of the archetype must, however, have been 'anlipige aldormenn,' as the
plural of the latter word appears in MSS. B, C, D and E.
It is curious that the scribe of MS. A should have changed
it to the singular.

**43.** From the Chronicle, with the addition that the terms
of the peace concluded with the Danes were that they
should leave Wessex. This seems to be the usual meaning
of the phrase 'friþ niman' in the Chronicle, for it does not
mean abject subjection to the Danes. In the present
instance the Danes are recorded under the next year as
going from Reading to London, where the Mercians made
peace with them, and where they wintered. It is evident
that they had quitted Wessex in consequence of the treaty,
'quod et impleverunt,' as the author says[2].

**44.** From the Chronicle.

**45.** From the Chronicle, omitting the mention of Tork-
sey (*Turecesieg*). This, however, occurs in the Annals of
St. Neots, which omits Lindsey[3]. The form used in the
Life, *Lindesig*, is a later one than the *Lindesse* of the
Chronicle, the name having been wrongly connected with
O.E. *īeg, īg,* 'island.' In Beda it is written *Lindissi*.

**46.** From the Chronicle, with a few amplifications, of
which the principal are that Hreopedun is in Mercia, and
that Burhred was king of that realm. Both are obvious
deductions from the language of the Chron., and Burhred
is described as king of Mercia in cc. 9, 11 ; 30, 6. Simi-

---

[1] See Introduction, p. lvii, § 34, and p. 104, above.
[2] Cf. c. 49, 10, where, however, the terms were dictated by Alfred.
[3] See Introduction, p. lviii, § 34, and p. 105, § 6, above.

larly the statement that he did not long survive his arrival
at Rome may be inferred from the Chron.

**46, 10 Schola Saxonum.** This was not a school, but
the body formed by the English Saxons dwelling in Rome
on the lines of the regional *scholae*, that is the later military
organization of the Roman militia[1]. The oldest of the
*scholae* of foreigners seem to have been those of the Greeks
and Jews[2]. In addition to the Saxons, the Frisians, Franks,
and Lombards were also formed into *scholae*. Father
Duchesne concludes that the Saxon School was, from the
early and intimate relations between Rome and the English
kings, the oldest of these Germanic bodies[3]. These four
*scholae* were formed by residents in the Trasteverene district
about the Vatican. Their positions are recorded by those of
the churches that served them as chapels. That of the Saxon
School was the church of St. Mary-in-Saxia, now known
as Santo Spirito in Sassia, the latter word still recording the
old connexion with the Saxons. As late as 848 the military
nature of these *scholae* is evident in the record that the
Saxons, Frisians, and the *schola* of the Franks were sent
out by Sergius II against the Saracens at Porto[4]. It was
possibly in their military capacity that the ' scolae peregri-
norum, videlicet Francorum, Frisonorum, Saxonorum, atque
Langobardorum,' met, with the rest of the population of
Rome, Leo III upon his return from his interview with
Charles the Great[5], in 799.

As the Schola Saxonum was thus a part of the military
organization of Rome, the statements in late chronicles that

---

[1] L. Duchesne, *Les premiers temps de l'État Pontifical*, Paris, 1898.
p. 42 ; Gregorovius, *Geschichte der Stadt Rom im Mittelalter*, ed. 4, ii.
409 sqq.

[2] Gregorovius, ii. 412.

[3] *Liber Pontificalis*, ii. p. 36, note 27. Gregorovius, ii. 413, also
describes the Saxon School as the oldest, but this is based upon the
statement of ' Matthew of Westminster' that it was founded by King Ine
of Wessex. See below, p. 244. A bull of John VI or VII, about 705,
records that the English clergy at Rome adopted, in an assembly of all
the English *proceres*, the Roman clerical dress (Jaffé-Wattenbach,
*Regesta Pontificum*, ed. 2, no. 2145 ; Haddan and Stubbs, *Councils*, iii.
p. 264).

[4] *Liber Pontificalis*, ii. p. 100, 6 ; Duchesne, *Les premiers temps*,
p. 107.

[5] *Liber Pontificalis*, ii. 6, 21 ; Duchesne, p. 85.

ascribe its foundation to King Ine of Wessex[1], or to King
Offa of Mercia[2], must be dismissed as unworthy of credence.
So also must be the story that Peter's Pence was established
for the maintenance of this school[3]. These accounts are
evidently based upon a misapprehension of the meaning of
*schola*. But we cannot accuse the author of the Life of
a similar blunder, although he does speak in this passage
of ' the church of St. Mary in the Schola Saxonum.' This,
in the first place, is merely a Latin rendering of the ' on
Sancta Marian ciricean on Angelcynnes scole ' (' in St. Mary's
church in the Englishmen's school ') of the Chronicle, and,
in the second place, the *schola* had before this time acquired
a local habitation, to which the word *schola* became attached[4].
The building was among the ruins of Nero's circus, then
known as the ' Naumachia,' on the Vatican Hill, and of the
adjoining buildings and gardens[5]. The *scholae* of the
Franks, Frisians, and Lombards had also their buildings
there, but either owing to the greater antiquity of the Saxon
settlement or to the larger size of their dwellings, nearly the
whole of the Vatican Hill and the region from Nero's circus
and its crypts, then known as the 'palatium' of Nero, to the
bank of the Tiber was called the 'Vicus Saxonum[6].' To
the crypts De Rossi refers an inscription, derived from
a later manuscript collection, which contains the lines—

Hic veneranda Dei consistunt membra piorum,
et clausa recubant operosa sub antra caconum.

The last word he emends into 'Saxonum,' explaining the

[1] Roger of Wendover, i. 215 ; Matthew Paris, *Chronica Maiora*, i.
331. Heinsch, *Die Reiche der Angelsachsen zur Zeit Karls des
Grossen*, p. 43 sqq., ascribes the foundation to Ine.
[2] Malmesbury, *Gesta Regum*, c. 109, p. 109 (see above, p. 194).
Matthew Paris, *Chronica Maiora*, i. 331, ascribes to Offa the restoration
of the school (cf. also p. 360). Gregorovius, ii. 414, note 1, adopts the
statement in the Life of St. Willegod, which was written after the commencement of the thirteenth century, that Offa bestowed upon the Saxon
School the grant of St. Peter's Pence.
[3] See above, p. 211, note 2.
[4] *Liber Pontificalis*, ii. 124, 27 ; 128, 14, both during the pontificate of
Leo IV, 847-55.
[5] De Rossi, *Inscriptiones Christianae Urbis Romae septimo saeculo
antiquiores*, ii. pars 1, p. 278.
[6] Gregorovius, ii. 414.

'operosa antra' as the vast substructures, crypts, and ruins of the Gaian circus and of the gardens of Nero.  He, however, regards the inscription as a forgery of the eleventh century [1].  The dwelling inhabited by the Saxons was called by them in their own tongue 'burh,' the 'Burgus Saxonum' of the *Liber Pontificalis* [2].  This appellation still survives in the Borgo, the name of the main street in front of the church and hospital of Santo Spirito, the famous hospital founded by Innocent III in 1204 on the site of the Saxon School.  The undefended district of the Vatican inhabited by the four Germanic *scholae* was enclosed with walls by Leo IV between 848 and 852 [3], and in the walls was a 'Porticus Saxonum [4].'  The habitation of the Saxons, 'which they call "burh,"' was destroyed by fire in the time of Pope Paschalis, who occupied the see from 817 to 824 [5].  The pope aided the 'peregrini' (which has probably not yet its later meaning of 'pilgrim') in rebuilding their houses (*domicilia*) [6].  This fire is recorded in the Chron. under 816, where the 'burh' is called 'Ongelcynnes scolu,' so that the term *schola* was already applied by the English to the buildings in which the Saxons forming the Schola Saxonum dwelt.  The 'Saxorum Vicus' was destroyed again by fire during the pontificate of Leo IV (847–855) when the 'houses' (*domos*) of the Saxons and Lombards and the 'porticus' bearing the name of the former were burnt [7].  The restoration of the Saxon School on this occasion is ascribed by William of Malmesbury to Æthelwulf during his visit to Rome [8].  But as this king did not reach Rome until the latter part of 855, the year of Leo's death,

[1] De Rossi, *loc. laud.*

[2] Ed. Duchesne, ii. 53, 29, under Paschalis, 817–24: 'per quorundam gentis Anglorum desidiam ita est omnis illorum habitatio, quae in eorum lingua " burgus" dicitur, flamma ignis exundante conbusta, ut etiam nec vestigia pristinae habitationis in eodem loco inveniri potuisset.'

[3] *Liber Pontificalis*, ii. 123–4; Duchesne, *Les premiers temps*, p. 110.

[4] *Liber Pontificalis*, ii. 124, 27.  Cf. also 54, 11; 111, 5; 331, 8.  See note 2.

[6] Ibid., ii. 53, 28.

[7] Ibid. ii. 111, 1.

[8] *Gesta Regum*, c. 109, p. 109.

and as the fire is described as happening early in the
pontificate of Leo, we can hardly place much trust in this
statement, more especially as the Schola Saxonum is mentioned as an existing building when Leo prayed upon the
completion of his new wall (the ' civitas Leoniana '), in 852,
on the postern of the Saxons[1]. We are also told that this
pontiff built the church of St. Mary over the Schola
Saxonum[2]. The story that Æthelwulf established the
English School to serve God night and day for the benefit
of his people, which occurs in a spurious Winchester
charter[3], is clearly a post-Conquest figment. Pope Marinus
(882–4) is recorded in the Chron. to have ' freed ' the School
of the English at Rome at the request of Alfred. In this
case the author of the Life describes it as ' Schola Saxonum
in Roma morantium ' (c. 71, 2). In the curious extract
from an alleged charter of Æthelstan given by William of
Malmesbury Alfred, the enemy of Æthelstan, is made to
die in the Schola Anglorum at Rome, after his failure to
clear himself of plotting against Æthelstan[4]. In the
itinerary of Archbishop Sigeric to Rome in 990[5], ' Sancta
Maria Scola Anglorum ' (apparently a merging of the church
and dwelling of the Schola) was the second place in Rome
visited by him, St. Peter's being the first. In 1053 the
right of burial in ' Scola Saxiae ' of Englishmen who died
therein was reserved by Leo IX in a confirmation of the

---

[1] *Liber Pontificalis*, ii. 124, 26 ; Duchesne, *Les premiers temps*,
p. 110.

[2] *Liber Pontificalis*, ii. 128, 13 : ' Nam et in ecclesia sanctae Dei
genetricis Mariae, quam ipse beatissimus pontifex a fundamentis supra
schola⟨m⟩ Saxonum noviter construxit, obtulit,' &c.

[3] *Cart. Sax.* ii. 96, 21, a charter that Kemble has described as bearing
' marks of forgery in every line ' (*Saxons in England*, ii. 487).

[4] *Gesta Regum*, c. 137, p. 153 ; *Gesta Pontificum*, c. 250, p. 402 ;
*Cart. Sax.* ii. 426, 25. The same account of Alfred's crimes is given in
a spurious Bath charter of Æthelstan founded upon one of King
Edmund, to whose reign the witnesses belong, not to Æthelstan's
(*Cart. Sax.* ii. 352, 25). See *Crawford Charters*, p. 137, note 1. The
text in the *Gesta Pontificum* is made up of three several charters in the
Malmesbury chartulary (*Cart. Sax.* ii. 355 ; 423; 425), with the addition
of the passage in the *Gesta Regum* about Alfred. It seems to have been
prepared and interpolated by Malmesbury, although he ascribes the
drawing up of this joint charter to Æthelstan himself (*Gesta Pontificum*,
*loc. laud.*).

[5] Printed by Stubbs, *Memorials of St. Dunstan*, p. 391.

rights of the canons of St. Martin's in Rome[1]. The Saxon
School came to an end in 1204, when the hospital of Santo
Spirito was founded upon its site[2], but its memory was still
strong enough for the Curia to found a claim for aid for the
hospital from the English[3].

**46, 16 Ceolwulf.** The name of this puppet king is
omitted in Chron. A, but is given in B, C, D and E.

**47.** From the Chronicle.

**47, 4 in duas se divisit turmas.** Kupferschmidt
suggests that the copy of the Chron. used by the author
of the Life had words corresponding to these, such as
the 'hie wærun on twæm gefilcum' of 871[4]. But they are
an obvious deduction from the information contained in
the Chron.

**48.** From the Chronicle, where all the MSS. give the
number of ships as seven, which is also the number given
in the Annals of St. Neots. Here again the latter work has
a better reading than the Cottonian MS. of the Life, and
may have derived it from a more correct text[5].

**49.** From the Chronicle, with the addition of the mention
of the *castellum* at Wareham (the great earthworks that still

---

[1] Jaffé-Wattenbach, *Regesta Pontificum*, no. 4292. The fragment
of the grant of Leo IV in 854 (Jaffé-Wattenbach, no. 2653), of which
this is a repetition, does not contain the reference to the Schola
Saxonum.

[2] Gregorovius, v. p. 607. Pope Alexander II refers to the school in
his letter to William the Conqueror (see p. 211, note 2, above).

[3] On March 25, 1204, John, at the request of Pope Innocent III,
granted the church of Writtle (in Essex) 'hospitali, quod idem dominus
papa construxit apud ecclesiam Sanctae Mariae in Saxonia, quae
Anglorum dicitur et Anglorum fuit hospitio deputata, ante basilicam
Beati Petri positam secus stratam' (*Rot. Chartarum*, p. 123 a). This
charter was confirmed by Edward III (*Rot. Chart.* 2 Ed. III, no. 9).
John granted, on December 10, 1213, permission to the brethren of the
hospital of St. Mary 'in Saxia,' lately founded at Rome by the pope,
permission to preach and collect alms in England (*Rot. Litterarum
Patentium*, p. 106 a). As late as 1290 the pope endeavoured to appro-
priate a prebend at York and another at Lincoln to the hospital of Santo
Spirito, a proceeding that met with vigorous resistance from Edward I
(Rymer, *Foedera*, i. p. 740; Prynne, *Records*, iii. pp. 417, 418, 625;
*Calendar of Close Rolls*, 1290, pp. 134–5; 1295, p. 450).

[4] *Ueber das HSS.-verhältniss der Winchester Annalen*, in *Englische
Studien*, xiii. p. 168.

[5] See Introduction, p. lvii, § 34, above.

exist[1]) and of the monastery there and its situation, the
British and Latin name of Exeter, the meaning of the name,
and the situation of that city. In the case of Wareham and
Exeter the author, no doubt, speaks from his own knowledge
of these places. Wareham was in the bishopric of Sherborne, which was Asser's see, and Exeter was under his
episcopal charge, according to the Life (c. 81, 28). The
verb *bestæl* of the Chron. is rendered *noctu exiens* in
lines 3, 4, probably on the strength of line 19, where the
Chron. has 'nihtes bestælon' ('they stole away in the
night'). The version of the Chron. used by the author
agreed with MSS. B, C, D and E, in containing a record of
the giving of hostages by the Danes, which is missing in
MS. A. The scribe of this last MS. has been probably,
here as in other cases, deceived by homoeoteleuton, his eye
wandering from 'ond him þa gislas' to 'ond him þa aþas'
in the next clause. The author substituted (probably from
what he had learnt in Wessex) a reference to relics for the
'on þam halgan beage' of the Chron., where the arm-rings
of the Danes are meant. It was these latter upon which
they had refused to swear to any people before this time.
They would have had little hesitation about taking an oath
upon the king's relics. There is probably an omission
here in the Cottonian MS. of the Life, for the Annals
of St. Neots has 'et super armillam, supra quam,' corresponding to the words of the Chron., which is another
feature supporting the theory that the compiler of the
Annals used a superior text of the Life. The author of the
Life could hardly have been so simple as to tell us that
the heathen Danes had up to this time steadily declined to
take an oath upon Alfred's relics to any people, for continental kings would not have had access to these relics
had they wished to extort an oath upon them from the
Danes.

**49,** 6 **Frauu,** the river Froom. This is a Welsh form,
which, as Mr. Henry Bradley has discovered, is easily
explained by the supposition that the river-name descends

---

[1] See the plan and description of these earthworks in G. T. Clark's
*Mediaeval Military Architecture in England,* ii. p. 513, where it is
stated, in agreement with what is said in the Life, that the west side is
the weak one.

from an early Celtic *Frāma*. In Welsh Celtic *ā* developed to *au*, Modern Welsh *aw*, and in such a position *m* became eventually *v*, so that by reading the form in the Life as *Frauv* we obtain a Welsh representative of *Frāma*, O.E. *Frōm*, which is recorded as the name of the Dorsetshire river in the Chron. under 998 and 1015. In Wales this river-name is recorded in *Aberffraw*, in Anglesey, a form that results from the vocalization of the *v* after *u*. As this specifically Celtic or Welsh change of *m* to *v* had not occurred at the time when the English occupied Dorset, as is proved by the form of this river-name, the author of the Life must either have detected the identity of *Frōm* and Welsh *Frau*, or have derived the latter from Welsh-speaking natives of the West of England who were acquainted with this Dorsetshire river. The latter is the more plausible origin. If we may trust the evidence of William of Malmesbury, the city of Exeter was divided between the Welsh and the English as late as the time of Æthelstan[1]. It is, therefore, not improbable that there were Celtic-speaking inhabitants nearer to Wareham than Exeter in 893. It is from them that the author most probably picked up this Celtic equivalent of the English name, for it is not very likely that without knowledge of the existence of this Celtic form he would convert English *Frōm* into this specifically Welsh *Frauu* or *Frauv*, although he might, as a Welshman acquainted with this mutation of *m* into *v*, recognize the identity of the Celtic and the English forms. The presence of Welsh-speaking people in Dorset or near enough to the Froom to know it by its Welsh name is more easily explicable at the end of the ninth century than the end of the tenth, and the existence of this undoubtedly Welsh form, with the equally Welsh *Durngueir* (c. 49, 7), *Guilou* (c. 42, 19), *Uuisc* (c. 49, 24), and *Cairuuisc* (c. 49, 23), is in our opinion an argument of some weight in favour of the authenticity of this work. Both these features fit in too well with the Welsh Asser, the Bishop of Sherborne, which diocese included Dorset, to be readily explained away as due to a later forger using his name.

[1] *Gesta Regum*, c. 134 (i. p. 148). This may have been derived from the Latin metrical Life of Æthelstan used by this chronicler. See above, p. 184, note 4.

**49, 7 Durngueir.** This form, which is restored for the *Durngueis* of the editions, which has clearly no basis beyond a typographical error in Parker's text caused by the easy confusion of *s* and *r* in O.E. types, is of interest. It is the regular Welsh descendant of the *Durnovaria*, which occurs in the Antonine Itinerary as the name of Dorchester. The changes in form are due to the regular loss of the stem-vowel of *Durno* in the compound, to the Welsh change of *w* to *gu*, and to the Welsh epenthesis and vowel-change, by which changes *waria* should yield regularly *gueir*. These changes had not taken place when Durnovaria came into the hands of the West Saxons, for they identified the latter part of the name with their own *ware*, 'inhabitants,' the O.E. name of the city being *Dornwarana-ceaster* or *Dornwara-ceaster* [1].

**49, 8 Thornsæta.** This form, instead of the usual *Dornsæte*, does not occur elsewhere, and is probably to be ascribed to an error in the MS., produced either by the *D* being read as Ð, or by false association of the name with 'thorn.'

**49, 20 omnes equites, quos habebat, occidit, versusque inde.** There is no mention in the Chron. of the slaying by the Danes of their horses, an inconceivable thing to do when on the point of flight. In the Chron. the corresponding passage is 'hie . . . nihtes bestælon þære fierde se gehorsoda here into Escanceastre' ('they, the mounted army, stole away from the *fierd* ⟨the English forces⟩ in the night into Exeter'). Here again the Annals of St. Neots have a reading that agrees with that of the Chron., 'omnes equites, quos habebat, occidentem versus in Domnaniam ad locum, qui dicitur Anglice Exanceastra,' which Gale has foolishly altered so as to agree with the reading of the Life. Florence of Worcester, who reproduces the erroneous reading of the Cottonian MS. of the Life, has added to the confusion by inserting *rex* after *quos*. This also appears in Gale's text of the Annals, but is not in the

---

[1] The former, embodying a weak genitive plural, occurs in a contemporary charter of 847 (Brit. Mus. *Facs.* ii. pl. 30; *Cart. Sax.* ii. 34, 8), and the latter in two Winchester charters of 863 and 868 (*Cart. Sax.* ii. 119, 7; 135, 34). *Dornwerecestre* occurs in a late Shaftesbury text dated 833 (ibid. i. 573, 16).

MS. It is upon this blundered and interpolated reading
that the mention of the slaying of Alfred's cavalry in histories of England is based[1]. The corruption was pointed
out by Dr. Steenstrup[2], who was able to correct it by the
reading from the MS. of the Annals of St. Neots given
in the *apparatus criticus* of the *Monumenta Historica
Britannica*.

49, 24 **Uuisc.** This is another Celtic form, and, like the
instances given above in the note to line 6, has undergone
Celtic sound-development that is later in date than the time
when the West Saxon invaders arrived at Exeter. The name
of the river Exe is recorded in the Roman name of Exeter
as *Isca* (*Dumnuniorum*) in the Antonine Itinerary and in the
Peutinger map, and it appears in some of the MSS. of
Ptolemy as Ἴσκα, which is clearly more accurate than Ἴσακα,
the reading of most of the MSS. and editions[3]. The initial
vowel was evidently Celtic *ē* (*ei*), which developed in Welsh
to *ui*, modern *wi*, so that the *Uuisc* of the present passage
represents an older *Ēsca*. It was evidently in the latter
form that the river-name first reached the English, for the
earliest spelling of Exeter is *Escancastre*, which occurs in
the middle of the eighth century[4], and from which *Exanceaster* has arisen by a not uncommon O.E. metathesis.
Thus the form *Uuisc* could not have been the English one
in the time of King Alfred, and the author must therefore
have heard it from Celtic inhabitants of Devon or have
recognized the identity of O.E. *Exe* with Welsh *Uuisc*. The
latter is more improbable than in the case of the *Frauu*[5],
and we may safely conclude that it was the name by which
the river was still known among the Welsh of Devon and
Cornwall at this time. The appearance of the river-name
in O.E. in the older form is another and important argu-

---

[1] Lappenberg, *Geschichte von England*, i. p. 315; Pauli, *König
Ælfred*, p. 116.

[2] *Normannerne*, ii. p. 70, note 1.

[3] The former is adopted by Müller in his edition of Ptolemy, lib. ii,
c. 3, § 3 (Paris, 1883).

[4] Willibrord's Life of St. Boniface, c. 1, ed. Jaffé, *Monumenta Mogun-
tina*, p. 433. He states that Boniface was educated in the monastery
*Adescancastre*, i.e. *æt Æscanceastre*, under Abbot Wulfhard.

[5] See p. 249, above.

ment in favour of the view that Devon was conquered by
the West Saxons at an earlier period than is given in our
histories [1]. *Cairuuisc*, which the author gives as the Welsh
name of Exeter, was, no doubt, derived from his local knowledge. In meaning it exactly agrees with the O.E. *Exanceaster.*

Florence of Worcester substituted ' eiusdem ' (referring to
*Exae,* for *Uuisc,* and the compiler of the Annals of St. Neots
similarly substituted *Exa.* The latter was not a result of
comparison with the wording of Florence, but was an alteration made independently. Both were evidently puzzled by
*Uuisc.* That this name was in the Life is proved, apart
from the evidence of Parker and Wise's editions, by the
occurrence of the interlinear gloss ' wisc, i⟨d est⟩ Eaxa ' in
the copy of Florence that belonged to the monastery of
Bury St. Edmunds [2], where it is written over *ripa* and
*fluminis* (line 24). This gloss was, no doubt, taken from
the present work, for it is not represented in the Annals of
St. Neots.

The words ' Exae, quae ' in line 23 are due to Florence,
and the Latin explanation of the meaning of the name of
Exeter seems also to have been lacking in the copy of the
Life used by the compiler of the Annals of St. Neots. The
explanation of the name as ' civitas aquae ' in both parts of
Simeon of Durham [3] is due to late twelfth-century alterations,
although no note of this fact is given in the unsatisfactory
editions of this work [4]. It seems to have grown out of
' exae quae ' of Florence.

    **50.** From the Chronicle.　Here occurs a remarkable gap

---

[1] See *Crawford Charters*, p. 44. The evidence of Willibrord is alone
sufficient to establish an English connexion with Exeter before the end
of the seventh century, unless we hold that the West Saxon Boniface
was educated among the Welsh of Cairuuisc in a monastery ruled by an
Englishman, and that Willibrord applied the English name to that city
proleptically.

[2] Bodley MS. 297. See page 101, above.

[3] The ' aquarum ' given in the printed texts of the first part is a misreading of the compendium for ' aquae ' in the MS.

[4] The latest edition by Arnold repeats many readings that do not
exist in the MS. but are due to blunders in Twysden's edition. An
example of this may be found in the treatment of the name of Ethandun
in all the printed texts of the Durham compilation. See p. 277, below.

in the Life as it has come down to us, the omission of the
events of the year 877, with the exception of the fragment
represented by c. 51. Florence has supplied the missing
portion from the Chron.[1], his version differing from that
in the Annals of St. Neots, which may possibly represent
the reading of the original of the Life. It is, however,
impossible to feel any certainty as to this. Parker, noticing
the omission, interpolated the passage from the Annals of
St. Neots (c. 50 d), and also that relating to these events
from the St. Albans compilation (c. 50 c). The omission
of the annal of 877 by the scribe of the Cottonian MS.
(or by the author of the Life) is, no doubt, due to oversight. Danish hostages are mentioned in the annals for
876 and 877, and the omission of the latter annal in the
Life seems to have arisen from confusion between the two.
Evidence of conflation exists in the 'quantos ipse solus
nominavit' of c. 49, 12, which is not represented in the
entry in the Chron. for 876, but renders the 'swa fela swa
he habban wolde' of 877. The mention of Exeter and
Wareham in both annals adds to the possibility of conflation.
It would therefore seem that the scribe, in resuming his
transcription (or the author in making his translation), carelessly regarded the passage relating to the hostages and
oaths in the annal for 876 as identical with that in 877, and
that he consequently altered the words rendering the 'þe
on þam here weorðoste wæron' ('who were of the greatest
dignity in the army') of 876 into the description of the
hostages of 877, and that he then copied (or translated)
the end of the annal for that year (c. 50).

**50 b, 1 Eodem anno Rollo cum suis Normanniam
penetravit.** This is the only one of the Parkerian interpolations that appears in the work bearing the name of
Florence of Worcester, where it occurs in the exact words
of the Norman Annals : 'Rollo cum suis Normanniam penetravit, xv. kal. Decembris.' It is in the text of the four
earliest existing MSS. of the Worcester work, but from its
position at the end of the entry for the year, it would seem
to be one of the interpolations made after Florence's time .

---

[1] See c. 49, 26 in the *apparatus criticus.*
[2] See above, pp. 108, 110. It was evidently in the copy of Florence

This entry appears in a translated form in MS. F of the Chron., where it is a late addition to the text of the Chron. Many difficulties have arisen from the acceptance of this date of the settlement of Rollo in Normandy, which is obviously wrong [1], although it found a wide acceptance in Normandy [2]. The presence of this entry would have condemned the Life as a later production than the time of Alfred, if we had not such clear proof that it is one of Parker's interpolations.

**51.** From the Chronicle.

**52.** From the Chronicle, with the addition of the description of the situation of Chippenham and of the statement that the Danes wintered there.

**52, 4 sinistrali parte,** 'north side.' See note to c. 35, 10.

**53.** From the Chronicle, with amplifications. The second section (lines 5–9) is due to the author.

**53, 3 fasellis.** A similar spelling occurs in *fassellis*, c. 55, 3. This O.E. spelling with *f* has been obliterated by Parker and the editors substituting *vassali*, which is probably derived from the Annals of St. Neots [3]. *Vasallus*

used by the author of the second part of Simeon of Durham, who reproduces it.

[1] The date appears already in Dudo of St. Quentin's work *De Moribus et Actis Normannorum*, in Duchesne, *Historiae Normannorum Scriptores Antiqui*, p. 75 D. This inaccurate writer is probably responsible for the impossible date, which was copied by Ordericus Vitalis from the Norman Annals in book v, c. 9, § 41 (ed. Le Prevost, ii. p. 360), where he repeats the words of the original, omitting the day. In book viii, c. 2 (iii. p. 268) Rollo's arrival is referred to this erroneous date, and in book iv, c. 8 (ii. p. 230) to about 880.

[2] Munch, *Det Norske Folks Historie*, i. part 1, p. 634, note 3, p. 636, note 1, proposed to correct the date to 897, while Steenstrup, *Normannerne*, ii. p. 282, note 3, prefers 896. The Norman traditions, as preserved by Dudo, make Rollo a friend of King Alstemus, a Christian king of England, meaning evidently Guthrum-Æthelstan, the Danish king of East Anglia, whose death is recorded in the Chron. under 890.

[3] The spelling *vassali* may represent that of the author of the Life, who would hardly be likely to anglicize it to *faselli*, which is more probably due to the copyist of the Cottonian MS. or to some intermediate scribe of English nationality. The Annals have several features that suggest that the author used a better text than the Cottonian MS. of the Life. In the present case we cannot feel any great confidence that he has preserved the original spelling of the Life, for it may be an alteration due to him.

was a Frankish legal expression[1], but it seems to have
been introduced into England shortly after the time of
Alfred and to have been used in the Latin of charters[2].
Hence its presence in the present work is a proof of
Frankish influence, but it is not, as has been said, a proof
that the Life is a twelfth-century fabrication[3], for the use
of the word in English writings later than the Norman
Conquest is exceedingly rare.

**53,** 3 **gronnosa,** ' marshy, swampy,' an adj. formed from
the sub. *gronna,* c. 97, 25, or *gronnia,* pl., c. 92, 9. Although
this word seems to be of Celtic origin[4] and its use has
been claimed as especially characteristic of Irish latinity[5],
no argument as to the nationality of the writer of the
present work can safely be founded upon it, for it was
known on the continent[6]. It is used in the ancient poem
*De Philomela,* which is based upon a work of Suetonius[7] :—

grus gruit in gronnis, cygni prope flumina drensant,
    accipitres pipant, milvus hiansque lupit.

---

[1] H. Brunner, *Deutsche Rechtsgeschichte,* i. p. 234; ii. p. 261;
Schröder, *Lehrbuch der deutschen Rechtsgeschichte,* p. 157.

[2] The *vassallus* of the Abingdon charter of 821 (*Cart. Sax.* i. 506,
20) comes from an obvious forgery. *Vasallus* occurs, in the sense of
*minister,* in a charter of 941 in the Shaftesbury register (ibid. ii. 502, 3),
which is condemned by Kemble, but which may be genuine. It is also
found in an Abingdon charter of 952 (ibid. iii. 55, 29), a Wilton charter
of about 956 (ibid. iii. 137, 27), and in an Exeter charter of 967, preserved in a late eleventh-century copy (Ordn. Survey *Facs.* ii. pl. 6;
*Cart. Sax.* iii. 473, 9). None of these texts is preserved in contemporary
copies, and some of them are open to doubt. But the use of the word
is so rare in England after the Norman Conquest that it would seem to
have been taken in these cases from genuine tenth-century charters.
The spelling *fasallus* in an Abingdon charter of 903 (*Cart. Sax.* ii. 254,
28) agrees with that of the Life, and thus seems to come from the tenth
century. In the early part of the eleventh century English scribes begin
to use *u* to express *v,* which had been previously represented by *f,* but
we cannot affirm that such a spelling as *fasallus* might not occur early
in that century.

[3] See Introduction, § 87, p. cxxiii, above.

[4] Stokes in Fick, *Vergleichendes Wörterbuch der indogerman.
Sprachen,* ed. 4, ii. 119; Holder, *Altceltischer Sprachschatz,* s. v. *gronna.*

[5] Zimmer, *Nennius Vindicatus,* Berlin, 1893, p. 111.

[6] It is found in Old High German glossaries. See Roediger's note to
Müllenhoff, *Deutsche Altertumskunde,* Berlin, 1890, i. 508.

[7] Aemilius Baehrhens, *Poetae Latini Minores,* v. 363; Reifferscheid,
*Suetonii . . . Reliquiae,* Lipsiae, 1860, pp. 247 sqq., 309.

It was introduced into England, probably from Fleury, with other Franco-Celtic Latin words in the tenth century. It is found in dubious charters of the years 854, 973, 1002 [1], and Florence of Worcester renders the ' on fen scēotan ' of the Chron. *an.* 1040 by ' in gronnam proicere.'

**53 b.** This is the most famous of the passages foisted into the Life by Parker. The Annals of St. Neots, from which he derived it, expressly state that it is taken from a ' Vita Sancti Neoti.' The appearance in the Life of the sentence conveying this information (c. 53, 9), which was not earmarked as an interpolation until the appearance of Petrie's text, led to the baseless conclusion that there was a Life of St. Neot in existence before this work was written in 893 [2], and, on the other hand, that the Life of Alfred was forged at the priory of St. Neots [3]. More mischief has been wrought by Parker's interpolation of this long passage than by any of his other falsifications of historic evidence.

The Life of St. Neot from which the compiler of the Annals of St. Neots copied this and the succeeding chapter is not now extant. It is evident from the nature of the extracts that he was, in accordance with his custom [4], transcribing them, and not reproducing their tenor in his own words. The two verses cited occur in a life of this saint in the Bodleian MS. 535, fo. 44 verso [5], an early twelfth-

---

[1] *Cart. Sax.* ii. 77, 1, 3, 18; iii. 613, 18; *Cod. Dipl.* iii. 324, 35.

[2] See *Acta Sanctorum*, Júlii tom. vii, pp. 315 B, 316 B, where the editors follow the English Benedictine, Edward Maihew. Hardy, *Descriptive Catalogue of Materials relating to the History of Great Britain*, i. p. 538, identifies one of the existing lives of St. Neot as ' seemingly that mentioned by Asser in his Life of Alfred,' quoting c. 53, 9.

[3] See Introduction, § 62, p. xcvii; § 66, p. ci; § 75, p. cix; § 78, p. cxiv, above.

[4] See p. 98, above.

[5] The text of this life has been printed by John Whitaker, the eccentric historian of Manchester, in *The Life of St. Neot, the oldest of the brothers of King Alfred*, London, 1809, p. 339 sqq. The statement that St. Neot was a brother of King Alfred arises from Whitaker's accepting the authority of the lives of this saint, and identifying him with Æthelstan, who is mentioned as the son of Æthelwulf in Chron. A, B, and C under 836, but who is called Ecgberht's son in D, E, and F. Portions of the Bodleian life are printed by G. C. Gorham, *The History*

century collection of saints' lives.  In this life the story is
told differently, although the verses are introduced by the
exclamation 'heus homo!' as in the present chapter.
Another Life of St. Neot was printed by Mabillon[1] from
a twelfth-century MS. then belonging to the monastery of
Le Bec Hellouin, in Normandy, of which the priory of
St. Neots was a cell.  The British Museum contains
another copy of this life in the Cottonian MS. Claudius
A v, a thirteenth-century text.  The life contained in the
two latter MSS. is clearly an expanded version of that in
the Bodleian MS., with considerable additions and embel-
lishments.  Traces of the phraseology of the Bodleian life
occur, while its arrangement of matter is closely followed.
In this the story of Alfred and the wife of the swineherd
(*subulcus*) is told in different words, and the two verses are
not quoted.  The verses recur in the account of this
incident given in the St. Albans compilation[2], the author of
which derived it from a life agreeing with that contained
in the Bodleian MS., and partly reproduces its phraseology.
There are some abridgements and paraphrases of these
lives, which are described in Hardy's *Descriptive Catalogue*.

The life used by the compiler of the Annals of St. Neots
cannot, from the date of the latter, be much later than the
end of the eleventh century.  So far as we can judge from
the fragments preserved in the Annals, it agreed in details
closely with the existing lives.  Like them, it describes
St. Neot as a kinsman of King Alfred[3]; depicts Alfred as
given to tyrannical courses in the early part of his reign,
for which he is reproved by St. Neot, and connects his
misfortunes with a prophecy of the saint; and recounts
the appearance of the saint to Alfred in a vision, in
which he promises to lead the king's army to victory[4].

---

and *Antiquities of Eynesbury and St. Neot's in Huntingdonshire, and
of St. Neot's in the County of Cornwall*, London, 1820, pp. 261, 266.
The extract on the former page is reproduced in the *Monasticon*, iii. p. 471.

[1] *Acta Sanctorum Ordinis S. Benedicti*, sect. iv, part 2, p. 324.  It is
printed more fully in the Bollandist *Acta Sanctorum*, Julii tom. vii,
p. 319.

[2] Roger of Wendover, ed. Coxe, i. p. 330; Matthew Paris, *Chronica
Maiora*, i. p. 411.

[3] See pp. 137, 20 (= c. 53 c, 20); 138, 17, above.

[4] Above, p. 138.

With the exception of the statement that St. Neot was a kinsman of Alfred, all these features appear in an O.E. homily on St. Neot, which is preserved in the Cottonian MS. Vespasian D xiv, fo. 145 verso[1]. This is a twelfth-century copy of a collection of homilies, most of which are known in older texts. In this homily the story of the cakes appears in a different form, for Alfred really turns the cakes in obedience to the orders of the *swān* or swineherd. Gorham has described this as the oldest existing Life of St. Neot[2], partly because he has wrongly assigned the MS. to the eleventh century, in which he is followed by Hardy. The assignment of royal descent to St. Neot in the Latin lives, and their treatment of the story of the cakes, are due to literary manipulation of the simple details given in the O.E. homily, which may therefore be regarded as containing an older form of the Life. The homily agrees with the two existing Latin lives in having an historical background that is evidently derived from the Chron., and in another remarkable feature, the statement that St. Neot was ordained at Glastonbury by Ælfheah, who subsequently became bishop of Winchester. There were two bishops of that see bearing this name, viz. Ælfheah the Bald, whose episcopate extended from 934 to 951, and St. Ælfheah, who was bishop from 984 to 1005, when he was translated to Canterbury. He was murdered by the Danes in 1012. The Bodleian life substitutes St. Dunstan for Ælfheah, and the expanded life does not say which Bishop Ælfheah is intended. It is, of course, impossible that either of them could have ordained St. Neot if he died, as the lives and the homily make him do, before 878[3]. The O.E. homily describes the bishop as St. Ælfheah, but this may be due to the scribe of the Cottonian MS., who has taken considerable liberties with the texts of other homilies in his collection[4]. Professor Wülcker has maintained that this

---

[1] Printed by Gorham, p. 256; in *The Shrine*, ed. Cockayne, London, 1864, p. 12, and by Wülcker, in *Anglia*, iii. p. 104.

[2] P. 250; adopted, with much other matter from this writer, by Hardy, *Descriptive Catalogue*, i. p. 539.

[3] See, however, p. 297 below.

[4] For this information we are indebted to Professor Napier, who has a minute knowledge of the MSS. of the O.E. homilies. He has assigned

homily is the work of Ælfric, but this historical blunder
about Bishop Ælfheah is fatal to any such claim. It is
impossible that Ælfric could have made either of the
bishops of this name ordain a man about the middle of the
ninth century, for he records that the earlier one lived in
the reign of King Æthelstan and ordained St. Dunstan
and St. Æthelwold[1], with both of whom he was himself
acquainted, while he knew St. Ælfheah personally[2]. The
O.E. homily adduces the testimony of 'the books,' so that
it is obviously founded upon some other work, no doubt
a Life of St. Neot. The blunder about Bishop Ælfheah's
date could hardly have been made in the century in which
he lived, and we may therefore reject the view that this
homily was composed at the end of the tenth century[3].
Its general agreement with the Latin lives is proof that it
is either based upon the original of the latter, or has been
very strongly influenced by it. The two existing Latin lives
contain strong presumptive evidence of Norman, or at least
non-English, authorship in the translation of English local
names into Latin[4], prefaced by such expressions as 'quod

this MS. to the early part of the twelfth century (*Academy*, Feb. 22,
1890, p. 134).

[1] *Vita S. Æthelwoldi*, ed. Stevenson, in *Chronicon Monasterii de
Abingdon*, ii. p. 256.

[2] Ibid. ii. p. 266. Cf. his Latin grammar, ed. Zupitza, p. 1, 16; 3, 15.

[3] Hardy, *Descriptive Catalogue*, i. p. 539, identifies the mention of
the bad times and of the death of cattle with the murrain of 986,
although he cites the record of another murrain in 1086. It is questionable whether there is a specific reference to any particular times of
trouble, for such endings are not uncommon in the O.E. homilies. In
the present case the author is dilating upon the evil nature of the times
in which he lived as a necessary proof that the end of the world was
approaching. Hardy advances this mention of the end of the world as
proof that the homily was written before 1000, but the view that the
end was expected in that year seems to rest upon misapprehension.
See Orsi, *Rivista Storica Italiana*, iv. p. 1 sqq.

[4] The widely-spread translation of Æthelinga-ig as 'Clitonum insula'
comes from the Bodleian life. This translation occurs in Alfred's
spurious charter to Athelney, dated 852 (*Cart. Sax.* ii. 164, 28). It
is rendered by 'regalis insula' in the expanded life. Bishop Clifford,
in his fantastic manner, explained the name as meaning 'isle of the
royal children,' because Alfred hid his wife and children in it in 878
(which is a mere guess), or because he permitted his nobles to accompany
him thither, according to Asser (*Somerset Archaeological and Nat. Hist.
Society's Proceedings*, 1876, part 2, p. 15; 1877, p. 13). The name

apud nos sonat,' 'quod apud nos exprimitur.' It is difficult
to believe that an English author of the eleventh century
could ascribe tyrannical conduct to King Alfred. These
Latin lives by foreign monks were probably composed
after the connexion of the priory of St. Neots with Le Bec
Hellouin, for before its enrichment by the De Clare
family, to whom the connexion with Bec is due, it was
a very small establishment. The date when it became
a cell of Bec is not known[1], but it was evidently late in
the eleventh century or early in the twelfth. We may
assign the expanded life to some period later than the
subordination of St. Neots to Bec. If we may trust the
authority of the Ely history, Gilbert de Clare (an obvious
mistake for his son Richard de Bienfaite or de Clare)
expelled the English monks from St. Neots soon after
the Norman Conquest and replaced them by monks from
Bec[2], a monastery with which his family was closely
connected. St Neots is mentioned in Domesday without
any hint of dependence upon Bec[3]. Richard's widow
bestowed upon it about 1113 the manor of Eynesbury[4].
From that time it became an important foundation. The
O.E. homily, which was composed in West Saxon, has no
direct connexion with the Huntingdonshire monastery
or with St. Neot in Cornwall[5], but was intended to be
delivered upon St. Neot's day. He does not appear in the
extant O.E. calendars, but he is found in a twelfth-century
calendar from Exeter[6]. The insertion of his name in the

from its formation may mean 'isle of the princes,' which is a very
unlikely O.E. local name, or, what is more probable, simply the island
of some person whose name began with the stem *Æthel.*

[1] The conclusions of Gorham, adopted in the *Monasticon*, are much
too definite for the nature of the evidence.

[2] *Liber Eliensis*, pp. 143, 239.

[3] Vol. i. p. 207, col. 2.

[4] *Monasticon*, iii. p. 473, No. xi.

[5] As assumed by Gorham, p. 250. The site of the saint's burial in
Cornwall is referred to and described in a way that would be unnecessary
in a homily used in the church covering his burial-place. This description of the position of 'St. Neotes Stoc' agrees closely with those in
the Latin versions, and has the appearance of having been translated
from a life composed in Latin.

[6] Harl. MS. 863, printed in Hampson, *Medii Aevi Kalendarium*,
London, 1841, p. 455, under July 31.

calendar would seem to be due to the vigorous pushing of
his claims by the monks of St. Neots. It is probable,
therefore, that the O.E. homily was compiled after the
Norman Conquest from one of the Latin lives, probably
the earliest of a series, much in the same way as Ælfric
founded a homily on St. Edmund upon Abbo's Latin
Passion of that saint.

If the foregoing conclusions are valid, it follows that we
have no evidence of the existence of this story of Alfred
and the cakes before the Norman Conquest. Many traditions concerning the O.E. kings were still current in the
early part of the twelfth century[1], and it is not impossible
that this anecdote was derived from tradition. It was
hardly necessary for the original author of the Life of
St. Neot to introduce it to show how low Alfred had fallen.
We are unable to suggest any other motive for its insertion
than that of emphasizing the depth of Alfred's decline.
It is conceivable that, in the form it appears under in the
O.E. homily, it is a tradition concerning Alfred that the
author of the Life of St. Neot dragged into his compilation
when wearied of filling up the gaps of his hero's life from
his imagination. But in view of the fraudulent character
of all the lives of St. Neot, it is impossible to feel any
certainty that the story is not a figment of the author of the
earliest Latin life, which has been embellished by the later
adaptors of the life.

**54.** The first clause is from the Chronicle, with the
additions that the Danish leader came from Dyfed (South
Wales), where the Danes had wintered, their ravages there,
the mention of the site of the fight, and the statement that
the king's ministers had taken refuge in the fortress. The
rest of the chapter is due to the author, and is probably
written from information gleaned on the spot, which was in
Asser's diocese of Sherborne. The statement that the
Danes had wintered in South Wales may also have come
from Asser, who would be living in Dyfed at this time
and who was a native of that principality.

**54,** 5 **cum mille et ducentis.** MSS. A, D and E of
the Chron. give the number of the Danes slain as eight

<hr>

[1] As may be seen from Malmesbury's *Gesta Regum.*

hundred and forty, B and C as eight hundred and sixty, the disparity arising from a transposition of the Roman numerals xl or lx. The number is given by Æthelweard as eight hundred[1]. The twelve hundred of the Life may perhaps be due to a misreading of D.CCC as M.CC, but this is not a very likely mistake. As the account is so much fuller than that given in the Chron. it is possible that it was drawn up from information gathered in the neighbourhood, and that the Danish losses had been gradually magnified by the inhabitants of the locality during the time that had elapsed between the battle and the time when it was related to the author of the Life.

**54, 6 ante arcem Cynuit.** The fortress is not mentioned in the Chron., but Æthelweard, writing in the latter part of the tenth century, states that the Danes besieged Odda, the ealdorman of Devon, in a castle. His account is noticeable for the statement that the Danes in the end were victorious, although they lost their 'king[2].' The site of Cynuit is unknown. The name seems to represent an old Welsh form of *Cunētio*, which still exists as a river-name in Wales in the later form *Cynwydd*. *Cunetio* is the older Celtic form of the name of the river Kennet, O.E. *Cynete*, but no river of this name is known in Devon.

Kenwith Castle, an ancient fortification in the parish of Abbotsham, near Bideford, co. Devon, is usually identified with Cynuit. A place known as 'Bloody Corner,' in Northam, is 'traditionally' regarded as the scene of a duel between two of the chieftains in 877[3], and a monument recording the battle has been erected. We have in this an instructive example of the worthlessness of 'tradition,' which is here, as so frequently happens elsewhere, the out-

---

[1] *Monumenta Historica Britannica*, p. 515 E.

[2] Ibid. p. 515 D: 'In eodem anno advectus est Healfdene ⟨et⟩ Iguuares tyranni frater, cum triginta moneribus, in occidentales Anglorum partes, obseditque Oddan, ducem provinciae Defenum, in quodam castro, incenderuntque Martem intus et foras. Barbarum rex ruit, octoginta quippe cum eo decades. Postremo victoriae obtinent locum etiam Dani.'

[3] Kelly's *Directory of Devonshire*. The Six-Inch Ordnance map of Devon marks Bloody Corner as the 'supposed site of a battle between the Danes and Saxons (A. D. 878).'

come of the dreams of local antiquaries, whose identifications become gradually impressed upon the memory of the
inhabitants.   The 'tradition' about Bloody Corner has
been produced by the suggestion of Mr. R. S. Vidal in
1804.   In a paper[1] in which he maintained that Cynuit
was, from the nature of the site, a fort formerly known as
Henniborough or Henni Castle, he argued that Bloody
Corner seemed by its name 'to be expressly pointed out as
the place where' the fight took place.   He identified 'Hub-
baslow' or 'Hubbastow,' the burial-place of Hubba, who is
assumed to have been the brother of Inguar and Healfdene
here referred to, with a place called 'Whibbelstone,' and he
associated this local name with an existing stone, which he
brought into connexion with Hubba's tumulus by the inadmissible assumption that the latter was a cairn of stones.
As a consequence of this paper, the name Kenwith (an
inaccurate form derived from Camden[2], who took it from
the *Flores Historiarum*[3]) has been foisted into the map, the
farm or hamlet bearing that name in the new Ordnance
map being called Woodtown on the old Ordnance map,
which was published in 1809.   The location of Cynuit in
this neighbourhood is the result of Camden's remark that
he had been unable to find any trace of Kenwith Castle
about Bideford, where he assumed the Danes must have
landed.   In 1630 Thomas Westcote writes, under Northam:
'Here may we see some remains of the Castle Hennaburgh
as it is said, as also that hereby was Kenith Castle, so
famous for that Hubba the Dane was vanquished at the
siege thereof and slain, and his ominous banner Refan
taken[4].'   He then mentions 'Whibbestow' as the cairn of
Hubba, but states that many other places in the county
claimed to be the site of the battle[5].   Tristram Risdon

---

[1] Printed in the *Archaeologia*, xv. p. 198 sqq.

[2] *Britannia*, ed. Gough, i. p. 30.

[3] Vol. i. p. 451.   It appears as *Cynwith* in the first part of Simeon
of Durham and in Roger of Howden, i. p. 43.

[4] *A View of Devonshire in* 1630, ed. by the Rev. Geo. Oliver, D.D.,
and Pitman Jones, Exeter, 1845, p. 342.

[5] Ibid.: 'In remembrance whereof (the Danish defeat) a great heap of
stones was there piled up together as a trophy of the victory gotten by
the natives, and the place yet remembered by the name Whibbestow;
not much exchanged from Asserius his word Hubbastow (a mistake

suggested that the castle of Kenwith was to be found in
'Hennaburgh, a fort not far hence' (from Northam), because of the resemblance ⟨!⟩ of the names, and because no
other fortification was to be found in that quarter[1]. A writer
in the *Gentleman's Magazine* for 1755 believed that Kenwith
was 'Henny Castle,' about a mile from Bideford, and states
that about two miles down the river from Bideford 'is
a place called Hubblestone, from a large stone of the same
name, of which they relate '·that Hubba came to Appledore,
was slain before Kenwith Castle, and buried under this
stone, which was in consequence called Hubba's Stone[2].''
Whibblestone, the name of the stone in question in 1797[3],
1804[4], and 1829[5], has now given place to Hubblestone
under the influence of these identifications. It is in the
parish of Appledore, and has obviously no possible etymo-
logical connexion with Ubba. This 'Hubba's Stone' has
been brought into the discussion in consequence of Camden's statement that the battle 'was ever since called by
our historians Hubbestow[6].' This form seems to have
arisen from an alteration of the *Ubbeslawe* of the fourteenth-
century Malmesbury *Eulogium Historiarum*[7], which is said
to be the site of Ubba's burial in Devon. The same
assertion is made in the English *Brut*, which calls the place
*Hubbeslugh*[8], and in the fifteenth-century compilation bearing the name of John Brompton, where it is called *Hubbe-
lowe.* They all state that this place was in Devonshire, and

arising through a misunderstanding of Camden). Though the heap of
stones be long since swept away by the continual encroaching of the sea.
But to tell you truly, I find as many places in this county claim the
honour of this victory, as cities in Greece for the birth of Homer.'
[1] *Survey of Devon*, published in London in 1714, p. 94.
[2] P. 446.
[3] Polwhele's *History of Devon*, 1797, p. 198, note *.
[4] As appears from Vidal's paper.
[5] *History of Devonshire*, by the Rev. Thomas Moore, 1829, i. p. 146,
where it is stated that the spot where Hubba was buried 'received the
name of Hubbastone,' that all vestiges of the cairn have been swept
away by the sea, but that 'the spot is now called Wibblestone.'
[6] Westcote seems to have substituted Whibbestow for Whibbestone
in order to agree more nearly with this Hubbestow.
[7] Vol. iii. p. 8, where it is called 'magna strues lapidum.'
[8] Cited by Hearne, in Spelman's *Life of Ælfred*, p. 60, note 2.

that the tumulus still existed. But they are all merely repeating Geoffrey Gaimar's account of the burial of Ubbe (who, he says, was slain in 'Pene Wood'), under a great 'how' or tumulus in Devon, which was called *Ubbelawe* [1]. The name of Hubba has been applied to a tumulus near Chippenham, although that is in Wilts, through connecting the death of Ubba with the Danes at Chippenham [2]. There is nothing in the accounts of the battle of Cynuit to prove that it was on the sea-coast. The mention of the Danes escaping to their ships is not incompatible with a long flight by land before they reached them [3].

**54 b, 2 vexillum, quod Reafan nominant.** It is curious that the copy of the Chron. used by the author did not contain a mention of the capture of the raven-banner of the Danes, if we may judge from his silence regarding it. Its capture is recorded in MSS. B, C, D and E: 'and þær wæs se guðfana genumen, þe hie "Hræfn" heton' ('and there was the war-banner taken that they called "Raven"'). Karl Horst has concluded that its

---

[1] *L'Estorie des Engles*, 3147:

Un frere Iware e Haldene
En fu oscis el bois de Pene;
Ubbe out a nun un mal fesant.
Sur li firent hoge mult grant
Li Daneis, quant l'ourent trové,
Ubbelawe l'unt apelé.
La hoge est en Deveneschire.

[2] Canon J. E. Jackson concluded that the name was imposed by Aubrey (*The Topographical Collections of John Aubrey*, 1659-70, Devizes, 1862, p. 75, Wilts Archaeological and Natural History Society).

[3] Professor Earle's suggestion that Cynuit may be Countesbury (*Two of the Saxon Chronicles Parallel*, p. 306) is impossible phonetically and formally, since the latter name occurs in the *Exon Domesday*, p. 374, as *Contesberia* and as *Contesberie* in the *Exchequer Domesday*, i. p. 110 b, col. 1. A compound of *Cynuit* and *burh*, as suggested by Mr. Plummer, *Two Saxon Chronicles*, ii. p. 93, 'Countesbury, *quasi* Cynwitesbyrig,' could not have had the gen. sing. *-es*. Bishop Clifford's attempt to prove that Cynuit was Cannington Park, Somerset, is one of the wildest freaks in his astounding paper (*Somersetshire Archaeological and Natural History Society's Proceedings*, 1877, p. 14). In the proceedings for 1876, part 2, p. 5, note 6, he alters the corrupt late form *Cynwith* into *Cynwich*, explains this is 'king's town' (an unrecorded O.E. *Cyne-wic*), and identifies it with Combwich!

omission in A is one of the numerous oversights of the
copyist of this MS.[1] As the next sentence begins with
'and þæs,' it would seem to be another instance of the
scribe's being misled by homoeoteleuton. But the silence
of the present work and of Æthelweard regarding this
banner renders the conclusion that its capture was recorded
in the archetype of the Chron. somewhat uncertain. It is
probable, therefore, that it was not in the version of the
Chronicle used by the author, and consequently not in the
archetype. But we must not lose sight of the possibility
that the author omitted it intentionally or inadvertently,
having otherwise deviated so widely from the Chronicle in
his account of this fight. The ancient copy of the Chron.
used by the compiler of the Annals of St. Neots seems to
have contained the entry. The source of the compiler's
description of this miraculous banner is unknown, and
his statement that it was the work of Lothbroc's daughters'
is peculiar to himself. It is probably of Norse origin.
Saxo Grammaticus ascribes two daughters only to Ragnar
Lothbroc[2]. The raven was an emblem of Odin[3], and
is figured on the coins of Anlaf, the Danish king of
Northumbria[4], and hence may have been in use in Alfred's
time. The story of the miraculous nature of the raven-
banner is referred to, in somewhat different terms, in
the eleventh-century *Gesta Cnuti*, otherwise known as the
*Encomium Emmae*, in connexion with the Danish army of
1016[5]. The raven-banner occurs again in the mythical
history of Earl Waltheof's family, in which Earl Siweard

[1] *Zur Kritik der altenglischen Annalen*, Daimstadt, 1896, p. 26.

[2] See Steenstrup, *Normannerne*, i. p. 114.

[3] Cf. Grimm, *Deutsche Mythologie*, p. 134; Müllenhoff, *Deutsche
Altertumskunde*, iv. p. 229, and Cleasby-Vigfússon, Icelandic Dictionary,
s. v. 'hrafn,' where instances of war-banners with ravens are cited.

[4] *Montague Sale Catalogue of Anglo-Saxon Coins*, pl. iv, no. 429;
*Brit. Mus. Catalogue of Anglo-Saxon Coins*, i. pl. xxix, 2.

[5] Cap. 9: 'Erat namque eis ⟨*scil.* Danis⟩ vexillum miri portenti, quod
licet credam posse esse incredibile lectori, tamen, quia verum est, verae
inseram lectioni. Enimvero dum esset simplissimo candidissimoque
intextum serico, nulliusque figurae in eo inserta esset imago, tempore
belli semper in eo videbatur corvus ac si intextus, in victoria suorum
quasi hians ore excutiensque alas, instabilisque pedibus; et suis devictis
quietissimus totoque corpore demissus.'

receives, when a young man, from an old man a banner
'Ravenlandeye, quod interpretatur "corvus terrae terror[1]."'

**55.** From the Chronicle, with the addition of the Latin
and British names of Selwood and of the statements that
Alfred encamped for one night at Ecgbriht's Stone and at
Æcglea. The latter are deduced from the Chronicle; see
note to line 15.

**55, 4 pagae.** The omission of this word in the
Cottonian MS. seems to be due to confusion with *paganos*,
the next word but one. Florence surmounted the difficulty
raised by its omission by converting *Summurtunensis* into
the abl. plural. Here again the Annals of St. Neots have
preserved a better reading than the Cottonian MS.[2]

**55, 6 Petram Ægbryhta.** Florence of Worcester has
more correctly *Petram Ecgbrihti*, a latinized genitive
corresponding to the *Ecgbryhtes Stan* of the Chron.[3]
This place is generally identified with Brixton Deverill,
co. Wilts, which was first suggested by Sir John Spelman[4].
The identification assumes the loss of the most strongly
accented part of the name, which is improbable. Brixton
Deverill is one of the group of Deverills mentioned in
Domesday. They derived their name from the river
Deverill[5], and Brixton is therefore a distinguishing addition.

---

[1] See the early thirteenth-century history by William, a monk of
Crowland, printed in Appendix C to Cooper's (unpublished) report
on Rymer's *Foedera*, p. 89; Francisque Michel, *Chroniques anglo-
normandes*, Rouen, 1836, ii. p. 107; Leland's *Itinerary*, iv. 142; Hearne's
appendix, and the somewhat different version in Brompton's *Chronicle*,
in Twysden, *Scriptores Quindecim*, col. 945. Upon this work see
Hardy's *Catalogue of Materials for British History*, ii. pp. 25, 26. The
'Ravenlandeye' of this story may be based upon acquaintance with the
banner of King Harald Hardrada, known as the 'landeyþa' or 'waster
of the land.' The references to this banner in the sagas are collected
by Kahle in the *Indogermanische Forschungen*, xiv. p. 211. The Old
Norse *eyða*, which has no cognate in O.E., has been replaced by O.E.
*ege*, 'terror.'

[2] See Introduction, §§ 25, 34, pp. xlvii, lvii, above.

[3] See Introduction, p. xlviii.

[4] *Life of King Ælfred*, p. 64. The wide diffusion of this identification is due to Gibson, in his edition of the Chronicle, 'Nominum
Locorum Explicatio,' p. 27.

[5] It occurs as *Defereal* in a charter of Edgar, dated 968, in the early
thirteenth-century Wilton chartulary, Harl. MS. 436, fol. 24 b, printed

It is in all probability derived from Brihtric, the alleged lover of Queen Matilda[1]. He held it in the time of Edward the Confessor. The Deverel recorded in Domesday as being held by 'Brictric' is there stated to have been given to the abbey of Le Bec Hellouin in Normandy by Queen Matilda[2], who received a grant of Brihtric's possessions. This is undoubtedly the *Brichtricheston* of the *Testa de Nevill*[3], where the donor to the abbey is confused with the Empress Matilda, the daughter of Henry I. The identification with *Ecgbrihtes Stan* must therefore be rejected. The new Ordnance survey marks an 'Ecgbright's Stone' as an antiquity by the side of the railway near Fairwood House, in the parish of Westbury, co. Wilts, on the borders of that county and Somerset[4]. The presence of the name on the map is due to Canon J. E. Jackson's suggestion that this stone was Ecgbriht's Stone[5]. On Adam and Dury's map of Wilts in 1773 it bears the name of 'Redbridge Stone,' and it is difficult to believe that this is a corruption of Ecgbrihtes Stan. Its position is hardly suitable, as the next stage of Alfred's march seems to have been south of Westbury. The O.E. records contain many mentions of stones that were known by men's names, but they have usually faded out of remembrance, except in a few cases where the stone was the meeting-place of a Hundred, when its name has been preserved, although its site has been forgotten. Thus *Wihtbrordes Stan*, where some of the laws of King Edgar were enacted[6], has perished without bequeathing any

---

in the *Monasticon*, ii. p. 323. This charter has been overlooked by Kemble and Birch.

[1] See Freeman, *Norman Conquest*, iv. pp. 165, 759 sqq.

[2] Domesday Book, i. p. 68 b, col. 1. It is curious that Hoare, who suggested that Brixton is derived from this Brihtric (*Modern Wilts*, 'Hundred of Heytesbury,' p. 4), states that it is 'undoubtedly' Ecgbrihtes Stan (ibid. p. 3, 'Hundred of Warminster,' p. 46).

[3] P. 154 a.

[4] On the Six-Inch map the 'Ecgbright's Stone' of the Twenty-five-Inch map (sheet xliv, 6) is miscopied as 'Erbright's Stone,' and is still further corrupted to 'Cebright's Stone' in the One-Inch map.

[5] *Wiltshire Archaeological and Natural History Magazine*, xiii. p. 109, note. Cf. also xxv. p. 59.

[6] *Laws of Edgar*, iv. c. 1, § 4 (Schmid, *Die Gesetze der Angelsachsen*, p. 194; Liebermann, *Die Gesetze der Angelsachsen*, i. p. 208).

memory of its site, but the Surrey *Brihtsiges Stan*[1], being
the meeting-place of a Hundred, has left its name to
Brixton Hundred and to the suburb of Brixton. In Smith's
County Atlas, published in 1804, a 'Bound Stone' is
marked in the maps of Somerset and Dorset at the point
where the boundaries of these counties meet those of Wilts
near Penzelwood[2]. This stone fulfils one requirement for
the identification with Ecgbrihtes Stan by being to the east
of Selwood or the 'West Wood[3],' which seems to have
formed the western boundary of Wilts. As Ecgbrihtes
Stan was Alfred's meeting-place with the *fyrds* of Hants
and Wilts, and as the Danes were in the north of the latter
county, the stone must have been in the south of the
county. It can hardly have been in Dorset, since the
Dorset men are not named as coming to the rendezvous.
The location of Ecgbrihtes Stan near Penzelwood agrees
with the identification of Igleah, Alfred's next stopping-
place, with a place in the parish of Warminster[4].

**55, 15–17 Diluculo sequenti illucescente . . ibi una
nocte castra metatus est.** The Chron. reads "he for
ymb ane niht of þam wicum to Iglea, and þas ymb ane to
Eþandun,' which means that 'he went in the course of one
day from the camp to Igleah, and afterwards in the course
of a day to Eþandun.' This passage is frequently misunderstood by historians as conveying that Alfred marched by
night, but it is merely an instance of the O.E. practice of
counting time by the nights instead of by days. Had
a night-march been meant, the adverb *nihtes* would have
been used. As the author of the Life mentions the
encampments for one night, he cannot have intended to
convey that the marches were made by night.

[1] Spelt *Bricsistan, Brixiestan, Brixistan* in Domesday.
[2] W. Phelps, *Modern Somerset*, i. p. 190, states that the 'three-shire
stones' were in the middle of a factory pond.
[3] See above, note to c. 12, 4, p. 197.
[4] See below, note to c. 55, 17. Bishop Clifford's identification of
Ecgbrihtes Stan with White Sheet Castle, between Mere and Stourton,
has no other foundation except the fanciful and erroneous idea that this
means 'castle of refuge,' which is based upon the assertions that a sheet
anchor is a safety anchor and a sheet is in nautical language a safety
rope (*Somerset Archaeological and Natural History Society's Proceedings*, 1876, part 2, p. 7; 1877, p. 20.) There are many other
equally fantastic arguments in these papers.

**55, 17 Æcglea.** This appears as *Iglea* in Chron. A, B
and C, but as *Æglea* in D and E. The former also occurs
in the Annals of St. Neots, which elsewhere shows signs of
the use of a better text of the Life than the Cottonian MS.[1]
Florence of Worcester agrees with the Cottonian MS.,
which seems to have been his immediate source[2]. Many
attempts have been made to identify this place. Bishop
Gibson suggested Leigh (Westbury Leigh), co. Wilts, under
the inadmissible theory that *Æglea* was a mistake for
*Æt Lea*[3]. Carte identified it with Oakley, near Basingstoke[4], but this was merely a violent attempt to find a place
that should agree with his other localizations of the names
mentioned in the Chron. at this time, and like them it
must be rejected. Dr. Milner suggested either Winsley or
Leigh (the latter the name of a tithing), both in Bradford-
on-Avon, co. Wilts[5]. Nothing can be said for either,
except that the identification is convenient for his theory
that the Danes were in Chippenham when Alfred arrived
upon the scene[6]. Gough thought that Cley Hill, in the
parish of Corsley, co. Wilts, 'by the sound might bid fair
to be this Æglea[7],' with which it cannot possibly be connected phonetically. This identification was rightly rejected
by Sir Richard Hoare, on the ground that Cley Hill is too
near Brixton· Deverill, which he erroneously held to be
Ecgbrihtes Stan[8]. Bishop Clifford placed it at Edgarley,
in Glastonbury, holding that King Edgar's name had been
substituted at a later time for the first part of the name[9].
This improbable theory is one of many desperate expedients

---

[1] See Introduction, § 34, p. lvii, above.
[2] See Introduction, §§ 25, 33, pp. xlvii, lv, above.
[3] In his edition of Camden's *Britannia*, i. p. 109.
[4] *History of England*, i. p. 300.
[5] *History of Winchester*, 1798, p. 129, note 3.
[6] See below, p. 274, note 3.
[7] Camden's *Britannia*, i. p. 100. The idea was first suggested by
Gibson in *Chron. Anglosaxonicum*, 'Nom. locorum Explicatio,' p. 33,
and in his edition of Camden's *Britannia*.
[8] *History of Modern Wilts*, 'Hundred of Heytesbury,' p. 46. He,
however, accepted the location of this place near Cley Hill (ibid.
'Hundred of Westbury,' p. 41; *Ancient History of South Wilts*, i.
pp. 59–64).
[9] *Somerset Archaeological and Natural History Society's Proceedings*,
1876, part 2, p. 21; 1877, p. 20.

into which he was driven in his attempt to locate the battle
of Ethandun in Somerset. Highleigh Common, in Melksham, which was suggested by Whitaker [1], has found many
adherents, but it seems to be merely one of the very
numerous Leighs in this part of the world, distinguished by
the adjective 'high.' Dr. Henry Beeke, Regius Professor
of Modern History in the University of Oxford, identified
Ægleah with the place (the site of which is unknown) from
which the Berkshire Hundred of *Eglei* in Domesday
derived its name [2]. He supported this by locating Ethandun
at Eddington, in Hungerford, which was in this Hundred.
The latter place was, however, not Ethandun [3], and the
Hundred appears under the more correct form of *Eg(g)eslea-
hundred* in the twelfth century [4], and would therefore seem
to be descended from an O.E. \**Ecges-lēah*. The spelling
in the Cottonian MS. of the Life suggests a form in *Ecg-*,
but it is probably miswritten for the *Æglea* of Chron. D
and E. From this we should expect a modern *Eiley* or
*Ailey*. An Eilly in the Hundred of Kinwardstone, co.
Wilts, occurs in 1275 [5], but this is too far to the east to be
identified with Alfred's camping-place. It is possible that
the form in the Life has been affected by local knowledge
of this place or of the Berkshire \**Ecges-lēah* on the part of
the scribe. The form *Æglea* may be merely a misreading
of \**Īeglēa*, which would be a more regular West Saxon

---

[1] *The Life of St. Neot*, by the Rev. John Whitaker, B.D., London,
1809, p. 266. This Highleigh is shown on the old Ordnance map,
but is not on the new ones. It was in Melksham, near Holbrook
Farm. In 1859 it was described as a 'grazing meadow a little above
the level of the river Avon called Iley' (*Wilts Archaeol. and Nat.
Hist. Mag.* v. p. 260). Canon Jackson in 1862 spoke of the 'rich land
of Iley in Melksham' (*The Topographical Collections of John Aubrey*,
1659–70, Devizes, 1862, p. 295, Wilts Archaeol. and Nat. Hist.
Society). In the modern dialect it would be impossible to distinguish
between the descendants of O.E. *Igleah* and High-leigh. Thus the
place called *Highsomley* in Westbury by Canon Jackson (*Wilts
Archaeol. and Nat. Hist. Mag.* xxv. p. 36) and *Hisomley* on the new
Ordnance map appears as *Isomley* on the old.

[2] Lysons, *Magna Britannia*, 1806, i. p. 162.

[3] See below, p. 274.

[4] Pipe Rolls, 17 Henry II, p. 90, *Egesleah⟨un⟩dr⟨ed⟩*, and 18 Henry II,
p. 15, *Eggesleah⟨un⟩dr⟨ed⟩*. It occurs with an inorganic *h* as
*Heggeleah⟨un⟩dr⟨ed⟩* in the roll for the sixteenth year, p. 72.

[5] *Rot. Hundred.* ii. p. 260 b.

spelling for Alfred's time than *Iglea*, if the first part of
the compound is derived from *ieg*, later *ig*, 'island, watery
land.' The balance of evidence is certainly in favour
of the form *Iglea*. This name, or one of identical formation,
seems to have been preserved until the seventeenth century
in the case of 'Iley Oak' or the 'Hundred Oak' near
Southleigh Wood, in the parish of Warminster, co. Wilts[1].
As the courts of the two Hundreds of Warminster and
Heytesbury met at a place called Ilegh in 1439[2], it is clear
that a place of that name then existed. It is probably an
older name of Southleigh Wood or of part of it, and that
*lēah* has in this case its older meaning of 'wood[3].' Southleigh Wood is bounded on one side by the river Deverill[4],
so that the application of *ieg* to it or a portion of it is
intelligible. We may accordingly conclude that this Ilegh
is the *Igleah* of the Chron., that *Æglea* of the Chron. D
and E is either a miscopying of an *\*Ieglea* in a lost early
copy of the Chronicle, or arises from an erroneous identification of *Ieglea* with some other local name, and that the
*Æcglea* of the Cottonian MS. of the Life and of Florence is
an attempt to rationalize the inexplicable *Æglea* by substituting for the first member of the compound the word *ecg*,
a late spelling of *ecg*, 'edge,' 'edge of a cliff.'

**56.** From the Chronicle, with amplifications and with
the additions that the king slew all the men found outside the fort and took the horses and cattle, the motives
of the Danes for surrender, and the statement that the

---

[1] Hoare, *Modern Wilts*, 'Hundred of Warminster,' p. 11; 'Hundred
of Heytesbury,' p. 2.

[2] Canon Jackson, *Wilts Archaeol. and Nat. Hist. Mag.* xiii. pp. 107,
114, 115. Writing in 1872, he states that Iley Oak 'was contiguous to
the camp called the Buries. A very old man told me that the exact site
of the oak (now gone) was close to Lord Heytesbury's Lodge at Sowley
Wood (of which wood, Iley forms the eastern part)' (ibid. p. 108).
This latter name does not appear in the new Ordnance map, which has,
however, an Eastleigh Wood adjoining Southleigh Wood on the north-
east. Canon Jackson rejected the identification of Iley with Æcglea
(ibid. p. 109, note). But it is the legitimate descendant of *Igleah*, and the
fifteenth-century form proves that it was not a compound of 'high.'

[3] Recorded in the case of *Andredesleah*, and proved by the continental
cognates of *lēah*, and by its Latin cognate *lucus*, older *loukus*.

[4] The meadow by South Leigh is marked on the new Ordnance map
as 'liable to flood.'

Danes gave to the king as many hostages as he wished, without receiving any from him, a form of peace that they had never before concluded with any one, and the description of Wedmor as a *villa regia*.

**56, 2 Ethandun.** Camden's location of the site of this battle at Edington, co. Wilts, has been frequently questioned in modern times. Several other sites have been suggested, but none of them satisfy the first requirement, that of having borne the name Ethandun. Edington, on the other hand, is well authenticated. King Alfred bequeathed *Eðandun* to Ealhswith, his wife[1]. In 957 King Eadwig executed a charter, of which the original is still in existence, at *Eðandun*[2]. So far there is nothing to prove the identity of this *Eðandun* with Edington, but as it was a royal possession, and as Edington was granted to the abbey of Romsey by King Edgar in 968[3], there can be little reason for questioning it. That Edgar's grant related to Edington appears clearly from the evidence of Domesday[4], the Hundred Rolls[5], and the chartulary of Romsey. In Domesday the name is written *Edendone*, a Norman spelling for the dative *Eðandune*. It is written *Ethendun* in 1280-1[6]. The position of Edington suits all the requirements of *Eðandun*. On the Downs above it is Bratton Castle, a camp that may be the fortress to which the Danes retreated (c. 56, 7). It is a noteworthy coincidence that there is a White Horse cut on the Downs below Bratton Castle, just as there is under Uffington Castle on the Berkshire Downs, the reputed site of Alfred's other great victory of Æscesdun[7], but there is no evidence to connect these horses with Alfred.

[1] *Cart. Sax.* ii. 178, 24. For the date of his will see Introduction, p. lxvii, note 3, above.

[2] *Crawford Charters*, no. v; *Cart. Sax.* iii. 688, 22.

[3] *Cart. Sax.* iii. 495, from the fifteenth-century chartulary, in which the copyist modernized the name to *Edyndon*.

[4] Vol. i. p. 68, col. 2.

[5] *Rotuli Hundredorum*, ii. 277 b.

[6] *Inquisitio post Mortem*, 1 Edward I, no. 42, an inquisition concerning the abbess's wood at Edington and Ashton.

[7] See hereon p. 237, above. Francis Wise, *Further Observations upon the White Horse*, Oxford, 1742, p. 48, stated that the Bratton White Horse had been made within the memory of people then living, but

In 1877 Bishop Clifford endeavoured to prove that Edington, co. Somerset, was the site of the battle of Eðandun, in a paper in which he described the imaginary plan of Alfred's campaign [1]. The whole article is of a very imaginative and unsatisfactory nature, built upon improbable assumptions, baseless identifications of sites, impossible etymologies, and shows a general lack of critical restraint. As this Somersetshire Edington occurs in the Domesday Survey as *Eduuinetune* [2], and as the scribes frequently omit the gen. -*s* in compound local names, it is evident that this name represents an O.E. *$\bar{E}$adwines-tūn*, and not *Eðan-dūn*. Heddington, co. Wilts, has also been suggested on the strength of the similarity of name [3]. This is the *Edintone* of Domesday [4], but it is evident from the majority of the mediaeval forms that the name began with an aspirate and was compounded with the suffix *ing*, and probably represents an O.E. *Hedding-tūn*. The claims of Eddington, in the parish of Hungerford, co. Berks, were advanced by Professor Beeke. He supported this identification by regarding the *Ecglea* of the Life as the place from which the Domesday Hundred of *Eglei*, in which Eddington was situate, derived its name, and by deducing Denford in Hungerford from the Danes, and contrasting it with Englewood in the

---

Gough, in his edition of Camden, i. p. 101, maintains that it is ancient despite Wise's statement. It was, unfortunately, 'new modelled' in 1778 by Mr. Gee, a surveyor (Hoare, *Modern Wilts*, 'Hundred of Heytesbury,' p. 46). This obliterated the ancient horse, and another 'restoration' occurred in 1853. See Rev. W. C. Plenderleath, 'White Horse Jottings,' in the *Wilts Archaeological and Natural History Magazine*, xxv. p. 57 sqq.

[1] *Somerset Archaeological and Natural History Society Transactions*, 1877, p. 20, part ii, pp. 1–27.

[2] Vol. i. p. 90, col. 1. It appears as *Edwinetona* in the fuller returns preserved in the Exon Domesday, p. 149. The disappearance of the *w* in the second syllable is phonetically regular. The name is written *Edinton* as early as 1208 (*Rotuli de Finibus*, p. 430).

[3] John Milner, *History of Winchester*, 1798, p. 129, note 3, adopted by Earle, *Two Saxon Chronicles Parallel*, p. 307. Milner's identification depends upon the assumption that the Danes were still in Chippenham on the eve of the battle. The words of Æthelweard upon which he lays stress do not mean this, and, if they did, his authority is too late to override that of the Chron.

[4] Vol. i. p. 69, col. 2.

adjoining parish of Kintbury[1]. He ascribes a march of something like forty miles in a day to Alfred in order to surprise the Danes, but it is difficult to believe that the shire levies constituting Alfred's army could have moved with anything like this speed. This Berkshire Eddington is written *Eddevetone* in Domesday[2], and *Edivetona, Edevetona* in the twelfth century[3]. From these forms it is clear that the O.E. form was *\*Eadgife-tun*, 'Eadgifu's town.' Joseph Stevenson regarded the *Eperedinge tun* of an Abingdon charter of 961[4] as referring to this Eddington, and the latter as the site of Eðandun[5]. But this clearly represents an O.E. *\*Æðeredinga-tun*, 'Æðelred's town.' Slaughterford, co. Wilts, was stated to be the site of the battle of Eðandun by Whitaker in 1809[6]. He was led to this conclusion by a statement in Gough's edition of Camden's *Britannia*[7] as to a tradition among the inhabitants that this village was the site of a great slaughter of the Danes, and by connecting the fight more closely

---

[1] Lysons, *Magna Britannia*, i. 162, published in 1806. See above, p. 271. It is not clear that Denford means 'ford of the Danes,' as it may be a compound of *ford* and *denu*, 'dean, valley.' It occurs in Domesday (i. 61, col. 1) as *Daneford*, and in 1199 as *Deneford* (*Rotuli Chartarum*, p. 14 a). If the name could be proved to mean 'Danes' ford,' it might with more probability be connected with the events of 1006, when the English *fyrd* attempted to defend the passage of the river Kennet against the Danes on their way from the Berkshire Downs to Winchester.

[2] Vol. i. p. 57 b, col. 1.

[3] Pipe Rolls, 13 Henry II, p. 9; 14 Henry II, p. 202; *Rot. Chart.* p. 23 b, an. 1200. In the *Chartulary of St. Frideswide*, Oxford Historical Society, i. 29; ii. 32, 324–6, it occurs as *Ediveton* (misprinted *Edineton*) in copies of documents dated 1147–58. The *Eduneton* of the *Testa de Nevill*, p. 125, must be miscopied or misprinted for *Ediueton*. The *Edinton* of a fine of 1195 (*Fines sive Pedes Finium*, p. 91; *Pipe Roll Society*, vol. xvii. p. 32), although endorsed Berkshire, relates to Addington, co. Surrey, since the road to Chelsham is mentioned, and William de Edinton, one of the parties, was an inhabitant of Surrey, as may be seen from the printed records of this time.

[4] *Cart. Sax.* iii. 307, 12. The identification, which has been accepted by Birch, seems to have been suggested by the writer of the rubric in the chartulary miscopying the name as *Æpedingetun*. Since no boundaries are given, it is hardly possible to identify this place.

[5] *Chronicon Monasterii de Abingdon*, ii. 516, note 3.

[6] *The Life of St. Neot*, by the Rev. John Whitaker, B.D., p. 269.

[7] Vol. i. p. 96.

with Chippenham than the words of the Chronicle or of the Life warrant. Gough's remark was a repetition of one of Gibson's in his edition of Camden[1], and it was derived by Gibson from the MSS. of John Aubrey, the Wiltshire antiquary[2]. Prior to the civil war of Aubrey's time most reputed battlefields were assigned by the rustic traditions to the Danes, and in this case the tradition was strengthened by the growth about Slaughterford of the plant known as ' Danes' Blood' (the dwarf elder), which is still popularly supposed to grow only on spots that have been the scene of fights with the Danes[3]. Tradition is of too unreliable a nature to have any weight in deciding the question of the sites of early battles, and is too frequently the product of the perfervid ingenuity of the local antiquary. In the present case there can be no doubt that the tradition is aetiological. As the word 'slaughter' is of Scandinavian origin, the corresponding West Saxon form being *slieht*, later *sliht*, it is impossible that this name could, if it means the 'ford of slaughter,' be old enough to be connected with the ninth century. The use of 'slaughter' in such a sense as this is even far more recent, and such a name is entirely unknown in O.E., where *slieht* means the act of slaying, not the result of the slaying. The name of the Wiltshire village was written Slaughtenford until the beginning of the nineteenth century, although earlier forms with *r* are known[4]. Both the *r* and the *n* would seem to have been part of the name, which therefore seems to be connected with O.E.

---

[1] Vol. i. p. 103 a.

[2] See the *Topographical Collections of John Aubrey*, p. 110, and the quotation from his *Monumenta Britannica* in the *Wilts Archaeological and Natural History Magazine*, iii. 78.

[3] Aubrey, as above, and his *Natural History of Wilts*, published in 1848, p. 50; Wright, *English Dialect Dictionary*, under ' Danes' Blood.'

[4] A. D. 1277, *Shlachtreford*, Close Rolls, p. 380; 1298, *Slaghteneford*, Close Roll, 26 Edward I, memb. 2; 1300, *Slaghtenford*, Patent Rolls, p. 532; 1341, *Sla(u)ghtenford*, *Inqq. Nonarum*, p. 165; 1468, *Slaghtneford*, Patent Rolls, p. 62; 1472, *Slaighteneford*, ibid. p. 328; 1385, *Slaghterford*, ibid., p. 24. The Gloucestershire Slaughterford occurs in an original charter of 779 as *Slohtranford* (*Cart. Sax.* i. 321, 19), which dissevers it from the Wilts name and from ' slaughter.' A Sussex *Sloghtreford* occurs in 1276 (*Rot. Hund.* ii. 202 b) and 1316 (Patent Rolls, p. 562), and thus seems to be of the same origin as the Gloucestershire name.

*slāhporn,* 'blackthorn.' Whitaker had the boldness to allege
that Yatton Keynell, the adjoining parish, is 'the fair
representative of *Ethandun*[1],' and this impossible equation
has found adherents in modern times.  It is the only name
near Slaughterford that even the ingenuity of local antiquaries could torture into *Eðandun*, and it has been backed
up by the illegitimate process of taking Ettone, one of the
forms in Domesday, and adding to it 'down,' and then
boldly claiming that this imaginary Etton-dun was Eðandun[2].  This Domesday form is one of the numerous cases
in which the scribes of the Survey have merged an initial
semi-vowel with the following vowel.  Such a process could
not have occurred in ninth-century O.E., in which the form
of this name must have appeared as *Geat-tun*, as proved
by the modern form and by the other and more correct
spelling *Getone* in Domesday.  Carte's identification of
Eðandun with Yattenden, co. Berks[3], is equally impossible,
for that name must have appeared in O.E. as *Geatinga-
denu*[4].  Eðandun could not possibly have developed into
either Yatton or Yattingdon[5].

The absurd form *Edderandun* given by Mr. Arnold for
*Eðandun* in both portions of Simeon of Durham in the
Rolls Series edition is due to the careless repetition of
the reading in Twysden's edition, which is reproduced in the
*Monumenta Historica Britannica.*  The MS. reads *Eððandun, Eððandun.*  It is obvious that Twysden's transcriber
mistook the ð for the compendium for *der, dre*, from which
it is hardly distinguishable in late twelfth-century MSS.
Canon Raine, who prepared the text for the Surtees Society's
edition of Simeon, printed *Ederderandun*, by a similar
error.  The careless collation of Twysden's text is respon-

[1] *Life of St. Neot,* p. 269.
[2] Dr. Thurnam and Mr. Scrope in the *Wilts Archaeological and
Natural History Magazine*, iii. pp. 81, 299.  It is stated at p. 300 that
Yatton 'is still pronounced Eaton or Etton,' which is even more
irrelevant than the Domesday form.
[3] *History of England*, i. p. 300.
[4] It occurs in the *Testa de Nevill*, in the early part of the thirteenth
century, as *Yetingeden, Yatingeden*, and *Yatingden* (pp. 111, 122, 132).
[5] It is not necessary to discuss the location of the battle of Ethandun
at Woeful Danes Bottom, near Minchinhampton, co. Gloucester, which
was suggested by J. M. Moffat in the *Graphic Illustrator*, 1834, p. 106.
He recognized Ethandun in *-hampton*!  See *Wilts Magazine*, iii. p. 81.

sible for the appearance in the first part of Simeon in the editions of *Cuderwine* (from c. 1, 14 of the Life) and *Fridrenwulf* (from c. 1, 21) for *Cuðwine* and *Friðuwulf,* which are given as *Cutherwine* and *Frithenulf* in the Surtees Society's edition, and of *aquarum* (from c. 49, 23). These blundered forms of Ethandun need not be cited any more in discussions as to the site of this battle.

**56,** 18 **suatim utens,** 'acting according to his natural disposition,' 'on his own initiative.' This strange expression occurs again at cc. 74, 21, and 106, 22. Florence of Worcester omitted the participle in the present chapter, retaining *suatim,* which the editors have tacitly altered to *suapte.* He omitted both words in the two latter passages. Parker treated the phrase in his usual radical manner. At c. 56, 18 he altered it to *sua ipsius*; c. 74, 21 to *sublevatus est*[1]; c. 106, 22 to *advocatos,* and these alterations are silently reproduced by the later editors. The true reading is recovered from the Corpus transcript and from the Annals of St. Neots. Probably the *suapte* of cc. 80, 8, 13 and 103, 10 is due to Parker, and may represent the same phrase. Both these chapters were omitted by the compiler of the Annals of St. Neots. In c. 56, 18 the reading *suatim utens* is supported by the addition in the margin of the Bury St. Edmunds copy of Florence of Worcester of the participle[2]. In both parts of Simeon of Durham the participle is omitted.

We have been unable to find an instance outside this work of the use of the phrase *suatim utens.* That the latter word is correct is proved by the evidence of the Annals of St. Neots and by the St. Edmunds marginal addition, so that it does not rest solely upon the somewhat uncertain testimony of the Corpus transcript of the Life. The word *suatim* was, however, in somewhat common use before and after the time of King Alfred. It was formed on the analogy of the early Latin *tuatim, nostratim*[3].

---

[1] Possibly this unmeaning phrase may be due to a blunder on the part of his copyist, for it appears in the British Museum transcript.

[2] See above, p. 101.

[3] See Carl Paucker, *Vorarbeiten zur lateinischen Sprachgeschichte* ('Materialien zur lateinischen Wortbildungsgeschichte'), Berlin, 1883, pp. vii, 132, 139.

Aldhelm uses it with the meaning 'after his (or her) manner or nature[1].' In the same sense it occurs in Odo of Cluny's *Occupatio*, a ninth-century work[2]; in Ælfric's *Vita Sancti Æthelwoldi*[3], and in Hincmar of Rheims[4].

**56,** 26 **triginta electissimis de exercitu suo viris.** This is a mistranslation of the words of the Chronicle : 'com se cyning to him Godrum þritiga sum þara monna þe in þam here weorþuste wæron' ('the king Godrum came to him one of the thirty of the most important men in the army'), a common O.E. locution which means that Godrum made up the number of thirty, so that he came not with thirty men but with twenty-nine.

**56,** 33 **beneficia.** The singular reading *aedificia*, which appears in the Annals of St. Neots, Florence and the Cottonian MS., seems also to have existed in the version used by the author of the first part of Simeon of Durham, for he represents the 'multa et optima aedificia' of the Life by ' multa et inedicibilia largita ⟨sic⟩ est dona,' where the *inedicibilia* seems to have been suggested by the *aedificia* of the original. *Aedificia* occurs again in c. 91, 20, but, from its position, it seems to be used in its proper sense of ' buildings.' In the present passage we have corrected *aedificia* to *beneficia*, following Lappenberg and Pauli[5]. It is, however, noticeable that Ducange contains a quotation from Anjou in which *edificamentum* is used in the sense of ' things acquired,' in reference to buildings and vineyards. But we have failed to find any instance of *aedificia* having the meaning of ' gifts.'

**57.** From the Chronicle, with the addition of the British name of Cirencester, and of the statement that the march thither was in pursuance of the promise of the Danes to

---

[1] *De Laudibus Virginitatis*, ed. Giles, c. 17, p. 17, 23 ; c. 36, p. 47, 7 ; c. 58, p. 77, 34.

[2] Ed. A. Swoboda, Leipzig, 1900, lib. vi. 385 ; vii. 625.

[3] Ed. Stevenson, *Chronicon Monasterii de Abingdon*, ii. p. 258. This is copied into the *Liber de Hyda*, p. 152, where it was regarded by the editor as a mistake for O.E. *swatum*, ' beer'! The passage, which is 'inebriatis Northanhymbris suatim,' lends some countenance to this.

[4] *Opera*, ed. Sirmond, ii. p. 548.

[5] See Introduction, § 86, p. cxxii, above.

quit Alfred's kingdom, which is a deduction from the annal
of the preceding year.

**58.** From the Chronicle, with the addition of the statement that the army of pagans came from beyond sea and
joined themselves to the army of Guthrum. This, if it
means physical union with Guthrum's forces, is contradicted
by cc. 60, 61. But the author says that the new army
'nevertheless wintered at Fulham,' so that he probably did
not mean to say that the two bodies of Danes united.

**59.** From the Chron., omitting the statement that the
eclipse lasted an hour, but with the addition of the time of
day when it occurred. This, as we have said [1], seems to
be a proof that the Life is the work of a man who saw this
eclipse, for the time can hardly be the result of a calculation made in the tenth century, and it is unlikely that it
is a guess, since there is little motive for the addition of
the time if the work is spurious. The indication of the
time of day is given in accordance with the custom in use
before and after the ninth century of measuring the time
by the canonical hours, and not by the hours of the day [2].
The time is indicated as closely as was possible at that
date.

If it could be proved that the time of day assigned for
the eclipse is accurate, it would be a conclusive proof of
the authenticity of the Life. But the question is sur-
rounded with uncertainties, for the author, following the
Chron., does not specify the time of the year when the
eclipse occurred or his place of observation, and both
are necessary before we can ascertain the time of the day
indicated by him. The Chron., followed by the author
in this passage, places the eclipse in 879, and states in
another place, which is also reproduced by the author
(c. 68, 8), that the eclipse occurred in the same year as
the death of Ludwig the Stammerer. This happened on
April 10, 879 [3]. In that year there was a partial eclipse of
the sun on March 26, but this does not seem to have been

---

[1] See Introduction, §§ 48, 90, pp. lxxviii, cxxviii.

[2] That is, time was said to be an hour after the ninth hour, instead of
the tenth hour. See Gustav Bilfinger, *Die antiken Stundenangaben*,
Stuttgart, 1888, pp. 45, 62.

[3] Dümmler, *Geschichte des ostfränkischen Reiches*, ed. 2, iii. p. 113.

visible in Wessex, where the entry in the Chron. was presumably written [1]. According to Pingré's tables [2] this eclipse
was visible in the north of Scotland only. He places the
time of conjunction at 4 p.m. Paris time, which is equivalent to about 3.50 p.m. Greenwich time. This, in accordance with astronomical practice, represents the time at the
centre of the earth of the nearest approach of the centres
of the sun and the moon viewed from that point. Owing
to the effects of parallax on the moon's place, the time when
the eclipse is visible at a given place on the surface of the
earth may be a few hours earlier or later than that at the
centre of the earth. Pingré's tables are so frequently misunderstood and misapplied by historical writers that it is
necessary to make this explanation. The more accurate
tables of Professor Oppolzer [3] assign 3 h. 48·1 m. p.m. Greenwich mean time as the time of conjunction. Mr. A. C. D.
Crommelin, of the Royal Observatory, Greenwich, has
been good enough to construct the eclipse graphically on
the basis of Newcomb's tables [4], and he makes the time of
conjunction 3 h. 37 m. 43·68 s. Greenwich mean time, from
which must be deducted 4 m. 44 s. for the equation of
time. He reaches the conclusion that the eclipse would
be visible over the whole of Scotland, the northern half of
England and Wales, and about three-quarters of Ireland,
the southern line of visibility running approximately from
Louth in Lincolnshire to Kilkenny. Oppolzer places the
southern limit about 1° 9′ farther south, thus bringing it
down to Greenwich. According to Mr. Crommelin's calculations the eclipse would be visible at Louth about
5 h. 27 m. p.m. mean time. He remarks that it is 'needless
to say that there is an uncertainty of several minutes of
arc in the moon's place a thousand years ago, so that

[1] There is always a possibility that a chronicler might record an
eclipse, although it was not visible in the monastery wherein he was
writing. But, considering the difficulties of intercommunication in the
ninth century, it is improbable that an annalist working very far beyond
the limit of visibility of an eclipse would hear of it and record it.
[2] In the second and later editions of *L'art de vérifier les dates.*
[3] In his *Canon der Finsternisse,* printed in the *Denkschriften der
kaiserlichen Akademie der Wissenschaften,* 'Mathematisch-naturwissenschaftliche Classe,' vol. lii, Vienna, 1887.
[4] Printed in the *Ephemeris Americana.*

there must in any case be a considerable probable error in the south limit.' This eclipse was a very small one in England, and it is impossible that it could have been visible for anything like an hour, while its duration on the limiting line of visibility was exceedingly short. We may therefore conclude, despite the evidence of the Chron. and of the Life, that the partial eclipse of the sun on March 26, 879, is not the one referred to, since it could not possibly be said of it that the sun was obscured for an hour, it could not be described as happening between the hours of. None and Vespers, and, finally, it may be doubted whether it would have been sufficiently visible without a telescope to ensure notice. There was no other solar eclipse in this year that was visible in England.

It is incredible that this small eclipse of March 26, 879, should have attracted the notice of the compiler of the Chron., and that he should have ignored the very remarkable total solar eclipse of October 29, 878[1]. The latter

---

[1] It has been maintained by Steenstrup, *Normannerne*, ii. 74, note 1, adopted by Plummer, *Two Saxon Chronicles Parallel*, ii. 95, that the Chronicle is a year too late in its dates relating to the Northmen between 878 and 896, but the instances are by no means conclusive. In 878 and 879 there is nothing to support this view beyond the eclipse in question; and the fact that Ludwig's death is referred by the Chron. under 885 to 879, which is the correct year, shows that we cannot correct all these dates by placing them a year back. The passage of the Northmen from England to Ghent, which is given in the Annals of St. Vaast under 879, and in the Chron. under 880, does not prove that the latter is wrong, for it mentions that they stayed there for a year, and hence the entry may have been written at the end of that time. Similarly in 882 the Chron. states that they ascended the Meuse into Frankland, where they remained a year. The ascent of the river occurred in November, 881. In 883 the Chron. states that the Danes went to Condé and remained a year. They arrived there in October or November, 882. Again, under 884 they are said to arrive at Amiens and remain a year. The date of their arrival was, apparently, November, 883. In 885 the Chron. says that Charles (meaning Carloman) died in this year before mid-winter. This happened on December 12, 884 (Dümmler, *Geschichte des ostfränkischen Reiches*, ed. 2, iii. 232). This entry suggests that the year of the Chron. began before December 25, the usual Frankish commencement, and hence some of the other discrepancies between the dates of the Chron. and those of the continental annalists may be due to a difference in the commencement of the year. Possibly also this may explain why the eclipse of October 29, 878, came to be entered under 879.

certainly made a great impression upon the continental chroniclers of the time. From them we learn that the sun was so obscured for half an hour or so that the stars became visible, causing men to think that night had commenced. The contemporary Annals of Fulda place this after the hour of None [1], while Regino, also a contemporary, states that it was 'about the hour of None [2].' This is a somewhat remarkable agreement with the assertion in the present chapter that the eclipse occurred 'between None and Vespers, but nearer to None,' and that in the Chron. that the sun was obscured for an hour of the day. Mr. J. R. Hind calculated the time of the eclipse at Fulda, and found that there was 'a total eclipse, totality commencing at 2 h. 9 m. 32 s. local mean time, and continuing 1 m. 41 s., with the sun at an altitude of 19°. The partial phase began at 0 h. 56 m. and ended at 3 h. 24 m. The Fulda annalist has "post horam nonam" for the time of the eclipse, but the times we found cannot be very much in error. The sun rose at Fulda on this day at 7 h. 12 m. apparent time, or at 6 h. 57 m. mean time, so that the ninth hour from sunrise would be 4 p.m.[3]' Here Mr. Hind and Dr. Hartwig of Leipzig, whom he cites, have been led into needless difficulties, through ignorance of the fact that in the ninth century the day was not divided into equal hours. The Greek and Roman system of dividing the time between

---

[1] Ed. Kurze, p. 92 : 'Eclipsis lunae facta est . . . sol quoque in iiii. kal. Novembris post horam nonam ita obscuratus est per dimidiam horam ut stellae in caelo apparerent, et omnes sibi noctem imminere putarent.'

[2] Ed. Kurze, p. 113 : 'eclipsis lunae facta est mense Octobrio, die xvi. Item eodem mense eclipsis solis accidit, die xxviiii. circa horam nonam.' The Prüm Annals, which are hereabouts based upon some lost annals that were used by Regino, have 'eclipsis magna lunae, uno eodemque mense similiter eclipsis solis ⟨h⟩orribilis' (Pertz, *Scriptores*, xv. part 2, p. 1291). Other references from continental chroniclers have been brought together by F. K. Ginzel, *Astronomische Untersuchungen über Finsternisse*, in the *Sitzungsberichte* of the Vienna Academy, 'Mathematisch-naturwissenschaftliche Classe,' vol. lxxxviii, 1884, p. 669. They are mostly based upon the Fulda Annals. His calculations of the eclipse are given at p. 673 and in vol. lxxxix, part 2, p. 514. According to him the southern limit of the zone of totality reached from Carnarvonshire to London and thence to Ypres.

[3] *Nature*, March 11, 1875, vol. xi, p. 365. For this reference we are indebted to Mr. A. M. W. Downing, the Superintendent of the *Nautical Almanac*.

sunrise and sunset and that between sunset and sunrise into twelve hours each prevailed until about the fourteenth century[1]. Except at the equinoxes the length of an hour of the day therefore differed from that of an hour of the night connected with it, and the length of the hour of both varied, strictly speaking, from day to day. It is inconceivable, however, that the imperfect time-measurers of the ninth century could have been so regulated as to represent with mathematical accuracy the length of these variable hours (ὧραι καιρικαί, 'horae temporales'). Apart from the somewhat primitive system of measuring time by the length of one's shadow[2], the only time-measurers in use seem to have been sun-dials and water-clocks, the latter being principally intended for measuring the hours of the night in the monasteries[3]. The sun-dials had not reached the perfection of the modern ones[4], so that minute divisions of the day were impossible. The water-clocks were probably regulated once a month[5], or at some other regular interval, and the indication of time given by them must have corresponded only roughly to the real time. It is therefore hardly possible to ascertain exactly the hour and minute of the day meant by None and Vespers on a given day in the ninth century, and the difficulties are enhanced by the modern astronomical use of mean time instead of

[1] Gustav Bilfinger, *Die mittelalterlichen Horen und die modernen Stunden*, Stuttgart, 1892, pp. 1 sqq., 141 sqq.; Franz Rühl, *Chronologie des Mittelalters und der Neuzeit*, Berlin, 1897, p. 211.

[2] Bilfinger, *Die antiken Stundenangaben*, p. 75 sqq. The length of the shadow, which was measured by the length of the foot of the observer, varied from month to month. The length is occasionally given in the O.E. calendars for each month, as, for example, in the eleventh-century calendar in Cott. MS. Vitellius A xviii, printed in Hampson, *Medii Aevi Calendarium*, 1841, p. 422 sqq., and in Leofric's *Missal*, p. 58, where the length of the third and the ninth hour, which were identical, are given. From these the other hours were reckoned by formula.

[3] Bilfinger, *Die mittelalterlichen Horen*, p. 147 sqq.

[4] Ibid. p. 143. They had an upright stylus, instead of a gnomon laid in the direction of the axis of the earth, as in the modern dials. Some interesting English dials from the eleventh century are figured in Hübner, *Inscriptiones Britanniae Christianae*, pp. 65, 66, nos. 179, 180, 181.

[5] As in the ancient customs of the monastery of St. Victor, Paris, cited by Bilfinger, *op. cit.* p. 148.

apparent time, the only one that could have been used in the ninth century. There is also the slight dislocation caused by the use of the Julian calendar. We may, however, approximately ascertain the time intended. If we divide the time between 6 h. 57 m. mean time, the hour of sunrise at Fulda according to Mr. Hind, and 4 h. 30 m., the time of sunset [1], by twelve, we obtain an hour of 47 m. 45 s. Adding nine of these hours to the time of sunrise, we arrive at 2 h. 6 m. 45 s. as the hour of None. By apparent local time it would be about quarter of an hour earlier. Vespers would be, on this calculation, at 3 h. 42 m. 15 s. local mean time. We thus see that the Fulda Annals and Regino are correct in their specification of time, and that, allowing for the uncertainty of the data and calculations, there is a remarkable agreement with the indication of time given in the present work. When the author tells us that the eclipse occurred between None and Vespers, but nearer to None, he is really limiting it to something less than 47 m. 45 s., which would have been, on the basis of this calculation, exactly halfway between None and Vespers. On the basis of the apparent local time at Fulda, he is telling us that the eclipse was nearer to 1 h. 51 m. 45 s. than to 3 h. 27 m. 15 s., and he seems to be correct [2].

It is to be regretted that the imperfect evidence at our command precludes our reaching a definite conclusion as to the time meant by the author. But, when all allowances have been made for the uncertainty of the calculations given above, there still remains such a remarkable approximation to what the author states that we can scarcely

---

[1] As given by Ginzel, *op. cit.* p. 673.

[2] The O.E. calendars frequently give the number of equinoctial hours (ὧραι ἰσημεριναί, 'horae aequinoctiales') in the day and in the night. For October they assign ten hours for the day and fourteen for the night, which would make the 'hora temporalis' for the day fifty minutes long. For November eight hours are assigned to the day, so that the 'hora temporalis' of the day would be forty minutes. For December they give only six hours to the day, which is much below the time between sunrise and sunset, which averages about eight hours. It is therefore difficult to use these data for the calculation of time, and we have no evidence to show that the time-measurers were altered to correspond with the change in the length of the 'hora temporalis' on the first day of each month.

doubt that the specification of time given by him is derived from personal observation. In that case, however, we should have to conclude that he was on the continent at no great distance from Fulda at the date of the eclipse. Such a conclusion is rendered plausible by the evidence of acquaintance with the Frankish empire[1]. Writing some fifteen years later in Wessex his memory might well have betrayed him into some slight error, but it does not appear that it has done so. He has, however, if our view be correct, been guilty of the error of assuming that the eclipse was visible in Wessex at the same time as it was in Frankland. But we could hardly expect a scholar of the ninth century to be aware of such an error. In England the time of the eclipse was somewhat earlier. Mr. Hind calculates that the time when totality commenced at St. Paul's, London, was 1 h. 16 m. 20 s. mean time, ending at 1 h. 18 m. 10 s. The eclipse in England was therefore, on any calculation, before the hour of None.

**60.** From the Chronicle.

**61.** From the Chronicle, with the addition of *Orientalem* to *Franciam*, a result, probably, of acquaintance with the political affairs of Frankland on the part of the author. Cf. note to c. 70.

**62.** From the Chronicle. The *superius* of line 3 is a somewhat too literal rendering of the *ufor* of the Chron., which in such constructions means 'farther from a point previously mentioned' (in this case Ghent), and hence with *faran* means 'to go up country,' 'to proceed inland.' Cf. c. 63. In the present case Florence substitutes *saepe-dictus*.

**63.** From the Chronicle. In line 4 *tanto longe* corresponds to the reading *feor* ('far') of MS. A, for which is substituted *ufor* in B, C, D and E. This latter is rendered *superius* in c. 62, 3.

**64.** From the Chronicle.

**65.** From the Chronicle, with the addition of the mention of the nunnery at Condé, which seems to be due to the author's acquaintance with Frankland[1].

The record of the gift by Pope Marinus to the king of a

---

[1] See Introduction, § 48, p. lxxviii, above.

part of the cross and of the sending of alms by the latter
to Rome and to India, which occurs in MS. B, C, D, E
and F of the Chron., is omitted in the Life. As the entire
annal for 884 has been overlooked by the author or copyist,
the omission of these details may be ascribed to carelessness. The omission of the annal for 884 seems to be due
to a clerical error, the eye of the writer having copied the
date for that year and then wandered to that for the following one [1], the entries for which he proceeded to copy
without discovering his mistake. The omission of the
pope's gift and of the king's mission cannot be explained
by any similar error caused by homoeoarcton [2], and it is
unlikely that the author would purposely omit such signal
proofs of his hero's piety. It would therefore seem that the
very early MS. of the Chron. used by him contained no
mention of these things. This conclusion is supported by
the fact that the oldest existing MS. A of the Chron. is
silent regarding them, and this agreement may be taken as
proof that they did not exist in the archetype of the Chron. [3]
The pope's gift is referred to in the Chron. under 885, a
passage that is reproduced in the Life (c. 71, 7). Hence
MSS. B, C, D and E have two entries of the gift of the
piece of the cross, which is suspicious. As the oldest of
these MSS. was written nearly a century after the date of
the composition of the present work, it is difficult to feel
any confidence that these details are not later interpolations
in the text of the Chron. Florence of Worcester, who
occasionally supplies from the Chron. matter omitted in the
Life, has nothing corresponding to the passages in question,
but his work contains what is clearly a later interpolation

[1] See Introduction, § 27, p. li, above. Both entries begin alike 'her
for se here up on,' and end alike 'ond þer sæt an gear,' the only differences between the two being that the river and town are the Scheldt and
Condé in the former and the Somme and Amiens in the latter, so that
it was easy to confuse one entry with the other.

[2] If the passages in question had followed the annal for 883, the
length of the latter would have been four times as great as without it,
and this increased length would probably have prevented the confusion
of the brief annal of 883 with the equally brief one of 884.

[3] They would also seem to have been absent from the version of the
Chron. used by Æthelweard, if we may safely argue from his silence
regarding them.

regarding the mission to India taken from William of Malmesbury[1]. The position of this interpolation, however, has been obviously determined by an entry in the Chron. corresponding to that in MSS. B, C, D, E and F. The silence of the Annals of St. Neots concerning this entry may be due to the close manner in which the compiler followed the Life, and can scarcely be adduced as proof that the important and early MS. of the Chron. used by him did not contain this entry.

The fact that Alfred sent a mission to India has been generally accepted on the strength of the passage in question. That his envoys should have penetrated into India appeared marvellous to William of Malmesbury in the twelfth century, and Gibbon evidently had his doubts as to the feasibility of such a mission[2]. The term India in Alfred's time was used in a much looser sense than we assign to it[3], and it may well be questioned whether it was possible to find the alleged resting-place of St. Bartholomew in the ninth century. Sir William Hunter has come to the con-

[1] See Introduction, § 41, p. lxix. above.

[2] *Decline and Fall of the Roman Empire*, c. 47 (ed. Bury, v. p. 151), where Gibbon 'almost suspects' that Alfred's envoys 'collected their cargo and legend in Egypt.'

[3] Alcuin is said to employ it to describe Asia (Sophus Ruge, *Geschichte des Zeitalters der Entdeckungen*, Berlin, 1881, p. 5). The *Martyrologium* of Beda (*Opera*, ed. Giles, iv. p. 112) connects Bartholomew with India. This is derived from a notice found in several eighth-century texts of the *Martyrologium Hieronymianum*. See R. A. Lipsius, *Die apocryphen Apostelgeschichten und Apostellegenden*, 1883–90, ii. part 2, p. 63, where the history of the apostle's connexion with 'India,' which began with Eusebius, is given. Ælfric's statement in his homily on St. Bartholomew (*Homilies*, ed. Thorpe, i. p. 454) as to the existence of three Indias, viz. one in Ethiopia, another in Media, and a third reaching to the great ocean and shrouded on one side in darkness, is derived from the Latin version of the *Passio Bartholomei* (see the quotation from the Greek version in Lipsius, p. 64, note 1). Aldhelm, in his poem on the Twelve Apostles (*Opera*, ed. Giles, p. 125, no. x), also refers to the three Indias ('quam tres in partes librorum scripta sequestrant'), using, no doubt, the same source. The O.E. poem on the Fate of the Apostles, which seems to be a composition of the eighth-century Northumbrian poet Cynewulf, places St. Bartholomew in India, where its Latin source, the *Breviarium Apostolorum*, has Lyc⟨a⟩onia (see Holthausen, in *Archiv für das Studium der neueren Sprachen und Litteraturen*, cvi. p. 343 sqq.). Lipsius, however, ascribes to the *Breviarium* the reading 'India' (p. 64).

clusion that Alfred's envoys could not have visited the
Coromandel coast, and that the India of his time never
meant the Indian peninsula[1]. He thinks that they may
have reached the shrine of St. Thomas at Edessa. It is
questionable, apart from the doubtful nature of the record,
whether this mission to St. Bartholomew and St. Thomas was
ever dispatched. The full form of the entry is preserved in
MSS. D and E, the entries in B and C being rendered
unintelligible through the omission of the sentences here
enclosed in square brackets: 'ond þy ilcan geare lædde
Sighelm ond Æþelstan þa ælmessan to Rome [þe Ælfred
cyning gehet þyder], ond eac on India to Sancte Thome
ond to Sancte Bartholomae, þa hi sæton wið þone here æt
Lundenne[2], ond hie þær, Godes þances, swiðe bentiþige
wurdan æfter þam gehate' ('and in the same year Sighelm
and Æthelstan took the alms to Rome [that King Alfred
promised ⟨to send⟩ thither], and also to St. Thomas in
India and to St. Bartholomew, at the time when they
⟨evidently meaning the king, Sighelm, and Æthelstan⟩
besieged the ⟨Danish⟩ army at London[2], and they were
very successful, thanks be to God, according to the
promise(s)'). This may be understood to convey that the
envoys carried the alms to Rome and to St. Thomas and
St. Bartholomew, but the construction is peculiar, and
seems rather to restrict the carrying of alms to Rome only.
The freeing of the Saxon School at Rome from tribute
(c. 71, 2) seems to have been one of the objects of this
mission. Malmesbury states that the jewels and other
things brought from India by Sighelm, whom he describes
as bishop of Sherborne, were in his time preserved in the
church at Sherborne[3]. But it is impossible to attach much
belief to this story, for the envoy can hardly have been the
Sighelm who became bishop of Sherborne between 918 and

---

[1] *The Indian Empire*, p. 290.

[2] It is one of the difficulties connected with this passage that the
Chron. does not record any siege of the Danes in London by Alfred
or Sighelm. Under 886 it records that Alfred 'restored' London (cf.
c. 83 below). Æthelweard, it is true, mentions a siege of London by
Alfred (*Mon. Hist. Brit.* 517 A), but the passage is evidently founded
upon this entry in the Chron., and his *obsidetur* has therefore arisen from
reading *gesette* as *besette*.

[3] *Gesta Regum*, c. 122 (p. 130); *Gesta Pontificum*, c. 80 (p. 177).

925–33, whom Malmesbury has boldly moved up three places in the list of bishops in order to bring him into connexion with the alleged mission to India. The entry in the Chron. suggests that Sighelm was an army-leader, and he was, in all probability, the Kentish ealdorman whose death is recorded in fighting against the Danes in the Chron. under 905. He witnesses a Kentish charter of 889[1]. His intimate connexion with Alfred is established by the fact that Eadgifu, his daughter, was the wife of Edward the Elder, as we learn from an interesting deed of hers written about 960[2]. Æthelstan is perhaps the Mercian priest who is mentioned in c. 77, 12 as an assistant of Alfred in his studies, for one of the two envoys to Rome would probably be a cleric.

**66.** From the Chronicle, with the addition of the statements that one portion of the Danish army went into East Frankland (representing the *east* of the Chron.), that the other came to Britain and Kent, with the description of the site of Rochester, that the Danish fort at Rochester was before the gates of the city, that the horses relinquished by the Danes had been brought by them from Frankland, and the mention of their captives. For the error in the Life assigning these events to 884 instead of 885, which Pauli[3] considered to be due to the damaged condition of the Cottonian MS., see note to previous chapter.

**66, 13 omnibus equis...derelictis.** This is a somewhat loose rendering of the 'hie wurdon þær behorsude' of the Chron., which, on the strength of the translation in the Life, is usually rendered : 'and they were there deprived of their horses.' The verb 'behorsian' is known only from this passage, and in it the prefix may have a deprivatory sense, as in the case of 'behēafdian' (to behead).

---

[1] Ordnance Survey *Facsimiles*, i. pl. 2 (10th cent. ?) ; *Cart. Sax.* ii. 202, 20. There is a grant to him in 898 (Ord. Sur. *Facs.* i. pl. 12 ; *Cart. Sax.* ii. 219, 18), written in a very singular and probably un-English hand, which seems to be somewhat later in date. He is probably the 'Sighelm minister' of a genuine charter of 875 relating to Kent (Brit. Mus. *Facs.* ii. pl. 40, in a slightly later hand ; *Cart. Sax.* ii. 159, 6), and the 'Sighelm dux' of a genuine Kentish charter of 889 (Ord. Survey *Facs.* i. pl. 11, tenth century copy ; *Cart. Sax.* ii. 202, 20).

[2] Ord. Sur. *Facs.* iii. pl. 29, contemporary ; *Cart. Sax.* iii. 284.

[3] *König Ælfred*, p. 11. Cf. Goscelin's date 885, p. 309, below.

**67.** From the Chronicle, with the addition of the statement that Alfred sent the ships to East Anglia for the sake
of spoil [1], and that the fleet that met the English on their
return had been gathered by the Danes dwelling in East
Anglia.

**67,** 9 **dormiret.** MSS. A, C and D of the Chron. have
here ' hamweard wendon' ('went homewards '), represented
by ' hamweard wæron' in B and E in error. It is evident
that the reading *dormiret* occurred in the MS. of the Life
used by the compiler of the first part of the chronicle
bearing the name of Simeon of Durham [2]. It is probably
a crasis of *domum rediret* or *domum iret.* Florence substitutes *rediret*, probably by collation with the Chron. This
variation in Florence is of so easily explicable a nature that
it is unnecessary to assume 'that he did not borrow from
Asser as we have it, but ⟨that⟩ both used some common
source [3].' Moreover, it seems clear that the Worcester
writer used the Cottonian MS. of the Life [4].

**68.** From the Chronicle, adding *Occidentalium* in line 2
(which may be a deduction from the words of the Chron.)
and the name of Charles's daughter Judith. From the
Chron. it repeats the loose statement that a year had
elapsed since the death of Ludwig III, which happened
on August 5, 882 [5], while Carloman's death occurred on
December 12, 884 [6]. It is noticeable that the author gives
Carloman's name correctly, as against the erroneous Carl of
the Chron. This may have been derived from the version
of the Chron. used by him, but may equally well be a correction of his own, founded upon personal acquaintance with

[1] See Introduction, § 86, p. cxxii. above.
[2] The ' dormiebant somno inerti' of the Durham writer is reproduced
in the St. Albans compilation (Roger of Wendover, i. p. 340; Matthew
Paris, *Chronica Maiora*, i. 417). Dr. Luard remarks that this passage
might suggest that Asser had been consulted, but he rejects this view,
holding that Florence was the only authority. The expression was
clearly borrowed from the Durham writer, who used a MS. of the Life
(see Introduction, § 35, p. lviii, above), and not from Florence.
[3] Plummer, *Two Saxon Chronicles Parallel*, ii. p. 97. See Introduction, p. lxxxiii, note 1, above.
[4] See Introduction, § 33, p. lvi. above.
[5] Dümmler, *Geschichte des ostfränkischen Reiches*, ed. 2, iii. p. 205.
[6] Ibid. iii. p. 232.

West Frankish history, such as is evinced by his account of
the succession of Charles III (c. 70, 5).

**68, 3 singularis,** 'boar.' Great confusion has arisen
from taking this Low Latin substantive as an adjective.
Florence added *ferus* (cf. Vulgate lxxix. (lxxx.) 13), and
Parker inserted in his text the gloss *aper* from the Annals
of St. Neots, altering in consequence *singularis* so as to
agree with *dente.*

**68, 8 eclipsis solis.** See note to c. 59.

**69.** From the Chronicle. The author has added that
the Danes came 'from Germany' into Old Saxony. This
seems to be another proof of his acquaintance with Frankish
history of the time, for the Danes wintered in Duisburg,
whence they set out about January, 884, and were defeated
in Saxony by an army under Henry of Saxony and Bishop
Arno of Würzburg[1]. The battle in Friesland, which was
about December, 884, was won by Rimbert, archbishop of
Bremen, against another Danish force[2]. It is curious that
the author should describe Old Saxony as not being in
Germany, a mistake that is avoided by Alfred in his version
of Orosius.

**70.** From the Chronicle, with the addition of the description of Charles as 'Alamannorum rex' and of the North
Sea. The Chron. speaks of the latter as 'this sea.' The
author's description of it as 'illum marinum sinum, qui
inter Antiquos Saxones et Gallos adiacet,' may be due to
knowledge of the continent. The use of *Galli* for the
inhabitants of modern France seems also to be due to
acquaintance with the Frankish learned Latinity. The
statement that Charles succeeded to the kingdom of the
East Franks 'voluntario omnium consensu' is probably due
to the author's personal knowledge. It agrees with the
facts[3], and can scarcely have been a mere guess added to
the Chron. account by a later forger.

**70, 10 antiqui, qui etiam fuit filius.** Here again the
Annals of St. Neots appear to have derived their reading

---

[1] Dümmler, *Geschichte des ostfränkischen Reiches,* ed. 2, iii. p. 222.
[2] Ibid. iii. p. 223. Dümmler regards this as a defeat inflicted upon
another Danish army, not the one that had wintered in Duisburg.
[3] See ibid., iii. p. 234, note 4.

from a better MS. of the Life than the Cottonian. The
latter had 'filius Pippini sive Caroli.' Florence omitted
the 'sive Caroli.' The 'antiqui' of the Annals represents
the 'aldan' of the Chron. The agreement of the second
part of Simeon of Durham with the Annals is somewhat
striking, and suggests that this may have been the reading
of the MS. of the Life[1] used by the compiler of the first
part of the Durham work, which would seem in this case
to have been consulted by the compiler of the second part,
who usually follows Florence[2].

**71.** From the Chronicle. The author has added that the
part of the cross sent to Alfred by the pope was 'non
parvam,' which may be due to his own knowledge of the
fragment or be merely another instance of his tendency to
exaggerate[3]. In one of the post-Conquest forgeries of the
monks of Westminster, Edward the Confessor is made to
say that he has given to the abbey on the day of its consecration 'reliquias, quas Martinus ⟨sic⟩ papa et Leo, qui
eum ⟨scil. Ælfredum⟩ consecravit, dederunt Ælfredo regi,
. . . quaeque ab ipso ad successorem eius Æthelstanum,
deinde ad Eadgarum, ad ultimum ad nos pervenerunt,
scilicet duas partes crucis Domini, et partem unius clavi,
partemque tunicae eius inconsutilis,' &c.[4] This is evidently
derived mainly from the Chron. or the present work, directly
or indirectly.

**71, 1 Marinus papa.** The present work is cited by the
learned editors of the *Regesta Pontificum Romanorum* for
the death of Pope Marinus in 884[5]. But as this chapter is
taken from the Chron., and the variation from the chronology
of the latter is due merely to a clerical error[6], the accuracy
of the date thus given accidentally by the present work
cannot be cited in its favour.

**72.** From the Chronicle, with the addition of the adverb
'opprobriose.'

---

[1] It is probable that the compiler of the Annals has substituted
*magni* for *famosi*.

[2] See Introduction, § 35, p. lix, above.

[3] See Introduction, § 92, p. cxxx, above.

[4] *Codex Diplomaticus*, iv. p. 176.

[5] Ed. Jaffé-Wattenbach, i. 426.

[6] See note to c. 65, p. 286, above.

**73.** This chapter is founded upon the preface to Einhard's
*Life of Charles the Great*, the author repeating or slightly
altering many of the sentences, as may be seen from the
following quotation : ' Vitam et conversationem et ex parte
non modica res gestas domini et nutritoris mei Karoli,
excellentissimi et merito famosissimi regis, postquam scribere
animus tulit, quanta potui brevitate complexus sum ; operam
impendens, ut de his, quae ad meam notitiam pervenire
potuerunt, nihil omitterem, neque prolixitate narrandi nova
quaeque fastidientium animos offenderem.'

**73, 2 portum optatae quietis.** See note to c. 21, 9,
above.

**74.** This chapter is supplied entirely by the author, and
it is an instructive specimen of his confused arrangement
and puzzling phraseology. It has hence given rise to misunderstandings, which have been advanced as arguments
against the authenticity of the work [1]. But even when these
have been cleared up, there remains much that it is difficult
to accept. These features are probably due to the author's
Celtic love of exaggeration and rhetoric, coupled with the
naïve credulity of his time. He has probably developed or
misunderstood what Alfred told him regarding his early life,
and has fallen a victim to the temptation besetting all
biographers—that of seeing in their hero their ideal of a
noble character. In this case the ideal is of a somewhat
morbidly religious nature.

The author starts by telling us that Alfred was seized
shortly after his prolonged wedding-feast, which is placed in
his twentieth year (line 9), as in c. 29, with an illness that
was unknown to his physicians [2]. From this he suffered
intermittently from his twentieth to his fortieth year and
beyond, which is more accurately defined as until his forty-
fifth year in line 65 and in c. 91, 4, the year in which the
Life was written (c. 91, 4). He suffered either from the
illness itself or from fear of it daily and hourly (line 65, and
c. 91, 6). The author then mentions the suggestions that
had been made as to its nature. Some ascribed it to ' favor

---

[1] See Introduction, § 67, p. ciii, above.
[2] The unknown nature of his ' infirmitates ' is also mentioned in
c. 25, 9.

et fascinatio' of the surrounding people, which, if the reading be correct, may mean something like the evil eye or
perhaps infection.   Others thought it was due to the envy
of the devil; others to an unusual sort of fever, while others
again thought that it was the *ficus*.   From the latter disease
Alfred had suffered from his infancy.   This leads the author
to relate how Alfred, when he was hunting in Cornwall
(evidently some time before his marriage), prayed by the
tomb of St. Gueriir that God would change his infirmity
into some lighter one, which should not appear outwardly
so as to render him an object of contempt to men.   The
author explains that Alfred feared leprosy or blindness[1].
Shortly afterwards Alfred's prayers were granted, and the
illness entirely disappeared, although, as the author explains,
Alfred was visited by this infirmity in answer to prayers
offered up by him in his youth.   The author then explains,
although (as he for once says) in reverse order, how Alfred
had prayed for some infliction that should enable him to
preserve chastity before his marriage, and that he had prayed
that the infliction might be one that should not make him
worthless or useless in the affairs of the world.   In answer
he was afflicted with the *ficus*, from which he suffered until
it was removed in response to his prayers before St. Gueriir's
tomb.   This is in flat contradiction to the statement in
line 17 that he had suffered from this disease from his
infancy, and there is a similarity about the requests contained
in the prayers.   The author then tells us that Alfred suffered
from this *ficus* long and severely for many years.   This,
again, is an obvious exaggeration, if, as we are told in the
second story, he incurred it in his youth and if it was
cured before his marriage, which happened in his twentieth
year.   The author then reverts to the mysterious affliction
with which Alfred was smitten at his wedding-feast.

Although there is a certain resemblance in outline between
the two stories of Alfred's prayers for a change of his infirmity and for a new infliction, there are too many differences to admit the suggestion that we have here two

[1] We may surely recognize a characteristic piece of exaggeration here.
Neither leprosy nor blindness could be described as 'lighter' afflictions
than the *ficus*; certainly no affliction could be greater than the former,
and few worse than the second.

alternative accounts of the same event. Both seem from the style to proceed from the same writer, so that there is little ground for the theory of interpolation or blundered copying[1]. But if the author did not intend one of these accounts to supersede the other, it is probable that he has applied the same details to both, although they probably belonged only to one of them.

The information concerning the final affliction is insufficient to identify it. It has been suggested that it was epilepsy, but this could hardly be mistaken for *ficus*. That name was applied amongst the English before the Norman Conquest to haemorrhoids[2], which may possibly have been the complaint from which Alfred suffered.

**74,** 18 **Cornubiam.** After the defeat of the united Danish and Cornish armies by Ecgberht at Hengestesdun (Hingston Down, co. Cornwall), which is entered in the Chron. under 835, we hear nothing of any warlike actions on the part of the Welsh inhabitants of Cornwall against Alfred's house in the ninth century. According to Dunstan's letter about the western bishoprics, Ecgberht gave three estates in Cornwall to the bishop of Sherborne[3], and these were still in the hands of the church in Dunstan's time. Alfred himself had estates in Cornwall[4]. In c. 81, 30 he is made to give to the author of the Life lands in Cornwall.

**74,** 20 **Gueriir.** The *Gueryr* of Camden, which is reproduced by the later editors, is, probably, an emendation. The name in Welsh is *Gwrhyr*, corresponding to the Irish *Ferghoir*, meaning apparently 'good shouter[5].'

**74,** 20 **et nunc etiam Sanctus Niot ibidem pausat.**

---

[1] Freeman, *Dict. Nat. Biography*, i. p. 159, remarks that these tales of sickness seem 'to have received legendary additions; but the general outline of the story seems to be trustworthy.' The agreement in style with the rest of the work is an objection to the suggestion here made.

[2] See Cockayne, *Leechdoms*, iii. p. 30, 16. It was also applied to other disorders, like the Greek σῦκον, συκέα.

[3] Crawford Charters, no. vii; *Cart. Sax.* ii. 277. See p. 322, below.

[4] See his will, *Cart. Sax.* ii. p. 178, 12.

[5] Rhys, *Lectures on the Origin and Growth of Religion as illustrated by Celtic Heathendom*, Hibbert Lectures, 1886, p. 489. Camden's explanation of the name of this saint as meaning 'physician' is based upon the Cornish *guerir*, 'to cure.' But this seems to be merely the French *guérir*, and hence was probably not introduced until after the Norman Conquest.

These words are clearly an interpolation[1]. We are unable
to decide whether they occurred in the MSS. used by the
compilers of the Annals of St. Neots and of the first part of
Simeon of Durham, as they both passed over this chapter
in silence. Nothing whatever is known of St. Gueriir beyond this mention of his place of burial in Cornwall. It is
evident that his fame was rapidly obscured by that of
St. Neot, for this place bore the name of Neotesstou in the
Domesday Survey[2], and is still known as St. Neot. The
date of St. Neot's death is unknown, but this interpolation,
which was made some time between 893, the date of the
composition of the Life, and 1000, the approximate date of
the Cottonian MS., harmonizes with the statements in the
lives of this saint that he was ordained by Bishop Ælfheah
of Winchester[3]. His death would, according to this, occur
in the latter part of the tenth century. Some time before
1020 his body is said to have been conveyed from Cornwall
to Eynesbury, co. Hunts[4], where the monastery of St. Neots
has made his name familiar. The monastery at Eynesbury
was founded some time between 978 and 984 by Leofric,
and Leoflæd his wife. This information was derived by
the twelfth-century compiler of the Ely history from a
contemporary deed then in the abbey[5]. He states, however,
that St. Neot had founded a monastery on this site, but this
is evidently an attempt to account for the monastery bearing
his name. It is clear that St. Neot was not connected with
the foundation at Eynesbury until the removal of his body
thither. This must have occurred some time after the
foundation by Leofric and Leoflæd. Mr. Gorham assigns
it to 974[6], but to do this he has to ignore the matter-of-fact
account of the foundation given by the Ely writer, and to
substitute the names of the founders given in the untrust-

[1] See Introduction, § 26, p. xlix, above.
[2] Vol. i p. 121, col. 2.
[3] See note to c. 53 b, p. 258, above.
[4] His body is described as lying there in the list of English saints
and their burial-places, which was compiled about 1020 (Liebermann,
*Die Heiligen Englands*, p. 13, ii. no. 24 ; *Liber Vitae* of Hyde, p. 90).
[5] *Liber Eliensis*, ed. Stewart, p. 143. The deed was written in Old
English in triplicate.
[6] *History and Antiquities of Eynesbury and St. Neot's*, p. 47 sqq.,
followed by the editors of the *Monasticon*, iii. p. 461.

worthy lives of St. Neot, and to date it by means of the
deed relating to Leofric and Leoflæd. This is a monstrous
mixture of true and false. It is probable that the body of
the saint was still reposing in Cornwall at the time when
the Cottonian MS. of the Life was written, for the writer
was evidently unaware of the removal of his relics to
Huntingdonshire[1]. Goscelin's Life of St. Ives mentions
the presence · of an 'inclyta matrona' named Ethelfledis
at the dedication of the church of Ramsey abbey in the
time of Abbot Eadnoth, 993–1008, and states that she
had founded the monastery at Eynesbury[2]. There were
several ladies bearing this name about this date[3], but it
is not possible to identify any of them with Goscelin's
Ethelfledis. Little reliance can be placed upon this late
eleventh-century writer of saints' lives, for he invented
such details as he lacked in compiling his lives of saints[4].
If the Crowland story preserved by Ordericus Vitalis can
be trusted, the body of St. Neot was at Eynesbury some
time before the end of the tenth century, and was handed
over by Leofgifu (*Leviova*), the lady of Eynesbury, to her
brother Turketul, abbot of Crowland, and it was said to
rest in that abbey at the time when Ordericus visited it[5].
This was about 1115[6]. It is a suspicious story, as, indeed,

[1] It is somewhat curious that the words ' sublevatus est' occur in the
British Museum transcript (B) and in Parker's and all the subsequent
editions of the Life, instead of the ' suatim utens' of the Corpus transcript, which was evidently the reading in the Cottonian MS. Was this
falsification of the text derived from a marginal note, which Parker
regarded as a gloss upon, or correction of, ' suatim utens'? As it stands
in the text, this interpolation is unintelligible.

[2] MS. Bodl. 285, fo. 102 verso, col. 1 (printed from a transcript in
Leland, *Itinerary*, iv. appendix, p. 22, ed. Hearne, p. 149). The text
in the *Acta Sanctorum*, Junii tom. ii. p. 290, does not contain this
passage.

[3] The Ramsey obituary records the death of ' Ethelfleda comitissa,'
wife of Ealdorman Æthelwine ' Dei Amicus,' in 977 (*Cartularium
Monasterii de Rameseia*, iii. pp. 165, cf. 166); and in 997 of another
countess of the same name, the wife of Ethelwold (an error for Ælfwold;
cf. *Vita S. Oswaldi*, p. 429), the brother of Æthelwine (ibid. i. 268;
iii. p. 167). The dates in the Ramsey obituary are seriously in error in
some cases.

[4] For an example of this see Introduction, p. c, note 2.

[5] Ordericus Vitalis, ed. Le Prevost, lib. iv. c. 16, ii. p. 283.

[6] Ibid. ii. p. 268; Delisle, in vol. v. p. xxxvi of Le Prevost's edition.

anything coming from that factory of fraud, Crowland, must be.

**75.** This chapter is due to the author, and its statements seem to be correct. Alfred mentions three daughters, the number here assigned to him, in his will [1]. In that instrument he also refers to his two sons, but the elder, Edward, is alone mentioned by name [2]. Florence of Worcester has an entry, not found in any existing MS. of the Chron., that the Clito Æthelweard, brother of King Edward, died on October 16, 922, and was buried at Winchester. An 'Æthelweard, frater regis,' witnesses a spurious Winchester charter bearing the name of King Alfred [3]. This is either derived from the present passage or from the 'Æthelweard, frater (*or* filius) regis,' who occurs frequently in the Winchester, Hyde, and Wilton charters ascribed to Edward the Elder [4]. Ælfthryth, who is here described as unmarried,

[1] *Cart. Sax.* ii. 178, 25, where he makes bequests to his eldest, his middle, and his youngest daughter.

[2] Ibid. ii. 177, 25; 178, 7.

[3] Ibid. ii. 207, 10. It contains a reference to payment of Danegeld, which was not known in Alfred's time.

[4] Ibid. ii. 232, 35; 241, 14; 242, 28; 244, 20; 247, 28; 249, 41; 251, 24; 253, 29; 257, 26; 261, 28; 262, 22 (Ealdereð); 271, 28; 273, 40; 275, 34; 285, 17; 289, 4; 293, 8; 295, 8; 298, 26; 301, 37 (called *episcopus* by a clerical error); 303, 33; 305, 7 (called *episcopus*). The Hyde *Liber Vitae* states that a son of Edward, named 'Ætheluuerdus Clito,' predeceased him (p. 6, 19). This is probably the Clito Æthelweard of Florence. Nothing is otherwise known of this son of Edward, the Ethelwardus of William of Malmesbury, *Gesta Regum*, c. 120 (p. 136), being probably an instance of the common confusion by twelfth-century writers of Æthel- and Ælf-. The death of Edward's son Ælfweard is entered in the Chron. under 924. It is possible that this Æthelweard, son of King Edward, may be due to the writer of the account in the Hyde book taking Edward's brother for his son, either through mistaking *frater* for *filius*, or because the latter witnessed as 'filius regis,' meaning son of King Alfred, not of the reigning king. Thus the 'Oswealdus, filius regis,' who witnesses a genuine charter of Alfred, dated 875 (Brit. Mus. *Facs.* ii. pl. 40, early tenth cent. ?; *Cart. Sax.* ii. 159, 2), would seem to have been the son of one of Alfred's brothers, unless he was one of Alfred's children who died in infancy (line 5 above). He occurs with the same description in a doubtful Winchester and a doubtful Abingdon charter bearing the name of King Æthelred (*Cart. Sax.* ii. 135, 37; 140, 11). On the other hand, it may be that Florence is in error in describing Æthelweard as brother of Edward the Elder. But he had probably some grounds for this, for if he met with 'Æthelweard Clito' without any other

became later the wife of Baldwin II of Flanders, the son of Judith, Alfred's step-mother[1]. Æthelflæd, the famous lady of the Mercians, is well known. Her marriage with Æthelred, ealdorman of the Mercians, is here referred to some date earlier than 893. She witnesses, as wife of Æthelred, a Worcester charter, dated 880, which, if genuine, must be a mistake for 887, with which year the Indiction agrees[2]. As Alfred's marriage occurred in 869 (c. 29), Æthelfled, who is described in the Life as the eldest child, could have been only eleven or twelve years of age in 880. She witnesses, next to Æthelred. another Worcester charter dated 889, which may be genuine[3]. Of Æthelgeofu little is known beyond this passage.

**75, 16 schola.** It is evident from c. 76, 33 that this was not a school in the modern sense of the term, but that it resulted from Alfred's causing the young nobles who were brought up, according to custom, in the court to be educated with his own children, and that he had added a sprinkling of promising youths of lowly origin, in accordance with his view expressed in the preface to his translation of Gregory's *Pastoral Care*[4]. His provision for the expenses of this school is described in c. 102, 17.

**76.** This chapter is the composition of the author. The interest of Alfred in Saxon literature, referred to in line 9, is in accordance with the evidence afforded by his works. Of his religious observances it is more difficult to procure proof, but his religious character, which is established independently of the Life by the testimony of his translations and his prefaces to them, renders it probable that the information conveyed by the author of the Life is true. It is easy also to believe that he was interested in the investigation of unknown things. We find evidences of this in his interviews with the Northmen Ohthere and Wulfstan, and in the

description he would naturally have concluded that he was the son of Edward.

[1] See Stubbs, William of Malmesbury, *Gesta Regum*, ii. p. xlv., note 4.

[2] *Cart. Sax.* ii. 167, 27, the date of which is accepted by Green, *Conquest of England*, p. 144, note 2.

[3] *Cart. Sax.* ii. 201, 15. Concerning this charter see Introduction, p. lxvi, note 3. and p. 151, note 2, and note to c. 22, 4, above.

[4] See Introduction, § 72, p. cvi, and § 89, p. cxxiv, above.

other additions of geographical information to his translation of Orosius. The improvement in the building of ships,
recorded in the Chron. under 897, which is directly ascribed
to him, is proof of his powers of observation and invention [1].
His interest in foreigners (line 21) is supported by the
independent evidence that he received Asser from Wales,
Grimbald from Frankland, and John the Old Saxon, while
we have proof of the employment of Frisians in his fleet in
the Chron. under 897. That work also records under 891
that three Scots from Ireland who landed in Cornwall
proceeded to his court, where they must have imparted to
the king the information given in this annal. Of his
reception of Danes we have evidence in the case of Ohthere
and Wulfstan. Thus we possess proof that he entertained
at his court or had in his service representatives of all the
races mentioned by the author of the Life, with the exception
of the Bretons (*Armorici*). The training of the sons of
the nobility at the court (line 32) seems to have been the
usual practice then as at later times, but the innovation of
teaching them letters (line 35 and c. 75, 13) was due to
Alfred's initiative.

**76, 31 ministeriales.** This is a Frankish-Latin term
not found in O.E. documents, and its use is due to the
Frankish element in the vocabulary of the author [2]. From
the time of Charles the Great the word was applied to
certain court officials, though not to those of the highest
rank, and has reference to the office (*ministerium*) about
the person of the emperor with which each of them was
charged [3]. The author uses the term correctly, for he
mentions the *ministeriales* after the *comites ac nobiles* and as
distinct from the *familiares*.

**76, 50 praestabuntur vobis.** This reading occurs in
the Old Latin version of the Bible in the St. Germain MS.[4],

---

[1] Cf. also the account in the present work of his invention of time-
candles, c. 104 sqq.

[2] See Introduction, § 58, p. xciv, above.

[3] See Waitz, *Deutsche Verfassungsgeschichte*, ed. 2, iii. 529; v. 323;
Brunner, *Deutsche Rechtsgeschichte*, i. 234 sqq.; R. Schröder, *Lehrbuch
der deutschen Rechtsgeschichte*, ed. 3, pp. 139, 433. The Frankish word
came into English after the Norman Conquest with a specialized sense,
and survives in the form 'minstrel.'

[4] Ed. Wordsworth, *Old Latin Biblical Texts*, no. 1, Oxford, 1883,

and in the eighth- or ninth-century Book of Armagh[1], and also in St. Hilary of Poitiers[2].

**76, 62 velut apis prudentissima.** The comparison of the gathering of information to the operations of bees in collecting honey occurs again in c. 88, 39. As we have suggested[3], the metaphor may be borrowed from Aldhelm, by whom it was elaborated even more than by the author of the Life[4]. The metaphor, which was common among classical[5] and later writers[6], was a favourite one with the writers of the Caroline renaissance. It is employed by Alcuin[7] and, in a passage that has several features in common with those in the Life, in the Life of St. Eloi[8]. It is also found in the ninth-century Life of St. Egil, abbot of Fulda, by Candidus[9],

[1] Wordsworth and White, *Novum Testamentum Latine*, Oxford, 1889–98.

[2] Sabatier, *Bibliorum Sacrorum Latinae Versiones Antiquae*, Remis, 1743.

[3] See Introduction, § 60, p. xcv, above.

[4] *De Laudibus Virginitatis*, c. 4 (ed. Giles, p. 3) : 'Attamen solertissimae apis industriam praedictis exemplorum formulis coaptari posse, uberrima rerum experimenta liquido declarant, quae roscido facessente crepusculo et exorto limpidissimi solis iubare densos extemplo tripudiantium turmarum exercitus per. patentes campos gregatim diffundunt. Modo melligeris caltarum frondibus seu purpureis malvarum floribus incubantes, mulsa nectaris stillicidia guttatim rostro decerpunt, et velut lento careni defruto, quod regalibus ferculis conficitur, avida viscerum receptacula certatim implere contendunt,' &c.

[5] Cf. Lucretius, iii. 9 ; Seneca, *Epist.* 84. § 3.

[6] Macrobius, *Saturnaliorum Praefatio*, § 5, which is merely a repetition of the words of Seneca.

[7] *Vita Sancti Willibrordi*, c. 4 : 'ex eorum propinquitate mellifluos pietatis carperet flores, et in sui pectoris alveario dulcissimos virtutum favos construeret.'

[8] Ed. Krusch, *Monumenta Germaniae Historica*, 'Scriptorum Rerum Merovingicarum' tom. iv. 679, 13 : 'quasi apis prudentissima diversos ex diversis flores legens, in alvearium sui pectoris optima quaeque recondebat.' It is possible that this is based upon the passage cited in the preceding note from Alcuin. Krusch believes that the Life of St. Eloi is a Carolingian production (p. 645).

[9] *Poetae Latini Aevi Carolini*, ii. 98, 20 :
Utque apis esuriens primo cum tempore veris
enitens paribus volitat per gramina pennis,
campigenosque sibi certat decerpere flores,
altius inde volans glaucas stridentibus alis
nunc salices, nunc namque pyrum platanumque nitentem
floribus ore legit, tiliam fervore recenti hinc
mellifluam satagit caeco sub condere tecto :

and is used by the Irish Sedulius[1], who wrote in Frankland about the middle of the century. In England it is found in the tenth century in Edgar's *Regularis Concordia Monachorum*[2], in the Life of St. Oswald of York[3], the Life of St. Dunstan[4], and in a letter written to Archbishop Æthelgar of Canterbury between 988 and 990[5].

**76, 68 quaerens extrinsecus quod intrinsecus non habebat, id est, in proprio regno.** This lack of scholars in Wessex is in accordance with what is stated in c. 24, 9, and is supported by Alfred's own evidence in the preface to his translation of Gregory's *Pastoral Care*[6].

**77.** This chapter is the composition of the author.

**77, 10 Plegmundum.** Plegmund became archbishop of Canterbury in 890, but it is probable that he was with Alfred some time before his election to the primacy. The Life is therefore probably correct in describing him as an instructor of the king before the latter had learned to read (c. 77, 10), that is before 887 (c. 87). The Life mentions Plegmund as one of the scholars who had been attracted by the king to his court before the arrival of the author, which seems to be referred to 884, but the date is not clear[7]. It is noticeable that Plegmund's name does not occur in Alfred's will, which was made between 873 and 888[8]. Werferth, bishop of Worcester, who is also mentioned by the Life as a literary assistant of the king, receives a considerable bequest. His arrival is assigned by

> haud secus hic iuvenis librorum carmine primum
> corticibus veluti rasis quis pascitur acris,
> donec vi quoque non propria, sed munere Christi
> proficiens aetate simul sensuque sagaci
> pasci promeruit umbrati nectaris haustu.

[1] *Liber de Rectoribus Christianis*, c. 20, ed. Mai, *Spicilegium Romanum*, Romae, 1842, viii, p. 67: 'sic et apes ex diversis floribus colligunt, quibus gratissimos favos artificiosa dispositione componunt, hos itaque apices velut enchiridion vestri sagacitas ingenii saepius transcurrendo perlegat.'

[2] *Cart. Sax.* iii. 423, 2; Selden, *Notae ad Eadmerum*, Opera, ii. 1614.

[3] Ed. Raine, *Historians of York*, i. 423.

[4] Ed. Stubbs, *Memorials of St. Dunstan*, p. 10.

[5] Ibid. p. 387.

[6] See below, p. 225, note 2.

[7] See Introduction, p. lxxii, above.

[8] See Introduction, p. lxvii, note 3, above.

the Life to an earlier date than that of Plegmund, and in this its testimony harmonizes with the evidence of the will, which would therefore seem to have been executed before Plegmund entered the king's service, or before he had been there long enough to earn Alfred's gratitude.

**77, 12 Æthelstan et Werwulfum, sacerdotes et capellanos.** The former is probably the alleged envoy of Alfred to Rome and India[1]. An 'Æðelstan presbiter' witnesses a Winchester charter dated 979, for 879[2], but he is described as 'dux' in another Winchester text[3]. An 'Æðelstan sacerdos' witnesses a Canterbury charter of 898[4], and an 'Æðelstan presbyter' occurs in a spurious Winchester charter of 901 in close proximity to a 'Werwulf presbyter[5],' and priests named Werwulf and Æthelstan witness side by side several other Winchester texts in 909[6]. But this raises a suspicion that the names may have been taken from the Life, and the Winchester chartulary is of such exceedingly bad repute that one cannot feel any confidence in the texts coming from it and bearing the name of Edward the Elder[7]. Æthelstan and Werwulf are mentioned in other charters[8], but there is not one that is

[1] See above. note to c. 65, p. 289.
[2] *Cart. Sax.* ii. 170, 15.
[3] Ibid. ii. 163, 12.
[4] Ord. Survey *Facs.* i. pl. 12 (see p. 290, note 1, above); *Cart. Sax.* ii. 220, 6.
[5] *Cart. Sax.* ii. 241, 19, 21; 242, 32, 34.
[6] Ibid. ii. 285, 25, 26; 289, 12, 13; 293, 16, 17; 295, 18, 19; 298, 34, 35; 300, 9, 10; 302, 5, 6; 303, 41, 42; 305, 7. Upon the first of these charters (Brit. Mus. *Facs.* iv. pl. 10), see p. 322, note 6, below.
[7] See p. 149, note 6, above.
[8] 'Æðelstan presbyter' occurs in a spurious Wilton charter of 901 (*Cart. Sax.* ii. 232, 26'), a Winchester one of 902 (ibid. ii. 252, 21, 23, 24, three of the name, evidently members of the monastery at Winchester), a Wilton text of 903 (ibid. ii. 253, 32, where he is described as 'mess(e-preost)'), and in Winchester charters of 904 and 909 (ibid. ii. 274, 3; 275, 39; 290, 26). An 'Æþelstan cle icus' of Winchester abbey is mentioned at ii. 280, 16; 290, 34. 'Werulf presbyter' witnesses a spurious Wilton charter of 892 (ibid. ii. 209, 23), a Malmesbury charter of about the same date, but without description (ibid. ii. 210, 23) and another of 901, where he is called 'minister' (ibid. ii. 228, 21). He occurs as 'presbyter' in a Hyde charter of 900 (ibid. ii. 261, 35, blundered into *Woenulf*), an Abingdon charter of 903 (ibid. ii. 255, 31), and in two from Winchester dated 904 (ibid. ii. 273, 41; 275, 37). In some of these the witnesses seem to have been taken from the Life.

altogether free from doubt. The Worcester chartulary, however, contains a demise for two lives to Werwulf the priest from Bishop Werfrith of Worcester, which was made in 899 'pro nostra antiqua sodalitate et sua fideli amicitia atque oboedientia[1].' This text seems to be genuine, and its evidence that Werwulf was a friend of Bishop Werfrith confirms the statement in the present chapter that he was a Mercian. Æthelstan is probably the person of that name who was consecrated bishop of Ramsbury upon the division of the West-Saxon sees in 909.

**77, 13 capellanos.** In c. 104, 2, 7, the 'capellani' are described as supplying the king with candles for measuring time. The word 'capellanus' is of exclusively Frankish origin, being at first the title of the clerks (*clerici capellani*) who were charged with the custody of the cope (*cappa*) of St. Martin[2], the most precious of the possessions of the Frankish kings. The place where it was kept was known as the 'capella.' From this has descended our meaning of 'chapel.' As early as 829 the term is applied to the emperor's private chapel in the palace at Aachen[3]. The early names for chapels were *oratoria, basilicae,* or *martyria*[4]. The chief chaplain, usually an eminent ecclesiastic, had naturally the care of the clerks of the palace, and filled the office represented later by the chancellor[5]. The imperial 'capella' remained long a school more for the service of the state than of the church, and many secular duties were discharged by its members[6]. The words 'chapel' and 'chaplain' do not appear to have reached England until the Norman Conquest[7], when the invaders brought with

---

[1] *Cart. Sax.* ii. 223, 7.
[2] See the quotation from Walafrid Strabo given in Waitz, *Deutsche Verfassungsgeschichte*, ed. 2, iii. p. 516, note 1, and Waitz's remarks on that and the following pages.
[3] Waitz, ibid. note 3, citing the annals ascribed to Einhard.
[4] E. Loening, *Geschichte des deutschen Kirchenrechts*, ii. 353.
[5] Waitz, vi. p. 345. See Schröder, *Lehrbuch der deutschen Rechtsgeschichte*, ed. 2, p. 483; Harry Bresslau, *Handbuch der Urkundenlehre*, i. p. 327.
[6] Waitz, vi. pp. 337, 340 sqq.
[7] *Capellae* in the modern sense are mentioned in clumsy Glastonbury forgeries bearing the dates 725 and 971 (*Cart. Sax.* i. 208, 41 ; 209, 20 ; iii. 575, 35), and in an equally clumsy Crowland fabrication bearing the date 1032 (*Cod. Dipl.* iv. 42, 8). Beda, *Hist. Eccl.* iii. c. 23, describes

them many other survivals of Frankish usages. With them 'chaplain' seems to have usually and predominantly its modern sense, but the tradition of the connexion with the chancery long existed[1]. It is, unfortunately, not clear whether the author of the Life uses the word in the later sense, or whether he applies it to clerks of Alfred's court, whom he found discharging duties corresponding roughly to those of the imperial 'capellani.' In both passages the word may be translated with either meaning without violating the sense. But from the date of the lost MS. it is probable that the word had the early meaning, and this seems to be supported by the description in the present passage of Æthelstan and Werwulf as 'sacerdotes et capellani,' which Florence of Worcester evidently considered as pleonastic, for he omitted the 'et capellanos.' But whatever may be the exact meaning to be given to the word in the Life, its appearance is clearly due to Frankish influence[2], a conclusion that holds good whether the Life be as old as it purports to be or as young as the date of the lost MS.

**78.** This chapter is due to the author.

**78, 3 Galliam.** Frankland was naturally the country that Alfred would send to for scholars. His father had in his service as secretary the Frank Felix[3]. The Frankish schools in Alfred's time were in a very efficient condition, and attracted scholars even from Ireland[4]. The selection of

a chaplain of a Northumbrian king as one 'qui ipsi ac familiae ipsius verbum et sacramenta fidei (erat enim presbyter) ministrare solebat.' In Leofric's *Missal*, p. 2 a, Leofric is described as a 'capellanus' of Edward the Confessor, but this passage was written after the Norman Conquest.

[1] The 'Constitutio Domus Regis,' which is in its present form as old as the beginning of the reign of Henry II, contains no trace of this connexion (*Liber Niger Scaccarii*, ed. Hearne, ed. 2, i. p. 341; *Red Book of the Exchequer*, ed. Hubert Hall, iii. 807). Eadmer, however, records under 1121 that Henry I appointed two clerks of his chapel, one of whom, Robert (de Sigillis), was keeper of his seal under the chancellor, to bishoprics (*Historia Novorum*, p. 290). It is more remarkable to find King John in 1207 describing Godfrey the Spigurnel (which was an office of the chancery connected with the sealing of the royal writs) as a 'servant of his chapel' (*Rot. Chartarum*, p. 169 a).

[2] See Introduction, § 58, p. xciv.

[3] See above, p. 225.

[4] See the passage in Heiric's preface to the *Vita Sancti Galli*, composed between 875-877, in which he dilates upon the eminence of the

scholars seems clearly to have been made with a view to the relationship of their native tongues to English [1].

A probable proof of Alfred's connexion with Frankish scholars is to be found in two anagrams in his honour, which have been printed from a ninth-century Berne MS. The first is written in the MS. in O.E. letters :

Admiranda mihi mens est transcurrere gesta
Ex arce astrifera cito si redis arbiter inde
Lex etiam docuit typice portendere Frede
Flagranti simul moles mundi arserit igne
Rex formasti habens melius gnarum, optime, flammis
Eripis atque chaos vincens, Christe, ipse necasti
Divino super astra frui per saecula vultu.

En tibi descendant e caelo Gratiae totae,
Laetus eris semper, Aelfred, per compita vitae
Fletus iam mentem sacris satiare querela,
Recte doces properans falsa dulcedine mure.
Ecce aptas clara semper lucrare taltan
Docte peregrinae transcurre rura sophiae [2].

**78, 4 Grimbaldum.** Goscelin, the eleventh-century hagiologist, who is said to have come from the famous Flemish monastery of St. Bertin of Sithiu [3], at St. Omer (Pas-de-Calais), wrote a Life of St. Grimbald, which has not come down to us [4]. In it he asserted that Grimbald came from the monastery of St. Bertin, and his statement is supported by the much higher authority of the *Liber Vitae* of Hyde Abbey [5], the monastery with which Grimbald was connected. This was written a century after Grimbald's

Frankish schools, by which, he says, even the Greeks were filled with envy (*Poetae Latini Aevi Carolini*, iii. p. 429).

[1] See note to c. 78, 4, p. 311, below.

[2] *Carmina Medii Aevi, maximam partem inedita . . . edidit Hermannus Hagen*, Bernae. 1877, p. 11, nos. 9, 10.

[3] Malmesbury, *Gesta Regum*, c. 342 (p. 389).

[4] An abstract of it is given by Leland in his *Collectanea*, ed. Hearne, i. p. 18, and portions of it are preserved in a lectionary of St. Bertin (Mabillon, *Acta Sanctorum Ordinis Sancti Benedicti*, sec. 5, p. 3). Abbot John of Ypres, who wrote in the fourteenth century a history of the monastery, cites a ' legenda, quam de ipso ⟨*scil.* Grimbaldo⟩ canimus in ecclesia Dei' (Martene and Durand, *Thesaurus Novus Anecdotorum*, iii. col. 510).

[5] Ed. Birch, p. 5.

death, but it is probably founded upon a tradition in the
monastery or upon some earlier record, and hence may be
accepted as true.  Grimbald was preceded or accompanied
by a letter from Fulco, archbishop of Rheims, 883–900,
recommending him to Alfred[1].  Fulco was abbot of
St. Bertin prior to his accession to the see of Rheims, and the
abbacy was afterwards conferred upon him, at the request
of the monks, in order to preclude Baldwin II, Count of
Flanders[2], who became the son-in-law of Alfred.  Baldwin
wished to become lay-abbot of the monastery, a position
subsequently obtained by him and handed on to his sons
Adalolf (who must surely have been named after King
Æthelwulf) and Arnulf the Old.  Upon the death of Abbot
Rodulf on January 4, 892, the monks of St. Bertin sent one
of their brethren named Grimbald to Fulco to seek his aid
against Baldwin.  The archbishop went to the king, and
eventually the abbacy was committed to him with the
consent of the monks[3].  Bishop Stubbs fixed the date
of Grimbald's arrival in England as subsequent to this
mission to Fulco[4].  But it is not certain that the envoy to

[1] Printed by Wise in his edition of Asser, p. 123, whence it is reprinted
in *Cart. Sax.* ii. p. 190.  Wise states in his notice to the reader that it
was communicated to him by Thomas Ford, M.A., rector of Banwell,
and that it was written 'in fine vetusti MS. Evangelii.'  Sir Thomas D.
Hardy has identified this as a tenth-century evangelary at Crowcombe
Court, Somerset, which contains Ford's autograph (*Second Report of the
Historical MSS. Commission*, appendix, p. 75).  He does not state that
the copy of the letter is in the same hand as the evangelary.  Stubbs
inferred that the copy was also written in a tenth-century hand, for he
states that the letter exists 'in manuscripts so ancient as to free it from
the taint of forgery' (Preface to Malmesbury, *Gesta Regum*, ii. p. xliv).
The only other MS. containing it is the late *Liber de Hyda*, pp. 31 sqq.
It, however, seems to be genuine.  There is no conceivable motive for
forging such a letter.  We can discover no grounds for Pauli's condemnation of it (*König Ælfred*, p. 195, note 2).  As Malmesbury, *Gesta
Regum*, c. 122 (p. 130), states that Grimbald was sent to Alfred at his
request by the archbishop of Rheims, he would seem to have been
acquainted with this letter.
[2] Folcwin, *Gesta Abbatum S. Bertini Sithiensium*, c. 98, ap. Pertz,
*Scriptores*, xiii. p. 624.  This work was written in 962.
[3] Ibid.
[4] Preface to Malmesbury, *Gesta Regum*, ii. p. xlv.  He had some
doubts as to the truth of the statements, for which he cites the
untrustworthy work of John of Ypres (ap. Martene and Durand, iii.
col. 533).

Fulco and Alfred's friend are one and the same, for Grimbald was not an uncommon name at St. Bertin's, and we
have, indeed, a record of a monk of this name who was
an old man in 944 [1], and may hence conceivably be the
same person as the envoy of 892. Goscelin placed Grimbald's arrival in England in 885, but no reliance can be
placed upon this date. He seems to have derived it from
the Life, and, it is worthy of note, from some copy that
was free from the error in the Cottonian MS. by reason of
which the events of 885, the last date mentioned previous
to this chapter, appear under 884 (c. 66). If we could
place any reliance upon the arrangement of the text by the
author of the Life, we should have to conclude that Grimbald came to Alfred's court at or about the same time as he
did himself, that is before 887 [2]. Archbishop Fulco writes
to Alfred, in the letter mentioned above, that he has unwillingly consented to accede to his request to send to him
Grimbald, a priest and monk (exactly the description given
of him in the Life), whom he highly valued. He does not
mention Grimbald's monastery, but as Fulco was abbot of
St. Bertin even after he became archbishop, it is probable
that Grimbald was a monk of that house. If Grimbald
was the envoy of the monks in 892 to Fulco, there might
be some reason for sending him to England to escape the
wrath of the violent Baldwin. John of Ypres makes him
flee thither out of fear of the count, but after the murder of
Fulco in 900.

Grimbald appears as a witness to a charter of 895 [3], but
it is a clumsy forgery of much later times [4]. He is thanked

[1] Folcwin, c. 107 (Pertz, xiii. p. 629, 22). This writer mentions two
monks of this name, 'quos ego iuvenculus et paene ultimus recordor in
hoc monasterio vixisse' (c. 111, ibid. p. 633, 1, 7, 12). As he did not
enter the monastery until 948 (c. 107, ibid. p. 629, 35), it is impossible
that either of these monks could be Alfred's 'magister,' for he died
in 902.

[2] See Introduction, p. lxxii, above. It is noticeable that the long
notices of Frankish events in the Chron. commence with 885, but there
is no proof that Grimbald or John the Old Saxon were the sources of
this information or the causes of the interest thus displayed in continental affairs. Possibly the author of the Life may have derived from
them some of the knowledge of Frankland displayed by him (Introduction, § 48, p. lxxviii, above).

[3] *Cart. Sax.* ii. 214, 5.          [4] See p. 201, note 4, above.

by Alfred in the preface to his translation of Gregory's
*Pastoral Care*[1], a fact that harmonizes with the statement
in the Life that Alfred sent to Gaul for him as a 'magister.'
This translation seems to have been written after the date
of the compilation of the Life[2], in which it is not mentioned.
Grimbald's death is entered as a 'mass-priest' (the description applied to him in the preface to the translation of
the *Pastoral Care*) in the Chron. under 903, an error for
902, the date preserved by the Annals of St. Neots[3].
Goscelin states that Grimbald became abbot of Newminster
(later Hyde), which was founded by Edward the Elder.
The history of the foundation of the abbey given in the
*Liber Vitae* informs us that Edward named him head of
the clerks in his new foundation[4]. He is not described
as abbot in the notice of his death in the Chron., and
his name does not appear in the list of abbots in the *Liber
Vitae*. The record of Grimbald's scholarship in the Life
caused him to be drawn into the apocryphal history of the
University of Oxford, which flourished and grew from the
fourteenth to the eighteenth century. It was this connexion
with the mythical history of Oxford that caused the fabri-
cator of Camden's interpolation (c. 83 b) to make him play
so important a part in his fraudulent attempt to prove that
the University existed long before Alfred's time.

Goscelin's statements that Alfred was received at St.
Bertin's by Grimbald on his first journey to Rome (in 853),
and that he afterwards sent John the priest (i. e. John the
Old Saxon) and Asser to bring him to England, are obviously inventions of this unscrupulous writer. He evidently
derived these names from the Life. It is possible that
Alfred became aware of Grimbald's character for learning
during the negotiations that preceded the marriage of his
daughter with Baldwin, which had not occurred at the time
when the Life was written[5].

[1] Ed. Sweet, p. 6, 21.
[2] See Introduction, p. cv, above.
[3] Page 143, above.
[4] Ed. Birch, p. 5 : ' Qui venerabilis pater, praefato rege astipulante,
clericorum huius ⟨monasterii⟩ praelatus congregationi, sanctae conversa-
tionis indesinenter dans operam, verbis operibusque eximiam vitam
agebat monasticam.'
[5] See p. 300, above.

The choice of John the Old Saxon and Grimbald as
literary assistants by the king was a very wise one, and
seems to have been largely dictated by the close relationship
of their native tongues with his own. An Old Saxon at
that time could have experienced little difficulty in understanding West Saxon. Grimbald, if he was a native of
the parts about St. Omer, would speak a mixed Frankish
and Saxon dialect[1], the former unaffected by the Old High
German sound-shift. His difficulties would be somewhat
greater than John's in understanding and speaking English,
but they could not have been very great. It is even
possible that his native tongue was little more removed
from English than Old Saxon, for St. Omer adjoins a
portion of Picardy (that round Boulogne), that seems from
the evidence of the local names to have been settled by
Saxons who were related to the conquerors of Britain even
more closely than the Old Saxons[2].

**78, 8 Iohannem.** This is, no doubt, the John who is
described as an Old Saxon in c. 94, 2. In his translation
of Gregory's *Pastoral Care*[3], Alfred thanks John, his 'mass-
priest,' for his assistance. Otherwise little is known of

---

[1] Archbishop Fulco, writing to the pope, describes the men of the
diocese of Térouanne (St. Omer) as 'barbaricae feritatis et linguae'
(Flodoard, *Hist. Remensis Ecclesiae*, c. iv. c. 3, ap. Pertz, *Scriptores*,
xiii. 561, 35). This was from the point of view of the Romance-speak-
ing people.

[2] See Waitz, *Das alte Recht der salischen Franken*, Kiel, 1846,
pp. 53 sqq. These names may be found in *Les Chartes de Saint-Bertin
. . . publiées par M. l'Abbé Daniel Haignerie*, Saint-Omer, 1886; in
Baron Tard's *Bibliographie historique de l'arrondissement de Saint-
Omer*, St. Omer, 1887; and in the *Cartulaires de l'église de Térouanne,
publiés par Th. Duchet et A. Giry*, St.-Omer, 1881; in the publications
of the Société des Antiquaires de la Morinie. M. Godefroi Kurth, *La
frontière linguistique en Belgique et dans le nord de la France*, published in the 'Mémoires couronnés et autres mémoires publiés par
l'Académie Royale . . . de Belgique,' collection in-8vo, vol. xlviii,
Brussels, 1895-8, i. 530 sqq., has collected forty-two instances of local
names ending with what he and other scholars conclude to be the
specifically English compound termination *-incthon, -incthun* (i e. O.E.
*-ingtun*). *Caestre, Caster, Chastre* (ib. i. 545), although not so described, seems to be quite as much peculiar to the English Saxons. The
frequency in English local names of *-ingham* renders it possible that
some of the Picard local names in *-eghem, -inghem*, &c. are not so exclusively Frankish as M. Kurth and other continental scholars hold.

[3] Ed. Sweet, 6, 22; 7, 22.

him [1]. His name occurs as a witness to several charters [2], but most of these are clearly spurious, and none of them can be accepted as evidence. His confusion with John Scotus is dealt with below [3].

**79.** This chapter is due to the author.

**79, 4 Dexteralium,** ' south.' See above, note to c. 35, 10.

**79, 7 Dene.** This *villa regia* in Sussex is, no doubt, the Dene (dat. sing.) of Alfred's will, in which it is bequeathed to Edward, the king's eldest son [4]. This seems to be Dean (Eastdean and Westdean), near Eastbourne, which in the time of Edward the Confessor was held by Goda, the king's sister [5].

**79, 9 famina,** ' words, conversation.' This word connects the work with the curious latinity of the *Hisperica Famina* [6], one feature of which is the excessive fondness for compounds in *-men*, very many of which are unknown to classical Latin [7]. *Famen* had a wide currency in Frankland in and after the time of Alfred, which was, no doubt, due to the influence of Celtic scholars. In the ninth century it is

---

[1] Mabillon, *Acta Sanctorum Ordinis Sancti Benedicti*, cent. iv, pars 2, p. 509, thinks that he came from the Westphalian monastery of Corvei, and that he was transferred to the mother-abbey of Corbie in Picardy, where many of the Old Saxons were educated after the conversion of their race.

[2] A.D. 892, *Cart. Sax.* ii. 209, 22, Wilton, spurious; 895, ibid. ii. 214, 7, Rochester, described as 'abbas,' spurious (see above, p. 201, note 4, upon this fabrication); 901, ibid. ii. 232, 26, Wilton, spurious; 904, ibid. ii. 261, 34, Hyde, spurious; ibid. ii. 273, 40, Winchester; ibid. ii. 275, 36, Winchester.

[3] See note to c. 95, p. 335, below.

[4] *Cart. Sax.* ii. 178, 7.

[5] *Domesday Survey*, i. 19, col. 1; 19 b, col. 1. Two tenants of Edward the Confessor in it are mentioned at 21, col. 2. See Introduction, p. lxxii, note 5, above.

[6] See Introduction, § 57, p. xci, above.

[7] The word is explained under *fare* ( = *fari* ) in a glossary printed by Cardinal Mai, *Classicorum Auctorum e Vaticanis Codicibus tom. VIII*, Rome, 1836, p. 215, 22, from a twelfth-century MS. The author of this glossary was strongly influenced by Hisperic Latinity. The glossary contains several French and English words, the entry of ' Anglia, nomen patriae; inde Anglus, et Anglicus, et Anglice, et Anglisso, id est Anglice loqui,' and a quotation from the Life of St. Edmund, p. 607, 9 (referring to c. 13 of Abbo of Fleury's *Passio S. Edmundi*, c. 13).

found in the metrical Life of St. Gall [1], the metrical *Gesta Apollonii* [2], Abbo's poem on the siege of Paris [3], in the tenth century *Gesta Abbatum St. Bertini* [4], &c. It is glossed by *locutio* by a late tenth-century Frankish scholar [5]. In England it was used by Aldhelm [6], and it came into use again in the tenth century with other Frankish-Latin words. Fridegoda employs it in the early part of this century in his life of St. Wilfrid [7], and it occurs in a charter of King Edgar, dated 964, the original of which was in existence at Worcester in Hickes' time [8]; in the contemporary life of St. Dunstan [9]; in a letter written to Æthelgar, archbishop of Canterbury, in 988–90 [1]; and in Æthelweard's Chronicle [2]. The word occurs in a curious long-winded formula, which seems to date from the middle of the eleventh century, although it appears under the name of Edgar [3]. A dubious charter of 1006–12 also uses it [4].

**79, 11 sinistrali... parte,** 'north side.' See above, note to c. 35, 10.

**79, 17 coronatus,** 'received the clerical tonsure.' Ducange has collected numerous instances of the use of *corona* in the sense of 'tonsure [5].'

**79, 33 Wintonia.** This has been usually taken to refer to Winchester. But this is difficult to reconcile with the statement in the previous line that the author had returned to his country ('ad patriam remeavimus'), and that he took counsel with 'nostri omnes' (line 45), evidently the religious

---

[1] Ed. Dümmler, *Poetae Latini Aevi Carolini*, ii. p. 446, 666; p. 458, 1156.

[2] Ibid. ii. p. 501, 593.

[3] Ed. Winterfeld, *Poetae Latini Aevi Carolini*, iii. p. 102, 144.

[4] Ed. Pertz, *Scriptores*, xiii. p. 614, 42.

[5] Ed. Schepps, in the *Neues Archiv*, ix. 183, glossing the *Gesta Apollonii*.

[6] *Opera*, ed. Giles, 138, 22; 156, 15; 180, 29; 194, 17; 198, 20. Cf. 109, 3; 112, 8, 9.

[7] Line 270, ed. Raine, *Historians of York*, i. p. 117.

[8] *Cart. Sax.* iii. 376, 19; Hickes, *Thesaurus*, i. p. 139.

[9] Ed. Stubbs, *Memorials of St. Dunstan*, pp. 16, 22.

[1] Ibid. p. 386, 5.

[2] *Mon. Hist. Brit.* 509 E.

[3] *Cart. Sax.* iii. 253, 29; 257, 5; 450, 24; 584, 14; 594, 9; *Cod. Dipl.* iii. 265, 13, 16.

[4] *Cod. Dipl.* iii. 354, 26, Chertsey.

[5] Cf. Aldhelm's letter to King Gerontius (*Opera*, ed. Giles, p. 85, 29).

of St. Davids, without any other mention of his proceeding
from Winchester to Wales, and of his returning to the
former. The improbability of his lying ill for twelve months
in Winchester without Alfred's having any knowledge of his
presence in his kingdom forms one of the chief articles in
the indictment against this work [1]. All the difficulties are
obviated if we identify Wintonia with Caerwent (*Venta
Silurum*) instead of Winchester (*Venta Belgarum*). We owe
this suggestion to George North, a capable antiquary of the
eighteenth century [2]. In its favour may be urged that in
the tenth century and, no doubt, in the ninth, Caerwent
was called *Guentonia* by Welshmen when writing Latin [3].
There was an abbey there [4], where a travelling ecclesiastic
would be likely to stay, and it was on the great Roman road
to South Wales, by which a traveller from Wessex to St.
Davids would proceed. The alteration of *Guentonia* into
*Wintonia* would be a natural one for an English scribe to
make [5], and the presence of the English form in the Cottonian
MS. may be taken as a proof that the latter was not the
autograph text of the Welsh author. Possibly some of the
other cases of initial *w* for *gu* are also due to alterations by
the English copyists. It is possible that Asser was a native
of the diocese of Llandaff [6], and may therefore have been
quite at home in Caerwent.

**79, 34 in qua.** This has been generally taken as

[1] See Introduction, § 74, p. cx, above.
[2] He has written in his copy of Wise's edition of the Life, which is
preserved in the Bodleian Library (Gough, *Sax. Lit.* 205), against this
passage : ' Nullus dubito, quin cuivis hanc paginam attente legenti mea
sententia perplacebit, quod civitatem Belgarum, hodie Winchester, ne-
quaquam innuebat Asserius, sed Ventam Silurum sive Caergwent, in
comitatu Monmouth, quae, quamvis hodie penitus diruta, ad tempus
Giraldi Cambrensis manebat.' In the reference to Giraldus he has
confused Caerwent with Caerleon-on-Usk.
[3] *Liber Landavensis*, ed. Rhys and Evans, p. 220, 11, from a record
of 955.
[4] Ibid. p. 222, 6, 'abbas Guentoniae urbis.' A ' lector urbis Guenti '
occurs at p. 243, 28. St. Malo was born in Gwent (*regio Wenti*,
according to the ninth-century life by Bili (*Vie inédite de Saint-Malo . . .
publiée . . . par le R. P. Fr. Plaine, O. S. B.*, Rennes, 1884, p. 36;
Leland, *Collectanea*, iv. p. 14).
[5] Giraldus Cambrensis uses the anglicized form *Winta* for Gwent
(*Opera*, iii. p. 386, 9).
[6] See Introduction, § 42, p. lxx, above.

referring to *Wintonia*, and stress has been laid upon the improbability of the author's lying ill of fever for twelve months in Winchester [1]. But it is equally possible that the antecedent is *febris* [2]. The statement that he suffered from the fever without hope of life for twelve months and a week, by day and by night, as he adds with his characteristic love of unnecessary detail, is certainly an exaggeration. We may suspect an error in the number of the months, but the time was evidently a long one, for six months (line 28) and a little more must have elapsed before Alfred sent to inquire after him, and he tells us that he was even then unable to ride to him.

**79, 38 indiculos,** 'letters.' So *indiculum* in line 40. The Frankish character of this word may be seen from the quotations given by Ducange, who, with his marvellous sagacity, recognized that this word lurked under the blundered *indiluculos, indiluculum* of the printed texts of the Life. It is used in its original sense of short list or index in a note written in 359 in reference to the number of verses in the Bible [3], and Symmachus employs it in the same sense [4]. The development from this meaning to that of 'letter' appears to be due to Frankish latinity. In England the word is seldom met with, but it was introduced into this country with other Frankish-Latin words in or before the early part of the tenth century. It is used in the attestation clause of Æthelstan in a contemporary charter of 931, where the deed itself is described as 'huius indiculi fulcimentum [5],' a formula that occurs in other charters of this king from later chartularies [6], and, with other words instead of *fulcimentum*, in several other texts derived from

---

[1] See note to c. 79, 33, on the preceding page.

[2] It has been so regarded by Joseph Stevenson in his translation, p. 467, and by Mr. Conybeare, p. 107. Dr. Giles, in his version, p. 71, refers it to Winchester.

[3] Printed from a ninth-century copy by Mommsen in *Hermes*, xxi. pp. 144, 146. Cf. Karl Dziatzko, *Untersuchungen über ausgewählte Kapitel des antiken Buchwesens*, Leipzig, 1900, p. 159, note 1.

[4] *Epist.* vi. 48; vii. 82, ed. Otto Seeck, *Mon. Germ. Hist.*, 'Auctores Antiquissimi,' vi. part 1.

[5] Brit. Mus. *Facs.* iii. pl. 3; *Cart. Sax.* ii. 364, 31.

[6] A.D. 931, *Cart. Sax.* ii. 361, 10, Abingdon; A.D. 932, ibid. ii. 379, 36, Winchester; 385, 2, Shaftesbury; 388, 4, Hyde.

chartularies [1], most of which seem to be genuine. It occurs
in the somewhat dubious 'indiculum libertatis de Osuualdes
Lauues Hundred' of about 964 [2], but this rubric may be
a later addition.

**79, 57 Nobis.** The death of Bishop Nobis of St. Davids
is recorded in the *Annales Cambriae* under 873 : 'Nobis et
Mouric moriuntur.' His accession to the see of St. Davids
is entered under 840 : 'Nobis episcopus in Miniu [3].' The
*Annales* are principally concerned with this diocese [4].

**80.** This chapter is due to the author.

**80, 3 Hemeid.** The death of Himeyd is entered in
the *Annales Cambriae* under 892 : 'Himeyd moritur.' He
was king of Dyfed [5], *Demetia* (in O.E. *Deomedum, Deomodum,*
dat. pl., of the inhabitants), which comprised Pembrokeshire
and part of Carmarthenshire [6].

**80, 5 Rotri.** Rhodri Mawr (the Great), king of
Gwyneth, who acquired the rule of the whole of North and
Mid-Wales and Cardigan. The account given by the
present work of his oppressions of Dyfed agrees with what
is known of Welsh history of this date, which, however,
mentions four sons of Rhodri only [7]. The Welsh evidence
is so very fragmentary that we cannot argue that the author
is wrong in the number of Rhodri's sons. The statement
that the South-Welsh princes sought the protection of Alfred
rests solely upon the authority of this work, but the frag-

---

[1] *Cart. Sax.* ii. 311, 32 ; 350, 20 ; 359, 10 ; 393, 12 ; 395, 19 ; 400, 12 ;
401, 30 ; 404, 4 ; 406, 33 ; 408, 19. In the texts at ii. 363, 3 ; 369, 5,
and 373, 21 *singraphae* is substituted for *indiculi,* and the entire phrase
is represented by *hunc indiculum* at ii. 317, 2 ; 424, 3 ; 425, 14.

[2] Ibid. iii. 382, 1.

[3] See Mr. Egerton Phillimore's admirable text of the Harleian MS.
3,859, a twelfth-century MS. that preserves the tenth-century form of
this compilation, in *Y Cymmrodor,* ix. p. 141 sqq.

[4] Phillimore, l. c., p. 145. The *Nouis* of the *Liber Landavensis,* ed.
Rhys and Evans, p. 216, 14, appears to be another bearer of this name.
'Nobis, episcopus Teiliau' (Llandaff) witnesses a grant entered in an
early ninth-century Welsh hand in the Book of St. Chad (see the
facsimile and text in *Liber Landavensis,* p. xlvi). It is not clear that
he is the person who became later bishop of St. Davids. See Introduction,
p. lxxi, note 3, above.

[5] See Rhys and Jones, *The Welsh People,* pp. 145, 150.

[6] See Mr. Phillimore's note in Owen's *Pembrokeshire,* i. 199, note 2.

[7] Rhys and Jones, *The Welsh People,* pp. 144 sqq. See also *Dict. of
Nat. Biography,* xlviii. p. 85.

mentary annals of Wales of this period show that the 'Saxons' had considerable relations with South Wales. Rhodri himself is recorded to have been slain by the Saxons in 876 in the *Annales Cambriae*.

**80, 6 Houil filius Ris, rex Gleguising.** Howel (Higuel) is recorded in the *Annales Cambriae* as dying in Rome in 885 [1], but his death is referred to 894 by the Gwentian *Brut* [2]. He witnesses deeds in the time of Bishop Cerenhir of Llandaff [3], and of Bishop Nud [4], and of Bishop Cyfeilog [5].

**80, 6 Brochmail atque Fernmail filii Mouric, reges Guent.** They witness, under the later Welsh forms Brochvail and Fernvail, with their father Mouric, a grant made to Llandaff in the time of Bishop Nud [6]. 'Brochmail filius Mouric' is recorded as a donor to Llandaff in the time of Bishop Cyfeiliog (*Cimeilliauc, Civeilliauc*, the successor of Nud), and he confirmed two grants made to that prelate [7]. This is the 'Camelgeac' who was redeemed from the Danes, who had captured him in Archenfield, by King Edward in 915 [8]. He is recorded, upon somewhat doubtful authority, to have been consecrated by Æthelred, archbishop of Canterbury, 870–89 [9].

---

[1] Ed. Phillimore, *Y Cymmrodor*, ix. p. 166.

[2] Haddan and Stubbs, *Councils*, i. p. 207. See Heinrich Zimmer, *Nennius Vindicatus*, Berlin, 1893, p. 70.

[3] *Liber Landavensis*, p. 212, 15.

[4] Ibid. pp. 227, 12 ; 229, 12, 23 ; 230, 6, 20 ; 231, 8.

[5] Ibid. p. 236, 20. The cross at Llantwit, co. Glamorgan, erected by Houelt to the memory of Res, his father, has been assigned to this king (Haddan and Stubbs, *Councils*, p. 626 ; Hübner, *Inscriptiones Britanniae Christianae*, p. 24, no. 63). But Professor Rhys has pointed out that Houelt is not the same name as Howel (*Archaeologia Cambrensis*, 1899, p. 155).

[6] *Liber Landavensis*, p. 226. The Welsh Annals record that Mouric was slain by the Saxons in 849. The death of another Mouric is entered in 873. The *Brut y Tywysogion* calls the latter a bishop, which may, however, be an erroneous extension of an abbreviation referring to Bishop Nobis, whose death is recorded in the same sentence.

[7] Ibid. pp. 232–5.

[8] Chron. C, D, and E, Florence of Worcester. Chron. A, which is three years in advance of the real dates hereabouts, enters it under 918.

[9] Ralph Diceto, *Abbreviatio Chronicorum*, ed. Stubbs, i. 138. See Haddan and Stubbs, *Councils*, i. 208. He was bishop before the death of King Howel (*Liber Landavensis*, p. 236), which seems to have occurred in 885 (*Annales Cambriae*, as in note 1, above).

**80, 8 Eadred, comitis.** This is clearly Æthelred, ealdorman of the Mercians, who is called Æthered[1] in line 22. The confusion of Æthered with Eadred is not uncommon in late records, and it must in this case be due to the carelessness of the scribe of the Cottonian MS.

**80, 10 Helised, filius Teudubr, rex Brecheniauc.** Teudur, son of Elised, king of Brecknock, is mentioned in the *Liber Landavensis* during the episcopacy of Bishop Libiau, 927–9[2].

**80, 13 Anaraut.** Anarawd, son of Rodri Mawr, king of Gwyneth. The Welsh Annals record that in 894 Anarawd with the English wasted Cardigan and Ystrat Towi, and that he died in 915. As the present work purports to have been written in 893 (c. 91, 4), Anarawd's submission to Alfred must have happened in or before that date, a conclusion that is confirmed by the Welsh evidence that he was acting with the English in 894, and by the record in the Chron. of the co-operation of some of the North-Welsh with the English in 894 (=893)[3]. Green's statement that the sons of Rodri submitted to Alfred in 897[4] is based upon some error.

**81.** This chapter is due to the author.

**81, 9 Leonaford.** In form this would seem to be a compound of the gen. plural of O.E. *lēo*, 'lion,' but such a name is highly improbable in England. It is likely that a second *n* has been omitted by the scribe of the Cottonian MS.[5], and that the name was really *Leonanford*, probably

---

[1] Upon this form of Æthelred see *Crawford Charters*, p. 109, where several ninth-century instances are given.

[2] Page 237, 27.

[3] No objection to the accuracy of the information conveyed by the author of the Life can well be founded upon the statement of Malmesbury, *Gesta Regum*, c. 134 (p. 148), that no English king before Æthelstan had reduced the North-Welsh princes to pay him tribute, even if this information was taken from the contemporary Latin Life of King Æthelstan that was used by Malmesbury, the source whence Malmesbury derived most of his information concerning this ruler (see p. 184, note 4, above).

[4] *Conquest of England*, p. 183.

[5] The *n* in such a position is frequently omitted about the date of this MS. Cf. for instance *Hlidaford* and *Beardastapol*, for *Hlidan-* and *Beardan-*, in the contemporary endorsement, 1016–20, in the *Crawford Charters*, no. IV, 131.

derived from a river or brook *Leone* (cf. the river Leen, co. Notts). The place has not been identified. Such a name would appear in Domesday as *Leneford*, or, with a common confusion therein of *en* and *an* due to French influence, as *Laneford*. In many cases this substitution of *an* for *en* (which would have regularly developed into *in*) has persisted in local names owing to the influence of written forms in legal documents. Hence we get compounds of O.E. *hēan-*, the weak dat. sing. of *heah*, 'high,' represented in modern local names by *Han-*, *Hen-*, and *Hin-*. In the first case an excrescent *d* is sometimes developed, as in the case of Handley, co. Dorset[1]. In like manner, Blandford, co. Dorset, has been produced from the *Bleneford* of Domesday[2], which may represent an O.E. *Bleonan-ford* or a similar compound with a different vowel or diphthong in the first syllable. It is therefore probable that Leonaford would now occur in the shape of Landford, more especially as this is a name that conveys a meaning to the ordinary Englishman. We may therefore suggest that Leonaford is the modern Landford, in the Hundred of Frustfield, co. Wilts. The growth of the *d* in this name can be proved, for the thirteenth and fourteenth century forms of it are *Laneford*[3]. It was a royal manor, but it is unfortunately not mentioned in Domesday. Early forms of it are difficult to discover, as it is seldom named in mediaeval records. The Hundred of Frustfield is constituted by Landford and Whiteparish. They both appear to be later divisions of Frustfield, Whiteparish being the Abbodestun of the *Nomina Villarum*. In 968 King Edgar granted to Wilton Abbey three hides in Frystesfeld or Fyrstesfeld[4], which is probably part of Whiteparish. The charter is proof that the royal house of Wessex possessed land in this neighbour-

---

[1] It appears in Domesday, i. 78 b, col. 2, as *Hanlege*, but the O.E. form was plainly *Heanleage* : cf. *Cart. Sax.* ii. 149, 1 (the *Hanlee* of ii. 148, 11, and iii. 159, 19 is due to the late scribe of the Shaftesbury Chartulary).

[2] It is written *Bleneford* six times and *Blaneforde* thrice.

[3] *Testa de Nevill*, p. 141 b; *Rot. Hund.* ii. 237 b; *Inquisitiones post Mortem*, 20 Edw. I, no. 21, and 18 Edw. III, no. 49.

[4] Dugdale's *Monasticon*, ii. 323, from the early thirteenth-century Wilton chartulary. This charter has been overlooked by Kemble and Birch.

hood, and we can hardly be wrong in concluding that Landford was part of Fyrstesfeld that was retained in the king's possession. Melchet Park or Forest, which is also in the Hundred, was a favourite hunting-place of the Plantagenets, and the facilities for sport afforded by the neighbourhood may have been the reason for Alfred's stay there. His house had many estates in South Wilts, and the identification of Landford with Leonaford has therefore much in its favour. We have, however, been unable to find any post-Conquest forms *Leneford*, and in their absence the identification must remain somewhat doubtful.

**81, 21 in duobus monasteriis.** This reference to the gift by the king of the two monasteries with everything in them to the author, is, in our opinion, an argument against the composition of the Life at the end of the tenth century. After the monastic reforms introduced by Æthelwold and Dunstan in the reign of King Edgar, such a disposition of a monastery would be, to say the least, unusual. Beda draws a picture of the state of religion in Northumbria in his time, in which one of the greatest abuses is the purchase and ownership of monasteries by laymen and others[1]. We have instances of the granting of monasteries by kings in the eighth century[2], but to members of religious orders. It is clear that the same system existed until the time of Æthelwold and Dunstan, for we find an instance of the purchase of a monastery as late as the time of Æthelstan[3].

**81, 22 Cungresbyri et Banuwille.** According to a statement written by Giso, bishop of Wells, 1061–88, Duduco, his predecessor, gave to the bishopric all the possessions that he had acquired in hereditary right from the king, including the towns of Congresbury and Banwell[4].

---

[1] *Epistola ad Ecgbertum Episcopum*, c. 12.

[2] *Cart. Sax.* i. 331, 23. Cf. the interesting case of Bath, ibid. i. 335, 23.

[3] *Vita S. Oswaldi*, ed. Raine, *Historians of York*, i. 411. Folcwin, *Gesta Abbatum S. Bertini*, c. 107, ap. Pertz, xiii. p. 629, records that King Æthelstan gave the monastery at Bath (*Ad Balneos*) to some of the monks who had left St. Bertin's as a protest against the introduction of reform.

[4] From the copy set out in the twelfth-century history of the bishopric printed by Joseph Hunter in *Ecclesiastical Documents*, Camden Society, 1840, p. 15.

They were taken into Harold's hands, and the former is returned in Domesday as being in the king's possession, while the latter is held by the bishop[1]. Nothing is known of them in the interval between the death of Asser and the gift to Duduco, but the latter is evidence that they were royal possessions, and hence may well have been given to the author by Alfred. Nothing is known of the monasteries there beyond the present passage.

**81, 28 Exanceastre, cum omni parochia . . . in Saxonia et in Cornubia.** The word *parochia* means in the latinity of this period 'ecclesiastical diocese.' Nothing, however, is known of a diocese of Exeter prior to the transference thither of the see of Crediton in 1050[2]. This portion of the Life was written in a hand some fifty years or so older than this date, a fact that puts out of court the attempts that have been made to prove that the work is a forgery of later date than the removal of the see to Exeter[3]. Apart from the Life, Asser is known as bishop of Sherborne[4], but we have no proof that he occupied that see so early as the date of the composition of the Life, although there is nothing except this passage to prove that he did not. Haddan has concluded that this passage means that Alfred organized a new diocese out of Devon and some small part of Cornwall, and that on Asser's succession to the see of Sherborne (which is categorically assigned to 900) this new diocese became merged in that of Sherborne[5]. Lingard thought that Asser became bishop of the western portion of the diocese of Sherborne, which, he holds, then extended to Land's End[6]. Freeman, who adopts Haddan's

---

[1] *Domesday Book*, i. 87, col. 1 ; 89 b, col. 1. For the details connected with Giso's claim to these estates see Freeman, *Norman Conquest*, ii. appendix SS.

[2] Bishop Leofric, who transferred the see, is described in his *Missal*, ed. Warren, p. 2, as 'primus episcopus factus est Exoniensis ecclesiae.'

[3] See Introduction, § 69, p. ciii ; § 76, p. cxi, above.

[4] See p. lxv, above.

[5] Haddan and Stubbs, *Councils*, i. pp. 673, 675.

[6] *History of the Anglo-Saxon Church*, ii. p. 423. He was led to make this suggestion under the erroneous impression that a copy of Alfred's version of Gregory's *Pastoral Care* was dedicated to 'Wulfsige, bishop of Sherborne,' Asser's predecessor. Asser is described as 'my bishop' by the king in his preface to this work, and therefore Lingard's conclusion was just if 'Wulfsige, bishop of Sherborne' had been men-

suggestion, states that 'whatever we may say about Devonshire, it is quite certain that the diocese of Sherborne did
not take in Cornwall[1].' This, however, is a mistake, for we
have evidence to the contrary. The profession of Kenstec
'⟨ad⟩ episcopalem sedem in gente Cornubia in monasterio,
quod lingua Brettonum appellatur *Dinnurrin*, electus,' made
to Ceolnoth, archbishop of Canterbury, 833–70, has been
preserved[2]. The site of his see is unknown[3], and nothing
else beyond this profession is known of him. It is possible
that Asser succeeded him as bishop of Devon and Cornwall. It was not until the time of Æthelstan, in or about
926, that we have a record of another bishop of these
shires. The first bishop of Crediton, Eadwulf, was then
consecrated as diocesan of these two counties[4]. It is
noticeable that his bishop-stool at Crediton was within
a few miles of Exeter, so that the causes that led Alfred to
place Asser at Exeter were still operative in his grandson's
time. The see of Crediton would thus seem to be a revival
of that held by Asser, and possibly that of Kenstec. We
have evidence in the letter of Dunstan concerning the
bishopric of Cornwall, which was written between 980 and
988[5], that Cornwall was in the diocese of Sherborne until
the consecration of the first bishop of Crediton. The letter is
a report concerning the disposition of three estates in Cornwall that were given by King Ecgberht to the church of Sherborne. It states that, upon the division of the West-Saxon
sees, they were assigned to the first bishop of Crediton.
There is no contemporary record of this division of the
sees, but some dubious Winchester charters refer it to 909[6].

tioned in the copy of the *Pastoral Care* referred to by him. But the
addition 'of Sherborne' does not occur in the MS. See Introduction,
p. cv, above.

[1] *King Ine*, part 2, p. 20 (in the *Somersetshire Archaeological and
Natural History Society's Proceedings*, vol. xx, 1874).

[2] Haddan and Stubbs, i. p. 674; reprinted in *Cart. Sax.* ii. p. 145.

[3] Haddan's suggestion that it is a mistake for Dingerein, the site of
which is also unknown, is not convincing.

[4] This appears from the letter of Dunstan cited below.

[5] *Crawford Charters*, no. vii, contemporary.

[6] *Cart. Sax.* ii. 283, 1 ( = 286, 4); 297, 9; 299, 12; 302, 27. These
texts, with the exception of the first, are derived from the Winchester
chartulary, and they are all of a very suspicious nature. Bishop Stubbs,
who accepts their evidence as fixing the division of the bishoprics in this

This was the year of Asser's death[1], and would thus be a suitable time for dividing the see of Sherborne[2]. From Dunstan's letter it is plain that the three estates in Cornwall were originally given to the bishop of Sherborne, for they were handed over to the first bishop of Crediton as diocesan, and Dunstan and the bishops recommended that they should be assigned to the recently consecrated bishop of Cornwall.

We have thus proof that Cornwall and Devonshire were in the diocese of Sherborne, and that in Dunstan's opinion the connexion was not severed until the division of the West Saxon dioceses after the death of Asser. Dunstan makes no mention of Kenstec, who was evidently not interested in the three Cornish estates, or of Asser. The latter, however, must, as bishop of Sherborne, have been in possession of these estates. Thus there would be no need to mention that he had held them as bishop of Devon and Cornwall before his succession to the see of Sherborne. There is nothing in the evidence at our disposal that conflicts with Lingard's suggestion that the present passage means that Alfred made Asser bishop of the western portion of the old diocese of Sherborne, an appointment for which his Welsh origin would peculiarly fit him, for Celtic was still spoken in Devonshire as well as in Cornwall[3].

year, states that the charter at p. 283 exists in an ' original tenth-century charter' (preface to Malmesbury, *Gesta Regum*, ii. p. lvi, note 3). It is reproduced in the Brit. Mus. *Facs.* iv, pl. 10, and is written in what must be a very late tenth-century hand, but is more probably an early eleventh-century one. It is one of the long series of forgeries intended to establish the reduction of the hidage of Chilcomb from a hundred hides to one. We have no indications that such reductions of hidation were known before the introduction of Danegeld, and no evidence beyond the Winchester charters that such reductions were made by royal charters. These suspicious texts speak not of the division of the West-Saxon dioceses into five bishoprics, but of that of Winchester into two.

[1] See Introduction, § 39, p. lxv, above.

[2] It is, however, noticeable that the letter and the other documents connected with this division (upon which see *Crawford Charters*, p. 103) state that the bishop appointed to Sherborne was Wærstan, who in the lists of bishops succeeds Æthelward, Asser's immediate successor.

[3] See above, p. 249. It is noticeable that Alfred in his will (*Cart. Sax.* ii. 178, 9', after mentioning his Devonshire estates at Axmouth, Branscombe, Cullompton, Tiverton, Exminster, Luton, and two others,

**82.** From the Chronicle, adding the description of the site of Paris, which is correctly placed in the realm of the West Franks, and of the lines of the Danish intrenchments [1], and the record of the failure of the attempt to capture Paris [2], which is not mentioned in the Chronicle. The version of the Chronicle used by the author agreed with MSS. B, C, D, and E, against A in mentioning that the winter quarters of the Danes were at Paris. It is obvious that the careless scribe of A overlooked 'æt Paris þære byrig' in his original.

**83.** From the Chronicle, adding the reference to the burning of towns and the slaying of men. The author translates the 'gesette' of the Chron. by 'restauravit et habitabilem fecit,' but it is not clear whether the first is intended as a rendering of the ambiguous O.E. verb, which may mean 'to settle with inhabitants' or 'to restore,' or is the result of a deduction by him that the 'burh' of London must have been restored before it could be repeopled or re-garrisoned. His reference to the condition of London is probably due to personal knowledge, for the MS. of the Chron. used by him contained no reference to its siege [3].

**83, 7 aut cum paganis sub captivitate erant.** This is a mistranslation of 'þæt buton Deniscra monna hæftniede was,' literally the part of the English folk 'who were without captivity to the Danish men,' i. e. who were not under Danish captivity.

**83 b.** This famous (or rather infamous) interpolation of Camden's is discussed in the Introduction [4]. Twyne's assertion that he had often seen it written separately at the beginning and end of many old books, such as Rosse and Richard of Cluni [5], is one of his desperate devices to

bequeaths also 'the lands that belong thereto, to wit, all that I have among the *Wealcyn* ⟨i. e. the Welsh of Cornwall and Devon⟩ except Triconscir' ⟨? the Hundred of Trigg, co. Cornwall⟩.

[1] This suggests that the author had been at Paris. It is one of several proofs of his acquaintance with Frankland. See Introduction, § 48, p. lxxviii, above. Cf. however p. 309, note 2, above.

[2] Cf. also c. 84, 3.

[3] See p. 289, above.

[4] See above, § 8, pp. xxiii sqq.

[5] *Antiquitatis Academiae Oxoniensis Apologia*, Oxford, 1608, lib. ii,

buttress up the authenticity of this passage. Rosse lived
at the end of the fifteenth century, and the addition, if it
ever existed, could hardly have been earlier than the
sixteenth century. Rosse's own account[1], which is founded
upon Higden and Thomas Rudbourne, is of even lower
value than the evidence of those writers. Richard of Cluni
was an eleventh-century Poitevin, and no MS. of his
chronicle is known to have been in England. Twyne
throughout his work frequently quotes marginal notes by
later writers as of equal value with the text to which they
were added. It is therefore probable that in this case
the 'most ancient hand' was little, if at all, older than
Elizabeth's time.

**84.** From the Chronicle, much expanded, adding the
mention of the mouth of the Marne and Yonne, and that
Chézy was a 'villa regia.' The latter is another proof of
the author's knowledge of Frankland[2].

**85.** From the Chronicle. The author has omitted the
mention in the Chronicle of the Danes passing beyond the
bridge at Paris, possibly regarding it as a repetition of that
represented in c. 84.

**85, 16 Hreni.** The substitution of this form for the
*Rin* of the Chron. is probably due to the Frankish preservation or revival of the classical form *Rhenus*[3].

**86.** From the Chronicle, adding that Æthelhelm was
ealdorman of the people of Wiltshire[4]. It is noteworthy
that the author has added that the mission to Rome occurred
in the same year as the Danes went from Paris to Chézy,

§ 81, p. 144 : 'Porro hunc Asserii locum non solum in iusto ⟨*leg.* isto⟩
exemplari, sed etiam in principiis ac fine multorum veterum librorum,
nominatim vero Rossi et Richardi Cluniacensis, seorsim antiquissima
manu scriptum saepe legi, ut nullus mihi de hoc loco dubitandi locus
restare videatur.'

[1] *Historia Regum Angliae*, ed. Hearne, p. 76. It is quoted by Twyne,
§ 172, p. 182.

[2] See Introduction, § 48, p. lxxviii, above.

[3] See the numerous quotations from Frankish sources given by Alfred
Holder, *Alt-Celtischer Sprachschatz*, ii, col. 1171 sqq.

[4] This is confirmed by the Chron. under 898, when Æthelhelm died.
Upon the alleged connexion between the alms carried to Rome and
Peter's Pence, see p. 211, note 2, above. As to Æthelhelm's possible
patronage of Archbishop Oda, see note to c. 94, 9, p. 334, below.

which is correct. The account in the Chronicle is somewhat obscured by the recounting under 887 of the proceedings of the Danes in France in the succeeding year.
**87.** This chapter is due to the author.
**88.** This chapter is due to the author.
**88, 6 libellum, quem in sinum suum sedulo porta-
bat.** This book is described in similar words in c. 24, 3.
The author does not state that this book of hours, psalms,
and prayers, was identical with the 'handbook' described
in c. 89, 20.
**88, 13 immensas . . . persolvi.** This seems to be
founded upon the words of Aldhelm : 'suscipiens, erectis
ad aethera palmis, immensas Christo pro sospitate vestra
gratulabundus impendere grates curavi [1].'
**88, 39 velut apis fertilissima.** See note to c. 76, 62,
above.
**89.** This chapter is due to the author.
**89, 11 in gabulo,** 'on the gallows or crucifix.' This is
a Celtic-Latin word (Old Irish *gabul*, Welsh *gafl*, 'fork ') [2],
which already occurs in Latin in Varro [3]. It is used by
Aldhelm [4], and occurs in an Abingdon charter of 1033 [5],
but is otherwise very rare in English Latin.
**89, 20 enchiridion, id est manualem librum.** This
was one of the Greek words in common use in the Frankish
Latin of this period [6]. The book itself seems to have been
still current in the time of William of Malmesbury, for he
cites it as 'Manualis Liber regis Elfridi' to prove the
relationship of Aldhelm to King Ine [7], and he also quotes

---

[1] *De Laudibus Virginitatis*, c. 2 (*Opera*, ed. Giles, p. 1, 20).
[2] See Brugmann, *Grundriss der vergleichenden Grammatik der indogermanischen Sprachen*, ed. 2, i. 575, § 638.
[3] Quoted in Nonius, ed. Lucian Müller, Leipzig, 1888, p. 166.
[4] *Opera*, ed. Giles, 7, 5; 42, 26; 180, 26.
[5] *Cod. Dipl.* iv. 47, 14.
[6] For example, the *Gesta Abbatum Fontanellensium*, ed. Löwenfeld,
c. 16, p. 47, c. 17, p. 54, 56, speak of the 'Enkiridion' of Saint Augustine
at Fontanelle. It was this work of St. Augustine's that gave the word
so great a currency. Regino recommends his abridgement of councils
to Archbishop Hatho, 'ut illum pro enkyridion habeatis, si quando
plenitudo librorum vestrorum in praesentia non est' (see Regino's
prefatory letter, printed in the introduction to Kurze's edition of his
Chronicle, p. xx).
[7] See p. 153, note 4, above. Faritius, abbot of Abingdon, who died

from it the story of Aldhelm's singing to the people in his
native tongue on the bridge at Malmesbury[1].

**90.** This chapter is due to the author.

**90, 3 Invigilant animi,** &c. We have been unable
to find the source of this verse, which expresses a sufficiently
common reflection[2]. From the use of the words *pia cura*
it would seem to be of Frankish origin, for the adjective
*pius* was, owing to its connexion with the imperial title,
an exceedingly favourite one with the Frankish writers of
Latin verse.

**91.** This chapter is due to the author. The king's
illness is described in almost the same words in c. 74.
He himself refers somewhat pathetically to the troubles of
his reign in his preface to his translation of Boethius[3].

**91, 15 Hiberniae.** This sentence is so corrupt that it
is difficult to decide whether Ireland or Spain (*Iberia*) is

in 1115 (*Chron. Monasterii de Abingdon*, ii. 290), seems also to refer
to the Handbook in the same connexion, for he says of King Ine that
Kenten ⟨Centwine, the father of Aldhelm⟩ was his brother, and that
he was 'virum probum, sanctitate lautum, honestate magnificum, anti-
quissimis Anglicanae linguae schedulis saepius ex interprete legendo
audivimus' (ed. Giles, *Sancti Aldhelmi Opera*, p. 356). Here the
Italian writer seems to have misunderstood the O.E. original, as appears
from Malmesbury's correction of the assertion that Centwine was brother
of Ine. Faritius was cellarer of Malmesbury before he became abbot of
Abingdon, and his Life of Aldhelm was, no doubt, written in the former
monastery, which seems to have possessed Alfred's Handbook or a copy
of it.

[1] In his Life of St. Aldhelm, in his *Gesta Pontificum*, c. 190, p. 336,
he says of Aldhelm: 'Litteris itaque ad plenum instructus, nativae
quoque linguae non negligebat carmina ; adeo ut, teste libro Elfredi, de
quo superius dixi ⟨in the quotation given at p. 153, note 4, above⟩, nulla
umquam aetate par ei fuerit quisquam. Poesim Anglicam posse facere,
cantum componere, eadem apposite vel canere vel dicere. Denique
commemorat Elfredus carmen triviale, quod adhuc vulgo cantitatur,
Aldelmum fecisse, adiciens causam, qua probat rationabiliter tantum
virum his, quae videantur frivola, institisse. Populum eo tempore
semibarbarum, parum divinis sermonibus intentum, statim cantatis missis
domos cursitare solitum. Ideo sanctum virum super pontem, qui iura et
urbem continuat, abeuntibus se opposuisse obicem, quasi artem cantitandi
professum. Eo plusquam semel facto, plebis favorem et concursum
emeritum.' The story is told somewhat differently by Faritius, who
alleges no authority for it.

[2] Cf. e. g. the *Iliad*, ii. 24, 61 ; Plato, *Leges*, 808 C.

[3] Ed. Sedgefield, Oxford, 1899, p. 1.

meant[1]. It would seem to be brought into connexion with the Mediterranean (if Wise's emendation of *Tyrreno* be accepted and extended to the Mediterranean), since the author adduces as final proof the correspondence with the patriarch of Jerusalem. But arguments from the arrangement of his material are somewhat uncertain. In favour of the reading *Hibernia* may be adduced the fact that the Chron. records under 891 the arrival in Cornwall of three Scots from Ireland, who proceeded to Alfred's court, and the sending by Alfred of gifts to that country mentioned in c. 102, 23.

**91, 16 de Hierosolyma ab El⟨ia⟩ patriarcha.** We have restored the original reading *patriarcha*, the form *patriarchae* in the printed texts being clearly an alteration made by Parker in order to make it agree with *Abel*, which he regarded as the genitive case. It is more natural to take *Abel*, as Canon Raine has done[2], as a confusion due to the scribes of *ab* and *El⟨ia⟩*. There is no record of a patriarch Abel at this time, but the records are so imperfect that Pagi[3] was prepared to accept him upon the authority of the Life. Le Quien held more probably that Abel was identical with Elias III, who was patriarch from about 879 to 907, and he explained the Abel of the Life as representing Ab-El, that is the name of Elias with a prefix of Abba[4]. This was a common prefix to the names of bishops who had been heads of monasteries. But this scarcely explains the presence of such a compound in the present work, for the author states that he had seen the gifts and letters of the patriarch, and the latter would, no doubt, bear his real name Elias.

It is a strong confirmation of the authenticity of the Life that we have proof that Elias sent to Alfred certain medical recipes[5], and that two letters of his to the rulers of western

---

[1] The Georgian Iberia seems to be out of the question, owing to its distance from the Mediterranean.

[2] In the Surtees Society's edition of Simeon of Durham, p. 60.

[3] In his edition of Baronius's *Annales Ecclesiastici*, an. 889.

[4] *Oriens Christianus*, Paris, 1740, iii. p. 462 C. In the list of patriarchs of Jerusalem given by Malmesbury, *Gesta Regum*, c. 368 (p. 425), the name appears in the nominative as *Ilia*.

[5] Cockayne, *Leechdoms*, &c., ii. p. 290, from MS. Reg. 12 D, xvii.

Europe are preserved. The first was brought by his envoys
Gispertus and Rainardus (who, from their names, would
seem to have been Lombards or Franks) to Charles the
Fat in 881 [1]. In this Elias begs for money for the rebuilding of churches, as he has raised all the money that was
possible in his own province. It was probably this letter
that reached Alfred, for the date of the other letter is
later than the composition of the Life. In it Elias prays
for help to raise the ransom demanded by the Turks for
some monks whom they had captured with Malacenus,
bishop of Amasia in Cappadocia [2]. The date of this letter
is established by the encyclical of Pope Benedict IV, 900–
903, recommending the object of the mission and asking
for safe conduct for the envoys from city to city and for
hospitality for them [3].

**91, 20 aedificiis aureis et argenteis.** The mention of
gold and silver buildings is somewhat surprising, but there
is no reason to suspect the accuracy of the reading, for the
preceding and following clauses treat of building operations.
The reference to gold and silver buildings must therefore
be ascribed either to rhetorical exaggeration on the part
of the author, or must have some narrower sense than the
literal one. Possibly he intended to refer to the use of the
precious metals in sacred edifices. We are told on the
doubtful authority of William of Malmesbury, that King
Ine built a chapel of gold and silver at Glastonbury [4]. A

---

written in the early part of the tenth century, ending ' þis eal het þus
secgean Ælfrede cyninge Domne Helias patriarcha on Gerusalem ' (' all
this Dominus Elias, patriarch of Jerusalem, ordered to be said to King
Alfred '). Cf. Cockayne's remarks, preface, p. xxiv.

[1] Printed by D'Achéry, *Spicilegium*, ed. 2, Paris, 1681, ii. p. 372.
Possibly it was this mission from the patriarch of Jerusalem that caused
Alfred to think of sending alms to ' India,' if the statement that he did
so is not entirely baseless. See p. 287 sqq. above. A few years before
the date of this mission the Frankish monk Bernard and his companions
visited Jerusalem. See his itinerary in *Itinera Hierosolymitana*, ed.
Tobler and Molinier, Geneva, 1879, p. 309, published by the Société de
l'Orient Latin.

[2] Printed by Mabillon, *Vetera Analecta*, ed. 1, iii. p. 434; ed. 2,
p. 428; and thence in Migne, *Patrologiae Cursus Completus*, cxxxi.
p. 43.

[3] Ibid.; Jaffé-Wattenbach, *Regesta Pontificum Romanorum*, no. 3530.

[4] *De Antiquitate Glastoniensis Ecclesiae*, ed. Hearne, *Adami de*

ninth-century writer records that Ansegis, abbot of Fontanelle, 806–833, partly decorated a spire of the abbey
with gilt metal [1], and another writer of that period mentions
the golden doors of the 'basilica' of St. Alban in his
description of the imperial palace at Ingelheim [2]. Giraldus
Cambrensis ascribes the use of golden roofs or roof-crests to
the Romans at Caerleon-on-Usk [3]. The idea that a king's
palace ought to be decorated with the precious metals is
probably an outcome of the late Roman rhetoric [4] and
Byzantine magnificence [5].

**91, 23 motatis.** Florence's alteration to *mutatis*, which
has been adopted by Wise and Petrie, is probably correct,
but we have refrained from placing it in the text because
*mutare* and its compounds are in the ninth and tenth
centuries frequently written *motare* [6], and the spelling is

*Domerham Historia*, i. p. 55 : ' Fecit etiam idem rex construere quandam
capellam ex auro et argento, cum ornamentis et vasis similiter aureis et
argenteis, ac infra maiorem collocavit.'

[1] *Gesta Abbatum Fontanellensium*, c. 17, ed. Löwenfeld, p. 55 : ' In
eadem autem Sancti Petri basilica piramidam quadrangulam ⟨sic⟩ altitu-
dinis triginta quinque pedum, de ligno tornatili compositam, in culmine
turris eiusdem aecclesiae collocari iussit ; quam plumbo, stagno ac cupro
deaurato cooperiri iussit, triaque ibidem signa posuit.'

[2] Ermoldus Nigellus (*Poetae Latini Aevi Carolini*, ed. Dümmler,
ii. p. 63, 187):
    Templa Dei Summi constant operata metallo,
      aerati postes, aurea hostiola.

[3] *Itinerarium Kambriae*, i. c. 5 (*Opera*, ed. Dimock, vi. p. 55):
' Videas hic multa pristinae nobilitatis adhuc vestigia ; palatia immensa,
aureis olim tectorum fastigiis Romanos fastus imitantia, eo quod a
Romanis principibus primo constructa et aedificiis egregiis illustrata
fuissent.'

[4] Cf. the fragment of an oration ascribed to Cassiodorus, ed. Traube,
in Mommsen's edition of the *Variae*, p. 483, 10 : ' fecisti quoque, Domina,
palatium. . . . Renidet crusta marmorum concolor gemmis, sparsum aurum
fulget in. . . .' Ibid. p. 483, 20 : ' Regis Persarum Cyri domus variis auro
lapidibus inligatis constructa perhibetur.'

[5] The great Swedish temple at Upsala was said to be covered with
gold. Cf. Adam of Bremen, *Gesta Hammaburgensis Ecclesiae Pontificum*, iv. c. 26.

[6] A.D. 811 Brit. Mus. *Facs.* ii. pl. 11, *Cart. Sax.* i. 462, 10, 31 ; 463,
13 (contemporary?) ; A.D. 869 Brit. Mus. *Facs.* ii. pl. 39, *Cart. Sax.* ii.
141,14(tenth cent.) ; A.D. 882 *Cart. Sax.* ii. 171, 23, Winchester (dubious ;
in this chartulary the word in this formula is in most other cases altered
to *mutare*) ; A.D. 892 ibid. ii. 211, 20, Worcester (genuine?) ; 904 ibid.

therefore probably that of the author, and is a proof of the
antiquity of the work.

**91**, 30 **navem suam.** The common classical comparison of the direction of a state to the steering of a ship [1]
was in great favour with the writers of the Middle Ages [2].
The metaphor is as elaborately worked out by St. Agobard [3],
a ninth-century Frankish writer, as by the author of the
present passage, who uses a similar figure in cc. 21, 9 ;
73, 2.

**91**, 49 **castellis.** In O.E. Latin this word is used in the
same sense as 'chester' and 'caster,' both from Latin
*castra* [4], and not in that of 'castle' or 'fort,' as it seems
to be in the present passage. In the *Liber Landavensis* it

---

ii. 260, 22, Hyde (dubious) ; A.D. 904 ibid. ii. 270, 32, Winchester ;
909 ibid. ii. 294, 14, Winchester ; A.D. 930 ibid. ii. 349, 3, Chichester
(genuine) ; 930 *Crawford Charters*, iv. 5, *Cart. Sax.* iii. 681, 5 (contemporary).

[1] *Exx. g.* Sophocles, *Oedipus Tyrannus*, 104 ; Aristophanes, *Ecclesiaz.*
109 ; Cicero, *In Pisonem*, ix. 20, *Ep. ad Famil.* i. 9, 21 ; Horace, *Carm.*
i. 14. Cf. Quintilian, viii. c. 6, § 44. In later times it is used by
Gregory of Nazianzus (Benedictine ed. of his works, Paris, 1840, ii.
pp. 76 B, 131 C, 206, 577).

[2] It is used in the Forged Decretals (*Decretales Pseudo-Isidorianae*,
ed. Paul Hinschius, Leipzig, 1863, pp. 34, 67, &c.).

[3] 'Tantis quippe in hoc loco huius mundi fluctibus quatior, ut
vetustam ac putrescentem navem, quam regendam occulta Dei dispensatione suscepi, ad portum dirigere nullatenus possim. Nunc ex adverso
fluctus irruunt, nunc ex latere cumuli spumosi maris intumescunt, nunc
a tergo tempestas insequitur ; interque haec omnia turbatus, cogor modo
in ipsa clavum adversitate dirigere, modo curvato navis latere minas
fluctuum ex obliquo declinare' (*Opera*, ed. Baluze, Paris, 1665, ii. p. 52).
Quite as elaborate is the form assumed by the metaphor in a suspicious
Malmesbury charter dated 675 (*Cart. Sax.* i. 61, 14).

[4] So in the Council of Hertford, in Beda, *Hist. Eccl.* iv. c. 5 : 'Putta,
episcopus castelli Cantuariorum, quod dicitur Hrofescæstir.' Beda's
*castella* of iii. c. 28, which are mentioned along with ' oppida, rura, casas,
vicos' as the scene of Chad's missionary labours, have probably the same
meaning. The term is applied to Rochester in a charter of 765 (*Cart.
Sax.* i. 278, 9), and in another of 788 (ibid. i. 352, 18), both of which
appear to be copied from genuine originals. In the eighth-century Life
of St. Guthlac by Felix, ed. Birch, 17, 4, it refers to the Roman camp
at Grantchester. In the late tenth-century Life of St. Oswald it is linked
with other words, such as 'towns,' 'villages,' 'houses,' relating to settlements of men, and hence cannot have the meaning of 'castle' (*Historians
of York*, pp. 425, 436, 472). In the O.E. glosses from the eighth-century
Corpus Glossary downwards *castellum* is glossed by ' wīc,' that is 'town.'

is applied to a *caer*[1] (which is supposed to be derived from *castra*), the Welsh name for Roman stations, few, if any of which, were inhabited at this time. Hence the sense 'castle' may be due to the Welsh origin of the author, or may perhaps be another Fránkish feature in his vocabulary.

**91, 59 eulogii.** This form seems to have arisen from confusion between *eloquium* and εὐλογία, of which there are other instances. In the present case it seems to have the meaning of 'text,' referring to the 'inanis poenitentia' mentioned in the preceding sentence on the authority of 'scripture.'

**92.** This chapter is due to the author.

**92, 9 gronna,** 'fens, moors.' See note to c. 53, 2.

**92, 11 cauticis.** This word seems to represent the Latin *caudica* (*navis*). The knowledge of it probably came indirectly from Isidore of Seville[2]. *Caudicae* are mentioned in the list of ship-names in Aulus Gellius[3]. A variant form *codicaria* occurs in Nonius[4], who cites Sallust and Varro. Further examples of *caudicae* may be found in Rönsch[5]. *Caudex* is glossed by O.E. *punt* in the glossaries[6]. William of Malmesbury similarly states that Athelney could only be reached by water[7].

**93.** This chapter is due to the author.

**93, 9 monasteria.** The description here given of the condition of the monasteries in England is, as Bishop Stubbs has remarked, true of the next half-century[8]. In

---

[1] Ed. Rhys and Evans, 226, 23. Cf. 205, 21.

[2] *Origines*, xix. c. 1, § 27: '*Trabariae* amnicae naves, quae ex singulis trabibus cavantur; quae alio nomine litorariae dicuntur. Hae et *caudicae* ex uno ligno cavato factae, et inde *caudicae*; quia a quatuor ad octo homines capiant.'

[3] *Noctes Atticae*, x. c. 25, 5 (ed. Hertz, ii. p. 49).

[4] Ed. Lucian Müller, 535 M (ii. p. 196).

[5] Hermann Rönsch, *Itala und Vulgata*, Marburg and Leipzig, 1869, p. 134.

[6] Wright-Wülcker, *Anglo-Saxon and Old English Vocabularies*, i. 181, 31; cf. 287, 33. The latter glossary seems to be based upon Isidore.

[7] *Gesta Pontificum*, c. 92, p. 199: 'Adelingea est non maris insula, sed ita stagnorum refusionibus et paludibus inaccessa, ut nullo modo nisi navigio adiri queat.'

[8] *Memorials of St. Dunstan*, p. lxxxiii, note 1.

his words, 'the churches and other buildings ⟨were⟩
standing, the libraries perhaps in a few cases continuing
entire, but the monastic life ⟨was⟩ extinct, the name preserved only as giving a title to the ownership of the lands,
and the abbots and monks, if there were any that called
themselves so, being really secular priests and clerks.' The
letter of Archbishop Fulco to Alfred refers to the disappearance of the 'ecclesiasticus ordo' in England, and to
Alfred's desire to restore it[1]. Ælfric, in his Life of St.
Æthelwold, describes the deserted condition of Abingdon
as late as the time of King Eadred[2], and Ely was in the
same condition[3]. Alfred's attempts to restore the monasteries do not appear to have been crowned with success,
and the story narrated in c. 96 sqq. suggests that his instru-
ments were not well chosen in all cases. The Frankish
monasteries from which he drew his helpers had not yet
felt the great monastic reform that was to spread from
Cluny. St. Bertin's itself was not reformed until the year
944[4]. We may learn from the Life of St. Oswald how low
the monastic life had fallen before the introduction of
reforms by Dunstan and Æthelwold. It must, however,
be borne in mind that the writer of this life was, like
Ælfric himself, a firm believer in the benefit of these
reforms, and that he was therefore likely to mete out scant
justice to the members of the unreformed monasteries. The
condemnation of the irregularities and vices of the canons
who were ousted from the monasteries by Dunstan and
Æthelwold and their followers is common in writings of the
end of the tenth and beginning of the eleventh centuries.
Thus a forger writing at that period might have written the
present passage from the point of view of that time, but in
that case we should expect him to have betrayed his enmity
to the canons. The fact that there is no hint of any such

---

[1] *Cart. Sax.* ii. 190, 18; 192, 1. Upon this letter see above, p. 308,
note 1.

[2] *Hist. Mon. de Abingdon,* ii. 257.

[3] Ibid. p. 262. Stubbs, *Memorials of St. Dunstan,* p. lxxxi, thinks
that Glastonbury was in a similar condition.

[4] Folcwin, *Gesta Abbatum S. Bertini,* c. 107 (Pertz, *Scriptores,* xiii.
p. 628).

feeling is an argument in favour of the authenticity of the Life.

**94.** This chapter is due to the author.

**94, 6 eiusdem gentis Gallicae,** referring to c. 78, 3.

**94, 9 unum paganicae gentis . . iuvenem.** It is a curious coincidence that Oda[1], who became bishop of Ramsbury between 925 and 927 and archbishop of Canterbury in 942, and who died in 958, was said to be the son of a Dane who came to England with Inguar and Ubba (in 866). This we learn from the life of his nephew Oswald, archbishop of York[2], which was written in the closing years of the tenth century. Oswald was also related to Oscytel[3], bishop of Dorchester 950, and archbishop of York 958, who died in 971. From his name Oscytel must have been of Danish origin[4]. It is not impossible that the pagan boy seen by the author of the Life in (presumably) a West-Saxon monastery was either Oda or Oscytel. From their occupancy of West Saxon bishoprics it is probable that both were educated in Wessex. Of Oda we are told in the life of Oswald that he left his parents and adhered to a knight named Æthelhelm[5], whom he accompanied to Rome, whence they returned after rendering alms[6]. They afterwards visited the king, who as a reward made Oda bishop of Ramsbury[7]. If this account is correct, it would refer the mission to Rome to about 925, but it is probably confused, for the biographer makes Oda spend ' perparvi spatii temporis ' at Ramsbury[8], instead of fifteen years or so. It is somewhat remarkable that the Chron. records under 887 the carrying of alms to Rome by Æthelhelm,

[1] The name is apparently an adaptation of O.N. Auði, Auðe (the cognate of O.E. Éada).
[2] Ed. Raine, *Historians of York*, i. 404.
[3] Ibid. i. p. 420.
[4] It is an adaptation of O.N. Ás-ketill. The second member of the compound was not used in native English personal names, and occurs only in adapted Scandinavian ones.
[5] *Historians of York*, i. p. 404, where an account of his education by Æthelhelm is given, which must not be taken too literally.
[6] Ibid. p. 405.
[7] Ibid. p. 406.
[8] Ibid., where his promotion to the primacy is ascribed to the king who nominated him to Ramsbury, which is impossible from the dates.

ealdorman of Wilts. It is hardly possible, however, that this can be the mission to Rome referred to in the life of St. Oswald, unless his story that Oda was already a priest be rejected.

**95.** This chapter is due to the author.

**95,** 1. This and the following chapters have been frequently misunderstood as relating the death of John the Old Saxon[1], although it is evident from line 21 that he survived the attack of the assassins. Further confusion has arisen from identifying this account of the attack upon John the Old Saxon with William of Malmesbury's relation of the murder of John Scotus by his pupils at Malmesbury[2]. But, as Mabillon[3] has remarked, William carefully distinguishes the two Johns, and he states that John Scotus 'is believed' to have flourished about the time of Alfred. The basis of his story was the existence in Malmesbury abbey of a tomb bearing a Latin epitaph to a 'sanctus Iohannes sophista,' who is therein said to have died 'martyrio[4].' He remarks that the latinity of this epitaph, which he quotes, is not up to the elegancy of his time. There is earlier evidence of the burial of a scholar named John at Malmesbury in the entry in the Corpus MS. of the list of burial-places of saints in England of the statement that 'Iohannes se wisa' (John the wise, or learned) was buried at Malmesbury[5]. This MS. was written about the middle of the eleventh century, and the entry does not appear in the older text of this list, which dates back to c. 1020. It is clear that William was in error in treating John of Malmesbury as the same person as John Scotus. Stubbs regards John of Malmesbury as distinct from John the Old Saxon, and cites as proof the appearance of John's name as a witness to charters of Edward the Elder[6]. But with the correction of his error in regarding the account in the Life as recording the death of John the Old Saxon, the

---

[1] See § 70, p. civ, and p. cxii, note 2, above.
[2] Ibid.
[3] *Acta Sanctorum Ordinis Sancti Benedicti*, cent. iv, pars 2, p. 511.
[4] *Gesta Regum*, c. 122, p. 132; *Gesta Pontificum*, c. 240, p. 394.
[5] *Die Heiligen Englands*, ed. Liebermann, ii. 41, p. 18.
[6] In his edition of Malmesbury's *Gesta Regum*, i. p. 131, note 1; ii. p. xlviii. Upon these charters see p. 312, note 2, above.

grounds for referring these attestations to some other John
disappear. As the date of John the Old Saxon's death is
unknown, it is even possible that the Malmesbury epitaph
is his, for no other John is known to us, and the person
described as 'Iohannes se wisa' must have been, like John
the Old Saxon, a great scholar. Whether Malmesbury's
account of the murder of John at Malmesbury accurately
reproduces a tradition then current in the abbey, or is some
account of the murder of John Scotus that he has imported
into his history in consequence of his identification of the
'Iohannes sophista' of the tomb with this famous scholar, it
is impossible to decide. Nothing is known of the end of
John Scotus or of John the Old Saxon. We should hardly
expect the murder of John Scotus by his pupils to be described as a 'martyrium,' a word that strongly suggests that
'Iohannes sophista' was slain by the Danes.

**96.** This chapter is due to the author.

**97.** This chapter is due to the author.

**97,** 25 **gronna,** 'fen, moor.' See note to c. 53, 2.

**98.** This chapter is due to the author.

**99.** This chapter is due to the author.

**99,** 5 **Dominum decimam sibi multipliciter redditurum,** &c. This obviously blundered sentence may
perhaps be derived from a draught [1], the copyist having
transcribed both the original reading and the emended
reading. The only passage resembling this that we have
been able to find is in a tract formerly ascribed to St.
Ambrose : 'Quia de omni substantia, quam Deus homini
donat, decimam partem sibi servavit, et ideo non licet
homini retinere illud, quod Deus sibi reservavit. Tibi
dedit novem partes, sibi vero reservavit decimam partem [2].'

**99,** 18 **Si recte offeras, recte autem non dividas,
peccas.** This is adapted from a reading in an Old-Latin
version, which represents the reading of the Septuagint [3],
and is quoted by Irenaeus, Jerome, and others [4].

**100.** This chapter is due to the author.

---

[1] See Introduction, p. cxxxi, above.
[2] *S. Ambrosii Opera,* Paris, 1690, ii, appendix, p. 425 B, 'Sermo xxv,
de sancta Quadragesima ix.'
[3] Gen. iv. 7 : Οὐκ ἐὰν ὀρθῶς προσενέγκῃς, ὀρθῶς δὲ μὴ διέλῃς, ἥμαρτες ;
[4] Sabatier, *Bibliorum Sacrorum Latinae Versiones Antiquae.*

**100,** 8 **in tribus namque cohortibus ... dividebantur,**
&c. The Chron. under 894 records that Alfred divided
his forces into two parts, one being on active service and
the other at home alternately, much as the author describes
the rotation of service among the warriors of his household.
Whether this rotation of service in the court was an innovation due to Alfred, or was an older custom, does not
appear. But it is a tempting theory that this rotation of
service is an outcome of the processes by which the *gesíðas*
ceased to be personal attendants upon the king and became
hereditary landed proprietors, by a similar process of
development to that undergone by the Merovingian *antru-
stiones* [1], who, like the *gesíðas*, represented the original
members of the king's *comitatus*. It is noticeable in the
present passage that Alfred's military attendants are no
longer landless *comites*, but have homes of their own at
which they spend two months out of every three. Alfred
makes a bequest in his will to the men who 'follow' him [2].

**100,** 9 **satellites.** The use of this term to describe the
king's military attendants is another proof of Frankish
influence in the vocabulary of the author [3]. In Frankish
Latin it was similarly used to describe what Waitz ventures
to call the emperor's body-guard [4]. The word is used in
the Vulgate, and hence must have been well known to most
scholars of the time [5], but in the present passage the author
uses it in a more technical sense that can only be due to
Frankish influence.

**101.** This chapter is due to the author.

---

[1] See Brunner, *Deutsche Rechtsgeschichte*, ii. p. 258.

[2] *Cart. Sax.* ii. 178, 30, whereby he bequeaths two hundred pounds
to the men who 'follow' (serve, form his *comitatus*) him and to whom
he made gifts at Eastertide. It was, no doubt, in these gifts, another
relic of the Germanic *comitatus*, that the money described in this chapter
as being given to the king's noble ministers was expended.

[3] See Introduction, § 58, p. xciv, above.

[4] *Deutsche Verfassungsgeschichte*, ed. 2, iii. 546.

[5] It occurs in a Worcester charter of 816 in Heming, which is of
somewhat unusual form (*Cart. Sax.* i. 495, 2), and in an Abingdon
charter of 964 (ibid. iii. 393, 26). The tenth-century instances in the
Life of St. Oswald, ed. Raine, *Historians of York*, i. p. 469, 6, and in
the Life of St. Dunstan ' auctore B,' in *Memorials of St. Dunstan*, ed.
Stubbs, p. 32, 21, may also from their date be due to Frankish influence.

**102.** This chapter is due to the author.

**102, 17 scholae.** The school is described in similar words in c. 75, 16. Cf. 76, 33.

**103.** This chapter is due to the author.

**104.** This chapter is due to the author.

**104, 6 sex candelas.** As these six candles weighed 72 pennyweights, each one was of the weight of 12d. The weight of the O.E. penny was $22\frac{1}{2}$ Troy grains [1], so that each candle would weigh roughly $\frac{5}{8}$ oz. avoirdupois. As the candles were twelve inches long, they would be very thin in proportion to their length. A modern beeswax candle burns at a considerable quicker rate than is here assumed, but we do not think this condemns the figures given in this chapter as imaginary. The candle of Alfred's time was probably not moulded, and the wick would not be made of cotton as in the modern ones. Rushes, tow [2], and the hards of flax [3] were used for wicks. Aldhelm refers to the use of linen or flax wicks [4], but also to those made of rushes [5]. It is therefore hardly possible to reproduce the candles used by Alfred for the purposes of testing this chapter. The fact that the later transcribers copied this chapter without hesitation cannot be adduced as proof that the details given in it are accurate. Nor, assuming that

---

[1] C. F. Keary, *British Museum Catalogue of English Coins*, Anglo-Saxon Series, i. p. xxxv ; Ruding, *Annals of the Coinage*, ed. 2, i. 277 note h, 280–1. There is great variation in the weight of the coins that have been preserved, and the weight given above seems to be rather a general average of a number of coins than the normal weight of each one.

[2] Moriz Heyne, *Fünf Bücher deutscher Hausaltertümer*, Leipzig, 1899, i. pp. 124–5.

[3] They were in use in the seventeenth century. See *Records of the Borough of Nottingham*, v. p. 175, 7.

[4] In his enigma on the candle (*Opera*, ed. Giles, p. 261) :

> Materia duplici palmis plasmabar apertis,
> interiora mihi candescunt viscera lino,
> seu certe gracili iunco spoliata nitescunt, &c.

[5] *De Laudibus Virginitatis*, c. 32 (*Opera*, p. 37, 32) : ‘ ut latex lucernarum cicindilibus infusus, in olei crassitudinem perniciter verteretur, et papirus in centro positus velut fomes arvina vel sevo madefactus solito clarius lucesceret.’ Other proofs of the use of rushes for wicks may be found in Bosworth-Toller's *Anglo-Saxon Dictionary*, s. v. ‘ wēoce.’

they are correct, can they be cited as proof that the work is
the production of a contemporary, for such details might
easily be supplied by a later writer.

**104, 10 per viginti quatuor horas die nocteque.**
It would seem that the author refers to a division of the
day and night taken together into twenty-four equal hours,
and not to the division of the day, the time between sunrise
and sunset, and the night, the time between sunset and
sunrise, into twelve hours each, the length of which, strictly
speaking, varied from day to day [1]. The author, who is so
exceedingly profuse in his explanations in this chapter,
does not hint at any device for accommodating the candles,
which he describes as being all of equal weight and length,
to the varying length of the hours or to the difference that
existed, except at the equinoxes, between the length of
the hour of the day and that of the night associated with it.
Apart from the mechanical difficulties involved in any such
attempt to represent these constantly varying hours, it is
obvious that Alfred could not obtain by their use any such
equal division of his time as is here described. It would
therefore seem that he is pictured as using the equinoctial
hours ; and he has, if this is so, the credit of anticipating
by several centuries the use of this, the modern, system,
which is so largely the result of the introduction of the
wheel-clock. This division into twenty-four hours may
have been suggested to Alfred by the system then in use of
dividing the day and the night into twelve hours each, or
by the astronomical division of the two into twenty-four
equal hours. This scientific usage is represented in the
O.E. calendars, which generally assign to each month so
many hours for the day and so many for the night, the
total of the two being twenty-four [2].

**104, 24 laternam ex lignis et bovinis cornibus.** On
the strength of this passage Alfred has been frequently

---

[1] See above, pp. 283-4.

[2] See above, p. 285, note 2. This use is represented in the famous
Bodleian MS. no. 63, written c. 850 by a Rægenbold, who, from his
name, was clearly not an Englishman, although he is therein said to be
a monk of ' Wentonia' (Winchester), which name is written in a ninth-
century hand over an erasure. See the account of this MS. given in the
Palaeographical Society's Publications, plate 168.

described as the inventor of the horn lantern. Ducange[1] objected that horn lanterns were known to the Greeks and Romans long before Alfred's time. But the passages adduced by Salmasius[2], to whom he refers, and such others[3] as we have been able to gather do not clearly describe a horn lantern lit by a candle, but rather screens formed of horn to place round oil lamps. It is possible therefore that Alfred may really be the inventor of the horn lantern as we know it. The door in the side, which would be rendered necessary by the change of the candles every four hours, is here described, and seems to be a new feature. The horn lamp-holders (λυχνοῦχοι) of the Greeks seem to have been screens that were placed over the lamp, but in a Roman example from Pompeii the lamp was inserted from the top, which was covered by a hinged lid[4]. Glass lamps for church use were known to Beda[5] and Aldhelm[6], and the latter mentions lanterns made of thin

---

[1] *Glossarium Latinitatis*, s. v. 'laterna.'

[2] *Exercitationes in Caii Iulii Solini Polyhistoria*, Paris, 1629, i. p. 166 b. He refers to Olympiodorus, *Commentaria in Aristotelis Meteorologica*, iv. 8, § 30 (ed. W. Stüve, Berlin, 1900, p. 321, 9) : ὥσπερ οἱ λαμπτῆρες, τούτεστι τὰ διαφανῆ κέρατα, ἐν οἷς ἐντίθενται αἱ λάμπαδες νύκτωρ, and to the fragment of the historian Philistus, preserved by Pollux, *Onomasticon*, x. 166 : Ἐκαλεῖτο δὲ καὶ λαμπτὴρ ὁ λυχνοῦχος. Ἐν γοῦν τῷ δευτέρῳ τῶν Φιλίστου βιβλίων εἴρηται " καὶ τὰς νύκτας ἐπαίρεσθαι λαμπτῆρας ἀντιπεφραγμένους "· ὑποδηλοῖ δὲ τὸν ἐκ κέρατος φανόν, where the explanation is due to Pollux. Salmasius also refers to Martial, xiv. 61.

[3] Phrynichus (Bekker, *Anecdota Graeca*, i. p. 50, 23) : Λυχνοῦχος, λαμπτήρ, φανὸς διαφέρει. λυχνοῦχος μέν ἐστι σκεῦός τι ἐν κύκλῳ ἔχον κέρατα, ἔνδον δὲ λύχνον ἡμμένον, διὰ τῶν κεράτων τὸ φῶς πέμποντα. Cf. also the quotation from an unnamed poet by Athenaeus, 699 A, of κεράτινος λύχνος, Pliny's statement that horns 'apud nos in lamnas secta tralucent atque etiam lumen inclusum latius fundunt' (*Hist. Nat.* xi. c. 37 (45), § 126, and xi. 16 (16), § 49), and Plautus, *Amphit.* 1, 1, 188 : 'quo ambulas tu, qui Volcanum in cornu conclusum geris?'

[4] See the engraving and explanation in A. Baumeister, *Denkmäler des klassischen Altertums*, Munich, 1887, ii. p. 812.

[5] *Historia Abbatum*, c. 5, where he says that the Angles learned from the Gaulish glassmakers imported by Benedict Biscop in the seventh century 'artificium nimirum vel lampadis aecclesiae claustris vel vasorum multifariis usibus non ignobiliter aptum.'

[6] *De Laudibus Virginum* (*Opera*, ed. Giles, p. 142, 4) :
Nec laterna tibi vilescat vitrea, Virgo,
tergore vel raso, et lignis compacta salignis,
seu membranarum tenui velamine facta, &c.

leather, by which he probably meant some transparent membrane. It is noteworthy that he does not refer to horn lanterns in this passage. It is clear that these lanterns were a novelty to the author of the Life. If they had been well-known objects it is inconceivable that even so circumstantial a writer as he was should have given such profuse details concerning them. It would seem that it was the planning of the lantern, not the use of it to shield his time-candles from the wind, that the author ascribes to Alfred, but his style is so involved and his thoughts generally so confused that it is conceivable that he meant merely that Alfred applied the lantern to this purpose. This use of candles as time-measurers seems to be, as the author says, a device of Alfred's own [1].

**105.** This chapter is due to the author.

**105, 4 permitteret.** The dependence of what follows this verb upon the preceding clauses is so obscure as to raise the presumption that the scribe of the Cottonian MS. has omitted some words or passages. The compiler of the Annals of St. Neots substitutes a sentence of his own for this passage, but it would be hazardous to conclude from this that the imperfection existed in the copy of the Life used by him, since the matter passed over by him here is such as he elsewhere omits. If the scribe of the Cottonian MS. has here faithfully reproduced his original, this chapter may be adduced as evidence that he was copying from the author's unrevised draught, of which there appear to be other traces elsewhere [2]. The imperfect sentence at the end of this chapter may perhaps also be further evidence of this. The missing verb in it may possibly be represented by the *studebat* with which the next chapter commences. Parker added *inhiabat* in order to complete the sentence, so that it is probable that he had some manuscript authority for making *studebat* the commencing word of the next chapter. A removal of the latter verb to the end of the

---

[1] There is no mention of any such device in G. S. Bilfinger's *Die Zeitmesser der antiken Völker* (in the *Festschrift zur Jubelfeier des Eberhard-Ludwigs-Gymnasiums in Stuttgart*), Stuttgart, 1886. We have not been able to see Kindler, *Die Zeitmesser bis zur Erfindung der Pendeluhr*, 1898.

[2] See Introduction, p. cxxxi, above.

present chapter would merely transfer the imperfection to the first sentence of the next one.

**106.** This chapter, which is due to the author, presents serious difficulties. Apparently it represents the king as receiving appeals from the judgements of lower courts, and as exercising considerable judicial powers. The right of appeal to a higher court did not come into use in England until long after the Norman Conquest[1], and the only way in which a suit could pass from one court to another was upon the failure of the lower one to do justice within a fixed time. Thus a suit might go from the Hundred Court to the Shire Moot. If the latter also failed to do justice (that is, to come to a decision of the suit within a prescribed time), the parties to the suit might appeal to the king for aid. In that case the king could remit the suit to the Shire Moot, with orders to render justice[2]. The author, perhaps from ignorance of West Saxon law, describes the ealdormen (*comites*) and sheriffs or reeves (*praefecti*) as judges, but, like the king, they had no judicial powers apart from the courts of which they formed part. The judges were really the whole body of the freemen who formed the Hundred Court, the Shire Moot, or the Witenagemot[3]. The Hundred Courts and the Shire Moots, which are evidently the courts referred to by the author, worked very slowly and inefficiently, and it is very probable that a great and influential noble could prevent justice being done in a suit brought against him. Such records as we have show great protraction of the proceedings in these courts, and it is clear that in many cases the parties to a suit agreed in the end to settle it by arbitration[4], in which the king was sometimes concerned. The author describes the parties as giving sureties (*subarabant*) to abide

---

[1] Pollock and Maitland, *History of English Law*, ii. p. 661.
[2] Henry Adams, *The Anglo-Saxon Courts of Law*, in *Essays in Anglo-Saxon Law*, Boston (U.S.A.), 1876, p. 24 sqq., where the whole question is admirably dealt with.
[3] Brunner, *Deutsche Rechtsgeschichte*, i. p. 152.
[4] It is noticeable that in the O.E. document concerning land at Fonthill, in which we catch a glimpse of Alfred washing his hands at Wardour and listening to suitors for advice, the king remitted the question of the disputed ownership of the land to arbitration (*Cart. Sax.* ii. p. 236).

by the decision of the king, and he adds that the party
who was conscious of having committed an injustice shrank
from facing so careful and upright a judge[1]. There is
nothing in this incompatible with an agreement to submit
their differences to the king, and it would seem that this,
and not an appeal to him against the judgement of a lower
court, is what the author intended to convey to us.
Kemble has noticed that Alfred is not described as revers-
ing unjust judgements[2]. The author tells us that Alfred
carefully examined into the conduct of the ealdormen and
sheriffs or reeves in the administration of justice, and that
he removed those whom he found incompetent or corrupt.
Under the legal organization of the time it is difficult to see
what other steps he could have taken to ensure the honest
and capable administration of justice, for he could hardly
punish the suitors of the popular courts, the real judges.
The ealdormen and sheriffs and reeves would, no doubt,
from their position have great influence in shaping the
decisions of these courts, more especially as they seem to
have supplied such legal and administrative knowledge as
was required. Thus a foreigner such as Asser might
imagine that they were judges. In later times we have a
record of the punishment of an ealdorman by deprivation of
office for unjust judgements[3], so that the ealdormen were
clearly held by that time to be responsible for the decisions
of the courts in which they presided[4].

**106, 12 quamvis per vim lege et stipulatione**, &c.
This is one of several corrupt passages that has the appearance of being copied from a draught bearing certain alterations, which the scribe copied along with the original words[5].
Thus we may assume that the ' contra voluntatem tamen '

---

[1] Kemble, *Saxons in England*, ii. p. 43, curiously refers this passage
to Alfred himself by what is a very forced translation and explanation.

[2] Ibid. ii. p. 44.

[3] In the case of Wulfgeat in Florence of Worcester under 1006.

[4] In connexion with this chapter may be quoted the words of Abbo
of Fleury in reference to St. Edmund of East Anglia : ' nec malignorum
hominum reciperet contra iustitiam sententias, rem quam nesciebat
diligentissime investigans ' (*Passio S. Eadmundi*, c. 4). This, of course,
is imaginary, and is written by a foreigner.

[5] See Introduction, p. cxxxi, above.

and the 'voluntarie nolebat,' the 'per vim' and the 'lege
et stipulatione' represent alternate phrases.

**106 d.** The Christian name John wrongly applied to
Asser by Bale, from whom Parker derived this chapter,
has obviously arisen from a mistake of Higden[1], who, in
abridging Matthew Paris[2] or the *Flores Historiarum*,
overlooked 'Asserum' at the end of the sentence corresponding to the beginning of c. 79 of the Life, so that his
text runs : 'Aluredus igitur . . . Sanctum Grimbaldum, monachum litteratura et cantu peritum, de partibus Galliae, ac
Iohannem monachum de ultimis Walliae finibus, scilicet de
monasterio Sancti David Meneviae, ad se vocavit,' where
Matthew Paris and the *Flores* have 'necnon et Iohannem,
presbyterum et monachum bonis moribus adornatum ; ex
ultimis etiam Walanorum finibus de monasterio Sancti
David, Asserum ad suum accivit consortium.' The *Liber
de Hyda*[4] makes matters worse by inserting 'Asserum'
before 'ac Iohannem,' so that both Asser and John are
made to come from St. Davids. John Rosse similarly brings
John and Asserus from Flanders with Grimbald, and, in
addition, a 'Iohannes Walensis' from St. Davids[5].

---

[1] *Polychronicon*, vi. p. 358.          [2] *Chronica Maiora*, i. p. 407.
[3] Ed. Luard, i. p. 448.                 [4] p. 29.
                    [5] Ed. Hearne, p. 76.

# INDEX

WORDS and figures in Clarendon type refer to the text of Asser (by chapter and line). Entries with a double dagger (‡) prefixed refer to the Annals of St. Neots. Figures denoting pages are set in ordinary type, and notes are indicated by superior figures.

‡Aachen, Aquisgran(um), death of Charles the Great at, p. 129.

Abbo of Fleury, p. 220; his 'Passion of St. Edmund,' pp. 232, 343[4]; excerpts from, in Florence of Worcester, p. 108[4]; and in the Annals of St. Neots, p. 104, p. 110, p. 133.

Abel, patriarch of Jerusalem. See Elias.

Abingdon, co. Berks, abbey of, p. 333; charters of, p. 150[2, 4], p. 151[2], p. 235[3], p. 236[4], p. 255[2], p. 299[4], p. 304[8], p. 315[6], p. 337[5]. Abbots of: see Faritius.

Abon, River (the Avon, at Chippenham, co. Wilts), 52, 6.

‡Acca, Eadweald, son of, slain, p. 144.

Acleah, 'id est in campulo quercus,' 5, 6; defeat of the Danes at, 5, 6, note on, p. 178; erroneously identified with Ockley, co. Surrey, p. 178.

— synod of, in 788, p. 208[3].

Aclee on West Sæxum, site of, p. 178.

Adam, 1, 41.

— of Bremen, cites Gesta Anglorum in his 'Gesta Hammaburgensis Ecclesiae Pontificum,' p. 112[5].

‡Adheluulfus. See Æthelwulf.

‡Adheluuoldus. See Æthelwold.

‡Adhered. See Æthelred.

‡Adhulfus. See Æthulf.

‡Adrian I, Pope, death of, p. 129.

Æcgleah. See Ægleah.

aedificia, 'gifts,' 56, 33; an error for 'beneficia,' p. 279.

‡Æduuoldus. See Eadweald.

Ægbryhta, Petra. See Ecgbrihtes Stan.

‡Ægelesthrep (co. Kent?), battle of, p. 119.

Ægleah, Æcgleah, Alfred arrives at, with his forces, 55, 17; notes on, p. lxxxvii[1], p. 270; probable site of, p. 272.

Ælfheah the Bald, bishop of Winchester 934-951, p. 258.

— St., bishop of Winchester 984-1005, archbishop of Canterbury 1005-1012, p. 258.

Ælflæd, daughter of Offa, married to Æthelred of Northumbria, p. 207.

Ælfred. See Alfred.

Ælfric, abbot, the Homilist, his Life of St. Æthelwold, p. 259, p. 333; renders into English Abbo of Fleury's 'Passion of St. Edmund,' p. 232.

Ælfthryth, third daughter of Alfred, 75, 3; education of, 75, 21; note on, p. 299.

— wife of King Edgar, adopts the title of queen, p. 202.

— alleged daughter of Offa, p. 208.

Ælfweard, son of Edward the Elder, death of, p. 299[4].

Ælla, usurper of throne of Northumbria, joins forces with his opponent, attacks the Danes at York, and is slain, 27, 6, 11, 25.

Æsc, king of Kent. *See* Oisc.

Æscesdun (Ashdown, i. e. the Berkshire Downs), defeat of the Danes at, 37–39 ; description of site of battle, 39, 1 ; thorn-tree centre of the fight, 39, 5, note on, p. 238; name erroneously explained as 'mons fraxini,' 37, 3 ; attempts to identify site of battle, p. 235.

— grant of land by, to Cuthred, son of Cwichelm, by Cenwealh, king of Wessex, in 648, p. 154, p. 236, p. 237 ; Cenwealh harries the Mercians as far as Æscesdun in 661, p. 237.

‡Æscuuine, king of Wessex, p. 123.

Æthelbeald, Æthelbaldus, son of Æthelwulf, king of Wessex, defeats with his father the Danes at Acleah, 5, 5; conspires against his father during his absence abroad, 12, 4, 17 ; receives from his father in consequence the western part of the realm, 12, 28 ; note on this conspiracy, p. 195; father's supporters wished to exile him, 13, 4 ; Æthelwulf divides his realm by his will between him and (Æthelberht), 16, 7 ; Æthelbeald marries Judith, his father's widow, 17, 5, note on, p. 212, p. 214; alleged separation from, p. 212 ; reign of, 17, 8, p.‡132, note on, p.195; death and burial of, 18, 2 (‡p. 132).

Æthelberht, son of King Æthelwulf, kingdom of Wessex divided between him and his brother Æthelbeald by his father's will, 16, 8 ; king of Kent, Surrey, Sussex, and Essex, 18, 4; origin of error in Life as to his accession to these kingdoms, p. 196, p. 215 ; succeeds Æthelbeald as king of Wessex, 18, 2, ‡p. 132 ; death and burial of, 19, 4; style of, p. 149[2] ; charters of, p. 163, p. 165.

Æthelberht, St., king of the East Angles, ‡death of, p. 128 ; life of, p. 208, used by compiler of the Annals of St. Neots, p. 104 ; life of, by Giraldus Cambrensis, p. lxiii.

— ‡Æthelbriht, king of Kent, p. 120 ; baptism of, p. 121 ; death of, ibid. ; described as a saint, ibid.

‡Æetheldritha. *See* Æthelthryth.

Æthelflæd, eldest child of Alfred, 75, 2 ; married to Eadred (*read* Æthelred), ealdorman of the Mercians, 75, 7 ; date of her marriage, p. 300 ; charters of, p. 147[2].

Æthelgeofu, second daughter of Alfred, 75, 3 ; becomes a nun, 75, 8 ; Alfred appoints her abbess of his newly-founded nunnery at Shaftesbury, 98, 4.

‡Æthelheard, Æthelherdus, king of Wessex, p. 126.

Æthelhelm, ealdorman of Wiltshire, carries Alfred's alms to Rome, 86, 3, note on, p. 325.

— a knight, patron of Archbishop Oda, p. 334.

Æthelingaeg (Athelney, co. Somerset), Alfred intrenches himself in, 55, 2 ; description of, 92, 8; Alfred founds a monastery at, ibid., ‡p. 143; spurious charter of Alfred relating to, p. 259[4] ; charters of, p. lxv[3] ; monastery filled with French monks, 94, 6 ; John, first abbot there, 94, 1 ; attempted murder of, 95 98; origin of translation of the name as 'island of nobles,' p. 259[4].

Alre near, 56, 27.

‡ Ethelm, Eathelmus, Mercian ealdorman, a commander at the battle of Buttingtun, p. 142.

‡ Ethelnoth, Eathelmnothus, Mercian ealdorman, a commander at the victory at Buttingtun, p. 142.

Æthelred, Æthered, king of Wessex, accession of, 21, 3, ‡p. 132; aids Burhred, king of Mercia, in attacking the Danes at Nottingham, 30, 8; attacks the Danes at Reading unsuccessfully, 36, 1, 10; defeats the Danes at Ashdown, 37–39; his devout behaviour before the battle, 37, 15; 38, 17; defeated by the Danes at Basing, 40, 5; death and burial of, 41, 1; source of the erroneous day of his death given in Florence of Worcester, p. 109³, p. 240; style of, p. 149², ³; charters of, p. 229⁴, p. 299⁴.

— the Unready, king of England, style of, p. 148², p. 150⁴; charters of, p. 148², p. 150⁴; coronation oath of, p. 182.

— ‡Athelredus, king of the Mercians, becomes a monk, p. 125.

— king of Northumbria, marries Ælflæd, daughter of King Offa, p. 207.

— archbishop of Canterbury 870–889, alleged consecration of Cyfeiliog, bishop of Llandaff, by, p. 317.

— ealdorman of the Gainas, father-in-law of Alfred, 29, 5, note on, p. 227; a Mercian noble, 73, 7; his surname Mucill, 29, 6, erroneously explained as meaning 'big,' p. 230; his wife Eadburh, 29, 7.

— ealdorman of the Mercians, Eadredus (for Ætheredus, p. 318), ‡Adhered, marries Æthelflæd, eldest child of Alfred, 75, 7; date of this marriage, p. 300; South Welsh princes seek protection of Alfred against, 80, 8; Alfred commits London to him, 83, 4; his subjection to Alfred, p. 147; ‡defeats the Danes at

Benfleet, p. 141; and at Buttingtun, p. 142; charters of, p. 147².

Æthelstan, son of King Ecgberht, or of King Æthelwulf, under-king of Kent, erroneously identified with St. Neot, p. 256⁵; defeats the Danes at Sandwich, 6, 1.

— king of England, Alfred confers upon him a scarlet cloak, a gemmed belt and a sword with golden sheath, p. 184; probably a repetition of the creation of Alfred as a consul at Rome by the pope, p. 185; bestows abbey of Bath upon monks of St. Bertin, p. 320³; Latin verse life of, used by William of Malmesbury, p. lxxx¹, p. 184⁴, p. 318³; style of, p. 148, p. 150, p. 151, p. 152; charters of, p. xcii, p. 148¹, ², p. 246 and ⁴, p. 315.

— (Guthrum), Danish king of East Anglia. See Guthrum.

— bishop of Ramsbury, p. 305.

— a Mercian priest, aids Alfred in his studies, 77, 12; is rewarded by Alfred, 77, 15; note on, p. 304.

— one of Alfred's envoys to Rome, and on alleged mission to India, p. 289, p. 290.

Æthelswith, sister of King Alfred and wife of Burhred of Mercia, called 'queen,' p. 201; death of, p. 209².

‡Æthelthryth, St., Ætheldritha, founds a monastery at Ely, p. 123; death of, p. 124.

Æthelweard, youngest son of Alfred, 75, 4; becomes a scholar, 75, 11; note on, p. 299.

— Clito, son of Alfred, notice of his death in Florence of Worcester, p. 299.

— Clito, son of Edward the Elder, death of, p. 299⁴.

— ealdorman, Chronicle of, p. lxxx¹; errors in, p. 154⁶, p. 262, p. 289²; describes Aldhelm's bishopric as Sealwudscir, p. 198; locates the battle of Acleah in Surrey, p. 178[1]; his account of the battles of Cynuit, p. 262, and of Ethandun, p. 274[3]; shares silence of the Life regarding the Raven banner of the Danes, p. 266; identifies English Jutes with the Danish Jutes, p. 166[4], p. 170.

Æthelwold, ‡Adheluuoldus, nephew of King Alfred, bequest to, in Alfred's will, p. 213; ‡elected king of Northumbria, p. 106, p. 143; ‡arrives in Essex, p. 144; ‡joined by East Saxons and East Anglians, ibid.; ‡ravages Mercia, ibid.; ‡crosses Thames at Cricklade, ibid.; ‡ravages country about Braden Forest, ibid.; ‡returns to Essex, ibid.; ‡defeats the English, but falls in the fight, ibid.

— St., bishop of Winchester, p. 259; reform of monasteries by, p. 320, p. 333.

Æthelwulf, ‡Adheluulfus, king of Wessex, accession of, ‡p. 130; father of Alfred, 1, 7; sends envoys to Frankland in 839, p. 185; his intention of journeying to Rome, ibid.; defeats the Danes at Acleah, 5, 4; aids Burgred, king of Mercia, in reducing the Welsh, 7, 3; sends Alfred, his son, to Rome, 8, 1; letter of pope concerning the visit, p. 180[1]; gives his daughter ⟨Æthelswith⟩ in marriage to Burgred, 9, 9; his Donation to the church, 11, 2, note on, p. 186; charters relating to it, p. lxvi[1], p. 216; his visit to Rome, 11, 6, note on, p. 194; his gifts there, p. 211; erroneous ascription to him of the foundation or restoration of the Saxon School there, p. 245, p. 246; marries Judith, daughter of Charles the Bald, 11, 11; 13, 8; 68, 11; ‡p. 139; note on marriage, p.

194; baseless suggestion that he repudiated Osburh, Alfred's mother, p. 222; seats Judith on the throne, contrary to the West Saxon usage, 13, 9, note on, p. 200; plot against him during his absence abroad, 12, 2, note on, p. 195; surrenders western part of his realm to his rebellious son Æthelbeald, 12, 28; received with joy on return, 13, 2; letter of Lupus of Ferrières to, p. 225; his devout nature, 16, 18; his will, 16, 5, note on, p. 210; his charitable bequests, 16, 18, note on, p. 210; his bequests to Rome, 16, 26, note on, p. 210, alleged origin of Peter's Pence, p. 211[2]; dies, 17, 1; date of death, p. 196[1]; his alleged burial at Steyning, ‡p. 132, note on, p. 213; perpetuation of his name in family of the Count of Flanders, p. 308; alleged education of, by Swithun, p. c[2]; style of, p. 149[2,3]; charters of, p. 175, p. 187, p. 188, p. 189, p. 191, p. 199, p. 216, p. 235[2]; charters of, Frankish elements in, p. 203[1]; his pincerna Oslac, comes, 2, 3, 4; his secretary Felix, p. 203[1], p. 225, p. 306.

Æthelwulf, ealdorman of Berkshire, defeats the Danes, 18, 11; attacks and defeats the Danes at Englefield, 35, 11; slain by them in attack upon Reading, 36, 11.

Æthered. See Æthelred.

Æthilwald, Northumbrian (?) poet, p. 163.

‡Æthulf, Adhulfus, ealdorman, brother of Queen Ealhswith, death of, p. 143.

‡Agamundus, Danish leader, slain at Wednesfield, p. 144.

‡Aidan, St., death of, p. 122.

Alamanni, king of the, Charles ⟨son of Ludwig the German⟩, 70, 1.

‡Alban, St., martyrdom of, p. 117.

‡Alchsuuitha. *See* Ealhswith.

Alcuin, his embassy from Charles the Great to Offa, p. 207.

‡Aldfrith, Aldfridus, king of Northumbria, p. 124; ‡death of, p. 125.

Aldhelm, St., p. 326; use of, by author of the Life, p. xcv, p. 302; death of, p. 125.

‡Alemannia, p. 128.

Alfred, Ælfred, birth of, 1, 2; note on, p. 152; genealogy of, 1, 6 *sqq.*; sent to Rome by his father, 8, 2, note on, p. 180; adopted by Pope Leo IV as his (spiritual) son, and 'anointed king' by him, 8, 4; meaning of this ceremony, p. 180; created a Roman consul by Pope Leo IV, p. 180; meaning of this title, p. 184; alleged coronation of, at Rome, origin of story, p. 181; crown alleged to have been used upon that occasion formerly preserved in Westminster Abbey, p. 182; second visit to Rome, in company with his father, 11, 7, note on, p. 193; refers to his visit to Rome in his version of St. Augustine's 'Soliloquies,' p. 185; childhood and youth, account of, 21, 17; 22–25; person of, described, 22, 5; remains ignorant of letters until his twelfth year, 22, 11, note on, p. 220; his powers of memory as a child, 22, 13; 23, 13, note on, p. 221; his mother shows him book of Saxon poems, 23, 2, note on, p. 221; learns book of hours and psalter, 24, 1; marries ⟨Æthelswith⟩, daughter of Æthelred, ealdorman of the Gaini, 29, 5, ‡p. 132; 73, 7; seized with illness at the marriage feast, 74, 1; goes with Æthelred, king of Wessex, to Nottingham to aid Burgred, king of Mercia, against the Danes, 30, 9; assists his brother King Æthelred in unsuccessful attack upon the Danes in Reading, 36, 2, 10; his exploits at the battle of Ashdown, 37, 12; 38, 8; 'Secundarius' under his brother King Æthelred, 29, 3; 42, 2; this title applied to him at battle of Ashdown, 38, 8; defeated with King Æthelred by the Danes at Basing, 40, 3; succeeds his brother Æthelred as king of Wessex, 42, 1; coronation of, in England, p. 181; his coronation oath, p. 181; defeated by the Danes at Wilton, 42, 18; defeats the Danes at sea, 48, 1; makes terms with Danes in Wareham, 49, 10, which they break, 49, 17 (cf. interpolation, 50 c, 50 d, ‡p. 136); takes refuge from the Danes in marshes of Somerset, 53, 1; story of his sojourn therein with cowherd's wife, interpolated (from ‡p. 136), 53, 9; 53 b; note on this story, p. 256; interpolated story (from ‡p. 136) of his relations with St. Neot, and of his pride in early part of reign, 53 c; intrenches himself at Athelney, 55, 1; warlike operations from thence, 55, 5; meets men of Somerset, Wilts, and Hants at Ecgbriht's Stone, 55, 6, note on, p. 267; proceeds thence to Æcgleah, 55, 17, note on, p. 270; marches to Ethandun, 56, 2, note on, p. 273; compels the Danes there to surrender, 56, 15; and their king to receive Christianity, 56, 22; subsequently entertains the Danish king, 56, 31; defeats the Danes at sea, 64, 1; repulses the Danes from Rochester, 66, 11; sends his fleet to East Anglia, 67, 3; which captures thirteen Danish ships, 67, 5; but it is surprised and defeated by the Danes of East Anglia, 67, 9; the Danes in East Anglia break peace with, 72, 1; obtains exemption of Saxon School at Rome from tribute to the Pope, 71, 4; Pope Marinus sends gifts, including a portion of the cross, 71, 5, note on, p. 286, p. 293; South Wales under his power, 80, 2, notes on, p. 316 sqq.; siege of London by, p. 289; restores London, and commits it to Æthelred, ealdorman of the Mercians, 83, 2, note on, p. 324; defeats the Danes at Farnham, ‡p. 141; and at Exeter, ‡ibid.; releases wife and sons of Hæsten, ‡ibid.; submission of Danes to, ‡p. 147; cares of his reign, 76, 1; his interest in Saxon literature, 76, 9, note on, p. 300; carries book of psalms, hours, &c., in his bosom, 24, 3; 88, 5; regrets his neglected education, 76, 40; his love of learning, 76, 45; acquires assistants in learning, 76, 59, from his own country and elsewhere, 76, 68; induces Werfrith, bishop of Worcester, to translate Gregory's 'Dialogues,' 77, 6; assisted in his thirst for learning by Plegmund, archbishop of Canterbury, and two other Mercian priests, Æthelstan and Werwulf, 77, 10, 13; honours and rewards these four Mercians, 77, 14; has sacred books recited before him, 76, 26; has books recited before him before he learns to read, 77, 20; 'recites' Saxon poems and books and learns Saxon poems by heart, 76, 9; sends abroad for foreign scholars, 78, 2; induces Grimbald and John to come to him from Gaul, 78, 4, 8; traces of his connexion with Frankish scholars, p. 307; induces Asser to come to him from Wales, 79, 1; receives him at Denu in Sussex, 79, 7; converses with him, and offers inducements to enter his service, 79, 15;

writes to Asser to inquire reason of his failure to return as promised, 79, 37; Asser agrees to devote half the year to his service, 79, 45; Asser hopes that Alfred will be induced to protect St. Davids against Welsh king, 79, 51; Asser reads books to, 81, 11; Alfred grants to Asser monasteries of Congresbury and Banwell, with all possessions in them, and other goods, 81, 20, note on, p. 320; and afterwards confers upon him the see of Exeter, 81, 28, note on, p. 321, and innumerable other gifts, 81, 30; grants him leave to return home, 81, 38; Asser reads to him, 88, 3; requests Asser to copy passages into his Handbook, 88, 9, 30; many other extracts added later, 88, 36; begins to read and interpret, 87, 1; reads and interprets in English, 89, 2; begins to read and interpret at Martinmas, 89, 14; has books read before him day and night, or reads them himself, 81, 12; has selected passages copied into book, which he called his ' Handbook,' 89, 19, note on, p. 326; his Handbook, p. 153, p. 326; ' Dicta Regis Elfredi,' p. 153[1]; his version of Boethius, p. lxviii, p. 327; ' Proverbs of,' p. lxxii[5]; his translation of Gregory's 'Pastoral Care,' p. lxv, p. cv, p. cvi, p. 225, p. 310, p. 311; MSS. of, p. xvi; date of, p. cv; his translation of Orosius, p. 169; Beda translation ascribed to, p. 153; his possible connexion with redaction of West Saxon royal genealogy, p. 153, and of the Chronicle, p. 181; alleged to have visited the University of Oxford to assuage disputes between Grimbald and the scholars, according to Camden's interpolation, 83 b, 8, notes on, § 8,

p. xxiii sqq., p. 324; tells Asser story of Eadburh, queen of Wessex, and Beorhtric, her husband, 13, 31; interest in investigation of unknown things, 76, 20, note on, p. 300; instructs goldsmiths and other craftsmen, 76, 5; instructs falconers and hounds, 76, 6; his skill as a hunter, 22, 15; 76, 4; visits church of St. Gueriir when hunting in Cornwall, 74, 18; his devotions, 76, 12; his religious nature, 92, 1; 99, 1; devotes half his time and revenue to God, 99, 9; 102, 1; 103, 7; a quarter of the revenue thus assigned allocated to relief of the poor, 102, 7, another to his monasteries, 102, 15, a third quarter to his school, 102, 17, and the remainder as gifts to monasteries in England, Wales, Cornwall, Gaul, Armorica, and Ireland, 102, 19; his division of his revenue, and allocation of it, 100, 1; carries relics of the saints about with him, 104, 11; frequent visitor to holy places from his infancy for prayer and almsgiving, 74, 22, 47; 76, 15; his chastity, 74, 42; founds monastery at Athelney, 92, 8; founds a monastery at Shaftesbury, 98, 1; his daughter Æthelgeofu first abbess, 98, 4; his care for the poor, 105, 6; almsgiving of, to foreigners and strangers, 76, 16; receives and adopts foreigners, noble and ignoble, who come to his court, 76, 21, note on, p. 301; his generosity to strangers flocking to his court, 101, 7; his care for his bishops and nobles, &c., 76, 30; educates sons of nobles in his court, 76, 32; his affability, 76, 19; his illness and infirmities, 91, 1; suffered from infancy from ficus, 74, 16, note on, p. 295; cured by intercession of St. Gueriir, 74, 17; story of origin of this illness, 74, 40, note on, p. 294; seized with another illness at his marriage, 74, 1, from which he suffers from his twentieth to his fortieth or forty-fifth year, 74, 9, 61; 91, 2; suppositions as to nature of illness, 74, 12, note on, p. 294; sufferings from, 74, 65; cares of government, 91, 9; his wars, 91, 12; missions to, from foreign nations, 91, 14; his alleged mission to India, p. lxix, p. 288, p. 329[1]; letters and gifts to, from the patriarch of Jerusalem, 91, 15, note on, p. 328; restores cities, and founds new ones, 91, 18; his beautiful buildings, 91, 20, note on, p. 329; constructs royal villae, 91, 21; receives lukewarm support from his subjects in his government, 91, 30, 45; orders erection of fortresses, 91, 49, 71; arranges that a third of his ministers shall reside at court for one month out of three, 100, 10, note on, p. 337; workmen, rewards to, 101, 4; employs workmen of many nationalities, 101, 5; uses candles to measure time by, 104, 6, 10, notes on, p. 338, p. 339; encloses them in horn lantern to secure equal combustion, 104, 25, note on, p. 339; divides the day and night into equal hours, p. 339; his supervision of judicial arrangements, 105, 5; 106, passim, note on, p. 342; threatens to deprive incompetent judicial officers of their offices, 106, 36, unless they learn to read, 106, 40; his estates in Devon and Cornwall, p. 323[3]; overlord of Mercia, p. 147; his style, p. 147; his charters, p. 151[2], p. 211, p. 259[4]; his alleged relationship to St. Neot, p. 256[5]; his relationship to Osweald, 'filius regis,' who

witnesses his charters, p. 299[4];
his will, p. lxii, p. lxvii, p. 151,
p. 154, p. 189, p. 210, p. 213,
p. 273, p. 299, p. 303, p. 323[3],
p. 337[2]; date of, p. lxvii[3]; his
death, interpolated notice of,
106 b; error as to date of his
death, p. 111, p.142; interpolated
verses on him, 106 c; description of his character, p. 142, p.
143; his tomb, p. 143; his family,
account of, 75, note on, p. 299.
Alfred, enemy of King Æthelstan,
p. 246.
Alfred of Beverley copies Florence
of Worcester, not the Life, p.
lxiv, p. 239.
Alfred's Camp, near Ashdown
Park, co. Berks, an antiquarian
figment, p. 235[2].
Alfrida. See Ælfthryth.
Allen, Thomas, M.A., of Trinity
College and Gloucester Hall,
p. xxvii, p. xxxvii.
Alre, near Athelney (Aller, co.
Somerset), Guthrum, the Danish
king, meets Alfred at, and receives baptism, 56, 27.
Althrida. See Ælfthryth.
‡Ambrose, St., bishop of Milan,
death of, p. 118.
Amesbury, nunnery of, granted to
abbey of Fontévrault, p. 156.
Anaraut, son of Rotri (Anarawd,
son of Rhodri Mawr), and his
brothers desert Northumbrian
alliance and submit to Alfred,
who becomes Anaraut's godfather, 80, 13; oppressions of
the six sons of Rotri in South
Wales, 80, 5, 12; notes on,
p. 316, p. 318.
‡Andreadesweald, Andredewal',
forest of, p. 140, p. 156[3].
Angli, all the, and Saxones not
under captivity to the Danes
submit to Alfred, 83, 6.
Anglorum, Gesta, referred to by
Adam of Bremen, p. 112.
Anglorum, Rex, origin of title,
p. 151.

Angul-Saxones, Dedication, 3
(p. 1); 1, 2; 13, 31; 21, 17;
64, 1; 67, 1; 71, 4; 73, 6;
83, 1; 87, 2; history of this
compound, p. 149.
Angul-Saxonum rex, use of title,
p. 149.
‡Anna, son of Eni, the brother
of Rædwald, king of East
Anglia, p. 122; death of, p. 110,
p. 123.
Annales Cambriae, chronology of,
p. lxv.
— Sancti Edmundi, p. 101, p. 102,
p. 103.
— Uticenses. See Ouche.
Annals of Lund, Latin version of
entries in the O.E. Chronicle in,
p. 105[1], p. 112[5]; author of, did not
use Annals of St. Neots, p. 112.
— Norman. See Norman Annals.
— of St. Neots. See St. Neots,
Annals of.
‡Anolafus niger, Danish leader,
slain at Wednesfield, p. 145.
‡Antiniacum (Attigny-sur-Aisne,
Ardennes, France), p. 128.
Antiqui Saxones. See Eald-
Saxones.
Anvind, Danish king, winters at
Cambridge, 47, 10.
‡Apuldre (Appledore, co. Kent),
Danes at, p. 140, p. 141.
‡Aquisgran⟨um⟩. See Aachen.
‡Arator, the poet, p. 120.
‡Archadius, the emperor, p. 118.
Ardington, co. Berks, p. 236[4].
Armorica, Brittany, Alfred's gifts
to monasteries in, 102, 22.
Armorici at Alfred's court, 76, 22.
Arnolf, the Emperor. See Ear-
nulf.
Arundel, Earl of, his transcript of
the Life, p. xxxix, p. liv.
Ashdown. See Æscesdun.
Ashdown Park, parish of Ashbury,
co. Berks, p. 235.
Ashendon, co. Bucks, erroneously
identified with Æscesdun, p.
235[1].
Assedone, Domesday manor in

Hundred of Compton, co. Berks, near Ashampstead, erroneously identified with Æscesdun, p. 238.

Asser, Dedication, 3 (p. 1); comes to Alfred at his solicitation from Wales, 79, 1; conducted to Alfred at Denu in Sussex, 79, 5; reception by Alfred, 79, 8; Alfred requests him to join his service and become his friend, 79, 10; Asser obtains leave to refer decision to his brethren, 79, 15; leaves Alfred under a promise to return in six months' time, 79, 29; on journey home is stricken down with fever in Wintonia (Caerwent, p. 313), 79, 33; writes to Alfred to inform him of reason for delay, 79, 40; decides, by advice of his brethren, to devote half the year to Alfred's service, in order to obtain his protection for St. Davids against depredations of King Hemeid, 79, 45; Asser's kinsman Nobis, archbishop of St. Davids, had been expelled thence by Hemeid, who had also expelled Asser, 79, 55; Asser's second visit to Alfred, whom he finds at Leonaford, 81, 7; stays in his court eight months, 81, 10; reads books to Alfred, 81, 10; seeks in vain for licence to return home, 81, 15; Alfred grants to him possessions in the monasteries of Congresbury and Banwell, and the two monasteries, and other gifts, 81, 20, note on, p. 320; afterwards confers upon him the see of Exeter, 81, 28, note on, p. 321; Alfred grants to him permission to return home, 81, 38; reads to Alfred, 88, 3; writes passages at Alfred's request in the latter's handbook, 88, 9, 30; adds later many other extracts, 88, 36; Bishop, account of, p. lxv; interpolated notice of, 106 d; origin of the Christian name

John applied erroneously to him, p. 344; ‡death of, p. 144; his Life of Alfred, extracts from, in Annals of St. Neots, p. 104; nature of copy used by compiler of Annals of St. Neots, p. lvii, p. 104; copy of, in monastery of Bury St. Edmunds?, p. 101.

Aston, near Wallingford, co. Berks, wrongly identified with Æscesdun, p. 235[1].

Athelney. See Æthelingaeg.

‡Athelredus. See Æthelred.

‡Audoenus (Ouen), St., death of, p. 123; translation of, p. 131.

‡Augustine, St., mission to Britain of, p. 121; Gregory sends pall to him, with Paulinus and other missionaries, p. 121.

‡— of Hippo, St., death of, p. 118; ‘Soliloquies’ of, King Alfred's version of, p. 185.

‡Autisiodorensium urbs.      See Auxerre.

‡Auxerre, Autisiodorensium urbs, battle between sons of Ludwig the Pius (at Fontenay-en-Puisaye, Yonne) near, p. 131.

Avon, River. See Abon.

Bægscecg, Danish king, slain at Ashdown, 39, 20.

‡Baioarii, the, p. 140.

Baldwin I, Count of Flanders, elopes with Judith, widow of Kings Æthelwulf and Æthelbeald, p. 223.

— II, Count of Flanders, son-in-law of Alfred, p. 308.

Bale, John, account of the Life by, p. xxxv, p. 115.

Banuwille (Banwell, co. Somerset), monastery of, granted by Alfred to Asser, 81, 22, note on, p. 320.

Barroc wood. See Berroc.

Bartholomew, St., shrine of, Alfred's alleged mission to, p. 288.

Basengas (Basing, co. Hants), defeat of King Æthelred and

Alfred at, by the Danes, **40**, 3, note on, p. 239.

Basing. *See* **Basengas.**

Bath abbey, bestowed by King Æthelstan upon ejected monks of St. Bertin, p. 320[3]; charters of, p. lxvi[1], p. 150[4], p. 246[4].

‡Bavaria, Bauuaria, Charles the Great in, p. 128; conquest of, by Franks, p. 128.

‡Beamfleot (Benfleet, co. Essex), Danes encamp at, p. 141; are defeated there by Ealdorman Æthelred, ibid.; Hæsten returns thither and restores the fort, ibid.

**Bearrocenses.** *See* Berkshire.

**Bearrocscir.** *See* Berkshire.

Beaw, **Beauu**, ancestor of the kings of Wessex, **1**, 36.

Bec Hellouin, Le, monastery of, Normandy, p. 257, p. 260, p. 268.

Beda, the Venerable, ‡p. 126; death of, ‡ibid.; his ' Historia Ecclesiastica,' use of, by author of the Life, p. xcv; extracts from, in the Annals of St. Neots, p. 104; Iutae, Iuti of, note on, p. 167; O.E. translation of, p. 153, p. 170.

Bedwig, **Beduuig**, ancestor of kings of Wessex, **1**, 38.

Behorsian, meaning of, in O.E., p. 290.

**Beldeag**, ancestor of kings of Wessex, **1**, 20.

‡Benedict, St. (of Nursia), p. 119.

Benfleet, co. Essex. *See* Beamfleot.

‡Bensingus, Danish leader, slain at Wednesfield, p. 144.

Beodrices-weorð, O.E. name of Bury St. Edmunds, p. 220.

**Beorhtric**, ‡Brihtricus, king of Wessex, accession of, ‡p. 128; marriage of, ‡ibid.; poisoned by his wife, Eadburh, **14**, 18; **15**, 1; his charters, p. 206.

Beorhtwulf, **Beorhtulfus**, king of Mercia, **4**, 8; defeated by the Danes, **4**, 8.

**Beorngar** (Berengar, king of Italy), receives rule of Lombardy, **85**, 18.

Beornnoð, error for Beorhtnoð in MS. A of Chron. an. 905, p. 106.

‡Beornwulf, Beornulfus, king of the Mercians, death of, p. 130.

Beowulf, Eotena, the (English) Jutes, of, p. 169; Hreðgotan of, p. 169[5]; meaning of ' nefa ' in, p. 172; ' þusend,' a denomination of value, in, p. 154[6].

Berkshire, **Bearrocscir, Berrocscir**, **1**, 4; **35**, 7; derivation of name, **1**, 4. Ealdorman of: *see* Æthelwulf. Men of, ' Bearrocenses,' **35**, 7. Alfred's estates in, p. 154.

— Downs, formerly known as Æscesdun, p. 235.

‡Berneardus, king of Lombardy, death of, p. 129.

**Berroc** wood, in Berkshire, **1**, 4; later occurrences of name, p. 156.

**Berrocscir.** *See* Berkshire.

Biblical quotations in the Life, source of, p. xciv.

Bishops, O.E. list of, p. lxvi, p. civ, p. 228[2].

Blandford, co. Dorset, p. 319.

Boethius, Alfred's version of, p. lxviii.

Bonnonia. *See* Boulogne.

Book (charter), the O.E., functions of, p. 189.

Bookland, p. 189.

Borough in local names sometimes derived from O.E. *beorge*, dat. sing. of *beorh*, p. 175.

‡Bosa, bishop of the Northumbrians, p. 124.

‡Botulf, St., founds monastery at Ycanhoh, p. 123.

‡Boulogne, Bonnonia, Danes at, p. 140.

Bowyer, Boyer (Sir George?), owns copy of the Life, p. xxxiii[3].

Box, growth of, in Berks, **1**, 4, note on, p. 157.

Boxford, co. Berks, p. 157.

Boxgrove, parish of Sulham, co. Berks, p. 157.

‡Bradena (Braden Forest, co. Wilts), Danes ravage country about, p. 144.

Bratton Castle, co. Wilts, White Horse under, p. 273.

Brecheniauc (Brecknock), Helised, son of Teudubr, king of, seeks protection of Alfred, 80, 11.

Bretwealda, use of title, p. 147.

‡Brichtnothus. See Byrhtnoth.

‡Brihtricus. See Beorhtric.

‡Brihtsige, Brihtsinus, son of Brichnoth, clito, slain, p. 144.

Britain, invaded by Julius Caesar, ‡p. 117; conquered by the Emperor Claudius, ‡ibid.; deserted by the Romans, ‡p. 118; settlements of the English in, ‡p. 119; arrival of Cerdic and Cynric in, ‡p. 119. Use of, in titles of O.E. Kings, p. 148, p. 151.

Britannia, Britain, 21, 6; 49, 25. — 'Wales,' 7, 9; 79, 2, 50; Britannia Dexteralis, 'South Wales,' under power of Alfred, 80, 2.

Britannica Insula, 61, 2.

Britannicus sermo, 'Welsh,' 9, 4; Britannice, 'in Welsh,' 30, 3; 49, 3, 22; 55, 8; 57, 5.

Britanny. See Armorica.

Britones, of the Isle of Wight, 2, 9. — (the Welsh), 1, 17; at Alfred's court, 76, 22. — Mediterranei, the inhabitants of Mid-Wales, reduced to submission by Æthelwulf, king of Wessex, and Burgred, king of Mercia, 7, 5.

‡Britons, the, invite English to Britain, p. 119; defeated by English at Ægelesthrep, ibid.; defeated at Cerdices ora by Cerdic and Cynric, p. 119.

Brixton Deverill, co. Wilts, erroneously identified with Ecgbrihtes Stan, p. 267; etymology of the name, p. 268.

Brochmail, son of Mouric, king of Gwent, seeks protection of Alfred, 80, 6, note on, p. 317.

Brompton, John, compilation bearing name of, p. lxiii[1], p. lxiv.

Brond, ancestor of kings of Wessex, 1, 19.

‡Brunichildis, queen of the Franks, p. 120.

Buildings, improvement in, by Alfred, 76, 6.

‡Burchardus, dux, slain, p. 145.

Bures St. Mary, co. Suffolk, alleged birthplace of St. Edmund, king of the East Angles, p. 215; coronation of St. Edmund at, p. 132.

Burgred, Burhred, king of Mercia, obtains assistance from Æthelwulf, king of Wessex, in reducing the Welsh, 7, 2; marries daughter of King Æthelwulf of Wessex, 9, 11; seeks aid of Æthelred, king of Wessex, and Alfred to repel Danes from Nottingham, where they besiege them in vain, 30, 6, 16; driven from his kingdom by the Danes, goes to Rome, 46, 7, where he dies and is buried, 46, 9.

‡Burh (Peterborough), foundation of monastery at, p. 125.

Burna. See Bures.

Burua, Edmund, king of East Anglia, interpolated account of coronation of, at, 17 b, 7 (from ‡p. 132), note on, p. 215.

Bury St. Edmunds, foundation of monastery at, p. 232; Annals of St. Neots probably compiled in, p. 101; probably owned a copy of Asser, 101; copy of Norman Annals owned by, 101. — Annals of. See Annales S. Edmundi.

‡Buttingtuna (Buttington, co. Montgomery), Danes defeated at, p. 142.

‡Byrhtnoth, Brichtnothus, clito, father of Brihtsige, p. 106, p. 144.

‡Byrinus, St., baptises King Cyne

gils of Wessex, p. 121; preaches to the East Saxons, p. 122.

Byrnstan, bishop of Winchester, story about, p. 108[4].

Caerwent (co. Monmouth)., *See* Wintonia.

‡Caesar Augusta. *See* Saragossa.

‡Caesar, Julius, conquest of Britain by, p. 116.

Cainan, 1, 41.

Cairceri, British name of Cirencester, 57, 5.

Cairuuisc, British name of Exeter, 49, 23, note on, p. 252.

Caius, Dr. John, uses the Life, p. xxxvi.

— Dr. Thomas, Master of University College, Oxford, his acquaintance with the Life, p. xxxvii.

Cambra, 'chamber,' 88, 1; 91, 21; note on, p. xciv.

Cambridge. *See* Grantebrycg.

Camden, William, his edition of the Life, p. xxi; a mere reprint of Parker's text, p. xxii, with a few arbitrary alterations, p. xxiii; interpolates in it a spurious passage regarding the University of Oxford, p. xxiii; his statement regarding the source of this interpolation, p. xxvi.

Camelgeac, bishop of Llandaff. *See* Cyfeiliog.

Candles, nature of, in Alfred's time, p. 338; Alfred uses them as time-measurers, 104, 6.

Cannington Park, co. Somerset, erroneous identification of, with Cynuit, p. 265[3].

Canterbury. *See* Dorubernia.

— archbishops of. *See* Ælfheah, Æthelred, Ceolnoth, Deusdedit, Dunstan, Plegmund, Sigeric, Tatwine, Theodore, Wulfred.

— Christ Church, charters relating to, p. 151[2], p. 165[2], p 290[1], p. 304; catalogue of library of, p. xxxv.

Canterbury, St. Augustine's abbey, charter relating to, p. 220.

Cantia (Kent), 3, 9; 5, 4; 6, 3; 66, 5; defeat of the Danes at Sandwich in, 6, 3; wasted by the Danes, 20, 9; Alfred sends fleet to East Anglia from, 67, 2: *see also* Kent. King of: *see* Æthelberht. Ealdorman of: *see* Ealhere.

Cantuarii (the men of Kent), 3, 8; purchase peace of the Danes in vain, 20, 3.

Cantwariorum civitas. *See* Dorubernia.

Capellani, 77, 13; 104, 2; note on, p. 305.

‡Capua, Charles the Great at, p. 128.

Carisbrooke, Isle of Wight, erroneously derived from Wihtgaraburh, p. 174; early forms of the name, p. 174[3].

‡Carisiacensis, synod. *See* Cérizy.

Carlomannus. *See* Karlmann.

‡Carnotensis. *See* Chartres.

Carolus. *See* Charles.

Castellum, 'fort,' 91, 49, note on, p. 331.

Cauticae = *caudicae* (*naves*), 92, 11, note on, p. 332.

Caziei (Chézy l'Abbaye, dep. of the Aisne, France), the Danes from Paris winter at, 84, 11; 86, 2.

‡Ceadda, bishop of the Northumbrians, p. 123.

‡Ceadwalla, king of Wessex, p. 124; death of, ibid.

Ceaster, 'chester,' occurrence of, in Picardy, p. 311[2].

Ceawlin, Ceaulin, king of Wessex, 1, 15; ‡p. 120; confused with Ceolwulf, p. 159.

Centwine, related to King Ine, p. 153.

‡— Kentuuine, king of Wessex, p. 123.

Cenwealh, king of Wessex, grants land in 648 by Æscesdun to Cuthred, son of Cwichelm, p. 154, p. 236, p. 237; harries the

Mercians as far as Æscesdun in 661, p. 237. *See* Koenwalh.

‡Ceol, king of Wessex, duration of reign of, p. 106, p. 120.

Ceolnoth, archbishop of Canterbury, 833–890, p. 322; death and burial of, 34, 1, note on, p. 233.

Ceolwald, grandfather of King Ine, 1, 14.

Ceolwulf, a king's thane, made king of Mercia by the Danes during their pleasure, 46, 16; Danes divide kingdom between themselves and him, 51, 2; portion of Mercia ruled by, p. 147².

‡— king of Northumberland, duration of reign of, p. 106, p. 126; erroneously said to have become bishop of Lindisfarne, p. 107, p. 126; origin of error, p. 107.

— king of Wessex, ‡p. 221; confused with King Ceawlin, p. 159.

Ceorl, ealdorman of Devon, defeats the Danes at Wicganbeorh, 3, 2, ‡p. 131; note on, p. 175.

Cerdic, king of Wessex, 1, 16; arrival of, in Britain, ‡p. 119; duration of his reign, ‡p. 120; grandfather, not father, of King Cynric according to lost archetype of the West Saxon royal genealogy, p. 157; captures Isle of Wight, p. 171; 'avunculus' of Stuf and Wihtgar, 2, 8, note on, p. 171.

‡Cerdices ora, arrival of Cerdic and Cynric at, p. 119; defeat of Britons at, ibid.

Cerenhir, bishop of Llandaff, p. 317.

‡Cérizy, Carisiacensis, synod of, in 741, p. 103, p. 127.

Challow, co. Berks, p. 157.

Chancery, connexion of, with royal chapel, p. 305.

Charles the Great, Carolus, the Emperor, 70, 10; receives Eadburh, the widow of Beorhtric, king of Wessex, 15, 4; story of his offer to her of choice between him and his son, and of her foolish answer, 15, 5; makes her abbess of a nunnery, 15, 14; ejects her for incontinence, 15, 22; his relations with King Offa, p. 206; ‡son of Pippin, king of the Franks, p. 127; ‡commencement of his reign, ibid.; ‡conquers Italy, p. 127; ‡his campaign in Spain, p. 128; ‡his second journey to Rome, p. 128; ‡his Bavarian expedition, p. 128; ‡his campaign against the Slaves, p. 128; ‡the wastes Hungary, p. 128; ‡created emperor, p. 129; ‡death of, p. 129.

Charles II (the Bald), the Emperor, ‡birth of, p. 130; ‡defeats his brother Lothaire, p. 131; interpolated note of his reign in Life, 10, 7; gives his daughter Judith in marriage to King Æthelwulf, 11, 12; 13, 8; 68, 10; ‡death of, p. 104, p. 136, p. 138.

— III ('the Fat'), the Emperor, commencement of reign (!), p. 131; succeeds to West Frankish kingdom, 70, 7, ‡p. 139; ‡vision of, p. 102, p. 140; dethronement and death of, 85, 1, 3, ‡p. 140.

— (son of Ludwig the German), king of the Alemanni, becomes king of the West Franks, 70, 1; son of Ludwig, 70, 6.

— ‡Martel, Maior Domus, p. 125; vision of, p. 126; death of, p. 126.

— ‡Puer ('the Simple'), king of West Frankland, accession of, p. 141.

‡Chartres, civitas Carnotensis, besieged by Rollo, p. 142; Walthelm, bishop of, ibid.

Cheke, Lady, her copy of the Life, p. xxxiii³, p. xxxv¹.

Chertsey abbey, spurious charter of Offa to, p. 208³; charters relating to, p. 151², p. 220⁷.

Chézy. *See* **Caziei.**

Chichester, charter relating to, p. 330[6].

‡Childebertus II, king of the Franks, p. 120.

— III, king of the Franks, p. 124.

‡Childericus I, king of the Franks, p. 119.

‡— II, king of the Franks, p. 124.

‡Chilpericus I, king of the Franks, p. 120.

‡— II (Daniel), king of the Franks, p. 125.

Chippenham, co. Wilts. *See* **Cippanhamme.** Tumulus of Ubba near, an antiquarian figment, p. 265.

Chronicle, the Old English, p. lxxxii, p. xcix ; traces of readings of archetype of, p. lxxxviii, p. 158, p. 171, p. 173, p. 175, p. 186, p. 231[1], p. 287 ; notes on variant readings of existing MSS. of, p. lxxxv, p. lxxxviii[1], p. 112[5], p. 157, p. 158, p. 160, p. 175, p. 177, p. 179, p. 198, p. 216, p. 217, p. 230, p. 231[1], p. 233, p. 239[3], p. 240, p. 242, p. 247, p. 248, p. 254, p. 261, p. 265, p. 270, p. 287, p. 289, p. 317[8], p. 324 ; version of, used by author of the Life, p. lxxxv, by Florence of Worcester (see under his name), by compiler of Annals of St. Neots, p. 104, p. 105 ; hypothetical Latin original of, p. lxxxiii, p. 105[1] : chronology of, p. lxxxii, p. lxxxviii[2], p. 280 sqq., p. 282[1]; possible traces of Alfred's influence in composition of, p. 153, p. 181, p. 217, p. 301 ; annals of 530 and 534 in, p. 171 ; notices of foreign affairs in, p. 309[2] ; modernizations of early forms in, by scribe of Parker MS. of, p. 173.

Chute Forest, co. Wilts, p. 156.

Cippanhamme (Chippenham, co. Wilts), marriage of Burhred, king of Mercia, with daughter

of Æthelwulf, king of Wessex, at, 9, 12, note on, p. 186; Danes from Exeter go to, 52, 4, and winter there, 52, 6, ‡p. 136 ; its site described, 52, 4 ; Danes leave, for Cirencester, 57, 3.

Cirrenceaster (Cirencester, co. Gloucester), called in British 'Cairceri,' 57, 5 ; situation of, ibid. ; Danes from Chippenham march to, and remain there for a year, 57, 4 ; leave, for East Anglia, 60, 3.

‡Claudius, the Emperor, conquest of Britain by, p. 117.

Cley Hill, parish of Corsley, co. Wilts, erroneous identification of, with Ægleah, Igleah, p. 270.

‡Clodio, second king of the Franks, p. 118.

‡Clodoveus I, king of the Franks, p. 119 ; baptism of, ibid.

‡— III, king of the Franks, p. 124.

‡Clotharius II, king of the Franks, p. 120.

‡— III, king of the Franks, p. 123.

Cluni, Richard of, chronicle of, p. 324.

Coenred, father of King Ine, 1, 13 ; note on this form, p. 160.

‡— Keonrædus, Kenredus, king of the Mercians, p. 125 ; goes to Rome and there dies, ibid.

Coit Maur, British name of Selwood Forest, 55, 7.

‡Columba, St., arrival in Britain of, p. 120.

Comes = ealdorman, 2, 6 ; 3, 3 ; 6, 2 ; 9, 1, 8 ; 12, 7, 10 ; 18, 10, 11 ; 29, 5 ; 75, 7 ; 86, 2 ; 106, 3, 40, 43 ; applied to Danish leaders, 35, 8, 12, 16 ; 37, 8 ; 39, 16, 20, 21, 22.

‡Commerciacum (Commercy, dep. of the Meuse, France), villa, p. 130.

Condé. *See* **Cundoth.**

Congresbury. *See* **Cungresbyri.**

‡Conrad I, son of Conrad, king of the Franks, p. 145.

‡Constantine, the Emperor, p. 117.

‡Constantius, the Emperor, p. 117.

Constitutio Domus Regis, the, p. 306[1].

Conybeare, Edward, translation of the Life by, p. xxxii.

Cornubia (Cornwall), church of St. Gueriir in (at St. Neot), visited by Alfred, 74, 19; diocese of Exeter in, granted to Asser by Alfred, 81, 30, note on, p. 321; Alfred's gifts to monasteries in, 102, 22.

Cornwall, King Ecgberht gives lands in, to bishopric of Sherborne, p. 296; possessions of Alfred in, p. 296, p. 323[3]; see of, p. 322; originally included in see of Sherborne, ibid. See also Cornubia. Bishop of: see Kenstec.

Coronation oath of the O.E. kings, p. 182.

Coronatus, 'tonsured,' 79, 17, note on, p. 313.

Corpus Christi College, Cambridge, Archbishop Parker's bequest of MSS. to, p. xviii[1], p. xxxvii; his transcript of the Life preserved there, p. li.

Cotton, Sir Thomas, obtains possession of the MS. of the Life, p. xl.

Countesbury, co. Devon, erroneously identified with Cynuit, p. 265[3].

Crediton, see of, transferred to Exeter in 1050, p. 321. Bishop of: see Eadwulf.

Creoda, king of Wessex, 1, 15; son of Cerdic, and father of Cynric according to the lost archetype of the West Saxon royal genealogy, p. 157.

‡Criccalada (Cricklade, co. Wilts), Danes under Æthelwold at, p. 144.

Cross, portion of the, presented to King Alfred by Pope Marinus, 71, 7, note on, p. 286, p. 293.

Crowland abbey, charters relating

to, p. 305[7]; story about St. Neot's body from, in Ordericus Vitalis, p. 298.

Cuda (Cuða), ancestor of Alfred, 1, 14.

Cultus, error in MS. for curtu(s), 100, 5, 11, 21, note on, p. 219.

Cundoth (Condé, dep. of the Nord, France), monastery at, 65, 4, note on, p. 286; Danes ascend the Scheldt to, 65, 4.

Cungresbyri (Congresbury, co. Somerset), monastery of, granted by Alfred to Asser, 81, 22, note on, p. 320.

Curtis, 'enclosure,' use of, in England, p. 220.

Curtu(s), 'court,' 22, 4; 75, 22; 81, 10; 100, 5, 6, 11, 21; note on, p. 219; written cultus in Cott. MS., p. xxix[5].

‡Cuthbert, author of letter concerning Beda's death, p. 126.

— St., p. 124.

Cuthburh, sister of King Ine and of Ingeld, queen of Bernicia, abbess of Wimborne, p. 155.

Cuthmann, St., buried at Steyning, p. 213; spurious life of, p. 213[6].

‡Cuthred, king of Wessex, date of accession of, p. 106, p. 126; probably a member of the West Saxon royal house, p. 155.

— son of Cwichelm, grant of land by Æscesdun to, by King Cenwealh, p. 154, p. 236.

Cuthwine, ancestor of Alfred, 1, 14.

— Cuthuuinus, addressee of letter of Cuthbert concerning Beda's death, p. 126.

Cwantawic, Quantauuic, Quentawich (Wicquinghem, dep. of Pas-de-Calais, France), p. 206[4]; ‡Danes at, p. 106, p. 131.

Cwichelmes-hlæw, now Scutchamfly Barrow, parish of East Hendred, co. Berks, p. 236; early forms of the name, ibid.; probably tumulus of Cwichelm, king of Wessex, who died in 593, ibid.

Cyfeiliog, bishop of Llandaff, p. lxx; alleged consecration of, by Æthelred, archbishop of Canterbury, p. 317.

‡Cynegils, Kynegylsus, king of Wessex, p. 121; baptism of, p. 121.

Cynete, the river (Kennet, co. Berks), 35, 10.

‡Cynewulf, Kyneuulfus, king of Wessex, p. 127.

Cynric, king of Wessex, 1, 15; ‡ arrives in Britain, p. 119; grandson, not son of, Cerdic, according to the lost archetype of the West Saxon royal genealogy, p. 157; captures with Cerdic the Isle of Wight, p. 171; ‡duration of reign of, p. 106, p. 120; 'consobrinus' of Stuf and Wihtgar, 2, 8.

Cynuit, arx, Danes besiege English in, and are defeated by garrison, 54, 6, 20, note on, p. 261; description of site of, 54, 10; attempts to identify, p. cxix, p. 262.

‡Dagobert I, king of the Franks, p. 121, p. 122.

‡— III, king of the Franks, p. 125.

Danes, pagani, ‡Normanni, ‡first arrival of, in Wessex, p. 128; ‡waste Rouen, p. 131; ‡battles against, at London, Cwantawic, and Rochester, ibid.; ‡in the Seine, ibid.; ‡in Frankland, p. 132; defeated at Wicganbeorh, 3, 4; winter in Sheppey, 3, 6; arrive in Thames, 4, 3; defeat Beorhtwulf, king of the Mercians, 4, 8; in Surrey, 5, 2; defeated at Acleah by King Æthelwulf, 5, 7; defeat and slay the ealdormen of Kent and Surrey in the Isle of Thanet, 9, 7; winter in the Isle of Sheppey, 10, 8; harry Winchester, 18, 8; subsequently defeated, 18, 12;

winter in the Isle of Thanet, 20, 2; waste East Kent, 20, 9; move from East Anglia to York, 26, 3; leave Mercia for Northumbria, 31, 3; march through Mercia to East Anglia, 32, 3; winter at Thetford, 32, 5; defeat and slay Edmund, king of East Anglia, 33, 4; defeated at Ashdown, 37–39; defeat the king of Wessex and Alfred at Basing, 40, 6; fresh army of, arrives from parts beyond sea, 40, 8; make peace with the West Saxons, 43, 1; go to London, where they winter, 44, 3; make peace with the Mercians, 44, 4; leave London and winter in Lindsey, 45, 3; again make peace with the Mercians, 45, 5; leave Lindsey, and winter at Repton, in Mercia, 46, 3; leave Repton, 47, 3; one half goes to Northumbria, the other to Cambridge, 47, 5; in Northumbria ravage the Picts and Strathclyde men, 47, 8; under Guthrum winter at Cambridge, 47, 10; defeated by Alfred at sea, 48, 1; leave Cambridge, and proceed to Wareham, where they make terms with Alfred, 49, 4, 10; which they break, stealing away by night to Exeter, 49, 17; where they winter, 49, 26, interpolated 50 c, 2, 9; under Healfdene settle in Northumbria, 50, 2; in Mercia divide that kingdom between themselves and their puppet-king Ceolwulf, 51, 2; winter in Dyfed (South Wales), 54, 2; under brother of Healfdene and Inwar defeated at Cynuit, 54; interpolated account of capture of raven-banner of, there (from ‡p. 138), 54 b, note on this story, p. 106, p. 265; defeated by Alfred at Ethandun, 56, 2; compelled by him to surrender, 56, 15; their king, Guthrum, baptized, **56**, 25 ; from Chippenham proceed to Cirencester, **57**, 4; march thence to East Anglia, **60**, 3 ; arrive from over sea at Fulham, where they winter, **58**, 2 ; leave Fulham, proceed to Ghent, **61**, 1, 5 ; march into Frankland, **62**, 3 ; proceed by the Meuse into Frankland, **63**, 4; and by the Scheldt to Condé, **65**, 4 ; divide into two armies, one of which goes to East Frankland, **66**, 4, and the other to Kent, **66**, 5 ; defeated at sea by Alfred, **64**, 1 ; from Frankland besiege Rochester, **66**, 6 ; repulsed by Alfred, **66**, 11 ; return to Frankland, **66**, 18 ; Alfred's fleet captures thirteen ships of the Danes in East Anglia, **67**, 5 ; but is afterwards surprised and defeated by the Danes of East Anglia, **67**, 9; from Germania march into Old Saxony and are defeated by the Old Saxons and Frisians, **69**, 5 ; in East Anglia break peace with Alfred, **72**, 1 ; leave land of East Franks and enter that of West Franks, proceeding down Seine to Paris, where they winter, **82**, 3 ; leave Paris, and proceed up the Marne to Chézy, **84**, 3, 11 ; after wintering at Chézy ascend the River Yonne, **84**, 12 ; besieged in London by Alfred, p. 289; ‡at Diusburg, p. 139; ‡at Boulogne, p. 140; ‡arrive in England, enter the River Limen, and encamp at Apuldre, ibid. ; ‡arrival in Thames under Hæsten, ibid.; ‡capture Évreux, p. 141; ‡camp at Benfleet, ibid. ; ‡defeated at Farnham by Alfred, ibid. ; ‡flight of, into Essex, ibid. ; ‡defeated at Benfleet, ibid. ; ‡Hæsten returns thither and restores the fort, ibid. ; ‡Hæsten erects fort at Shoebury, and is there joined by Danes from Appledore and by East Anglians and Northumbrians, ibid.; ‡cross the Thames, and are defeated at Buttingtun, ibid. ; ‡in Northumbria received Æthelwold, cousin of King Edward, and elect him king, p. 143; at Alfred's court, **76**, 22 ; as ecclesiastics in Alfred's time, p. 334; a pagan boy seen by Asser in monk's habit in one of Alfred's monasteries, **94**, 9, note on, p. 334.

Danes' Blood (Dwarf Elder), popular connexion of, with sites of battles with the Danes, p. 276.

‡Daniel (Chilperic II), king of the Franks, p. 125.

**Danubia**, Danes come from, to England, **21**, 5, note on, p. 217.

Day, division of the, in Alfred's time, p. 339.

**Degui**, St. (St. Davids, co. Pembroke', brethren of, counsel Asser to enter service of Alfred in order to protect them against depredations of King Hemeid, **79**, 51 ; account of Hemeid's persecutions of the bishops, **79**, 54 ; Nobis, archbishop of, expelled by him, **79**, 57 ; Asser (also archbishop ?) also expelled by him, **79**, 59.

**Demetica regio**, Dyfed (South Wales), Danes winter in, **54**, 2 ; inhabitants of, submit to Alfred, **80**, 4. King of: see **Hemeid**.

Dena, meaning of, p. 156[3].

Den-bera, meaning of, in O.E., p. 156[6].

Denewulf, bishop of Winchester, story of his lowly origin, p. 108[4].

Denford, parish of Hungerford, co. Berks, p. 274.

**Denu**, in Sussex, Asser conducted to Alfred at, **79**, 7 ; site of, p. lxxii[5], p. 312.

‡Desiderius, king of the Lombards, captured by Charles the Great, p. 127.

‡Deusdedit, St., archbishop of
Canterbury, death of, p. 123.
Deverill, River, co. Wilts, p. 267[5].
Devon, probable survival of Welsh-
speaking inhabitants in, in
Alfred's time, p. 241 (cf. p. 262);
Alfred's estates in, p. 323[3];
diocesan history of, p. 322.
See also Domnonia, Domnonii.
Dexterales Saxones, 'South
Saxons,' 79, 5. See also Suth
Seaxe.
Dextralis, ' southern,' 35, 10; 79,
4; note on, p. 233.
Diceto, Ralph de, chronicle of,
p. 102.
‡Diocletian, the Emperor, p. 117.
‡Dionysius, St., p. 127.
‡— ⟨Exiguus⟩, paschal cycle of,
p. 120.
‡Diusburg, Germany, Danes at,
p. 139.
Domesday Survey, treatment of
English names in, p. 176[2], p.
319.
Domnonia, Devon, Ceorl, eal-
dorman of, 3, 2; 'Domnonia'
interpolated, 49, 21; Danes
come to, from South Wales, 54,
4; are defeated in attack upon
fortress of Cynuit, 54, 5, 20.
Domnonii, the inhabitants of
Devon, 3, 3.
Dorcacestra. See Dorchester, co.
Oxford.
Dorchester, co. Dorset. See Durn-
gueir.
‡— Dorcacestra, co. Oxford, baptism of King Cynegils of Wessex
at, p. 121.
Dorset, Thornsæta, called in
British Durngueir, 49, 7; note
on form, p. 250; probable survival of Welsh-speaking inhabitants in, in Alfred's time, p. 249.
Dorubernia (Canterbury), 'id
est Cantwariorum civitas,' Danes
at, 4, 4, note on, p. 177.
Dudo of St. Quentin, chronicler,
p. 103; inaccuracy of, p. 254[1].
Duduco, bishop of Wells, p. 320.

Dunstan, St., archbishop of Canterbury, p. 259; reform of monasteries by, p 320, p. 333; letter
of, regarding estates of bishopric
of Cornwall, p. 322; alleged to
have ordained St. Neot, p. 258.
Durham Ritual, note in, p. 178.
Durngueir, British name of Dorchester, co. Dorset, 49, 7; note
on the form, p. 250.
Dux = ealdorman, 42, 36.
Dyfed. See Demetica regio

Eadburh, daughter of Offa,
king of Mercia, married to
Beorhtric, king of Wessex, 14,
6, ‡p. 128, notes on, p. 201,
p. 205, p. 207; her tyranny and
crimes, 14, 10; poisons her
husband in mistake, 14, 18, note
on, p. ci; crosses to Frankland,
and is received by Charles the
Great, 15, 4; story of choice
between him and his son offered
to her by him, and of her foolish
answer, 15, 6, note on, p. 206;
Charles makes her abbess of a
nunnery, 15, 14; detected in
incontinence there, and ejected
by him, 15, 20; reduced to
beggary, and dies in Pavia, 15,
25, note on, 208.
— wife of Æthelred Mucill, ealdorman of the Gaini, mother-in-
law of Alfred, 29, 7.
Eadgifu, wife of Edward the Elder,
daughter of Ealdorman Sighelm
of Kent, p. 290.
‡Eadhæd, Eadhead, bishop of the
Northumbrians, p. 124.
Eadmund. See Edmund.
Eadred, King, style of, p. 148[2];
p. 150[2]; charters of, p. 148[2],
150[2], 235[2]; will of, p. 154.
Eadredus. See Æthelred.
‡Eadweald, Eadwoldus, son of
Acca, slain, p. 144.
‡— Æduuoldus, bishop, slain, p.
144.
Eadwerd. See Edward.
Eadwig, King, style of, p. 148[2],

p. 150²; charters of, p. 148², p. 150², p. 273.

Eadwulf, bishop of Crediton, c. 926, p. 322.

Eafa, ancestor of Ecgbert, king of Wessex, 1, 8.

‡Eagellus, Danish leader, slain at the battle of Wednesfield, p. 107, p. 145.

Eald-Saxones, the Old Saxons, 94, 2; Eald Seaxum (sic), Antiqui Saxones, 69, 2; 70, 4; defeat the Danes, 69, 5; Old Saxony regarded by Asser as outside Germany, p. 292.

Ealhere, ealdorman of Kent, defeats the Danes at Sandwich, 6, 2; defeated and slain by the Danes in Thanet, 9, 1.

Ealhmund, father of Ecgberht, king of Wessex, 1, 8.

Ealhstan, bishop of Sherborne, conspires against Æthelwulf during the latter's absence abroad, 12, 5, 10, note on, p. 195; death and burial of, 28, 1; character of, p. 198, p. 227; length of episcopate, p. 227.

Ealhswith, wife of Alfred, p. lx; bequests of Alfred to, p. 154, p. 273; ‡death of, p. 144.

Eanwulf, ealdorman of Somerset, conspires against King Æthelwulf during absence abroad, 12, 6, 10; note on, p. 198.

Eardulfes-leah (? Ardington, co. Berks), p. 236⁴.

Earnulf, Arnolf the Emperor, ‡p. 145; deprives his uncle Charles (III) of the imperial throne, and succeeds, 85, 2, 7, 14; retains the direct government of land east of the Rhine, 85, 16; ‡death of, p. 142.

East Angles, East Engle, Orientales Angli, Orientales Saxones (in error), ‡mission of Felix to, p. 122; ‡slay Beornwulf and Ludeca, kings of Mercia, p. 130; Danes arrive among, 21, 5; Danes leave, for

York, 26, 3; 35, 3; Danes from Northumbria arrive among, 32, 4; Danes slay Edmund, king of, 33, 4; Danes from Cirencester march to, 60, 4; Danes divide country of, among themselves, and settle there, 60, 4; Alfred sends a fleet against, 67, 3; which is surprised and defeated, 67, 5, 9; Danes in, break treaty with Alfred, 72, 1; ‡join Danes under Hæsten at Shoebury, p. 141; ‡join Æthelwold, king of the Danes, p. 144. Bishop of: see Hunberht. Kings of: see Anna, Ecgric, Edmund, Guthrum-Æthelstan, Offa, Sigeberht.

East Saxons, Orientales Saxones, East Seaxum (sic), 3, 8, 10; 4, 6, 7; 21, 6; ‡conversion of, p. 121; ‡St. Birinus preaches to, p. 122; ‡join Æthelwold, king of the Danes, p. 144. See also Essex. King of: see Sębercht.

‡Eata, bishop of the Northumbrians, p. 124.

‡Eathelmnothus. See Æthelnoth.

‡Eathelmus. See Æthelm.

‡Ebalus, count of Poitou, aids in raising siege of Chartres, p. 142.

Eboracum. See York.

‡Ebroacensis civitas. See Évreux.

Ecgberht, ‡Ecgbrychtus, king of Wessex, 1, 7, ‡p. 129; received by Charles the Great when driven into exile, p. 207; adopts title of Bretwealda, p. 147¹; gives lands in Cornwall to bishopric of Sherborne, p. 296, p. 322; charters of, p. 199, p. 227; ‡death of, p. 130.

— archbishop of York, Pontifical of, p. 182.

— ‡Egbrychtus, St., death of, p. 126.

Ecgbright's Stone in New Ordnance Map, origin of name, p. 268.

Ecgbrihtes Stan, Petra Egbryhta, Alfred meets forces of

Somerset, Hants, and Wilts, at, 55, 6; note on, p. 267.

‡Ecgfrith, Ecgfridus, king of the Mercians, p. 129.

— king of Northumbria, p. 124; death of, ibid.

Ecgric, Ecgricus, king of the East Angles, p. 122.

Eclipse of sun in Alfred's reign, date of, p. 280.

Eddington, parish of Hungerford, co. Berks, erroneously identified with Ethandun, p. 271, p. 274; early forms of name, p. 275.

Edgar, King, story of his being rowed on the River Dee by tributary kings, p. 108[4]; coronation oath of, p. 182; style of, p. 150; charters of, p. 150, p. 202, p. 216[3], p. 229[4], p. 273, p. 313.

Edgarley, in Glastonbury, co. Somerset, erroneously identified with Ægleah, Igleah, p. 270.

Edington, co. Somerset, erroneously identified with Ethandun, p. 274; early forms of name, p. 274[2].

— co. Wilts. See Ethandun.

Edmund, Eadmund, king of the East Angles, notice of commencement of his reign (interpolated from, ‡p. 131), 10, 2; coronation of (interpolated from ‡p. 131), 17 b, 5; slain by the Danes, 33, 4; rapid rise of his cult as a saint, p. 231; account of, ‡p. 133; Abbo of Fleury's 'Passion' of, p. 104.

— King, style of, p. 148[2], p. 150[2]; charters of, p. 246[4].

— illegitimate son of King Edgar, p. 158 note. ·

Education of Alfred's children, 75 passim; school at court for royal children and young nobles and other youths, 75, 13; 76, 32; hunting formed part of education of young nobles, 75, 19. See also School.

Edward, Eadwerd, the Elder,

King, eldest son of Alfred, 75, 3; education of, 75, 21; ‡accession of, p. 143; takes Mercia into his own hands, p. 147[2]; his wife Eadgifu, p. 290; style of, p. 149; charters of, p. lxv[3], p. 149, p. 210, p. 299, p. 304, p. 335.

Edward the Confessor, crown of, among the Regalia, alleged to have been the one used at the pretended coronation of Alfred at Rome, p. 183; style of, p. 150[4]; charters of, p. 150[4], p. 156[4], p. 293; laws of, 170[6].

‡Edwin, king of Northumbria, p. 122.

Eglei, Domesday Hundred, co. Berks, erroneously identified with Ægleah, Igleah, p. 271.

Einhard's Life of Charles the Great, character of, p. lxxvii, p. xcviii; adaptation of part of, by author of the Life, p. lxxx, p. xcv, p. 294.

Elesa, father of Cerdic, king of Wessex, 1, 16.

El⟨ias⟩, patriarch of Jerusalem, sends letters and gifts to Alfred, 91, 16, note on, p. 328.

Ely, Elig, abbey, p. 333; ‡foundation of, p. 123.

Enchiridion, 89, 20, note on, p. 326.

Encomium Emmae, p. lxxx, p. 266.

Englafeld (Englefield, co. Berkshire), Danes defeated at, 35, 13, note on, p. 233.

England, absence of monastic life in, 93.

‡English, Angli, arrive in Britain, p. 119; mission of St. Augustine to, p. 121.

‡Eni, brother of Redwald, the king of East Anglia, ‡p. 122.

Enoch, 1, 40.

Enos, 1, 41.

‡Eohricus, Danish king, slain, p. 144.

Eoppa, ancestor of Ecgberht, king of Wessex, 1, 8.

Eotan, the (English) Jutes in Beowulf, p. 169.

Eotas, or Eote, late Anglian form of the name of the (English) Jutes, p. 168; become Geotas in late O.E. dialects, p. 170.

‡Eouuils, Danish king, slain at Wednesfield, p. 144.

Esla, ancestor of the West Saxon kings, 1, 16.

Esne, Bishop, p. lxvii.

‡Essex, East Seaxa, Danes in, p. 141; ‡flee into, after their defeat by Alfred at Farnham, p. 141[8]; ‡Æthelwold arrives with Danish fleet in, p. 144. See also East Saxons.

Ethandun (Edington, co. Wilts), Alfred marches to, 56, 2; fights and defeats the Danes there, 56, 6; receives their surrender and grants them terms, 56, 16; causes their king to be baptized, 56, 21; and acts as his godfather, 56, 28; subsequently entertains him, 56, 32; note on identification, p. 273.

Ethelred of Rievaulx, p. lxxii[5].

Eþeredingetun, erroneously identified with Ethandun, p. 275.

Eulogium, 'text (of scripture),' 91, 59, note on, p. 332.

Euthiones, the, of Venantius Fortunatus, p. 169.

‡Évreux, Ebroacensis civitas, captured by Danes, p. 141.

Exanceaster (Exeter), called in British 'Cairwisc,' on river Wisc (Exe), 49, 23; English monastery at, in seventh century, p. 251[4], p. 252[1]; Danes escape from Wareham and reach, 49, 22; interpolated (from ‡p. 136) 50 c, 2, 9; Danes leave, for Chippenham, 52, 3; granted, with all its diocese in Wessex and Cornwall, to Asser by Alfred, 81, 28, note on, p. ciii, p. 321; Alfred pursues Danes to, p. 141; partly occupied by Welsh until Æthelstan's time,

p. 249; charters relating to, p. 255[2].

Exe, River, co. Devon, history of name, p 251. See Wisc.

Exeter. See Exanceaster.

Eynesbury, co. Huntingdon, foundation of monastery at, p. 297; alleged removal thither of body of St. Neot, and consequent change of name to St. Neots, ibid. See also St. Neots.

Famina,'words, conversation,' 78, 9, note on, p. 312.

‡Faramundus, king of the Franks, p. 118.

Faran ufor, meaning of, in O.E., p. 286.

Faritius, abbot of Abingdon, ob. 1115, acquainted with Alfred's Handbook, p. 326[7].

Farnham, co. Surrey. See Fearnham.

Faselli, vassals, 53, 3; 55, 3; note on this form, p. 254.

Fawley, co. Berks, p. 157.

— South, co. Berks, p. 157.

‡Fearnham (Farnham, co. Surrey), Alfred defeats the Danes at, p. 141.

Fécamp, abbey of (Seine-Inférieure, Normandy), grant of Steyning to, p. 213.

‡Felix, St., preaches to the East Angles, p. 122.

— Frankish secretary of King Æthelwulf, p. 203[1], p. 225, p. 306.

Fens of Cambridgeshire, Huntingdonshire, &c., Edward the Elder ravages the country up to, p. 144.

Fernmail, son of Mouric, king of Gwent, seeks protection of Alfred, 80, 6, note on, p. 317.

Ferrières, Lupus Servatus of, letter of, to King Æthelwulf, p. 225.

Fingodwulf, error for 'Finn, filius Godwulf,' 1, 21.

Finn, ancestor of the kings of Wessex, 1, 21.

Fleury-sur-Loire (Dep. of the Loiret, France), abbey of St. Benedict at, relations of scholars of, with England, p. xcii, p. 256.

‡Flodoveus (Clovis II), son of Dagobert, king of the Franks, p. 122.

Florence of Worcester, chronicler, character of, p. xiv; his extracts from the Life, p. xiv, p. lxxxiii[1]; his alterations in text of the Life, p. l, p. lvii, p. lxxxvii[1], p. 217, p. 219, p. 250, p. 252, p. 278, p. 286, p. 291, p. 292, p. 293; retains many errors in MS. of the Life, p. xlvii; his additions to the Life, p. xlvii; uses the lost Cottonian MS. of the Life, ibid.; rearranges material derived from Life, p. lvi; adds to extracts from the Life passages from Abbo of Fleury's 'Passion of St. Edmund,' p. 232; probable source of the date therein supplied, p. 232[5]; MS. of Chronicle used by, p. 173, p. 177; his addition to Chronicle, p. 213; usually calculates the day of the week upon which calendar dates fell, p. 232; worthlessness of dates so supplied for historical purposes, ibid.; omits reference to Offa's tyrannical behaviour, p. 205 (cf. p. 110); probable error of, regarding date of death of King Æthelwulf, p. 196[1], p. 240; adds date of St. Edmund's death to Life, p. 232; source of the date thus supplied, ibid.; his note of death of Æthelweard, brother of Edward the Elder, p. 299; interpolations in text of, p. lxix, p. 253, p. 287; interpolation in, concerning death of Asser and Alfred's mission to India, p. lxix; interpolations in text of, from William of Malmesbury, p. 108; notices of bishops in, probably later interpolations, p. 108; uses Goscelin's Life of

St. Swithun, p. c[2]; used by the compiler of the second part of Simeon of Durham, p. lix; and by William of Malmesbury, p. lx; MS. of, from abbey of Bury St. Edmunds, p. 101; relations between him and the Annals of St. Neots, p. 107; inaccuracies in printed texts of, p. 158[2].

Florence of Worcester, Appendix to chronicle of, relationship to text of his chronicle. p. 110, and to the Annals of St. Neots, p. 110; genealogy of West Saxon royal house in, p. 153[4]; Scandinavian influence in, p. lxii[5], p. 170[4]; erroneous statement in, regarding Offa's daughters, p. 208[3]; list of bishops in, p. 228[2]; used by William of Malmesbury, p. lxii.

Fontenelle, Picardy, abbey of St. Wandrille, p. 102[2].

Fontévrault, abbey of (Dep. of the Maine-et-Loire, France), p. 155.

Fontibus, Geoffrey de, author of 'Liber de Infantia S. Eadmundi,' p. 215; borrows from Annals of St. Neots, ibid.

Fortresses, building of, by Alfred, 91, 49, 71.

‡Fossae (the Cambridgeshire Ditches), p. 144.

Fræna, Danish 'comes,' slain at Ashdown, 39, 21.

Francia, Frankland, 62, 3; Danes from Ghent march into, 62, 3; 63, 4; divide themselves into two armies, one of which comes to Kent, 66, 5; the latter repulsed by Alfred from Rochester, 66, 11; thence return to Frankland, 66, 18.

— East, Orientales Franci, Danes from England arrive in, 61, 3; leave, for the land of the West Franks, 82, 3.

— West, Occidentalium Francorum Regio, Danes from East

Frankland enter, and winter at Paris, **82**, 3.

‡Franco, archbishop of Rouen, p. 103 ; baptizes Rollo, p. 135.

‡Frankfort, Frankonoford, p. 130.

Frankish Annals, the, used by compiler of the Annals of St. Neots, p. 103.

Frankland, envoys of King Æthelwulf to, in 839, p. 185.

Franks, **Franci**, fight against the Danes, **61**, 4 ; Franks at Alfred's court, **76**, 21 ; ‡commencement of kingdom of, p. 118. Kings of : *see* Charles, Karlmann, Ludwig, Pipin.

— West, **Franci Occidentales**, Karlmann, king of, slain by a boar, **68**, 1 ; Charles, son of Ludwig (the German), king of, **70**, 1.

**Frauu**, River (the Froom, co. Dorset), **49**, 6 ; note on the form, p. 248.

**Frealaf**, ancestor of the kings of Wessex, **1**, 21.

**Freawine**, ancestor of the kings of Wessex, **1**, 18.

**Freothegar**, ancestors of the kings of Wessex, **1**, 19.

Frisians received by Alfred, **76**, 21.

**Frisones**, the Frisians, defeat the Danes, **69**, 5.

Friþ niman, meaning of, in O.E., p. 242.

‡Frithestan, bishop of Winchester, p. 144.

**Frithowald**, ancestor of the kings of Wessex, **1**, 20.

**Frithuwulf**, ancestor of the kings of Wessex, **1**, 21.

Froom, River, co. Dorset. *See* Frauu.

Frustfield, Hundred of, co. Wilts, p. 319.

Fulco, archbishop of Rheims, letter of, to Alfred, p. 308, p. 333.

**Fullonham** (Fulham, co. Middlesex), Danes winter at, **58**, 4 ; leave, for Ghent, **61**, 1.

**Gaini**, in Mercia, Æthelred, ealdorman of, **29**, 5 ; erroneous connexion of the name with Gainsborough, p. 228.

Gainsborough, erroneously derived from the Gaini of the Life, p. 228.

Gale, Roger, transcript of the Life belonging to, p. liv.

— Dr. Thomas, his account of the MS. of the Life, p. xliii ; his edition of the Annals of St. Neots, p. 115.

**Galli**, inhabitants of France, **70**, 4 ; at Alfred's court, **76**, 21 ; use of term by the author of the Life, p. 292.

**Gallia**, France, **49**, 25 ; **78**, 3, note on, p. 306 ; Alfred sends to, for masters, **78**, 3 ; priests and deacons from, introduced by Alfred into his newly-founded monasteries, **94**, 3 ; plot of a Gaulish priest and deacon to murder abbot of Athelney, **96**, 2 ; they engage two Gaulish servants to commit murder of abbot, **96**, 7 ; Alfred's gifts to monasteries in, **102**, 22.

‡Gascony, Wasconia, Charles the Great in, p. 128.

**Geata, Geta**, ancestor of the kings of Wessex, **1**, 22, 36, note on, p. 160.

Gēatas = O.N. Gautar, the Γαυτοί of Procopius, confused with the (English) Jutes, p. 170 ; in O.E. translation of Beda applied to the (English) Jutes, p. 170.

**Geguuis**, Welsh name for the West Saxons, **1**, 17, note on, p. 161.

**Gendi** (Ghent), in East Frankland, Danes from Fulham proceed to, **61**, 5.

Geoffrey of Monmouth, p. cxxix, p. 111, p. 162.

Geotas, written for Eotas, p. 170.

Gerard of Cornwall, 'De Gestis Regum Westsaxonum,' character of this work, p. 212[4].

Germania, 69, 2 ; the term ex-
cludes Old Saxony, 69, note on,
p. 292.

Germanus, St. (of Auxerre), alleged to have studied at Oxford
according to Camden's interpolation, 83 b, 21.

Gesettan, meaning of, in O.E.,
p. 324.

Gesīthas, change in status of,
p. 337.

Geata. See Geata.

Gewis, Geguuis, ancestor of the
kings of Wessex, 1, 17.

Gewisse, the West Saxons, called
by this name by the Welsh, 1,
17, note on, p. 161.

Ghent. See Gendi.

— St. Peter's monastery, charters
relating to, p. 156³.

Gildas, St., alleged to have studied
in Oxford in Camden's interpolation, 83 b, 19.

Giles, Dr. J. A., translation of the
Life by, p. xxxi.

Giraldus Cambrensis refers to the
Life, p. lxiii, p. lxxix¹.

‡Giruuinense monastery (Yarrow,
co. Northumberland), p. 126.

Giso, bishop of Wells, 1061–88,
p. 320.

Glastonbury, Glastonia, foundation
of monastery at, ‡p. 126; charters
relating to, p. lxxvii¹, p. 150²,
p. 151², p. 235², p. 305⁷.

Gleguising (Glywyssing, old name
of Glamorgan and part of Mon-
mouthshire), Houil, son of Ris,
king of, seeks protection of
Alfred, 80, 6.

Gloucester abbey, foundation
charter of, p. 154⁶.

Glywyssing. See Gleguising.

Gnavewic, Parker's error for Suanewic, interpolated, 50 c, 19.

‡Godefrid and another Godefrid,
Danish leaders, slain at Wednesfield, p. 145.

Godrum. See Guthrum.

Godwulf, ancestor of the kings of
Wessex, 1, 22.

Goldsmiths and other craftsmen
instructed by Alfred, 76, 5.

Goscelin, his life of St. Grimbald,
p. 307 ; his life of St. Ives, p.
298 ; his Life of St. Swithun,
p. c², p. 108⁴.

Gotan, the Goths, use of this form
by Alfred, p. 167.

Gothrum. See Guthrum.

‡Goths capture Rome, p. 118.

Gothus = Jute, 2, 4, 5, note on,
p. 166.

Grantebrycg (Cambridge), Danes
under Guthrum winter at, 47,
11 ; leave, 49, 3.

Graphium, 11, 4, note on, p. 191.

Gregory the Great, Pope, ' Dialogues' of, translated into English by Werfrith, bishop of
Worcester, at suggestion of
Alfred, 77, 6; ‡his mission to
Britain, p. 120, p. 121 ; ‡sends
pall to St. Augustine, p. 121 ;
‡dispatches St. Paulinus and
others to Britain, ibid. ; ‡death
of, ibid.

Grimbald, priest and monk, comes
to Alfred from Gaul by invitation, 78, 4 ; date of his arrival,
p. lxxii, p. 308 ; his learning
and skill as a chanter, 78, 5,
note on, p. 307 ; interpolated
passage concerning pretended
disputes between him and the
scholars of the University of
Oxford in the time of Alfred,
83 b, 2 ; according to this interpolation he erected the church
and crypt of St. Peter's in the
East, 83 b, 32 ; retires, according to this interpolation, in dis-
gust to Winchester, 83 b, 31 ;
notes on this interpolation, § 8,
p. xxiii sqq., p. 310 ; ‡death of,
p. 143.

Gronna, 97, 25, note on, p. 255.

Gronnosa, 'swampy,' 53, 3, note
on, p. 255.

Guent, Gwent (in co. Monmouth),
kings of, Brochmail and Fernmail, sons of Mouric, 80, 7.

Gueriir, St., **74**, 20, note on, p. cii, p. cix, p. 296; church of, in Cornwall (St. Neot), **74**, 20; visited by Alfred, **74**, 19; St. Neot buried therein, **74**, 20.

Guilou, River (Wiley, co. Wilts), **42**, 19, note on form, p. 241.

‡Guirthegirnus. *See* Vortigern.

‡Guntrannus, king of Orleans, p. 120.

‡Guthlac, St., death of, p. 125.

Guthrum, **Gothrum, Godrum,** Danish king, winters at Cambridge, **47**, 10; surrenders with his army to Alfred, **56**, 21; receives baptism, **56**, 22; Alfred becomes his godfather, and entertains him subsequently, **56**, 28, 32; receives the name of Æthelstan, p. 140; said to have been a friend of Rollo, p. 254[2]; death and burial of, p. 140; coins of, p. 231.

Gutland, Sweden, island of, Goths of, p. 170; trade of island with England, p. 170[6].

**Guuihtgaraburhg.** *See* Wihtgaraburh.

Gwent. *See* **Guent.**

Gwyneth, king of. *See* **Rotri.**

‡Hadleigh (co. Suffolk ?), King Guthrum buried at, p. 100, p. 140.

‡Hæsten, Hastengus, Danish leader, arrives in the Thames, p. 140; encamps at Middeltun, ibid.; his wife and children captured at Benfleet are released by Alfred, p. 141; returns to Benfleet and repairs the fort, ibid.; crosses the Thames, ibid.; proceeds to the Severn and is defeated at Buttington, p. 142; returns to Essex, ibid.; leaves England, ibid.

‡Hagano, 'miles' of Charles 'the Simple,' king of the West Franks, p. 141.

Hampshire, Jutes of, cease to call themselves by that name, p. 167.
— men of, **Hamtunenses,** Osric,

ealdorman of, defeats the Danes, **18**, 10; meet Alfred at Ecgbriht's Stone, **55**, 10.

Hareld, 'comes' of the Danes, slain at Ashdown, **39**, 22.

‡Haribertus (Caribert), king of Paris, p. 120.

Hariulf, his 'Chronicon Centulense,' p. 104, p. 140.

‡Hastengus. *See* Hæsten.

Hathra, ancestor of the kings of Wessex, **1**, 38.

‡Headlega. *See* Hadleigh.

Healfdene, **Healftene, Halfdene,** brother of Inwar, and of another unnamed brother, **54**, 1; leader of the Danes in Northumbria, **47**, 5; divides Northumbria among his army, and settles it, **50**, 1.

— Danish king, slain at Wednesfield, p. 144.

Hean, alleged first abbot of Abingdon, p. 235[3].

Hearne, Thomas, p. xxv[1].

Hecana, the, p. 228; the Westan Hecani, p. 229.

‡Hedda, St., bishop (of the West Saxons), death of, p. 124.

Heddington, co. Wilts, erroneously identified with Ethandun, p. 274.

‡Helena, Queen, mother of the Emperor Constantine, p. 117.

Helised, **son of Teudubr,** king of Brecheniauc, seeks protection of Alfred, **80**, 10; note on, p. 318.

Hemeid, king of Dyfed, p. lxxi; oppresses St. Davids, **79**, 54; expels archbishop Nobis and Asser from St. Davids, **79**, 57, 58; submits to Alfred's lordship, **80**, 3; note on, p. 316.

‡Hengest, Hencgistus, king of Kent, p. 119; father of Oisc, ibid.

Henniborough or Henni Castle, older name of Kenwith Castle, parish of Abbotsham, co. Devon, p. 263.

Heremod, ancestor of the kings of Wessex, **1**, 37.

**Hibernia,** missions (?) from, to Alfred, **91,** 15, note on, p. 327.
— (Ireland), Alfred's gifts to monasteries in, **102,** 23 (cf. p. 328).
Hidage, charters granting reduction of, p. 322[6].
— Tribal, the, p. 173[3].
Higden, Ranulph, author of 'Poly chronicon,' p. 325, p. 344.
Highleigh Common, parish of Melksham, co. Wilts, erroneously identified with Egleah, Igleah, p. 271.
Hii. *See* Iona.
‡Hilarius, bishop of Poitiers, death of, p. 118.
‡Hilda, St., abbess of Streaneshealh (Whitby), death of, p. 124.
Hill, James, of Trinity College, Oxford, collates MS. of the Life for Wise's edition, p. xxix; supplies the facsimile of the MS. to Wise, p. xxxii.
‡Hilpericus, king of Soissons, p. 120.
Hinguar. *See* **Inwar.**
Hisperica Famina, the, Latinity of, p. xcii, p. 312.
**Hlothuuicus.** *See* Ludwig.
‡Honorius, the Emperor, p. 118.
‡Horsa, slain at battle of Ægelesthrep, p. 119.
**Houil, son of Ris,** king of Gleguising, seeks protection of Alfred, **80,** 6; notes on, p. lxx, p. 317.
Hounds, Alfred trains, **76,** 6.
Howden, Roger of, immediate source of matter in his chronicle derived from the Life, p. lxiv.
Howorth, Mr. (now Sir) Henry, attack of, upon authenticity of the Life, p. cx sqq.
Hreið-Gota-land of the Norsemen, p. 169.
**Hreni,** River (the Rhine), **85,** 16; note on, p. 325.
**Hreopedun** (Repton, co. Derby), Danes winter at, **46,** 5; Danes leave, **47,** 3.

Hreðgotan of Beowulf, p. 169[5].
**Hrofesceaster** (Rochester, co. Kent), besieged unsuccessfully by the Danes, **66,** 6, 15; battle against the Danes at, p. 131; charters relating to, p. 151[2], p. 201[4], p. 211, p. 227, p. 312[2]. Bishop of: *see* Paulinus.
**Hrothuulf** (Rudolf I), king of Burgundy, accession of, **85,** 16.
Hubba. *See* Ubba.
Hubblestone, parish of Appledore, co. Devon, an antiquarian perversion of Whibblestone, alleged cairn of Ubba, the Danish leader, at, p. 263, p. 264[5].
**Huda,** ealdorman of Surrey, defeated and slain by the Danes in Thanet, **9,** 2.
**Huiccii** (inhabitants of the kingdom of the Hwicce, cos. Gloucester, Worcester, &c.), **57,** 6, note on, p. 228, p. 229.
Hunberht, Hunberchtus, bishop of East Anglia, crowns Eadmund, king of East Anglia (interpolated from, ‡p. 131), **17 b,** 4.
‡Hungri, the, campaign of Charles the Great against, p. 128.
Huntingdon, Henry of, chronicler, p. c[2]; not acquainted with the Life, p. lxiv.
‡Husa (River Ouse, co. Bedford), p. 144.
**Hwala, Huala,** ancestor of the kings of Wessex, **1,** 38.
Hwicce, kingdom of the. *See* **Huiccii.**
Hyda, Liber de, error in, p. 344.
Hyde abbey, co. Hants, charters relating to, p. lxv[3], p. 149[6], p. 152, p. 201, p. 299, p. 304[8], p. 312[2], p. 315[6], p. 330[6].
Hynguar. *See* **Inwar.**
‡Hysopa, Danish 'baro,' slain, p. 144.

**Iared, 1,** 40.
Igleah, camping-place of Alfred, note on, p. 270; probable site of, p. 272.

India, alleged mission of Alfred to, p. lxix, p. 107, p. 288, p. 329[1]; application of the name India, p. 288[2].

Indiculi, 'letters,' 79, 38, 40, note on, p. 315.

Ine, king of Wessex, 1, 9; his pilgrimage to Rome, 1, 10, p. 106, ‡p. 125; alleged foundation of Saxon school there by, p. 244; death of, 1, 10; charters of, p. 216[3]; his brother Ingild, 1, 9, p. 155; his sister Cuthburh, p. 155.

Ingild, brother of Ine, king of Wessex, 1, 9; ancestor of Alfred, p. 155.

Inwar, ‡Hinguarus, leader of the Danes, brother of Healfdene, and of another unnamed brother, 54, 1, ‡p. 133; death of the latter, 54 b, 24; son of Lodebrochus (Ragnar Lothbroc), interpolated (from ‡p. 138), 54 b, 3; sisters of, ibid., note on, p. 266.

‡Iona, Hii, island of, arrival of St. Columba at, p. 120.

Iona, River (the Yonne, France), the Danes from Chézy enter, 84, 14.

Ireland. See Hibernia.

Itermod, ancestor of the kings of Wessex, 1, 37.

Iuthitta, Iuthitha. See Judith.

Iuti or Iutae = the (English) Jutes, 2, 5, note on, p. 166.

James, Dr. Thomas, First Bodley's Librarian, his description of the MS. of the Life, p. xxxvii.

‡Jerome, St., death of, p. 118.

Jerusalem, Elias, patriarch of, Alfred receives letters and gifts from, 91, 16, note on, p. 328.

Jocelyn, John, secretary of Archbishop Parker, p. xlii; composite MS. chronicle compiled by, p. xxviii[4]; list of writers on English history by, p. xxxiii[3];

his extracts from the Annals of St. Neots, p. 115.

John, an Old Saxon, comes to Alfred by invitation from Gaul, 78, 8, ‡p. 143, notes on, p. 311, p. 335; his learning, 78, 9; his skill in arts, 78, 11; Alfred makes him abbot of his newly-founded abbey at Athelney, 94, 1; account of attempted murder of, by Gaulish priests there, 95-98; erroneous confusion of this account with Malmesbury's story of the murder of John the Scot, p. civ, p. cxii[2], p. 335.

— the Scot, confusion of, with John the Old Saxon, p. civ, p. cxii[2], p. 335.

— the Wise, Iohannes Sophista, of Malmesbury, p. 335.

Judith, Iuthitha, daughter of Charles the Bald, marries Æthelwulf, 11, 11; 13, 8; 68, 11; 70, 8; ‡p. 139; note on, p. 194; is seated by him at his side on throne, contrary to custom of the West Saxons, 13, 9; crowned before leaving home, p. 200; after his death marries his son Æthelbeald, 17, 5, note on, p. 212, p. 214; alleged separation from him, p. 212; not the 'mater' of the story regarding Alfred and the book of poems, p. 222; her elopement with Baldwin of Flanders, p. 223.

‡— the Empress, wife of Ludwig the Pious, p. 130.

Jutes of Denmark, confusion of name of, with that of the English Jutes, p. 169.

— the (English), called (erroneously) Gēatas in O.E. version of Beda, p. 170; of Hampshire and the Isle of Wight, traces of the name, p. 167, p. 168; of Kent, cease to call themselves by that name, p. 167.

‡Karlmann, Karolomannus, son of Charles Martel, Maior Domus,

p. 126; becomes a monk at Mons Soracte and Monte Cassino, p. 127; death of, ibid.

Karlmann, ‡son of Pepin the Short, king of the Franks, p. 127.

— ‡son of Ludwig the German, king of Bavaria and Italy, p. 136.

— Carlomannus, king of the West Franks, ‡p. 139; death of, 68, 1.

Karolus. *See* Charles.

Kennet, River. *See* Cynete.

Kenstec, bishop of Cornwall, p. 322.

Kent, Danes arrive in, from Frankland, and besiege Rochester unsuccessfully, 66, 6, 15; ‡Edward the Elder awaits army of, p. 144; Jutes of, cease to call themselves by that name, p. 167. *See also* Cantia, Cantuarii. Kings of: *see* Hengest, Oisc. Ealdormen of : *see* Ealhere, Sighelm.

Kentigern, alleged to have studied at Oxford according to Camden's interpolation, 83 b, 19.

‡Kentuuine. *See* Centwine.

‡Kenuulfus, abbot of Peterborough, slain, p. 144.

Kenwith Castle, parish of Abbotsham, co. Devon, a modern antiquarian figment, p. 262; older name of, p. 263.

‡Keonrædus. *See* Coenred.

Kintbury, co. Berks, p. 157.

‡Koenwalh, king of Wessex, accession of, in 642, p. 122; succeeded by his wife Sexburch in 672, p. 123; older form of name than that in Chron. preserved by the Annals of St. Neots, p. 105. *See* Cenwealh.

‡Kynegylsus. *See* Cynegils.

‡Kyneuulfus. *See* Cynewulf.

‡Kynricus. *See* Cynric.

Lamech, 1, 39.

Landford, in the Hundred of Frustfield, co. Wilts, probably the Leonaford of the Life, p. 319.

Landfred's Life of St. Swithun, p. c².

Lantern, horn, constructed by Alfred to secure equal combustion of candles used by him in measuring time, 104, 25, note on, p. 339.

Latin books used in court school by Alfred's children, 75, 16.

Law courts in Alfred's time, p. 342.

Learning, low state of, in England in Alfred's youth, 24, 9, notes on, p. 225, p. 303.

Leigh in Bradford-on-Avon, co. Wilts, suggested identification of, with Ægleah, Igleah, p. 270.

Leland, John, the antiquary, owner of MS. of the Life, p. xxxiv; his account of the work and its author, ibid. ; notes in his hand in MS. of the Annals of St. Neots, p. 114.

‡Leo III, Pope, expulsion from Rome and mutilation of, p. 129; consecrates Charles the Great as emperor, ibid. ; death of, ibid.

— IV, Leo, Pope, receives Alfred at Rome, adopts him as his spiritual son, and ' anoints him king,' 8, 4; his letter to King Æthelwulf concerning this ceremony, p. 180¹.

Leofric and Leoflæd, his wife, founders of monastery at St. Eynesbury, afterwards known as St. Neots, p. 297.

Leonaford, royal town, Asser visits Alfred at, 81, 9; probable site of, p. 318.

Letcomb, co. Berks, p. 157.

‡Limen, River (cos. Kent and Sussex), the Danes enter, p. 140, p. 142.

Lindesig (Lindsey, co. Lincoln), in Northumbria, Danes winter in, 45, 5; Danes leave, and winter at Repton, in Mercia, 46, 3; origin of this form, p. 242.

‡Lindisfarne, bishop of. *See* Ceolwulf (*sic*).

Lindsey. *See* **Lindesig**.

Llandaff, bishops of. *See* Cerenhir, Cyfeiliog, **Nobis**, Nud.

**Loco funeris dominati sunt**, version of O.E. 'wælstowe geweald ahton,' p. 178.

Lodbrochus (Ragnar Lothbroc), daughters of, make magic banner of the Danes called Ræfan, interpolated (from ‡p. 138), 54 b, 3.

‡Lodouuicus. *See* Ludwig.

London, **Lundonia**, ‡battle against the Danes at, in 842, p. 131 ; Danes at, 4, 4 ; site of, described, 4, 4, note on, p. 177 ; Danes winter at, 44, 3 ; leave it, 45, 3 ; siege of, by Alfred, p. 289 ; restored by Alfred, and committed to Æthelred, ealdorman of the Mercians, 83, 2, note on, p. 324 ; ‡citizens of, with Ealdorman Æthelred, defeat the Danes at Benfleet, p. 141. St. Paul's, charters of, p. 229⁴. Bishop of : *see* Theodred.

‡Lothaire, Lotharius, the Emperor, p. 130, p. 131 ; note of his death interpolated (from ‡p. 131) in the Life, 10, 5.

‡Ludeca, king of Mercia, death of, p. 109, p. 130.

Ludwig, **Hlothuuicus** (the Pious), the Emperor (10, 6, interpolated from ‡p. 131), 70, 10, ‡p. 129, ‡p. 130, ‡p. 139 ; ‡death of, p. 131 ; Life of, by Thegan, p. lxxx.

— the German, king of the Norici or Bavarians, 70, 6, ‡p. 140 ; ‡death of, p. 135.

— (II) the Stammerer, son of Charles the Bald, king of the West Franks, death of, 68, 7, ‡p. 139.

— (III), son of Ludwig the Stammerer, king of the West Franks, dies, 68, 5 ; ‡defeats the Northmen ⟨at Saucourt⟩, p. 139.

Ludwig, the Younger, king of the Saxons, enters Bavaria, p. 139.

— the Child, son of the Emperor Arnulf, king of the East Franks, p. 142 ; death of, p. 145.

Lumley, Lord, library of, included Parker's MS. of the Life, p. xxxvii.

**Lundonia**. *See* London.

Mæil Brith Mac Durnan, gospel of, p. 152.

Magesætan, kingdom of the, p. 228, p. 229.

Magister, an unnamed, teaches Alfred Saxon poems, 23, 14.

**Malaleel**, 1, 41.

Malmesbury abbey, charters relating to, p. lxvii, p. 151², p. 246, p. 304⁸.

— William of, chronicler, source of the material derived from the Life in his 'Gesta Regum Anglorum' probably Florence of Worcester, p. lx ; errors of, regarding Alfred's family, p. lxi ; uses Appendix to Florence, p. lxii ; his account of Asser, p. lxviii ; acquainted with Alfred's 'Handbook,' p. 326 ; acquainted with Archbishop Fulco's letter to Alfred, p. 308¹ ; uses Goscelin's Life of St. Swithun, p. c² ; borrows from Æthelweard, p. 166¹ ; Latin verse life of Æthelstan used by, p. lxxx¹, p. 184⁴, p. 318³ ; borrows from Hariulf's 'Chronicon Centulense,' p. 102², p. 140 ; his works not used by compiler of the Annals of St. Neots, p. 111 ; his story of murder of John the Scot, confusion of, with account of attack upon John the Old Saxon in the Life, p. civ, p. cxii², p. 335 ; his story of Bishop Sighelm's mission to India, p. 289 ; interpolations from, in text of Florence of Worcester, p. lxix, p. 108 ; errors of, p. 244², p. 245,

p. 299[4]; his work on the history of Glastonbury, p. 329.

‡Marcianus, the Emperor, p. 119.

Mare Occidentale, the sea to the west of Wales, 7, 6.

Marinus, Pope, death of, 71, 1; exempts Saxon school at Rome from tribute, 71, 2; sends gifts to King Alfred, including portion of the Cross, 71, 5, notes on, p. 286, 293.

Marne, River. See Materne.

‡Martin of Tours, St., death of, p. 118.

Materne, River (the Marne), the Danes from Paris ascend the Seine to the mouth of the Marne, which they ascend as far as Chézy, 84, 7, 9.

Mathusalem, 1, 40.

‡Maximinianus, the Emperor, p. 117.

‡Medeshamstede (Peterborough), foundation of monastery at, p. 125. Abbot of: see Kenuulfus.

Medwæg, River (the Medway, co. Kent), 66, 7.

Melchet Forest. co. Wilts, p. 320.

Melkin, St., alleged to have studied in Oxford according to Camden's interpolation, 83 b, 19.

‡Mellitus converts the East Saxons, p. 121.

Mercia, Merciorum Regnum, 7, 6; 14, 1; 29, 4; 30, 2, 13; 74, 1; ‡conversion of, p. 123; Danes from Northumbria march through, on their way to East Anglia, 32, 3; subdued by Danes, 46, 13, who appoint Ceolwulf king during their will, 46, 16; Danes divide, between themselves and Ceolwulf, their puppet-king, 51, 2; scholars from, assist Alfred in his studies, 77; apparently in subjection to Alfred, p. 147; ravaged by Æthelwold, king of Northumbria, and the Danes, p. 144. Kings of: see Æthelred, Beorhtwulf, Beornwulf, Burgred,

Coenred, Ecgfrith, Ludeca, Offa, Penda. Ealdorman of: see Æthelred.

Mercia, men of, Mercii, make peace with the Danes, 44, 3; 45, 5; power of, over Middle and South Welsh, 7, 5; 80, 8.

‡Mereseig (Mersea, co. Essex), Danes winter in, p. 142.

Meretun, battle of, reasons for omission of, from the Life, p. 239.

‡Meroveus, king of the Franks, p. 119.

Mersea. See Mereseig.

Mese, River (the Meuse), in Frankland, 63, 4.

Middel Seaxum (sic), the inhabitants of Middlesex, 4, 6.

‡Middeltun (Milton, co. Kent), Hæsten encamps at, p. 140.

‡Milan, Mediolanum, St. Ambrose, bishop of, death of, p. 118.

Milton, co. Kent. See Middeltun.

Ministerialis, ' thane holding an office about the king,' 76, 31, note on, p. 301.

Minster, Isle of Sheppey, monastery at, c. 3, 10; date of destruction of, p. 176.

Monasteries, deserted condition of, in England, 93, 9, note on, p. 333; Alfred founds a monastery at Athelney, 92, 8, and a nunnery at Shaftesbury, 98, 2; is compelled to send abroad for monks, 93, 1, 94, 2; portion of his revenue assigned to the monasteries founded by him, 102, 15; another portion as gifts to monasteries elsewhere in England, Wales, Cornwall, and abroad, 102, 19; gifts of, p. 320; reform of, by Æthelwold and Dunstan, p. 320, 333.

Monks, lack of native, in England, compels Alfred to send abroad for others, 93, 1; 94, 2.

Monmouth, Geoffrey of. See Geoffrey.

‡Monte Cassino, Mons Cassinus, monastery of St. Benedict at, p. 127, p. 128.

Motatus = mutatus, 91, 23, note on, p. 330.

Mouric, father of Brochmail and Fernmail, kings of Gwent, 80, 7, note on, p. 317.

Mucill, nickname of Æthelred, ealdorman of the Gaini, 29, 5; erroneously explained as meaning 'big,' p. 230; note on, p. 229.

Mul, wergeld for, paid by men of Kent in 694, p. 154⁶.

Nachededorne, Domesday Hundred of, co. Berks, p. 238.

‡Narbonne, p. 128.

Nefa in O.E., meaning of, p. 171.

Nennius, alleged to have studied at Oxford according to Camden's interpolation, 83 b, 19; borrowings from, in Life, p. lxxvii, p. 186; Frankish influence in, p. xciii.

Neot, Niot, St., note on, p. 297; lives of, p. 256; extract from life of, in Annals of St. Neots, p. 104, pp. 136-8, whence they have been interpolated in the Life, 53, 9, 53 b, 53 c, 54 b; erroneous statement that he was a brother of Alfred, origin of, p. 256⁵; his alleged relationship to Alfred, p. 257; interpolated reference to his place of burial, 74, 21, note on, p. xlix, p. 297.

Nephew and uncle, intimate relationship between, among the Germans and English, p. 172.

Newdigate, co. Surrey, erroneously identified with Wudigan-gæt, p. 178; early forms of name of, p. 178⁵.

Nobis, bishop of St. Davids, 79, 57, note on, p. lxxi, p. 316.

Noe (Noah), 1, 39.

‡Norici, p. 140.

Norman Annals, the, p. 103¹; used by compiler of the Annals of St. Neots, p. 101, p. 103; used by compiler of the Annales S. Edmundi, p. 101¹; translations of entries in, interpolated in text of MS. E of the Old-English Chronicle, p. 112⁵.

Normandy, arrival of Rollo in, interpolated (from ‡p. 134), 50 b, 1.

‡Normanni. See Danes.

Northanhymbri. See Northumbria.

Northumbria, Northanhymbri, Northanhymbrorum Regio, dispute among men of, regarding succession to the throne, 27, 4; men of, defeated by the Danes at York, 27, 24; Danes leave, for Mercia, 30, 2; return to, 31, 3; winter in, near the Tyne, 47, 7; settled by Danes under Healfdene, 50, 2; Danes winter at Lindsey in, 45, 3; Alfred's gifts to monasteries in, 102, 22; submission of, to him, p. 147; men of, join the Danes under Hæsten at Shoebury, p. 141. Kings of: see Ælla, Aldfrith, Ceolwulf, Ecgfrith, Edwin, Osbyrht, Oswald, Oswine, Oswiu. Bishops of: see Eadhæd, Wilfrid.

Nottingham. See Snotengaham.

Nud, bishop of Llandaff, p. 317.

Oakley, near Basingstoke, co. Hants, erroneously identified with Ægleah, Igleah, p. 270.

‡Ochter, Danish jarl, slain at Wednesfield, p. 144.

Ockley, co. Surrey, erroneously identified with Acleah, p. 178; early forms of name, p. 178².

Oda (Odo), king of the West Franks, accession of, 85, 17.

— bishop of Ramsbury, 925-942. archbishop of Canterbury, 942-958, p. 334.

Odda, ealdorman of Devon, 262.

Offa, king of Mercia, 14, 1; ‡p. 110; constructs Offa's Dyke,

14, 3, note on, p. 204 ; his relations with Charles the Great,
p. 206 ; his yearly grant, to
Rome, p. 211[2]; his alleged
foundation of Saxon school at
Rome, p. 244; ‡slays St. Æthel-
briht, king of the East Angles,
p. 128 ; ‡his death, p. 129;
spurious charter of, to Chertsey
abbey, p. 208[3] ; daughters of,
p. 207.

‡Offa, king of East Anglia, goes
to Rome, p. 106, p. 125.

Offa's Dyke, 14, 3 ; p. lxxv[2], p. 204.

Ohthere, voyage of, p. 300 ; not
mentioned in the Life, § 84, p.
cxxi ; Jutland called Gotland in
Alfred's account of his voyage,
p. 169.

‡Oisc, king of Kent, accession of,
in 455, p. 119; an older form
of his name than the Æsc of
the existing MSS. of the Chron.
p. 105.

Old Saxons. See Eald-Saxones.

Ordericus Vitalis, West Saxon
royal genealogy used by him,
p. 158[2]; reproduces errors of
Dudo of St. Quentin, p. 254[1];
Crowland story about body of
St. Neot in, p. 298.

Ordlaf, Ealdorman, p. 199.

Orientales Angli. See East
Angles.

Orientales Saxones. See East
Angles, East Saxons.

Orosius, Alfred's translation of,
p. 301.

Osbern, Danish ' comes,' slain at
Ashdown, 39, 21.

Osburh, mother of Alfred, 2, 1 ;
her descent, ibid. ; baseless suggestion that she was cast off by
Æthelwulf, p. 222 ; date of her
death, p. 224.

Osbyrht, king of Northumbria,
joins forces with usurper Ælla,
attacks Danes at York, and is
slain, 27, 5, 10, 25.

Oscytel, archbishop of York, 958–
971, p. 334.

Osferth, kinsman of Alfred, p. 163[5].

‡Osfridus, Danish leader, slain at
Wednesfield, p. 144.

‡Oskytellus, Danish ' baro,' slain,
p. 144.

Oslac, maternal grandfather of
Alfred, 2, 3, note on, p. 163 ;
his descent, ibid.

Osric, ealdorman of Hampshire,
defeats the Danes, 18, 10, notes
on, p. 163[5], 216.

Osscytil, Danish king, winters in
Cambridge, 47, 10.

‡Oswald, Saint, king of Northumbria, p. 121 ; death of, p. 122.

— archbishop of York, 972-992,
p. 334.

Osweald, the king's son, witness
of Alfred's charters, p. 299[4].

‡Oswine, Osuuinus, St., king of
Northumbria, death of, p. 122.

‡Oswiu, Osuiuus, king of Northumbria, death of, p. 123.

‡Othulfus, Danish leader, slain at
Wednesfield, p. 144.

Ouche, Normandy (Dep. of the
Eure), monastery of St. Évroul,
version of the Norman Annals
(' Annales Uticenses '), agreement with version used by compiler of Annals of St. Neots,
p. 103.

Ouse. See Husa.

Oxford, Camden's interpolated
passage concerning disputes in
University in time of Alfred,
in which church and crypt of
St. Peter's in the East are alleged
to be the work of Grimbald,
83 b, 33.

Paga, ' shire,' 1, 3, 4 ; 5, 2 ; 12, 7 ;
35, 6 ; 42, 19 ; 45, 5 ; 49, 6 ;
53, 4 ; 55, 4, 10, 11 ; note on
form, p. 155.

‡Pampeluna (Pampilonia), captured and destroyed by Charles
the Great, p. 128.

Papa universalis, 16, 37, note on
use of title, p. 211.

Paris, Matthew, chronicler, use of

St. Albans compilation by, p. lxiv, p. 162, p. 173, p. 212[4], p. 236[3], p. 244[1, 2], p. 257[2], p. 291[2], p. 344.

**Parisia** (Paris), Danes winter at, 82, 6 ; description of site of, 82, 9, note on, p. 324 ; Danes leave, 84, 3 ; 86, 2.

**Parker, Matthew,** archbishop of Canterbury, his edition of the Life, p. xii, p. xiv ; his falsifications and interpolations of the text, p. xiv, p. xvii, p. xviii, p. xix (cf. lxvii[1]), p. 278, p. 292 ; his modernization of forms in, p. 172 ; careless preparation of his text, p. xx ; his account of the MS., p. xxxiii ; his transcript of, p. li ; owner of MS. of Annals of St. Neots, p. 113 ; his transcript of, p. 114.

‡**Paschalis I,** Pope, crowns ⟨Lothaire⟩ as Emperor, p. 130.

‡**Paul, St.,** p. 127.

‡**Paulinus, St.,** sent to Britain by St. Gregory, p. 121 ; death of, p. 122.

**Pavia,** ‡captured by Charles the Great, p. 127 ; Eadburh, widow of Beorhtric, king of Wessex, dies in beggary at, 15, 25, note on, p. 208 ; frequented by English pilgrims on their way to Rome, p. 209.

**Pedesecus,** use of the title, p. 165.

‡**Penda,** king of Mercia, p. 122, p. 123 ; death of, p. 123.

‡**Peter, St.,** p. 127.

**Peterborough.** *See* Medeshamstede.

**Peter's Pence,** alleged origin of, in bequest of King Æthelwulf, p. 211[2] : cf. p. 244.

**Petra Egbryhta.** *See* Ecgbrihtes Stan.

**Petrie, Henry,** editor of the ' Monumenta Historica Britannica,' his edition of the Life, p. xxxi.

‡**Philip,** the Emperor, p. 117.

**Picardy,** Saxon names in, p. 311[2].

**Picts, Picti,** ‡defeat and slay Ecgfrith, king of Northumbria, p. 124 ; ‡mission of St. Columba to, p. 120 ; their country ravaged by the Danes, 47, 8.

**Pincerna,** use of the title, p. 164.

**Pipinus,** Pippinus, ‡Frankish Maior Domus, father of Charles Martel, p. 124.

— (the Short), ‡succeeds Charles, his father, as Maior Domus, p. 126 ; ‡becomes king of the Franks, p. 127 ; father of Charles the Great, 70, 10 ; death of, p. 127.

**Plegmund,** archbishop of Canterbury, a Mercian, aids Alfred in his studies, 77, 10, notes on, p. lxviii, p. lxxii, p. 303 ; rewarded by Alfred, 77, 15.

**Plympton,** co. Devon, monastery at, p. lxvi.

‡**Portland,** Isle of, arrival of Danes in, p. 128.

‡**Priscian,** the grammarian, p. 120.

**Procopius,** Γότθοι of, = the Jutes, p. 166[3] ; Γαυτοί of, = O. N. *Gautar,* O.E. *Gēatas,* p. 170.

**Quantauuic.** *See* Cwantawic.

**Queen,** title not applied to consorts of West Saxon kings, 13, 12 ; origin of this custom, 13, 17, note on, p. 200.

**Rædigam, Rædigum,** *for* Rædingum (Reading, co. Berks), Danes entrench themselves at, 35, 5 (cf. p. 239) ; repulse attack of West Saxons there, 36, 3, 10.

**Ræfan, Reafan,** magic banner of the Danes, interpolated account (from ‡p. 138) of its manufacture, and of its capture by the English, 54 b, 2 ; note on, p. 265.

**Ramsbury,** bishop of. *See* Oda.

**Ramsey** abbey, obituary of, p. 298[3].

**Raven Banner** of Danes. *See* Ræfan.

**Ravenlandeye,** banner of the Danes, p. 267.

Reading. *See* **Rædigam.**

Reafan (for Ræfan). *See* **Ræfan.**

Reiðgotaland of the Norsemen, p. 169[5].

‡Rémi, St., baptizes Clodoveus (Clovis), king of the Franks, p. 119.

Repton. *See* **Hreopedun.**

Rhine, the river. *See* **Hreni.**

Rhodri Mawr, king of Gwyneth. *See* **Rotri.**

‡Richard, duke of Burgundy, raises siege of Chartres, p. 142.

Ridan upp, meaning of, in O.E., p. 233.

Rievaulx, Ethelred of, chronicler, does not borrow directly from the Life, p. lxiv.

**Ris,** father of **Houil,** king of Gleguising, 80, 6.

Rochester. *See* **Hrofesceaster.**

Rök, in East Götland, Sweden, runic inscription at, p. 169[5].

Rollo, arrival of, in Normandy, interpolated, **50 b,** 1 (from ‡p. 134), note on, p. 253; vision of, in England, **50 b,** 2 (referring to ‡pp. 134–5), note on, p. 103, p. 112; ‡besieges Chartres, p. 142.

‡Romans, end of dominion of, in Britain, p. 118.

Rome, **Roma, 12,** 8; **13,** 1; **16,** 2; ‡captured by the Goths, p. 118; journey of King Ine to, **1,** 11; visit of Alfred to, **8,** 3, note on, p. 180; visit of King Æthelwulf to, **11,** 7; his gifts there, p. 211; second visit of Alfred to, **11,** 7, note on, p. 193; Burgred, king of Mercia, goes to, upon his expulsion from his realm, **46,** 9; Æthelhelm, ealdorman of Wilts, carries alms of Alfred and of the Saxons to Rome, **86,** 4; Alfred's mission to, p. 289. St Paul's church at, bequest by King Æthelwulf to, **16,** 35. Schola Saxonum in, history of, p. 243; liberated from tribute by Pope, **71,** 2,

note on, p. 289; church of St. Mary in, **46,** 10.

Romsey abbey, co. Hants, p. 273.

Rosse, John, the Warwick antiquary, p. 324, p. 344.

Rothley, Temple, co. Leicester, p. 157.

**Rotri** (Rhodri Mawr, king of Gwyneth), six sons of, oppressions by, in South Wales, 80, 5, 12; they submit to Alfred, 80, 14, note on, p. 316. *See also* **Anaraut.**

‡Rouen, Rothomagum, wasted by the Danes, p. 131; submits to Rollo, p. 135.

Rudborne, Thomas, his 'Annales Ecclesiae Wintoniensis,' p. 325; nature of this work, p. 212[1].

Rudolf I, king of Burgundy. *See* **Hrothuulf.**

**Ruim,** British name of the Isle of Thanet, **9,** 4, note on, p. 186.

St. Albans Compilation, the basis of the chronicles of Roger of Wendover and of Matthew of Paris, p. 102, p. 236[3], p. 257, p. 291; embodies matter from the Life, p. 161, p. 173, p. 212[4], p. 244[1]; this matter derived from Florence of Worcester or Simeon of Durham, not immediately from the Life, p. lxiv.

St. Davids, **Sanctus Deguui,** monastery of, **79,** 52; suffers from ravages of King Hemeid, ibid.

— Nobis, bishop of, p. lxx.

St. Denis, near Paris, monastery of, O.E. charters to, p. 155.

St. Neot, formerly Neotesstou, co. Cornwall, Alfred at, p. 260, p. 297; burial-place of St. Gueriir, 74, 20.

St. Neots, Annals of, character of, p. cx, p. 97 sqq.; origin of name, p. 98; falsely ascribed to Asser, p. 97, p. 98[3]; date of compilation of, p. 98, p. 102; probably composed at Bury St. Edmunds, p. 101; MS. of, p.

113; Parker's transcript of, p. 114; Joscelyn's extracts from, p. 115; Gale's edition of, p. 115; sources of, p. 101 sqq.; embody much of the Life, p. xiv, p. lvii; nature of copy of Life used by compiler of, p. lvii, p. 104; his treatment of the text of the Life, p. lviii; uses the O.E. Chronicle, p. 105; nature of version used by him, ibid.; origin of his Latin version of, ibid.; his relations with work of Florence of Worcester, p. 107, p. 109, and with the Appendix to this writer, p. 110; he does not use William of Malmesbury or Geoffrey of Monmouth, p. 111; are used by author of the St. Albans Compilation, p. 111, and by Geoffrey de Fontibus in his 'Liber de Infantia S. Eadmundi,' p. 215; not used by the author of the Lund Annals, p. 112.

St. Neots, priory of, co. Huntingdon, p. cii, p. cix, p. 257, p. 260, p. 297.

Sandwic (Sandwich, co. Kent), defeat of the Danes at, 6, 3.

‡Saracens of Spain, subjugated by Charles the Great, p. 128.

‡Saragossa, Caesar Augusta, Charles the Great at, p. 128.

‡Sarepte. See Soracte.

Satelles, 100, 9, note on, p. 337.

Savile, Henry, probably the author of the interpolation in the Life regarding the University of Oxford, p. xxvii.

Saxon names in Picardy, p. 311[2].

Saxon, Saxonicus, poems learned by Alfred as a child, 22, 13; 23, 13; he has Saxon books read before him, 106, 54; Saxon books and poems used by Edward and Ælfthryth, Alfred's children, in their youth, 75, 29; Saxon books used by other children and by the court school, 75, 17.

Saxones, all the Angli and, not in captivity under the Danes submit to Alfred, 83, 6.
— = West Saxons, 86, 3.

Saxonia, Wessex, 12, 21, 22, 31; 13, 29; 79, 2, 50; 81, 29; 102, 20.

Saxonica lingua, 9, 4; 77, 8; 89, 2.

Saxonice, 21, 7; 49, 7, 22; 66, 6; 81, 22.

‡Saxons (Old), conversion of, p. 127.

Saxonum rex, use of title, p. 149.

‡Saxony (Old), conquest of, p. 128.

Scald, River (Scheldt), the Danes ascend, to Condé, 65, 4.

Scaldingi, the Danes, origin of this form, p. 218[1].

Sceaf, in error Seth, ancestor of the kings of Wessex, 1, 39.

Sceapieg, Scepieg, 'Insula Ovium' (Sheppey, co. Kent), Danes winter in, 3, 6; description of site of, 3, 7; monastery in, 3, 10, note on, p. 176; Danes winter in, 10, 8, ‡p. 131.

Sceftesburg (Shaftesbury, co. Dorset), Alfred founds a nunnery there, 98, 2; Æthelgeofu, his daughter, appointed abbess, 98, 4.

Sceldwea, ancestor of the kings of Wessex, 1, 37.

‡Sceobyrig (Shoebury, co. Essex), Hæsten erects fort at, and is there joined by East Anglians and Northumbrians, p. 141.

Scheldt. See Scald.

Schola Saxonum, Rome. See under Rome.

Scholars, lack of, in Wessex, in Alfred's youth, 24, 10, notes on, p. 225, p. 303.

School established by Alfred, 75, 16; 76, 33, note on, p. cxxv, p. 300; Alfred assigns a portion of his revenue to the school established by him, 102, 17. See also Education.

Scireburna. *See* Sherborne.

‡Sclavi. *See* Slaves.

Scotti at Alfred's court, 76, 22.

‡Scurfa, Danish jarl, slain at Wednesfield, p. 144.

Scutchamfly Barrow, co. Berks. *See* Cwichelmes-hlæw.

Seaford, co. Sussex. *See* Sevorde.

‡Sebar, bishop of Evreux, p. 141.

‡Sebercht, king of the East Saxons, p. 121.

Secundarius, title or office of Alfred in reign of his brother Æthelred, 29, 3, note on, p. 227.

Sedulius, Christian poet, 1, 24, note on, p. 162.

Segnius, use of this word by the author of the Life, p. 179.

Seine. *See* Signe.

— ‡Sequana, Danes in, p. 131; Rollo enters, p. 135; Hæsten enters, p. 142.

Selwudu (Selwood Forest, co. Somerset, &c.), 12, 3, note on, p. 197; in Latin 'Sylva Magna,' in British 'Coit Maur,' 55, 8; Ecgbriht's Stone, near, 55, 7.

Sequana. *See* Seine.

Seth, 1, 41.

— error for Sceaf, ancestor of the kings of Wessex, 1, 39.

Sevorde (Seaford, co. Sussex), Alfred at, p. lxxii⁵.

Sexburh, queen of Wessex, p. 200, ‡p. 123.

‡Sexwulf, Sexuulfus, Bishop, founder of monastery at Medeshamstede (Peterborough), death of, p. 125.

Shaftesbury abbey. *See* Sceftesburg.

— charters relating to, p. 223, p. 241³, p. 255², p. 315⁶.

Sheppey, Isle of. *See* Sceapieg.

Sherborne, co. Dorset, Scireburna, Æthelbeald, king of Wessex, buried at, 18, 4; Æthelbeorht, king of Wessex, buried at, 19, 4; Bishop Ealhstan, buried at, 28, 4. Bishops of: *see* Asser, Ealhstan, Sighelm,

Swithelm, Wærstan, Wulfsige. Bishopric of, included Cornwall, p. 322; gift of lands in Cornwall to, by Ecgberht, p. 296, p. 322.

Shoebury. *See* Sceobyrig.

Sidroc the elder, 'comes' of the Danes, slain at Ashdown, 39, 20.

— the younger, 'comes' of the Danes, slain at Ashdown, 39, 20.

Sigeberht, Sigeberchtus, Sigebrychtus, king of East Anglia, slain, death of, p. 110, p. 122.

— king of Wessex, p. 127.

— son of Sigewulf, slain, p. 144.

‡Sigebert I, king of the Franks, death of, p. 120.

‡ — bishop of Metz, p. 120.

‡Sigehelm. *See* Sighelm.

Sigeric, archbishop of Canterbury, itinerary of, to Rome, p. 209, p. 246.

‡Sigeuulf (Ealdorman), slain, p. 144.

Sighelm, one of Alfred's envoys to Rome and on alleged mission to India, p. 289, p. 290.

— bishop of Sherborne, alleged mission of, to India, p. 289.

— ealdorman of Kent, father-in-law of Edward the Elder, p. 290; ‡slain, p. 144.

‡Sigila, daughter of Pipin, king of the Franks, p. 127.

Signe, Sigona, River (the Seine), Danes descend to Paris, 82, 5; ascend to the Marne, 84, 6. *See also* Seine.

Simeon of Durham, chronicles bearing the name of, the compilers of, borrow from the Life, p. xiv; alterations of text of the Life in, p. 278, p. 279, p. 291; interpolations in text of, p. 230, p. 252; inaccurate nature of printed texts of, p. 277. First part of (SD I), p. lix; compiler of, probably used Cott. MS. of the Life, p. xlvii⁴, p. xlviii, p. lix; possible influence of Florence of Worcester on, by means of the second part, p. lix. Second part of (SD 2), p. lix; founded upon Florence of Worcester, not upon the first part, which borrowed directly from Life, ibid.; influenced, however, by the first part, ibid., p. 293.

Singularis, 'boar,' 68, 3; note on, p. 292.

Sinistralis, 'north,' 52, 4; 79, 11, note on, p. 234.

Sister's son, intimate connexion between a man and his, among the English, p. 172.

Siweard, earl of Northumbria, p. 266.

Slaughterford, co. Gloucester, early forms of name of, p. 276⁴.

— co. Wilts, erroneously identified with the site of the battle of Ethandun, p. 275; early forms of the name, p. 276.

‡Slaves, Sclavi, called 'Wilti,' campaign of Charles the Great against, p. 128.

Smith, William, Fellow of University College, Oxford, condemns Camden's interpolation in the Life as a forgery, p. xxv¹.

Snotengaham (Nottingham), in Mercia, called in British 'Tigguocobauc,' in Latin 'Speluncarum Domus,' 30, 3, note on, p. 231; Danes arrive at, and are besieged there, 30, 3, 16.

Somerset. See Summurtunensis paga.

‡Soracte, Sarepte (sic), Mons, Italy, death of Carloman, son of Charles Martel, at, p. 127.

‡Spain, Hispanias, campaign of Charles the Great in, p. 128.

Spelman, Sir John, describes the MS. of the Life, p. xliii.

Stemruga, error in printed texts for 'Steningam,' in interpolation, 17, 2.

‡Steningam (Steyning, co. Sussex), Æthelwulf buried at, p. 132 (cf. p. 213).

‡Stephen, St., invention of body of, p. 118.

‡— — pope, blesses King Pipin, p. 127.

Stepmother, marriage with, p. 214.

Stevenson, Father Joseph, translation of the Life by, p. xxxi.

Steyning, co. Sussex, owned by Alfred, p. 213; descent of, ibid.; alleged burial of King Æthelwulf at, 17 note, p. 132, 6; note on, p. 213; monastery of St. Cuthman at, p. 213. See also ‡Steningam.

Stowe, John, transcript of the Life by, p. xxxiii³.

Stratclutenses (the people of Strathclyde, the valley of the River Clyde), ravaged by the Danes under Healfdene, 47, 8.

‡Streanesheala (Whitby), St. Hilda, abbess of, death of, p. 124.

Stuf, 'nepos' of King Cerdic and Cynric, joint-conqueror of the Isle of Wight, 2, 6, p. 163; note on, p. 170; meaning of 'nepos,' p. 171.

Stur, River (Stour, cos. Suffolk and Essex), 67, 4.

Suanevine, Parker's error for Suanewic, in interpolation, 50 d, 3. See Swanage.

Suanewic. See Swanage.

Suatim utens, 56, 18; 74, 21 (note on alteration of text, p. 298¹); 106, 22; meaning of, p. 278.

Subarrare, 'to give earnest or security,' 29, 6; 106, 8, note on, p. 230.

Sudbury, William de, monk of Westminster, attempts to prove that the crown wherewith Alfred was alleged to have been crowned at Rome was still preserved in the abbey, p. 183.

Summurtunensis paga (Somerset), Alfred hides in, 53, 4; his warlike operations in, 55, 4; he meets men of, at Ecgbriht's

Stone, **55**, 6. Ealdorman of:
see Eanwulf.
Sun, total eclipse of, in Alfred's
reign, **59** ; date of, p. 280.
Surrey. *See* **Suthrie.**
Suth Seaxe (Sussex), **Suth Se-
axum** (*sic*), **79**, **5** ; Alfred at
Denu in Sussex. **79**, 7 ; Æthelberht, king of, **18**, 5. *See*
**Dexterales Saxones.**
**Suthrii, Suthrie** (O.E. Suð-
rige) **Suthriga** (O.E. gen. pl.),
the men of Surrey, **9**, 2 ; situation of Surrey, **5**, 2 ; Danes in,
**5**, 2. King of: *see* **Æthelberht.**
Ealdorman of : *see* **Huda.**
Sussex. *See* Suth Seaxe.
Swæbhard, king of Kent, charter
of, p. 220.
Swanage, Suanewic, Suanauuic,
Danes defeated in sea-fight near,
interpolated, **50 c**, 16 ; **50 d**, 3
(from ‡p. 136).
Swithelm, bishop of Sherborne,
alleged envoy of Alfred to India,
p. lxix.
Swithun, St., bishop of Winchester,
alleged education of King Æthelwulf by, p. c² ; alleged to have
caused King Æthelbeald to separate from Judith, p. 212⁴ ; lives
of, by Landfred, Wulfstan, and
Goscelin, p. c², p. 108⁴.

Tætwa, **Tætuua**, ancestor of the
kings of Wessex, **1**, 36.
**Tamesis** (the River Thames), **3**,
8 ; **4**, 5 ; **5**, 3 ; **35**, 6, 10 ; **58**,
5.; arrival of Danes in, **4**, 3 ;
**58**, 2.
**Tanet.** *See* **Tenet.**
Tarrant, River, co. Dorset. *See*
**Terente.**
‡Tassilio dux, p. 128.
Tatwine, St., archbishop of Can-
terbury, death of, p. 126.
**Tenet, Tanet** (Thanet, co. Kent),
Isle of, Danish victory in, **9**, 4 ;
Danes winter in, **20**, 2 ; **Ruim,**
British name for, **9**, 4, note on,
p. 186.

**Terente**, River (Tarrant, co. Dor-
set), **49**, 6.
**Teudubr,** father of Helised, king
of Brecheniauc, **80**, 11, note
on, p. 318.
Textus Roffensis, p. lxvi³, p. 151²,
p. 158, p. 160, p. 162.
Thames, River. *See* **Tamesis.**
Thanet, Isle of. *See* **Tenet.**
‡Theodebald, king of the Franks,
p. 119.
‡Theoderic I, king of the Franks,
p. 119.
‡— III, king of the Franks, p.
124.
**Theodford** (Thetford, co. Nor-
folk), Danes winter at, **32**, 5.
‡Theodore, St., archbishop of Canterbury, p. 123.
‡Theodosius, the Emperor, p. 118.
‡ — son of Arcadius, the Emperor,
p. 118.
Theodred, bishop of London, 926–
951, will of, p. 209, p. 232.
**Theotisci,** German races, **13**, 29 ;
notes on the use of this term,
p. xciii, p. 202.
Thetford. *See* **Theodford.**
Thomas, St., shrine of, Alfred's
alleged mission to, p. 289.
Thoresby, Ralph, the Leeds antiquary, p. xxvii⁵.
**Thornsæta,** Dorset, **49**, 8 ; note
on form, p. 250. *See also* Dor-
set.
Thousand, a denomination of
value, p. 154⁶.
‡Thurfridus, Danish leader, slain
at Wednesfield, p. 145.
**Tigguocobauc,** Welsh interpreta-
tion of Snotengaham, in Latin
'Speluncarum Domus,' **30**, 3,
note on, p. 231.
Time, methods of measuring and
expressing, p. 280, p. 284, p.
338, p. 339.
Tine, River (co. Northumberland),
Danes winter by, **47**, 7.
Trinoda Necessitas, p. 189.
‡Tullense territorium (Toul,
France), p. 130.

Twyne, Brian, Fellow of Corpus Christi College, Oxford, interviews Camden regarding the latter's interpolation of the Life, p. xxv; inspects the MS. of the Life, p. xxxix; his attempt to support its authenticity, p. 324.

Tyrrenum Mare, 91, 15.

(Ubba?) brother of Inwar and Healfdene, slain at Cynuit, 54, 1, 22; his alleged cairn called Hubbleston, parish of Appledore, co. Devon, an antiquarian figment, p. 263; his name similarly connected with a tumulus near Chippenham, co. Wilts, p. 265; Hubba, son of Lodebrochus (Ragnar Lothbroc), interpolated (from ‡p. 138), 54 b.

Uffington Castle, co. Berks, White Horse below, p. 237.

Uhtred, king of the Hwiccii, charter of, p. 164.

Universalis Papa, 16, 37, note on use of this title, p. 211.

Ussher, James, archbishop of Dublin, condemns Camden's interpolation of the Life, p. xxv; states that Camden had never seen a MS. source of this interpolation, and that it came from Henry Savile, p. xxviii; testimony as to a reading of the Cott. MS. of the Life, p. xxx, p. 166; collates MS. of the Life, p. xl; his description of the MS., p. xli.

Uuanating. See Wanating.

Uuecta. See Wecta.

Uuicganbeorg. See Wicganbeorh.

Uuisc. See Wisc.

Uuoden. See Woden.

‡Valentinianus, the Emperor, ‡p. 119.

Venantius Fortunatus, the Euthiones of, 169.

Villa regia, 1, 2; 9, 12; 35, 5; 52, 4; 56, 30; 79, 7; 81, 9; 91, 23; note on, p. 154.

Vitae, blundered form of Iutae, origin of, p. 166².

‡Vortigern, Guirthegirnus, leader of the Britons, p. 119.

Wædmor (Wedmore, co. Somerset), a royal town, 56, 31; chrism-loosing of Guthrum, the Danish king, at, ibid.

Wærstan, bishop of Sherborne, p. 323².

‡Walthelmus, bishop of Chartres, defends city against Rollo, p. 142.

Waltheof, Earl, mythical history of his family, p. 266.

Wanating, Uuanating (Wantage, co. Berks), birthplace of Alfred, 1, 3, note on, p. 154.

Wanley, Humphrey, p. 148²; his assignment of date to the lost MS. of the Life, p. xliv; his accuracy in dating MSS., ibid.; his method in doing so, p. xlv².

Wareham. See Werham.

‡Wasconia. See Gascony.

Wealwudu, blundered form of Sealwudu, p. 198¹.

Wecta, Uuecta, Insula (the Isle of Wight), 2, 7. See also Wight.

Wednesfield. See Wodnesfeld.

Weekaborough, Wickaborough, parish of Berry Pomeroy, co. Devon, erroneously identified with Wicganbeorh, p. 176.

Weights, use of pennies in, 104, 3.

Welewe-stoc, co. Somerset (Wellow), p. 241.

Wellow, co. Somerset, origin of name, p. 241.

Wells, charters relating to, p. lxv. Bishops of: see Duduco, Giso.

Welsh, probable survival of, in Wiltshire in Alfred's time, p. 241; and in or near Dorsetshire, p. 249; and in Devon, p. 251 (cf. p. 262): cf. p. lxxvi.

Welwe, River, co. Somerset, probably name of an affluent of the Avon, p. 241.

Wembury, co. Devon, erroneously

identified with Wicgan-beorh, p. 175; early forms of name of, p. 176.

Wendover, Roger of, use of St. Albans compilation by, p. lxiv, p. 162, p. 173, p. 212[4], p. 236[3], p. 244[1], p. 257[2], p. 291.

Werfrith, bishop of Worcester, p. lxvii, p. 305; a Mercian, translates at Alfred's suggestion Gregory's 'Dialogues,' 77, 5; helps Alfred in his studies, and is rewarded by him, 77, 15, note on, p. 303.

Werham (Wareham, co. Dorset), Danes from Cambridge march to, 49, 4; they make terms with Alfred, 49, 10; which they break, stealing away to Exeter, 49, 17, cf. Parker's interpolations, 50 c, 50 d (from ‡p. 136); description of site of castle, 49, 8, note on, p. 248.

Werwulf, a Mercian priest, aids Alfred in his studies, 77, 13; is rewarded by Alfred, 77, 15; note on, p. 304.

Wessex, Occidentalium Saxonum Regnum, 24, 10; 35, 4; 77, 16; lack of teachers in, 24, 10; foundation of, p. 159. See also Saxonia, West Saxons.

Westbury, co. Wilts, origin of Ecgbright's Stone of New Ordnance Map in, p. 268.

Westbury Leigh, co. Wilts, suggested identification of, with Ægleah, p. 270.

Westminster Abbey, charters relating to, p. 182, p. 293; monks of, claim that kings of England were crowned there before the Norman Conquest, and support this by series of forgeries, p. 182; tract of William de Sudbury in support of claim, p. 183; pretend that crown wherewith Alfred was alleged to have been crowned at Rome was still preserved by them, p. 182.

Westminster, Matthew of, errors in the chronicle ('Flores Historiarum') of the so-called, p. 243[3].

West Saxons, Occidentales Saxones, 1, 9; 7, 4; 9, 10; 12, 13; 14, 6; 17, 8; 21, 3; 68, 11; make peace with the Danes, 43, 1; custom of not allowing their king's wife to sit upon the throne or be called queen, 13, 12; origin of custom, 13, 17; note upon it, p. 200. See also Saxones. Kings of: see Æscuuine, Æthelbeald, Æthelheard, Æthelred, Æthelwulf, Alfred, Brihtricus, Ceadwalla, Cenwealh, Ceol, Ceolwulf, Cerdic, Creoda, Cuthred, Cynegils, Cynewulf, Cynric, Ecgberht, Ine, Kentuuine, Sigeberht (see also Sexburh, queen of). Style of kings of, p. 149. Regnal table of, p. 152, p. 157. Genealogy of royal house, p. 157; possible connexion of Alfred with its redaction, p. 153. See also Saxonia, Wessex.

Whibblestone, parish of Appledore, co. Devon, altered into Hubbastone and Hubbastow by antiquarian influence, p. 263, p. 264[1].

Whitby, co. York. See Streanesheala.

White Horse, below Uffington Castle, co. Berks, p. 237.

—— below Bratton Castle, near Edington, co. Wilts, p. 273.

White Lackington, co. Somerset, origin of name, p. 174.

Whiteparish, co. Wilts, p. 319.

White Sheet Castle, co. Wilts, erroneously identified with Ecgbrihtes Stan, p. 269[1].

Wicganbeorh, Uuicganbeorg, defeat of the Danes at, 3, 4; site of, wrongly identified with Wembury, co. Devon, p. 175; possibly Wigborough, parish of South Petherton, co. Somerset, p. 176.

Wido, king of Italy. See Witha.

‡Widukind, Witichingis (king of the Old Saxons), baptism of, p. 128.

Wig, ancestor of the kings of Wessex, 1, 18.

Wigborough, parish of South Petherton, co. Somerset, possibly Wicganbeorh of the Chronicle, p. 176; early forms of name of, p. 176[2].

Wight, Isle of, English conquest of, p. 171; Jutes of, cease to call themselves by that name, p. 167; erroneous derivation of name from the Jutes, p. 166[2]. See also Wecta.

Wiht, O.E. compound personal names in, treatment of, in local names, p. 174.

Wihtgar, 'nepos' of Kings Cerdic and Cynric of Wessex, p. 163; joint-conqueror of the Isle of Wight, 2, 6; note on, p. 170; meaning of 'nepos,' p. 171; buried at Guihtgaraburh (Wihtgaraburh) in the Isle of Wight, 2, 11.

Wihtgaraburh, Guihtgaraburh, in the Isle of Wight, 2, 11; explanation of form, p. 172; battle at, 2, 11, note on, p. 171; burial-place of Wihtgar, 'nepos' of Cerdic and Cynric, p. 173; meaning of 'nepos,' p. 171; wrongly identified with Carisbrooke, 173; erroneously explained as fort of the men of Wight, the Wiht-ware, p. 173.

Wiley, River, co. Wilts, origin of name, p. 241. See Gwilou.

‡Wilfrid, St., bishop of the Northumbrians, p. 123; expelled from bishopric, ibid.

Willibrord's Life of St. Boniface, p. 251[4].

‡Wilti, Sclavi called, p. 128.

Wiltshire. See Wiltunscir.

Wiltunscir (Wiltshire), 52, 5; Wiltunensis paga, men of, meet Alfred at Ecgbriht's Stone, 55, 10; probable existence of

Welsh-speaking inhabitants in Alfred's time, p. 241. Wiltunenses, ealdorman of; see Æthelhelm.

Wiltun (Wilton, co. Wilts), defeat of Alfred by the Danes at, 42, 18.

— abbey, charters relating to, p. lxv[3], p. 151[2], p. 220[7], p. 241[3], p. 255[2], p. 267[5], p. 299, p. 304[8], p. 312[2], p. 319.

Wimborne. See Winburna.

Winburna (Wimborne Minster, co. Dorset), King Æthelred buried at, 41, 4; Cuthburh, sister of King Ine, abbess of, p. 155.

Winchcombe Abbey, co. Gloucester, foundation charter of, p. 229[1].

Winchester, Wintonia, harried by Danes, 18, 8; King Æthelwulf buried at, 17, 2. Bishops of: see Æthelwold, Ælfheah, Denewulf, Frithestan, Hedda, Swithun. Chartulary of, charters derived from, p. lxv[3], p. 149[6], p. 151[2,3], p. 216[3], p. 227, p. 229[4], p. 241[3], p. 246, p. 250[1], p. 299 and note [4], p. 304, p. 312[2], p. 315[6], p. 322[6], p. 330[6]; Ælfsin's Winchester calendar, p. 232[5], p. 240.

Windsor Forest, p. 156.

Winsley in Bradford-on-Avon, co. Wilts, suggested identification of, with Ægleah, Igleah, p. 270.

Wintonia (Caerwent), Asser stricken down by fever at, on his return from his first visit to Alfred, 79, 33; erroneously identified with Winchester, p. lxxiii, p. 313.

Wisc, Uuisc, River (the Exe, co. Devon), 49, 24; note on this form, p. 251.

Wise, Francis, M.A., Fellow of Trinity College, Oxford, his edition of the Life, p. xxviii; inaccuracy of, p. xxix, p. 166; his description of the MS. of the Life, p. xliii.

Wistan, St., account of, p. 108[4].
Witha (Wido, king of Italy), receives Lombardy on division of Empire, 85, 18.
‡Witichingis. See Widukind.
Wittering, co. Sussex, origin of name, p. 174[1].
Wittersham, co. Kent, origin of name, p. 174[1].
Wixford, co. Warwick, origin of name, p. 174[1].
Woden, Uuoden, ancestor of the kings of Wessex, 1, 20.
Wodnesfeld (Wednesfield, co. Stafford), battle of, p. 107, p. 144.
Wood, Anthony à, his account of the MS. of the Life, p. xlii.
Woodyates, co. Devon, probably the 'Wudigan-gæt' of the Durham Ritual, p. 178.
Worcester, bishop of. See Werfrith.
— monastery at, charters relating to, p. lxvi[3], p. 148[2], p. 150[2], p. 151[2], p. 164[3], p. 219[6], p. 220[7], p. 300, p. 305, p. 313, p. 316, p. 330[6], p. 337[5]. Calendar from, in Hatton MS. 113, probably used by Florence of Worcester, p. 232[5].
Worr, Ealdorman (ob. 800), wrongly alleged to be the victim of Queen Eadburh described in 14, 15, p. 205.
Wright, Thomas, impugns the authenticity of the Life, p. xcvi.
Writtle, co. Essex, p. 247[1].
Wudigan gæt at Aclee on West Sæxum, site of, p. 178.

Wulfheard, ealdorman of Hampshire, apparently an error in Chron. B and C for Osric, p. 216.
Wulfred, archbishop of Canterbury, charter of, p. 220.
Wulfsige, bishop of Sherborne, p. lxvi.
Wulfstan, account of voyage of, in Alfred's 'Orosius,' p. 169[4], p. 300.
— bishop of Worcester, p. 232[5].
Wulfstan's Life of St. Swithun, p. c[2].
Wulfthryth, queen (of Wessex?), p. 201[4].

Yarrow. See Giruuinense monasterium.
Yattenden, co. Berks, erroneously identified with Ethandun, p. 277.
Yatton Keyneli, co. Wilts, erroneously identified with Ethandun, p. 277.
‡Ycanhoh, St. Botulf founds a monastery at, p. 123.
Yonne, the River. See Iona.
York, Eboracum, 26, 4; Danes arrive at, from East Anglia, 26, 4; besieged there by Northumbrians, 27, 10, whom they defeat, 27, 20; defences of, 27, 17, note on, p. 226; Danes winter at, 31, 4. Archbishops of: see Oscytel, Oswald, Paulinus.
Ȳte, West Saxon form of the name of the Jutes, p. 168.
Ytene, name of the New Forest, preserves the name of the (English) Jutes, p. 168.

| ISBN 0–19– | Author | Title |
|---|---|---|
| 8143567 | ALFÖLDI A. | The Conversion of Constantine and Pagan Rome |
| 6286409 | ANDERSON George K. | The Literature of the Anglo-Saxons |
| 8228813 | BARTLETT & MacKAY | Medieval Frontier Societies |
| 8114222 | BROOKS Kenneth R. | Andreas and the Fates of the Apostles |
| 8148348 | CAMPBELL J.B. | The Emperor and the Roman Army 31 BC to 235 AD |
| 826643X | CHADWICK Henry | Priscillian of Avila |
| 826447X | CHADWICK Henry | Boethius |
| 8219393 | COWDREY H.E.J. | The Age of Abbot Desiderius |
| 8148992 | DAVIES M. | Sophocles: Trachiniae |
| 825301X | DOWNER L. | Leges Henrici Primi |
| 8143109 | FRAENKEL Edward | Horace |
| 8201540 | GOLDBERG P.J.P. | Women, Work and Life Cycle in a Medieval Economy |
| 8140215 | GOTTSCHALK H.B. | Heraclides of Pontus |
| 8266162 | HANSON R.P.C. | Saint Patrick |
| 8224354 | HARRISS G.L. | King, Parliament and Public Finance in Medieval England to 1369 |
| 8581114 | HEATH Sir Thomas | Aristarchus of Samos |
| 8140444 | HOLLIS A.S. | Callimachus: Hecale |
| 8212968 | HOLLISTER C. Warren | Anglo-Saxon Military Institutions |
| 8223129 | HURNARD Naomi | The King's Pardon for Homicide – before AD 1307 |
| 8140401 | HUTCHINSON G.O. | Hellenistic Poetry |
| 8142560 | JONES A.H.M. | The Greek City |
| 8218354 | JONES Michael | Ducal Brittany 1364–1399 |
| 8271484 | KNOX & PELCZYNSKI | Hegel's Political Writings |
| 8225253 | LE PATOUREL John | The Norman Empire |
| 8212720 | LENNARD Reginald | Rural England 1086–1135 |
| 8212321 | LEVISON W. | England and the Continent in the 8th century |
| 8148224 | LIEBESCHUETZ J.H.W.G. | Continuity and Change in Roman Religion |
| 8141378 | LOBEL Edgar & PAGE Sir Denys | Poetarum Lesbiorum Fragmenta |
| 8152442 | MAAS P. & TRYPANIS C.A . | Sancti Romani Melodi Cantica |
| 8148178 | MATTHEWS John | Western Aristocracies and Imperial Court AD 364–425 |
| 8223447 | McFARLANE K.B. | Lancastrian Kings and Lollard Knights |
| 8226578 | McFARLANE K.B. | The Nobility of Later Medieval England |
| 8148100 | MEIGGS Russell | Roman Ostia |
| 8148402 | MEIGGS Russell | Trees and Timber in the Ancient Mediterranean World |
| 8142641 | MILLER J. Innes | The Spice Trade of the Roman Empire |
| 8147813 | MOORHEAD John | Theoderic in Italy |
| 8264259 | MOORMAN John | A History of the Franciscan Order |
| 8116020 | OWEN A.L. | The Famous Druids |
| 8143427 | PFEIFFER R. | History of Classical Scholarship (vol 1) |
| 8111649 | PHEIFER J.D. | Old English Glosses in the Epinal-Erfurt Glossary |
| 8142277 | PICKARD–CAMBRIDGE A.W. | Dithyramb Tragedy and Comedy |
| 8269765 | PLATER & WHITE | Grammar of the Vulgate |
| 8213891 | PLUMMER Charles | Lives of Irish Saints (2 vols) |
| 820695X | POWICKE Michael | Military Obligation in Medieval England |
| 8269684 | POWICKE Sir Maurice | Stephen Langton |
| 821460X | POWICKE Sir Maurice | The Christian Life in the Middle Ages |
| 8225369 | PRAWER Joshua | Crusader Institutions |
| 8225571 | PRAWER Joshua | The History of The Jews in the Latin Kingdom of Jerusalem |
| 8143249 | RABY F.J.E. | A History of Christian Latin Poetry |
| 8143257 | RABY F.J.E. | A History of Secular Latin Poetry in the Middle Ages (2 vols) |
| 8214316 | RASHDALL & POWICKE | The Universities of Europe in the Middle Ages (3 vols) |
| 8148380 | RICKMAN Geoffrey | The Corn Supply of Ancient Rome |
| 8141076 | ROSS Sir David | Aristotle: Metaphysics (2 vols) |
| 8141092 | ROSS Sir David | Aristotle: Physics |
| 8264178 | RUNCIMAN Sir Steven | The Eastern Schism |
| 814833X | SALMON J.B. | Wealthy Corinth |
| 8171587 | SALZMAN L.F. | Building in England Down to 1540 |
| 8218362 | SAYERS Jane E. | Papal Judges Delegate in the Province of Canterbury 1198–1254 |
| 8221657 | SCHEIN Sylvia | Fideles Crucis |
| 8148135 | SHERWIN WHITE A.N. | The Roman Citizenship |
| 8642040 | SOUTER Alexander | A Glossary of Later Latin to 600 AD |
| 8222254 | SOUTHERN R.W. | Eadmer: Life of St. Anselm |
| 8251408 | SQUIBB G. | The High Court of Chivalry |
| 8212011 | STEVENSON & WHITELOCK | Asser's Life of King Alfred |
| 8212011 | SWEET Henry | A Second Anglo-Saxon Reader—Archaic and Dialectical |
| 8148259 | SYME Sir Ronald | History in Ovid |

| 8143273 | SYME Sir Ronald | Tacitus (2 vols) |
| 8200951 | THOMPSON Sally | Women Religious |
| 8201745 | WALKER Simon | The Lancastrian Affinity 1361–1399 |
| 8161115 | WELLESZ Egon | A History of Byzantine Music and Hymnography |
| 8140185 | WEST M.L. | Greek Metre |
| 8141696 | WEST M.L. | Hesiod: Theogony |
| 8148542 | WEST M.L. | The Orphic Poems |
| 8140053 | WEST M.L. | Hesiod: Works & Days |
| 822799X | WHITBY M. & M. | The History of Theophylact Simocatta |
| 8114877 | WOOLF Rosemary | The English Religious Lyric in the Middle Ages |
| 8119224 | WRIGHT Joseph | Grammar of the Gothic Language |